SwiftUI

for Masterminds

How to take advantage of Swift and SwiftUI
to create insanely great apps for
iPhones, iPads, and Macs

J.D Gauchat

www.jdgauchat.com

SwiftUI for Masterminds
Copyright © 2022 John D Gauchat
All Rights Reserved

The source code for this book is available at **www.formasterminds.com**

Copyright Registration Number: 1165896

ISBN: 978-1-7779782-2-8

1st Edition 2020 John D Gauchat
2nd Edition 2022 John D Gauchat
3rd Edition 2022 John D Gauchat

Table of Contents

Chapter 7—Lists

Chapter 8—Navigation

Chapter 9—Concurrency

Chapter 10—Storage

Chapter 11—Graphics and Animations

Conventions

This book explores basic and advanced topics required to develop professional applications. Depending on your current level of knowledge and experience, you may find some of these topics easy or difficult to learn. To help you navigate the book, we have identified each section with a label. The following is a description of what these labels represent.

Basic
The Basic label represents topics you can ignore if you already know the basics of Swift and app development. If you are learning how to develop applications for Apple devices for the first time, these sections are required.

Medium
The Medium label represents topics that are not required for every app. You can ignore the information presented in these sections until they are applied in practical situations later or when you need them in your own applications.

Advanced
The Advanced label represents topics that are only required in advanced applications or API development. The information presented in these sections is not required for the development of most applications, but it can be helpful if you want to improve your understanding of how Apple technologies work.

If you are new to app development, read all the Basic sections first, and only read the Medium sections later when you need to understand how the examples work.

Examples

Every single topic presented in this book is explained through examples that you can try yourself. We recommend that you open Xcode and try the examples as you learn, but you can download the codes and projects from our website to save time (**www.formasterminds.com**).

The examples in this book only apply the technologies you already know, so they don't always follow best practices. There are several programming patterns and best practices you can follow. What applies to you depends on the characteristics of your application and what you want to achieve with it. We recommend you explore all the possibilities presented in this book but also experiment and try your own.

 IMPORTANT: Apple technologies are extensive, and a book cannot teach you everything. After each topic is introduced, you should read the official specifications provided by Apple and look for additional examples on the Web. The links to the specifications, additional information, tutorials, and videos are available on our website **www.formasterminds.com**. Apple's official documentation is available at **developer.apple.com**. Frameworks and APIs references are available at **developer.apple.com/documentation**.

Chapter 1
App Development

Basic **1.1 Overview**

Apple has provided tools for developers to create apps for its devices since the introduction of the first iPhone in 2007. But the Apple ecosystem has grown significantly since then. Developers now need to consider that users own many devices, including iPhones, iPads, Mac computers, the Apple Watch, and Apple TV. Having all these devices available with such distinctive features is great for users, but difficult for developers. Creating apps that work across multiple platforms is demanding and involves a steep learning curve. This resulted in many applications being distributed exclusively for one system or another. Apple engineers quickly realized that the tools were not ready to meet the demands of modern developers, and in June 2019, they released SwiftUI.

SwiftUI is an abstraction layer that sits on top of previous tools to simplify the construction of the user interface and revamp the way developers create applications for Apple devices. With SwiftUI, we can easily develop apps that share data and work seamlessly on all devices and any screen size.

Basic **Requirements**

Apple requires developers to develop the applications with software provided by the company, and this software only works on Apple computers. For this reason, the options are limited, but the good news is that the tools and accounts we need are provided by the company for free.

Mac Computer—This in theory could be any Mac computer, but the development software always requires the latest operating system (currently macOS Ventura), so in practice we need a relatively new computer with a recommended 16GB of memory.

Xcode—This is the software provided by Apple for development. The latest version is number 14. It's free and the package comes with everything we need to create our apps, including an editor, the SDK (Software Development Kit), and a simulator to test the applications.

Apple Developer Account—This is a basic account we can get for free. From this account, we can manage our membership, create certificates, app identifiers and other information we need to test and publish our apps.

Apple Membership—This is the membership required to publish our apps in the App Store. As of this writing, the cost of this membership is $99 US dollars per year.

Mobile Device—This could be any of the devices available in the market that support the current versions of Apple's mobile operating systems (currently iOS 16, tvOS 16, watchOS 9, iPadOS 16, and macOS Ventura). Testing our applications on a real device is not required but highly recommended.

In short, to develop applications for Apple devices we need a Mac Computer capable of running the operating system required by the latest version of Xcode (currently macOS Ventura), make sure that we have an Apple ID to access our Developer Account (**developer.apple.com**), and install the latest version of Xcode (currently 14).

1.2 Xcode

Xcode is a general-purpose IDE (Integrated Development Environment). It includes a very powerful editor with graphic tools to help us write our code, the SDKs (Software Development Kits) for the creation of software for the iOS, iPadOS, macOS, watchOS, and tvOS operating systems, and compilers for the C, C++, Objective-C and Swift programming languages. From Xcode, we can program software for every Apple platform using any of these tools and programming languages.

Xcode is available as an app in the Mac App Store. To download this application, we must open the App Store from Launchpad (the application organizer that comes with macOS) or double click the App Store icon inside the Applications folder in Finder (macOS's file explorer).

If we search for the term "Xcode" in the App Store, the window shows Xcode's icon at the top and a button to download it (Figure 1-1, number 1).

Figure 1-1: Xcode in the Mac App Store

Once the application is downloaded, the software is automatically installed. To start Xcode, we open Launchpad and click on the icon or double-click the program from the Applications folder in Finder. Figure 1-2 shows Xcode's welcome screen.

Figure 1-2: Xcode's welcome screen

The welcome screen offers a list of recent projects on the right and buttons on the left to create a new project, open a project on our computer, or clone one stored in a repository.

Basic **1.3 Development**

Even though some simple projects could be developed without programming a single line of code, we always need to write our own code if we want to create a useful application, and for that, we need programming languages, frameworks, and APIs.

(Basic) Programming Languages

Several years ago, Apple adopted and implemented a language called Objective-C to allow developers to create applications for its devices. Due to the technical level required to work with this language, the spectacular success of Apple's mobile devices did not impress developers the same way as consumers. The demand for more and better applications was growing fast, but the complicated nature of the system did not appeal to most developers who were used to working with more traditional tools. To solve this problem, in 2014 the company introduced a new programming language called *Swift*. Swift presents a simpler syntax that developers find familiar, while at the same time preserves that low-level nature necessary to take advantage of every aspect of Apple's devices. Swift was designed to replace Objective-C and, therefore, it is the language recommended to new developers.

(Basic) Frameworks and APIs

Programming languages by themselves cannot do much. They provide all the elements to interact with the system but are basic tools for data management. Because of the complexity of the information required to control sophisticated technologies and access every part of a system, it could take years to develop an application from scratch working with just the instructions of a programming language. Doing simple things like printing graphics on the screen or storing data in files would become a nightmare if programmers had to depend on the tools provided by programming languages alone. For this reason, these languages are always accompanied by pre-programmed routines grouped in libraries and frameworks that through a simple interface called *API* (Application programming interface) allow programmers to incorporate to their apps amazing functionality with just a few lines of code. Apple provides all this functionality, including frameworks and their APIs, in a set of tools called SDK (Software Development Kit) that comes with Xcode.

Frameworks and APIs are fundamental to app development. As developers, we must learn and apply these tools if we want to create useful applications and, therefore, they will become the main subject of study in the following chapters.

(Basic) Compiler

Computers do not understand Swift or any other programming language. These languages were created for us to give machines instructions we can understand. Our code must be converted to elemental orders that work at an electronic level, turning multiple switches on and off to represent the abstraction humans work with. The translation from the language humans understand to the language computers understand is done by a program called *compiler*.

Compilers have specific routines to translate instructions from programming languages to machine code. They are language and platform specific, which means that we need a specific compiler to program in one language and platform. There are a few compilers available to Apple systems, but the one currently implemented by Xcode is called *LLVM*. LLVM is capable of compiling code written in Swift, C, C++, and Objective-C.

With the compiler, the machinery to build an app is complete. Figure 1-3, below, shows all the elements involved. There are three main sources of code the compiler uses to build the application: our code in Swift, the frameworks our program requires, and a set of basic routines necessary for the app to run (called Application Loop in Figure 1-3). The process begins with Xcode. In this program, we write our code, access frameworks through their APIs, and configure the app to be compiled (built). Combining our code, the codes from the frameworks our app requires, and the basic routines (Application Loop), the compiler creates an executable program that may be run in a simulator, a device, or submitted to the App Store for distribution.

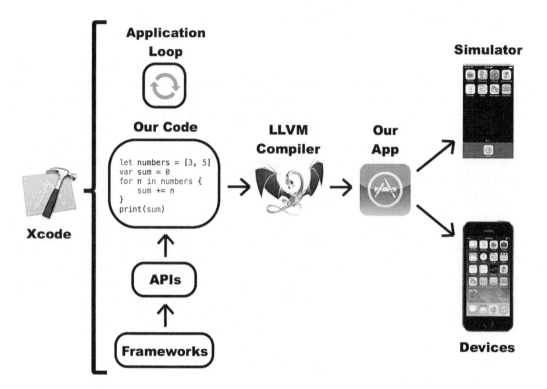

Figure 1-3: Building an App

 IMPORTANT: The Application Loop is a group of elemental routines, common to every program, that connect the app to the operating system and provide a loop (a code that executes itself over and over again) to constantly check for events produced by the user or coming from the system. Although you never work directly with these routines, they are connected to your code to report the state of the application, as we will see Chapter 14.

Chapter 2
Introduction to Swift

Basic **2.1 Computer Programming**

Computers can't do anything unless we write a program. A program is a succession of instructions that the computer must follow. We write the program using the instructions provided by a specific programming language, then a compiler translates these instructions into orders the computer can understand, and when we tell the computer to run the program, the orders are executed sequentially one by one.

The instructions are always listed in sequential order, but programming languages offer different ways to group them together and organize the code and the data that is going to be processed. Developing an app demands a deep understanding of these instructions and the combinations required to achieve the results we want. Since this may be daunting for beginners, Xcode includes a tool called *Playground* to learn how to program and test our code.

Basic **Playground**

As the name suggests, Playground offers a place to experiment and play around with our code before including it in our applications. Although we could start an Xcode project to create an application right away, it is better to work with Playground first to learn how to program and how to take advantage of some of the fundamental frameworks included in the SDK. Playground files are created from the Playground option in the File menu at the top of the screen.

Figure 2-1: *Playground option*

This opens a window with a list of icons to select the template we want to use. Templates are files with pre-programmed code to help us get started with our project. The ones available at this time are called Blank (with just a few lines of code to start from scratch), Game (with basic code to program a video game), Map (with the code to display a map), and Single View (with the same code required to create the user interface for an application).

Figure 2-2: *Playground templates*

After the template is selected, Xcode asks for the name of the Playground file and where we want to store it. Next, Xcode shows the Playground's interface on the screen. Figure 2-3, below, shows what we see when we create a Blank template.

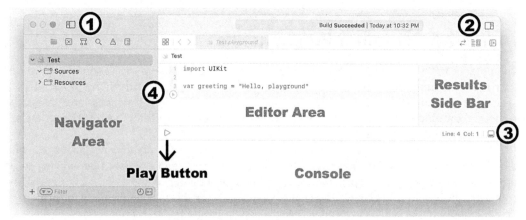

Figure 2-3: *Playground's interface*

Playground presents a simple interface with a toolbar at the top and four areas: the Navigator Area where we can see the resources included in our Playground project, the Editor Area where we write our code, the *Results Side Bar* on the right where the results produced by our code are displayed, and the Console at the bottom where we can read the errors produced by the code and print our own messages.

The interface includes buttons to open and remove some of these panels. The button in the upper left corner removes the Navigator Area (number 1), the one in the upper right corner controls a panel called Utilities Area with information about the selected resource, and the button in the lower right corner opens or removes the Console.

As illustrated in Figure 2-3, the Editor Area includes a button at the bottom of the panel to run and stop the code (Play Button). There is also a play button on the left side of the Editor Area that we can press if we want to execute parts of the code instead (number 4). When this button is pressed, the code is executed up to the line in which the button is located.

Playground can run the code automatically or wait until we press the Play button. By default, the mode is set to Automatically Run, but we can press and hold the Play button to access a menu that allows us to modify this behavior.

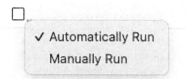

Figure 2-4: *Playground's running mode*

In the Editor Area, we can see the code we have programmed so far. When a new Playground file is created, Xcode offers a template that includes a few basic lines of code to start with. Listing 2-1, below, is the code currently generated for the Blank template.

```
import UIKit

var greeting = "Hello, playground"
```

Listing 2-1: *Playground template*

A computer program is just text written with a specific syntax. Each line of text represents an instruction. Sometimes a single line includes several instructions, and therefore each line is usually called *statement*. Every statement is an order, or a group of orders, required for the computer to perform a task. In the code of Listing 2-1, the first statement uses the instruction **import** to include in our code the pre-programmed codes from the UIKit framework, and the second statement uses the instruction **var** to store the text "Hello, playground" in memory.

If we press the Play Button to execute the code, we see the result inside the Results Side Bar. (In this case, the bar shows the text stored in memory by the **var** instruction.) When we move the mouse over the text on the bar, two small buttons show up, as illustrated below.

Figure 2-5: Show Result and Quick Look buttons

The button on the right is called *Quick Look*, and it shows a popup window with a visual representation of the result produced by the execution of the code, such as formatted text or an image. In this case, no visual effect is generated by the code, so we only see plain text.

Figure 2-6: Quick Look window

The button on the left is called *Show Result*, and what it does is to open a window within our code with a visual representation of the results of the execution of the code over time. In this case, nothing changes, so only the "Hello, playground" text is shown.

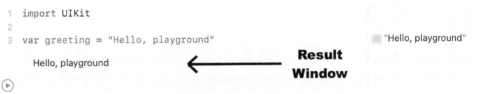

Figure 2-7: Result window

The code provided by Xcode for the Blank template is useless, but it shows the basic syntax of the Swift language and how to do elemental things in a program such as importing frameworks to add functionality and storing data in memory. The reason why one of the statements is storing data in memory is because this is the most important task of a program. A program's main functions are storing, retrieving, and processing data. Working with data in the computer's memory is a delicate process that demands meticulous organization. If we are not careful, data may be accidentally deleted, corrupted, or completely overwritten. To make sure this does not happen, programming languages introduce the concept of variables.

(Basic) 2.2 Variables

Variables are names representing values stored in memory. Once a variable is defined, its name remains the same but the value in memory it represents may change. This allows us to store and retrieve a value from memory without having to remember where in the memory the value was stored. With just mentioning the name of the variable we used to store the value, we can get it back or replace it with a new one.

When we use variables, the system takes care of managing the memory for us, but we still need to understand how memory works in order to know what kind of values we can store.

Memory

The computer's memory is like a huge honeycomb, with consecutive cells that can be in two possible states: activated or deactivated. They are electronic switches with on and off positions established by low and high energy levels.

Figure 2-8: *Memory cells*

Because of their two possible states, each cell is a small unit of information. One cell may represent two possible states (switch on or off), but by combining a sequence of cells we can represent more states. For example, if we combine two cells, we have four possible states.

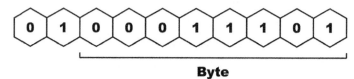

Combination 1   Combination 2   Combination 3   Combination 4

Figure 2-9: *Combining two cells*

With these two cells, we can now represent up to four states (4 possible combinations). If we had used three cells instead, then the possible combinations would have been 8 (eight states). The number of combinations doubles every time we add another cell to the group. This can be extended to represent any number of states we want. Because of this characteristic, this system of switches is used to represent binary numbers, which are numbers expressed by only two digits: 0 and 1. An **on** switch represents the value **1** and an **off** switch represents the value **0**. Basic units were determined with the purpose of identifying parts of this endless series of digits. One cell was called a *bit* and a group of 8 bits was called a *Byte*. Figure 2-10, below, shows how a Byte looks like in memory, with some of its switches **on** representing the binary number 00011101.

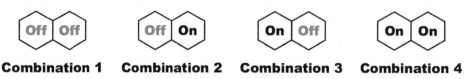

Byte

Figure 2-10: *Representation of one Byte in memory*

Numbers of one numeral system, like binary, can be converted to any other numeral system, like decimal. The binary system is the one a computer can understand because it translates directly to the electronic switches they are built with, but humans find this difficult to read, so we use other systems to express numbers, like the decimal system. For instance, the possible combinations of 8 bits are 256, therefore, a Byte can represent decimal numbers from 0 to 255. (If the Byte in our example is converted to the decimal system, we get the number 29).

To represent larger numbers, Bytes are grouped together. For example, if we take two Bytes from memory, we get a binary number composed of a total of 16 bits (16 zeros and ones). A binary number of 16 bits can represent decimal numbers from 0 to 65535 (a total of 65536 possible combinations). To establish clearly defined data structures, every programming language declares its own units of data of a predetermined size. These units are usually called *primitive data types*.

Basic **Primitive Data Types**

Primitive data types are units of data defined by the programming language. They are always the same size, so when we store a value of one of these data types, the computer knows exactly how much memory to use. The following are the most basic data types provided by Swift.

Int—This data type defines integer numbers, which are numbers with no fractional component. In 64 bits systems, the size of this data type is 8 Bytes and therefore it can store values from -9,223,372,036,854,775,808 to 9,223,372,036,854,775,807.

Although it is recommended to use the **Int** data type to store integers, some frameworks require a very specific type of integer. For this reason, Swift also defines the following data types.

Int8—This data type defines integer numbers of a size of 1 Byte (8 bits). Because of its size, it can store values from -128 to 127.

Int16—This data type defines integer numbers of a size of 2 Bytes (16 bits). Because of its size, it can store values from -32,768 to 32,767.

Int32—This data type defines integer numbers of a size of 4 Bytes (32 bits). Because of its size, it can store values from -2,147,483,648 to 2,147,483,647.

Int64—This data type defines integer numbers of a size of 8 Bytes (64 bits). Because of its size, it can store values from -9,223,372,036,854,775,808 to 9,223,372,036,854,775,807.

If we calculate the size of each type presented so far and determine the possible combinations of bits, we will discover that the maximum values don't match. For example, an **Int8** uses 1 Byte, which means it is composed of 8 bits, and for this reason it should be able to store numbers from 0 to 255 (256 possible combinations). The reason why an **Int8** has a positive limit of 127 is because it only uses 7 bits to store the value, the first bit on the left is reserved to indicate the sign (positive or negative). Although these limits are not restrictive, the language also provides the unsigned versions of these types in case we need to store larger positive values.

UInt—This is the same as **Int** but for unsigned values. Because it does not reserve a bit for the sign, in 64-bit systems it can store values from 0 to 18,446,744,073,709,551,615.

The specific data types for **UInt** are **UInt8**, **UInt16**, **UInt32**, and **UInt64**. These data types work exactly like the equivalents for **Int**, but they are intended to store only positive numbers.

Although all these data types are very useful, they are only good for storing binary values that can be used to represent integer numbers. Arithmetic operations also require the use of real numbers (e.g., 3.14 or 10.543). Computers cannot reproduce these types of values, but they can work with an approximation called *floating-point* numbers. The following are the most frequently used floating-point data types defined in the Swift language.

Float—This data type defines 32 bits floating-point numbers with a precision of 6 digits.

Double—This data type defines 64 bits floating-point numbers with a precision of at least 15 digits.

Floating-point types can handle large numbers using scientific notation, but because of their precision, it is recommended to declare a variable of type **Double** when performing calculations and use **Float** for minor tasks, such as storing coordinates to position graphics on the screen.

(Basic) Declaration and Initialization

If we want to store data in memory, the first thing we need to do is to select the right type from the data types provided by the language and then create a variable of that type. This action is called *Declaration*, and it is done using the **var** instruction and the syntax **var name: type**.

```
var mynumber: Int
```

***Listing 2-2:** Declaring variables*

This example creates a variable called **mynumber** of type **Int**. When the system reads this statement, it reserves a space in memory 8 Bytes long (64 bits) and assigns the name **mynumber** to that space. After the execution of this statement, we can use the variable **mynumber** to store in memory any integer value from -9,223,372,036,854,775,808 to 9,223,372,036,854,775,807.

 IMPORTANT: You can use any character you want to declare the name of a variable, except for spaces, mathematical symbols, and some Unicode characters. Also, the name cannot start with a number, and Swift distinguishes between lowercase and uppercase characters (**MyInt** is considered a different variable than **myint**). You must also make sure that the name does not match any reserved word. If you declare a variable with an illegal name, Xcode will show you an error.

The memory is a reusable resource. The space reserved for a variable may have been used before by another variable or a piece of code may have been stored in the same location. For this reason, after the declaration of a variable we must always store a value in it to clear the space. This action is called *Initialization*.

```
var mynumber: Int
mynumber = 5
```

Listing 2-3: *Initializing variables*

In the new example of Listing 2-3, we first declare the variable as we did before, and then initialize it with the value 5 (we store the number 5 in the space of memory reserved for this variable). To store the value, we use the **=** (equal) symbol and the syntax **name = value**, where **name** is the name of the variable and **value** is the value we want to store (once the variable was declared, we do not have to use the **var** instruction or specify its type anymore).

Most of the time, we know what the variable's initial value will be right away. In cases like this, Swift allows us to declare and initialize the variable in just one line of code.

```
var mynumber: Int = 5
```

Listing 2-4: *Declaring and initializing variables in the same statement*

 Do It Yourself: If you haven't done it yet, create a new Playground file with the Blank template. Replace all the statements in the template by the code in Listing 2-4 and press the Play button. You should see the value 5 on the Results Side Bar. Repeat this process for the following examples.

Variables are called variables because their values are not constant. We can change them any time we want. To store a new value in the space of memory reserved for a variable, we must implement the same syntax used for initialization.

```
var mynumber: Int = 5
mynumber = 87
```

Listing 2-5: *Assigning a new value to a variable*

The process of storing a value in a variable is called *assignment*. In these terms, we can say that in the example of Listing 2-5 we "initialize the variable **mynumber** with the number 5 and then assign the value 87 to it". The value 87 replaces the value 5 in memory. After that second statement is executed, every time we read the **mynumber** variable from other statements in the code it will return the value 87 (unless another value is assigned to the variable later).

 IMPORTANT: Once a variable is declared, the values stored in that variable must be of the same data type. If we declare a variable of type **Int**, we cannot store floating-point values in it later (e.g., 14.129).

Of course, we can create all the variables we want and of the data type we need.

```
var mynumber: Int = 5
var myfavorite: Float = 14.129
```

Listing 2-6: Declaring variables of different data types

The first statement in Listing 2-6 declares an integer variable and initializes it with the value 5. The second statement does the same but for a floating-point variable. When the data type of a value is easy to identify, Swift can infer it and the syntax may be simplified, as shown next.

```
var mynumber = 5
var myfavorite = 14.129
```

Listing 2-7: Declaring variables without specifying the data type

Swift infers the variable's data type from the value we are trying to assign to it. In this last example, the value 5 is clearly an integer and the value 14.129 is clearly a floating-point value, so Swift creates the variable **mynumber** of type **Int** and the variable **myfavorite** of type **Double** (it selects the most comprehensive type).

 IMPORTANT: Xcode offers a simple tool you can use to see the data type assigned to a variable and get additional information. All you need to do is click on the name of the variable while holding down the Option key. This opens a popup window with the full declaration of the variable, including its data type, and any information we may need to identify the code's functionality. As we will see later, this not only applies to variables but also to instructions, including properties and methods.

An important feature of variables is that the value of one may be assigned to another.

```
var mynumber = 5
var myfavorite = mynumber
```

Listing 2-8: Assigning variables to variables

The second statement in Listing 2-8 reads the value of the **mynumber** variable and assigns it to the **myfavorite** variable. The type of **myfavorite** is inferred to be **Int** (the same of **mynumber**). After this code is executed, we have two integer variables, each with its own space in memory containing the value 5.

Basic Arithmetic Operators

Storing values in memory is what variables allow us to do, but those values do not have to be declared explicitly, they can also be the result of arithmetic operations. Swift supports the operations: + (addition), − (subtraction), * (multiplication), / (division) and % (remainder).

```
var mynumber = 5 + 10   // 15
```

Listing 2-9: Assigning the result of an operation to a variable

When the system reads the statement in Listing 2-9, it adds 10 to 5 and assigns the result to **mynumber** (15).

 IMPORTANT: The text added at the end of the statement in Listing 2-9 is a comment that we used to show the value produced by the statement. Comments are ignored by the compiler but useful for programmers to remember vital information. They are introduced after the characters **//** (e.g., **//** `comment`) or in between the characters **/* */** (e.g., **/*** `comment` ***/**). You can write the characters yourself or use Xcode's shortcut by selecting the lines of code you want to turn into a comment and press the keys Command and /.

Of course, we can perform not only addition but any operation we want.

```
var mynumber = 2 * 25   // 50
var anothernumber = 8 - 40 * 2   // -72
var myfraction = 5.0 / 2.0   // 2.5
```

Listing 2-10: Performing operations in variables of different type

The first two statements in Listing 2-10 are easy to read. They perform arithmetic operations over integer numbers that produce an integer value, so the variables **mynumber** and **anothernumber** will be of type **Int**. A problem arises when we work with operations that may produce floating-point numbers. That is why in the third statement we specifically declared the values as floating-point numbers by adding the fractional part (**.0**). This forces Swift to infer the variable's type as **Double** and produce a result of that type.

When the compiler finds an operation with two or more numbers and has to infer the data type of the result, it converts the number of the less comprehensive type to the most comprehensive type. For example, when we declare an **Int** and a **Double** in the same operation (e.g., 5 + 2.0), the **Int** value is converted and processed as **Double**, and therefore the result will also be **Double**.

```
var myfraction1 = 5.0 / 2.0   // 2.5
var myfraction2 = 5 / 2.0   // 2.5
var myfraction3 = 5 / 2   // 2
```

Listing 2-11: Inferring the data type from an operation

This example declares and initializes three variables. In the first statement both numbers were declared as floating-point values, so the compiler infers a **Double** and creates the **myfraction1** variable of that type. In the second statement, we have an integer value and a floating-point value. Because of the floating-point value, the compiler interprets the integer (5) as a **Double** (5.0) and creates the **myfraction2** variable of type **Double**. But in the last statement there is no clear floating-point value. Both numbers were declared as integers (with no fractional part). In this case, the compiler does not know what we want to do, so it interprets both numbers as integers and creates the **myfraction3** variable of type **Int**. When an operation produces a result that is expected to be an integer, any fractional part is discarded. In this example, the system gets rid of the decimal 5 from the result and only assigns the integer 2 to the variable. If we don't want to lose the fractional part, we must avoid inference and declare the data type explicitly as **Float** or **Double**.

Dividing integer numbers is pointless most of the time, except in some circumstances when we need to know the remainder. The remainder is the amount left over by a division between two numbers and it is calculated using the **%** symbol.

```
var remainder1 = 11 % 3   // 2
var remainder2 = 20 % 8   // 4
var remainder3 = 5 % 2   // 1
```

Listing 2-12: Calculating the remainder

Each statement in Listing 2-12 calculates the remainder of dividing the first number by the second number and assigns the result to the variable. For instance, the first statement produces the remainder 2. The system divides 11 by 3 and finds a quotient of 3. Then, to get the remainder, it calculates 11 minus the multiplication of 3 times the quotient (`11 - (3 * 3) = 2`).

The second statement produces a remainder of 4 and the third statement produces a remainder of 1. This last statement is particularly useful because it allows us to determine whether a value is odd or even. When we calculate the reminder of an integer divided by 2, we get a result according to its parity. If the number is even, the remainder is 0, and if the number is odd, the remainder is 1 (or -1 for negative values).

Performing arithmetic operations becomes useful when instead of numbers we use variables.

```
var mynumber = 5
var total = mynumber + 10   // 15
```

Listing 2-13: Adding numbers to variables

This example declares the **mynumber** variable and initializes it with the value 5. In the next statement, the **total** variable is declared and initialized with the result of the addition of the current value of **mynumber** plus 10 (5 + 10).

In Listing 2-13, we used a new variable to store the result of the operation, but when the old value is not important anymore, we can store the result back into the same variable.

```
var mynumber = 5
mynumber = mynumber + 10   // 15
```

Listing 2-14: Performing operations on the variable's current value

In this example, the current value of **mynumber** is added to 10 and the result is assigned to the same variable. After the execution of the second statement, the value of **mynumber** is 15.

Working with values previously stored in a variable allows our program to evolve and adapt to new circumstances. For instance, we could add 1 to the current value of a variable and store the result in the same variable to create a counter. Every time the statement is executed, the value of the variable is incremented by one unit. Recurrent increments and decrements of the value of a variable are very important in computer programming. Because of this, Swift supports two operators that were specifically designed for this purpose.

- **+=** is a shorthand for **variable = variable + number**, where **number** is the value we want to add to the variable's current value.

- **-=** is a shorthand for **variable = variable - number**, where **number** is the value we want to subtract from the variable's current value.

With these operators, we can easily add or subtract a value to the current value of the variable and assign the result back to the same variable.

```
var mynumber = 5
mynumber += 4   // 9
```

Listing 2-15: Modifying the value of a variable using incremental operators

The process generated by the code in Listing 2-15 is straightforward. After the value 5 is assigned to the **mynumber** variable, the system reads the second statement, gets the current value of the variable, adds 4 to that value, and stores the result back to **mynumber** (9).

 IMPORTANT: Swift also offers Overflow operators (**&+**, **&-**, **&***, **&/** and **&%**). These operators are useful when we think that an operation could produce a result that goes over the limit the data type can handle. For more information, visit our website and follow the links for this chapter.

Basic Constants

As we already mentioned, the memory of a computer is a sequence of switches. There are millions and millions of switches, one after another, with no clear delimitations. To be able to know where the space occupied by a variable starts and ends, the system uses addresses. These addresses are just consecutive numbers that correspond to each Byte of memory (8 bits). For example, if one Byte is at the address 000000, the next Byte will be at the address 000001, the next one at 000002, and so on. If we declare a variable of 4 Bytes, the system reserves the four consecutive Bytes and remembers where they are so as not to overwrite them with the value of another variable. The task is easy when working with primitive data types because their sizes are always the same, but the size of variables of more complex or custom data types depends on the values we assign to them. For example, the space in memory required to store the text "Hello" is smaller than the space required for the text "Hello World". Managing the memory for data of inconsistent sizes takes time and consumes more resources than working with fixed sizes. This is one of the reasons why Swift includes the concept of constants.

Constants are the same as variables, but their values cannot change. Once a constant is declared and initialized, we cannot change its value. Therefore, constants provide a secure way to store a value and help the system to manage memory. To declare them, we must apply the same syntax used for a variable but replace the **var** keyword by the **let** keyword.

```
let mynumber = 5
```

Listing 2-16: *Declaring and initializing a constant*

All the rules for variables also apply to constants; with the exception that we cannot assign a new value after the constant was already initialized. The **mynumber** constant declared in Listing 2-16 will always have the value 5.

 IMPORTANT: When to use constants or variables depends on your application. As guidance, you can follow what Apple recommends: if a stored value in your code is not going to change, always declare it as a constant with the **let** keyword. Use variables only for storing values that need to be able to change.

Basic 2.3 Swift Data Types

Besides primitive data types, Swift defines additional data types to allow us to work not only with numbers but also more complex values such as logical values (true or false), characters, or text.

Basic Characters

Because of their nature, computers cannot store decimal numbers, characters, or text. As we have seen in the previous section, the computer memory is only capable of storing 1s and 0s (switches on and off), but they can work with more complex values using tables that contain the information necessary to represent those values (numbers, letters, symbols, etc.). What the system stores in memory is not the character but the value corresponding to the index of the character on the table. For example, if we use the letter A, the value stored in memory will be the decimal number 65 (in its binary representation) because that's the position of the letter A on the table used by Swift to define these characters.

There are several standard tables of characters available. Swift is compliant with a table called *Unicode*. This is a comprehensive table that includes every character from almost any language in the world, and special characters, such as emojis. Due to its broad range, the space in memory required to store a single character varies from one character to another. For this reason, Swift provides a data type called **Character** to store these values.

```
var myletter: Character = "A"
```

Listing 2-17: Declaring and initializing a `Character` *variable*

A character is declared using the **Character** data type and initialized with the value between double quotes. In Listing 2-17, we declare a variable called **myletter** with the value A.

In addition to the characters on the keyboard, Unicode allows us to store emojis and symbols. Xcode offers a handy tool to select the graphics we want. By pressing the combination of keys Control + Command + Space, we can open a popup window and select a graphic with a click of the mouse.

Figure 2-11: Emojis and symbols

(Basic) Strings

Individual characters are barely used in computer programming. Instead, we usually store strings of characters. The **String** type was created for this purpose.

```
let mytext: String = "My name is John"
```

Listing 2-18: Declaring and initializing a `String` *variable*

A string is a sequence of **Character** values. It is declared with the **String** type and the value between double quotes. These types of variables are very flexible; we may replace a string by another one of different length, concatenate two or more, or even modify parts of it. Concatenation is a common operation, and it is done with the **+** and **+=** operators.

```
var mytext = "My name is "
mytext = mytext + "John"   // "My name is John"
```

Listing 2-19: Concatenating strings

In Listing 2-19, the **mytext** variable is created with the value "My name is " and then the string "John" is added at the end of the current value to get the string "My name is John". The **+=** operator works in a similar way, and we can also combine them to get the string we want.

```
let name = "John"
var mytext = "My name is "
mytext += name   // "My name is John"
```

Listing 2-20: Concatenating strings with the + and += operators

With the + and += operators we can concatenate strings with strings. To concatenate strings with characters and numbers we must implement a procedure called *String Interpolation*. The variables must be included inside the string between parentheses and prefixed by a backslash.

```
let age = 44
let mytext = "I am \(age) years old"  // "I am 44 years old"
```

Listing 2-21: Including variables in strings

In this code, we read the **age** variable and add its current value to the string. The string "I am 44 years old" is then assigned to **mytext**. Using this tool, we can insert any value we want inside a string, including **Character** and **String** values, numbers, and arithmetic operations. In the following example, the value of **age** is multiplied by 12 and the result is included in the string.

```
let age = 44
let mytext = "I am \(age * 12) months old"  // "I am 528 months old"
```

Listing 2-22: Performing operations inside strings

Sometimes we need to include special characters in the string, like backslashes or quotes. Swift offers two ways to achieve this purpose. We can prefix the special character with another backslash, or enclose the entire string in hash characters, as shown next.

```
let text1 = "This is \"my\" age"  // "This is "my" age"
let text2 = #"This is "my" age"#  // "This is "my" age"
```

Listing 2-23: Including special characters in a string

Another important feature of strings is the possibility to create multiple lines of text. Again, Swift offers two alternatives. We can include the special characters \n where we want to generate a new line or we can use triple quotes ("""") and the compiler will consider the original format of the text and automatically insert the \n characters when required, as shown next.

```
let twolines = "This is the first line\nThis is the second line"
let multiline = """
This is the first line
This is the second line
"""
```

Listing 2-24: Generating multiple lines of text

The **twolines** constant defined in this example includes the \n characters between sentences, which asks the compiler to generate two lines of text. If we press the Show Result button on the Results Side Bar, Xcode introduces a box below the code showing the two lines of text, one on top of the other. Something similar happens with the value of the **multiline** constant, although in this case the """ characters tell the compiler that it must add the \n characters at the end of each line for us.

(Basic) **Booleans**

Boolean variables are a type of variables that can only store two values: **true** or **false**. These variables are particularly useful when we want to execute an instruction or a set of instructions only if a condition is met. To declare a Boolean variable, we can specify the data type as **Bool** or let Swift infer it from the value, as in the following example.

```
var valid = true
```

Listing 2-25: Declaring a Boolean variable

The purpose of these variables is to simplify the process of identifying a condition. By using a Boolean variable instead of an integer, for example, we just need to check whether the value is equal to **true** or **false** to verify the condition. We will see some practical examples later.

(Basic) **Optionals**

As mentioned at the beginning of this chapter, after a variable is declared, we must provide its initial value. We cannot use a variable if it was not initialized. This means that a variable has a valid value all the time. But this is not always possible. Sometimes we do not have an initial value to assign to the variable during development or need to indicate the absence of a value because the current one becomes invalid. For these situations, Swift defines a modifier that turns every data type into an optional type. This means that the variable marked as optional may have a value or be empty. To declare an optional, we add a question mark after the type's name.

```
var mynumber: Int?
```

Listing 2-26: Declaring an optional variable of type Int

New values are assigned to optionals as we do with normal variables.

```
var mynumber: Int?
mynumber = 5
```

Listing 2-27: Assigning new values to optional variables

The empty state is represented by the keyword **nil**. Therefore, when an optional variable is declared but not initialized, Swift assigns the **nil** keyword to the variable to indicate the absence of a value. Thus, if later we need to empty the variable, we can assign the keyword **nil** to it.

```
var mynumber: Int?
mynumber = 5
mynumber = nil
```

Listing 2-28: Using nil *to empty an optional variable*

This example declares an optional integer, assigns the value 5 to it, and then declares the variable as empty with the keyword **nil**. Although optionals seem to work like regular variables, they do not expose their values. To read the value of an optional, we must unwrap it by adding an exclamation mark at the end of the name.

```
var mynumber: Int?
mynumber = 5
var total = mynumber! * 10   // 50
```

Listing 2-29: Unwrapping an optional variable

The last statement in Listing 2-29 unwraps **mynumber** to get its value, multiplies this value by 10, and assigns the result to the **total** variable. This is only necessary when we need to use the value. If we just want to assign an optional to another optional, the process is as always.

```
var mynumber: Int?
mynumber = 5
var total = mynumber
```

Listing 2-30: Assigning an optional to another optional

In this example, the system infers the type of the **total** variable to be an optional of type **Int** and assigns the value of **mynumber** to it. If we want to read the value of **total** later, we must unwrap it as we did with **mynumber** before.

 IMPORTANT: Before unwrapping an optional, we need to make sure it contains a value (it is not equal to **nil**). If we try to unwrap an empty optional, the app will return an error and crash. Later in this chapter we will learn how to use conditional statements to check this condition.

There are times when we know that an optional will always have a value, but we do not know what the initial value is. For example, we could have a variable that receives a value from the system as soon as the application is executed. When the variable is declared in our code, we do not have a value to assign to it, but we know that the variable will have a value as soon as the user launches the app. For these situations, Swift includes *Implicitly Unwrapped Optionals*. These are optional variables declared with the exclamation mark instead of the question mark. The system treats these variables as optionals until we use them in a statement, as in the following example.

```
var mynumber: Int!
mynumber = 5
var total = mynumber * 10   // 50
```

Listing 2-31: Declaring Implicitly Unwrapped Optionals

In this code, the **mynumber** variable was declared as an implicitly unwrapped optional and it was later initialized with the value 5. Notice that it was not necessary to write the exclamation mark when reading its value anymore. The system unwraps the **mynumber** variable automatically to uses its value in the multiplication (this is only available for implicitly unwrapped optionals).

(Basic) **Tuples**

A tuple is a type of variable that contains a group of one or more values of equal or different data type. It is useful when we need to store values that are somehow related to each other. Tuples are declared with their values and data types in parentheses and separated by commas.

```
var myname: (String, String) = ("John", "Doe")
```

Listing 2-32: Declaring a tuple with two values

In this example, the **myname** variable is declared to be a tuple that contains two **String** values. The values of this tuple are of the same type, but we can use any combination of values we want.

```
var myname = ("John", "Doe", 44)
```

Listing 2-33: Declaring a tuple with values of different type

To be able to read the values later, an index is automatically assigned to each of the values of the tuple. The first value will be at index 0, the second at index 1, and so on. Using the corresponding index and dot notation we can access the value we want to read.

Chapter 2 - Introduction to Swift

```
var myname = ("John", "Doe", 44)
var mytext = "\(myname.0) is \(myname.2) years old" // "John is 44 years
old"
```

Listing 2-34: Reading the values of a tuple

In Listing 2-34, we read the values of the **myname** tuple at index 0 and 2 to include them in a new string and assign the string to **mytext**. The same syntax may be used to modify a value.

```
var myname = ("John", "Doe", 44)
myname.0 = "George"
var mytext = "\(myname.0) is \(myname.2) years old"
```

Listing 2-35: Modifying the value of a tuple

The second statement in Listing 2-35 assigns a new string to the first value of the tuple. The data type of the new value must be of the same as the old one or we will get an error. After the code is executed, the value of **mytext** is "George is 44 years old".

Indexes are a quick way to access the values of a tuple, but they do not help us remember what the values represent. To identify the values in a tuple, we can assign a name to each one of them. The name must be declared before the value and separated with a colon, as shown next.

```
var myname = (name: "John", surname: "Doe", age: 44)
var mytext = "\(myname.name) is \(myname.age) years old"
```

Listing 2-36: Declaring names for the values of a tuple

Swift also provides a way to copy the values of the tuple into independent variables.

```
var myname = ("John", "Doe", 44)
var (name, surname, age) = myname
var mytext = "\(name) \(surname) is \(age) years old"
```

Listing 2-37: Creating multiple variables from the values of a tuple

The names of the variables are declared between parentheses. The values are assigned to the variables in the same order they are in the tuple. If only some of the values are required, the rest may be ignored with an underscore, as shown next.

```
var myname = ("John", "Doe", 44)
var (name, _, age) = myname
var mytext = "\(name) is \(age) years old"
```

Listing 2-38: Ignoring some of the values of a tuple

Only the variables **name** and **age** are created in this last example. (Notice the underscore in the place of the second variable.) The string assigned to **mytext** is "John is 44 years old".

(Basic) 2.4 Conditionals and Loops

Up to this point, we have written the instructions in sequence, one after the other. In this programming pattern, the system executes each statement once. It starts with the one at the top and goes on until it reaches the end of the list. The purpose of Conditionals and Loops is to break this sequential flow. Conditionals allow us to execute one or more instructions only when a condition is met, and Loops execute a group of instructions repeatedly.

If and Else

A simple but handful conditional statement available in Swift is **if**. With **if** we can check a condition and execute a group of instructions only when the condition is true. The instructions that are going to be executed are declared after the condition between braces.

```
var age = 19
var message = "John is old"
if age < 21 {
    message = "John is young"
}
```

Listing 2-39: Comparing two values with `if`

Two variables are declared in this code. The **age** variable contains the value we want to check, and the **message** variable is the one we are going to modify depending on the state of the condition. The **if** statement compares the value of **age** with the number 21 using the character < (less than). This comparison returns the state of the condition (true or false). If the condition is true (the value of **age** is less than 21), the instruction between braces is executed, assigning a new value to the **message** variable, otherwise, the instruction is ignored and the execution continues with the instruction after the braces. In this case, the value of **age** is less than 21 and therefore the string "John is young" is assigned to the **message** variable.

 IMPORTANT: One or more lines of code enclosed in braces is usually called *block*. As illustrated by the example in Listing 2-39, the instructions inside a block are displaced to the right. The whitespace on the left is used to help us differentiate the statements in the block from the rest of the statements. This whitespace is automatically generated for you by Xcode, but you can add it yourself, when necessary, by pressing the Tab key on your keyboard.

The < symbol we used in the last example to compare values is part of a group of operators called *Comparison Operators*. The following is the list of comparison operators available in Swift.

- **==** checks whether the value on the left is equal to the value on the right.
- **!=** checks whether the value on the left is different from the value on the right.
- **>** checks whether the value on the left is greater than the value on the right.
- **<** checks whether the value on the left is less than the value on the right.
- **>=** checks whether the value on the left is greater or equal than the value on the right.
- **<=** checks whether the value on the left is less or equal than the value on the right.

All these operators are applied as we did with the < operator in the previous example. For instance, the following code modifies the value of **message** when the value of **age** is less or equal than 21.

```
var age = 21
var message = "John is old"
if age <= 21 {
    message = "John is young"
}
```

Listing 2-40: Comparing two values with the <= operator

When only two results are required, we may define the condition using a Boolean. These values do not need to be compared with the expected value; they already return true or false.

Chapter 2 - Introduction to Swift

```
var underage = true
var message = "John is allowed"
if underage {
   message = "John is underage"
}
```

Listing 2-41: Conditions with Boolean values

This code checks whether the value of the **underage** variable is **true** or **false**. If it is **true** (which means the condition is true), a new string is assigned to the **message** variable.

If what we want is to execute the statements when the value is **false**, Swift offers a logical operator to toggle the condition. All we need to do is to precede the condition with an exclamation mark.

```
var underage = true
var message = "John is underage"
if !underage {
   message = "John is allowed"
}
```

Listing 2-42: Using logical operators

The original value of the **underage** variable in the code of Listing 2-42 is **true**, so when the **if** statement toggles the condition, the resulting condition is false and therefore the value of the **message** variable is not modified.

The exclamation mark is part of a group of logical operators provided by Swift.

- **!** (logical NOT) toggles the state of the condition. If the condition is true, it returns false, and vice versa.
- **&&** (logical AND) checks two conditions and returns true if both are true.
- **||** (logical OR) checks two conditions and returns true if one or both are true.

Logical operators work with any kind of conditions, not only Booleans. To work with complex conditions, it is recommended to enclose the condition between parentheses.

```
var smart = true
var age = 19
var message = "John is underage or dumb"

if (age < 21) && smart {
   message = "John is allowed"
}
```

Listing 2-43: Using logical operators to check multiple conditions

The **if** statement in Listing 2-43 compares the value of the **age** variable with 21 and checks the value of the **smart** variable. If **age** is less than 21 and **smart** is **true**, then the overall condition is true, and a new string is assigned to **message**. If any of the individual conditions is false, then the overall condition is false, and the block of instructions is not executed. In this case, both conditions are true and therefore the "John is allowed" string is assigned to **message**.

 IMPORTANT: Using **&&** (AND) and **||** (OR) you can create a logical sequence of multiple conditions. The system evaluates one condition at a time from left to right and compares the results. If you want to make sure that the expressions are evaluated in the correct order, you can declare them within parentheses, as in **(true && false) || true**. The expression within the parentheses is evaluated first, and the result is then evaluated against the rest of the expression.

Although we can use comparison operators and logical operators in most of the data types available, optionals are slightly different. Their values are wrapped, so we cannot compare them with other values, or check their state as we do with Booleans. Optionals must be first compared against the **nil** keyword and then unwrapped before working with their values.

```
var count = 0
var myoptional: Int? = 5
if myoptional != nil {
   let uvalue = myoptional!
   count = count + uvalue   // 5
}
```

Listing 2-44: Checking whether an optional contains a value or not

This example introduces the process we must follow to read the value of an optional variable. The optional is first compared against **nil**. If it is different from **nil** (which means it contains a value), we unwrap the optional inside the block of statements using an exclamation mark, assign its value to a constant, and use the constant to perform any operation necessary.

We must always make sure that an optional has a value before unwrapping it. For this reason, Swift introduces a convenient syntax that checks the optional and unwraps its value at the same time. It is called *Optional Binding*, and we can use it in an **if** statement, as shown next.

```
var count = 0
var myoptional: Int? = 5
if let uvalue = myoptional {
   count = count + uvalue   // 5
}
```

Listing 2-45: Using Optional Binding to unwrap an optional variable

This code is cleaner and easy to read. The optional is unwrapped as part of the condition. If it is different from **nil**, its value is assigned to the **uvalue** constant and the statements in the block are executed, otherwise, the statements inside the block are ignored.

As we will see later, variables and constants declared inside a block are only available to the code in the block. This also means that variables and constants declared in different blocks are independent (their values are stored in different locations in memory). An interesting consequence of this is that we can declare the constant for the Optional Binding with the same name as the variable, and they will be considered by Swift to be different.

```
var count = 0
var myoptional: Int? = 5
if let myoptional = myoptional {
   count = count + myoptional   // 5
}
```

Listing 2-46: Using the same name to unwrap a value

The **myoptional** constant declared by the **if** statement is only accessible by the code inside the block and therefore is different from the **myoptional** variable declared outside the block. The code can be simplified even more by only declaring the name of the constant, as shown next.

```
var count = 0
var myoptional: Int? = 5
if let myoptional {
   count = count + myoptional   // 5
}
```

Listing 2-47: Unwrapping an optional value of the same name

In this example, Swift looks for an optional variable called **myoptional**, unwraps the value, and assigns it to the constant. The result is the same as before, but the code has been simplified.

 IMPORTANT: The constants and variables declared inside and outside blocks have different scopes, which means they are independent and their values are stored in different locations in memory, even when they share the same name. We will learn more about the scope of variables in Chapter 3.

If we want to unwrap several optionals at the same time using Optional Binding, we must declare the expressions separated by comma. This also applies when we want to check for other conditions in the same statement. For instance, the following example unwraps an optional and only executes the code between braces if its value is equal to 5.

```
var count = 0
var myoptional: Int? = 5
if let uvalue = myoptional, uvalue == 5 {
    count = count + uvalue   // 5
}
```

Listing 2-48: Checking multiple conditions with Optional Binding

The **if** statement in Listing 2-48 unwraps the optional first and, if there is a value, compares it with the number 5. The statements in the block are executed only if both conditions are true (the **myoptional** variable contains a value and the value is equal to 5).

Sometimes, a group of instructions must be executed for each state of the condition. For this purpose, Swift includes the **if else** statement. The instructions are declared in two blocks. The first block is executed when the condition is true, and the second block when the condition is false.

```
var mynumber = 6
if mynumber % 2 == 0 {
    mynumber = mynumber + 2   // 8
} else {
    mynumber = mynumber + 1
}
```

Listing 2-49: Using if else *to respond to both states of the condition*

This is a simple example that checks whether a value is odd or even using the remainder operator. The condition gets the remainder of the division between the value of the **mynumber** variable and 2 and compares the result against 0. If true, it means that the value of **mynumber** is even, so the first block is executed. If the result is different from 0, it means that the value is odd and the condition is false, so the block corresponding to the **else** instruction is executed instead.

The statements **if** and **else** may be concatenated to check as many conditions as we need. In the following example, the first condition checks whether **age** is less than 21. If not true, the second condition checks whether **age** is over 21. And if not true, the final **else** block is executed.

```
var age = 19
var message = "The customer is "
if age < 21 {
    message += "underage"   // "The customer is underage"
} else if age > 21 {
    message += "allowed"
} else {
    message += "21 years old"
}
```

Listing 2-50: Concatenating if else *instructions*

If all we need from an **if** statement is to assign a value to a variable depending on a condition, we can use a shortcut provided by Swift called *Ternary Operator*. A ternary operator is a construction composed by the condition and the two values we want to return for each state separated with the characters **?** and **:**, as in the following example.

```
var age = 19
var message = age < 21 ? "Underage" : "Allowed"   // "Underage"
```

Listing 2-51: Implementing a ternary operator

The first value is returned if the condition is true, and the second value is returned if the condition is false. The advantage of using a ternary operator is that it reduces the size of the code significantly, but the result is the same as using an **if else** statement. In our example, the string "Underage" is assigned to the variable **message** because the value of **age** is less than 21.

Ternary operators can also be implemented to unwrap optionals. For instance, we can check whether an optional variable contains a value and assign it to another variable or give the variable a default value if the optional is empty.

```
var age: Int? = 19
var realage = age != nil ? age! : 0   // 19
```

Listing 2-52: Unwrapping an optional with a ternary operator

This code defines an optional variable called **age** with the value 19. Next, we unwrap it with a ternary operator and assign its value to a new variable called **realage**. If the optional contains a value, its value is assigned to the variable, otherwise, the value 0 is assigned instead.

Assigning values by default when the optional is empty is very common. To simplify our work, Swift offers the nil-coalescing operator, which is represented by the characters **??**. This operator works like the ternary operator implemented in Listing 2-52; it unwraps the optional and returns its value or returns another value if the optional is empty. In the following example, we create an empty optional called **age** and use the nil-coalescing operator to assign its value to the **maxage** variable or the value 100 if the optional is empty.

```
var age: Int?
var maxage = age ?? 100   // 100
```

Listing 2-53: Unwrapping an optional with the nil-coalescing operator

(Basic) **Switch**

We can keep adding **if** and **else** statements to check as many conditions as we need, but this pattern can make the code impossible to read and maintain. When several conditions must be verified, it is better to use the **switch** instruction instead. This instruction compares a value with a list of values and executes the statements corresponding to the value that matches. The possible matches are listed between braces using the **case** keyword, as in the following example.

```
var age = 19
var message = ""

switch age {
   case 13:
      message = "Happy Bar Mitzvah!"
   case 16:
      message = "Sweet Sixteen!"
```

```
   case 21:
      message = "Welcome to Adulthood!"
   default:
      message = "Happy Birthday!"   // "Happy Birthday!"
}
```

Listing 2-54: Checking conditions with `switch`

The cases must be exhaustive. If we do not include a **case** statement for every possible value, we must add a **default** statement at the end that is executed when no match is found. In Listing 2-54, we compare the value of the **age** variable with a small set of values corresponding to special dates. If no **case** matches the value of the variable, the **default** statement is executed and the string "Happy Birthday!" is assigned to **message**.

When we need to execute the same set of instructions for more than one value, we can declare the values separated by comma.

```
var age = 6
var message = "You go to "
switch age {
   case 2, 3, 4:
      message += "Day Care"
   case 5, 6, 7, 8, 9, 10, 11:
      message += "Elementary School"   // "You go to Elementary School"
   case 12, 13, 14, 15, 16, 17:
      message += "High School"
   case 18, 19, 20, 21:
      message += "College"
   default:
      message += "Work"
}
```

Listing 2-55: Checking multiple conditions per case

The **switch** statement can also work with more complex data types, such as strings and tuples. In the case of tuples, **switch** provides additional options to build complex matching patterns. For example, the following code checks the second value of a tuple to determine the difference in age.

```
var message = ""
var ages = (10, 30)
switch ages {
   case (10, 20):
      message = "Too close"
   case (10, 30):
      message = "The right age"   // "The right age"
   case (10, 40):
      message = "Too far"
   default:
      message = "Way too far"
}
```

Listing 2-56: Matching a tuple in a `switch` *statement*

This example always compares the first value of the tuple against 10 but checks different matches for the second value. If a value does not matter, we can use an underscore to ignore it.

```
var message = ""
var ages = (10, 30)
```

```
switch ages {
   case (_, 20):
      message = "Too close"
   case (_, 30):
      message = "The right age"   // "The right age"
   case (_, 40):
      message = "Too far"
   default:
      message = "Way too far"
}
```

Listing 2-57: Matching only the second value of a tuple

An alternative offered by the **switch** statement to create complex matching patterns is to capture a value in a constant to be able to access it from the instructions of the **case**.

```
var message = ""
var ages = (10, 20)

switch ages {
   case (let x, 20):
      message = "Too close to \(x)"   // "Too close to 10"
   case (_, 30):
      message = "The right age"
   case (let x, 40):
      message = "Too far to \(x)"
   default:
      message = "Way too far"
}
```

Listing 2-58: Capturing values with constants

In this example, when the **switch** statement checks the first and third cases, it creates a constant called **x** and assigns the first value to it, so we can access and use the value from the statements inside the **case**. (In this example, we just add the value to a string.)

There is an even more complex matching pattern that involves the use of a clause called **where**. This clause allows us to check additional conditions. In the following example, we capture the values of the tuple with another tuple and compare them against each other.

```
var message = ""
var ages = (10, 20)

switch ages {
   case let (x, y) where x > y:
      message = "Too young"
   case let (x, y) where x == y:
      message = "The same age"
   case let (x, y) where x < y:
      message = "Too old"   // "Too old"
   default:
      message = "Not found"
}
```

Listing 2-59: Comparing values with where

Every time the **switch** statement tries to match a **case** in this example, it creates a tuple and assigns the values of **ages** to it. The **where** clause compares the values and when the condition is true, it executes the statements inside the **case**.

Chapter 2 - Introduction to Swift

While and Repeat While

The conditionals studied so far execute the statements only once. Sometimes the program requires executing a block of instructions several times until a condition is satisfied. An alternative offered by Swift to create these loops is the **while** statement (and its sibling **repeat while**).

The **while** statement checks a condition and executes the statements in the block while the condition is true. The following example initializes a variable with the value 0 and then checks its value in a **while** statement. If the value of the variable is less than 5, the statements inside the block are executed. After this, the condition is checked again. The loop keeps running until the condition is false (the value of the **counter** variable is equal or greater than 5).

```
var counter = 0
while counter < 5 {
    counter += 1
}
```

***Listing 2-60:** Using* while *to create a loop*

If the first time the condition is checked it returns false, the statements in the block are never executed. If we want to execute the statements at least once, we must use **repeat while**.

```
var counter = 10
repeat {
    counter += 1
} while counter < 5
```

***Listing 2-61:** Using* repeat while *to create a loop*

In this case, the initial value of the **counter** variable is declared as 10. This is greater than 5, but since we are using the **repeat while** instruction, the statements in the block are executed before the condition is checked, so the final value of **counter** will be 11. (Its value is incremented once and then the condition returns false, ending the loop.)

For In

The purpose of the **for in** loop is to iterate over collections of values, like the strings of characters studied before. During the execution of a **for in** loop, the system reads the elements of the collection one by one in sequential order and assigns their values to a constant that can be used by the statements inside the block. In this case, the condition that must be satisfied for the loop to be over is reaching the end of the collection.

The syntax of a **for in** loop is **for constant in collection {}**, where **constant** is the name of the constant that we are going to use to capture the value of each element in the collection, and **collection** is the name of the collection of values that we want to iterate over.

```
var mytext = "Hello"
var message = ""

for letter in mytext {
    message += message != "" ? "-" : ""
    message += "\(letter)"
}
```

***Listing 2-62:** Using* for in *to iterate over the characters of a string*

The code in Listing 2-62 defines two **String** variables: **mytext** with the text "Hello" and **message** with an empty string. Next, we use a **for in** loop to iterate over the characters of the string in **mytext** and add each character to the current value of **message**. In each cycle of the loop, the **for in** instruction takes one character from the value of **mytext**, assigns it to the **letter** constant, and executes the statements in the block. The first statement uses a ternary operator to check whether the value of **message** is an empty string. If not, it adds the – character at the end of it, otherwise, it adds an empty string. Finally, the second statement adds the current value of **letter** to the end of **message**.

The code works as follows: in the first cycle, the character "H" is assigned to the **letter** constant. Because at this moment the **message** string is empty, nothing is added by the first statement in the block. Then, the second statement adds the value of **letter** to the current value of **message** and the next cycle is executed. In this new cycle, the character "e" is assigned to the **letter** constant. This time, the **message** string already contains the letter "H", so the character "-" is added at the end by the first statement ("H-"), and then the second statement adds the letter "e" at the end of this new string ("H-e"). This process continues until all the characters in the **mytext** variable are processed. The final value of **message** is "H-e-l-l-o".

When the constant is not required inside the block, we can replace it with an underscore.

```
var mytext = "Hello"
var counter = 0

for _ in mytext {
   counter += 1
}
var message = "The string contains \(counter) letters"   // 5
```

Listing 2-63: Iterating over a string without reading the characters

In this example, we iterate over the value of **mytext** to count the number of characters in the string. The value of the **counter** variable is incremented by 1 in each cycle, giving a total of 5.

A **for in** instruction may include the **where** clause to perform the next cycle only when a condition is met. For instance, the following code checks the value of **letter** and only performs the cycle when the letter is not an L. In consequence, only the letters H, e, and o are counted.

```
var mytext = "Hello"
var counter = 0

for letter in mytext where letter != "l" {
   counter += 1
}
var message = "The string contains \(counter) letters"   // 3
```

Listing 2-64: Adding a condition to a loop

(Basic) Control Transfer Statements

Sometimes loops must be interrupted, independently of the state of the condition. Swift offers instructions to break the execution of loops and conditionals. The following are the most frequently used.

continue—This instruction interrupts the current cycle and moves to the next. The system ignores the rest of the statements in the block after the instruction is executed.

break—This instruction interrupts the loop. The rest of the statements in the block and any pending cycles are ignored after the instruction is executed.

The **continue** instruction is applied when we do not want to execute the rest of the statements in the block, but we want to keep the loop running. For instance, the following code counts the letters in a string but ignores the letters "l".

```
var mytext = "Hello"
var counter = 0
for letter in mytext {
   if letter == "l" {
      continue
   }
   counter += 1
}
var message = "The string contains \(counter) letters"   // 3
```

Listing 2-65: Jumping to the next cycle of the loop

The **if** statement inside the **for in** loop of Listing 2-65 compares the value of **letter** with the letter "l". If the characters match, the **continue** instruction is executed, the last statement inside the loop is ignored, and the loop moves on to the next character in **mytext**. In consequence, the code counts all the characters that are different from "l" (H, e, and o).

Unlike the **continue** instruction, the **break** instruction interrupts the loop completely, moving the execution of the program to the statements after the loop. The following example only counts the characters in the string that are placed before the first letter "l".

```
var mytext = "Hello"
var counter = 0
for letter in mytext {
   if letter == "l" {
      break
   }
   counter += 1
}
var message = "The string contains \(counter) letters"   // 2
```

Listing 2-66: Interrupting the loop

Again, the **if** statement of Listing 2-66 compares the value of **letter** with the character "l", but this time it executes the **break** instruction when a match is found. If the character currently processed by the loop is "l", the **break** instruction is executed, and the loop is over, no matter how many characters are left in the string. In consequence, only the characters located before the first letter "l" are considered (H and e).

The **break** instruction is also useful to cancel the execution of a **switch** statement. The problem with the **switch** statement in Swift is that the cases must be exhaustive, which means that every possible value must be contemplated. When this is not possible or necessary, we can use the **break** instruction to ignore the values that are not applicable. For example, we can declare the cases for the values we need and then break the execution in the **default** case for the rest of the values that we do not care about.

```
var age = 19
var message = ""
switch age {
   case 13:
      message = "Happy Bar Mitzvah!"
   case 16:
      message = "Sweet Sixteen!"
```

```
case 21:
   message = "Welcome to Adulthood!"
default:
   break
}
```

Listing 2-67: Ignoring values in a `switch` *statement*

After the execution of this code, the **message** variable is empty because there is no **case** that matches the value of the **age** variable and therefore the code in **default** is executed and the **break** instruction returns the control to the statements after the **switch**.

(Basic) **Guard**

The **guard** instruction is intended to prevent the execution of the code that follows the statement. For example, we can break the execution of a loop when a condition is satisfied, as we do with an **if else** statement.

```
var mytext = "Hello"
var counter = 0
for letter in mytext {
   guard letter != "l" else {
      break
   }
   counter += 1
}
var message = "The string contains \(counter) letters"   // 2
```

Listing 2-68: Interrupting a loop with `guard`

The **guard** instruction works along with the **else** instruction and therefore it is very similar to the **if else** statement, but the code is only executed when the condition is false. In the example of Listing 2-68, the **for in** loop reads the characters of the string in **mytext** one by one, as done before. If the characters are different from the letter "l", we increment the value of **counter** by 1, but when the value of **letter** is equal to "l", the condition of the **guard** instruction is false and therefore the **break** instruction is executed, interrupting the loop.

 IMPORTANT: The advantage of **guard** over the **if else** statement is that the variable or constant defined in the condition outlives the statement, and therefore we can read its value outside the **else** block. Although you can implement the **guard** instruction to break or continue a loop, the instruction was introduced to work along with the **return** instruction to interrupt the execution of a function. We will study the **return** instruction and functions next.

Chapter 3
Swift Paradigm

Basic **3.1 Programming Paradigms**

Programs wouldn't be very useful if we were only able to write them as a consecutive set of instructions. At first, this was the only way to write a program, but soon programming languages incorporated tools to allow programmers to group instructions together and execute them every time necessary. The way instructions are organized is called *paradigm*. Different paradigms are now available, with the most common being Object-Oriented Programming, or OOP. This paradigm emerges from the construction and integration of processing units called *objects*. Swift adopts OOP, but it is not focused as much on objects as other languages do. Instead, it implements other types of processing units called *structures* and *enumerations* along with blueprints called *protocols* to conform a new paradigm called *Protocol-Oriented Programming*. The Swift paradigm unifies objects, structures, and enumerations through protocols that define how these units behave and the type of functionality they provide.

Do It Yourself: The examples in this chapter were designed to be tested in Playground. You need to create a Playground file with a Blank template and then replace the code with the example you want to try.

Basic **3.2 Functions**

The processing units that define the Swift paradigm (objects, structures, and enumerations) are capable of encapsulating data along with functionality. The data is stored in the same variables studied before, but the functionality is provided by functions. Functions are blocks of code delimited by curly braces and identified by a name. The difference between functions and the block of codes used in loops and conditional statements is that there is no condition to satisfy; the statements inside a function are executed every time the function is called (executed). Functions are called by writing their names followed by parentheses. This call may be performed from anywhere in the code and every time necessary, which completely breaks the sequential processing of a program. Once a function is called, the execution of the program continues with the statements inside the function and only returns to the section of the code that called the function once the execution of the function is over.

Basic **Declaration of Functions**

Functions are declared with the `func` keyword followed by a name, parentheses, and the code enclosed in braces.

```
var mynumber = 5
func myfunction() {
    mynumber = mynumber * 2   // 10
}
myfunction()
```

Listing 3-1: Declaring and calling functions

The code in Listing 3-1 declares the `mynumber` variable, initializes it with the value 5, and then declares a function called `myfunction()`. The statements in a function are only processed when the function is called, so after the `myfunction()` function is declared, we call it with the

myfunction() instruction. When our function is called, it multiplies the current value of **mynumber** times 2 and assigns the result back to the variable. Once all the statements inside the function are processed, the execution continues from the statement after the call.

As we already mentioned, once the function is declared, we can call it any time necessary. For example, the following code runs a **while** loop that calls **myfunction()** a total of 5 times (the loop runs while **counter** is less than 5). Every time the function is executed, **mynumber**'s current value is multiplied by 2, getting a result of 160.

```
var mynumber = 5
var counter = 0
func myfunction() {
    mynumber = mynumber * 2   // 160
}
while counter < 5 {
    myfunction()
    counter += 1
}
```

Listing 3-2: Calling functions from a loop

The functions in these examples are modifying the value of an external variable (a variable that was not declared inside the function). Creating a function that works with values and variables that do not belong to the function itself can be dangerous; some variables may be modified by accident from other functions, the function may be called before the variables were even declared or initialized, or the variables that the function tries to modify may not be accessible by the function (functions have limited scope, as we will see later). To make sure that a function processes the right values, they must be sent to the function when it is called. The type of values the function can receive and the names they are going to take are specified within the function's parentheses separated by a comma. When the function is executed, these parameters are turned into constants that we can read inside the function to get their values.

```
func doubleValue(number: Int) {
    let total = number * 2
    let message = "Result: \(total)"   // "Result: 10"
}
doubleValue(number: 5)
```

Listing 3-3: Sending values to a function

In this example, we don't use external variables anymore. The value to be processed is sent to the function when it is called and received by the function's parameter. The parameters are declared within the function's parentheses with the same syntax used for constants and variables. We must write the name and the data type separated by a colon. In Listing 3-3, the function is declared with one parameter of type **Int** called **number**.

The call must include the name of the parameter and the value we want to send to the function. When the function of Listing 3-3 is called, the value between the parentheses of the call (5) is assigned to the **number** constant, the value of the constant is multiplied by 2, and finally the result is included in a string with string interpolation.

Of course, we can include as many parameters as we need. The following example multiplies two values and creates a string with the result.

```
func multiply(number1: Int, number2: Int) {
    let result = number1 * number2
    let message = "The result is \(result)"   // "The result is 80"
}
```

```
multiply(number1: 20, number2: 4)
```

Listing 3-4: Sending multiple values to a function

Functions may not only be called every time we need them, but also the values we provide to the function in the call may be different each time. This makes functions reusable.

```
func doubleValue(number: Int) {
   let total = number * 2
   let message = "Result: \(total)"
}
doubleValue(number: 5)    // "Result: 10"
doubleValue(number: 25)   // "Result: 50"
```

Listing 3-5: Sending different values to a function

The constants and variables declared inside a function, like **total** and **message**, are not accessible from other parts of the code. This means that a function can receive values, but the result produced by processing those values is trapped inside the function. To communicate the result of an operation to the rest of the code, functions can return a value using an instruction called **return**. The **return** instruction finishes the processing of the function, so we must declare it after all the required statements have been processed, as in the following example.

```
func doubleValue(number: Int) -> Int {
   let total = number * 2
   return total
}
let result = doubleValue(number: 25)
let message = "The result is \(result)"   // "The result is 50"
```

Listing 3-6: Returning a value from a function

When we create a function that returns a value, the data type of the value returned is specified in the declaration after the parentheses with the syntax **-> type**, where **type** is just the data type of the value that is going to be returned by the function. A function can only return values of the type specified in its definition. For instance, the function in Listing 3-6 can only return integer values because we declared the returned type as **-> Int**.

When a function returns a value, the system calls the function first and then the value returned is processed inside the statement that made the call. For instance, in the code of Listing 3-6, we create the **result** variable and assign to it a call to the **doubleValue()** function. When the system processes this statement, the function is executed first and then the value returned (50) is assigned to the variable.

The values received and returned by a function may be of any available data type. The following example takes a string and returns a tuple with a string and an integer.

```
func sumCharacters(word: String) -> (String, Int) {
   var characters = ""
   var counter = 0
   for letter in word {
      characters += "\(letter) "
      counter += 1
   }
   return (characters, counter)
}
var (list, total) = sumCharacters(word: "Hello")
var message = "There are \(total) characters (\(list))"
```

Listing 3-7: Returning a tuple

The **sumCharacters()** function in Listing 3-7 receives a string (**word: String**) and returns a tuple composed of a string and an integer (**-> (String, Int)**). The function adds the characters to the **characters** variable and counts them with the **counter** variable, as we did before (see Listing 2-63). At the end, the tuple is returned, its values are assigned to the **list** and **total** variables, and then incorporated into a string ("There are 5 characters (H e l l o)").

Besides returning the result of an operation, the **return** instruction can also be used to interrupt the execution of a function. The **guard** instruction introduced in Chapter 2 is perfect for cases like this, as illustrated by the following example.

```
func doubleValue(number: Int) -> Int {
    guard number < 10 else {
        return number
    }
    return number * 2
}
let result = doubleValue(number: 25)
let message = "The result is \(result)"   // "The result is 25"
```

Listing 3-8: Interrupting the execution of a function with guard

The **doubleValue()** function in Listing 3-8 is similar to previous examples. It receives a number, multiplies it by 2, and returns the result, but this time we first check that the value received by the function is less than 10. If the value is equal or higher than 10, the **guard** instruction calls the **return** instruction with the value received by the function, otherwise, the statements of the function are executed as normal. In this case, the value sent to the function is 25, therefore the condition is false, and the same value is returned.

Notice that in the example of Listing 3-8 we simplified our code including the multiplication in the **return** instruction. The **return** instruction can take single values or expressions like this and it takes care of solving the expression and returning the result. For this reason, sometimes we may find functions with only one statement in charge of returning a value. If this is the case, we can remove the **return** keyword. In the following example, the call sends the number 25 to the function, the value is multiplied by 2, and returned, as in previous examples, but this time we didn't have to declare the **return** keyword because there is only one statement inside the function and therefore the compiler knows what to return.

```
func doubleValue(number: Int) -> Int {
    number * 2
}
let result = doubleValue(number: 25)
let message = "The result is \(result)"   // "The result is 50"
```

Listing 3-9: Removing the return *keyword*

A related keyword is **inout**. This keyword is used to preserve a value after the function finishes processing. When a parameter is marked with **inout**, any changes performed on the value are stored in the original variable. This is useful when we call a function from another function, and we want the modifications introduced by the second function to persist.

```
func first() {
    var number = 25
    second(value: &number)
    print("The result is \(number)")   // "The result is 50"
}
func second(value: inout Int) {
    value = value * 2
}
```

```
first()
```

Listing 3-10: Modifying external variables from a function

This code defines two functions: **first()** and **second()**. The **second()** function receives an **inout** parameter called **value**, which means that any modification on its value is stored in the original variable. The **first()** function defines a variable called **number** and then executes the **second()** function with it, so when the **second()** function multiplies this value times 2, the result (50) is stored in **number**. At the end, we execute the **first()** function to start the process. Notice that in the call to the **second()** function we include an ampersand before the variable's name (&). This tells the system that the variable is going to be modified by the function.

An important aspect of the definition of a function are the names of the parameters. For example, the function **doubleValue()** of previous examples includes a parameter called **number**. Every time we call this function, we must include the parameter's name (e.g., **doubleValue(number: 50)**). These names are called *Argument Labels*. Swift automatically generates argument labels for every parameter using their names. Sometimes the names assigned to the parameters of a function may be descriptive enough for the statements of the function but may be confusing when we perform the call. For cases like these, Swift allows us to define our own argument labels in the function's definition; we just need to declare them before the name of the parameter separated by a space.

```
func doubleValue(years number: Int) -> Int {
    number * 2
}
let result = doubleValue(years: 8)
let message = "The result is \(result)"   // "The results is 16"
```

Listing 3-11: Declaring argument labels

The **doubleValue()** function in Listing 3-11 declares an argument label called **years** for the **number** parameter. From now on, the name of the parameter (**number**) is the one used by the statements of the function to access the value received from the call, while the argument label (**years**) is the one used when calling the function.

If what we want instead is to remove an argument label, we can define it with an underscore.

```
func multiply(number1: Int, _ number2: Int) -> Int {
    number1 * number2
}
let result = multiply(number1: 25, 3)
let message = "The result is \(result)"   // "The result is 75"
```

Listing 3-12: Removing argument labels

In this example, we preserved the behavior by default for the first parameter and removed the argument label for the second parameter. Now the call only has to include the argument label of the first parameter (**multiply(number1: 25, 3)**).

Every function we have defined so far requires the values to be specified in the call. We cannot omit any of the values that the function expects to receive, but Swift allows us to declare a default value for any of the parameters to avoid this requirement.

```
func sayhello(name: String = "Undefined") -> String {
    return "Your name is " + name
}
let message = sayhello()   // "Your name is Undefined"
```

Listing 3-13: Declaring default values for parameters

The code in Listing 3-13 declares the function **sayhello()** with one parameter of type **String** called **name** and with the string "Undefined" as the default value. When the function is called without a value, the string "Undefined" is assigned to **name**.

(Medium) **Generic Functions**

Although creating two or more functions with the same name is not allowed, we can do it if their parameters are not the same. This is called *Overloading* and allows us to define multiple functions with the same name to process different types of values.

```
func getDescription(value: Int) -> String {
   let message = "The value is \(value)"
   return message
}
func getDescription(value: String) -> String {
   let message = "The value is \(value)"
   return message
}
let result1 = getDescription(value: 3)   // "The value is 3"
let result2 = getDescription(value: "John")   // "The value is John"
```

Listing 3-14: Declaring different functions with the same name

The functions in Listing 3-14 have the same name, but one receives an integer and the other a string. We can say that the function that receives the string overloads the function that receives the integer. When we call the **getDescription()** function, the system selects which function is going to be executed depending on the value of the argument. (When we call the function with an integer, the first function is executed, and when we call it with a string, the second function is executed.)

The advantage of creating functions with the same name is that there is only one name to remember. We call the function and Swift takes care of executing the right one depending on the values assigned to the arguments. But when the functions perform the same task and only differ in the type of value received, we end up with two or more pieces of code to maintain, which can introduce errors. In cases like this, we can declare only one function with a generic data type.

Generic data types are placeholders for real data types. When the function is called, the generic data type is turned into the data type of the value received. If we send an integer, the generic data type turns into an **Int**, if we send a string, it becomes a **String**. To define a generic function, we must declare the generic data type using a custom name between angle brackets after the function's name, as in the following example.

```
func getDescription<T>(value: T) -> String {
   let message = "The value is \(value)"
   return message
}
let result1 = getDescription(value: 3.5)   // "The value is 3.5"
let result2 = getDescription(value: "George")   // "The value is George"
```

Listing 3-15: Defining generic functions

This function is a generic function. The generic data type was called **T** (this is a standard name for a generic data type, but we can use any name we want). The function performs the same task, and it has the same name than the two functions from the previous example, but now we have reduced the amount of code in our program. When the function is called, the **T** generic data type is converted into the data type received and the value is processed. (The first time the function is called in our example, **T** is turned into a **Double** and the second time into a **String**.)

Chapter 3 - Swift Paradigm

In our example, we only use one parameter and therefore the function can only work with one data type, but we can declare two or more generic data types separated by commas (e.g., `<T, U>`).

 IMPORTANT: Although we can send any value of any type we want to a generic function, the operations we can perform on them are very limited due to the impossibility of the compiler to know the nature of the values received. For example, we can add two integers, but we cannot add two Boolean values. To solve these issues, we can constrain the generic data types with protocols. We will study how to define protocols and how to use them later in this chapter.

(Basic) Standard Functions

The main advantage of functions is that we can call them from other parts of the code and they will always perform the same operations. We don't even need to know how the function does it, we just send to the function the values we want to process and read the result. Because of this feature, functions can be shared, and programmers can implement pre-programmed functions provided by libraries and frameworks to incorporate additional functionality that would take them too long to code themselves.

All the features of the Swift language we have implemented so far are included in a library called *Standard Library*. The Standard Library includes everything, from operators to primitive data types, as well as predefined functions. The following are some of the most frequently used.

print(String**)**—This function prints a string on the Xcode's console.

abs(Value**)**—This function returns the absolute value of an integer.

max(Values**)**—This function compares two or more values and returns the largest.

min(Values**)**—This function compares two or more values and returns the smallest.

There are also functions available to stop the execution of the application in case of an unrecoverable error.

fatalError(String**)**—This function stops the execution of the application and prints on the console the message provided by the argument.

precondition(Bool, String**)**—This function stops the execution of the application and prints a message on the console if a condition is false. The first argument is the condition to be checked and the second argument is the message we want to print on the console.

Of all the functions in the Swift Standard Library, `print()` is probably the most useful. Its purpose is to print messages on the Xcode's console that may help us fix bugs in our code. In the following example, we use it to print the result of two operations.

```
let absolutenumber = abs(-25)
let minnumber = min(absolutenumber, 100)
print("The number is: \(minnumber)")   // "The number is: 25"
```

Listing 3-16: Printing values on the console with `print()`

The code in Listing 3-16 implements the **abs()** function to calculate the absolute value of -25, then gets the smallest value between **absolutenumber** and the number 100 with the **min()** function, and finally prints a message on the console with the result.

As we will see later, sequences and collections of values are very important in computer programming. The strings studied in Chapter 2 are a clear example. A string is a sequence of values of type **Character**. The Swift Standard Library includes a few functions to quickly create sequences of values our application may need to process information. The following are some of the most frequently used.

stride(from: Value, **through:** Value, **by:** Value)—This function returns a collection of values from the value specified by the **from** argument to the value specified by the **through** argument in intervals specified by the **by** argument.

stride(from: Value, **to:** Value, **by:** Value)—This function returns a collection of values from the value specified by the **from** argument to the value specified by the **through** argument in intervals specified by the **by** argument. The last value is not included.

repeatElement(Value, **count:** Int)—This function returns a collection with the number of elements specified by the **count** argument and with the value specified by the first argument.

zip(Collection, Collection)—This function returns a collection of tuples containing the values of the collections provided by the arguments in sequential order.

The following example applies some of these functions to create a list of tuples that contain a string and an integer.

```
let sequencetext = repeatElement("Hello", count: 5)
let sequencenumbers = stride(from: 0, to: 10, by: 2)
let finalsequence = zip(sequencetext, sequencenumbers)
for (text, number) in finalsequence {
   print("\(text) - \(number)")
}
```

Listing 3-17: Creating collections of values

The code in Listing 3-17 calls the **repeatElement()** function to create a collection of 5 elements, all of them with the string "Hello" ("Hello", "Hello", "Hello", "Hello", "Hello"). Next, the **stride()** function creates another collection with integers from 0 to 10, increased by 2, and without including the last one (0, 2, 4, 6, 8). Next, the **zip()** function merges these two collections in one collection of tuples (the first tuple contains the first value of the **sequencetext** collection along with the first value of the **sequencenumbers** collection, and so on). Finally, we use a **for in** loop to iterate over the values of the **finalsequence** collection and print them on the console ("Hello - 0", "Hello - 2", "Hello - 4", "Hello - 6", "Hello - 8").

(Basic) Scopes

The conditionals and loops studied in Chapter 2 and the functions studied in this chapter have a thing in common; they all use blocks of code (statements in braces) to enclose their functionality. Blocks are independent processing units; they contain their own statements and variables. To preserve their independence and avoid conflicts between these units and the rest of the code, their variables and constants are isolated. Variables and constants declared inside a block are not accessible from other parts of the code; they can only be used inside the block in which they were created.

The space in the code where a variable is accessible is called *scope*. Swift defines two types of scopes: the global scope and the local scope (also referred as global space or local space). The variables and constants outside a block have global scope, while those declared inside a block have local scope. The variables and constants with global scope are accessible from any part of the code, while those with local scope are only accessible from the statements inside the block in which they were created (and the statements from blocks created inside their block). To better understand how scopes are defined in code, here is a practical example.

```
var multiplier = 1.2
var total = 0.0

func first() {
   let base = 10.0
   total += base * multiplier
}
func second() {
   let multiplier = 5.0
   let base = 3.5
   total += base * multiplier
}
first()
second()

print("Total: \(total)")   // "Total: 29.5"
```

Listing 3-18: Using variables and constants of different scopes

This example declares two variables in the global space, **multiplier** and **total**, and two functions with local constants. The **multiplier** and **total** variables are global and therefore they are accessible from anywhere in the code, but the constants defined inside the functions are available only to the statements inside the function in which they were created. Therefore, the **base** constant declared inside the **first()** function is only accessible from this function (neither the statements in the global space nor other functions or blocks outside **first()** have access to it), but we can modified the value of **total** from this function because it is a global variable.

The next function, **second()**, declares a new constant called **multiplier**. This constant has the same name as the **multiplier** variable declared before in the global space, but they have different scopes and therefore they are assigned different locations in memory and can contain different values. When we read the value of **multiplier** in the **second()** function to add a new value to the **total** variable, the **multiplier** that the system reads is the one declared inside the function because in that space this constant has precedence over the global variable with the same name, which shows that we can declare variables and constants with the same name as long as they have different scopes.

Medium Closures

Blocks of code, such as those used to create functions, conditionals, and loops, have their own scope, and know the variables that are available to them. Because of this, we can generate independent processing units that do not interfere with the operations of other units. This feature is so important in computer programming that Swift offers the possibility to create independent blocks called *Closures* to take advantage of it.

Closures are simple blocks of code with the syntax **{ (parameters) -> Type in statements }**. They are like functions (functions are closures with a name), but they are wrapped with braces and the **in** keyword is included to separate the data types from the statements.

Closures can be assigned to variables and executed using the name of the variable, as we do with functions. The name of the variable becomes the name of the closure, as shown next.

```
let multiplier = { (number: Int, times: Int) -> Int in
   let total = number * times
   return total
}
print("The result is \(multiplier(10, 5))")   // "The result is 50"
```

Listing 3-19: Assigning closures to variables

This example defines a closure and assigns it to the **multiplier** constant. After this, the name of the constant may be used to execute the closure. Notice that the parameters of the closure and the return type are declared with the same syntax as functions (**(number: Int, times: Int) -> Int**), but the parameters' names are not turned into argument labels and therefore they are ignored in the call.

An advantage of being able to assign closures to variables is the possibility to initialize the variables with the result of complex operations. The closure is assigned to the variable and executed right away adding parentheses at the end of the declaration. When the system reads the statement, it executes the closure and then assigns the value returned by the closure to the constant or variable.

```
let myaddition = { () -> Int in
   var total = 0
   let list = stride(from: 1, through: 9, by: 1)

   for number in list {
      total += number
   }
   return total
}()
print("The total is \(myaddition)")   // "The total is 45"
```

Listing 3-20: *Initializing a variable with the value returned by a closure*

The closure declared in Listing 3-20 doesn't receive any value and returns an integer (**() -> Int**). The code in the closure adds the values of a collection (1 to 9) and returns the result, but because we included the parentheses at the end of the definition, the value assigned to the **myaddition** constant is the one returned by the closure (45), not the closure itself.

If the closure does not receive any parameter, we can simplify the syntax by declaring the constant's data type to be the same than the data type of the value returned by the closure. Notice that in this case, the **in** keyword can also be removed.

```
let myaddition: Int = {
   var total = 0
   let list = stride(from: 1, through: 9, by: 1)

   for number in list {
      total += number
   }
   return total
}()
print("The total is \(myaddition)")   // "The total is 45"
```

Listing 3-21: *Simplifying a closure*

Closures cannot only be assigned to constants and variables but also sent and returned from functions, as any other value. When a function receives a closure, the parameter's data type only has to include the data types the closure receives and returns, as in the following example.

```
let multiplier = { (number: Int, times: Int) -> Int in
   let total = number * times
   return total
}
func processclosure(myclosure: (Int, Int) -> Int) {
   let total = myclosure(10, 2)
   print("The total is: \(total)")   // "The total is: 20"
}
```

```
processclosure(myclosure: multiplier)
```

Listing 3-22: Sending a closure to a function

The first statement in Listing 3-22 defines a closure that multiplies two integers and returns the result. A function that receives a closure of this type is defined next. Notice that the data type of the value received by the function was declared as **(Int, Int) -> Int**. This indicates to the compiler that the **processclosure()** function can receive a closure that in turn receives two integer values and returns another integer. When the **processclosure()** function is called in the last statement, the value of the **multiplier** variable is sent to the function. The function assigns the closure to the **myclosure** constant, and the closure is executed inside the function using this name and the values 10 and 2, producing the result 20.

The closure in the previous example was defined in the global space and was executed inside the **processclosure()** function, but we don't need to assign the closure to a variable, we can just define it in the function's call.

```
func processclosure(myclosure: (Int, Int) -> Int) {
   print("The total is: \(myclosure(10, 2))")  // "The total is: 20"
}
processclosure(myclosure: { (number: Int, times: Int) -> Int in
   return number * times
})
```

Listing 3-23: Assigning the closure to the function's argument

The code in Listing 3-23 works the same way as the previous example, but it was simplified by assigning the closure directly to the function's argument. This can be simplified even further by using a pattern called *Trailing Closures*. When the final argument of a function is a closure, we can declare the closure at the end of the call, as in the following example.

```
func processclosure(myclosure: (Int, Int) -> Int) {
   print("The total is: \(myclosure(10, 2))")  // "The total is: 20"
}
processclosure() { (number: Int, times: Int) -> Int in
   number * times
}
```

Listing 3-24: Using Trailing Closures

When we pass the closure this way, the call does not include the **myclosure** argument anymore. The closure declared after the parentheses is considered to be the last argument of the function and therefore the argument label is not necessary.

The code in Listing 3-24 works the same way as previous examples, the only advantage is the reduction in the amount of code we have to write. And that can be simplified even further. In the last example we already removed the **return** keyword. As explained before, when the content of a function (or in this case a closure) includes only one statement, the compiler implies that the value produced by that statement is the one to return and therefore the **return** keyword is not required anymore. But when we are passing the closure to a function, Swift can also infer the data types of the values received by the closure and therefore we don't have to declare that either. Instead, we can represent these values using shorthand argument names. These are special placeholders made up of the $ symbol and an index starting from 0. The first value received by the closure is represented by $0, the second value by $1, and so on.

```
func processclosure(myclosure: (Int, Int) -> Int) {
   print("The total is: \(myclosure(10, 2))")  // "The total is: 20"
}
```

```
processclosure() { $0 * $1 }
```

Listing 3-25: Inferring the closure's data types

Again, the code is the same, but now the closure is extremely simple. When it is executed from the **processclosure()** function, it receives the values 10 and 2 and assigns them to the placeholders $0 and $1, respectively. Then, it multiplies their values and returns the result.

So far, we have executed the closure received by the function inside the same function, but there are situations in which a closure must be executed outside the function. This usually applies to asynchronous operations, as we will see later. If we want to execute a closure received by the function from outside the function, we must declare it as an *escape* closure. Escape closures are closures that remain in memory after the execution of the function is over. They are declared preceded by the **@escaping** keyword, as in the following example.

```
var myclosure: () -> Void = {}
func passclosure(closure: @escaping () -> Void) {
   myclosure = closure
}
passclosure() { () -> Void in
   print("Closure Executed")
}
myclosure()
```

Listing 3-26: Declaring escaping closures

In the code of Listing 3-26, we declare a variable called **myclosure** that stores a closure that doesn't receive or return any values (**() -> Void**), and then assign an empty closure to it. After that, we define a function called **passclosure()** that receives an escaping closure and all it does is to assign that closure to the **myclosure** variable. Next, we call the **passclosure()** function with a closure that prints a value on the console, so now the **myclosure** variable contains that closure. Finally, we execute the closure in **myclosure** and the message is printed on the console.

 IMPORTANT: When we define the data type of a closure, we must declare the data types of the values it receives and the data type of the values it returns. Therefore, if the closure doesn't return any value, we must declare the return type as **Void**, as we did in Listing 3-26.

(Basic) **3.3 Structures**

Structures are an essential part of the organizational paradigm proposed by Swift. They are custom data types that include not only data but also the code in charge of processing that data. When we define a structure, what we are doing is declaring a data type that may contain variables and constants (called *properties*) and functions (called *methods*). Later we can declare variables and constants of this type to store information with the characteristics defined by the structure. These values (called *instances*) will be unique, each one with its own properties and methods.

(Basic) **Definition of Structures**

To define a new structure, we must use the **struct** keyword and enclose the data and functionality in braces.

```
struct Item {
   var name: String = "Not defined"
```

```
   var price: Double = 0
}
```

Listing 3-27: Defining a structure

This example defines a structure called **Item** with two properties (variables): **name** and **price**. The definition is just delineating the elements of the data type (also called *members*), like a blueprint that will be later used to create the real structures. What we need to do to store values of this new data type is to declare a variable or a constant, as we did for any other data type before. In this case, the data type is the name of the structure and the initialization value is a special initializer with the syntax **Name()** (where **Name** is, again, the name of the structure).

```
struct Item {
   var name: String = "Not defined"
   var price: Double = 0
}
var purchase: Item = Item()
```

Listing 3-28: Declaring a variable of type Item

The code in Listing 3-28 creates a variable of type **Item** that stores an instance of the **Item** structure containing the properties **name** and **price**. The instance is created by the **Item()** initializer and then assigned to the **purchase** variable.

In this last example, the properties of a new instance always take the values declared in the structure's definition (**"Not Defined"** and **0**), but we can modify them as we do with any other variable. The only difference is that the properties are inside a structure, so every time we want to access them, we must mention the structure they belong to. The syntax implements dot notation, as in **variable.property**, where **variable** is the name of the variable that contains the instance of the structure and **property** is the name of the property we want to access.

```
struct Item {
   var name = "Not defined"
   var price = 0.0
}
var purchase = Item()
purchase.name = "Lamps"
purchase.price = 10.50

print("Product: \(purchase.name) $ \(purchase.price)")
```

Listing 3-29: Assigning new values to the properties of a structure

In this example, the properties of the **Item** structure and the **purchase** variable are declared as before, but this time we let Swift infer their data types. After the instance is created, new values are assigned to its properties using dot notation. Dot notation is not only used to assign new values but also to read the current ones. At the end, we read and print the values of the **name** and **price** properties on the console ("Product: Lamps $ 10.5").

 IMPORTANT: Notice that we have stored the structure in a variable (**var**). This is to be able to assign new values to its properties later. When the values of the properties in a structure are modified, instead of modifying the properties of the instance, the system creates a new instance and assigns the values to the properties of that instance. For this to be possible, the structure must be stored in a variable so it can be replaced by the new structure later.

Structures may be instantiated inside other structures, as many times as necessary. The dot notation is extended in these cases to reach every element in the hierarchy.

```
struct Price {
    var USD = 0.0
    var CAD = 0.0
}
struct Item {
    var name: String = "Not defined"
    var price: Price = Price()
}
var purchase = Item()
purchase.name = "Lamps"
purchase.price.USD = 10.50
```

Listing 3-30: Structures inside structures

Listing 3-30 defines two structures: **Price** and **Item**. The **Item** structure contains the same properties as before, but now the data type of the **price** property is **Price**, which means that instead of storing a single value, this property can now store a structure that in turn contains two properties: **USD** and **CAD**. When the **Item** structure is created and assigned to the **purchase** variable, the **Price** structure for the **price** property is also created with its values by default.

By concatenating the names of the variables and properties we can read and modify any value we want. For instance, the last statement in the code of Listing 3-30 accesses the **USD** property of the **price** structure inside the **purchase** structure to assign a price to the item in American Dollars (**purchase.price.USD = 10.50**).

In this example, the **price** structure is created during instantiation, but this is not usually the case. Sometimes the values of the properties containing structures are defined after the instance is created and therefore those properties must be declared as optionals. The problem with optionals is that we always need to check whether the variable or property has a value before we use it. To simplify this task, Swift introduces Optional Chaining.

Optional chaining makes it easy to access properties and methods in a hierarchical chain that contains optional components. As always, these components are accessed using dot notation, but a question mark is added to the names of the properties that have optional values. When the system finds an optional, it checks whether it contains a value and continues reading the expression only in case of success. Here is the same example, but with the **price** property turned into an optional.

```
struct Price {
    var USD = 0.0
    var CAD = 0.0
}
struct Item {
    var name: String = "Not defined"
    var price: Price?
}
var purchase = Item()
purchase.name = "Lamps"
purchase.price?.USD = 10.50   // nil
```

Listing 3-31: Accessing optional properties

The **price** property in this code is declared as an optional (its initial value is not defined). Every time we read this property, we must unwrap its value, but if we use Optional Chaining, we can just concatenate the values with dot notation and add a question mark after the name of the optional property (**purchase.price?.USD**). The system reads every component in the instruction and checks their values. If any of the optionals have no value, it returns **nil**, but when all the optionals have values, the instruction performs the task. (In this case, it assigns the number 10.50 to the **USD** property.)

Key Paths

Besides using dot notation to read and write a property, we can use key paths. A key path is a reference to a property that we can use to read and modify its value. The advantage of using key paths instead of dot notation is that they are stored in structures and therefore we can pass them to other parts of the code and then use them to access the values of the properties they are referencing without even knowing what those properties are. This can be useful when we need to interact with frameworks, or when we are extending code to include our own functionality.

Swift defines several structures to store key paths. For instance, a read-only key path is stored in an instance of a structure of type `KeyPath` and read-and-write key paths are stored in a structure of type `WritableKeyPath`.

The syntax to define a key path includes a backward slash and the name of the data type followed by the name of the property we want to reference. To access the value of a property using a key path, Swift uses a syntax that includes square brackets after the instance's name and the `keypath` keyword, as illustrated in the following example.

```
struct Item {
    let name: String
    let price: Double
}
var purchase: Item = Item(name: "Lamps", price: 27.50)
let keyPrice = \Item.price
print(purchase[keyPath: keyPrice])   // "27.5"
```

Listing 3-32: Creating key paths

This code defines a structure with two properties: **name** and **price**. Next, we create a key path to reference the **price** property. Because the properties are defined as constants, the key path is created of type **KeyPath** (a read-only key path). In the last statement, we use this key path to access the value of the **price** property of the **purchase** instance and print it on the console.

We can easily create a read-and-write key path by defining the structure's properties as variables. In the following example, we turn the **name** and **price** properties into variables and modify the value of **price** using our **keyPrice** key path.

```
struct Item {
    var name: String
    var price: Double
}
var purchase: Item = Item(name: "Lamps", price: 27.50)
let keyPrice = \Item.price
purchase[keyPath: keyPrice] = 30.00
print(purchase.price)
```

Listing 3-33: Using read and write key paths

Basic **Methods**

If we could only store properties, structures would be just complex data types, like tuples, but structures can also include code. This is done through functions. Functions inside structures are called *methods*, but the definition and functionality are the same.

The syntax to execute a method is **variable.method()**, where **variable** is the name of the variable that contains the instance of the structure and **method** is the name of the method we want to call inside that structure, as shown in the following example.

```
struct Item {
   var name = "Not defined"
   var price = 0.0

   func total(quantity: Double) -> Double {
      return quantity * price
   }
}
var purchase = Item()
purchase.name = "Lamp"
purchase.price = 10.50

print("Total: \(purchase.total(quantity: 2))")   // "Total: 21.0"
```

Listing 3-34: Defining methods

In Listing 3-34, a method is declared as part of the definition of the **Item** structure. The method receives a value representing the number of items sold and calculates the total money spent in the transaction. We could have performed this operation outside the structure by reading the value of the **price** property, but having a method in the structure itself presents some advantages. First, we don't have to worry about how the method calculates the value; we just call the method with the right value and let it perform the task, no matter how complex it is. And second, we do not have to write the operation over and over again, because it is always part of the instance of the structure we are working with.

A method can read the values of the instance's properties but cannot assign new values to them. If we want a method to be able to modify the values of the properties of its own instance, we must declare the **mutating** keyword before the **func** keyword in the structure's definition.

```
struct Item {
   var name = "Not defined"
   var price = 0.0

   mutating func changename(newname: String) {
      name = newname
   }
}
var purchase = Item()
purchase.changename(newname: "Lamps")

print("Product: \(purchase.name)")   // "Product: Lamps"
```

Listing 3-35: Assigning new values to properties from inside the structure

The **changename()** method of the **Item** structure in Listing 3-35 is declared as a mutating method so it can assign a new value to the **name** property. Therefore, we do not need to modify the **name** property directly, we can call this method with the value we want to store, and the method takes care of assigning the value to the property.

(Basic) **Initialization**

Every instance created from the structure's definition has the purpose to store and process specific data. For example, we can create multiple instances of our **Item** structure to store information about different products. Each product will have its own name and price, so the properties of each instance must be initialized with the proper values. The initialization of an instance is a very common task and it would be far too cumbersome if we had to assign the values one by one every time a new one is created. For this reason, Swift provides different alternatives to initialize the values of a structure. One of them is called *Memberwise Initializer.*

Memberwise initializers detect the properties of the structure and declare their names as argument labels. Using these argument labels, we can provide the values for initialization between the parentheses of the initializer. The following code implements a memberwise initializer to initialize an instance of the **Item** structure declared in previous examples.

```
struct Item {
   var name = "Not defined"
   var price = 0.0
}
var purchase = Item(name: "Lamp", price: 10.50)
print("Purchase: \(purchase.name) $ \(purchase.price)")
```

Listing 3-36: Initializing properties

Memberwise initializers reduce the amount of code and simplify initialization. Also, if we use the memberwise initializer, we don't need to assign values by default, as shown next.

```
struct Item {
   var name: String
   var price: Double
}
var purchase = Item(name: "Lamp", price: 10.50)
print("Purchase: \(purchase.name) $ \(purchase.price)")
```

Listing 3-37: Using memberwise initializers to provide the initial values of a structure

The two forms of initialization we have seen so far are not customizable enough. Some structures may have multiple properties that require initialization or even methods that must be executed right away to get the proper values for the instance to be ready. To add more alternatives, Swift provides a method called **init()**. The **init()** method is called as soon as the instance is created, so we can use it to initialize the properties any way we want.

```
struct Price {
   var USD: Double
   var CAD: Double

   init() {
      USD = 5
      CAD = USD * 1.29
   }
}
var myprice = Price()
```

Listing 3-38: Initializing properties from the init() method

When the instance is generated by the initializer, the properties are created first and then the **init()** method is executed. Inside this method we can perform any operation we need to get the properties' initial values. In the example of Listing 3-38, we assign an initial value of 5 to the **USD** property and then multiply this value by the corresponding exchange rate to get the value of the **CAD** property (the same price in Canadian dollars).

As well as with any other method or function, the **init()** method may include parameters. These parameters are used to specify initial values from the initializer.

```
struct Price {
   var USD: Double
   var CAD: Double
```

```
    init(americans: Double) {
        USD = americans
        CAD = USD * 1.29
    }
}
var myprice = Price(americans: 5)
```

Listing 3-39: Declaring the parameters to initialize the structure

This is similar to what Swift creates for us in the background when we use memberwise initializers, but the advantage of declaring the `init()` method ourselves is that we can specify only the parameters we need (as in the last example) or even declare multiple `init()` methods to present several alternatives for initialization, as shown next.

```
struct Price {
    var USD: Double
    var CAD: Double

    init(americans: Double) {
        USD = americans
        CAD = USD * 1.29
    }
    init(canadians: Double) {
        CAD = canadians
        USD = CAD * 0.7752
    }
}
var myprice = Price(canadians: 5)
```

Listing 3-40: Declaring multiple `init()` methods

As explained before, Swift identifies each function by its name and parameters, so we can declare functions with the same name as long as they have different parameters. In the example of Listing 3-40, two `init()` methods were declared to initialize the instance of the structure. The first method receives a **Double** value with the name **americans** and the second method also receives a **Double** value but with the name **canadians**. The right method will be executed according to the argument included in the initializer. In this example, we use the argument **canadians** with the value 5, so the instance is initialized by the second `init()` method.

(Medium) **Computed Properties**

The properties we have declared up to this point are called *Stored Properties*. Their function is to store a value in memory. But there are other types of properties called *Computed Properties*. These properties do not store a value of their own, instead they have access to the rest of the properties of the structure and can perform operations to set and retrieve their values.

Two methods are available for computed properties to be able to set and retrieve a value: **get()** and **set()**. These methods are also called *getters* and *setters* and are declared in braces after the property's name. Although both methods are useful, only the **get** method is required.

```
struct Price {
    var USD: Double
    var ratetoCAD: Double

    var canadians: Double {
        get {
            return USD * ratetoCAD
        }
    }
}
```

```
var purchase = Price(USD: 11, ratetoCAD: 1.29)
print("Price in CAD: \(purchase.canadians)")   // "Price in CAD: 14.19"
```

Listing 3-41: Declaring computed properties

The structure defined in Listing 3-41 contains a stored property called **USD** to store the price in American dollars, a stored property called **ratetoCAD** to store the exchange rate for Canadian dollars, and a computed property called **canadians** that converts the US dollars into Canadian dollars and returns the result. Computed properties are like methods, they calculate the value every time the property is read. No matter if the value of the **ratetoCAD** property changes, the **canadians** property will always return the right price in Canadian dollars.

Computed properties with only a getter are called read-only properties because we can only read their values. When we declare a read-only property, we can omit the **get** method. In addition, as we have seen before, when a block contains only one statement, it knows what to return, so we can omit the **return** keyword as well. The previous example can therefore be simplified as follows.

```
struct Price {
   var USD: Double
   var ratetoCAD: Double

   var canadians: Double {
      USD * ratetoCAD
   }
}
var purchase = Price(USD: 11, ratetoCAD: 1.29)
print(purchase.canadians)   // "14.190000000000001"
```

Listing 3-42: Defining read-only properties

By including the **set** method for the **canadians** property we can, for example, set a new price using the same currency.

```
struct Price {
   var USD: Double
   var ratetoCAD: Double
   var ratetoUSD: Double

   var canadians: Double {
      get {
         USD * ratetoCAD
      }
      set {
         USD = newValue * ratetoUSD
      }
   }
}
var purchase = Price(USD: 11, ratetoCAD: 1.29, ratetoUSD: 0.7752)
purchase.canadians = 500
print("Price: \(purchase.USD)")   // "Price: 387.6"
```

Listing 3-43: Adding the set *method to set a new value*

The new structure defined in Listing 3-43 can retrieve and set a price in Canadian dollars. When we set a new value for the **canadians** property, the value is stored in a constant called **newValue** (the constant is created automatically for us). Using this constant, we can process the new value and perform the operations we need. In this example, the value of **newValue** is multiplied by the exchange rate to get the price in American dollars. The price is always stored in American dollars but using the **canadians** property we can set it and retrieve it in Canadian dollars.

If we want to use a different name for the new value, we can set the parameter's name between parentheses. In the following example, the parameter was called **CAD** and used instead of **newValue** to calculate the value for the **USD** property.

```
struct Price {
    var USD: Double
    var ratetoCAD: Double
    var ratetoUSD: Double

    var canadians: Double {
        get {
            USD * ratetoCAD
        }
        set(CAD) {
            USD = CAD * ratetoUSD
        }
    }
}
var purchase = Price(USD: 11, ratetoCAD: 1.29, ratetoUSD: 0.7752)
```

Listing 3-44: Using a different name for the parameter of the set *method*

(Medium) **Property Observers**

The properties of an instance of a structure may be modified at any moment by different processes, such as in response to user interaction or events triggered by the system. To inform an instance that one of its properties was modified, Swift introduces Property Observers.

Property Observers are special methods, similar to **get()** and **set()**, that we can include within a property to execute code before and after a value is assigned to it. The methods are called **willSet()** and **didSet()**, and are declared in braces after the property's name.

```
struct Price {
    var increment: Double = 0
    var oldprice: Double = 0

    var price: Double {
        willSet {
            increment = newValue - price
        }
        didSet {
            oldprice = oldValue
        }
    }
}
var product = Price(price: 15.95)
product.price = 20.75
print("New price: \(product.price)")     // "New price: 20.75"
print("Old price: \(product.oldprice)")  // "Old price: 15.95"
```

Listing 3-45: Adding observers to a store property

The **Price** structure in Listing 3-45 includes three properties: **increment**, **oldprice**, and **price**. We use the **price** property to store the value of an item, the **oldprice** property to store the previous price, and the **increment** property to store the difference between the old price and the new one. To set this last value, we declare property observers for the **price** property. Every time a new value is assigned to the property, the **willSet()** and **didSet()** methods are executed.

Swift automatically creates a parameter called **newValue** for the **willSet()** method to provide access to the value that is going to be assigned to the property, and a parameter called

oldValue for the **didSet()** method to provide access to the property's old value after the new value was assigned. (We can change the names of these parameters as we did for the **set()** method in Listing 3-44.) In our example, when the **willSet()** method is executed, the current value of **price** is subtracted from **newValue** to get the difference, and the result is assigned to the **increment** property. And in the **didSet()** method, we assign the old price provided by **oldValue** to the **oldprice** property to have access to the item's previous price later.

(Basic) Type Properties and Methods

The properties and methods declared above are accessible on the instances created from the definition of the structure. This means that we must create an instance of the structure to be able to read and modify their values. But there are times when being able to execute properties and methods from the definition itself makes sense. We might need, for example, to get information related to all instances, or call methods to create instances with standard values. In Swift, this is possible by declaring type properties and methods. These are properties and methods accessible from the data type, not the instance created from that type.

Type properties and methods for structures are declared adding the **static** keyword to the definition. Once a property or method is declared with this keyword, they are only accessible from the definition itself. In the following example, we include a type property called **currencies** to inform how many currencies the structures can handle.

```
struct Price {
   var USD: Double
   var CAD: Double

   static var currencies = 2
}
print(Price.currencies)   // 2
```

Listing 3-46: Defining type properties

As illustrated by the code in Listing 3-46, there is no need to create an instance to access a type property or method. After the definition, the **currencies** property is read using the name of the structure and dot notation (**Price.currencies**). If we create an instance from this definition, the only properties accessible from the instance will be **USD** and **CAD**. The **currencies** property is a type property, only accessible from the type itself. The same happens with methods, as shown next.

```
struct Price {
   var USD: Double
   var CAD: Double

   static func reserved() -> Price {
      return Price(USD: 10.0, CAD: 11.0)
   }
}
var reservedprice = Price.reserved()
print("Price in USD: \(reservedprice.USD) CAD: \(reservedprice.CAD)")
```

Listing 3-47: Defining type methods

The structure in this example includes a type method called **reserved()**. The method creates and returns an instance of the **Price** structure with standard values. This is a common procedure and another way to create our own initializer. If we use the initializer by default, the values must be provided every time the instance is created, but with a type method all we need to do is to call the method on the type to get in return an instance configured with specific values. In our example, the values correspond to a reserved price. We call the **reserved()** method on the **Price** type, the method creates an instance of the **Price** structure with the values 10.0 and 11.0, and then this instance is assigned to the **reservedprice** variable. At the end, the values of both properties are printed on the console to confirm that their values were defined by the **reserved()** method. (Again, the method is not accessible from the instance, only from the data type.)

Advanced Generic Structures

At the beginning of this chapter, we explained how to create generic functions. These are functions that can process values of different data types. The function defines a placeholder for the data type and then adopts the data type of the value it receives. But generics data types are not exclusive to functions, we can also turn data types themselves, such as structures, into generic types. The advantage is that we can create independent processing units that can handle different types of values. To create a generic structure, we must declare the generic data type after the name of the structure and between angle brackets, as we did for functions.

```
struct MyStructure<T> {
   var myvalue:T

   func description() {
      print("The value is: \(myvalue)")   // "The value is: 5"
   }
}
let instance = MyStructure<Int>(myvalue: 5)
instance.description()
```

Listing 3-48: Defining generic structures

This example defines a generic structure called **MyStructure** with one generic type called **T**. The structure contains a generic property called **myvalue** and a method that prints a message with the property's value. After the definition of the structure, we create an instance with an integer. The system replaces the **T** with the **Int** type, creates the instance, and assigns the value 5 to the **myvalue** property. In the last statement, we call the **description()** method to print it.

When we create an instance of a generic structure, the data type we want the structure to work with is included after the name and between angle brackets, but this is only required when the initialization doesn't include any value. For example, the following code creates an instance of the same structure but with a string and let Swift infer the generic data type from the value.

```
struct MyStructure<T> {
   var myvalue:T

   func description() {
      print("The value is: \(myvalue)")   // "The value is: Hello"
   }
}
let instance = MyStructure(myvalue: "Hello")
instance.description()
```

Listing 3-49: Using generic structures

 IMPORTANT: These are basic examples of how to create and work with generic data types. As with functions, generics only become useful when we constrain the data using protocols. We will learn more about generics in the following sections and study protocols at the end of this chapter.

Primitive Type Structures

Including properties and methods inside a structure and then assigning an instance of that structure to a variable is a simple way to wrap data and functionality in a single portable unit of code. Structures are usually used this way, as practical wrappers of code, and Swift takes advantage of this feature extensively. In fact, all the primitive data types defined in Swift are structures. The syntax `variable: Int = value`, for example, is a shortcut provided by Swift for the initializer `variable = Int(value)`. Every time we assign a new value to a variable of a primitive data type, we are assigning a structure that contains that value. The following are the initializers of some of the primitive data types studied in Chapter 2.

Int(Value**)**—This is the initializer of the `Int` data type. The argument is the value we want to assign to the instance. If no value is provided, the value 0 is assigned by default. Initializers for similar types are also available (`Int8()`, `Int16()`, `Int32()`, and `Int64()`).

UInt(Value**)**—This is the initializer of the `UInt` data type. The argument is the value we want to assign to the instance. If no value is provided, the value assigned is 0. Initializers for similar types are also available (`UInt8()`, `UInt16()`, `UInt32()`, and `UInt64()`).

Float(Value**)**—This is the initializer of the `Float` data type. The argument is the value we want to assign to the instance. If no value is provided, the value 0.0 is assigned by default.

Double(Value**)**—This is the initializer of the `Double` data type. The argument is the value we want to assign to the instance. If no value is provided, the value assigned is 0.0.

The structures for these data types are defined in the Swift Standard Library. All we need to do to create an instance is to implement the initializer with the value we want to store.

```
var mynumber = Int(25)
var myprice = Double(4.99)
```

Listing 3-50: Initializing variables with standard initializers

This is the same as assigning the values directly to the variable (e.g., **var myprice = 4.99**), but these initializers become useful when the value we want to assign to the structure is of different type. The definitions of these structures include several initializers that convert the value to the right type. This is called *Casting*, and we can use it to turn a variable of one data type into another. For example, when we divide numbers, the system converts those numbers to the most comprehensive type and performs the operation, but variables are already of a specific type and therefore they must be explicitly converted before the operation is performed or we get an error. (The process does not really convert the variable; it creates a new value of the right type.)

```
var number1: Int = 10
var number2: Double = 2.5
var total = Double(number1) / number2   // 4.0
```

Listing 3-51: Casting a variable

The variables **number1** and **number2** defined in Listing 3-51 are of type **Int** and **Double**. To perform a division between them we must cast one of them to the data type of the other (arithmetic operations cannot be performed on values of different data type). Using the **Double()** initializer, we create a new value of type **Double** from the value of **number1** and perform the operation. (The value 10.0 created by the initializer is divided by the value 2.5 of **number2** to get the result 4.0.) The process is described as "casting the **number1** variable to a **Double**".

These initializers are also useful when working with **String** values. Sometimes the characters of a string represent numbers that we need to process. The problem is that strings cannot be processed as numbers. We cannot include a string in an arithmetic operation without first converting the string into a value of a numeric data type. Fortunately, the initializers for numeric types such as **Int** and **Double** can convert a value of type **String** into a number. If the operation cannot be performed, the initializer returns **nil**, so we can treat it as an optional value. In the following example, we convert the string "45" into the integer 45 and add the value 15 to it.

```
var units = "45"
if let number = Int(units) {
   let total = number + 15
   print("The total is \(total)")   // "The total is 60"
}
```

Listing 3-52: Extracting numbers from strings

The structures defined for primitive data types also have their own properties and methods. This includes type properties and methods. For instance, the following are the most frequently used properties and methods provided by the structures that process integer values (e.g., **Int**).

min—This type property returns the minimum value the data type can handle.

max—This type property returns the maximum value the data type can handle.

random(in: Range**)**—This type method returns a random number. The value is calculated from a range of integers provided by the **in** argument.

negate()—This method inverts the sign of the value.

isMultiple(of: Int**)**—This method returns **true** if the value is a multiple of the value provided by the **of** argument (this is similar to what we can achieve with the % operator).

The **min** and **max** properties are especially useful because they allow us to determine whether an operation could overflow a variable (produce a result that is greater or lesser than the minimum and maximum allowed).

```
var mynumber: Int8 = 120
let increment: Int8 = 10
if (Int8.max - mynumber) >= increment {   // (127 - 120) >= 10
   mynumber += increment
}
print(mynumber)   // "120"
```

Listing 3-53: Checking the maximum possible value for the Int8 type

This example takes advantage of the **max** property to make sure that incrementing the value of a variable will not overflow the variable (the result will not be greater than the maximum value the variable can handle). The code starts by defining a variable of type **Int8** to store the result of the operation and another to store the number we want to add. Then, we calculate how far the current value of **mynumber** is from the maximum value admitted by an **Int8** variable (**Int8.max — mynumber**) and compare this result with the value of **increment**. If the number of units we have left is greater or equal than the value of **increment**, we know that the operation can be performed without going over the limit. (In this example, the operation is not performed because the addition of 120 + 10 produces a result greater than the limit of 127 admitted by **Int8**.)

The type **Double** also includes its own selection of properties and methods. The following are the most frequently used.

Chapter 3 - Swift Paradigm

pi—This type property returns the value of the constant pi.

infinity—This type property returns an infinite value.

minimum(Double, Double)—This type method compares the values provided by the arguments and returns the minimum.

maximum(Double, Double)—This type method compares the values provided by the arguments and returns the maximum.

random(in: Range)—This type method returns a random number. The value is calculated from a range of values of type `Double` provided by the `in` argument.

negate()—This method inverts the sign of the value.

squareRoot()—This method returns the square root of the value.

remainder(dividingBy: Double)—This method returns the remainder produced by dividing the value by the value specified by the **dividingBy** argument.

rounded(FloatingPointRoundingRule)—This method returns the value rounded according to the rule specified by the argument. The argument is an enumeration with the values `awayFromZero`, `down`, `toNearestOrAwayFromZero`, `toNearestOrEven`, `towardZero` and `up`.

In this case, the most useful method is probably `rounded()`. With this method, we can round a floating-point value to the nearest integer.

```
var mynumber: Double = 2.890
mynumber = mynumber.rounded(.toNearestOrAwayFromZero)
print("The round number is \(mynumber)")   // "The round number is 3.0"
```

Listing 3-54: Rounding floating-point values

Of course, Boolean values are also structures. Among others, the `Bool` data type offers the following methods.

toggle()—This method toggles the value. If the value is `true`, it becomes `false` and vice versa.

random()—This type method returns a random `Bool` value.

The following example checks the current value of a variable and assigns the value `false` if it is `true`, or vice versa.

```
var valid: Bool = true
if valid {
   print("It is Valid")
   valid.toggle()
}
print(valid)   // false
```

Listing 3-55: Modifying the value of a `Bool` variable

(Basic) **Range Structures**

The `random()` method provided by some of the structures introduced above work with ranges of values (collections of values in sequential order). These are structures included in the Swift Standard Library that can manage open and close ranges of values. For instance, we can create a range from 1 to 5. If the range is open, it will include the values 1, 2, 3, and 4, but if the range is closed, it will include the values 1, 2, 3, 4, and 5. Swift includes two operators to generate ranges.

- ... (three dots) creates a range from the value on the left to the value on the right, including both values in the range (e.g., 1...5 creates a range that includes the values 1, 2, 3, 4 and 5). The value on the right can be omitted to create a one-sided range. A one-sided range goes from the value on the left to the maximum value allowed for the data type.
- ..< (two dots and the less than character) creates a range from the value on the left to the value before the value on the right (e.g., 1..<5 creates a range that includes the values 1, 2, 3 and 4).

When we declare a range using these operators, Swift creates the proper structure according to the operator involved. A structure of type **Range** is created for an open range and a structure of type **ClosedRange** is created for a closed range. These structures provide common properties and methods to work with the range. The following are the most frequently used.

lowerBound—This property returns the range's lower value (the value on the left).

upperBound—This property returns the range's upper value (the value on the right).

contains(Element)—This method returns a Boolean value that determines if the value specified by the argument is inside the range.

clamped(to: Range)—This method compares the original range with the range specified by the **to** argument and returns a new range with the part of the ranges that overlap.

reversed()—This method returns a collection with the values in reversed order.

Ranges are useful in a variety of situations. For instance, if we need a loop with a fixed number of cycles, we can implement a **for in** loop with a range. The following example iterates over a closed range of integers from 0 to 10, generating a total of 11 cycles.

```
var total = 0
for value in 0...10 {
    total += value
}
print("The total is \(total)")   // "The total is 55"
```
Listing 3-56: Using for in *to iterate over a range*

We can also invert the loop with the **reversed()** method.

```
var message = ""
var range = 0..<10

for item in range.reversed() {
    message += "\(item) "
}
print(message)   // "9 8 7 6 5 4 3 2 1 0 "
```
Listing 3-57: Inverting a range

This example creates a range from 0 to 9 with the **..<** operator and then calls the **reversed()** method to invert it. This method creates a collection with the values in reversed order, so we can read it with a **for in** loop. The statement inside the loop adds the values to the **message** string, and this string is printed on the console to confirm that the values were effectively reversed.

Ranges can also simplify **switch** statements that have to consider multiple values per case.

Chapter 3 - Swift Paradigm

```
var age = 6
var message = "You have to go to "

switch age {
   case 2...4:
      message += "Day Care"
   case 5...11:
      message += "Elementary School"
   case 12...17:
      message += "High School"
   case 18..<22:
      message += "College"
   case 22...:
      message += "Work"
   default:
      message += "Breastfeeding"
}
print(message)   // "You have to go to Elementary School"
```

Listing 3-58: Using range operators in a `switch` *statement*

In this example, we compare an age with different ranges of values. If the value of **age** is within one of the ranges, the instructions for that **case** are executed. As illustrated by this example, we can also declare only one side of a range and let the system determine the other. The last **case** creates a one-sided close range from the value 22 to the maximum value allowed for the data type.

As mentioned before, ranges are used by the **random()** method to get a random value. The following example generates a loop that calculates multiple random values from 1 to 10. The condition stops the loop when the number returned by the method is equal to 5. Inside the loop, we also increment the value of the **attempts** variable to calculate the number of cycles required for the **random()** method to return our number.

```
var mynumber: Int = 0
var attempts = 0

while mynumber != 5 {
   mynumber = Int.random(in: 1...10)
   attempts += 1
}
print("It took \(attempts) attempts to get the number 5")
```

Listing 3-59: Calculating random numbers

(Basic) **String Structures**

Not only primitive data types and ranges are structures, but also the rest of the data types defined in the Swift Standard Library, including the **String** data type. As we have seen in Chapter 2, we can initialize a **String** structure by simply assigning a string (a text between double quotes) to a constant or a variable. This is another shortcut. In the background, instances of the **String** structure are created from the initializer included in the structure's definition.

String(Value)—This initializer creates a string from the value provided by the argument. The **String** structure defines multiple versions of this initializer to create strings from different types of values, including other strings, characters, and numbers.

Once the string is created, we can manipulate it with the properties and methods provided by the **String** structure. The following are the most frequently used.

isEmpty—This property returns a Boolean that indicates whether the value is an empty string. This is the same as comparing the string with an empty string (`string == ""`).

count—This property returns the total number of characters in the string.

first—This property returns the first character in the string.

last—This property returns the last character in the string.

lowercased()—This method returns a copy of the string in lowercase letters.

uppercased()—This method returns a copy of the string in uppercase letters.

hasPrefix(String**)**—This method returns a Boolean value that indicates whether the string begins with the text specified by the argument or not.

hasSuffix(String**)**—This method returns a Boolean value that indicates whether the string ends with the text specified by the argument or not.

contains(String**)**—This method returns a Boolean value that indicates whether the character or string specified by the argument exists in the string or not.

Most of the time, we will assign a string directly to a variable as we have done so far, but the `String()` initializer is useful when we need to convert values into strings. For instance, the following example converts the number 44 into a string and counts the number of digits.

```
var age = String(44)
var mytext = "Total digits \(age.count)"   // "Total digits 2"
```

Listing 3-60: Converting a number into a string

Swift strings are composed of Unicode characters, which occupy different amounts of memory. Because of this, it is not possible to establish the position of a character using integer values. The index of the first character is always 0, but the indexes of the consecutive characters depend on the size of their predecessors. Swift solves this problem by defining a data type called `Index`. This is a structure defined inside the `String` structure that was designed to manage string indexes. The `String` structure includes properties and methods to work with indexes and access the characters of a string. The following are the most frequently used.

startIndex—This property returns the index value of the first character of the string.

endIndex—This property returns the index value of one position after the last character of the string. It is useful to manipulate range of characters, as we will see later.

firstIndex(of: Character**)**—This method returns the index where the character specified by the **of** argument appears for the first time in the string.

lastIndex(of: Character**)**—This method returns the last index where the character specified by the **of** argument appears in the string.

insert(Character, **at:** Index**)**—This method inserts into the string the character provided by the first argument at the position determined by the **at** argument.

insert(contentsOf: String, **at:** Index**)**—This method inserts into the string the value of the **contentsOf** argument at the position determined by the **at** argument.

remove(at: Index**)**—This method removes and returns the character at the position determined by the **at** argument.

prefix(Int**)**—This method returns a string created from the first character of the original string to the maximum length determined by the attribute.

prefix(through: Index)—This method returns a string created from the first character of the original string to the character at the index indicated by the **through** argument.

prefix(upTo: Index)—This method returns a string created from the first character of the original string to the character at the index indicated by the **upTo** argument, but without including this last character.

replaceSubrange(Range, **with:** String)—This method replaces the characters in the position determined by the range provided as the first argument with the string provided by the **with** argument.

removeSubrange(Range)—This method removes the characters in the positions determined by the range specified by the argument.

Strings are collection of values. To access a specific character in a string, we must declare the **Index** structure with the index of the character we want to read after the name of the variable that contains the string, enclosed in square brackets, as in the following example.

```
var text = "Hello World"
if !text.isEmpty {
   let start = text.startIndex
   let firstChar = text[start]

   print("First character is \(firstChar)")   // "First character is H"
}
```

Listing 3-61: Processing the string's characters

The first thing we do in this example is to check the value of the **isEmpty** property to make sure the string is not empty and there are characters to read (notice the **!** operator to invert the condition). Once we know that there are characters to work with, we get the index of the string's first character from the **startIndex** property and read the character in that position using square brackets.

If we want to access a character in a different position, we must increment the value returned by **startIndex**. The trick is that, since **Index** values are not integers, we cannot just add a number to them. Instead, we must use the methods provided by the **String** structure.

index(after: Index)—This method increments the index specified by the **after** argument one unit and returns a new **Index** value with the result.

index(before: Index)—This method decrements the index specified by the **before** argument one unit and returns a new **Index** value with the result.

index(Index, **offsetBy:** Int)—This method increments the index specified by the first argument the amount of units specified by the **offsetBy** argument and returns a new **Index** value with the result.

The following example advances the initial index 6 positions to get a different character.

```
var text = "Hello World"
if text != "" {
   let start = text.startIndex
   let newIndex = text.index(start, offsetBy: 6)

   print("The character is \(text[newIndex])")   // "The character is W"
}
```

Listing 3-62: Calculating a specific index

The **index()** method applied in Listing 3-62 takes an integer to calculate the new index. The original index is incremented the number of units indicated by the integer and the resulting **Index** value is returned. With this index, we get the character at the position 6 (indexes start from 0).

If we wanted to get the previous index, we could have specified a negative number of units for the offset value, but another way to move forward and backward is to implement the other versions of the **index()** method. The following example gets the next index after the initial index and prints the corresponding character on the console.

```
var text = "John"
let start = text.startIndex
var next = text.index(after: start)

print("Second letter is \(text[next])")   // "Second letter is o"
```

Listing 3-63: Getting the next index

Once the right index is calculated, we can call some of the **String** methods to insert or remove characters. The **insert()** method, for instance, inserts a single character at the position indicated by the second argument. In the following example, we call it with the value of **endIndex** to add a character at the end of the string (**endindex** points to the position after the last character).

```
var text = "Hello World"
text.insert("!", at: text.endIndex)

print("New string is \(text)")   // "New string is Hello World!"
```

Listing 3-64: Inserting a character in a string

If we do not know where the character is located, we can find the index with the **firstIndex()** method. The value returned by this method is an optional containing the **Index** value of the first character that matches the argument or **nil** if no character is found. In the following example, we implement it to find the first space character and remove it with the **remove()** method.

```
var text = "Hello World"
var findIndex = text.firstIndex(of: " ")

if let index = findIndex {
    text.remove(at: index)
    print("New string is \(text)")   // "New string is HelloWorld"
}
```

Listing 3-65: Removing a character

If we want to work with groups of characters, we must implement ranges of **Index** values.

```
var text = "Hello World"
var start = text.startIndex
var findIndex = text.firstIndex(of: " ")

if let end = findIndex {
    print("First word is \(text[start..<end])")   //"First word is Hello"
}
```

Listing 3-66: Getting a range of characters

The **firstIndex()** method in Listing 3-66 looks for a space character and returns its index. With this value, we can create a range from the first character to the space character and get the first word. But we must be careful because the **end** index is pointing to the space character, not to the last character of the word. To get the word without the space, we create an open range with the **..<** operator, so the character on the right is not included.

We can also use ranges to replace or remove parts of the text. The **String** structure offers the **replaceSubrange()** and **removeSubrange()** methods for this purpose.

```
var text = "Hello World"
var start = text.startIndex
var findIndex = text.firstIndex(of: " ")

if let end = findIndex {
    text.replaceSubrange(start..<end, with: "Goodbye")   // "Goodbye World"
}
findIndex = text.firstIndex(of: " ")
if let start = findIndex {
    text.removeSubrange(start...)   // "Goodbye"
}
```

Listing 3-67: *Working with ranges of characters*

The **replaceSubrange()** method in Listing 3-67 replaces the characters from the beginning of the string up to the character before the space character ("Hello") with the string "Goodbye", and the **removeSubrange()** method uses an open range to remove the characters of this sentence from the space character to the end of the string (" World"), getting the final string "Goodbye". Notice that after applying the methods over the same string, the indexes are lost and therefore they must be recalculated. That's why before calling the **removeSubrange()** method we search for the position of the space character once more and update the **findIndex** variable.

The rest of the methods provided by the **String** structure are straightforward. For instance, the following example implements two of them to check if a string contains the word "World" at the end and converts all the letters into uppercase letters.

```
let text = "Hello World"

if text.hasSuffix("World") {
    print(text.uppercased())   // "HELLO WORLD"
}
```

Listing 3-68: *Implementing* String *methods*

Basic Array Structures

The strings studied before and the values we have created in previous examples with functions such as **stride()** or **repeatElement()** are collections of values. Collections do not represent a value; they are containers for other values. A value of type **String** does not contain the string "Hello", it contains a collection of variables of type **Character**, with the values H, e, l, l, and o. Swift includes several collections like this, some were defined to contain specific values, like **String**, and others are generic (they can store values of any data type we need). One of those collections is **Array**.

Arrays are collections that contain an ordered list of values. They are generic structures that have the capacity to store all the values we need of any data type we want, but with the condition that once a data type is selected, all the values must be of that same type. For example, if we create an array of type **Int**, we will only be able to store values of type **Int** in it. Swift offers multiple syntaxes to create an array, including the following initializers.

Array<Type>()—This initializer returns an empty **Array** structure of the data type indicated by the value of **Type**.

Array(repeating: Value, **count:** Int)—This initializer returns an **Array** structure with copies of the same value. The **repeating** argument determines the value to copy, and the **count** argument determines how many copies the array will contain.

A shortcut to create an array is declaring the data type between square brackets followed by parentheses (e.g., **var list = [Int]()**), but the most frequently used is declaring the array with initial values enclosed in square brackets and separated by comma.

```
var list: [Int] = [15, 25, 35]
```

Listing 3-69: Declaring arrays

As with any other variable, Swift can infer the data type from the values.

```
var list = [15, 25, 35]
```

Listing 3-70: Declaring arrays with type inference

The **list** array declared in this example is initialized with three integer values, 15, 25 and 35. The values of an array are usually called *elements* or *items*. On these terms, we can say that the code in Listing 3-70 declares an array of three elements of type **Int**.

An index is automatically assigned to each value starting from 0, and as with strings, we must specify the index of the value we want to read surrounded by square brackets.

```
var list = [15, 25, 35]
print(list[1])  // 25
```

Listing 3-71: Reading the array's elements

The last statement in Listing 3-71 prints the value of the second element of the **list** array on the console (the element at index 1). We can also use indexes to modify the values.

```
var list = [15, 25, 35]
list[0] = 400
print(list)  // [400, 25, 35]
```

Listing 3-72: Assigning a new value to an element

Assigning new values is only possible for elements that already exist in the array. If we try to access an element with an index that doesn't exist, we get an error. One way to add a new element, or several, is with the **+=** operator.

```
var list = [15, 25, 35]
list += [45, 55]
print(list)  // [15, 25, 35, 45, 55]
```

Listing 3-73: Adding new elements to an array

The **+=** operator adds an array at the end of another array. In Listing 3-73, we use it to add two more elements to the array declared in the first statement. The **+=** operator concatenates the two arrays and assigns the result back to the same variable. If we want to use two or more arrays to create a new one, we can apply the **+** operator.

```
var list1 = [15, 25, 35]
var list2 = [45, 55, 65]
var final = list1 + list2  // [15, 25, 35, 45, 55, 65]
```

Listing 3-74: *Concatenating two arrays*

It is possible to declare arrays of arrays. These types of arrays are called *Multidimensional Arrays*. Arrays inside arrays are listed separated by comma.

```
var list: [[Int]] = [[2, 45, 31], [5, 10], [81, 12]]
```

Listing 3-75: *Creating multidimensional arrays*

This example creates an array of arrays of integers. (Notice the declaration of the array inside another array `[[Int]]`.) To access the values, we must declare the indexes of each level in square brackets, one after another. The following example returns the first value (index 0) of the second array (index 1). The instruction looks for the array at index 1 and then gets the number at index 0.

```
var list: [[Int]] = [[2, 45, 31], [5, 10], [81, 12]]
print(list[1][0])  // 5
```

Listing 3-76: *Reading values from a multidimensional array*

To remove all the elements from an array, we can assign to the variable one of the initializers introduced before or just the square brackets with no values.

```
var list = [15, 25, 35]
list = []
```

Listing 3-77: *Removing the elements of an array*

Arrays are collections of values and therefore we can iterate over their values with a **for in** loop, as we did with strings before.

```
var total = 0
let list = [15, 25, 35]
for value in list {
   total += value
}
print("The total is \(total)")  // "The total is 75"
```

Listing 3-78: *Reading an array with a* for *in loop*

The code in Listing 3-78 implements a **for in** loop to add the numbers in the **list** array to the **total** variable. At the end, we print the result. Although this is a legit way to do it, arrays offer multiple properties and methods to read and process their values.

count—This property returns the total number of elements in the array.

isEmpty—This property returns a Boolean value that indicates if the array is empty.

first—This property returns the first element of the array or **nil** if the array is empty.

last—This property returns the last element of the array or **nil** if the array is empty.

append(Element**)**—This method adds the value specified by the argument at the end of the array.

insert(Element, at: Int)—This method adds a new element to the array. The first argument is the value we want to assign to the new element, and the **at** argument represents the position of the array where we want to insert the element.

remove(at: Int)—This method removes an element from the array at the index specified by the **at** argument.

removeFirst()—This method removes the first element of the array. It returns the value of the element deleted.

removeLast()—This method removes the last element of the array. It returns the value of the element deleted.

removeAll(where: Closure)—This method removes the elements in the array that meet the condition established by the closure assigned to the `where` argument.

removeSubrange(Range)—This method removes a range of elements from the array. The argument is a range of integers representing the indexes of the elements to remove.

replaceSubrange(Range, with: Array)—This method replaces a range of elements with the elements of the array provided by the **with** argument. The first argument is a range of integers corresponding to the indexes of the elements we want to replace.

dropFirst(Int)—This method removes the number of elements specified by the argument from the beginning of the array. If no amount is declared, only the first element is removed.

dropLast(Int)—This method removes the number of elements specified by the argument from the end of the array. If no amount is declared, only the last element is removed.

enumerated()—This method is used to iterate over the elements of the array. It returns a tuple containing the index and the value of the current element.

min()—This method compares the values of the elements and returns the smallest.

max()—This method compares the values of the elements and returns the largest.

sorted()—This method returns an array with the elements of the array in ascending order.

sorted(by: Closure)—This method returns an array with the elements of the array in the order determined by the closure provided to the **by** argument.

randomElement()—This method randomly selects an element from the array and returns it. If the array is empty, the value returned is `nil`.

shuffled()—This method returns an array with the elements of the array in random order.

reversed()—This method returns an array with the elements of the array in reverse order.

swapAt(Int, Int)—This method exchanges the values of the elements at the indexes specified by the arguments.

joined(separator: String)—This method returns a string that includes all the values in an array of strings joined by the string specified by the **separator** argument.

filter(Closure)—This method filters an array and returns another array with the values that passed the filter. The argument is a closure that processes the elements and returns a Boolean value indicating whether the value passed the filter or not.

map(Closure)—This method returns a new array containing the results of processing each of the values of the array.

compactMap(Closure)—This method returns a new array containing the results of processing each of the values of the array, but ignores the values that produce a `nil` result.

reduce(Value, Closure)—This method sends the values of the array to the closure one by one and returns the result of the operation. The first argument is the value that is going to be processed with the first value of the array.

contains(where: Closure)—This method returns a Boolean that determines if the array contains an element that meets the condition in the closure.

allSatisfy(Closure)—This method returns a Boolean value that determines if all the elements in the array comply with the requisites of a closure.

difference(from: Array)—This method returns a `CollectionDifference` structure containing all the changes that have to be performed to synchronize the array with the array provided by the **from** argument. This method can work in conjunction with the `applying()` method to apply all the changes in the array at once.

In the previous example, we have seen how to iterate over the elements of an array with the **for in** loop, but that iteration only returns the value of the element, not its index. An alternative is provided by the **enumerated()** method, designed to work with these types of loops. Each cycle returns a tuple with the index and the value of the current element.

```
let fruits = ["Banana", "Orange", "Apple"]
var message = "My fruits:"
for (myindex, myfruit) in fruits.enumerated() {
   message += " \(myindex + 1)-\(myfruit)"
}
print(message)   // "My fruits: 1-Banana 2-Orange 3-Apple"
```

Listing 3-79: Reading indexes and values of an array

This example uses the constants **myindex** and **myfruit** to capture the values produced by the **enumerated()** method and generates a string. Notice that since the array's indexes start from 0, we added 1 to **myindex** to start counting from 1.

Another useful property is **count**. As mentioned before, we can access each element of the array with the index between square brackets. But trying to read a value in an index that has not yet been defined will produce an error. To make sure that the index exists, we can check whether it is greater than 0 and less than the total amount of elements in the array using this property.

```
let ages = [32, 540, 12, 27, 54]
let index = 3
if index > 0 && index < ages.count {
   print("The value is: \(ages[index])")   // "The value is: 27"
}
```

Listing 3-80: Checking whether an array contains a value in a specific index

The methods to add and remove elements from an array are straightforward. The following example illustrates how to implement them.

```
var fruits = ["Banana", "Orange"]
if !fruits.isEmpty {
   fruits.append("Apple")   // ["Banana", "Orange", "Apple"]
   fruits.removeFirst()   // "Banana"
   fruits.insert("Pear", at: 1)   // ["Orange", "Pear", "Apple"]
```

```
fruits.insert(contentsOf: ["Cherry", "Peach"], at: 2)
// ["Orange", "Pear", "Cherry", "Peach", "Apple"]
}
```

Listing 3-81: Adding and removing elements

 IMPORTANT: Every time an array is modified, its indexes are reassigned. For instance, if you remove the first element of an array of three elements, the index 0 is reassigned to the second element and the index 1 to the third element. The system makes sure that the indexes are always consecutive and start from 0.

A more complex method is **removeAll(where:)**. This method removes several elements at once, but only those that meet a condition. The condition is established by a closure that processes each of the values in the array and returns **true** or **false** depending on whether the value meets the condition or not. In the following example, we compare each value with the string "Orange" and therefore all the values "Orange" are removed from the array.

```
var fruits = ["Banana", "Orange", "Apple", "Orange"]
fruits.removeAll(where: { value in
   value == "Orange"
})
print(fruits)  // ["Banana", "Apple"]
```

Listing 3-82: Removing all the elements that meet a condition

Another method that works with a closure is **contains(where:)**. In the following example, we use this method to determine whether an array contains a value greater than 60 or not.

```
var list = [55, 12, 32, 5, 9]
let found = list.contains(where: { value in
   value > 60
})
print(found)  // false
```

Listing 3-83: Finding if an element meets a condition

We can also select a random value with the **randomElement()** method. This method selects a value from the array and returns an optional, so we must compare it against **nil** or use optional binding before processing it, as in the following example.

```
let fruits = ["Banana", "Orange", "Apple"]
if let randomValue = fruits.randomElement() {
   print("The selected value is: \(randomValue)")
}
```

Listing 3-84: Selecting a random value from an array

Another random operation is performed by the **shuffled()** method. With this method we can randomly sort the elements of an array.

```
var fruits = ["Banana", "Orange", "Apple"]
fruits = fruits.shuffled()
print(fruits)  // e.g., ["Orange", "Apple", "Banana"]
```

Listing 3-85: Changing the order of the elements of an array

Besides working with all the elements of an array, we can do it with a range of elements.

Chapter 3 - Swift Paradigm

```
var fruits = ["Banana", "Orange", "Apple", "Cherry"]
var someFruits = fruits[0..<2]  // ["Banana", "Orange"]
print("The new selection has \(someFruits.count) fruits")
```

Listing 3-86: Reading a range of elements

This example gets the elements at the indexes 0 and 1 from the **fruits** array and assigns them to the new **someFruits** array. Now we have two arrays: **fruits** with 4 elements and **someFruits** with 2.

Arrays created from a range of indexes are of type **ArraySlice**. This is another collection type provided by Swift to store temporary arrays that are composed of elements taken from other arrays. We can iterate over these types of arrays with a loop or read its elements as we do with normal arrays, but if we want to assign them to other array variables or use them for persistent storage, we must cast them as **Array** types using the **Array()** initializer. The initializer takes the values in the **ArraySlice** variable and returns a normal array, as shown next.

```
var fruits = ["Banana", "Orange", "Apple", "Cherry"]
var someFruits = fruits[0..<2]  // ["Banana", "Orange"]
var newArray = Array(someFruits)
```

Listing 3-87: Casting arrays of type ArraySlice

The **Array** structure also offers the **removeSubrange()** and **replaceSubrange()** methods to remove and replace a range of elements.

```
var fruits = ["Banana", "Orange", "Apple", "Banana", "Banana"]
fruits.removeSubrange(1...2)
fruits.replaceSubrange(0..<2, with: ["Cherry", "Cherry"])
print(fruits)  // "["Cherry", "Cherry", "Banana"]"
```

Listing 3-88: Removing and replacing elements

In Listing 3-88, we call the **removeSubrange()** method to remove the range of elements from index 1 to 2 (getting an array filled with the value "Banana"), and then we call the **replaceSubrange()** method to replace the elements from index 0 to 1 with another array filled with "Cherries". This is just to illustrate how the methods work, but it shows a recurrent situation in app development where sometimes we need to fill a collection with elements of the same value. When working with arrays, this is easy to achieve. The **Array** structure includes an initializer that takes two arguments, **repeating** and **count**, and generates an array with the number of elements indicated by **count** and the value indicated by **repeating**.

```
var fruits = ["Banana", "Orange", "Apple"]
let total = fruits.count
let newArray = Array(repeating: "Cherry", count: total)
fruits.replaceSubrange(0..<total, with: newArray)
print(fruits)  // "["Cherry", "Cherry", "Cherry"]"
```

Listing 3-89: Initializing an array with elements of the same value

In this example, we create an array with the same amount of elements as the **fruits** array and then use the **replaceSubrange()** method to replace every element with a new one.

The methods to remove and replace elements of an array are not selective enough; they affect the elements in a specific index or a range of indexes without considering their values. If we want to perform a more specific job, we can use the **filter()** method. This method takes a closure and sends each element to the closure for processing. If the closure returns **true**, the element is included in the new array, otherwise it is ignored, as shown next.

```
var fruits = ["Apple", "Grape", "Banana", "Grape"]
var filteredArray = fruits.filter({ $0 != "Grape" })
print(filteredArray)  // "["Apple", "Banana"]"
```

Listing 3-90: *Filtering the values of an array*

The **filter()** method sends the values one by one to the closure, the closure replaces the placeholder (**$0**) with the current value, compares it with the value "Grape", and returns a Boolean with the result. If the value is **true**, the element is included in **filteredArray**.

If what we need is to modify the elements of an array all at once, we can use the **map()** method. This method sends to a closure the values of the array one by one and returns another array with the results produced by the closure.

```
let list = [2, 4, 8, 16]
let half = list.map({ $0 / 2 })
print(half)  // "[1, 2, 4, 8]"
```

Listing 3-91: *Mapping an array*

The example in Listing 3-91 defines a list of integers and then calls the **map()** method on the array to divide each value by 2. The **map()** method sends the values of the array to the closure one by one, the closure replaces the placeholder (**$0**) with the current value, divides the number by 2, and returns the result. All the results are stored in a new array and that array is returned by the **map()** method when the process is over.

Of course, we can perform any kind of operations we want on the values in the closure. For instance, the following code converts the values into strings with the **String()** initializer.

```
let list = [1, 2, 3, 4, 5]
let listtext = list.map({ String($0) })
print(listtext)  // "["1", "2", "3", "4", "5"]"
```

Listing 3-92: *Converting the elements of an array into strings*

When all we want to do is to initialize a new structure with the value received by the closure, instead of a closure, Swift allows us to provide the structure's initializer. The value received by the closure is sent to the initializer and a new structure of that type is returned.

```
let list = [1, 2, 3, 4, 5]
let listtext = list.map(String.init)
print(listtext)  // "["1", "2", "3", "4", "5"]"
```

Listing 3-93: *Using a structure initializer with the* map() *method*

This example produces the same result as before, but instead of using a closure, we use a reference to the **String** initializer. The **map()** method sends the value to the initializer, the initializer returns a new **String** structure with that value, and the process continues as always.

Another way to process all the values of an array at once is with the **reduce()** method. This method works like **map()**, but instead of storing the results in an array, it sends the result back to the closure to get only one value in return. For instance, the following code uses the **reduce()** method to get the result of the addition of all the numbers in an array.

```
let list = [2, 4, 8, 16]
let total = list.reduce(0, { $0 + $1 })
print(total)  // "30"
```

Listing 3-94: *Reducing an array*

The code in Listing 3-94 defines an array of integers and then calls the **reduce()** method on it. This method sends two values at a time to the closure. In the first cycle, the values sent to the closure are the ones provided by the first argument (**0**) and the first value of the array (**2**). In the second cycle, the values sent to the closure are the value returned by the closure in the first cycle (0 + 2 = **2**), and the second value of the array (**4**). The loop goes on until all the values of the array are processed.

When it comes to sorting the elements of an array, there are several options available. The most frequently used are **reversed()** and **sorted()** (and its variant **sorted(by:)**). The **reversed()** method takes the elements of an array and returns a new array with the same elements in reversed order. The value returned by the method is stored in a structure of type **ReversedCollection**. As we did before with the **ArraySlice** type, we can cast these values as **Array** structures with the **Array()** initializer.

```
var fruits = ["Apple", "Blueberry", "Banana"]
var array = Array(fruits.reversed())   // ["Banana", "Blueberry", "Apple"]
```

Listing 3-95: Reversing the elements of an array

The **sorted()** method sorts the array in ascending order and returns a new array.

```
var fruits = ["Blueberry", "Apple", "Banana"]
let basket = fruits.sorted()
print(basket)   // ["Apple", "Banana", "Blueberry"]
```

Listing 3-96: Sorting the elements of an array

If we want to sort the elements in a custom order, we can use the **sorted(by:)** method. This method works in a similar fashion to the **filter()** method studied before. It takes a function or a closure that receives the value of two elements and returns **true** if the first element should appear before the second element, or **false** otherwise.

```
var fruits = ["Apple", "Raspberry", "Banana", "Grape"]
var newArray = fruits.sorted(by: { $0 > $1 })
print(newArray[0])   // "Raspberry"
```

Listing 3-97: Sorting the elements of an array in a custom order

When the **sorted()** method is executed, it performs a loop. On each cycle, two values of the **fruits** array are sent to the closure. The closure compares the values and returns **true** or **false** accordingly. This indicates to the **sorted()** method which value should appear before the other in the new array, effectively sorting the elements. Unlike the example we programmed for the **filter()** method, this one does not compare the argument against a specific value. This allows us to order arrays of any data type. For example, we can use the closure to sort an array of integers.

```
var numbers = [55, 12, 32, 5, 9]
var newArray = numbers.sorted(by: { $0 < $1 })
print(newArray[0])   // 5
```

Listing 3-98: Sorting an array of integers

If we decide to work with specific data types, we can perform custom tasks. For example, we can count the characters in the strings and sort them according to their length.

```
var fruits = ["Apple", "Blueberry", "Banana", "Grape"]
var newArray = fruits.sorted(by: { $0.count < $1.count })
print(newArray)  // ["Apple", "Grape", "Banana", "Blueberry"]
```

Listing 3-99: Sorting strings according to the number of characters

Arrays also include two powerful methods to compare elements: **min()** and **max()**. These methods compare the values and return the smallest or largest, respectively.

```
let ages = [32, 540, 12, 27]
if let older = ages.max() {
   let digits = String(older)
   print("The maximum age is \(digits.count) digits long")
}
```

Listing 3-100: Getting the largest element

The code in Listing 3-100 takes the largest value from an array of integers and counts the number of digits in the value returned. Because the **max()** method returns an optional, we use optional binding to read the value. The rest of the code turns this value into a string and counts its characters to print the number of digits on the console.

Besides selecting the largest or smallest value with the **max()** and **min()** methods, we can also fetch values from the array using the **first** and **last** properties.

```
let ages = [32, 540, 12, 27]
if let firstAge = ages.first {
   print("The first person is \(firstAge) years old")  // 32
}
```

Listing 3-101: Getting the first value of an array

The value returned by the **first** property is also an optional, so we use optional binding again to read the value and store it in the **firstAge** constant. The **first** and **last** properties only get the first and last values, respectively. To search for any value in the array or its index, the **Array** structure offers the following methods.

firstIndex(of: Element)—This method performs a search from the beginning of the array and returns the index of the first element that matches the value of the **of** argument.

lastIndex(of: Element)—This method performs a search from the end of the array and returns the index of the first element that matches the value of the **of** argument.

firstIndex(where: Closure)—This method returns the index of the first value that meets the condition in the closure assigned to the **where** argument.

lastIndex(where: Closure)—This method returns the index of the last value that meets the condition in the closure assigned to the **where** argument.

first(where: Closure)—This method returns the first value that meets the condition in the closure assigned to the **where** argument.

last(where: Closure)—This method returns the last value that meets the condition in the closure assigned to the **where** argument.

If we only need the index of a particular element, we can use the **firstIndex(of:)** method. For instance, we can look for the first appearance of a number in an array and get the index.

```
let ages = [32, 540, 12, 27, 54]
if let index = ages.firstIndex(of: 540) {
    print("The value is at the position \(index)")   // 1
}
```

Listing 3-102: Getting the index of a specific value

If what we need instead is to get the index of a value that meets a condition, we can use methods like **firstIndex(where:)** or **lastIndex(where:)** depending on whether we want to search from the beginning or the end of the array.

```
let ages = [32, 540, 12, 27, 54]
let first = ages.firstIndex(where: { $0 < 30 })
if first != nil {
    print("The first value is at index \(first!)")   // 2
}
```

Listing 3-103: Getting the index of a value that meets a condition

In this example, we look for the index of a value smaller than 30. The **firstIndex(where:)** method reads every value of the array from the beginning and sends them to the closure assigned to the **where** argument. The closure takes the current value returned by the placeholder and compares it against the number 30, if the value is greater than 30, the closure returns **false**, otherwise it returns **true** and the index of that value is assigned to the **first** variable. In this case, the first number in the array smaller than 30 is 12, and therefore the index assigned to the variable is 2.

Basic Set Structures

If we store two elements in an array, one element automatically receives the index 0 and the other the index 1. This correlation between indexes and values never changes, allowing elements to be listed always in the right order and have elements with the same value at different indexes. But if we don't care about the order, we can create a set. Sets are like arrays, but they do not assign an index to their values, therefore there is no order and all the values are unique. Sets are created from the **Set** structure.

> **Set<Type>()**—This initializer returns an empty **Set** structure of the data type indicated by the value of **Type**.

This initializer can be used to create an empty set (e.g., **let myset = Set<Int>()**), but we can also use square brackets, as we do with arrays. The difference with arrays is that we must specify that we are creating a set with the **Set** keyword, as shown next.

```
var ages: Set<Int> = []
```

Listing 3-104: Creating an empty set of integers

If we initialize the set with some values, Swift can infer its type from their data type, simplifying the declaration.

```
var ages: Set = [15, 25, 35, 45]
```

Listing 3-105: Creating a set of integers

To access and process the elements of a set, we can use a **for in** loop, as we did before with strings and arrays, but sets also provide their own properties and methods for this purpose.

count—This property returns the number of elements in the set.

isEmpty—This property returns a Boolean value that indicates whether the set is empty or not.

contains(Element**)**—This method returns a Boolean value that indicates whether there is an element in the set with the value specified by the argument.

contains(where: Closure**)**—This method returns a Boolean value that determines if the set contains an element that meets the condition in the closure.

min()—This method compares the elements in the set and returns the smallest.

max()—This method compares the elements in the set and returns the largest.

sorted()—This method returns an array with the elements of the set in ascending order.

sorted(by: Closure**)**—This method returns an array with the elements of the set in the order determined by the closure specified by the **by** argument.

randomElement()—This method randomly selects an element from the set and returns it. If the set is empty, the value returned is `nil`.

shuffled()—This method returns an array with the elements of the set in random order.

insert(Element**)**—This method inserts a new element in the set with the value provided by the argument.

union(Collection**)**—This method returns a new set created with the values of the original set plus the values provided by the argument (an array or another set).

subtract(Collection**)**—This method returns a new set created by subtracting the elements provided by the argument to the original set.

intersection(Collection**)**—This method returns a new set created with the values of the original set that match the values provided by the argument (an array or another set).

remove(Element**)**—This method removes from the set the element with the value provided by the argument.

isSubset(of: Set**)**—This method returns a Boolean value that indicates whether or not the set is a subset of the set specified by the **of** argument.

isSuperset(of: Set**)**—This method returns a Boolean value that indicates whether or not the set is a superset of the set specified by the **of** argument.

isDisjoint(with: Set**)**—This method returns a Boolean value that indicates whether or not the original set and the set specified by the **with** argument have elements in common.

Using these methods, we can easily access and modify the values of a set. For instance, we can implement the `contains()` method to search for a value.

```
var fruits: Set = ["Apple", "Orange", "Banana"]

if fruits.contains("Apple") {
   print("Apple exists!")
}
```

Listing 3-106: Using contains() *to find an element in a set*

To insert a new element, we just have to execute the `insert()` method.

```
var fruits: Set = ["Apple", "Orange", "Banana"]
if !fruits.contains("Grape") {
    fruits.insert("Grape")
}
print("The set has \(fruits.count) elements")  // 4
```

Listing 3-107: Inserting a new element in a set

In listing 3-107, we use the **contains()** method again to check if an element with the value "Grape" already exists in the set. But this is not really necessary. If the value is already part of the set, the **insert()** method does not perform any action.

To remove an element, we must call the **remove()** method.

```
var fruits: Set = ["Apple", "Orange", "Banana"]
if let removed = fruits.remove("Banana") {
    print("\(removed) was removed")  // "Banana was removed"
}
```

Listing 3-108: Removing an element from a set

The **remove()** method removes the element which value matches the value of its argument and returns an optional with the value that have been removed or **nil** in case of failure. In the code of Listing 3-108, we get the value returned by the method and print a message if the value was successfully removed.

Sets are collections without order. Every time we read a set, the order in which its values are returned is not guaranteed, but we can use the **sorted()** method to create an array with the values of the set in order. The following example sorts the elements of the **fruits** set in alphabetical order, creating a new array we call **orderFruits**.

```
var fruits: Set = ["Apple", "Orange", "Banana"]
var orderFruits = fruits.sorted()
if let lastItem = orderFruits.last {
    print(lastItem)  // "Orange"
}
```

Listing 3-109: Sorting the elements of a set

The rest of the methods available are straightforward. The following example joins two sets with the **union()** method and then subtracts elements from the result with **subtract()**.

```
var fruits: Set = ["Apple", "Banana"]
var newSet = fruits.union(["Grapes"])  // "Banana", "Grapes", "Apple"
newSet.subtract(["Apple", "Banana"])  // "Grapes"
```

Listing 3-110: Combining sets

The **Set** structure also offer methods to compare sets. We can determine if a set is a subset or a superset of another set with the **isSubset()** and **isSuperset()** methods, or check if two sets have elements in common with the **isDisjoint()** method. The following example implements the **isSubset()** method to check if the fruits in a basket come from the store. The code checks if the elements in the **basket** set are found in the **store** set and returns **true** in case of success.

```
var store: Set = ["Banana", "Apple", "Orange", "Pear"]
var basket: Set = ["Apple", "Orange"]
```

```
if basket.isSubset(of: store) {
    print("The fruits in the basket are from the store")
}
```

Listing 3-111: Comparing sets

Basic | Dictionary Structures

There is only one way to access the elements of an array and that is through their numeric indexes. Dictionaries offer a better alternative. With dictionaries, we can define the indexes ourselves using any custom value we want. Each index, also known as *key*, must be explicitly declared along with its value. Swift offers multiple syntaxes to create a dictionary, including the following initializers.

Dictionary<Type1: Type2**>()**—This initializer returns an empty **Dictionary** structure with the keys and values of the data type indicated by **Type1** and **Type2**.

Dictionary(grouping: Collection, **by:** Closure)—This initializer returns a **Dictionary** structure with the values provided by the **grouping** argument grouped in arrays according to the keys returned by the closure provided by the **by** argument.

If the data types are explicitly defined, we can also declare a dictionary with a simplified syntax, as in **var list: [String: String] = Dictionary()**, or use square brackets with a colon, as in **var list: [String: String] = [:]**. The latest is also used to define a dictionary with initial values. In this case, the keys and values are separated by a colon and the items are separated by comma, as in the following example.

```
var list: [String: String] = ["First": "Apple", "Second": "Orange"]
```

Listing 3-112: Declaring a dictionary with initial values

The first value of each item is the key and the second is the value. Of course, if the keys and the values are of a clear data type, Swift can infer them.

```
var list = ["First": "Apple", "Second": "Orange"]
```

Listing 3-113: Declaring a dictionary with type inference

As with arrays, if we want to read or replace a value, we must declare the key (index) in square brackets after the name of the dictionary.

```
var list = ["First": "Apple", "Second": "Orange"]
list["Second"] = "Banana"
```

Listing 3-114: Assigning a new value to an element of a dictionary

The second statement in Listing 3-114 assigns a new value to the element identified with the "Second" key. Now, the dictionary contains two elements with the values "Apple" and "Banana". If the key used to assign the new value exists, the system updates the value, but if the key does not exist, a new element is created, as shown next.

```
var list = ["First": "Apple", "Second": "Orange"]
list["Third"] = "Banana"
print(list)  // "["Second": "Orange", "First": "Apple", "Third":
"Banana"]"
```

Listing 3-115: Adding a new element to a dictionary

Chapter 3 - Swift Paradigm

In this example, the second statement assigns the value "Banana" to a key that does not exist, and therefore the system creates the new element with the specified key and value.

Dictionaries return optional values. If we try to read an element with a key that does not exist, the value returned is **nil**.

```
var list = ["First": "Apple", "Second": "Orange"]
print(list["Third"])   // nil
```

Listing 3-116: Reading an element that does not exist

The code in Listing 3-116 tries to read a value with the "Third" key in the **list** dictionary that does not exist. As a result, the value **nil** is printed on the console. If the element exists and we want to read its value, we must unwrap it.

```
var list = ["First": "Apple", "Second": "Orange"]
if let first = list["First"], let second = list["Second"] {
   print("We have \(first) and \(second)")   // "We have Apple and Orange"
}
```

Listing 3-117: Reading a value in a dictionary

Since dictionary elements are optionals, we can assign the value **nil** to remove them. The following example removes the element with the "First" key.

```
var list = ["First": "Apple", "Second": "Orange"]
list["First"] = nil
```

Listing 3-118: Removing an element from a dictionary

As with arrays and sets, we can also iterate over the values of a dictionary with a **for in** loop. The value produced by each cycle of the loop is a tuple containing the element's key and value.

```
var fruits = ["First": "Apple", "Second": "Orange"]
var message = "My fruits:"
for (mykey, myfruit) in fruits {
   message += " \(mykey)-\(myfruit)"
}
print(message)   // "My fruits: First-Apple Second-Orange"
```

Listing 3-119: Using for in to iterate over a dictionary

The **for in** loop in Listing 3-119 reads the elements of the **fruits** dictionary one by one, assigns the index and the value to the **mykey** and **myfruit** constants, and adds their values to the **message** variable. At the end, we get a string with all the keys and values in the dictionary.

Of course, dictionaries may also contain arrays as values. The declaration is simple, the key is declared as always, and the single value is replaced by an array.

```
var fruits: [String: [String]] = ["A": ["Apple", "Apricot"], "B":
["Banana", "Blueberries"]]
```

Listing 3-120: Combining dictionaries with arrays

Reading the values of a dictionary like this is a bit more complicated. Because dictionaries return optionals, we cannot just specify the indexes as we do for multidimensional arrays (see Listing 3-76). The array returned by the dictionary must be unwrapped before reading the values.

```
var fruits: [String: [String]] = ["A": ["Apple", "Apricot"], "B":
["Banana", "Blueberries"]]
if let list = fruits["A"] {
   print(list[0])   // "Apple"
}
```

Listing 3-121: Reading arrays inside dictionaries

In this example, we create a dictionary with two values. The values are arrays of strings with a string as key. The code gets the array corresponding to the "A" key, unwraps it, and stores it in a constant. The `list` constant now contains the array assigned to the "A" key, and therefore when we read the element at index 0, we get the value "Apple".

What we have created in the last example is what the `Dictionary(grouping:, by:)` initializer does. It takes the values of a collection and groups them together in arrays according to the value of a key returned by the closure, as shown next.

```
let list = [15, 25, 38, 55, 42]
let group5 = Dictionary(grouping: list, by: {$0 % 5 == 0 ? "Yes" : "No"})
print(group5)   // "["No": [38, 42], "Yes": [15, 25, 55]]"
```

Listing 3-122: Grouping values by a key

The `Dictionary` initializer implemented in Listing 3-122 takes the values of the `list` array, sends them to the closure one by one, and creates a new dictionary with the keys returned by the closure. The closure receives the value and returns the strings "Yes" or "No" depending on whether the current value is multiple of 5. If the value is multiple of 5, it is included in an array with the "Yes" key, otherwise it is included in an array with the "No" key.

Dictionaries also include properties and methods to manage the values. The following are the most frequently used.

count—This property returns the total number of elements in the dictionary.

isEmpty—This property returns a Boolean value that indicates if the dictionary is empty.

keys—This property returns a collection with the keys in the dictionary.

values—This property returns a collection with the values in the dictionary.

sorted(by: Closure)—This method returns an array of tuples with each element of the dictionary (key and value) in the order determined by the closure.

randomElement()—This method randomly selects an element from the dictionary and returns a tuple with its key and value. If the dictionary is empty, the value returned is `nil`.

shuffled()—This method returns an array of tuples containing the keys and values of each element of the dictionary in random order.

updateValue(Value, **forKey:** Key)—This method updates the value of an element with the value and key specified by its arguments. If the key does not exist, the method creates a new element. If the key exists, it returns the previous value, otherwise, the value returned is `nil`.

removeValue(forKey: Key)—This method removes the element with the key equal to the value of the **forKey** argument. It returns an optional containing the value of the deleted element or `nil` if no element with the specified key was found.

contains(where: Closure)—This method returns a Boolean value that determines if the dictionary contains an element that meets the condition in the closure.

Some of the methods provided by the **Dictionary** structure are like those included in the **Array** and **Set** structures, but others are more specific. For example, the **updateValue()** and **removeValue()** methods require the element's key to process the values.

```
var fruits = ["one": "Banana", "two": "Apple", "three": "Pear"]
fruits.updateValue("Banana", forKey: "three")  // "Pear"
fruits.removeValue(forKey: "one")  // "Banana"
print(fruits)  // "[["three": "Banana", "two": "Apple"]"
```

Listing 3-123: Adding and removing elements from a dictionary

The **updateValue()** method updates the value of an element when there is already an element with that key or creates a new one if the key does not exist. This is the same as assigning a value directly to an element (see Listings 3-114 and 3-115), but the method returns the previous value, which may be useful sometimes.

Like sets, dictionaries are an unordered collection of values, but we can create an array with their elements in a specific order using the **sorted()** method. The method returns the values as tuples, with the element's key first and the value second.

```
var fruits = ["one": "Banana", "two": "Apple", "three": "Pear"]
var list = fruits.sorted(by: { $0.1 < $1.1 })
print(list)
```

Listing 3-124: Sorting the values of a dictionary

As with arrays, the **sorted()** method sends to the closure two values at a time, but the values in a dictionary are sent as tuples containing the key and value of each element. For instance, the first values sent to the closure in Listing 3-124 are ("one", "Banana") and ("two", "Apple"). These values replace the placeholders **$0** and **$1**, so if we want to order the elements according to the names of the fruits, we must compare the values of the tuples at index 1 (**$0.1 < $1.1**). The array returned is a collection of tuples in alphabetical order, with every element containing the keys and values of the dictionary (**[(key: "two", value: "Apple"), (key: "one", value: "Banana"), (key: "three", value: "Pear")]**).

Earlier, we saw how to iterate over the elements of a dictionary with a **for in** loop (see Listing 3-119). The loop gets each element and generates a tuple with the key and value. But there are times when we only need the element's key or the element's value. The **Dictionary** structure provides two properties for this purpose: **keys** and **values**. These properties return a collection containing only the keys or the values of the elements, respectively.

```
var fruits = ["one": "Banana", "two": "Apple", "three": "Pear"]
for key in fruits.keys {
   if key == "two" {
      print("We have an element with the key 'two'")
   }
}
```

Listing 3-125: Iterating over the dictionary's keys

The collections returned by the **keys** and **values** properties are structures of type **Keys** and **Values** defined inside the **Dictionary** structure. As we did before with other collection types, we can turn them into arrays with the **Array()** initializer.

```
var fruits = ["one": "Banana", "two": "Apple", "three": "Pear"]
let keys = Array(fruits.keys)
print(keys)
```

Listing 3-126: Reading the keys of a dictionary

3.4 Enumerations

Enumerations are a way to create data types with a limited set of values. An enumeration type is like the **Bool** type but with the possible values defined by the programmer. They are declared with the **enum** keyword, and the values are defined in braces with the **case** keyword.

```
enum Number {
   case one
   case two
   case three
}
```
Listing 3-127: Defining an enumeration type

This example defines an enumeration call **Number** with three possible values: **one, two,** and **three**. We can assign any names we want for the enumeration and its values. The values may also be declared just in one **case** statement separated by comma.

```
enum Number {
   case one, two, three
}
```
Listing 3-128: Declaring the enumeration values in one statement

An enumeration is a custom data type. As we did with structures, we must create a variable of this type and assign to that variable one of the possible values using dot notation.

```
enum Number {
   case one, two, three
}
var mynumber: Number = Number.one
```
Listing 3-129: Initializing an instance of an enumeration

Variables of this data type can only store the values allowed by the type (**one, two,** or **three**). To assign a value, we must use the name of the enumeration and dot notation. The **mynumber** variable declared in Listing 3-129 is of type **Number** and has the value **one**.

Once the data type of the variable was already defined, only the dot and the value are necessary to modify its value.

```
enum Number {
   case one, two, three
}
var mynumber = Number.one
mynumber = .two
```
Listing 3-130: Assigning a new value to a variable of type Number

In the last statement of Listing 3-130, we assign a new value to **mynumber**. The value **.two** may have been written as **Number.two**. Both syntaxes are valid, but Swift infers that the new value is of the same data type, so it is not necessary to declare the name anymore.

Like Booleans, enumeration types may be used as signals to indicate a state that can be checked later to decide whether to perform a certain task. Therefore, they are frequently used with conditionals and loops. The following example checks the value of an enumeration variable with a **switch** statement. This statement is particularly useful when working with enumerations because these data types have a limited set of values, making it easy to define a **case** for each one of them.

```
enum Number {
   case one
   case two
   case three
}
var mynumber = Number.two
switch mynumber {
   case .one:
      print("The number is 1")
   case .two:
      print("The number is 2")   // "The number is 2"
   case .three:
      print("The number is 3")
}
```

Listing 3-131: Using `switch` *with an enumeration type*

In this example, the **Number** enumeration is defined and then the **mynumber** variable is declared with the value **two**. Next, a **switch** statement compares the value of this variable with the three possible values of its type and prints a message on the console.

(Medium) **Raw Values**

The cases of an enumeration can have values by default. These values are called *Raw Values*. Swift assigns values by default to every case, starting from 0, but we can assign our own.

```
enum Number: String {
   case one = "Number One"
   case two = "Number Two"
   case three = "Number Three"
}
var mynumber = Number.one
```

Listing 3-132: Assigning raw values to enumeration values

Enumerations behave like structures. We can define our own properties and methods inside an enumeration, and they also include initializers, properties, and methods by default. The most useful property is called **rawValue**, which lets us read the raw value of each **case**.

```
enum Number: String {
   case one = "Number One"
   case two = "Number Two"
   case three = "Number Three"
}
var mynumber = Number.one
print("The value is \(mynumber.rawValue)")   // "The value is Number One"
```

Listing 3-133: Reading raw values

Additionally, enumerations include an initializer to create an instance from a raw value. Instead of declaring the variable using the value's name (**one**, **two** or **three**), we can use the initializer and the raw value. The initializer includes the **rawValue** argument to specify the value used to create the instance.

```
enum Number: String {
   case one = "Number One"
   case two = "Number Two"
   case three = "Number Three"
}
```

```
var mynumber = Number(rawValue: "Number Two")
if mynumber == .two {
   print("Correct Value")   // "Correct Value"
}
```

Listing 3-134: Creating an enumeration from a raw value

We can read the **case** value or the raw value to identify an instance of an enumeration type. In Listing 3-134, we create an instance of **Number** with the raw value "Number Two" and then check that the variable contains the proper **case** value with an **if** statement.

What makes enumerations part of the programming paradigm proposed by Swift is not their capacity to store different types of values but the possibility to include custom methods and computed properties. The following example adds a method to our **Number** enumeration that prints a message depending on the instance's current value.

```
enum Number: Int {
   case one
   case two
   case three

   func getMessage() -> String {
      switch self {
         case .one:
            return "We are the best"
         case .two:
            return "We have to study more"
         case .three:
            return "This is just the beginning"
      }
   }
}
var mynumber = Number.two

print(mynumber.getMessage())   // "We have to study more"
```

Listing 3-135: Adding methods to an enumeration

When we need to check the current value of the instance from inside a method, we must use the **self** keyword. This keyword refers to the instance where the method is being executed (in our case, **mynumber**), and this is how we can check for the instance's current value and return the right message. (We will learn more about the **self** keyword later.)

Medium Associated Values

Enumerations include the possibility to associate values to a case. These are values we can attach to a case when variables of that type are initialized. For instance, in the following example we create an enumeration that can store information about a character, but it differentiates between letters and numbers.

```
enum MyCharacters {
   case number(Int, String)
   case letter(Character, String)
}
var character = MyCharacters.number(1, "Number One")

switch character {
   case .number(let value, let description):
      print("\(description) - \(value)")   // "Number One - 1"
```

```
case .letter(let letter, let description):
    print("\(description) - \(letter)")
}
```

Listing 3-136: Associating values

This example defines an enumeration called **MyCharacters** that includes two cases. The first case is called **number** and it takes two associated values: an integer and a string. The second case is called **letter** and it also takes two associated values: a character and a string. When we create a value of this type, we must select the case value, as always, but we must also specify the associated values. If the value of the enumeration is **number**, we must provide an integer and a string, and if the value is **letter**, we must provide a character and a string. In this example, we create an instance with the value **number** and the associated values 1 and "Number One".

In each case of the **switch** statement, we test whether the value is **number** or **letter** and extract their associated values with constants between parenthesis, similar to what we did with tuples before (see Listing 2-37).

If we need to check a single case, we can use an **if** or a **guard** statement and assign the value to the case we want to check.

```
enum MyCharacters {
    case number(Int, String)
    case letter(Character, String)
}
var character = MyCharacters.number(1, "Number One")

if case .number(let number, let text) = character {
    print("Number: \(number)")   // "Number: 1"
    print("Text: \(text)")   // "Text: Number One"
}
```

Listing 3-137: Reading associated values from an if *statement*

This syntax includes the **case** keyword and the necessary constants to receive the values. The statement is saying something like "Assign the value to this case, if not possible, return false". In our example, if the **character** variable doesn't contain a **MyCharacters** enumeration with the value **number**, the statement returns **false** and nothing is done, otherwise, the associated values in the **character** variable are assigned to the constants and printed on the console.

(Basic) # 3.5 Objects

Objects are data types that encapsulate data and functionality in the form of properties and methods, but unlike the structures and enumerations introduced before they are stored by reference, which means that more than one variable can reference the same object in memory.

(Basic) ## Definition of Objects

Like structures and enumerations, objects are defined first and then instances are created from their definition. The definitions of objects are called *Classes*, and what we called objects are the instances created from those classes. Classes are declared the same way as structures or enumerations, but instead of the **struct** or **enum** keywords we must use the **class** keyword.

```
class Employee {
    var name = "Undefined"
```

```
   var age = 0
}
```

Listing 3-138: Defining a class

This example defines a simple class called **Employee** with two properties: **name** and **age**. As always, this does not create anything, it is just defining a new custom data type. To store data in memory in this format, we must assign an instance of this class to a constant or variable.

```
class Employee {
   var name = "Undefined"
   var age = 0
}
let employee1 = Employee()
employee1.name = "John"
employee1.age = 32
```

Listing 3-139: Creating an object from a class

In Listing 3-139, the **Employee()** initializer creates a new instance of the class **Employee**. The words instance and object are synonyms, so we can say that in this example we have created a new object called **employee1** containing two properties, **name** and **age**.

Of course, we can also modify the values of the properties of an object from its methods, but unlike structures, these methods can modify the properties of their own object without adding anything to the definition (they do not need to be declared as **mutating**).

```
class Employee {
   var name = "Undefined"
   var age = 0

   func changename(newname: String, newage: Int) {
      name = newname
      age = newage
   }
}
let employee1 = Employee()
employee1.changename(newname: "Martin", newage: 32)

print("Name: \(employee1.name)")   // "Name: Martin"
```

Listing 3-140: Modifying properties from the object's methods

In Listing 3-140, the **changename()** method is added to the **Employee** class to modify the values of the properties. After the instance is created, we call this method to assign the values "Martin" and 32 to the **name** and **age** properties, respectively.

 IMPORTANT: As well as structures, we can create all the objects we need from the same definition (class). Each object will have its own properties, methods, and values.

(Basic) Type Properties and Methods

We have studied type properties and methods before with structures. These are properties and methods accessible from the data type, not from the instances. They work in classes the same way as in structures, but instead of the **static** keyword we must use the **class** keyword to define them.

```
class Employee {
    var name = "Undefined"
    var age = 0

    class func description() {
        print("This class stores the name and age of an employee")
    }
}
Employee.description()
```

Listing 3-141: *Declaring a type method for a class*

This example defines an **Employee** class with two properties: **name** and **age**. The type method declared next is just describing the purpose of the class. Every time the **description()** method is executed on the class, a description is printed on the console. Again, we don't have to create an instance because the method is executed on the class itself.

 IMPORTANT: Classes can also use the **static** keyword to define type properties and methods. The difference between the **static** and **class** keywords is that properties and methods defined with the **static** keyword are immutable and those defined with the **class** keyword can be modified by subclasses. (We will learn about subclasses and inheritance later in this chapter.)

(Basic) Reference Types

Structures and enumerations are value types. This means that every time we assign a variable of any of these data types to another variable, the value is copied. For example, if we create an instance of a structure and then assign that instance to another variable, we end up with two instances of the same structure in memory, as illustrated below.

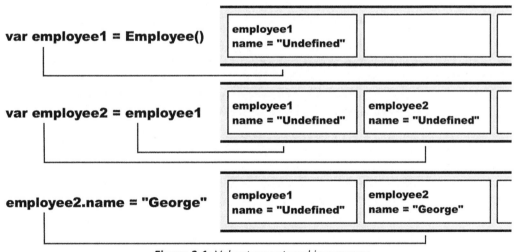

Figure 3-1: *Value types stored in memory*

Figure 3-1 shows how two different copies of the **Employee** structure, one referenced by the **employee1** variable and the other referenced by the **employee2** variable, are stored in memory. Any modification to the values of one of the instances will not affect the other, because they occupy different spaces in memory.

Objects, on the other hand, are passed by reference. This means that when we assign an object to constants or variables, they receive a reference to the object, not the object itself. In the following example, the object in **employee2** is the same as the object in **employee1**. Any change in the **name** property is reflected in the other because both variables point to the same object in memory (they reference the same instance).

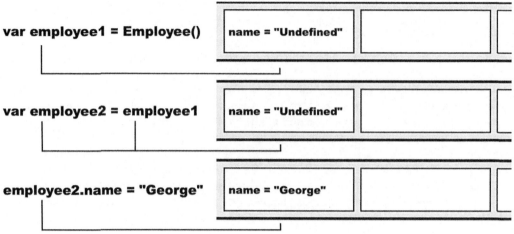

Figure 3-2: *Objects stored in memory*

Constants or variables that were assigned an object do not store the object; they store the value of the memory address where the object is located. When a constant or a variable containing this address is assigned to another constant or variable, only the address is copied, and therefore the object is not duplicated. This is the most important characteristic of objects, and what makes them suitable for situations in which data in memory must be accessed and shared by different parts of the code.

IMPORTANT: Because constants and variables store a reference to an object (a memory address), two or more variables in your code may reference the same object. If you need to know whether this is the case, you can compare the variables with the operators **===** (identical to) and **!==** (not identical to) provided by Swift. If what you need is to know whether two objects contain different information, you can use the basic operators **==** and **!=**, but you can only do this when the objects conform to the **Equatable** protocol; a protocol that determines how the objects will be compared. We will study protocols and the **Equatable** protocol later in this chapter.

(Basic) **Self**

Because the same object may be referenced by multiple constants or variables, every language that works with objects offers a way for the object to reference itself. In Swift, this is done automatically, but there are situations in which this reference must be declared explicitly. For this purpose, Swift defines a special keyword called **self**. We have introduced this keyword earlier to read the current value of an enumeration from inside the instance (see Listing 3-135). In structures and objects, the **self** keyword works the same way; it references the instance to which the values belong.

The most common situation in which the use of this keyword is required is when we need to declare the names of the parameters of a method equal to the names of the object's properties. If the names are the same, the system doesn't know whether we are trying to modify the property or the parameter. The **self** keyword clarifies the situation.

```
class Employee {
    var name = "Undefined"

    func changename(name: String) {
        self.name = name
    }
}
let employee1 = Employee()
employee1.changename(name: "Martin")

print("Name: \(employee1.name)")   // "Name: Martin"
```

Listing 3-142: *Referring to the object with* `self`

The **self** keyword in the **changename()** method of Listing 3-142 represents the object created from the **Employee** class and helps the system understand what we are trying to access when we use the word **name**. When we call the **changename()** method in the **employee1** object, the value of the **name** parameter is assigned to the object's **name** property (**self.name**).

The **self** keyword in this example is a reference to the object stored in the **employee1** variable. This would be the same as declaring **employee1.name**, but since we do not know the name of the variable that is going to store the instance when the class is defined, we must use **self** instead.

Another useful application of the **self** keyword is to reference the data type itself. The value generated by reading the **self** keyword on a data type is called *Metatype*. A metatype refers to the type itself, not an instance of it. For example, the value **Int.self** refers to the definition of the **Int** data type, not an integer number created from that type, as shown in the following example.

```
let reference = Int.self
let newnumber = reference.init(20)
print(newnumber)   // "20"
```

Listing 3-143: *Referring to the data type with* `self`

The code in Listing 3-143 stores a reference to the **Int** data type in a constant and then uses that constant to create an instance of **Int** with the value 20. Notice that when working with metatypes we must call the **init()** method implicitly to create an instance. Metatypes are widely used to pass references of data types to methods and initializers of other types, as we will see in further chapters.

Advanced Memory Management

Because objects are stored by reference, they can be referenced by several variables at the same time. If a variable is erased, the object that the variable is referencing cannot be erased from memory because another variable could still be using it. This creates a situation in which the device's memory is filled with objects that are no longer necessary. The solution provided by Apple is an automatic system that counts the number of variables referencing an object and only removes the object from memory when all the references are erased (all the variables were erased, set to **nil**, or they were assigned a reference to another object). The system is called *ARC* (Automatic Reference Counting). ARC automatically erases the objects when there is no longer a constant or a variable containing a reference to that space in memory.

In an ideal scenario, this system works like magic, counting how many references we create to the same object and erasing that object when none of those references exist anymore. But there are situations in which we can create something called *Strong Reference Cycle*. This happens when two objects have a property that references the other object.

```
class Employee {
   var name: String?
   var location: Department?
}
class Department {
   var area: String?
   var person: Employee?
}
var employee: Employee? = Employee()
var department: Department? = Department()

employee?.name = "John"
employee?.location = department

department?.area = "Mail"
department?.person = employee
```

Listing 3-144: Referencing one object from another

This example defines two classes: **Employee** and **Department**. Both classes contain a property that references an object of the other class (**location** and **person**). After the definition, objects of each class are created and stored in the **employee** and **department** variables. The reference in the **department** variable is assigned to the **location** property of the **employee** object, and the reference in the **employee** variable is assigned to the **person** property of the **department** object. After this, each object contains a reference to the other.

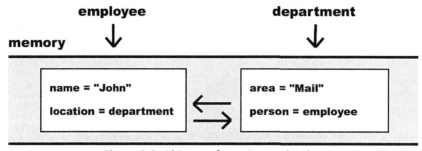

Figure 3-3: Objects referencing each other

At this point, each object is referenced by a variable and a property. The object of the **Employee** class is referenced by the **employee** variable and the **person** property, and the object of the **Department** class is referenced by the **department** variable and the **location** property. If, for some reason, we do not need to access these objects from our code anymore and erase or modify the values of the **employee** and **department** variables, ARC will not erase the objects from memory because their properties still have a reference that keeps them alive.

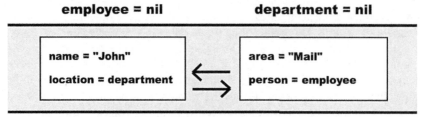

Figure 3-4: Objects preserved in memory

In this example, we assume that the value **nil** was assigned to the **employee** and **department** variables, and in consequence the objects are not accessible anymore, but they are preserved in memory because ARC has no way to know that they are no longer required.

Swift solves this problem by classifying the references into three categories: strong, weak, and unowned. Normal references are strong; they are always valid and the objects associated to them

Chapter 3 - Swift Paradigm

are preserved in memory for as long as they exist. These are the kind of references we have been using so far, and that is why the cycle created by our example is called Strong Reference Cycle. The solution to break this cycle is to define one of the references as **weak** or **unowned**. When ARC encounters one of these types of references to be the last reference to an object, the object is erased from memory as if the reference had never existed.

```
class Employee {
   var name: String?
   var location: Department?
}
class Department {
   var area: String?
   weak var person: Employee?
}
var employee: Employee? = Employee()
var department: Department? = Department()

employee?.name = "John"
employee?.location = department

department?.area = "Mail"
department?.person = employee
```

Listing 3-145: *Assigning weak references*

In the code of Listing 3-145, the **person** property was declared as **weak**. Now, when the references from the variables are erased, the object created from the **Employee** class is erased from memory because the only reference left is the weak reference from the **person** property. After this object disappears, the object created from the **Department** class does not have any other strong reference either, so it is also erased from memory.

The unowned reference works the same way, but it differs from the weak reference on the type of values it applies to. Weak references apply to variables with optional values (they can be empty at some point) and unowned references apply to non-optional values (they always have a value).

 IMPORTANT: Closures can create strong reference cycles if we try to access properties or methods defined outside the closure. If we need to reference properties or methods with **self** inside a closure, we can declare the reference to **self** as weak with the syntax **[weak self]** or **[unowned self]**. The expression must be declared before the closure's parameters. For more information on ARC and how to avoid strong reference cycles, visit our website and follow the links for this chapter.

(Medium) **Inheritance**

One of the main purposes of structures and objects is to define pieces of code that can be copied and shared. The code is defined once and then instances (copies) of that code are created every time they are required. This programming pattern works well when we define our own code but presents some limitations when working with code programmed by other developers and shared through libraries and frameworks. The programmers creating the code for us cannot anticipate how we are going to use it and all the possible variations required for every application. To provide a solution to this problem, classes incorporate inheritance. A class can inherit properties and methods from another class and then improve it by adding properties and methods of its own. This way, programmers can share classes and developers can adapt them to their needs.

To illustrate how inheritance works, the following examples present a situation in which a class must be expanded to contain additional information that was not initially contemplated.

```
class Employee {
   var name = "Undefined"
   var age = 0

   func createbadge() -> String {
      return "Employee \(name) \(age)"
   }
}
```

The **Employee** class declared in Listing 3-146 is a normal class, like those we have defined before. It has two properties and a method called **createbadge()** that returns a string with the values of the properties. This class would be enough to create objects that generate the string of text necessary to print a badge for every employee with his or her name and age. But for the sake of argument, let's say that some of the employees require a badge that also displays the department they work in. One option is to define another class with the same properties and methods and add what we need, but this produces redundant code, and it is difficult to do when the class was taken from a library (they are usually not accessible or too complex to modify or duplicate). The solution is to create a new class that inherits the characteristics of the basic class and adds its own properties and methods to satisfy the new requirements.

To indicate that a class inherits from another class, we must write the name of the basic class after the name of the new class separated by a colon.

```
class Employee {
   var name = "Undefined"
   var age = 0

   func createbadge() -> String {
      return "Employee \(name) \(age)"
   }
}
class OfficeEmployee: Employee {
   var department = "Undefined"
}
```

The **OfficeEmployee** class added to our code in Listing 3-147 only has one property called **department**, but it inherits the **name** and **age** properties, and also the **createbadge()** method from the **Employee** class. All these properties and methods are available in any of the objects created from the **OfficeEmployee** class, as shown next.

```
class Employee {
   var name = "Undefined"
   var age = 0

   func createbadge() -> String {
      return "Employee \(name) \(age)"
   }
}
class OfficeEmployee: Employee {
   var department = "Undefined"
}
let employee = OfficeEmployee()
employee.name = "George"
employee.age = 25
employee.department = "Mail"

var badge = employee.createbadge()
```

```
print("Badge: \(badge)")   // "Badge: Employee George 25"
```

Listing 3-148: Creating objects from a subclass

A class like **Employee** is called *Superclass*, and a class that inherits from another class like **OfficeEmployee** is called *Subclass*. In these terms, we can say that the **OfficeEmployee** class is a subclass that inherits the properties and methods of the **Employee** superclass. A class can inherit from a superclass that already inherited from another superclass in an infinite chain. When a property is accessed, or a method is called, the system looks for it on the object's class and, if it is not there, it keeps looking in the superclasses up the hierarchical chain until it finds it.

 IMPORTANT: Inheritance does not work the other way around. For example, considering the code in Listing 3-148, objects created from the class **OfficeEmployee** have access to the **department** property of this class and the properties and methods of the **Employee** class, but objects created from the **Employee** class do not have access to the **department** property.

Because of this hierarchical chain, sometimes a method does not have access to all the properties available to the object. For example, the **createbadge()** method called on the **employee** object created in Listing 3-148 have access to the properties declared on the **Employee** class but not those declared in the **OfficeEmployee** class. If we want the method to also print the value of the **department** property, we must implement it again in the **OfficeEmployee** class with the appropriate modifications. This is called *Overriding*. To override a method of a superclass, we prefix it with the **override** keyword.

```
class Employee {
    var name = "Undefined"
    var age = 0

    func createbadge() -> String {
        return "Employee \(name) \(age)"
    }
}
class OfficeEmployee: Employee {
    var department = "Undefined"

    override func createbadge() -> String {
        return "Employee \(department) \(name) \(age)"
    }
}
let employee = OfficeEmployee()
employee.name = "George"
employee.age = 25
employee.department = "Mail"

var badge = employee.createbadge()
print("Badge: \(badge)")   // "Badge: Employee Mail George 25"
```

Listing 3-149: Overriding an inherited method

The new **OfficeEmployee** subclass of Listing 3-149 overrides the **createbadge()** method of its superclass to generate a string that includes the value of the **department** property. Now, when the method is called from an object of this class, the system executes the one defined in **OfficeEmployee** (the old method from the superclass is ignored), and therefore the badge includes the values of the three properties.

Using inheritance, we have created a new class without modifying previous classes or duplicating any code. The **Employee** class can create objects to store the name and age of an employee and generate a badge with this information, and the **OfficeEmployee** class can create objects to store the name, age, and the department of the employee and generate a more complete badge with the values of all these properties.

When we call the **createbadge()** method on the **employee** object created from the **OfficeEmployee** class in Listing 3-149, the method executed is always the one defined in the **OfficeEmployee** class. If we want to execute the method on the superclass instead, we must use a special keyword called **super**. The **super** keyword is like the **self** keyword, but instead of representing the object, **super** represents the superclass. It is often used when we have overridden a method but we still need to execute the method on the superclass.

```
class Employee {
   var name = "Undefined"
   var age = 0

   func createbadge() -> String {
      return "Employee \(name) \(age)"
   }
}
class OfficeEmployee: Employee {
   var department = "Undefined"

   override func createbadge() -> String {
      let oldbadge = super.createbadge()
      return "\(oldbadge) \(department)"
   }
}
let employee = OfficeEmployee()
employee.name = "George"
employee.age = 25
employee.department = "Mail"

var badge = employee.createbadge()
print("Badge: \(badge)")   // "Badge: Employee George 25 Mail"
```

Listing 3-150: Calling a method on the superclass

This is the same as the previous example, but now, when the **createbadge()** method of an object created from the **OfficeEmployee** class is called, the method calls the **createbadge()** method of the superclass first and assigns the result to the **oldbadge** constant. The value of this constant is later added to the value of the **department** property to generate the final string.

(Medium) **Type Casting**

Inheritance not only transfers functionality from one class to another but also connects the classes together. The superclasses and their subclasses are linked together in a hierarchical chain. Because of this, whenever we declare a variable of the type of the superclass, objects of the subclasses can be assigned to that variable too. This is a very important feature that allows us to do things like creating arrays of objects that are of different classes but belong to the same hierarchy.

```
class Employee {
   var name = "Undefined"
   var age = 0
}
class OfficeEmployee: Employee {
   var deskNumber = 0
}
class WarehouseEmployee: Employee {
   var area = "Undefined"
}
var list: [Employee] = [OfficeEmployee(), WarehouseEmployee(),
OfficeEmployee()]
```

Listing 3-151: Creating an array of objects from different subclasses

This example defines a superclass called **Employee** and then two subclasses of **Employee** called **OfficeEmployee** and **WarehouseEmployee**. The purpose is to have the information for every employee in one class and then have classes for specific types of employee. Following this organization, we can create objects that contain the **name**, **age**, and **deskNumber** properties to represent employees working at the office and objects that contain the **name**, **age**, and **area** properties to represent employees working at the warehouse.

No matter the differences between one object and another, they all represent employees of the same company, so sooner or later we will have to include them on the same list. The class hierarchy allows us to do that. We can declare a collection of the data type of the superclass and then store objects of the subclasses in it, as we did in Listing 3-151 with the **list** array.

This is all good until we try to read the array. The array was declared of type **Employee**, so we can only access the properties defined in the **Employee** class. Also, there is no way to know what type of object each element is. We could have an **OfficeEmployee** object at index 0 and later replace it with a **WarehouseEmployee** object. The indexes do not provide any information to identify the objects. Swift solves these problems with the **is** and **as** operators.

is—This operator returns a Boolean value indicating whether the value is of a certain data type.

as—This operator converts a value of one class to another class when possible.

Identifying an object is easy with the **is** operator. This operator returns a Boolean value that we can use in an **if** statement to check the object's class.

```
var countOffice = 0
var countWarehouse = 0

for obj in list {
   if obj is OfficeEmployee {
      countOffice += 1
   } else if obj is WarehouseEmployee {
      countWarehouse += 1
   }
}
print("We have \(countOffice) employees working at the office")  // 2
print("We have \(countWarehouse) employees working at the warehouse") //1
```

Listing 3-152: Identifying the object's data type

In Listing 3-152, we create the **list** array again with objects from the same classes defined in the previous example, but this time we add a **for in** loop to iterate over the array and count how many objects of each class we have found. The **if** statement inside the loop implements the **is** operator to check if the current object stored in the **obj** constant is of type **OfficeEmployee** or **WarehouseEmployee** and increments the counter respectively (**countOffice** or **countWarehouse**).

Counting objects is not really what these operators are all about. The idea is to figure out the type with the **is** operator and then convert the object with the **as** operator to be able to access their properties and methods. The **as** operator converts a value of one type to another. The conversions are not always guaranteed, and that is why this operator comes in two more forms: **as!** and **as?**. These versions of the **as** operator work like optionals. The **as!** operator forces the conversion and returns an error if the conversion is not possible, and the **as?** operator tries to convert the object and returns an optional with the new object or **nil** in case of failure.

```
for obj in list {
   if obj is OfficeEmployee {
      let temp = obj as! OfficeEmployee
      temp.deskNumber = 100
```

```
    } else if obj is WarehouseEmployee {
        let temp = obj as! WarehouseEmployee
        temp.area = "New Area"
    }
}
```

Listing 3-153: Casting an object

When we use the **as!** operator we are forcing the conversion, so we need to make sure that the conversion is possible or otherwise the app will crash. (This is the same that happens when we unwrap optionals with the exclamation mark.) In the code of Listing 3-153, we only use this operator after we have already checked with the **is** operator that the object is of the right class. Once the object is casted (converted) into its original data type, we can access its properties and methods. In this example, the objects returned by the **as!** operator are stored in the **temp** constant and then new values are assigned to the **deskNumber** and **area** properties.

Checking for the type before casting is redundant. To simplify the code, we can use the **as?** operator. Instead of forcing the conversion and crashing the app, this version of the **as** operator tries to perform the conversion and returns an optional with the result.

```
for obj in list {
    if let temp = obj as? OfficeEmployee {
        temp.deskNumber = 100
    } else if let temp = obj as? WarehouseEmployee {
        temp.area = "New Area"
    }
}
```

Listing 3-154: Casting an object with the as? *operator*

In this example, we use optional binding to cast the object and assign the result to the **temp** constant. First, we try to cast **obj** as an **OfficeEmployee** object. If we are successful, we assign the value 100 to the **deskNumber** property, but if the value returned is **nil**, then we try to cast the object to the **WarehouseEmployee** class and modify its **area** property.

Casting can also be performed on the fly if we are sure that the conversion is possible. The statement to cast the object is the same but it must be declared between parentheses.

```
let myarea = (list[1] as! WarehouseEmployee).area
print("The area of employee 1 is \(myarea)")   // "Undefined"
```

Listing 3-155: Casting an object on the fly

In this example, we do not assign the object to any variable; we just cast the element of the **list** array at index 1 as a **WarehouseEmployee** object inside the parentheses and then access its **area** property. The value of this property is stored in the **myarea** constant and then printed on the console. All we need to remember is that conversions performed with the **as!** operator are only possible when we are sure it is going to be successful.

 IMPORTANT: The **as!** operator is applied when the conversion is guaranteed to be successful, and the **as?** operator is used when we are not sure about the result. But we can also use the basic **as** operator when the Swift compiler can verify that the conversion will be successful, as when we are casting some primitive data types (e.g., **String** values into **NSString** objects).

The **as** operator works on objects that belong to the same class hierarchy. Because sometimes the objects that require casting are not in the same hierarchy, Swift defines several generic data types to represent values of any kind. The most frequently used are **Any** (structures), **AnyObject** (objects), and **AnyClass** (classes). By taking advantage of these generic types, we can create collections with values that are not associated with each other.

```
class Employee {
   var name = "Undefined"
}
class Department {
   var area = "Undefined"
}
var list: [AnyObject] = [Employee(), Department(), Department()]

for obj in list {
   if let temp = obj as? Employee {
      temp.name = ""
   } else if let temp = obj as? Department {
      temp.area = ""
   }
}
```

Listing 3-156: Working with objects of AnyObject *type*

The **list** array declared in Listing 3-156 is of type **AnyObject** and therefore it can contain objects of any data type. To populate the array, we created two simple and independent classes: **Employee** and **Department**. A few objects are created from these classes and included in the array. The objects are later casted by the **as?** operator inside a **for in** loop and their corresponding properties are modified following the same procedure used in previous examples.

(Basic) ## Initialization

We have been initializing the properties during definition in every class declared so far. This is because classes do not provide memberwise initializers as structures do. The properties of a class have to be initialized explicitly in the definition or during instantiation with the **init()** method.

```
class Employee {
   var name: String
   var age: Int

   init(name: String, age: Int) {
      self.name = name
      self.age = age
   }
}
let employee1 = Employee(name: "George", age: 28)
```

Listing 3-157: Declaring a Designated Initializer

The **init()** method declared for the **Employee** class in Listing 3-157 initializes every property of the class with the values specified in the **Employee()** initializer. This type of initializer is called *Designated Initializer*. When we declare a Designated Initializer, we need to make sure that all the properties are initialized.

If we know that in some circumstances our code will not be able to provide all the values during initialization, we can also declare a Convenience Initializer. A Convenience Initializer is an initializer that offers a convenient way to initialize an object with values by default for some or all of its properties. It is declared with the **init()** method but preceded by the **convenience** keyword. A Convenience Initializer must call the Designated initializer in the class with the corresponding values.

```
class Employee {
   var name: String
   var age: Int
```

```
init(name: String, age: Int) {
   self.name = name
   self.age = age
}
convenience init() {
   self.init(name: "Undefined", age: 0)
}
}
let employee1 = Employee()
```

Listing 3-158: Declaring a Convenience Initializer

When we create an instance of **Employee**, the system detects the number and type of arguments and executes the corresponding initializer. For example, if we provide the values for the **name** and the **age** parameters, the system executes the Designated Initializer because this is the initializer that contains the necessary parameters to receive those values, but if the initialization does not include any **argument**, the Convenience Initializer is executed instead and then the Designated Initializer is called with values by default ("Undefined" and 0).

Unlike structures, classes can inherit properties and methods from other classes, and this includes the **init()** method. When a subclass does not provide its own Designated Initializer, the initializer of its superclass is used instead.

```
class Employee {
   var name: String
   var age: Int

   init(name: String, age: Int) {
      self.name = name
      self.age = age
   }
}
class OfficeEmployee: Employee {
   var department: String = "Undefined"
}
let employee1 = OfficeEmployee(name: "George", age: 29)
```

Listing 3-159: Inheriting the Designated Initializer

The code in Listing 3-159 defines the subclass **OfficeEmployee** that inherits from the **Employee** class. The **OfficeEmployee** class does not provide any initializer, so the only initializer available is the one provided by its superclass. This initializer only initializes the properties **name** and **age**. The **department** property of **OfficeEmployee** is explicitly initialized with the value "Undefined". To provide an initializer that also includes this property, we must declare a new Designated Initializer in the **OfficeEmployee** class.

```
class Employee {
   var name: String
   var age: Int

   init(name: String, age: Int) {
      self.name = name
      self.age = age
   }
}
class OfficeEmployee: Employee {
   var department: String
   init(name: String, age: Int, department: String) {
      self.department = department
      super.init(name: name, age: age)
   }
}
```

```
let employee1 = OfficeEmployee(name: "John", age: 24, department: "Mail")
```

Listing 3-160: Declaring a Designated Initializer for the subclass

The Designated Initializer of a subclass must initialize the properties of its own class first and then call the initializer of its superclass. This is done by calling the **init()** method on **super**. The **super** keyword refers to the superclass, so when the system executes the **super.init()** statement in the code of Listing 3-160, the **init()** method of the superclass is executed and the **name** and **age** properties of this class are initialized.

 IMPORTANT: There are different ways to combine Designated and Convenience initializers. The possibility of classes to inherit from other classes in an unlimited chain can turn initialization into a very complex process. This book does not explore all the possibilities provided by Swift for initialization. For more information, visit our website and follow the links for this chapter.

(Medium) **Deinitialization**

There is a counterpart of the initialization process called *Deinitialization*. Despite its name, this process is not directly related to the initialization process but rather to the ARC system. ARC, as we studied previously in this chapter, is an automatic system adopted by Swift to manage memory. Letting the system manage the memory and take care of removing the objects our program no longer needs presents a huge advantage, but it also means that we do not always know when an object is going to be removed. There are times when an object is using resources that must be released or information that needs to be stored. Whatever the task, Swift offers the **deinit** method to execute any last-minute instructions we need before the object is erased from memory.

```
class Item {
    var quantity = 0.0
    var name = "Not defined"
    var price = 0.0

    deinit {
        print("This instance was erased")
    }
}
var purchase: Item? = Item()
purchase = nil
```

Listing 3-161: Declaring a deinitializer

This example defines a simple class with a deinitializer. The object is created and assigned to an optional variable. Right after that, the **nil** value is assigned to the same variable to erase the reference and test the **deinit** method, which prints a message on the console.

(Medium) **Access Control and Modifiers**

Swift defines keywords (also called *modifiers*) that can be applied to entities (classes, structures, properties, methods, etc.) to confer them special attributes. We have already seen the **mutating** and **override** keyword, but there are more available, like the following.

lazy—This keyword defines a property whose initial value is not assigned until the property is used for the first time.

final—This keyword is used on a class when we don't want to allow the code to create subclasses of it. It must be declared before the **class** keyword.

The **lazy** keyword is frequently used when the property's value may take time to be determined and we don't want the initialization of the structure or the class to be delayed. For example, we may have a property that stores a name retrieved from a server, which is a resource intensive task that we should perform only when the value is required.

```
class Employee {
    lazy var name: String = {
        // Loading name from a server
        print("Loading...")
        return "Undefined"
    }()
    var age = 0
}
let employee = Employee()
```

Listing 3-162: Defining `lazy` *properties*

The **Employee** class in Listing 3-162 defines two properties, **name** and **age**, but this time a closure is assigned to the **name** property to get the employee's name from a server (we will see how to retrieve information from the Web in Chapter 17). Because we declared this property as **lazy**, the closure will only be executed when we try to read it. If we execute the example as it is, we get nothing in return, but if we read the **name** property with a statement at the end, we will see the text "Loading..." printed on the console.

The Swift language also includes keywords to define the level of access for each entity in our code. Access control in Swift is based on modules and source files, but it also applies to single properties and methods. Source files are the files we create for our application, the properties and methods are the ones we have created for our structures and classes in previous examples, and modules are units of code that are related with each other. For instance, a single application and each of the frameworks included in it are considered modules (we will introduce frameworks in Chapter 4). Considering this classification, Swift defines five keywords to determine accessibility.

open—This keyword determines that an entity is accessible from the module it belongs to and other modules.

public—This keyword determines that an entity is accessible from the module it belongs to and other modules. The difference between **public** and **open** is that we can't create subclasses of **public** classes outside the module in which they were defined. This also applies to methods and properties (e.g., **public** methods can't be overridden outside the module in which they were declared).

internal—This keyword determines that an entity is accessible only inside the module in which it was created. This is the default access mode for applications. By default, every entity defined in our application is only accessible from inside the application.

private—This keyword determines that an entity is accessible only from the context in which it was created (e.g., a **private** property in a class will only be accessible from methods of the same class).

fileprivate—This keyword determines that an entity is accessible only from the file in which it was declared (e.g., a **fileprivate** property in a class will only be accessible by other entities defined inside the file in which it was declared).

As we will see later, most of these keywords apply to frameworks and are rarely used in single applications. By default, the properties and methods we include in our classes and structures are declared **internal**, which means that our classes and structures are only available from inside our application (module). Unless we are creating our own frameworks, this is all we need for our applications, and is the reason why we didn't have to specify any keyword when we defined our structures and classes before. All our classes and structures are accessible by the rest of the code inside our application, but if we want to have a level of control in our data types or avoid modifying values by mistake, we can declare some of them as **private**, as shown next.

```
class Employee {
   private var name = "Undefined"
   private var age = 0

   func showValues() {
      print("Name: \(name)")
      print("Age: \(age)")
   }
}
let employee = Employee()
employee.showValues()
```

Listing 3-163: Declaring `private` *properties*

The code in Listing 3-163 defines the **name** and **age** properties of our **Employee** class as **private** and adds a method called **showValues()** to access their values. Due to access control, these properties are only accessible by the method in the class. If we try to read their values from outside the object using dot notation, Xcode will return an error (**employee.name**).

If what we want is to be able to read the property from outside the object but not allow assigning new values to it, we can declare it with a public getter but a private setter.

```
class Employee {
   private var name = "Undefined"
   public private(set) var age = 0

   func setAge(newAge: Int) {
      age = newAge
   }
}
let employee = Employee()
employee.setAge(newAge: 25)
print(employee.age)
```

Listing 3-164: Declaring a public getter and private setter

The **age** property in the **Employee** class of Listing 3-164 was declared as public, so everyone can read its value, but with a private setter (**private(set)**), so only the methods inside the class can modify it. To change the value, we defined the **setAge()** method. The code creates an instance of the class and calls the method, but this time we can read the value of the **age** property and print it on the console because it was declared with a public getter.

Medium Singletons

As already mentioned, we can create as many objects as we want from a single class. These objets are independent from one another; they have their own properties and methods and process their own values. But sometimes our code needs only one object to be created from a class, so every piece of code will have access to the same object and working on the same values. To guarantee that only one instance of a class is created and the instance is available from anywhere in our code, the class needs to implement two things: a type property to create the only instance available, and a private initializer that doesn't allow the code to create more, as shown in the following example.

```
class Employee {
   var name: String
   var age: Int

   static let shared = Employee(newName: "Undefined", newAge: 0)

   private init(newName: String, newAge: Int) {
      name = newName
      age = newAge
   }
}
let employee1 = Employee.shared
let employee2 = Employee.shared
employee1.name = "George"
print("\(employee1.name) - \(employee2.name)")   // "George - George"
```

Listing 3-165: Defining a singleton

The `Employee` class in this example defines a type property called `shared` and initializes it with an instance of the same class, so every time we read this property from anywhere in the code, we get the same `Employee` object in return. For instance, in this example, we define two constants called `employee1` and `employee2`, and initialize them with the instance returned by the `shared` property. Because this is the same object, when we modify a value in the `employee1` object, the same value is returned by the `employee2` object.

Because the purpose of this class is to only allow the creation of one instance (one object), we prefix the initializer with the `private` keyword. As a result, only the single instance created by the `shared` property is available. That is the reason why the object created from this class is called *Singleton*.

Basic 3.6 Protocols

The main characteristics of classes, and therefore objects, are the capacity to encapsulate data and functionality and the possibility to share and improve code through inheritance. This introduced an advantage over previous paradigms and turned the Object-Oriented Programming paradigm into the industry standard for a while. But that changed with the introduction of protocols in Swift. Protocols define properties and methods that structures can have in common. This means that Swift's structures not only can encapsulate data and functionality, just like objects, but by conforming to protocols they can also share code. Figure 3-5 illustrates the differences between these two paradigms.

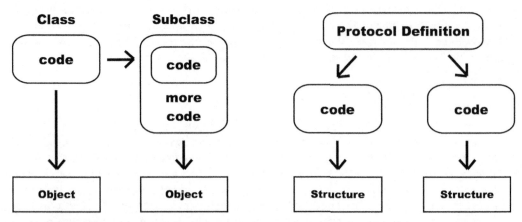

Figure 3-5: Object-Oriented Programming versus Protocol-Oriented Programming

In OOP, the code is implemented inside a class and then objects are created from that class. If we need to create objects with additional functionality, we must define a subclass that inherits the code from the superclass and adds some of its own. Protocols offer a slightly different approach. The properties and methods we want the structures to have in common are defined in the protocol and then implemented by the structures' definitions. This allows us to associate different structures together through a common pattern. The code implemented by each structure is unique, but they follow a blueprint set by the protocol. If we know that a structure conforms to a protocol, we can always be sure that besides its own definitions, it will also include the properties and methods defined by the protocol. In addition, protocols can be extended to provide their own implementations of the properties and methods we want the structures to have in common, allowing the paradigm to completely replace classes and objects.

 IMPORTANT: The Swift paradigm is built from the combination of structures and protocols, but protocols may also be adopted by enumerations and classes. For instance, many frameworks use protocols to offer a programming pattern called *Delegation*. We will study how classes conform to protocols and how to implement delegation later.

(Basic) Definition of Protocols

Protocols are defined with the **protocol** keyword followed by the name and the list of properties and methods between braces. No values or statements are assigned or declared inside a protocol, only the names and the corresponding data types. Because of this, methods are defined as always, but they omit the braces and the statements, and properties must include the **get** and **set** keywords between braces to indicate whether they are read-only properties, or we can read and assign values to them (see Listing 3-43 for an example of getters and setters). To indicate that the structure conforms to the protocol, we must include the protocol's name after the structure's name separated by a colon, as shown in the following example.

```
protocol Printer {
   var name: String { get set }
   func printdescription()
}
struct Employees: Printer {
   var name: String
   var age: Int

   func printdescription() {
      print("Description: \(name) \(age)")   // "Description: John 32"
   }
}
let employee1 = Employees(name: "John", age: 32)
employee1.printdescription()
```

Listing 3-166: Defining protocols

A protocol tells the structure what properties and methods are required, but the structure must implement them. In the example of Listing 3-166, we define a protocol called **Printer** that includes the **name** property and the **printdescription()** method. The **Employees** structure defined next conforms to this protocol, and along with the protocol's property and method it also implements its own property called **age**. Although this property was not defined in the protocol, we can read it inside the **printdescription()** method and print its value.

The advantage of this practice is evident when structures of different types conform to the same protocol, as shown in the following example.

```
protocol Printer {
    var name: String { get set }
    func printdescription()
}
struct Employees: Printer {
    var name: String
    var age: Int

    func printdescription() {
        print("Description: \(name) \(age)")
    }
}
struct Offices: Printer {
    var name: String
    var employees: Int

    func printdescription() {
        print("Description: \(name) \(employees)") // "Description: Mail 2"
    }
}
let employee1 = Employees(name: "John", age: 32)
let office1 = Offices(name: "Mail", employees: 2)
office1.printdescription()
```

Listing 3-167: *Defining multiple structures that conform to the same protocol*

Although the structures created in Listing 3-167 from the **Employees** and **Offices** definitions are different (they have different properties), they both conform to the **Printer** protocol and provide their own implementation of the **printdescription()** method. The common functionality defined by the protocol ensures that no matter what type of structure we are working with, it will always have an implementation of **printdescription()**.

Protocols are also data types. This allows us to associate structures by the common functionality.

```
let employee1 = Employees(name: "John", age: 32)
let office1 = Offices(name: "Mail", employees: 2)
var list: [Printer] = [employee1, office1]
for element in list {
    element.printdescription()
}
```

Listing 3-168: *Using protocols as data types*

Listing 3-168 uses the same protocol and structures defined in the previous example, but this time it stores the instances in an array. The type of the array was defined as **Printer**, which means the array may contain structures of any type as long as they conform to the **Printer** protocol. Because of this, no matter the element's data type (**Employees** or **Offices**) we know that they always have an implementation of the **name** property and the **printdescription()** method.

When we process a structure or an object as a protocol type, we can only access the properties and methods defined by the protocol. If we need to access the instance's own properties and methods, we must cast it using the **as** operator as we did with classes before. The following example prints the value of the **age** property if the element of the array is of type **Employees**.

```
let employee1 = Employees(name: "John", age: 32)
let office1 = Offices(name: "Mail", employees: 2)
```

Chapter 3 - Swift Paradigm

```
var list: [Printer] = [employee1, office1]
for element in list {
   if let employee = element as? Employees {
      print(employee.age)   // "32"
   }
   element.printdescription()
}
```

Listing 3-169: Accessing the instance's own properties

Because protocols are data types, we can use them to define variables, or return them from functions. The following example declares a function that returns a value of type **Printer**.

```
func getFile(type: Int) -> Printer {
   var data: Printer!
   if type == 1 {
      data = Employees(name: "John", age: 32)
   } else if type == 2 {
      data = Offices(name: "Mail", employees: 2)
   }
   return data
}
let file = getFile(type: 1)
file.printdescription()   // "Description: John 32"
```

Listing 3-170: Returning values of a protocol type

The **getFile()** function in Listing 3-170 creates an instance of a structure depending on the value received. If the **type** parameter is equal to 1, it returns an instance of **Employees**, but if the value is equal to 2, it returns an instance of **Offices**. But because the value returned by the function is of type **Printer** we know it will always include the **printdescription()** method.

(Advanced) **Generic Protocols**

Protocols can also define generic properties and methods, but they work slightly different than the generic types studied before. When we want to define a protocol with a generic property or method, we first must define the name of the generic type with the **associatedtype** keyword.

```
protocol Printer {
   associatedtype protype
   var name: protype { get set }
}
struct Employees: Printer {
   var name: String
}
let employee = Employees(name: "John")
print(employee.name)   // "John"
```

Listing 3-171: Defining generic protocols

This example defines a generic protocol called **Printer** and a structure that conforms to that protocol called **Employees**. The protocol defines a generic type with the name **protype** and then declares a property of that type. The property's real data type is defined by the structure or the class that conforms to the protocol. In this case, the **Employees** structure defines the **name** property as type **String**, and that's the type of values we can use in the instances of this structure, but we could have declared the property as type **Int** or any other necessary.

Swift Protocols

The Swift language makes use of protocols extensively. Almost every API includes protocols that define common features and behavior. But there are also important protocols defined in the Swift Standard Library that we can use to improve our custom data types. The following are the most frequently used.

Equatable—This protocol defines a data type which values can be compared with other values of the same type using the operators == and !=.

Comparable—This protocol defines a data type which values can be compared with other values of the same type using the operators >, <, >=, and <=.

Numeric—This protocol defines a data type that only works with values that can participate in arithmetic operations.

Hashable—This protocol defines a data type that provides the hash value (unique identifier) required for the value to be included in collections, such as sets and dictionaries.

CaseIterable—This protocol defines a data type, usually an enumeration without associated values, that includes a property called `allCases` that contains the collection of all the cases included in the data type.

These protocols are responsible of elemental processes performed by the system and the Swift language. For example, when we compare two values with the == or != operators, the system checks whether the values conform to the **Equatable** protocol and then calls a type method in the data type to compare them and solve the condition (true or false, depending on whether the values are equal or not). Swift primitive data types conform to the **Equatable** protocol and implement its methods, but we can also implement them in our own data types to compare their values. For this purpose, we must declare that the data type conforms to the protocol and implement the methods required by it. The **Equatable** protocol requires only one method called == to check for equality. (The system infers that if two values are not equal, they are different, and therefore the method for the != operator is optional.) This method must have a name equal to the operator (==), receive the two values to compare, and return a Boolean value to communicate the result. For instance, we can make our **Employees** structure conform to the **Equatable** protocol and implement a method with the == name to be able to compare two different instances of the same structure.

```
struct Employees: Equatable {
   var name: String
   var age: Int

   static func == (value1: Employees, value2: Employees) -> Bool {
      return value1.age == value2.age
   }
}
let employee1 = Employees(name: "John", age: 32)
let employee2 = Employees(name: "George", age: 32)

let message = employee1 == employee2 ? "Equal" : "Different"
print(message)   // "Equal"
```

Listing 3-172: *Conforming to the* `Equatable` *protocol*

In this example, we use the == method to compare the values of the **age** properties and therefore the structures are going to be equal when the employees are the same age. In this case, both instances are created with the value 32 and therefore the value "Equal" is assigned to the **message** constant when we compare the objects with the ternary operator.

Chapter 3 - Swift Paradigm

If what we want is to compare each of the properties in the structure, then we can omit the method. When we conform to the **Equatable** protocol, the compiler automatically generates the method for us to compare all the values of the structure (in this case, **name** and **age**).

```
struct Employees: Equatable {
   var name: String
   var age: Int
}
let employee1 = Employees(name: "John", age: 32)
let employee2 = Employees(name: "George", age: 32)
let message = employee1 == employee2 ? "Equal" : "Different"
print(message)   // "Different"
```

Listing 3-173: Letting the compiler create the protocol methods for us

Because we did not declare the **==** method in the example of Listing 3-173, the system creates the method for us and compares the values of all the properties. As a result, the system determines that the objects are different (the ages are the same, but the names are not).

Of course, we could have compared the properties directly (**employee1.name == employee2.name**) but being able to compare the objects instead simplifies the code and allows us to use our structures (or objects) in APIs that require the values to be comparable. For example, when we created a generic function earlier in this chapter, we could not perform any operations on the values (see Listing 3-15). Because the data type used in those functions is generic, Swift is incapable of knowing the capabilities of the data type and therefore Xcode returns an error if we try to perform operations on the values, but we can easily solve this problem by making the generic type conform to a protocol. This feature is called *Type Constraint* because it constrains the generic type to a data type with certain capabilities. For instance, the function in the following example receives two generic values, but only of a data type that conforms to the **Equatable** protocol, and therefore we can compare the values inside the function.

```
struct Employees: Equatable {
   var name: String
   var age: Int
}
func compareValues<T: Equatable>(value1: T, value2: T) -> String {
   let message = value1 == value2 ? "equal" : "different"
   return message
}
let employee1 = Employees(name: "George", age: 55)
let employee2 = Employees(name: "Robert", age: 55)
let result = compareValues(value1: employee1, value2: employee2)
print("The values are \(result)")   // "The values are different"
```

Listing 3-174: Adding a type constraint to a generic function

The conformance to the protocol is specified inside the angle brackets after the name of the generic type. The **compareValues()** function in Listing 3-174 declares the **T** type to conform to **Equatable** and then compares the values with a ternary operator and returns the result. In this case, the ages of the employees are the same (55), but the names are different ("George" and "Robert"), and therefore the system considers the structures to be different.

Another protocol used as a type constraint is **Numeric**. This protocol determines that the data types of the values received by the function must support arithmetic operations.

```
func calculateResult<T: Numeric>(value1: T, value2: T) {
   print(value1 + value2)   // 7.5
}
```

```
calculateResult(value1: 3.5, value2: 4)
```

Listing 3-175: Using the `Numeric` *protocol to set a type constraint*

The **calculateResult()** function in Listing 3-175 is a generic function and therefore it can receive any value of any type, but because we set a type constraint with the **Numeric** protocol, the function can only receive values of data types that can participate in arithmetic operations.

Besides comparing for equality with the **Equatable** protocol, we can also compare magnitudes with the **Comparable** protocol. This protocol is like **Equatable**, but the system does not offer a default implementation of the type methods, we must implement them ourselves. The protocol requires four methods to represent the operations >, <, >= and <=. In the following example, we compare the ages of the employees.

```
struct Employees: Comparable {
   var name: String
   var age: Int

   static func > (value1: Employees, value2: Employees) -> Bool {
      return value1.age > value2.age
   }
   static func < (value1: Employees, value2: Employees) -> Bool {
      return value1.age < value2.age
   }
   static func >= (value1: Employees, value2: Employees) -> Bool {
      return value1.age >= value2.age
   }
   static func <= (value1: Employees, value2: Employees) -> Bool {
      return value1.age <= value2.age
   }
}
let employee1 = Employees(name: "George", age: 32)
let employee2 = Employees(name: "Robert", age: 55)

if employee1 > employee2 {
   print("\(employee1.name) is older")
} else {
   print("\(employee2.name) is older")   // "Robert is older"
}
```

Listing 3-176: Conforming to the `Comparable` *protocol*

When we compare two instances of the **Employees** structure, the system calls the corresponding type method and the method returns **true** or **false** according to the values of the **age** property. Because in this example the value of **age** in the **employee1** structure is not greater than the value of **age** in the **employee2** structure, we get the message "Robert is older".

Another useful protocol is **Hashable**. Every time we include a structure or an object in a set or use them as the index of a dictionary, the system requires the data type to provide a hash value that can be used to uniquely identify each element. This is a random integer that is created based on the values of the properties. The purpose of the **Hashable** protocol is to define properties and methods to handle this value. Most of the data types defined by Swift conform to this protocol and that is why we do not have any problems when including these values in a set or as the index of dictionaries, but for custom structures and objects we must provide the hash value ourselves. Fortunately, if the values in our data type are already Hashable, we do not need a specific property to be used to create the hash value, all we need to do is conform to the protocol and the system creates the value for us. The following example makes the **Employees** structure conform to the **Hashable** protocol, so we can include the instances in a set.

```
struct Employees: Hashable {
   var name: String
   var age: Int
}
let employee1 = Employees(name: "John", age: 32)
let employee2 = Employees(name: "Robert", age: 55)
let list: Set<Employees> = [employee1, employee2]
for item in list {
   print(item.name)
}
```

Listing 3-177: Conforming to the Hashable *protocol*

Hash values are random integers created based on the values of the properties. If we just conform to the protocol, the system uses the values of all the properties in the instance to create it (all the properties must be hashable), but we can specify which properties should be included by implementing the properties and methods defined by the protocol.

hashValue—This property returns the instance's hash value. It is of type Int.

hash(into: inout Hasher)—This method defines the properties that are going to be included in the hasher to create the hash value.

To calculate the hash value, the Swift Standard Library includes a structure called **Hasher**. This is the structure received by the **hash(into:)** method and it contains a method called **combine()** to tell the hasher which properties should be used to create the value. The following example illustrates how to implement the **hash(into:)** method and call the **combine()** method on the hasher to create a hash value from the value of the **name** property.

```
struct Employees: Hashable {
   var name: String
   var age: Int

   func hash(into hasher: inout Hasher) {
      hasher.combine(name)
   }
}
let employee = Employees(name: "George", age: 32)
print(employee.hashValue)   // e.g., 7722685913545470055
```

Listing 3-178: Defining our own hash value

At the end of Listing 3-178, we print the value of the **hashValue** property. Because the resulting value is always an integer calculated randomly every time the app is executed, we won't notice any difference, but this procedure may be useful when we manage sensitive information.

The last protocol from our list is called **CaseIterable**. This is a simple protocol that defines a property called **allCases** to store a collection with all the cases in an enumeration. Again, the system automatically initializes this property, so all we need to do is to declare that the enumeration conforms to the protocol. In the following example, we define an enumeration with three cases and then iterate through the collection in the **allCases** property to print the names.

```
enum Departments: CaseIterable {
   case mail
   case marketing
   case managing
}
var message = ""
```

```
for department in Departments.allCases {
   message += "\(department) "
}
print(message)  // "mail marketing managing "
```

Listing 3-179: Conforming to the `CaseIterable` *protocol*

(Medium) **Extensions**

Protocols only define the properties and methods that the data types will have in common, but they do not include any implementation. However, we can implement properties and methods that will be common to all the data types that conform to the protocol by taking advantage of a feature of the Swift language called *Extensions*. Extensions are special declarations that add functionality to an existing data type. We can use them with structures, enumerations, and classes, but they are particularly useful with protocols because this is the way protocols can provide their own functionality. The syntax includes the **extension** keyword followed by the name of the data type we want to extend. The following example recreates the **Printer** protocol introduced in previous examples and extends it with a method.

```
protocol Printer {
   var name: String { get set }
}
extension Printer {
   func printdescription() {
      print("The name is \(name)")
   }
}
struct Employees: Printer {
   var name: String
   var age: Int
}
struct Offices: Printer {
   var name: String
   var employees: Int
}
let employee = Employees(name: "John", age: 45)
let office = Offices(name: "Mail", employees: 2)

employee.printdescription()  // "The name is John"
office.printdescription()  // "The name is Mail"
```

Listing 3-180: Extending a protocol

In this example, we define a **Printer** protocol with just the **name** property and then extend it to include a common implementation of the **printdescription()** method. Now, the **Employees** and **Offices** structures in our example share the same implementation and produce the same result when their **printdescription()** methods are executed.

As we already mentioned, extensions are not only available for protocols but also for any other data type. We can use them to extend structures, enumerations, and classes. This is particularly useful when we do not have access to the definitions of the data types and need to add some functionality (like when they are part of a library or a framework). In the following example, we extend the **Int** structure to provide a method that prints a description of its value.

```
extension Int {
   func printdescription() {
      print("The number is \(self)")
   }
}
```

Chapter 3 - Swift Paradigm

```
let number = 25
number.printdescription()   // "The number is 25"
```

Listing 3-181: Extending data types

The **Int** data type is a structure defined in the Swift Standard Library. We cannot modify its definition, but we can extend it to add more functionality. In this example, we add a method called **printdescription()** to print a message with the current value. (Notice the use of the **self** keyword to refer to the instance.) This method is not included in the original definition, but it is now available in our code.

Of course, we can also extend our own data types if we consider it appropriate. The following example extends our **Employees** structure to add a new method.

```
struct Employees {
   var name: String
   var age: Int
}
extension Employees {
   func printbadge() {
      print("Name: \(name) Age: \(age)")
   }
}
let employee = Employees(name: "John", age: 50)
employee.printbadge()   // "Name: John Age: 50"
```

Listing 3-182: Extending custom data types

Extensions can also be conditional. For instance, if we have a generic structure, we can add an extension only for specific types of values. The condition is determined by the **where** clause. The clause works like an **if** statement, so the extension is only applied if the condition is met.

```
struct Employees<T> {
   var value: T
}
extension Employees where T == Int {
   func doubleValue() {
      print("\(value) times 2 = \(value * 2)")
   }
}
let employee = Employees(value: 25)
employee.doubleValue()   // "25 times 2 = 50"
```

Listing 3-183: Defining a conditional extension

In this example, we define a generic structure called **Employees** with a generic property called **value** and then define an extension for this structure with a method called **doubleValue()**, but this method will only be added to the instance if the data type used to create the instance is **Int**. At the end, we create an instance with the value 25 and call the method, which multiplies the value by 2 and prints a string with the result. This works because we created the instance with an integer, but if we try to use another type of value, Xcode will show an error.

Another useful implementation of extensions is the customization of string interpolation. We have introduced string interpolation in Chapter 2 and have been using it in almost every example to insert values in strings (e.g., **print("My name is \(name)")**). What we haven't mentioned is that these values are managed by a structure called **StringInterpolation** (a typealias of **DefaultStringInterpolation**) and that by extending this structure we can customize how the system processes the values. The **StringInterpolation** structure includes the following methods for this purpose.

appendInterpolation(Value**)**—This method interpolates the value provided by the argument into the final string.

appendLiteral(String**)**—This method adds the string provided by the argument to the interpolation.

To customize the interpolation, we extend the **StringInterpolation** structure with an overload of the **appendInterpolation()** method, process the value inside this method, and finally append the result to the interpolation with the **appendLiteral()** method.

```
extension String.StringInterpolation {
    mutating func appendInterpolation(celsius value: Double) {
        let fahrenheit = ((value * 9)/5) + 32
        appendLiteral(String(fahrenheit))
    }
}
print("Temperature in Fahrenheit \(celsius: 25)")
```

Listing 3-184: Customizing string interpolation

The **appendInterpolation()** method can take as many parameters as we need. In this example, we define only one parameter with the name **value** and a label called **celsius**. When we create a string with this label and a number, the method is executed. Inside, we use the formula to turn Celsius degrees into Fahrenheit and then add the result to the interpolation with the **appendLiteral()** method to get the string "Temperature in Fahrenheit 77.0".

Medium Delegates

As we have already seen, an instance of a structure or an object can be assigned to the property of another instance. For example, we could have an instance of a structure called **Employees** with a property that contains an instance of a structure called **Offices** to store information about the office where the employee works. This opens the door to new programming patterns where the instances adopt different roles. The most useful pattern is called *Delegation*. A structure or object delegates responsibility for the execution of certain tasks to another structure or object.

```
struct Salary {
    func showMoney(name: String, money: Double) {
        print("The salary of \(name) is \(money)")
    }
}
struct Employees {
    var name: String
    var money: Double
    var delegate: Salary

    func generatereport() {
        delegate.showMoney(name: name, money: money)
    }
}
let salary = Salary()
var employee1 = Employees(name: "John", money: 45000, delegate: salary)
employee1.generatereport()  // "The salary of John is 45000.0"
```

Listing 3-185: Delegating tasks

The **Employees** structure in Listing 3-185 contains three properties. The properties **name** and **money** store the employee's data, but the **delegate** property stores the instance of the **Salary** structure in charge of printing that data. The code creates the **Salary** instance first and then uses this value to create the **Employees** instance. When we call the **generatereport()** method on the **employee1** structure at the end, the method calls the **showmoney()** method on **delegate**, effectively delegating the task of printing the data to this structure.

This pattern presents two problems. First, the structure that is delegating needs to know the data type of the structure that is going to become the delegate (in our example, the **delegate** property always has to be of type **Salary**). Following this approach, not every structure can be a delegate, only the ones specified in the definition. The second problem is related to how we know which are the properties and methods that the delegate must implement. If the structure is too complex or is taken from a library, we could forget to implement some methods or properties and get an error when the structure tries to access them. Both problems are solved by protocols. Instead of declaring a specific structure as the delegate, we define a protocol and declare the **delegate** property to be of that type, as shown in the following example.

```
protocol SalaryProtocol {
    func showMoney(name: String, money: Double)
}
struct Salary: SalaryProtocol {
    func showMoney(name: String, money: Double) {
        print("The salary of \(name) is \(money)")
    }
}
struct Employees {
    var name: String
    var money: Double
    var delegate: SalaryProtocol

    func generatereport() {
        delegate.showMoney(name: name, money: money)
    }
}
let salary = Salary()
let employee1 = Employees(name: "John", money: 45000, delegate: salary)
employee1.generatereport()   // "The salary of John is 45000.0"
```

Listing 3-186: *Delegating with protocols*

The **delegate** property of the **Employees** structure is now of type **SalaryProtocol**, which means that it can store any instance of any type providing that it conforms to the **SalaryProtocol** protocol. As illustrated by this example, the advantage of protocols is that we can use structures of different types to perform the task. It doesn't matter what type they are as long as they conform to the delegate's protocol and implement its properties and methods. For example, we could create two different structures to print the data of our last example and assign to the delegate one instance or another depending on what we want to achieve.

```
protocol SalaryProtocol {
    func showMoney(name: String, money: Double)
}
struct Salary: SalaryProtocol {
    func showMoney(name: String, money: Double) {
        print("The salary of \(name) is \(money)")
    }
}
struct BasicSalary: SalaryProtocol {
    func showMoney(name: String, money: Double) {
        if money > 40000 {
            print("Salary is over the minimum")
        } else {
            print("The salary of \(name) is \(money)")
        }
    }
```

```
    }
}
struct Employees {
    var name: String
    var money: Double
    var delegate: SalaryProtocol

    func generatereport() {
        delegate.showMoney(name: name, money: money)
    }
}
let salary = Salary()
var employee1 = Employees(name: "John", money: 45000, delegate: salary)
employee1.delegate = BasicSalary()
employee1.generatereport()   // "Salary is over the minimum"
```

Listing 3-187: Using different delegates

The **BasicSalary** structure added in Listing 3-187 conforms to **SalaryProtocol** and implements its **showMoney()** method, but unlike the **Salary** structure, it produces two different results depending on the employee's salary. The output produced by the execution of the **generatereport()** method on the **Employees** structure now depends on the type of structure we previously assigned to the **delegate** property.

Medium **3.7 Errors**

Errors are common in computer programming. Either our code or the code provided by libraries and frameworks may return errors. No matter how many precautions we take, we can't guarantee success and many problems may be found as our code tries to serve its purpose. For this reason, Swift introduces a systematic process to handle errors called *Error Handling*.

Medium **Throwing Errors**

When a method produces an error, it is said that it *throws* an error. Several frameworks provided by Apple are already programmed to throw errors, as we will see in further chapters, but we can also do it from our own structures and classes. To throw an error, we must use the **throw** and **throws** keywords. The **throw** keyword is used to throw the error and the **throws** keyword is specified in the method's declaration to indicate that the method can throw errors.

Because a method can throw multiple errors, we also must indicate the type of error found with values of an enumeration type. This is a custom enumeration that conforms to the **Error** protocol. For instance, let's consider the following example.

```
struct Stock {
    var totalLamps = 5
    mutating func sold(amount: Int) {
        totalLamps = totalLamps - amount
    }
}
var mystock = Stock()

mystock.sold(amount: 8)
print("Lamps in stock: \(mystock.totalLamps)")   // "Lamps in stock: -3"
```

Listing 3-188: Getting an error inside a method

The code in Listing 3-188 defines a structure called **Stock** that manages the stock of lamps available in the store. The class includes the **totalLamps** property to store the number of lamps we still have available and the **sold()** method to process the lamps sold. The method updates the stock by subtracting the number of lamps we have sold from the value of the `totalLamps` property. If the number of lamps sold is less than the number of lamps in stock, everything is fine, but when we sell more lamps than we have, as in this example, there is clearly a problem.

To throw an error from a method, we must define the types of errors available, add the `throws` keyword to the definition (between the arguments and the returning data types), detect the error, and throw it with the `throw` keyword.

```
enum Errors: Error {
    case OutOfStock
}
struct Stock {
    var totalLamps = 5
    mutating func sold(amount: Int) throws {
        if amount > totalLamps {
            throw Errors.OutOfStock
        } else {
            totalLamps = totalLamps - amount
        }
    }
}
var mystock = Stock()
```

Listing 3-189: Throwing errors

In this example, we declare an enumeration called `Errors` that conforms to the `Error` protocol and includes a case called `OutOfStock`. By declaring `sold()` as a throwing method with the `throws` keyword, we can now throw the `OutOfStock` error every time we try to sell more lamps than we have. If the lamps sold are more than the number of lamps in stock, the method throws the error, otherwise the stock is updated.

(Medium) ## Handling Errors

Now that we have a method that can throw errors, we must handle the errors when the method is executed. Swift includes the `try` keyword and the `do catch` statements for this purpose. The `do catch` statements create two blocks of code. If the statements inside the `do` block return an error, the statements in the `catch` block are executed. To execute a method that throws errors, we must call the method inside the `do` statement with the `try` keyword in front of it.

```
enum Errors: Error {
    case OutOfStock
}
struct Stock {
    var totalLamps = 5
    mutating func sold(amount: Int) throws {
        if amount > totalLamps {
            throw Errors.OutOfStock
        } else {
            totalLamps = totalLamps - amount
        }
    }
}
var mystock = Stock()
do {
    try mystock.sold(amount: 8)
} catch Errors.OutOfStock {
    print("We do not have enough lamps")
}
```

Listing 3-190: Handling errors

This code expands the previous example to handle the error thrown by the **sold()** method. Because of the addition of the **try** keyword, the system tries to execute the **sold()** method in the **mystock** structure and check for errors. If the method returns the **OutOfStock** error, the statements inside the **catch** block are executed. This pattern allows us to respond every time there is an error and report it to the user or correct the situation without having to crash the app or produce unexpected results.

Do It Yourself: Create a new Playground file. Copy the code in Listing 3-190 inside the file. You should see the message "We do not have enough lamps" printed on the console. Replace the number 8 with the number 3. Now the message should not be printed because there are enough lamps in stock.

IMPORTANT: You can add as many errors as you need to the **Errors** enumeration. The errors can be checked later with multiple **catch** statements in sequence. Also, you may add all the statements you need to the **do** block. The statements before **try** are always executed, while the statements after **try** are only executed if no error is found.

If the error is not one of the types we are expecting, we can print information about it. The information is stored in a constant called **error** that we can read inside the **catch** block.

```
enum Errors: String, Error {
   case OutOfStock = "Hello"
}
struct Stock {
   var totalLamps = 5
   mutating func sold(amount: Int) throws {
      if amount > totalLamps {
         throw Errors.OutOfStock
      } else {
         totalLamps = totalLamps - amount
      }
   }
}
var mystock = Stock()
do {
   try mystock.sold(amount: 8)
} catch {
   print(error)   // OutOfStock
}
```

Listing 3-191: Getting information about the error

On the other hand, if we do not care about the error, we can force the **try** keyword to return an optional with the syntax **try?**. If the method throws an error, the instruction returns **nil**, and therefore we can avoid the use of the **do catch** statements.

```
enum Errors: Error {
   case OutOfStock
}
struct Stock {
   var totalLamps = 5
   mutating func sold(amount: Int) throws {
      if amount > totalLamps {
         throw Errors.OutOfStock
      } else {
         totalLamps = totalLamps - amount
      }
   }
}
```

Chapter 3 - Swift Paradigm

```
var mystock = Stock()
try? mystock.sold(amount: 8)   // nil
```

Listing 3-192: Catching errors with `try?`

The instruction at the end of Listing 3-192 returns the value **nil** if the method throws an error, or an optional with the value returned by the method if everything goes right.

Sometimes, we know beforehand that a throwing method is not going to throw an error and therefore we want to avoid writing unnecessary code. In cases like this, we can use the syntax **try!**. For instance, the following code checks if there are enough lamps before calling the **sold()** method, so we know that the instruction will never throw the **OutOfStock** error.

```
enum Errors: Error {
    case OutOfStock
}
struct Stock {
    var totalLamps = 5
    mutating func sold(amount: Int) throws {
        if amount > totalLamps {
            throw Errors.OutOfStock
        } else {
            totalLamps = totalLamps - amount
        }
    }
}
var mystock = Stock()
if mystock.totalLamps > 3 {
    try! mystock.sold(amount: 3)
}
print("Lamps in stock: \(mystock.totalLamps)")
```

Listing 3-193: Ignoring the errors

Medium **Results**

Sometimes we need to return more than just an error. For this purpose, the Swift Standard Library defines the **Result** enumeration. This enumeration defines two cases with associated values to use in case of success or failure called **success()** and **failure()**. The Result enumeration is generic, which means that the data types of the associated values can be anything we want. For instance, in the following examples we define a **Result** enumeration of type **<Int, Errors>** to return an integer and the **OutOfStock** error defined in the previous example.

```
enum Errors: Error {
    case OutOfStock
}
struct Stock {
    var totalLamps = 5

    mutating func sold(amount: Int) -> Result<Int, Errors> {
        if amount > totalLamps {
            return .failure(.OutOfStock)
        } else {
            totalLamps = totalLamps - amount
            return .success(totalLamps)
        }
    }
}
var mystock = Stock()
```

```
let result = mystock.sold(amount: 3)
switch result {
   case .success(let stock):
      print("Lamps in stock: \(stock)")
   case .failure(let error):
      if error == .OutOfStock {
         print("Error: Out of Stock")
      } else {
         print("Error")
      }
}
```

Listing 3-194: Returning an error with a Result *enumeration*

The **sold()** method in Listing 3-194 now returns a **Result** value of type **<Int, Errors>**, so if an error occurs, the method can return a **failure()** value with the associated value **OutOfStock**, but if we have enough lamps to fulfill the order, we can return a **success()** value with the remaining number of lamps. The result can be processed by a **switch** statement. We check whether the value returned by the method is **failure()** or **success()**, get the associated value with a constant, and proceed accordingly. In this case, there are enough lamps available, so a message is printed on the console with the remaining stock.

Instead of using a **switch** statement, we can use the following method defined by the **Result** enumeration.

get()—This method returns the associated value of the **success()** case or throws an error with the associated value of the **failure()** case.

The only purpose of the **get()** method is to simplify the code. Now, instead of a **switch** statement, we can use a **do catch**.

```
enum Errors: Error {
   case OutOfStock
}
struct Stock {
   var totalLamps = 5

   mutating func sold(amount: Int) -> Result<Int, Errors> {
      if amount > totalLamps {
         return .failure(.OutOfStock)
      } else {
         totalLamps = totalLamps - amount
         return .success(totalLamps)
      }
   }
}
var mystock = Stock()
let result = mystock.sold(amount: 2)
do {
   let stock = try result.get()
   print("Lamps in stock: \(stock)")
} catch Errors.OutOfStock {
   print("Error: Out of Stock")
}
```

Listing 3-195: Processing an error with the get() *method*

The result is the same, but now all we need to do is to call the **get()** method. If the method doesn't return an error, the remaining stock is printed on the console, otherwise, the **catch** block is performed, and an error is printed instead.

Chapter 4
Introduction to Frameworks

Basic) **4.1 Frameworks**

The programming tools introduced in previous chapters are not enough to build professional applications. Creating an app requires accessing complex technologies and performing repetitive tasks that involve hundreds or even thousands of lines of code. Faced with this situation, developers always implemented pre-programmed codes that perform common tasks. These pieces of code are organized according to their purpose in what we know as frameworks.

Frameworks are libraries (pre-programmed code) and APIs (Application Programming Interfaces) that we can use to add functionality to our applications. This includes managing databases, creating graphics on the screen, storing files, accessing resources on the Web, sharing data online, and more. These frameworks are essential for building professional applications for Apple devices and are therefore part of the SDK (Software Development Kit) included with Xcode.

Do It Yourself: The examples in this chapter are designed for Playground. You just need to create a Playground file with a Blank template, as in the previous chapters, and then replace the code with the example you want to try.

Basic) **Importing Frameworks**

The Swift Standard Library implemented in previous chapters is automatically loaded for us and available everywhere in our code, but when additional frameworks are required, we must tell the compiler what we need. This is done by adding the **import** instruction at the beginning of each file followed by the name of the framework we want to include (e.g., **import Foundation**). Once the framework is imported, it is included with our file, giving us access to all the structures, classes, functions, and any of the values defined by it.

Basic) **4.2 Foundation**

Foundation is one of the oldest frameworks provided by Apple. It was written in Objective-C and developed by Steve Jobs's second company NeXT. It was created to manage basic tasks and store data. The framework provides its own data types (structures and classes) to store any value we want, including numbers, strings, arrays and dictionaries, and a primary class called **NSObject** with basic functionality that every other class inherits from. Most of these definitions are now obsolete, replaced by Swift's data types, but others remain useful, as we will see next.

Basic) **More Standard Functions**

As we have seen in Chapter 3, the Swift Standard Library includes a few standard functions, such as **print()** and **abs()**, but others are provided by frameworks like Foundation. The following are some of the basic functions available when we import the Foundation framework.

pow(Float, Float)—This function returns the result of raising the first value to the power of the second value. The arguments may be numbers of type **Float** or **Double**.

sqrt(Float)—This function returns the square root of the value of its argument. The argument may be of type **Float** or **Double**.

log(Float)—This function returns the natural logarithm of a value. Similar functions are **log2()**, **log10()**, **log1p()**, and **logb()**. It can take a value of type **Float** or **Double**.

sin(Float**)**—This function returns the sine of a value. Similar functions are `asin()`, `sinh()`, and `asinh()`. The argument may be of type `Float` or `Double`.

cos(Float**)**—This function returns the cosine of a value. Similar functions are `acos()`, `cosh()`, and `acosh()`. The argument may be of type `Float` or `Double`.

tan(Float**)**—This function returns the tangent of a value. Similar functions are `atan()`, `atan2()`, `tanh()`, and `atanh()`. The argument may be of type `Float` or `Double`.

The application of these functions is straightforward, as shown in the following example.

```
import Foundation

let square = sqrt(4.0)
let power = pow(2.0, 2.0)
let maximum = max(square, power)
print("The maximum value is \(maximum)")   // "The maximum value is 4.0"
```

Listing 4-1: Applying math functions

The first thing we do in the code of Listing 4-1 is to import the Foundation framework. After this, we can implement any of the tools defined inside the framework, including the basic functions introduced above. This example gets the square root of 4.0, calculates 2.0 to the power of 2.0, and compares the results using the `max()` function from the Swift Standard Library.

(Basic) **Strings**

Foundation defines a class called **NSString** to store and manage strings of characters. The **String** structure offered by the Swift Standard Library for this same purpose adopts most of its functionality, turning the class obsolete, but because Swift coexists with old frameworks and data types, **NSString** objects are still required in some circumstances. The **NSString** class includes several Initializers to create these objects. The one usually implemented in Swift takes an argument called **string** with the string of characters we want to assign to the object.

```
import Foundation

var text: NSString = NSString(string: "Hello")
print(text)   // "Hello"
```

Listing 4-2: Creating an NSString object

If we already have a **String** value in our code, we can cast it into an **NSString** object with the **as** operator.

```
import Foundation

var text = "Hello World"
var newText = text as NSString
print(newText)   // "Hello World"
```

Listing 4-3: Casting a String value into an NSString object

A **String** structure can be turned into an **NSString** object with the **as** operator because they are interconnected. It is said that the **String** structure bridges with the **NSString** class. This means that we can access the functionality offered by the **NSString** class from a **String** structure, including the following properties and methods.

capitalized—This property returns a string with the first letter of every word in uppercase.

length—This property returns the number of characters in the string of an **NSString** object. (For **String** values, we should use the **count** property instead.)

localizedStringWithFormat(String, Values**)**—This type method creates a string from the string provided by the first argument and the values provided by the second argument. The first argument is a template used to create the string, and the second argument is the list of values we want to include in the string separated by comma.

contains(String**)**—This method returns a Boolean value that indicates whether or not the string specified by the argument was found inside the original string. The class also includes the **localizedCaseInsensitiveContains(String)** method to perform a case insensitive search that considers local conventions.

trimmingCharacters(in: CharacterSet**)**—This method erases the characters indicated by the **in** argument at the beginning and the end of the string and returns a new string with the result. The argument is a **CharacterSet** structure with type properties to select the type of characters we want to remove. The most frequently used are **whitespaces** (spaces) and **whitespacesAndNewlines** (spaces and new line characters).

compare(String, **options:** CompareOptions, **range:** Range?, **locale:** Locale?**)** —This method compares the original string with the string provided by the first argument and returns an enumeration of type **ComparisonResult** with a value corresponding to the lexical order of the strings. The **orderedSame** value is returned when the strings are equal, the **orderedAscending** value is returned when the original string precedes the value of the first argument, and the **orderedDescending** value is returned when the original string follows the value of the first argument. The **options** argument is a property of the **CompareOptions** structure. The properties available are **caseInsensitive** (it considers lowercase and uppercase letters to be the same), **literal** (performs a Byte-to-Byte comparison), **diacriticInsensitive** (ignores diacritic marks such as the visual stress on vowels), **widthInsensitive** (ignores the width difference in characters that occurs in some languages), and **forcedOrdering** (the comparison is forced to return **orderedAscending** or **orderedDescending** values when the strings are equivalent but not strictly equal). The **range** argument defines a range that describes the portion of the original string we want to compare. Finally, the **locale** argument is a **Locale** structure that defines localization. Only the first argument is required.

caseInsensitiveCompare(String**)**—This method compares the original string with the string provided by the argument. It works exactly like the **compare()** method but with the option **caseInsensitiveSearch** set by default.

range(of: String, **options:** CompareOptions, **range:** Range?, **locale:** Locale?**)** —This method searches for the string specified by the first argument and returns a range to indicate where the string was found or **nil** in case of failure. The **options** argument is a property of the **CompareOptions** structure. The properties available for this method are the same we have for the **compare()** method, with the difference that we can specify three more: **backwards** (searches from the end of the string), **anchored** (matches characters only at the beginning or the end, not in the middle), and **regularExpression** (searches with a regular expression). The **range** argument defines a range that determines the portion of the original string where we want to search. Only the first argument is required.

As we already mentioned, the **String** structure is bridged to the **NSString** class and therefore we can call these methods from **String** values, but because they are defined in the **NSString** class, we still must import the Foundation framework to be able to use them. Some of them are like those offered by the **String** structure but allow us to perform additional operations on the values. For instance, we can incorporate values into strings with string interpolation, but the `localizedStringWithFormat()` method offers a different approach. This method takes a string with placeholders and replaces them with a list of values. The placeholders are declared with the % symbol followed by a character that represents the type of value we want to include. For example, if we want to replace the placeholder by an integer, we must use the characters %d.

```
import Foundation

var age = 44
var mytext = String.localizedStringWithFormat("My age is %d", age)
print(mytext)   // "My age is 44"
```

Listing 4-4: Creating a formatted string

There are different placeholders available. The most frequently used are %d for integers, %f for floating-point numbers, %g to remove redundant 0 (zeros), and %@ for objects and structures. We can use any of these characters and as many times as necessary. This is like what we would get with string interpolation, but with this method we can also format the values. For instance, we can determine the number of digits a value will have by adding the amount before the letter.

```
import Foundation

let length = 12.3472
let total = 54
let decimals = String.localizedStringWithFormat("Decimals: %.2f", length)
let digits = String.localizedStringWithFormat("Digits: %.5d", total)
print(decimals)   // "Decimals: 12.35"
print(digits)   // "Digits: 00054"
```

Listing 4-5: Formatting numbers

The code in Listing 4-5 formats two numbers, a double and an integer. The double is processed with the %.2f placeholder, which means that the value is going to be rounded to two decimals after the point, and the integer is processed with the %.5d placeholder, which means that the number in the string is going to contain a total of five digits.

Other **NSString** class methods perform operations that are already available for **String** values, but they produce a more comprehensive result. For example, the **compare()** method compares strings like the == operator does, but the value returned is not just **true** or **false**.

```
import Foundation

var fruit = "Orange"
var search = "Apple"

var result = fruit.compare(search)
switch result {
  case .orderedSame:
    print("Fruit and Search are equal")
  case .orderedDescending:
    print("Fruit follows Search")   // "Fruit follows Search"
  case .orderedAscending:
    print("Fruit precedes Search")
}
```

Listing 4-6: Comparing String *values*

The **compare()** method takes a string, compares it to the original string, and returns a **ComparisonResult** value to indicate the order. The **ComparisonResult** enumeration contains three values: **orderedSame**, **orderedDescending**, and **orderedAscending**. After comparing the values of the **fruit** and **search** variables in our example, the **result** variable contains one of these values according to the lexical order of the strings. In this case, the value "Orange" assigned to **fruit** is larger (follows alphabetically) the value "Apple" assigned to **search**, so the value returned is **orderedDescending** (the order is descending from **fruit** to **search**).

The **compare()** method implemented in Listing 4-6 and the **==** operator studied in Chapter 2 consider a lowercase string different from an uppercase string. Adding an option to the **compare()** method we can compare two strings without considering lower or uppercase letters.

```
import Foundation

var fruit = "Orange"
var search = "ORANGE"

var result = fruit.compare(search, options: .caseInsensitive)
switch result {
   case .orderedSame:
      print("The values are equal")   // "The values are equal"
   case .orderedDescending:
      print("Fruit follows Search")
   case .orderedAscending:
      print("Fruit precedes Search")
}
```

Listing 4-7: Comparing `String` *values with options*

The strings stored in the **fruit** and **search** variables in Listing 4-7 are different, but because of the **caseInsensitive** option, they are considered equal. This type of comparison is very common, which is why the class includes the **caseInsensitiveCompare()** method that all it does is calling the **compare()** method with the **caseInsensitive** option already set.

Despite this being the most common scenario, we can perform more precise comparison by providing the range of characters we want to compare.

```
import Foundation

var phone = "905-525-6666"
var search = "905"

var start = phone.startIndex
var end = phone.firstIndex(of: "-")

if let endIndex = end {
   let result = phone.compare(search, options: .caseInsensitive, range:
start..<endIndex)
   if result == .orderedSame {
      print("The area code is the same")   // "The area code is the same"
   } else {
      print("The area code is different")
   }
}
```

Listing 4-8: Comparing only a range of characters

This example compares only the initial characters of a string to check the area code of a phone number. The code defines a range that goes from the first character of the **phone** variable to the position before the **-** character. This range is provided to the **compare()** method and in consequence the value of the **search** variable is compared against the first three characters.

We can also use ranges to search for strings using the **range()** method. This method searches for a string inside another string and returns a range that determines where the string was found.

```
import Foundation

var text = "The Suitcase is Black"
var search = "black   "
search = search.trimmingCharacters(in: .whitespacesAndNewlines)

var range = text.range(of: search, options: .caseInsensitive)
if let rangeToReplace = range {
    text.replaceSubrange(rangeToReplace, with: "Red")
}
print(text)   // "The Suitcase is Red"
```

Listing 4-9: Searching and replacing characters in a string

The **range()** method returns an optional value that contains the range where the string was found or **nil** in case of failure. In Listing 4-9, we search for the value of the **search** variable inside the **text** variable and check the optional value returned. When we have a range to work with (which means that the value was found) we use it to call the **replaceSubrange()** method of the **String** structure to replace the characters in the range with the string "Red" (see Listing 3-67). Notice that because search values are usually provided by the user, we trim the value of the **search** variable with the **trimmingCharacters()** method to make sure that there are no space characters at the beginning or the end of the string (the two spaces after the word "black" are removed).

(Basic) Ranges

Although Swift includes structures to store ranges of values, some frameworks programmed in Objective-C still implement an old Foundation class called **NSRange**. The **NSRange** class is slightly different than the Swift's **Range** structure. Instead of storing the initial and final values of the range, **NSRange** objects store the initial value and the length of the range.

NSRange(Range**)**—This initializer creates an **NSRange** object from a **Range** value.

NSRange(Range, **in:** String**)**—This initializer creates an **NSRange** object to represent a **Range** structure with string indexes.

Range(NSRange**)**—This initializer creates a **Range** structure from an **NSRange** value.

Range(NSRange, **in:** String**)**—This initializer creates a **Range** structure to represent an **NSRange** object with string indexes.

The **NSRange** class includes two properties to retrieve the values: **location** and **length**. The following example initializes an **NSRange** object from a Swift range and prints its values.

```
import Foundation

let range = NSRange(4..<10)
print("Initial: \(range.location)")   // "Initial: 4"
print("Length: \(range.length)")   // "Length: 6"
```

Listing 4-10: Creating and reading an NSRange value

The initializer implemented in this example is for countable ranges. If we work with string indexes, we must use the initializer defined for strings. This is because the **String** structure works with Unicode characters while **NSString** objects work with a less comprehensive character encoding called *UTF-16*. Working with different character encodings means that the space the characters occupy in memory varies. A range that represents a series of characters in a **String** value may differ from a range that represents the same series of characters in an **NSString** value. The following example illustrates how to work with this initializer.

```
import Foundation

let text = "Hello World"
if let start = text.firstIndex(of: "W") {
   let newRange = NSRange(start..., in: text)
   print("Initial: \(newRange.location)")  // "Initial: 6"
   print("Length: \(newRange.length)")  // "Length: 5"
}
```

Listing 4-11: Converting a range of string indexes

(Basic) # Numbers

Foundation offers a class called **NSNumber** to represent and store numbers. With the introduction of the Swift's primitive data types, the use of this class is no longer necessary, but there are a few old frameworks that still require these types of values. The class includes the following initializer.

NSNumber(value: Value**)**—This initializer creates an **NSNumber** object with the value specified by the **value** argument. The argument may be a value of any of the data types available in Swift for numbers.

The class also provides properties to perform the opposite operation, getting Swift data types from **NSNumber** objects. The following are the most frequently used.

intValue—This property returns an **Int** value with the object's number.

floatValue—This property returns a **Float** value with the object's number.

doubleValue—This property returns a **Double** value with the object's number.

The following example shows how to create **NSNumber** objects and how to get them back as Swift data types to perform operations.

```
import Foundation

var mynumber = NSNumber(value: 35)
var mydouble = mynumber.doubleValue * 2  // 70
```

Listing 4-12: Working with NSNumber objects

Besides its own data type, Foundation also provides the means to format numbers. Every time we print a number, all the digits are shown on the screen, including all the decimal digits. In Listing 4-4, we explained how to specify how many digits of a number we want to include in a string using placeholders (e.g., **%.2f**), but this is not customizable enough. To provide a better alternative, the framework includes the following formatting method.

formatted(FormatStyle**)**—This method formats the number according to the styles provided by the argument.

To format a number, we must call this method from the instance with the styles we want to apply to it. The styles are defined by a structure that conforms to the **FormatStyle** protocol. For numbers, the framework defines the **IntegerFormatStyle** and the **FloatingPointFormat-Style** structures. These structures include the following methods to style a number.

precision(Precision**)**—This method defines the number of digits included in the integer and decimal parts of the number. The argument is a **Precision** structure, which includes the **integerLength(Int)** and **fractionLength(Int)** methods to specify the number of digits in the integer and decimal parts, and the **integerAndFraction-Length(integer: Int, fraction: Int)** method to specify both.

rounded(rule: FloatingPointRoundingRule)—This method rounds the number to the nearest value. The **rule** argument is an enumeration with the values **up, down, awayFromZero, toNearestOrAwayFromZero, toNearestOrEven**, and **towardZero**.

grouping(Grouping)—This method determines if the digits of a number are going to be separated in groups (e.g., 9,000,000). The argument is a structure with the properties **automatic** (default) and **never**.

notation(Notation)—This method determines the number's notation. The argument is a structure with the properties **automatic** (default), **compactName**, and **scientific**.

sign(strategy: SignDisplayStrategy)—This method determines if the sign will be included (+ and -). The **strategy** argument is a **SignDisplayStrategy** structure, which includes the **automatic** (default) and **never** properties, and also the **always(includingZero: Bool)** method to determine if the sign is displayed or not.

decimalSeparator(strategy: DecimalSeparatorDisplayStrategy)—This method determines if a separator is going to be included after the number. The **strategy** argument is a structure with the properties **automatic** (default) and **always**.

The **FormatStyle** protocol defines the **number** property, which contains an instance of the **IntegerFormatStyle** or the **FloatingPointFormatStyle** structures, depending on the number's data type. From this instance, we can apply all the styles we want to a number.

```
import Foundation

let mynumber: Double = 32.56789
let text = mynumber.formatted(.number.precision(.fractionLength(2)))
print(text)   // "32.57"
```

Listing 4-13: Formatting a number

The styles are provided one by one with dot notation. We first get the styling structure from the **number** property. (In this case, the number is a **Double** so the value of the property is an instance of the **FloatingPointFormatStyle** structure.) Next, we call the **precision()** method, and send to this method the value returned by the **fractionLength()** method, which formats the number with 2 decimal digits. As a result, we get a string with the value "32.57" (the value is rounded up).

Styles can be concatenated, one after another, with dot notation. For instance, in the previous example, the number was rounded up by default, but we can change this behavior by applying the **rounded(rule:)** method, as shown next.

```
import Foundation

let mynumber: Double = 32.56789
let text =
mynumber.formatted(.number.precision(.fractionLength(2)).rounded(rule: .d
own))
print(text)   // "32.56"
```

Listing 4-14: Rounding a number

In this example, the **rounded(rule:)** method is called after the number is formatted with 2 decimal digits, so the rest of the digits are rounded down.

The grouping, notation, and decimal separator styles usually apply to large numbers. For instance, by default, the digits of large numbers are separated in groups, as in 32,000,000, but we can change this behavior with the **grouping()** method.

```
import Foundation

let mynumber: Int = 32000000
let text = mynumber.formatted(.number.grouping(.never))
print(text)   // "32000000"
```

Listing 4-15: Disabling grouping

We can also show the sign in front of the number (+ or -). In the following example, we always show the sign except when the number is equal to 0.

```
import Foundation

let mynumber: Int = 32000000
let text =
mynumber.formatted(.number.sign(strategy: .always(includingZero: false)))
print(text)   // "+32,000,000"
```

Listing 4-16: Adding the sign

In addition to **number**, the **FormatStyle** protocol defines the **percent** property to style the number as a percentage, and the **currency(code:)** method to format monetary values. The **percent** property is a **Percent** structure that all it does is to add the % sign to the number.

```
import Foundation

let mynumber: Int = 32
let text = mynumber.formatted(.percent)
print(text)   // "32%"
```

Listing 4-17: Formatting the number as a percentage value

On the other hand, the **currency(code:)** method can produce a number with any format and currency symbol we want. The currency is defined by the string assigned to the argument. There are values for any currency available. For instance, the USD string is for American Dollars, the CAD string is for Canadian Dollars, EUR for Euros, and so on. The following example gets the number expressed in Canadian dollars.

```
import Foundation

let mynumber: Double = 32.55
let text = mynumber.formatted(.currency(code: "CAD"))
print(text)   // "CA$32.55"
```

Listing 4-18: Formatting currency values

 **Dates**

Foundation defines multiple classes and structures to create and process dates, including **Date**, **Calendar**, **DateComponents**, **DateInterval**, **Locale**, and **TimeZone**. The data type in charge of creating the structure to store the actual date is **Date**. The following are some of the initializers.

Date()—This initializer creates a **Date** structure with the system's current date.

Date(timeIntervalSinceNow: TimeInterval)—This initializer creates a **Date** structure with a date calculated from the addition of the current date plus the time specified by the **timeIntervalSinceNow** argument. The argument is a value of type **TimeInterval** that indicates how many seconds the date is from the initial date.

Date(timeInterval: TimeInterval, **since:** Date)—This initializer creates a `Date` structure with a date calculated from the addition of the date specified by the **since** argument plus the time specified by the **timeInterval** argument. The argument is a value of type `TimeInterval` that indicates how many seconds the date is from the initial date.

Date(timeIntervalSinceReferenceDate: TimeInterval)—This initializer creates a `Date` structure with a date calculated from a reference date in the past plus the time interval in seconds specified by the argument.

The following example shows different ways to initialize a date.

```
import Foundation

var currentdate = Date()
var nextday = Date(timeIntervalSinceNow: 24 * 60 * 60)
var tendays = Date(timeInterval: -10 * 24 * 3600, since: nextday)
```

Listing 4-19: *Storing dates with* Date *structures*

If the initializer requires an interval, as those in the code of Listing 4-19, the value is specified in seconds. An easy way to calculate the seconds is multiplying every component. For example, the date for the **nextday** object created in our example is calculated adding 1 day to the current date. The number of seconds in 1 day are calculated by multiplying the 24 hours of the day by the 60 minutes in an hour by the 60 seconds in a minute (24 * 60 * 60). For the **tendays** object, we apply the same technique. This initializer adds the interval to a specific date (**nextday**). The seconds are calculated by multiplying the components, albeit this time it multiplies the previous result by -10 to get a date 10 days before **nextday**. (We will see better ways to add components to a date later.)

 IMPORTANT: These methods require a value of type **Double** to declare the interval in seconds, but instead of **Double** the framework calls it **TimeInterval**. This is a typealias (an alternative name for an existing type). Once defined, aliases are used exactly like regular data types. To create your own type aliases, you can use the instruction **typealias** (e.g., **typealias Myinteger = Int**).

Besides the initializers, the class also includes type properties that return special dates. Some of these properties produce values that are useful to set limits and sort lists, as the following.

distantFuture—This type property returns a **Date** structure with a value that represents a date in a distant future.

distantPast—This type property returns a **Date** structure with a value that represents a date in a distant past.

The **Date** structure also includes properties and methods to calculate and compare dates. The following are the most frequently used.

timeIntervalSinceNow—This property returns a **TimeInterval** value representing the difference in seconds between the date in the **Date** structure and the current date.

timeIntervalSinceReferenceDate—This property returns a **TimeInterval** value representing the difference in seconds between the current date and a reference date in the past (In current systems, this is January 1st, 2001). The structure also includes the **timeIntervalSince1970** property to return the interval between the current date and January 1st 1970.

Chapter 4 - Introduction to Frameworks

compare(Date**)**—This method compares the date in the **Date** structure with the date specified by the argument and returns an enumeration of type **ComparisonResult** with a value corresponding to the order of the dates. The possible values are **orderedSame** (the dates are equal), **orderedAscending** (the date is earlier than the value), and **orderedDescending** (the date is later than the value).

timeIntervalSince(Date**)**—This method compares the date in the **Date** structure with the date specified by the argument and returns the interval between both dates in seconds.

addingTimeInterval(TimeInterval**)**—This method adds the seconds specified by the argument to the date in the **Date** structure and returns a new **Date** structure with the result.

addTimeInterval(TimeInterval**)**—This method adds the seconds specified by the argument to the date in the **Date** structure and stores the result in the same structure.

Comparing dates and calculating the intervals between dates is a constant requirement in app development. The following example compares the current date with a date calculated from a specific number of days. If the resulting date is later than the current date, the code prints a message on the console to show the time remaining in seconds.

```
import Foundation
var days = 7
var today = Date()
var event = Date(timeIntervalSinceNow: Double(days) * 24 * 3600)
if today.compare(event) == .orderedAscending {
    let interval = event.timeIntervalSince(today)
    print("We have to wait \(interval) seconds")
}
```

Listing 4-20: Comparing two dates

The dates in **Date** structures are not associated to any calendar. This means that to get the components in a date (year, month, day, etc.) we must decide first in the context of which calendar the date is going to be interpreted. The calendar for a date is defined by the **Calendar** structure. This structure provides properties and methods to process a date according to a specific calendar (Gregorian, Buddhist, Chinese, etc.). To initialize a **Calendar** structure, we have the following initializer and type property.

Calendar(identifier: Identifier**)**—This initializer creates a **Calendar** structure with the calendar specified by the argument. The **identifier** argument is a property of a structure called **Identifier** defined inside the **Calendar** structure. The properties available are **gregorian**, **buddhist**, **chinese**, **coptic**, **ethiopicAmeteMihret**, **ethiopicAmeteAlem**, **hebrew**, **ISO8601**, **indian**, **islamic**, **islamicCivil**, **japanese**, **persian**, **republicOfChina**, **islamicTabular** and **islamicUmmAlQura**.

current—This type property returns a structure with the current calendar set in the system.

A **Calendar** structure includes the following properties and methods to manage the calendar and to get and set new dates.

identifier—This property returns the value that identifies the calendar.

locale—This property sets or returns the **Locale** structure used by the **Calendar** structure to process dates. The value by default is the **Locale** structure set by the system.

timeZone—This property sets or returns the `TimeZone` structure used by the `Calendar` structure to process dates. The value by default is the `TimeZone` structure set by the system.

dateComponents(Set, from: Date)—This method returns a `DateComponents` structure with the components indicated by the first argument from the date indicated by the **from** argument. The first argument is a set with properties of a structure called `Unit` that represent each component (**year, month, day, hour, minute, second**, etc.).

dateComponents(Set, from: Date, to: Date)—This method returns a `DateComponents` structure with the components indicated by the first argument. These components represent the difference between the dates specified by the **from** and **to** arguments. The first argument is a set with properties of a structure called `Unit` that represent each component. The most frequently used are **year, month, day, hour, minute**, and **second**.

date(byAdding: DateComponents, to: Date)—This method returns a `Date` structure with the value obtained by adding the components indicated by the **byAdding** argument to the date indicated by the **to** argument.

date(from: DateComponents)—This method returns a date created from the components provided by the **from** argument.

The `Calendar` structure works along with the `DateComponents` structure to read and return components from a date. The instances created from the `DateComponents` structure include the properties **year, month, day, hour, minute, second**, and **weekday** to read and set the values of the components. The following example combines these tools to get the year of the current date.

```
import Foundation

var today = Date()
let calendar = Calendar.current
var components = calendar.dateComponents([.year], from: today)
print("The year is \(components.year!)")
```

Listing 4-21: Extracting components from a date

In Listing 4-21, we get a reference to the calendar set in the system from the **current** property and then use the **dateComponents()** method to get the year from the current date.

Several components may be retrieved at once by adding the corresponding properties to the set. The following example gets the year, month, and day from the current date.

```
import Foundation

var today = Date()
let calendar = Calendar.current
var comp = calendar.dateComponents([.year, .month, .day], from: today)
print("Today \(comp.day!)-\(comp.month!)-\(comp.year!)")
```

Listing 4-22: Extracting multiple components from a date

DateComponents structures are used to retrieve the components of existing dates and to set the values for new dates. In the following example, a new **Date** structure is created from the values of a **DateComponents** structure.

```
import Foundation
```

```
let calendar = Calendar.current
var comp = DateComponents()
comp.year = 1970
comp.month = 8
comp.day = 21
var birthday = calendar.date(from: comp)   // "Aug 21, 1970, 12:00 AM"
```

Listing 4-23: Creating a new date from single components

The **date(from:)** method of the **Calendar** structure returns a new date with the values provided by the **DateComponents** structure. The components which values are not explicitly defined take values by default (e.g., 12:00 AM).

Generating a new date requires a specific calendar. For example, in the code of Listing 4-23, the values of the components are declared with the format established by the Gregorian calendar. In this case, we rely on the calendar returned by the system, but if we want to use the same calendar no matter where the app is executed, we must set it ourselves from the **Calendar** initializer.

```
import Foundation
let id = Calendar.Identifier.gregorian
let calendar = Calendar(identifier: id)

var comp = DateComponents()
comp.year = 1970
comp.month = 8
comp.day = 13
var birthday = calendar.date(from: comp)   // "Aug 13, 1970 at 12:00 AM"
```

Listing 4-24: Using a Gregorian calendar

Declaring a specific calendar is not only recommended when creating new dates but also when calculating dates by adding components, as in the following example.

```
import Foundation
let id = Calendar.Identifier.gregorian
let calendar = Calendar(identifier: id)
var comp = DateComponents()
comp.day = 120

var today = Date()
var appointment = calendar.date(byAdding: comp, to: today)
```

Listing 4-25: Adding components to a date

The **date()** method implemented in Listing 4-25 adds components to a date and returns a new **Date** structure with the result. The component **day** was set to 120. The **date()** method takes this value, adds it to the date in the **today** structure, and returns the result.

A common task when working with multiple dates is getting the time between dates, such as the hours remaining for a process to complete or the days remaining for an event to begin. The **Calendar** structure includes a version of the **dateComponents()** method that allows us to compare two dates and get the difference expressed in a specific component.

```
import Foundation
let calendar = Calendar.current
var comp = DateComponents()
comp.year = 1970
comp.month = 8
comp.day = 21
```

```
var today = Date()
var birthdate = calendar.date(from: comp)
if let olddate = birthdate {
   let components = calendar.dateComponents([.day], from: olddate, to:
today)
   print("Days between dates: \(components.day!)")
}
```

Listing 4-26: Comparing dates

This example calculates the days between a birthdate and the current date. The value returned by the **date()** method used to generate the birthdate returns an optional, so we unwrap it before calculating the difference. We assign this value to the **olddate** constant and then compare it with the current date. The number of days between dates is returned and printed on the console.

Another way to specify intervals between dates is with the **DateInterval** structure. This structure allows us to create an interval with **Date** values. The following are the initializers.

DateInterval(start: Date, **end:** Date)—This initializer creates a **DateInterval** structure with the interval between the values provided by the **start** and **end** arguments.

DateInterval(start: Date, **duration:** TimeInterval)—This initializer creates a **DateInterval** structure with an interval that starts at the date specified by the **start** argument and last as long as the time specified by the **duration** argument.

The **DateInterval** structure also offers the following properties and methods.

start—This property sets or returns the initial **Date** of the interval.

end—This property sets or returns the final **Date** of the interval.

duration—This property sets or returns the duration of the interval in seconds.

contains(Date)—This method returns a Boolean value that indicates whether the date specified by the argument is inside the interval or not.

intersects(DateInterval)—This method returns a Boolean value that indicates if the interval intersects with the interval specified by the argument.

intersection(with: DateInterval)—This method returns a **DateInterval** value with the interval in which the original interval and the one provided by the **with** argument overlap.

A typical use of the **DateInterval** structure is to create an interval from two dates and check if a specific date falls within the interval, as in the following example.

```
import Foundation

let calendar = Calendar.current

var components = DateComponents()
components.year = 1970
components.month = 8
components.day = 21
var birthday = calendar.date(from: components)

components.year = 2020
components.month = 8
components.day = 21
var future = calendar.date(from: components)

if birthday != nil && future != nil {
   let today = Date()
```

Chapter 4 - Introduction to Frameworks

```
    let interval = DateInterval(start: birthday!, end: future!)
    if interval.contains(today) {
        print("You still have time")   // "You still have time"
    }
}
```

Listing 4-27: Finding a date in an interval

The code in Listing 4-27 creates two dates, **birthday** and **future**, and then generates an interval from one date to another. The **contains()** method is used next to check whether the current date is within the interval or not.

As with numbers, Foundation also provides the tools to format dates. The **Date** structure defines two versions of the **formatted()** method for this purpose.

formatted(date: DateStyle, **time:** TimeStyle**)**—This method formats the date with the styles specified by the arguments. The **date** argument defines the style for the date. It is a structure with the type properties **abbreviated**, **complete**, **long**, **numeric**, and **omitted**. And the **time** argument defines the style for the time. It is a structure with the type properties **complete**, **omitted**, **shortened**, and **standard**.

formatted(FormatStyle**)**—This method formats the date with the styles specified by the argument.

If all we need is a standard format, we can call the **formatted(date:, time:)** method with the styles we want for the date and time. The method takes these values and returns a string with a date in the format defined by the current locale (the user's language and location).

```
import Foundation

let mydate = Date.now
let text = mydate.formatted(date: .abbreviated, time: .omitted)
print(text)   // "Jun 18, 2021"
```

Listing 4-28: Formatting dates

The code in Listing 4-28 gets the current date from the **now** property and then calls the method with the **abbreviated** and **omitted** values. This creates a string that contains a date with abbreviated text and no time ("Jun 18, 2021").

Standard styles include all the components of the date, but the **Date** structure includes an additional version of the **formatted()** method that takes a **FormatStyle** structure to format the date any way we want. The following are some of the methods included for customization.

day(Day**)**—This method includes the day. The argument defines the style for the day. It is a structure with the properties **defaultDigits**, **ordinalOfDayInMonth**, and **twoDigits**.

month(Month**)**—This method includes the month. The argument defines the style for the month. It is a structure with the properties **abbreviated**, **defaultDigits**, **narrow**, **twoDigits**, and **wide**.

year(Year**)**—This method includes the year. The argument defines the style for the year. It is a structure with the properties **defaultDigits** and **twoDigits**.

hour(Hour**)**—This method includes the hour. The argument defines the style for the hour. It is a structure with the properties **defaultDigitsNoAMPM** and **twoDigitsNoAMPM**.

minute(Minute**)**—This method includes the minutes. The argument defines the style for the minutes. It is a structure with the properties **defaultDigits** and **twoDigits**.

second(Second**)**—This method includes the seconds. The argument defines the style for the seconds. It is a structure with the properties `defaultDigits` and `twoDigits`.

weekday(Weekday**)**—This method includes the weekday. The argument defines the style for the day. It is a structure with the properties `abbreviated`, `narrow`, `oneDigit`, `short`, `twoDigits`, and `wide`.

The `FormatStyle` structure includes the following properties to configure the parameters used to format the date.

calendar—This property sets or returns the calendar used to format the date. It is of type `Calendar`.

locale—This property sets or returns the locale used to format the date. It is of type `Locale`.

timeZone—This property sets or return the time zone used to format the date. It is of type `TimeZone`.

Although we can create our own `FormatStyle` structure, the structure includes a type property called `dateTime` to return an instance with the calendar and standard values set by the device. If the configuration by default is enough, we can use this property to format the date, as shown next.

```
import Foundation

let mydate = Date.now
let text = mydate.formatted(.dateTime.weekday(.wide))
print(text)   // "Friday"
```

Listing 4-29: Specifying a custom format

The code in Listing 4-29 calls the `weekday()` method from the `FormatStyle` structure returned by the `dateTime` property to get the day of the week. In this case, we call the method with the value `wide`, which returns the day's full name ("Friday"). Only one component is included in this example, but we can add more by concatenating the methods with dot notation, as we did before for numbers.

```
import Foundation

let mydate = Date.now
let text = mydate.formatted(.dateTime.day().hour().month(.wide))
print(text)   // "June 18, 6 PM"
```

Listing 4-30: Including multiple date components

In this code, we implement the `day()`, `month()`, and `hour()` methods. The result is a string with a date that includes the month (full name), the day, and the hour ("June 18, 6 PM").

Notice that the order in which the methods are called doesn't matter. The date and time are always formatted with a standard format that depends on the user's locale (language and country). This is because the `formatted()` method processes dates according to local conventions, including the language, symbols, etc. This means that the components of a date are interpreted according to the conventions currently set on the device. For example, the same date will look like this "Tuesday, August 6, 2021" for a user in the United States and like this "2021年8月6日 星期二" for a user in China. How dates are processed is determined by an object of the `Locale` structure. Every device has a `Locale` structure assigned by default, and our code will work with it unless we determine otherwise. To get a reference to the current structure or create a new one, the `Locale` structure includes the following initializer and type property.

Locale(identifier: String)—This initializer creates a `Locale` structure configured for the region determined by the value of the argument. The argument is a string that represents a language and a region (e.g., en_US for the United States, zh_CN for China).

current—This type property returns the `Locale` structure assigned by default to the device or defined by the user in the Settings app.

The `FormatStyle` structure includes the following method to format a date for a locale.

locale(Locale)—This method specifies the locale to use by the formatter.

Although it is recommended to use the `Locale` structure set by the system and keep the values by default, there are times when our application must present the information with a specific configuration. For example, we may need to create an application that always shows dates in Chinese, no matter where the user is located. We can do this by defining a `Locale` structure and then include the `locale()` method in the formatter with this value.

```
import Foundation

let mydate = Date.now
let chinaLocale = Locale(identifier: "zh_CN")
let text =
mydate.formatted(.dateTime.locale(chinaLocale).day().month().year())
print(text)  // "2021年6月18日"
```

Listing 4-31: Specifying a different locale

This example creates a new `Locale` structure with the zh_CN identifier, which corresponds to China and the Chinese language, and then formats the date with this locale and the **day()**, **month()**, and **year()** methods. The result is a string with the date in Chinese.

 IMPORTANT: The list of identifiers you can use to create a `Locale` structure is extensive. You can print the type property `availableIdentifiers` from the `Locale` structure to get an array with all the values available.

The date stored in a `Date` structure is not a date but the number of seconds between the date represented by the object and an arbitrary date in the past (January 1st, 2001). To process these values and get the actual date, the `Calendar` structure needs to know the user's time zone. Foundation includes the `TimeZone` structure to manage time zones. An object is assigned by default to the system containing the time zone where the device is located (that is why when we display a date it coincides with the date in our device), but we can define a different one as we did with the `Locale` structure. To get a reference to the current structure or create a new one, the `TimeZone` structure includes the following initializer and type property.

TimeZone(identifier: String)—This initializer creates a `TimeZone` structure configured for the time zone determined by the value of the **identifier** argument. The argument is a string that represents the name of the time zone (e.g., "Europe/Paris", "Asia/Bangkok").

current—This type property returns the `TimeZone` structure assigned by default to the device or defined by the user in the Settings app.

The `FormatStyle` structure does not include a method to provide a specific time zone to format the date. For this purpose, we must create a custom instance and then assign the time zone to the structure's `timeZone` property, as in the following example.

```
import Foundation

if let tokyoTimeZone = TimeZone(identifier: "Asia/Tokyo"), let
madridTimeZone = TimeZone(identifier: "Europe/Madrid") {
   let mydate = Date.now
   let mytime = mydate.formatted(.dateTime.hour().minute().second())

   var dateTimeStyle = Date.FormatStyle()
   dateTimeStyle.timeZone = tokyoTimeZone
   let tokyoTime =
mydate.formatted(dateTimeStyle.hour().minute().second())

   dateTimeStyle.timeZone = madridTimeZone
   let madridTime =
mydate.formatted(dateTimeStyle.hour().minute().second())

   print("My Time: \(mytime)")      // "My Time: 9:25:19 PM"
   print("Tokyo Time: \(tokyoTime)")    // "Tokyo Time: 10:25:19 AM"
   print("Madrid Time: \(madridTime)")    // "Madrid Time: 3:25:19 AM"
}
```

Listing 4-32: Working with different time zones

The code in Listing 4-32 creates two **TimeZone** structures, one for Tokyo's time zone and another for Madrid's. If successful, we initialize a **FormatStyle** structure and format the date twice, first for Tokyo and then for Madrid. Notice that the **TimeZone** structure is assigned to the **timeZone** property of the **FormatStyle** structure before using it to format each date.

 IMPORTANT: The list of names for the time zones is stored in a database. The **TimeZone** structure offers the **knownTimeZoneIdentifiers** type property that you can print to see all the values available.

(Medium) **Measurements**

Some applications require the use of units of measurement, such as pounds, miles, liters, etc. Defining our own units present some challenges, but Foundation includes the **Measurement** structure to simplify our work. This structure includes two properties, one for the value and another for the unit. The initializer requires these two values to create the structure.

Measurement(value: Double, **unit:** Unit)—This initializer creates a **Measurement** structure with the values specified by the **value** and **unit** arguments. The **unit** argument is a property of a class that inherits from the **Dimension** class.

The value declared for the **Measurement** structure is a number that determines the magnitude, like 55 in 55 km, and the unit is a property of a subclass that inherits from the **Dimension** class and represents the unit of measurement, like km in 55 km. The **Dimension** class contains all the basic functionally required for measurement but is through its subclasses that the units of measurement are determined. Foundation offers multiple subclasses for this purpose. The following are the most frequently used.

UnitDuration—This subclass defines the units of measurement for duration (time). It includes the following properties to represent the units: **seconds**, **minutes**, and **hours**, with **seconds** defined as the basic unit.

UnitLength—This subclass defines the units of measurement for length. It includes the following properties to represent the units: **megameters**, **kilometers**, **hectometers**, **decameters**, **meters**, **decimeters**, **centimeters**, **millimeters**, **micrometers**, **nanometers**, **picometers**, **inches**, **feet**, **yards**, **miles**, **scandinavianMiles**,

lightyears, **nauticalMiles**, **fathoms**, **furlongs**, **astronomicalUnits**, and **parsecs**, with **meters** defined as the basic unit.

UnitMass—This subclass defines the units of measurement for mass. It includes the following properties to represent the units: **kilograms**, **grams**, **decigrams**, **centigrams**, **milligrams**, **micrograms**, **nanograms**, **picograms**, **ounces**, **pounds**, **stones**, **metricTons**, **shortTons**, **carats**, **ouncesTroy**, and **slugs**, with **kilograms** defined as the basic unit.

UnitVolume—This subclass defines the units of measurement for volume. It includes the following properties to represent the units: **megaliters**, **kiloliters**, **liters**, **deciliters**, **centiliters**, **milliliters**, **cubicKilometers**, **cubicMeters**, **cubicDecimeters**, **cubicMillimeters**, **cubicInches**, **cubicFeet**, **cubicYards**, **cubicMiles**, **acreFeet**, **bushels**, **teaspoons**, **tablespoons**, **fluidOunces**, **cups**, **pints**, **quarts**, **gallons**, **imperialTeaspoons**, **imperialTablespoons**, **imperialFluidOunces**, **imperialPints**, **imperialQuarts**, **imperialGallons**, and **metricCups**, with **liters** defined as the basic unit.

The **Measurement** structure includes the following properties and methods to access the values and convert them to different units.

value—This property sets or returns the structure's value. It is of type **Double**.

unit—This property sets or returns the structure's unit of measurement. It is represented by a property of a subclass of the **Dimension** class.

convert(to: Unit)—This method converts the values of the **Measurement** structure to the unit specified by the **to** argument.

converted(to: Unit)—This method converts the values of the **Measurement** structure to the unit specified by the **to** argument and returns a new **Measurement** structure with the result.

The initialization of a **Measurement** structure is simple, we just need to provide the value for the magnitude and the property that represents the unit of measurement we want to use. The following example creates two structures to store a measurement of 30 centimeters and another of 5 pounds.

```
import Foundation
var length = Measurement(value: 30, unit: UnitLength.centimeters) // 30.0 cm
var weight = Measurement(value: 5, unit: UnitMass.pounds)   // 5.0 lb
```

Listing 4-33: Initializing Measurement *structures*

If the measurements are of the same dimension (e.g., length), we can perform operations with their values. The **Measurement** structure allows the operations +, -, *, /, and also the use of the comparison operators ==, !=, <, >, <=, and >= to compare values. The following example adds two measurements in centimeters.

```
import Foundation
var length = Measurement(value: 200, unit: UnitLength.centimeters)
var width = Measurement(value: 800, unit: UnitLength.centimeters)
var total = length + width   // 1000.0 cm
```

Listing 4-34: Adding the values of two Measurement *structures*

If the units are different, the **Measurement** structure returned by the operation is defined with the dimension's basic unit. For example, if we are working with lengths, the basic unit is **meters**.

```
import Foundation
var length = Measurement(value: 300, unit: UnitLength.meters)
var width = Measurement(value: 2, unit: UnitLength.kilometers)
var total = length + width  // 2300.0 m
```

Listing 4-35: *Adding two values of different units*

The code in Listing 4-35 adds two lengths of different units (meters and kilometers). The system converts kilometers to meters and then performs the addition, returning a **Measurement** structure with a value in meters (the basic unit).

If we want everything to be performed in the same unit, we can convert a value to a different unit using the **convert()** or **converted()** methods. In the following example, we convert the unit of the **length** variable to kilometers and perform the addition again in kilometers.

```
import Foundation
var length = Measurement(value: 300, unit: UnitLength.meters)
var width = Measurement(value: 2, unit: UnitLength.kilometers)
length.convert(to: UnitLength.kilometers)

var total = length + width  // 2.3 km
```

Listing 4-36: *Converting units*

The values of a **Measurement** structure are printed as they are stored and with the units they represent, but this is usually not what we need to show to users. To prepare the value for display, the **Measurement** structure defines the **formatted()** method.

formatted(FormatStyle**)**—This method formats the measurement with the styles specified by the argument.

This method requires a **FormatStyle** structure to format the value. The structure includes the following initializer and type method to create an instance for every type of unit.

FormatStyle(width: UnitWidth, **locale:** Locale, **usage:** MeasurementFormatUnitUsage, **numberFormatStyle:** FloatingPointFormatStyle**)**—This initializer creates a **FormatStyle** structure with the format set by the arguments. The **width** argument specifies how the unit is going to be displayed. It is a structure with the properties **abbreviated**, **narrow**, and **wide**. The **locale** argument specifies the locale. The **usage** argument specifies the purpose of the measurement. The structure to declare this value includes properties for any type of measurement, including **asProvided** (UnitType), **food** (UnitEnergy), **general** (UnitType), **person:** (UnitLength), **personHeight** (UnitLength), **personWeight** (UnitMass), **road** (UnitLength), **weather** (UnitTemperature), and **workout** (UnitEnergy). Finally, the **numberFormatStyle** argument specifies the format of the value.

measurement(width: UnitWidth, **usage:** MeasurementFormatUnitUsage, **numberFormatStyle:** FloatingPointFormatStyle**)**—This method returns a **FormatStyle** structure with the format set by the arguments (the same required by the initializer).

The **FormatStyle** structure also includes an additional initializer and method specific to format temperatures.

FormatStyle(width: UnitWidth, **locale:** Locale, **usage:** Measurement-FormatUnitUsage, **hidesScaleName:** Bool, **numberFormatStyle:** FloatingPointFormatStyle)—This initializer creates a `FormatStyle` structure with the format set by the arguments. The **width** argument specifies how the unit is going to be displayed. It is a structure with the properties `abbreviated`, `narrow`, and `wide`. The **locale** argument specifies the locale. The **usage** argument specifies the purpose of the measurement. The structure to declare this value includes properties for any type of measurement. The ones available at the moment are `asProvided` (UnitType), `food` (UnitEnergy), `general` (UnitType), `person` (UnitTemperature), `personHeight` (UnitLength), `personWeight` (UnitMass), `road` (UnitLength), `weather` (UnitTemperature), and `workout` (UnitEnergy). The **hidesScaleName** argument determines if the name of the unit is going to be displayed, and the **numberFormatStyle** argument specifies the format of the value.

measurement(width: UnitWidth, **locale:** Locale, **usage:** Measurement-FormatUnitUsage, **hidesScaleName:** Bool, **numberFormatStyle:** FloatingPointFormatStyle)—This method returns a `FormatStyle` structure with the format set by the arguments. The arguments are the same required by the initializer.

Most of the arguments in these initializers and methods are optional. If an argument is not declared, the formatter uses values by default. For instance, if we just want to show the full name of the unit, we can implement the **measurement()** method with the **width** argument and the value **wide**.

```
import Foundation

let length = Measurement(value: 40, unit: UnitLength.kilometers)
let text = length.formatted(.measurement(width: .wide,
usage: .asProvided))
print(text)  // "40 kilometers"
```
Listing 4-37: Formatting a measurement

In this example, we have also included the **usage** argument with the **asProvided** value to tell the formatter to use the original units (kilometers). If this argument is not declared, the formatter uses the value by default, which formats the measurement with the configuration and locale set in the device. For instance, if we specify the **road** value instead, the formatter will format the value to represent a distance using the device's locale, which for a device running in the United States means that the original value will be expressed in miles.

```
import Foundation

let length = Measurement(value: 40, unit: UnitLength.kilometers)
let text = length.formatted(.measurement(width: .wide, usage: .road))
print(text)  // "25 miles"
```
Listing 4-38: Formatting a measurement for a specific purpose

By default, the formatter rounds the number. That's why in this example the result of converting 40 kilometers to miles is 25, when it should've been 24.8548. If we want to specify a different format, we can add the **numberFormatStyle** argument and implement the methods provided by the `IntegerFormatStyle` and `FloatingPointFormatStyle` structures introduced before. For instance, we can specify a precision of 2 digits for the decimal part with the **fractionLength()** method, as shown next.

```
import Foundation

let length = Measurement(value: 40, unit: UnitLength.kilometers)
let text = length.formatted(.measurement(width: .wide, usage: .road,
numberFormatStyle: .number.precision(.fractionLength(2))))
print(text)   // "24.85 miles"
```

Listing 4-39: Formatting the measurement's value

The **formatted()** method in this example includes the **width** argument to get the unit's full name, the **usage** argument to format the value to represent a distance, and the **numberFormatStyle** argument to format the value. The value is expressed in miles again, but with better accuracy.

If our application has to display a value always with the same unit of measurement independently of the device's location, we can set a specific locale. The **formatted()** method doesn't include an **argument** to designate a locale, but the initializers included in the **FormatStyle** structure do. The following example formats the measurements in Chinese, no matter where the device is located.

```
import Foundation

let length = Measurement(value: 40, unit: UnitLength.kilometers)
let chinaLocale = Locale(identifier: "zh_CN")
var format = Measurement<UnitLength>.FormatStyle(width: .wide, locale:
chinaLocale, usage: .asProvided)
let text = length.formatted(format)
print(text)   // "40.00公里"
```

Listing 4-40: Formatting a measurement for a specific locale

The code in Listing 4-40 initializes a **FormatStyle** structure with the locale configured for China and then calls the **formatted()** method with this structure to format the value. Notice that the **FormatStyle** structure is defined inside the **Measurement** structure, which is a generic structure and therefore we must specify the type of values the structure is going to process. In this case, we are working with units of length so we must specify the **UnitLength** data type.

Medium Timer

Timers are objects that perform an action after a specific period of time. There are two types of timers: repeating and non-repeating. Repeating timers perform the action and then reschedule themselves to do it again in an infinite loop. Non-repeating timers, on the other hand, perform the action one time and then invalidate themselves. Foundation defines the **Timer** class for this purpose. The class includes the following properties and methods to create and manage timers.

isValid—This property returns a Boolean value that indicates if the timer can still be fired, or it was invalidated.

timeInterval—This property returns the time interval in seconds for repeating timers.

tolerance—This property sets or returns a period of tolerance in seconds to provide the system with more flexibility. It is a value of type **TimeInterval**. The value by default is 0.

scheduledTimer(withTimeInterval: TimeInterval, **repeats:** Bool, **block:** Closure)—This type method returns repeating and non-repeating timers depending on the values of its arguments. The **withTimeInterval** argument represents the seconds the timer must wait before performing the action, the **repeats** argument is a Boolean value that determines if the timer is repeating (**true**) or non-repeating (**false**), and the **block** argument is the closure to be execute when the time is up.

fire()—This method fires the timer without considering the time remaining.

invalidate()—This method invalidates the timer (stops the timer).

The **scheduledTimer()** method creates a timer according to the value of the arguments and automatically adds it to an internal loop that will process it when the time is up. The time is set in seconds with a **TimeInterval** value (a typealias of **Double**), and we can declare the closure as a trailing closure to simplify the code, as in the following example.

```
import Foundation

print("Wait 5 seconds...")
Timer.scheduledTimer(withTimeInterval: 5.0, repeats: false) { (timer) in
    print("The time is up")
}
```

Listing 4-41: *Creating a non-repeating timer*

The code in Listing 4-41 creates a non-repeating timer. It prints a message and then initializes a timer with the **scheduleTimer()** method. The timer is set to 5 seconds, non-repeating, and the closure just prints a message on the console. When we execute the code, the first message appears on the console and 5 seconds later the message "The time is up" is printed below.

The closure receives a reference to the **Timer** object that we can use to access the timer's properties or invalidate it. It was not required in the last example, but it may be useful when working with repeating timers, as in the following example.

```
import Foundation

var counter = 0

func startTimer() {
    Timer.scheduledTimer(withTimeInterval: 1.0, repeats: true)
{ (timerref) in
        report(timer: timerref)
    }
}
func report(timer: Timer) {
    print("\(counter) times")
    counter += 1
    if counter > 10 {
        print("Finished")
        timer.invalidate()
    }
}
startTimer()
```

Listing 4-42: *Creating a repeating timer*

In this code, we define two functions. The **startTimer()** function schedules the timer, and the **report()** function is executed when the time is up. In this last function, we count how many times the code is executed with the **counter** variable and print a message on the console with the number. If the value is greater than 10, we print the text "Finished" and invalidate the timer, so the function is not executed anymore. (Repeating timers keep running indefinitely until they are invalidated.)

4.3 RegexBuilder Framework

With the methods provided by Foundation and the **String** data type, we can modify a string, remove or insert a string from another one, and determine whether a string contains another string, or the characters match a specific pattern. For instance, we can check if a string contains an email address. For simple patterns, like finding a word at the beginning or the end of the string, these tools are more than enough, but determining if a string represents a phone number, an email address, or extracting the values of more complex structures like the content of a spreadsheet, requires looping through the characters one by one and comparing them with previous characters to recognize valid or invalid patterns. This process is generally cumbersome and error-prone. To simplify our work, Swift implements regular expressions.

Medium **Regular Expressions**

A regular expression is a sequence of characters that represent the pattern we want to identify on a string. It is composed of common characters that match the characters in the string one by one, and also special characters that describe specific patterns or matches. For instance, the expression **/message/** will match any string that contains the word "message", but we can add the special characters **\s+** at the end to match a string that contains the word "message" followed by one or more spaces (**/message\s+/**).

To differentiate special characters from common characters, they are preceded by a backward slash, as in **\s** (the **s** represents a white space). There are dozens of special characters to represent anything we need. The following are the most frequently used.

- **\s** and **\t** match a whitespace. The **\s** character matches any whitespace character, and the **\t** character matches only tab characters.
- **\d** match a digit (any number from 0 to 9).

To match a character from a group of characters, regular expressions include the following special characters.

- **[ ]** match any character in the square brackets (e.g., **[abc]** matches the character **a** or **b** or **c**). It can also match a character in a range of consecutive characters. The range is defined with a hyphen, as in **[a-z]** to match a lowercase letter from **a** to **z**, or **[a-zA-Z]** to match a lowercase or uppercase letter from **a** to **z**.
- **[^]** match any character different from those in the square brackets (e.g., **[^abc]** matches any character that is not **a** or **b** or **c**).
- **.** (dot) matches any character except a new line (new lines are represented by the special character **\n**).
- **|** (or) matches the character on the left or the right (e.g., **a|b** matches the character **a** or the character **b**).

These special characters match a single character. To specify quantity, regular expressions include the following.

- ***** specifies 0 or more occurrences of the previous character.
- **+** specifies 1 or more occurrences of the previous character.
- **?** specifies 0 or 1 occurrences of the previous character.
- **{min, max}** specifies the minimum and maximum occurrences of the previous character (e.g., **{3, 5}** matches 3, 4, or 5 characters). If the maximum value is ignored, the expression matches the character at least the times specified by the minimum value (e.g., **{2,}** matches the character at least two times). And if only one value is declared, the expression matches the character exactly the times specified by the value (e.g., **{2}** matches the characters only two times).

There are also special characters to delineate the expression. The following are the most frequently used.

- ^ matches the beginning of the string.
- $ matches the end of the string.
- () define a subexpression (useful when we want to capture the value).

Regular expressions are defined by a combination of these special characters and also common characters, as we have seen before. For instance, if we have a string like "Name: John" and we want to know whether the string contains any name, we can match it against the regular expression /Name:\s+[a-zA-Z]+/. The slashes at the beginning and the end are the way to tell Swift that this is a regular expression. The string "Name:" matches exactly the same sequence of characters in the original string. The \s+ characters tell the system that the string "Name:" must be followed by one or more spaces. And the [a-zA-Z]+ characters indicate that after the space there should be one or more lowercase or uppercase letters. If the original string doesn't contain the string "Name:" followed by one or more spaces and one or more letters, we won't get a match.

To match the regular expression against a string, the Swift Standard Library includes the following methods.

firstMatch(of: Regex)—This method finds the first sequence of characters in the string that match the regular expression specified by the **of** argument.

wholeMatch(of: Regex)—This method matches the whole string against the regular expression.

prefixMatch(of: Regex)—This method matches the beginning of the string against the regular expression.

matches(of: Regex)—This method finds all the sequences of characters in the string that match the regular expression.

These methods take a value of type **Regex** (a structure defined to contain a regular expression) and return a value of type **Match** if a match is found or **nil** otherwise. The **Match** structure contains two properties: **output** with the strings that matched the regular expression, and **range** with a **Range** value that represents the range of the overall match.

For instance, the following code processes the string and regular expression mentioned before with the **firstMatch()** method to check if the string contains a name.

```
let message = "Name: John"
let regex = /Name:\s+[a-zA-Z]+/

if let match = message.firstMatch(of: regex) {
   let found = match.output
   print("Found: \(found)")   // "Found: Name: John"
}
```

Listing 4-43: Using regular expressions

This code defines a regular expression and assigns it to a constant. The compiler detects that the value is a regular expression and creates a **Regex** structure with it. Next, the **firstMatch()** method matches the string in the **message** constant against the regular expression and returns a value with the result. In this case, the string contains the string "Name:"followed by one or more spaces and one or more letters, so the match is successful. The part of the string that matches the regular expression is assigned to the **output** property of the **Match** structure returned by the method, so we assign it to a constant and print it on the console.

IMPORTANT: Declaring the regular expression between slash characters, as we did in our example, allows Xcode to recognize it and provide feedback. If the expression is invalid, it is displayed in a single color, otherwise, the special characters are highlighted. This is the recommended notation in Swift, but the language provides others. For instance, we can create the **Regex** structure directly with the structure's initializer and the regular expression in quotes. Swift also allows us to declare the regular expression using different syntaxes, including an extended syntax that can be used to provide names and define the data types of the values we captured. For more information, visit our website and follow the links for this chapter.

The values returned in the **Match** structure depend on the expression. In the previous example, the **output** property returns a single string with the sequence of characters that match the regular expression, but we can define subexpressions to capture specific values. For instance, if we want to get back the name, we can define a subexpression with parentheses.

```
let message = "Name: John"
let regex = /Name:\s+([a-zA-Z]+)/

if let match = message.firstMatch(of: regex) {
   let found = match.output.1
   print("The name is: \(found)")   // "The name is: John"
}
```

Listing 4-44: *Capturing values with subexpressions*

In this example, the **output** property returns a tuple. The first element of the tuple is the string that matches the regular expression, as before, but the second value is the string that matches the expression between parenthesis. (In this case, one or more letters after a space.)

The **firstMatch()** method finds the first sequence of characters that match the regular expression and returns that value. If we want to get all the matches in a string, we must implement the **matches()** method.

```
let message = "Name: John, Name: George, Name: David"
let regex = /Name:\s+([a-zA-Z]+)/
let matches = message.matches(of: regex)
if !matches.isEmpty {
   let names = matches.map({ value in
      return value.output.1
   })
   let list = names.joined(separator: ", ")
   print("Names are: \(list)")   // "Names are: John, George, David"
}
```

Listing 4-45: *Capturing multiple values*

The **matches()** method returns an array of **Match** structures. Again, we use a subexpression to capture the names, so we loop through the array with the **map()** function, return the name from each match, and then join them with the **joined()** method to get the list of names separated by comma.

The Swift Standard Library includes a few more methods to take advantage of regular expressions. The following are the most frequently used.

split(separator: Regex)—This method divides a string by a separator and returns an array with the parts. The **separator** argument specifies the regular expression that matches the characters used to split the string.

Chapter 4 - Introduction to Frameworks

replacing(Regex, with: String)—This method replaces the sequence of characters that match the regular expression specified by the first argument with the string specified by the **with** argument.

The `split()` method is useful when we have to process long texts or a text file line by line. In the following example, we use triple quotes to tell the compiler to add the characters \n after each line of text to generate a new line (see Listing 2-24). This is how usually text files are structured. To read each line, we define a regular expression with the special character \n and then call the `split()` method to get each line of text in an array.

```
let message = """
John
George
Martin
"""
let separator = /\n/
let lines = message.split(separator: separator)
print(lines)   // ["John", "George", "Martin"]
```

Listing 4-46: Processing multiple lines of text with a regular expression

The `replacing()` method could be implemented in a similar fashion, but instead of using the regular expression as a separator, we can use it to replace the sequence of characters with another one. For instance, we can replace each new-line character in our string (\n) with a comma to get all the lines of text in a single string.

```
let message = """
John
George
Martin
"""
let separator = /\n/
let result = message.replacing(separator, with: ", ")
print(result)   // "John, George, Martin"
```

Listing 4-47: Replacing the characters that match a regular expression

(Medium) **Regex Builder**

The regular expressions implemented so far match simple characters, like whitespaces or letters, but the complexity of regular expressions increases when we try to match patterns that can take many combinations of characters. For instance, if we want to know whether a string represents an email address, we must determine if the string begins with a set of valid characters, such as letters and numbers, followed by the @ character, followed by the characters valid for a domain, including the right number of characters for the extension. The complexity of this type of regular expressions goes from something like /[A-Z0-9._%+-]+@[A-Z0-9.-]+\.[A-Z]{2,}/, which is capable of validating approximately 98% of email addresses, to regular expressions that extend for three or four lines of text to match all the possible email addresses. Constructing and understanding these regular expressions is not an easy task. For this reason, the Swift Standard Library introduces the RegexBuilder framework.

The RegexBuilder framework defines structures to represent every special character in a regular expression and more. The following are the structures included to specify characters.

CharacterClass(Characters**)**—This structure represents a group of characters and also special characters like whitespaces and new lines (similar to square brackets in literal notation). The initializer takes ranges of characters separated by comma, and also type properties to represent common characters, such as `any` (any character), `digit` (digits from 0 to 9), `whitespace`, and `newlineSequence`.

Anchor—This structure defines an anchor character, like the ^ and $ characters used in literal notation to match the beginning and end of the string. The instances are created from the type properties `startOfLine`, `endOfLine`, `startOfSubject`, `endOfSubject`, `endOfSubjectBeforeNewline`, `firstMatchingPositionIn-Subject`, `textSegmentBoundary`, and `wordBoundary`.

Lookahead(Closure**)**—This structure matches the characters returned by the argument without capturing them. (They are not returned by the expression.)

ChoiceOf(Closure**)**—This structure matches different values, like the | (OR) in literal notation.

There are also structures to represent quantifiers.

One(Characters**)**—This structure matches only one occurrence of the group of characters specified by the attribute.

Optionally(RegexRepetitionBehavior, Closure**)**—This structure matches a character that may or may not be present. The first argument determines the type of matching. It is a structure with the type properties `eager` (default), `possessive`, and `reluctant`. The second argument specified the characters we want to match.

ZeroOrMore(RegexRepetitionBehavior, Closure**)**—This structure matches zero or more characters (similar to the * character in literal notation). The first argument determines the type of matching. It is a structure with the type properties `eager` (default), `possessive`, and `reluctant`. The second argument specified the characters we want to match.

OneOrMore(RegexRepetitionBehavior, Closure**)**—This structure matches one or more characters (similar to the + character in literal notation). The first argument determines the type of matching. It is a structure with the type properties `eager` (default), `possessive`, and `reluctant`. The second argument specified the characters we want to match.

Repeat(Characters, **count:** Int**)**—This structure matches the characters specified by the first argument the number of times specified by the **count** argument (similar to the { } characters in literal notation). The **count** argument can be replaced by a range of values to specify multiple quantities (2...4).

The framework also includes structures to capture values from the string.

Capture(Closure, **transform:** Closure**)**—This structure captures the sequence of characters that matches the expression provided by the first argument. The **transform** argument is a closure used to transform the captured value into any data type we want.

TryCapture(Closure, **transform:** Closure**)**—This structure captures the sequence of characters that matches the expression provided by the first argument, but unlike `Capture`, the structure returns a no-match if the value cannot be transformed.

The Regex Builder is built from a `Regex` structure. The structure includes an initializer that takes strings, structures, and regular expressions in literal notation to define the final expression. For instance, the following Regex Builder defines the same regular expression used before to determine if a string contains a name.

```
import RegexBuilder

let regex = Regex {
   "Name:"
   OneOrMore(.whitespace)
   OneOrMore {
      CharacterClass("a"..."z", "A"..."Z")
   }
}
let message = "Name: John"
let result = message.matches(of: regex)
if !result.isEmpty {
   print(result[0].output)
}
```

Listing 4-48: Defining a regular expression with a Regex Builder

In this example, we first import the RegexBuilder framework to have access to the framework's structures and then initialize the **Regex** structure to build our regular expression. In this case, we are looking for a sequence of characters that begins with the string "Name:", followed by one or more whitespaces, and one or more lowercase or uppercase letters. The patterns are declared one per line. We first declare the string "Name:", then use the **OneOrMore** structure with the **CharacterClass** structure returned by the **whitespace** property to match one or more whitespaces, and finally we include another **OneOrMore** structure, this time with a **CharacterClass** defined with two ranges, one for lowercase letters and another for uppercase letter. The result is the same as before. The **matches()** method returns an array with a **Match** structure that contains the string that matches the entire expression ("Name: John").

If we want to capture the name, as we did in the example in Listing 4-44, we must include the **Capture** structure. In the following example, we use the **One** structure to ensure that the name is capitalized, and capture the name with the **Capture** structure.

```
import RegexBuilder

let regex = Regex {
   "Name:"
   OneOrMore(.whitespace)
   Capture {
      One(CharacterClass("A"..."Z"))
      OneOrMore {
         CharacterClass("a"..."z")
      }
   }
}
let message = "Name: John"
let result = message.matches(of: regex)
if let name = result.first?.output.1 {
   print("The name is: \(name)")   // "The name is: John"
}
```

Listing 4-49: Capturing a value from a Regex Builder

The regular expression matches the string "Name:" followed by one or more spaces, as before, but now the name's first character is matched against an uppercase letter, so the string is captured only if the name is capitalized. The rest of the code is the same as before; we match the expression against the string and print the value captured by the **Capture** structure.

The **Match** structure returns substrings. These are instances of a **Substring** structure defined in the Swift Standard Library to store a slice of a string. But we can transform these values to any data types we want. For this purpose, the initializer of the **Capture** structure includes an argument called **transform**. The closure assigned to this argument is called with the value that matches the expression and from it we can convert it to a different data type and return it. For instance, in the following example we convert two values into integers.

```
import RegexBuilder
let message = "09 units, stock 190"
let regex = Regex {
   Capture {
      OneOrMore(.digit)
   } transform: { value in
      Int(value)
   }
   OneOrMore(.any, .reluctant)
   Capture {
      OneOrMore(.digit)
   } transform: { value in
      Int(value)
   }
}
let result = message.matches(of: regex)
if let units = result.first?.output.1, let stock = result.first?.output.2
{
   let total = units + stock
   print("Final Stock: \(total)")   // "Final Stock: 199"
}
```

Listing 4-50: Transforming values to the right data type

The string we are processing includes numbers at the beginning and the end. The first number represents the units to be added to the stock, and the last number represents the current stock. To get the first number as an integer, we capture one or more digits. (The **digit** property returns a **CharacterClass** structure that represents numbers between 0 and 9.) Capturing the last number is a bit tricky. Because we may have any characters in between, to match the text we use the **any** property, which returns a **CharacterClass** structure that represents any character. But this includes numbers, which means that the number at the end will also be matched by this pattern and the last **Capture** structure won't have anything else to match. By default, the behavior of the **OneOrMore** structure is determined by the **RegexRepetitionBehavior** structure returned by the **eager** property. This structure tells the system to match as many characters as it can. But we can change this behavior by assigning the **reluctant** property instead, as we did in our example. The structure returned by this property asks the system to match the current expression until any character matches the next expression, so when the number is found, the system moves to the next **OneOrMore** structure that matches digits and we are able to capture our second number.

Although we can transform any value we want, some like dates and complex numbers may require long patterns. To simplify our work, the Foundation framework includes properties and methods we can use to match these values. The following are the most frequently used.

localizedDecimal(locale: Locale**)**—This method returns a **FormatStyle** structure to match decimal numbers. The **locale** argument specifies the locale.

localizedCurrency(code: Currency, **locale:** Locale**)**—This method returns a **FormatStyle** structure to match currency values. The **code** argument can be specify as a string to represent the currency (e.g.: "USD"). The **locale** argument specifies the locale.

date(DateStyle, locale: Locale, **timeZone:** TimeZone, **calendar:** Calendar?**)**
—This method returns a `ParseStrategy` structure to match a date. The first argument is a `DateStyle` structure that specifies the date's format. The structure includes the type properties `abbreviated`, `complete`, `long`, `numeric`, and `omitted`. The **locale** argument specifies the locale, the **timeZone** argument the time zone, and the **calendar** argument the calendar we want to use to interpret the date.

dateTime(date: DateStyle, **time:** TimeStyle, **locale:** Locale, **timeZone:** TimeZone, **calendar:** Calendar?**)**—This method returns a `ParseStrategy` structure to match date and time. The **date** argument is a structure that specifies the date's format. The structure includes the type properties `abbreviated`, `complete`, `long`, `numeric`, and `omitted`. The **time** argument is a structure that specified the time's format. The structure include the type properties `complete`, `omitted`, `shortened`, and `standard`. The **locale** argument specifies the locale, the **timeZone** argument the time zone, and the **calendar** argument the calendar we want to use to interpret the date and time.

The following example shows how to match dates and currency. In this case, we process a string with multiple items and split the content in lines of text to process each value, as we did in Listing 4-46.

```
import Foundation
import RegexBuilder

let separator = /\n/
let content = """
06/15/2020 Lamp $35.00
06/21/2020 Desk $250.50
06/29/2020 Chair $129.00
"""
let regex = Regex {
   Capture {
      One(.date(.numeric, locale: .current, timeZone: .current))
   }
   OneOrMore(.whitespace)
   Capture {
      OneOrMore(CharacterClass("a"..."z", "A"..."Z"))
   }
   OneOrMore(.whitespace)
   Capture {
      One(.localizedCurrency(code: "USD", locale: .current))
   }
}
let lines = content.split(separator: separator)
for line in lines {
   if let result = line.firstMatch(of: regex) {
      print("Date: \(result.output.1.formatted(date: .complete,
time: .omitted))")
      print("Item: \(result.output.2)")
      print("Price: \(result.output.3)")
   }
}
```

Listing 4-51: Matching dates and currency

The first pattern matches one occurrence of a date using the numeric format and the current locale and time zone. After that, we match a string of lowercase and uppercase letters, and finally match one occurrence of a currency value in US Dollars. The three values are captured by `Capture` structures and printed on the console. Notice that because we get a `Date` value in return we are able to format the date using the `formatted()` method introduced before.

IMPORTANT: This introduction to regular expressions only scratches the surface. The topic is beyond the scope of this book. For more information, visit our website and follow the links for this chapter.

(Basic) 4.4 Core Graphics

Core Graphics is an old framework programmed in the C language. It was developed to provide a platform-independent two-dimensional drawing engine for Apple systems. The framework is composed of drawing tools and its own data types. Due to its characteristics, instead of being replaced, the framework was integrated with newer frameworks and, therefore, it remains in use.

(Basic) Data Types

What modern applications require the most from this old framework are its data types. In Swift, Core Graphics' data types are implemented as structures, with their own initializers, properties, and methods. They can store values that represent attributes of elements on the screen, such as position or size. For instance, the following is the structure used to specify coordinate values.

CGFloat—This structure is used to store values of type `Double` for drawing purposes.

A more complex structure is `CGSize`, designed to store values that represent dimensions (width and height). This data type includes the following initializer and properties.

CGSize(width: CGFloat, **height:** CGFloat)—This initializer creates a `CGSize` structure with the values specified by the **width** and **height** arguments. The structure defines initializers to create instances from values of type `Int`, `CGFloat`, and `Double`.

zero—This type property returns a `CGSize` structure with its values set to zero.

width—This property sets or returns the structure's width.

height—This property sets or returns the structure's height.

Another structure included in the framework is `CGPoint`, which is used to define points in a two-dimensional coordinate system. It includes the following initializer and properties.

CGPoint(x: CGFloat, **y:** CGFloat)—This initializer creates a `CGPoint` structure with the coordinates specified by the **x** and **y** arguments. The structure defines initializers to create instances from values of type `Int`, `CGFloat`, and `Double`.

zero—This type property returns a `CGPoint` structure with its values set to zero.

x—This property sets or returns the structure's x coordinate.

y—This property sets or returns the structure's y coordinate.

There is also a more complex structure called `CGRect` that we can use to define and work with rectangles. This data type includes the following initializers and properties.

CGRect(origin: CGPoint, **size:** CGSize)—This initializer creates a `CGRect` structure to store the origin and size of a rectangle. The **origin** argument is a `CGPoint` structure with the coordinates of the rectangle's origin, and the **size** argument is a `CGSize` structure with the rectangle's width and height.

CGRect(x: CGFloat, **y:** CGFloat, **width:** CGFloat, **height:** CGFloat)—This initializer creates a **CGRect** structure to store the origin and size of a rectangle. The **x** and **y** arguments define the coordinates of the rectangle's origin, and the **width** and **height** arguments its size. The structure defines initializers to create instances from **Int**, **CGFloat**, and **Double** values.

zero—This type property returns a **CGRect** structure with its values set to zero.

origin—This property sets or returns a **CGPoint** structure with the coordinates of the rectangle's origin.

size—This property sets or returns a **CGSize** structure with the rectangle's width and height.

midX—This property returns the value of the rectangle's **x** coordinate located at the horizontal center of the rectangle. The framework also include the **minX** and **maxX** properties to return the smallest and largest value in the x-coordinate for the rectangle.

midY—This property returns the value of the rectangle's **y** coordinate located at the vertical center of the rectangle. The framework also include the **minY** and **maxY** properties to return the smallest and largest value in the y-coordinate for the rectangle.

The structures provided by Core Graphics are declared and initialized as any other structures in Swift, but we must import the Core Graphics framework first for the types to be recognized.

```
import CoreGraphics
var myfloat: CGFloat = 35
var mysize: CGSize = CGSize(width: 250, height: 250)
var mypoint: CGPoint = CGPoint(x: 20, y: 50)
var myrect: CGRect = CGRect(origin: mypoint, size: mysize)
```

Listing 4-52: Initializing Core Graphics' structures

The **CGSize** and **CGPoint** structures may be initialized with their member initializers, but the **CGRect** structure provides an additional initializer to create the instance from the values of its internal structures.

```
import CoreGraphics
var myrect = CGRect(x: 30, y: 20, width: 100, height: 200)
print("The origin is at \(myrect.origin.x) and \(myrect.origin.y)")
print("The size is \(myrect.size.width) by \(myrect.size.height)")
```

Listing 4-53: Using the CGRect convenience initializer

The **origin** and **size** properties of a **CGRect** value are **CGPoint** and **CGSize** structures, respectively, so they can be copied into other variables or properties as any other values.

```
import CoreGraphics
var myrect = CGRect(x: 30, y: 20, width: 100, height: 200)
var mypoint = myrect.origin
var mysize = myrect.size
print("The origin is at \(mypoint.x) and \(mypoint.y)")
print("The size is \(mysize.width) by \(mysize.height)")
```

Listing 4-54: Accessing the structures inside a CGRect structure

When we don't have initial values for the coordinates or the size, we can use the **zero** type property to create a structure with all the values initialized to 0.

```
import CoreGraphics

var myrect = CGRect.zero

print("The origin is at \(myrect.origin.x) and \(myrect.origin.y)")
print("The size is \(myrect.size.width) by \(myrect.size.height)")
```

Listing 4-55: Assigning empty structures to a CGRect *variable*

The **myrect** variable in Listing 4-55 is a **CGRect** structure with all its properties initialized with the value 0. Assigning the value of the **zero** property to a variable is the same as using the initializer **CGRect(x: 0, y: 0, width: 0, height: 0)**.

The **CGRect** structure also includes properties to calculate values from the coordinates and size. For example, the **midX** and **midY** properties return the coordinates at the center.

```
import CoreGraphics

var rect = CGRect(x: 0, y: 0, width: 100, height: 100)

print("The horizontal center is \(rect.midX)")   // 50.0
```

Listing 4-56: Calculating the coordinate at the center of the rectangle

 IMPORTANT: In this chapter, we have explored the part of Core Graphics used by modern frameworks to build user interfaces, but the framework is extensive and includes tools for the creation of custom graphics. For more information, visit our website and follow the links for this chapter.

Chapter 5
SwiftUI Framework

Basic) **5.1 Xcode**

Up to this point, we have been working with a simplified interface called *Playground*. Playground was designed to reduce the learning curve and to allow developers to test code, but to build functional applications we must move to the Xcode's main interface. This is a toolset that comprises an editor, a canvas for displaying previews, resource managers, configuration panels, and debugging tools, all integrated into a single workspace where we can create our applications.

Basic) **Projects**

Applications are built from several files and resources, including our own codes, frameworks, images, databases, and more. Xcode organizes this information in projects. An Xcode project includes all the information and resources necessary to create an application. The welcome window, illustrated in Figure 1-2, presents a button called *Create a new Xcode project* to initiate a project. When this button is clicked, a window appears to select the type of project we want to create.

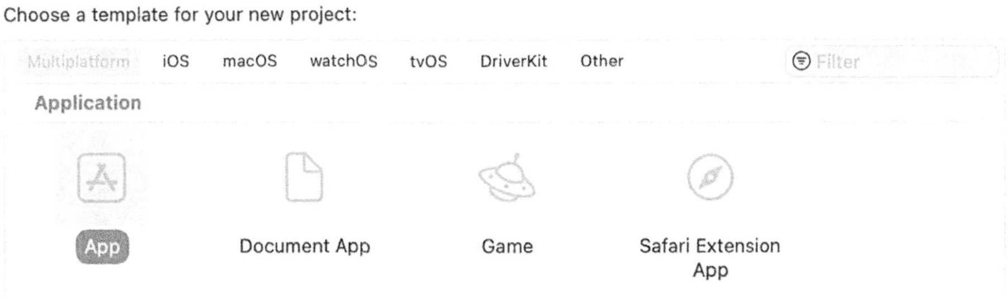

Choose a template for your new project:

Multiplatform	iOS	macOS	watchOS	tvOS	DriverKit	Other	⊛ Filter

Application

App	Document App	Game	Safari Extension App

Figure 5-1: Selecting the type of project

There are technologies to create applications for all available Apple devices. For instance, to create applications for iPhones and iPads, Apple provides the UIKit framework, and for Mac computers we have the AppKit framework. The project window includes options for each one of them, including iOS for iPhones and iPads, macOS for Mac computers, watchOS for the Apple Watch, and tvOS for Apple TV. With the introduction of SwiftUI, we can now build apps for every device using the same framework, and this is why there is an additional option called Multiplatform. A Multiplatform project comes set up to create an application for iPhones, iPads and Mac computers using SwiftUI (although we can add more platforms later). All we need to do is to select the Multiplatform section and the App option, as shown in Figure 5-1. Once this option is selected, we must configure the project, as shown below.

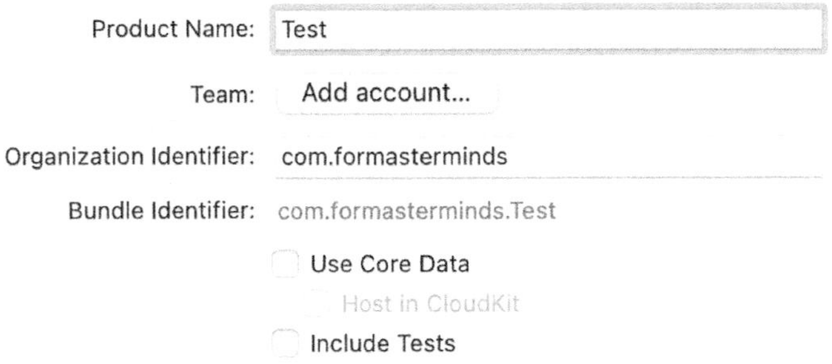

Product Name:	Test
Team:	Add account...
Organization Identifier:	com.formasterminds
Bundle Identifier:	com.formasterminds.Test
	☐ Use Core Data
	Host in CloudKit
	☐ Include Tests

Figure 5-2: Project configuration window

The Product Name is the name of the project. By default, this is the name of our app, so we should write a name that is appropriate for our application (this value can be modified later). Next is the Team's account. This is the developer account created with our Apple ID or our company's account. If we haven't yet registered our account with Xcode, we will see the Add Account button to add it. The next value is the Organization Identifier. Xcode uses this value to create a unique identifier for our app and therefore it is recommended to declare it with an inverted domain, as we did in our example (com.formasterminds). Using the inverted domain ensures that only our app will have that identifier. And finally, there is a list of options we can select to incorporate additional functionality to our project, such as Core Data and Tests. We will explore these alternatives in further chapters, but should be left unchecked if we are not planning to use them.

As mentioned above, the Team's field shows a list of developer accounts registered with Xcode. If we haven't yet inserted our account, we will see the Add Account button instead. Pressing this button opens Xcode preferences and a window to insert our Apple ID. (This is the same ID used to initialize our computer, but we can create a new one if necessary.)

Figure 5-3: *Registering our Apple account in Xcode*

Once we insert our Apple ID, the Apple account is configured to work with our copy of Xcode and we can select it from the list. With the account selected and all the information inserted in the form, we can now press the Next button to select the folder where our project is going to be stored. Xcode creates a folder for each project, so we only have to designate the destination folder where we are going to store all our projects and everything else is generated for us.

Do It Yourself: Open Xcode. In the welcome screen, click on the option Create a new Xcode project (Figure 1-2). You can also go to the File menu at the top of the screen and select the options New/Project. After this, you should see the projects window (Figure 5-1). Select the Multiplatform tab, click on the App icon, and press Next. Now you should see the form of Figure 5-2. In Product Name, Insert the name of your app. In the Team option, select your developer account or press the Add Account button to add it to Xcode. In Organization Identifier insert the inverted domain of your website or blog. Make sure that the rest of the options are disabled. Finally, press Next and select a folder where to store the project.

IMPORTANT: Although it's not mandatory, you should get your own domain and website. Apple not only recommends the use of an inverted domain to generate the Bundle Identifier, but at the time of submitting your app to the App Store you will be asked to provide the web page used for promotion and where the users should go for support (see Chapter 20).

Once the project is created, Xcode generates some files according to the selected template and presents the main interface on the screen. Figure 5-4 shows what this interface looks like.

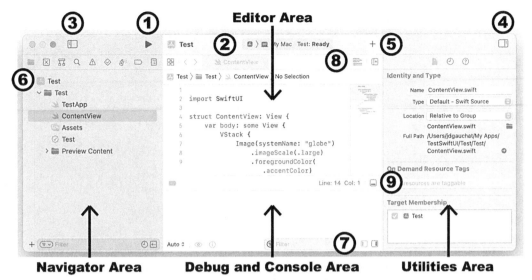

Figure 5-4: Xcode's interface

Like the Playground interface, the Xcode's main window is organized in several areas. There is a toolbar at the top, an area to edit the files at the center called *Editor Area*, and three removable panels on the sides called *Navigator Area*, *Debug and Console Area*, and *Utilities Area*.

Toolbar—This is the area at the top with buttons to control the appearance of the interface, and a display to show warnings, errors, and the app's status. It provides buttons to run and stop the app (number 1), a drop-down list to select the device or the simulator where we want to run the app (number 2), a button that opens a popup window with tools to create the user interface (number 5), and two buttons to show or hide the removable panels (number 3 and number 4).

Navigator Area—This is a removable area that provides information about the files that comprise the application and tools for debugging (identify and remove errors in the code). From here, we can select the files to edit, create groups to organize them, add resources, check for errors, and more. In addition to the files, this area shows an option at the top to configure the app (number 6).

Editor Area—This is the only non-removable area and is the one where we will do much of the work. The content of files and configuration panels are displayed here. Although the Editor Area cannot be removed, it includes buttons at the top to split the area into multiple editors or panels, as we will see later (number 8).

Debug and Console Area—This is a removable area with two sections. The section on the left provides information for debugging, while the section on the right is a console to display the results of the execution of our code, including warnings and errors. The panel can be shown or hidden from the button at the top-right corner (number 9), and each section can be shown or hidden from the buttons at the bottom-right corner (number 7).

Utilities Area—This is a removable area that provides additional information about the app and tools to edit the interface.

Basic Editor Area

The Editor Area is the only non-removable area in the interface. By default, this area always displays the content of the selected file, but we can modify the layout from the buttons in the upper right corner (Figure 5-4, number 8). The button on the right adds more editor panels to the area (Figure 5-5, number 2). New editors are placed on the right side of previous editors, but we can place them below by pressing and holding the Option key. Figure 5-5, below, shows what we see when we press the Add Editor button. Two editors are shown side by side.

Figure 5-5: *Multiple editors in the Editor Area*

These inner panels are useful when we need to edit two or more files at the same time. We can divide each editor as many times as we want, resize them by dragging the lines between them, and close them by pressing the X button in the upper left corner.

On the other hand, the button on the left (Figure 5-5, number 1) shows a popup menu with options to expand the editor, as shown below.

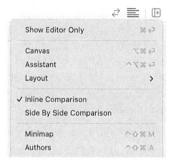

Figure 5-6: *Adjust Editor Options*

In SwiftUI, the most useful options are the Canvas, the Layout, and the Minimap. The Canvas option displays a panel where we can see a preview of the views as they are created, the Layout option allows us to place the preview on the right or at the bottom of the code, and the Minimap option shows a visual representation of our code that we can use for reference and navigation.

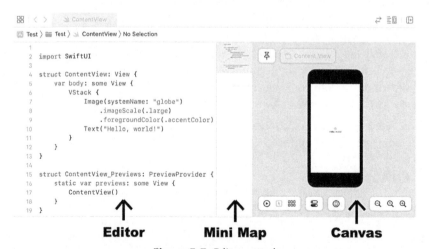

Figure 5-7: *Editor panel*

In addition to the previews offered by the Canvas, there are two other ways to run and test our application from Xcode: the simulator and a real device. The buttons to select these options, run and stop the application, are located on the toolbar (Figure 5-4, number 1 and number 2).

Applications always run on a specific destination and can have different configurations called *Schemes*. The destination could be multiple things, from real devices to windows or simulators, and the scheme defines things like the region where the device is located, or the human language used by the app to display the information on the screen. To set the scheme and destination, Xcode's toolbar includes two buttons (Figure 5-4, number 2). If we click on the button on the left (the one with our app's name), a menu appears with options to edit the current scheme, create a new one, or select the one we want to use.

Figure 5-8: *Scheme menu*

On the other hand, the button on the right allows us to select the destination. The Multiplatform template includes a target configured to create an application for iPhones, iPads, and Mac computers. Therefore, when we want to run our application, all we need to do is to click this button to open the drop-down list (Figure 5-4, number 2) and select a simulator or a device, as shown below.

Figure 5-9: *Options available to run the app*

After the destination is selected, we can press the Play button to run the application (Figure 5-4, number 1). If we use a simulator, a new window opens where we can see our app and interact with it, as shown below.

Figure 5-10: App running in the simulator

The simulator works out of the box, but to run the application on a device, we must connect the device to the computer with a USB cable, select it from the list, and then open the Settings app on the device, select the Privacy & Security option, open the Developer Mode option at the bottom, and turn Developer Mode on, as shown below.

Figure 5-11: Developer mode

 Do It Yourself: If you haven't done it yet, create a new Multiplatform project with the App template following the steps described above. From the toolbar, select an iPhone simulator (Figure 5-9). Press the Play button to run the app (Figure 5-4, number 1). You should see the simulator on the screen with an icon and the text "Hello World" at the center (Figure 5-10).

The app's configuration is stored on a target. The target includes things like the app's name and version, the systems it will support, and the capabilities the app will have, such as access to the camera or iCloud servers. The option to change these values is available in the Navigator Area (Figure 5-4, number 6). Once we click on it, a series of panels are displayed in the Editor Area (Figure 5-12, number 1).

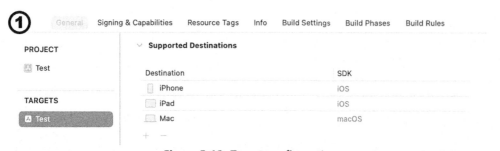

Figure 5-12: Target configuration

From the General panel we can change basic aspects of the application such as the devices the app will support, the app's name, version, available orientations for iPhones and iPads, and the deployment target (the operating systems the app supports). In the Signing & Capabilities panel we can set up the signing certificates required for distribution (usually set up automatically by Xcode) or assign capabilities to the app, such as access to the camera or iCloud servers. Another useful panel is called Info. Here we can find a list of configuration values and insert new ones.

Key		Type	Value	
Bundle version string (short)	◇	String	$(MARKETING_VERSION)	
Bundle identifier	◇	String	$(PRODUCT_BUNDLE_IDENTIFIER)	
⌄ Supported interface orientations (iPad)	◇	Array	(4 items)	
Item 0		String	Portrait (bottom home button)	◇
Item 1		String	Portrait (top home button)	◇
Item 2		String	Landscape (left home button)	◇
Item 3		String	Landscape (right home button)	◇
Bundle name	◇	String	$(PRODUCT_NAME)	
InfoDictionary version	◇	String	6.0	
Localization native development region	◇	String	$(DEVELOPMENT_LANGUAGE)	◇
Executable file	◇	String	$(EXECUTABLE_NAME)	

Figure 5-13: App configuration

The information in this panel is stored in a plist file; which is a file with a format that allows us to store keys and values. The keys represent configuration options and the values are what we want to assign to our app. These configuration options include those declared from other panels, like the available orientations set in the General panel, and also custom options, like the image we want to show when the app is launched, as we will see later.

(Basic) **SwiftUI Files**

The Multiplatform App template includes two Swift files: one with the code to initialize the app (TestApp.swift in our example) and another to define the user interface (ContentView.swift). Figure 5-14, below, shows the Navigator Area with all the items created by the template.

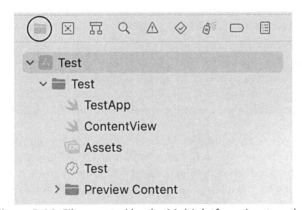

Figure 5-14: Files created by the Multiplatform App template

The first file is named after the application and includes the App suffix to indicate that the code it contains is in charge of initializing the app (TestApp in our example). The following is the code generated by the template for this file.

```
import SwiftUI
@main
struct TestApp: App {
   var body: some Scene {
      WindowGroup {
         ContentView()
      }
   }
}
```

Listing 5-1: *Initializing the app*

Everything in SwiftUI is created inside structures. As illustrated by the code in Listing 5-1, the initial configuration of the application is defined inside a structure that conforms to the **App** protocol. This is a protocol declared in the SwiftUI framework to define the structure and behavior of an application. The protocol's only requirement is the definition of a computed property called **body** that determines the app's content and returns a Scene (window).

The **App** structure must be preceded by the **@main** attribute, which indicates the app's point of entry. When the app is launched, the system looks for a structure that conforms to the **App** protocol and is preceded by the **@main** attribute, creates an instance of that structure, and then executes the code in the **body** property.

In Apple devices, we can open multiple instances of an app. For instance, in iPads and Mac computers, we can open two or more copies of the same app to process different information, such as two windows of the Text editor to process two different documents. To manage these instances, the system implements Scenes.

A Scene is a structure that conforms to the **Scene** protocol; a SwiftUI protocol defined to manage the app's interface and adapt it to every platform. Although we can create our own Scenes by defining a structure that conforms to this protocol, SwiftUI includes several structures to create standard Scenes for every system. The currently available are **WindowGroup**, **Window**, **DocumentGroup**, **Settings**, and **MenuBarExtra**. Some of these structures are designed to create Scenes for Mac computers, as we will see later, and others are more generic. For instance, the **WindowGroup** structure can manage multiple windows for iPhones, iPads and Macs, and therefore it is the one recommended for most projects. The following is the structure's initializer.

WindowGroup(Text, **id:** String, **content:** Closure**)**—This initializer creates a Scene to manage all the windows of an instance of the application. The first argument defines the window's title, the **id** argument specifies the window's identifier, and the **content** argument is a closure that defines what the windows are going to display.

Due to its capacity to create applications for every device, the **WindowGroup** structure is the one implemented in the template of a Multiplatform project, as illustrated in Listing 5-1. Notice that the argument is declared with a trailing closure and because there is only one statement in the block, we didn't have to include the **return** keyword. This is common practice in SwiftUI to simplify the code and make it easy to read.

The **WindowGroup** structure creates a Scene with a window. Windows determine the space where the graphics are displayed, but they do not generate any visible content. The user's interface is built inside a window from similar containers called *Views*. These views are rectangular areas of custom size, designed to display graphics on the screen. Some views are used as containers while others present graphic tools, such as buttons and switches, and graphic content, such as images and text. The views are organized in a hierarchy, one within the other.

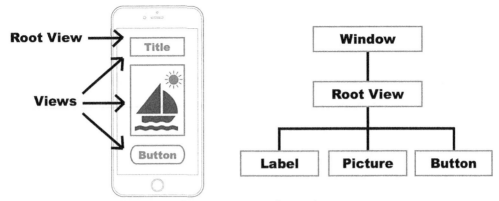

Figure 5-15: *Views hierarchy*

SwiftUI views are defined by structures. In the example provided by the App template, the closure assigned to the **WindowGroup** structure initializes and returns a structure called **ContentView**. This is a custom structure included by the template to define the initial view. (The initial view represents the initial content the user sees on the screen when the app is launched.) The structure is defined in the ContentView.swift file, as shown next.

```
import SwiftUI

struct ContentView: View {
    var body: some View {
        VStack {
            Image(systemName: "globe")
                .imageScale(.large)
                .foregroundColor(.accentColor)
            Text("Hello, world!")
        }
    }
}
```

Listing 5-2: *Defining a structure that conforms to the* View *protocol*

As illustrated by the code in Listing 5-2, a structure that defines a SwiftUI view must conform to the **View** protocol. This is another protocol defined in the SwiftUI framework which only requirement is the implementation of a computed property called **body** that returns at least one view. Within the closure assigned to this property is where we declare all the views we need to design the user interface, as we will see later.

When the system processes a **View** structure, it creates a view called *root view*, and then determines its size from the size of its container. This container can be the window or another view. For instance, the **ContentView** view created by the App template is assigned as the window's root view by the **WindowGroup** structure, and therefore its size is going to be determined by the size of the window.

The views defined in the **body** property follow a different path. They determine their size from the size of the container, but then they propose that size to their content and it is the content that finally decides which size the view is going to take.

We can see this at work when we preview on the canvas the interface produced by the **ContentView** structure created by the template. The structure creates a white view that occupies the entire screen and then two small views inside, one with an icon and another with the text "Hello World!", as shown below.

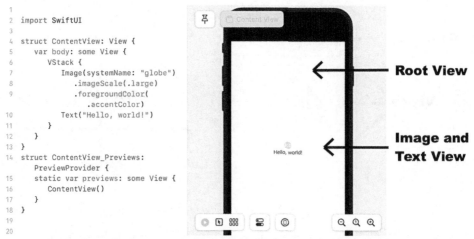

Figure 5-16: *Views created by the App template on the Canvas*

Canvas

SwiftUI files include the definition of two structures, one to declare the view and another to create the preview on the canvas. This second structure conforms to the **PreviewProvider** protocol which requires the implementation of a type property called **previews** that returns the view or group of views to display on the canvas. The following is the preview structure defined by the App template for the **ContentView** view.

```swift
struct ContentView_Previews: PreviewProvider {
    static var previews: some View {
        ContentView()
    }
}
```

Listing 5-3: *Defining the Canvas preview*

When a preview structure is present in our file, Xcode compiles the application and shows a preview on the canvas. The content of the preview is defined by the closure assigned to the **previews** property. The code included by the App template defines the content of this property as an instance of the **ContentView** view, so what we see on the canvas is what the user will see on the device when the app is launched.

Xcode automatically generates the previews, but it cannot always determine when our code is ready to do it. If we introduce significant changes to the code, we must tell Xcode when it can resume the previews. For this purpose, the canvas displays a banner at the top with a refresh button that we must press once all the modifications have been made.

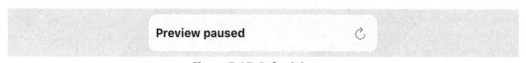

Figure 5-17: *Refresh button*

The preview always matches the destination device selected from the toolbar (see Figure 5-9). Once we set the device, the canvas shows options at the bottom to configure the preview.

Figure 5-18: *Preview configuration*

There is the Live button (number 1) to start a live preview (enabled by default), the Selectable button (number 2) to disable live preview and enable selection, the Variants button (number 3) to show the app in multiple configurations, such as portrait and landscape orientation, the Settings button (number 4) to set the device's configuration, such as the color scheme and orientation, the Preview on Device button (number 5) to run the application on the device connected to the computer, and the Zoom buttons (number 6) to select the preview's size.

Do It Yourself: Click on the ContentView.swift file. You should see the code of Listing 5-2 and 5-3 in the Editor Area. If you don't see the canvas, click on the Adjust Editor button at the upper right corner (Figure 5-5, number 1) and select the Canvas option (Figure 5-6). If you want to see what the interface looks like in a different device, select the target and the device you want from the toolbar (Figure 5-9). Press the Refresh button if necessary. You should see something like Figure 5-16. To test the application on a device, connect the device to a USB port and press the Preview on Device button (Figure 5-18, number 5). Remember to activate Developer Mode on the device (see Figure 5-11).

(Advanced) **Opaque Types**

The value produced by the **body** property is a view (a structure that conforms to the **View** protocol), but because the views assigned to the property may be different each time, it is declared as an opaque type (**some View**). Opaque types are data types that hide the value's data type from the programmer. They are usually required when working with generic data types, like the generic structures introduced before (see Listing 3-48). For example, the **reversed()** method included in **Array** structures returns a **ReversedCollection** structure, and this structure is generic, so the definition of the type depends on the type of values we are processing. An array of strings will generate a structure of type **ReversedCollection <Array<String>>** and an array of integers will return a structure of type **Reversed-Collection<Array<Int>>**, as in the following example.

```
func reverseit(mylist: [Int]) -> ReversedCollection<Array<Int>> {
    let reversed = mylist.reversed()
    return reversed
}
let reversedlist = reverseit(mylist: [1, 2, 3, 4, 5])
print(Array(reversedlist))    // "[5, 4, 3, 2, 1]"
```

Listing 5-4: Returning values of complex data types

The code in Listing 5-4 defines a function called **reverseit()** that receives an array of integers and returns a **ReversedCollection** value with the values in reverse order, and then casts the collection returned by the function into an array and print it on the console.

This code runs fine and there are no issues with it, until we decide to work with different value types, such as strings. Instead of **ReversedCollection<Array<Int>>**, the return data type would have to be defined as **ReversedCollection<Array<String>>**. Although in this case it may seem easy to switch types, the generic data types used to create SwiftUI views can be complex and replacing them repeatedly in generic properties and methods can be time consuming and error prone. But if we know that the values we want to return conform to the same protocol, we can declare the return type as opaque and let the compiler figure out the data type for us. When the compiler finds an opaque type, it takes care of determining the real data type of the value and process it as such.

Opaque types are declared with the **some** keyword followed by the name of the protocol to which the type conforms. For instance, collections such as the one returned by the **reversed()** method, conform to a protocol called **Collection**, so we can define the return type as **some Collection** and let the compiler figure out the real data type.

```
func reverseit(mylist: [String]) -> some Collection {
   let reversed = mylist.reversed()
   return reversed
}
let reversedlist = reverseit(mylist: ["One", "Two", "Three", "Four",
"Five"])
print(Array(reversedlist))   // "["Five", "Four", "Three", "Two", "One"]"
```

Listing 5-5: Returning opaque types

This example defines the same **reverseit()** function as before, but this time the function receives an array of strings and returns the opaque type **some Collection**. The value returned by the function is of type **some Collection**, but the compiler detects the value's data type as **ReversedCollection<Array<String>>** and process it as such, which means that we are still able to turn it into an **Array** and print it on the console.

 IMPORTANT: Functions, methods and closures that return an opaque type must always return a value of a specific type. When the compiler finds an opaque type, it determines the value's real data type from the value returned. If we, for instance, use an **if else** statement to select the view we want to assign to the **body** property, the compiler won't be able to determine the right data type of the value returned and will show an error. Possible solutions are to wrap the views in a **Group** view (see Listing 5-81), or implement the **@ViewBuilder** property wrapper (see Listing 5-89).

Basic 5.2 User Interface

The user interface is the most important aspect of an application. In SwiftUI, the interface is declared in the definition of a structure, one view at a time, and then the compiler takes care of generating the code necessary to display it on the screen and adapt it to every device.

All SwiftUI views are defined by structures, including those defined by the developer and the system. The framework includes several structures to produce standard views. For instance, the **Image** and **Text** structures implemented in the example defined by the App template create views to display images and text, respectively. These are the most basic views in SwiftUI, but there are many more, including some to contain other views and many to display graphics.

Basic Text View

The **Text** structure takes a string and returns a view that displays the text on the screen. The structure defines multiple initializers. The following are the most frequently used.

Text(String**)**—This initializer creates a **Text** view with the text defined by the argument.

Text(Date, **style:** DateStyle**)**—This initializer creates a **Text** view to present a date. The first argument defines the date, and the **style** argument is a structure that determines the format. The structure includes the type properties **date**, **offset**, **relative**, **time**, and **timer** to define this value.

Because of text being the primary means of communication, **Text** views are implemented all the time in SwiftUI applications, and that is why the **ContentView** view generated by the App template includes one. The **Text** view included in the template is created with a **String** value to display the text "Hello World!" on the screen (see Listing 5-2), but a **Text** view can also include values with string interpolation.

```
struct ContentView: View {
    let number: Float = 30.87512

    var body: some View {
        Text("My Number: \(number)")
    }
}
```

Listing 5-6: Displaying values with a Text *view*

This example displays the value as it is, but we can use the **formatted()** method to format the value, as we did in Chapter 4. For instance, we can turn the number into currency to represent US Dollars.

```
struct ContentView: View {
    let number: Float = 30.87512

    var body: some View {
        Text("My Number: \(number.formatted(.currency(code: "USD")))")
    }
}
```

Listing 5-7: Formatting the value for the Text *view*

My Number: $30.88

Figure 5-19: Text *view with formatted values*

Of course, we can include and format other types of values. For instance, we can use the **formatted()** method on a **Date** value to show a date.

```
struct ContentView: View {
    let today = Date()

    var body: some View {
        Text(today.formatted(date: .abbreviated, time: .omitted))
    }
}
```

Listing 5-8: Displaying a date with a Text *view*

Nov 17, 2021

Figure 5-20: Date displayed with a Text *view*

The **Text** structure defines a specific initializer to show dates. The initializer includes an argument that takes a **DateStyle** structure to format the date. The formats available are not as comprehensive as those provided by the **formatted()** method, but the advantage of using this formatter is that some of the styles available can update the values as they change. For instance, one of the type properties included by the `DateStyle` structure is called `timer`. This formatter displays the date as a counter that starts counting from the current date.

```
struct ContentView: View {
   let today = Date()

   var body: some View {
      Text(today, style: .timer)
   }
}
```

Listing 5-9: Displaying a timer with a `Text` view

 Do It Yourself: Update the `ContentView` view in your ContentView.swift file with the example you want to try. If the canvas is not visible, click on the Adjust Editor button and select the Canvas option. If necessary, press the refresh button to resume the preview. You should see the text produced by the `Text` view on the canvas (Figure 5-16). The last example should display a counter on the screen counting up from 0.

(Basic) Modifiers

Views are presented with attributes by default, such as a standard font and color, but the `View` protocol defines methods to modify their aspect. These methods are called *Modifiers*, and they are executed right after the instance is created, as in the following example.

```
struct ContentView: View {
   var body: some View {
      Text("Hello World")
         .font(.largeTitle)
   }
}
```

Listing 5-10: Applying modifiers to a view

When the system reads the **body** property of the example in Listing 5-10 to build the interface, it creates an instance of the **Text** structure with the string "Hello World", and then calls the **font()** method on this structure. This method creates a new view with the **largeTitle** attribute applied to the text and returns that view. As a result, the **body** property produces a view with a large title. If we open the canvas, we can see the change in real time.

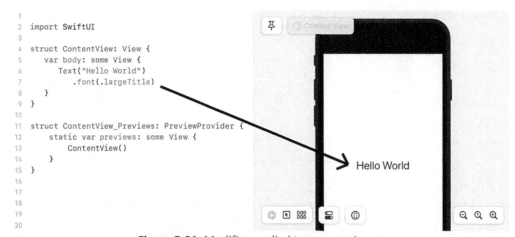

Figure 5-21: Modifier applied to a `Text` view

Do It Yourself: Update the `ContentView` view with the code in Listing 5-10. Press the refresh button on the canvas to refresh the preview. You should see something similar to Figure 5-21.

The code and the canvas are interconnected. If we add a modifier to a view, as we did in Listing 5-10, the changes are automatically performed on the canvas, but we can also edit the views from the canvas. By default, the canvas is in Live Preview mode, but we can change it to Selectable mode by pressing the Selectable button at the bottom (see Figure 5-22, number 1). Once the canvas enters the Selectable mode, there are two ways to edit a view. One alternative is to click on the view (Figure 5-22, number 2) and then open the Attributes Inspector panel in the Utilities Area (Figure 5-4, number 4). The panel shows a list of all the attributes we can change for that view (Figure 5-22, number 3).

Figure 5-22: *View's attributes*

The Attributes Inspector panel shows the attributes currently assigned to the view. In our example, the option Large Title is already selected because we added the `font()` modifier in Listing 5-10. If we remove the modifier, the panel is updated to show the current values. The same happens the other way around. if we change any value on this panel, the change is reflected on the canvas and the corresponding modifier is added to the code.

Another way to modify our views is with a context menu. If we move the mouse over a view on the canvas or in our code and click on it while holding down the Command key, we will see a menu with multiple options to modify the view. One of those options is called *Show SwiftUI Inspector*, which opens a panel with all the same options we can find in the Attributes Inspector panel. Changing the options in this window produces the same effect as before.

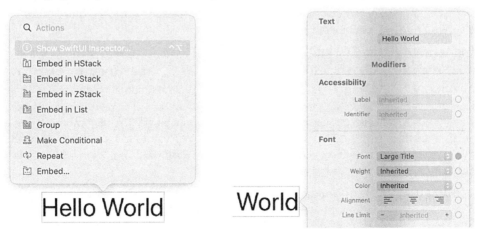

Figure 5-23: *View's context menu*

Additionally, Xcode offers a library with a list of views and modifiers that we can incorporate to our interface by dragging and dropping them onto the canvas or the code. The library is activated from the Library button in the toolbar (Figure 5-4, number 5), and the lists of views and modifiers are selected from the buttons at the top of the window. The first button presents a list with all the views we can add to the interface and the second button opens a list with all the modifiers available. We can also use the search bar at the top of the window for a quick search. Figure 5-24, below, illustrates how to add a modifier from this library to change the color of the text.

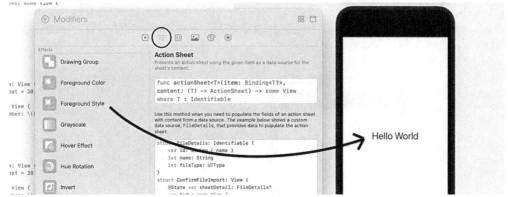

Figure 5-24: Adding a modifier from the Library

 Do It Yourself: Click on the ContentView.swift file and open the canvas. Press the Selectable button to activate the Selectable mode (Figure 5-22, number 1). Move the mouse to the "Hello World" text on the canvas, press and hold the Command key and click on it. You should see a context menu (Figure 5-23, left). Select the Show SwiftUI Inspector option. In the next window, click on the Text field, change the text to "Goodbye World", and press Enter. You should see the text changing on the canvas and the code. Experiment with different values and try to add modifiers to the view from the Library, as shown in Figure 5-24.

Most modifiers are defined by the **View** protocol and then implemented by the structures that conform to it. There are common modifiers that apply to most views and others that are more specific. The following are some of the modifiers used to determine the size of the view.

frame(width: CGFloat?, **height:** CGFloat?, **alignment:** Alignment)—This modifier assigns a new size and alignment to the view. The **alignment** argument determines the alignment of the view's content. It is a structure of type **Alignment** with the type properties **bottom**, **bottomLeading**, **bottomTrailing**, **center**, **leading**, **top**, **topLeading**, **topTrailing**, and **trailing**.

frame(minWidth: CGFloat?, **idealWidth:** CGFloat?, **maxWidth:** CGFloat?, **minHeight:** CGFloat?, **idealHeight:** CGFloat?, **maxHeight:** CGFloat?, **alignment:** Alignment)—This modifier assigns a minimum and a maximum size to the view. We can also define an ideal width and height that will be taken into consideration when the available space must be distributed among the views. The **alignment** argument determines the alignment of the view's content. It is a structure of type **Alignment** with the type properties **bottom**, **bottomLeading**, **bottomTrailing**, **center**, **leading**, **top**, **topLeading**, **topTrailing**, and **trailing**.

padding(CGFloat)—This modifier adds a padding between the view's content and its frame. The argument determines the width of the padding. We can provide a **CGFloat** value to specify the padding for all sides. (If we do not specify a value, the system assigns a standard padding that adapts to each device.) The modifier can also take an **EdgeInsets** value to specify a padding for each side, or a set of **Edge** values along with a **CGFloat** value to declare which sides we want to modify and for how much (**padding([Edge], CGFloat)**). The **Edge** type is an enumeration with the values **bottom**, **leading**, **top**, **trailing**, **horizontal** (left and right), and **vertical** (top and bottom).

The screen of a device is composed of a grid of hundreds of dots called *pixels*, ordered in rows and columns. The number of pixels varies from one device to another. To compensate for the disparities between devices, Apple adopted the concept of points (sometimes called *logical pixels*). The goal is to have a unit of measurement that is independent of the device and the density of the pixels on the screen. A point occupies a square of one or more pixels, depending on the device. For instance, the screen of an iPhone 13 has a grid of 1170 pixels by 2532 pixels, but the views are positioned and sized according to the grid in points (390 by 844). Using this reference, we can determine the appropriate size of a view for every device. In the following example, we implement the **frame()** modifier to give the **Text** view a size of approximately two thirds the width of the screen (250 points).

```
struct ContentView: View {
    var body: some View {
        Text("Hello World!")
            .frame(width: 250, height: 100, alignment: .leading)
    }
}
```

Listing 5-11: *Assigning a fixed size to a view*

In this example, we take advantage of the **alignment** argument provided by the initializer to align the text to the left. Notice that the value does not specify the side. Instead, the side is represented by the **leading** value. There are two values available, **leading** and **trailing**. These values represent the left or the right side of the view depending on the language. For instance, if the language set on the device is left-to-right, like English, the **leading** value is associated to the left side of the view and the **trailing** value to the right.

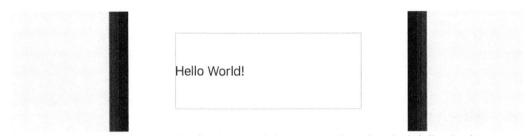

Figure 5-25: *View with a fixed size and the content aligned to the left (leading)*

 Do It Yourself: Update the **ContentView** view with the code in Listing 5-11. Press the Selectable button to activate the Selectable mode on the canvas. Click on the **Text** view in the code or in the canvas to select it. You should see a blue rectangle indicating the area occupied by the view, as illustrated in Figure 5-25.

The arguments in the **frame()** modifier are optional. We can declare only the width or the height, and the rest of the arguments will be defined with the values set by the view. This is particularly useful when we want to turn one side of the view flexible. Flexible views are defined with the **maxWidth** and **maxHeight** arguments. For instance, we can apply the **maxWidth** argument to extend the view to the left and right side of the window, and let the content determine the height.

```
struct ContentView: View {
   var body: some View {
      Text("Hello World!")
         .frame(minWidth: 0, maxWidth: .infinity)
   }
}
```

Listing 5-12: Creating flexible containers

The value **infinity** is a type property defined in the **CGFloat** structure that asks the system to expand the view to occupy all the space available in its container. In our example, we applied this value to the **maxWidth** argument, so the **Text** view extends to the edges of the screen.

Figure 5-26: Flexible view

 IMPORTANT: Notice that for a flexible view to work properly it is recommended to always declare the minimum size as well. If you are declaring a flexible width, you should set the **minWidth** argument, and if you are declaring a flexible height, you should also include the **minHeight** argument.

Another way to specify a custom size is with the **padding()** modifier. The padding is inserted between the content and the edges of the view. There are different ways to determine the padding's thickness. For instance, if we don't specify any value, the system assigns one by default, depending on the device, but we can also provide a **CGFloat** value to declare a specific thickness in points.

```
struct ContentView: View {
   var body: some View {
      Text("Hello World")
         .padding(25)
   }
}
```

Listing 5-13: Adding a padding to the view

The code in Listing 5-13 assigns a padding of 25 points to the **Text** view. The padding is applied between the text and the view's frame, as shown below.

Figure 5-27: View with padding

The **View** protocol defines a structure called **EdgeInsets** that we can use to specify a width for each side of the view.

EdgeInsets(top: CGFloat, **leading:** CGFloat, **bottom:** CGFloat, **trailing:** CGFloat)—This initializer returns an **EdgeInsets** structure with the values specified by the arguments.

The following example implements this structure to assign a padding of 40 points only to the left and right sides.

```
struct ContentView: View {
    var body: some View {
        Text("Hello World")
            .padding(EdgeInsets(top: 0.0, leading: 40.0, bottom: 0.0,
trailing: 40.0))
    }
}
```

Listing 5-14: Assigning a specific padding for each side

Figure 5-28: Padding only on the sides

The code in Listing 5-14 assigns padding to specific sides of the view. Another way to achieve the same is with the values of an enumeration provided by SwiftUI called **Edge**. This enumeration includes the values **bottom, leading, top**, and **trailing** to represent each side. We must declare a set with the values that represent the sides we want to modify and a second argument with the thickness we want to assign to the padding. The following example adds a padding of 50 points at the view's top and bottom.

```
struct ContentView: View {
    var body: some View {
        Text("Hello World")
            .padding([.top, .bottom], 50)
    }
}
```

Listing 5-15: Assigning padding with Edge *values*

Figure 5-29: Padding at the top and bottom

In addition to the view, we can also style its content. For instance, the **View** protocol defines modifiers that are especially useful with **Text** views. The following are the most frequently used.

font(Font**)**—This modifier assigns a font to the text. The argument is a **Font** structure that provides type properties and methods to select the font we want.

bold(Bool**)**—This modifier assigns the bold style to the text. The argument is a Boolean value to dynamically enable or disable the modifier.

italic(Bool**)**—This modifier assigns the italic style to the text. The argument is a Boolean value to dynamically enable or disable the modifier.

fontWeight(Weight**)**—This modifier assigns a weight to the text. The argument is a structure with the type properties **black**, **bold**, **heavy**, **light**, **medium**, **regular**, **semibold**, **thin**, and **ultraLight**.

textCase(Case**)**—This modifier transforms the text to lowercase or uppercase letters. The argument is an enumeration with the values **lowercase** and **uppercase**.

dynamicTypeSize(DynamicTypeSize**)**—This modifier sets the dynamic type size to apply to the text. The argument is an enumeration with the values **large**, **medium**, **small**, **xLarge**, **xSmall**, **xxLarge**, and **xxxLarge**. It can be declared as a range of values to determine the minimum and maximum size allowed.

underline(Bool, **color:** Color**)**—This modifier underlines the text. The first argument is a Boolean value that indicates whether the text has an underline or not, and the second argument defines the color of the line.

strikethrough(Bool, **color:** Color**)**—This modifier draws a line through the text. The first argument is a Boolean value that indicates whether the text is strikethrough or not, and the second argument defines the color of the line.

shadow(color: Color, **radius:** CGFloat, **x:** CGFloat, **y:** CGFloat**)**—This modifier assigns a shadow to the text. The arguments define the color of the shadow, its size, and the horizontal and vertical offsets.

The most important aspect of a text is the font. The system defines standard fonts and sizes to show the text produced by a **Text** view, but we can specify our own with the **font()** modifier. The **font()** modifier assigns the font to the view, but the font is defined by an instance of a structure included in the SwiftUI framework called **Font**. With this structure, we can create custom and dynamic fonts. Custom fonts are fonts provided by the system or the developer, and dynamic fonts are the fonts Apple recommends using because they adapt to the font size selected by the user from Settings.

The easiest to implement are dynamic fonts. They are defined by type properties provided by the **Font** structure, so all we have to do is to apply the **font()** modifier with the property that represents the font type we want to assign to the text. We have done this before with the **largeTitle** property (see Listing 5-10), but the structure also includes the properties **title**, **headline**, **subheadline**, **body**, **callout**, **caption**, and **footnote**.

```
struct ContentView: View {
    var body: some View {
        Text("Hello World")
            .font(.body)
    }
}
```

Listing 5-16: Assigning dynamic font types

The **body** property produces a font similar to the standard font provided by the system, but we can use other properties to get fonts with different styles and sizes. Figure 5-30, below, shows some of the fonts returned by these properties compared to the system's standard font.

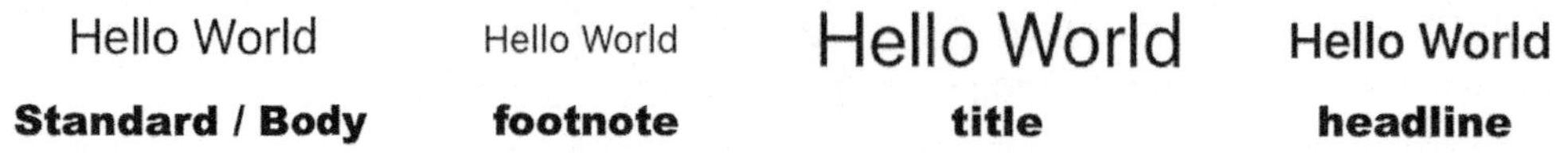

Hello World	Hello World	Hello World	Hello World
Standard / Body	**footnote**	**title**	**headline**

Figure 5-30: Dynamic font types

Do It Yourself: Dynamic fonts have a predefine size, but they change according to the size set by the user from Settings. If you want to see how your text looks like in different sizes, run the app in the simulator or a device, open the Settings app, go to Accessibility / Display & Text Size / Large Text, activate Large Accessibility Sizes, and then change the size from the slider at the bottom.

Although it is recommended to use dynamic fonts, so the interface automatically adapts to the size set by the user, the **Font** structure also includes the following type methods to implement the font defined by the system or to load custom fonts when necessary.

system(size: CGFloat)—This type method returns the system font with the size defined by the **size** argument.

custom(String, **size:** CGFloat)—This type method returns a font of the type specified by the first argument and with the size specified by the **size** argument.

With the **system()** method, we can get the standard font provided by the system but of any size we want. The font and size defined by this method are not affected by the choices the user makes from Settings.

```
struct ContentView: View {
   var body: some View {
      Text("Hello World")
         .font(Font.system(size: 50))
   }
}
```

Listing 5-17: *Using the system font*

This example displays a text with a size of 50 points that always remains at that size no matter the changes performed by the user, but the font type is the one defined by the system. If we want to use a custom font, we have to implement the **custom()** method.

Operating systems come with a set of standard fonts. If the font we want to use is already included in the system, we just need to specify its name and size, as in the following example.

```
struct ContentView: View {
   var body: some View {
      Text("Hello World")
         .font(Font.custom("Georgia", size: 50))
   }
}
```

Listing 5-18: *Using standard fonts*

Figure 5-31: *Text with the Georgia font*

If the font we want to include is not provided by the system, we must copy the file into the project. Including the file in our project is easy; we must drag it from Finder to the Navigator Area, as shown below.

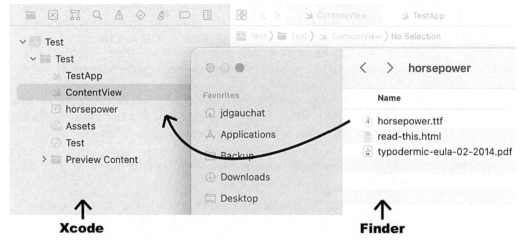

Figure 5-32: *Dragging files from Finder to our Xcode's project*

When we drop the files into our Xcode project, a window asks for information about the destination and the target. If we want the files to be copied to the project's folder (recommended), we must activate the option *Copy items if needed*, as shown in Figure 5-33 below. We must also indicate that the files are going to be added to the target created for our project from the *Add to targets* option.

Destination: ☑ Copy items if needed

Added folders: ○ Create groups
○ Create folder references

Add to targets: ☑ 🅰 Test

Figure 5-33: *Options to add files to the project*

After these options are selected and the Finish button is pressed, Xcode includes the files with the rest of the files in our project. But to be able to use our custom font, we must modify the app's configuration from the Info panel (see Figure 5-13). Every option on the list includes a + button. By pressing any of these buttons, we can add a new key (Figure 5-34, number 1). The key we need in this case is called "Fonts provided by application". This key already includes an item (Item 0), so all we need to do to add a font is to press the arrow on the left to expose the item (Figure 5-34, number 2) and then replace its value with the name of the file that contains our font (Figure 5-34, number 3).

General	Signing & Capabilities		Resource Tags	Info	Build Settings	Build Phases	Build Rules

Key		Type	Value
Bundle name	↕ ⊕ **①** String		$(PRODUCT_NAME)
② ∨ Fonts provided by application	↕ Array		(1 item)
Item 0	String		horsepower.ttf **③**
Bundle identifier	↕ String		$(PRODUCT_BUNDLE_IDENTIFIER)
InfoDictionary version	↕ String		6.0

Figure 5-34: *Custom fonts declared in the Info panel*

In this example, we include the horsepower.ttf file, which defines a font called *Horse Power*. Now, we can use this font from our application, as shown next.

```
struct ContentView: View {
    var body: some View {
        Text("Hello World")
            .font(Font.custom("Horsepower-Regular", size: 50))
    }
}
```

Listing 5-19: Using custom fonts

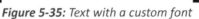

Figure 5-35: Text with a custom font

 Do It Yourself: Download the horsepower.ttf file from our website or provide your own. Drag the file from Finder to the project's Navigator Area (Figure 5-32). Make sure to check the option "Copy items if needed" and the target (Figure 5-33). Go to the app's settings (Figure 5-4, number 6), open the Info panel, click on the + button in any of the rows, and select the "Fonts provided by the application" key. Click on the arrow at the option's left hand side to reveal the items. You should see the Item 0 with no value. Click on the value field to change it. Copy and paste the name of your font's file, including the extension. Modify the **ContentView** view with the code in Listing 5-19. Press the Resume button to see the text with the new font on the canvas.

 IMPORTANT: The names we have to provide to the **custom()** method are the PostScript names. To find the PostScript name of the font you want to add to your project, open the Font Book application from the Applications folder, go to the View menu, and select the option Show Font Info. Click on the font. The PostScript name is shown in the panel on the right.

Applying the rest of the modifiers available for **Text** views is straightforward, as shown next.

```
struct ContentView: View {
    var body: some View {
        Text("Hello World")
            .font(.largeTitle)
            .underline()
            .fontWeight(.heavy)
            .shadow(color: Color.gray, radius: 1, x: 1, y: 1)
    }
}
```

Listing 5-20: Applying multiple styles to a text

The structure in Listing 5-20 defines a **Text** view with a **largeTitle** font, a weight of type **heavy**, a shadow, and underlines the text. In this example, we define the **radius**, **x**, and **y** arguments of the **shadow()** modifier to 1 to cast a subtle shadow that extends to the right and bottom of the text.

Hello World

Figure 5-36: Multiple styles applied to a text

`Text` views can be provided as the content of other `Text` views, which allows us to assign different styles to each portion of the text, as shown below.

```
struct ContentView: View {
    var body: some View {
        Text("Hello \(Text("World").underline())")
            .font(.largeTitle)
    }
}
```
Listing 5-21: Nesting `Text` views

In this example, we applied the **largeTitle** and **underline** modifiers, but because the **underline** modifier was applied to the second **Text** view, only the text in this view is underlined.

Figure 5-37: Nested `Text` views with different styles

The **Font** structure also includes the following modifiers to style the font.

bold()—This modifier adds the bold style to the font.

italic()—This modifier adds the italic style to the font.

weight(Weight**)**—This modifier assigns a weight to the font. The argument is a structure of type **Weight** with the properties **black**, **bold**, **heavy**, **light**, **medium**, **regular**, **semibold**, **thin**, and **ultraLight**.

Because these modifiers are defined by the **Font** structure, they are applied to the font, not the view. For instance, we can apply the **weight()** modifier to the **Font** structure returned by the **largeTitle** property to get a bold text.

```
struct ContentView: View {
    var body: some View {
        Text("Hello World")
            .font(.largeTitle.weight(.semibold))
    }
}
```
Listing 5-22: Styling the font

Figure 5-38: Semibold text

By default, **Text** views can show multiple lines of text, but we can implement modifiers provided by the **View** protocol to set a limit on the number of lines allowed or to format the text.

lineLimit(Int**)**—This modifier determines how many lines the text can contain. The argument is an optional that indicates the number of lines we want. By default, the value is set to **nil**, which means the view will extend to include the number of lines necessary to show the full text.

multilineTextAlignment(TextAlignment**)**—This modifier defines the alignment of multiline text. The argument is an enumeration with the values **center**, **leading** (default), and **trailing**.

lineSpacing(CGFloat**)**—This modifier determines the space between lines.

truncationMode(TruncationMode**)**—This modifier determines how the text is truncated when it doesn't fit inside the view's frame. The argument is an enumeration with the values **head**, **middle**, and **tail** (default).

textSelection(TextSelectability**)**—This modifier determines if the text is selectable by the user (the user can copy the text and paste it somewhere else). The argument is a structure with the type properties **enabled** and **disabled**.

privacySensitive()—This modifier indicates that the view contains sensitive information. It is used to prevent the system from exposing private data.

The following example displays a text aligned to the center and with a space of 5 points between lines.

```
struct ContentView: View {
    var body: some View {
        Text("Monsters are real, and ghosts are real too. They live inside
us, and sometimes, they win. Stephen King.")
            .padding()
            .multilineTextAlignment(.center)
            .lineSpacing(5)
            .textSelection(.enabled)
    }
}
```

Listing 5-23: Formatting text

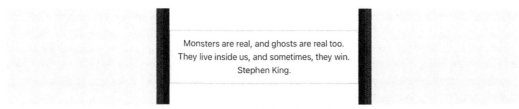

Figure 5-39: Multiline text

If we limit the number of lines, we must consider how the text is going to be displayed to the user when it is too long or does not fit within the view. By default, the system truncates the text and adds ellipsis at the end to indicate that part of the text is missing, but we can move the ellipsis to the beginning or the middle with the **truncationMode()** modifier.

```
struct ContentView: View {
    var body: some View {
        Text("Monsters are real, and ghosts are real too. They live inside
us, and sometimes, they win. Stephen King.")
            .padding()
            .lineLimit(1)
            .truncationMode(.middle)
    }
}
```

Listing 5-24: Truncating text

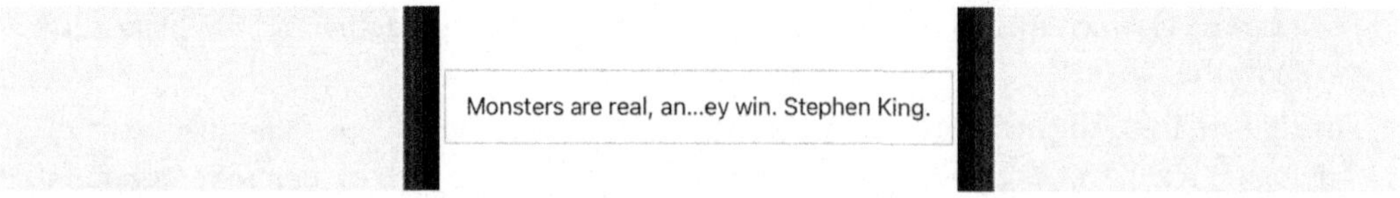

Monsters are real, an...ey win. Stephen King.

Figure 5-40: *Truncation mode*

(Basic) ## Color View

Some modifiers can change the colors of the view and the content. Colors in SwiftUI are defined by a **Color** view. The following are some of the structure's initializers.

Color(RGBColorSpace, **red:** Double, **green:** Double, **blue:** Double, **opacity:** Double**)**—This initializer returns a **Color** view with the color and opacity defined by the arguments. The first argument defines the color system used to interpret the values. It is an enumeration with the values **sRGB**, **sRGBLinear**, and **displayP3**. If ignored, the color system set on the device is used instead. The **red**, **green**, and **blue** arguments determine the levels of red, green, and blue with values from 0.0 (no color) to 1.0 (full color). And the **opacity** argument determines the level of opacity with a value from 0.0 (transparent) to 1.0 (opaque). The opacity may be ignored.

Color(RGBColorSpace, **white:** Double, **opacity:** Double**)**—This initializer returns a **Color** view with the color defined by the arguments. The first argument defines the color system used to interpret the values. It is an enumeration with the values **sRGB**, **sRGBLinear**, and **displayP3**. If ignored, the color system set on the device is used instead. The **white** argument determines the level of white with a value from 0.0 to 1.0 (black to white), and the **opacity** argument determines the level of opacity with a value from 0.0 (transparent) to 1.0 (opaque). The opacity may be ignored.

Color(hue: Double, **saturation:** Double, **brightness:** Double**)**—This initializer returns a **Color** view with the color defined by the arguments. The arguments determine the level of hue, saturation, and brightness of the color with values from 0.0 to 1.0.

The **Color** structure also offers an extensive list of type properties that return a **Color** view with a predefined color that adapts to the interface mode (light or dark). The properties available are **black**, **blue**, **brown**, **cyan**, **gray**, **green**, **indigo**, **mint**, **orange**, **pink**, **purple**, **red**, **teal**, **white**, and **yellow**. There is also a property to make the element transparent called **clear**, a property to get the color set for the app by default called **accentColor**, and two properties called **primary** and **secondary** that return predefined colors that also change depending on the mode set for the interface (light or dark).

Most of the time, **Color** views are used to define a color for the content of other views, but they are views on their own right and therefore can be included in the interface like any other.

```
struct ContentView: View {
    var body: some View {
        Color(red: 0.9, green: 0.5, blue: 0.2)
            .frame(width: 250, height: 100)
    }
}
```

Listing 5-25: *Implementing* Color *views*

Figure 5-41: Color *view*

The code in Listing 5-25 creates an orange **Color** view with a size of 250 by 100 points. In this case, the **Color** initializer was implemented with values from 0.0 to 1.0 to determine the levels of red, green and blue, but RGB colors (Red, Green, Blue) are usually determined with integer values from 0 to 255. If we want to work with these values, we can divide the number by 255. For instance, the following initializer assigns an RGB color with the values 100, 228, 255 (cyan).

```
struct ContentView: View {
    var body: some View {
        Color(red: 100/255, green: 228/255, blue: 255/255)
            .frame(width: 250, height: 100)
    }
}
```

Listing 5-26: *Defining the color with RGB values*

Colors defined with the initializers are static colors, which means they are always the same, independent of the interface appearance (light or dark), but we can assign dynamic colors with the structure's properties. Dynamic colors adapt to the appearance. The following example creates a **Color** view with the **red** property. In dark mode this color will look slightly different than in light mode.

```
struct ContentView: View {
    var body: some View {
        Color.red
            .frame(width: 250, height: 100)
    }
}
```

Listing 5-27: *Assigning a dynamic color*

In addition to the SwiftUI files, the App template includes a file called Assets (see Figure 5-14). This is a tool called Asset Catalog that makes it easy to access resources, including images, icons, colors, and more. When selected, Xcode shows a visual interface in the Editor Area to manage and configure the content. The interface includes two columns: the column on the left presents a list of sets of resources, such as images and colors, and the column on the right displays the content of the selected set, as shown below.

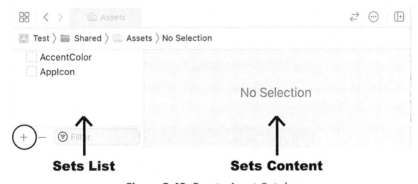

Figure 5-42: *Empty Asset Catalog*

The type properties provided by the **Color** structure, like the **red** property implemented in Listing 5-27, define colors that adapt to the appearance (light or dark). With the Asset Catalog, we can define our own sets of adaptive colors. The set is added from the Editor menu (Add New Asset / Color Set), or by pressing the + button at the lower left corner (circled in Figure 5-42). Once we select the Color Set option, Xcode creates a set with two placeholders for the colors, one for the color to show in Any appearance, and another for the Dark mode.

Figure 5-43: *Colors for Light and Dark appearances*

The name of the set is the name we use to reference the color from code. In this example, we call it *MyColor*. To assign the color, we must select the placeholder we want to change and define the color from the Attributes Inspector panel. For instance, in the following example we change the color for the dark appearance to orange.

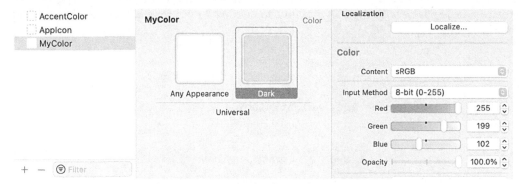

Figure 5-44: *New color for Dark appearance*

Once the set is defined, we can assign it to a view, as shown next.

```
struct ContentView: View {
    var body: some View {
        Color("MyColor")
            .frame(width: 250, height: 100)
    }
}
```

Listing 5-28: *Assigning a custom color*

In this example, the `Color` view will be white in light appearance, but orange when the appearance is changed to dark.

Figure 5-45: *Custom color in Dark appearance*

 Do It Yourself: Click on the Assets item in the Navigator Area to open the Asset Catalog. Click on the + button and select the option Color Set (Figure 5-42). Click on the set to select it, open the Attributes Inspector panel and change its name to MyColor (Figure 5-43). Click on the squares that represent the colors in the Editor Area and set a different color for each one of them from the Attributes Inspector panel. Modify the **ContentView** view with the code in Listing 5-28. To change the appearance, click on the Device Settings button (Figure 5-18, number 4), activate Color Scheme and select the Dark Appearance option. You should see something like Figure 5-45.

The Asset Catalog includes two predefined sets called *AccentColor* and *AppIcon*. The AppIcon set defines the icons we must provide to represent the application. (Icons are the little images the user taps or clicks to launch the app.) On the other hand, the AccentColor set defines the color used by some views, such as buttons and other controls, to style their content. The color by default is blue, but we can modify this set to define a new one. In the example below, we change the accent color to green. From now on, all the controls that use the accent color will be green.

Figure 5-46: *Accent color*

As we already mentioned, the most common application of **Color** views is to define the colors of other views. The following are some of the modifiers that implement **Color** views to define the color of the views or are useful when working with colors.

foregroundColor(Color**)**—This modifier assigns a color to the view's content.

border(Color, **width:** CGFloat**)**—This modifier assigns a border to the view. The first argument determines the border's color and the **width** argument determines its width.

cornerRadius(CGFloat**)**—This modifier rounds the corners. The argument determines the radius of the corners.

background(View, **alignment:** Alignment**)**—This modifier assigns a view as the view's background. The first argument is a SwiftUI view, including **Color** views, and the **alignment** argument determines how the view is going to be aligned within the bounds of the parent view.

foregroundStyle(ShapeStyle**)**—This modifier assigns a style to the view's content. The argument is a value that conforms to the **ShapeStyle** protocol, such as the **Color** structure for colors, the **AngularGradient** and **LinearGradient** structures for gradients, and the **Material** structure for materials.

overlay(View, **alignment:** Alignment**)**—This modifier displays a view in front of the view that is being modified. The first argument is a SwiftUI view, including **Color** views, and the **alignment** argument determines how the view is going to be aligned within the bounds of the view we are modifying.

Using these modifiers, we can apply colors to different parts of the view. For instance, the **foregroundColor()** modifier assigns a color to the view's content. In the following example, we use it to change the color of the text in a **Text** view.

```
struct ContentView: View {
    var body: some View {
        Text("Hello World")
            .font(.largeTitle)
            .foregroundColor(Color.red)
    }
}
```

Listing 5-29: Assigning a color to the text of a Text *view*

Figure 5-47: Text in different color

Besides changing the color of the text, we can assign a color to the view's background. The **background()** modifier can take any view, but it is usually applied with a **Color** view.

```
struct ContentView: View {
    var body: some View {
        Text("Hello World")
            .font(.largeTitle)
            .background(Color.gray)
    }
}
```

Listing 5-30: Assigning a background color to a Text *view*

Figure 5-48: View with a background

As we already mentioned, the area occupied by the view is determined by a rectangular frame. In **Text** views, the size of this rectangle is determined by the size of the text. If we want to extend the background, we can set the frame's size with the **frame()** modifier or add a padding with the **padding()** modifier, as we do next.

```
struct ContentView: View {
    var body: some View {
        Text("Hello World")
            .font(.largeTitle)
            .padding(20)
            .background(Color.gray)
    }
}
```

Listing 5-31: Assigning a background color to the view and the padding

Notice that the padding was applied before the background. This is important because the order of the modifiers matters. Every time a modifier is executed, a new view is created with the characteristics of the previous view plus the changes requested by the modifier. For example, the code in Listing 5-31 creates a **Text** view with the text "Hello World", then the **font()** modifier creates a new view with a larger font, after that the **padding()** modifier creates another view with the characteristics of the previous one but with a padding of 20 points, which expands the view's frame 20 points on each side, and finally the **background()** modifier creates another view with a background that covers the whole area occupied by the previous view, which includes the padding. If we had declared the background before the padding, the background color would have been applied to the view generated by the **font()** modifier, which didn't include the padding, as illustrated below.

Figure 5-49: Background applied before and after the padding

In addition to the background, we can assign a border to the view with the **border()** modifier. This modifier takes a view that represents the style of the border (usually a **Color** view) and the width, and adds a border with those characteristics.

```
struct ContentView: View {
    var body: some View {
        Text("Hello World")
            .font(.largeTitle)
            .padding(20)
            .background(Color.gray)
            .border(Color.yellow, width: 10)
    }
}
```

Listing 5-32: Assigning a border to the view

Figure 5-50: Background and border applied to the view

If we have a view with a background or content that fills the view's frame, such as a **Color** view or an image, we can round its corners with the **cornerRadius()** modifier.

```
struct ContentView: View {
    var body: some View {
        Text("Hello World")
            .font(.largeTitle)
            .padding(20)
            .background(Color.gray)
            .cornerRadius(20)
    }
}
```

Listing 5-33: Rounding corners

Hello World

Figure 5-51: Round corners

The **overlay()** modifier works like the **background()** modifier but instead of displaying the view in the background, it does so on the front. For instance, the following code adds a translucent yellow view in front of the view generated by the previous example.

```
struct ContentView: View {
    var body: some View {
        Text("Hello World")
            .font(.largeTitle)
            .padding(20)
            .background(Color.gray)
            .cornerRadius(20)
            .overlay(
                Color(red: 1, green: 1, blue: 0.3, opacity: 0.2)
                    .frame(width: 160, height: 40)
            )
    }
}
```

Listing 5-34: Displaying a view in front of another view

Figure 5-52: Overlay

The **Color** view also includes the following property and method to apply simple effects to the views.

gradient—This property applies a gentle gradient to the color.

opacity(Double**)**—This method defines the color's opacity. The argument takes values from 0.0 (fully transparent) to 1.0 (fully opaque).

The **gradient** property returns a gentle gradient generated from the original color. It can be applied anywhere a **Color** view is implemented. For instance, in the following example, we apply it to the background of our **Text** view.

```
struct ContentView: View {
    var body: some View {
        Text("Hello World")
            .font(.largeTitle)
            .padding(20)
            .background(Color.gray.gradient)
            .cornerRadius(20)
    }
}
```

Listing 5-35: Applying a predefined gradient to a view

Figure 5-53: Gradient

Materials

Modern interfaces make extensive use of blur effects and transparency. Although we can set the opacity of a `Color` view to make it translucent, as we did in the example of Listing 5-34, the SwiftUI framework offers a better alternative with Materials. Materials apply a blur effect to the background of a view, producing an effect that resembles frosted glass. SwiftUI includes the `Material` structure to create these materials, and this structure defines the following type properties to produce standard effects: `ultraThinMaterial`, `thinMaterial`, `regularMaterial`, `thickMaterial`, and `ultraThickMaterial`.

Materials are applied to the view with the `background()` modifier. The translucent effect they produce is useful when the view appears on top of other views (they overlap), but we can test it with a single view, as shown next.

```
struct ContentView: View {
    var body: some View {
        Text("Hello World")
            .font(.largeTitle)
            .background(.thickMaterial)
    }
}
```

Listing 5-36: Applying a material

Because we only have one view and the root view is white, the effect is barely visible, but materials become useful when working with multiple views and images, as we will see later.

Figure 5-54: Material applied to a view

Materials can also be applied to the view's content with the `foregroundStyle()` modifier, as in the following example.

```
struct ContentView: View {
    var body: some View {
        Text("Hello World")
            .font(.largeTitle)
            .background(.red)
            .foregroundStyle(.thickMaterial)
    }
}
```

Listing 5-37: Applying a material to the view's content

Figure 5-55: Material applied to the text

Images

Images are used for everything in modern applications, from backgrounds and patterns to the creation of customized controls. But before incorporating images into our projects, we must consider that they are stored in files with a resolution in pixels, while the user interface is defined in points. As we already mentioned, the screens of Apple devices have different resolutions and scales. In some devices, one point represents one pixel and in others more. At this moment, three scales have been defined: 1x, 2x, and 3x. The 1x scale defines one point as one pixel, the 2x scale defines 1 point as a square of 2 pixels, and the 3x scale defines one point as a square of three pixels. For this reason, every time we want to show images in our interface, we must consider the conversion between pixels and points. For example, if we have an image of 300 pixels wide and 400 pixels tall, in a device with a scale of 1x the image will almost fill the screen, but in a device with a scale of 2x the image will look half its size. The image is occupying the same space, 300 by 400 pixels, but because of the higher resolution the pixels represent a smaller area on the screen in devices with scales of 2x or 3x, as shown below.

Figure 5-56: *Same image in devices with different scale*

One solution to this problem is to scale up a small image in devices with higher resolution or scale down a big image in devices with lower resolution. For example, we can expand an image of 300 x 400 pixels to 600 x 800 pixels and make it look like the same size in a screen with a scale of 2x (a space of 300 x 400 points represents 600 x 800 pixels at this scale), or we could start with an image of 600 x 800 pixels and reduce it to 300 x 400 pixels for devices with half the scale. One way or another, we have a problem. If we expand a small image to fill the screen, it loses quality, and if we reduce it, it occupies unnecessary space in memory because the image is never shown in its original resolution. Fortunately, there is a more efficient solution. It requires us to include in our project three versions of the same image, one for every scale. Considering the image of our example, we will need one picture of the husky in a size of 300 x 400 pixels for devices with a scale of 1x, another of 600 x 800 pixels for devices with a scale of 2x, and a third one of 900 x 1200 for devices with a scale of 3x. Now, the images can be shown in the same size and with the same quality no matter the device or the scale.

Figure 5-57: *Different images for specific scales*

Chapter 5 - SwiftUI Framework

Providing the same image in different resolutions solves the problem but introduces some complications. We must create three versions of the same image and then select which one is going to be shown depending on the scale of the device. To help us select the right image, Apple systems detect the scale that corresponds to the image by reading a suffix on the file's name. What we need to do is to provide three files with the same name but with suffixes that determine the scale for which they were designed. The file containing the image for the 1x scale (300 x 400 pixels in our example) only requires the name and the extension (e.g., **husky.png**), the name of the file with the image for the 2x scale (600 x 800) must include the suffix @2x (e.g., **husky@2x.png**), and the name of the file with the image for the 3x scale (900 x 1200) must include the suffix @3x (e.g., **husky@3x.png**). Every time the interface requires an image, the system reads the suffixes and loads the one corresponding to the scale of the screen.

 IMPORTANT: There is a useful application in the App Store for Mac computers called *Prepo* that can take an image of a scale of 3x and reduce it to create the versions for the rest of the scales. It can also help you generate the icons for your app. (We will learn more about icons in Chapter 20.)

There are two ways to incorporate images into our project. We can drag the files to the Navigator Area, as we did before for the font type (see Figure 5-32), or we can add the images to the Asset Catalog. The latter is the preferred option because it simplifies the management of a large number of images. The images are added to the Asset Catalog and then referenced from code by name. This is similar to what we have done to create custom colors (see Figure 5-43). We create an Image Set and then fill the placeholders with the images we want to add to the project.

New sets are added from the + button in the lower left corner (circled in Figure 5-42) or the Editor menu at the top of the screen. If we open the Editor menu and click on the option Add New Asset / *Image Set*, a new empty set is created.

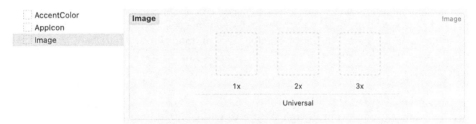

Figure 5-58: New set of images

The name of the set is the name we are going to use to get the image from code. Xcode calls the new set *Image* but we can click on it and rename it, as we did for colors. Once the set is created, we can drag the files from Finder to the corresponding squares. For example, the file husky.png mentioned before goes inside the 1x square, the file husky@2x.png goes inside the 2x square, and the file husky@3x.png goes inside the 3x square. Figure 5-59, below, shows the Editor Area after the images of a husky are dragged from Finder to the Asset Catalog and the name of the set is changed to "husky".

Figure 5-59: The husky set is ready

Although we can add all of our images one by one, as we did in this example, the process soon becomes tedious. An easy way to create a new set is to drag the three images for the set to the Asset Catalog. Xcode creates a new set with the images and assigns their names as the name of the set. The creation and configuration of the set is done automatically when we drag the files and drop them inside the Asset Catalog. In fact, we can drag several files at the same time and Xcode takes care of extracting the information and creating all the sets for us.

In addition to the image for every scale, we can also add versions for different devices and appearances. By default, the set of images is assigned to a Universal device, which means that the images of the set are going to be display on every device, but we can add to the set images for a specific device by selecting the options in the Attributes Inspector panel.

Figure 5-60: *Images for iPhones*

When a set is selected, the Attributes Inspector panel shows the list of properties assigned to the set, including Devices and Appearance. If we check the box of a device or select a different value for the appearance (Dark or Light), the interface adds placeholders where we can drag and drop the images for that specific attribute. For instance, in Figure 5-60, we checked the box for iPhones and now we have three placeholders to add images for that specific device. After the images are incorporated into the Asset Catalog, we can load the image from our code using its name and the system will pick the right version according to the characteristics of the device where the app is running.

 IMPORTANT: The Multiplatform App template includes an additional Asset Catalog to incorporate images into the project that are only going to be used for previews during development. The item is called Preview Assets and it is inside a group called Preview Content. The resources added to this Asset Catalog are available during development but not included in the app's final build.

Once the images are incorporated into our project, we can show them in our application. SwiftUI includes the **Image** view for this purpose. The following are some of the view's initializers.

Image(String**)**—This initializer creates an **Image** view with the image indicated by the argument. The argument is a string with the name of the file or the set in the Asset Catalog.

Image(systemName: String, **variableValue:** Double**)**—This initializer creates an **Image** view with an SF symbol. The **systemName** argument is the name of the symbol, and the **variableValue** argument is a value between 0.0 and 1.0 that determines the symbol's appearance.

Image(uiImage: UIImage**)**—This initializer creates an **Image** view from a **UIImage** object.

An **Image** view can load and display any image that was incorporated into our project or added to the Asset Catalog. All we need is to specify its name. For instance, the following example creates an **Image** view with an image we put in the Asset Catalog called *Toronto*.

```
struct ContentView: View {
    var body: some View {
        Image("Toronto")
    }
}
```

Listing 5-38: Displaying an image

 Do It Yourself: Download the Toronto image from our website or provide your own. Drag the files to the Asset Catalog in your project. Modify the **ContentView** view with the code in Listing 5-38. You should see a picture of Toronto on the canvas.

By default, **Image** views are the size of their content. If the image is larger than the window, as in this case, the view will extend beyond the limits of the screen.

Figure 5-61: Image view larger than the screen

The image is independent of the view. If we resize the view with the **frame()** modifier, the image remains in its original size. To adapt the image to the space provided by the view, we must apply the following modifiers.

clipped()—This modifier clips the image to the view's frame.

resizable()—This modifier resizes the image to fit within the view's frame.

aspectRatio(CGSize, **contentMode:** ContentMode**)**—This modifier changes the image's aspect ratio to the values specified by the first argument and resizes the image according to the mode specified by the **contentMode** argument. This argument is an enumeration of type **ContentMode** with the values **fill** and **fit**. If we want to use the original aspect ratio, we can declare the first argument as **nil** or just ignore it.

scaledToFit()—This modifier scales the image to fit within the view. It works like the **aspectRatio()** modifier with the aspect ratio set to **nil** and the mode to **fit**.

scaledToFill()—This modifier scales the image to fill the view. It works like the **aspectRatio()** modifier with the aspect ratio set to **nil** and the mode to **fill**.

There are several transformations we can apply to the image with these modifiers. One alternative is to clip the image to the view's frame with the **clipped()** modifier.

```
struct ContentView: View {
    var body: some View {
        Image("Toronto")
            .frame(width: 250, height: 100)
            .clipped()
    }
}
```

Listing 5-39: Clipping the image

The **clipped()** modifier creates a new view that only shows the part of the image that is within the view's frame.

Figure 5-62: Image clipped

This reduces the size of the visible image, but the image is still presented in its original size, independent of the size of the view. To adapt the size of the image to the size of the view, we have to make the image flexible with the **resizable()** modifier.

```
struct ContentView: View {
    var body: some View {
        Image("Toronto")
            .resizable()
            .frame(width: 250, height: 100)
    }
}
```

Listing 5-40: Resizing the image

The **resizable()** modifier creates a view that adjusts the size of the image to fit the space available within the view's frame.

Figure 5-63: Image resized

 IMPORTANT: As we already mentioned, modifiers return a new view and therefore the order in which they are applied matters. The **resizable()** modifier applied in the example of Listing 5-40 is implemented by the **Image** structure and therefore it must be applied first. If we try to declared this modifier after the **frame()** modifier, we will get an error because the **frame()** modifier does not return an **Image** view, it returns a view of type **some View**.

In the previous example, we didn't have to clip the image because the **resizable()** modifier resizes the image to the size of the view. But this creates another problem. The image is squashed. If we want to resize the image but keeping its original aspect ratio, we must define the content mode with the **aspectRatio()** modifier. The values available are **fit** (Aspect Fit) and **fill** (Aspect Fill).

```
struct ContentView: View {
    var body: some View {
        Image("Toronto")
            .resizable()
            .aspectRatio(contentMode: .fit)
            .frame(width: 250, height: 100)
    }
}
```

Listing 5-41: Resizing an image to fit the view

In this example, we create an **Image** view with the same image as before, but this time we resize it with the **resizable()** modifier and make it fit within the space available preserving its original aspect ratio with the **aspectRatio()** modifier. The same effect can be achieved with the **scaledToFit()** modifier.

```
struct ContentView: View {
    var body: some View {
        Image("Toronto")
            .resizable()
            .scaledToFit()
            .frame(width: 250, height: 100)
    }
}
```

Listing 5-42: Resizing the image to fit within the view with the scaledToFit() *modifier*

There are two modes available: **fit** and **fill** (**scaledToFit()** and **scaledToFill()**) Figure 5-64, below, shows what happens when we apply these content modes to the image of our example.

Figure 5-64: Aspect fit (left) and aspect fill (right)

In **fit** mode, the image is resized to fit within the view, even when that leaves some parts of the frame empty (Figure 5-64, left). In **fill** mode, the image is resized to fill the view, even when parts of the image may lie outside the view (Figure 5-64, right). If we want to use the **fill** mode to fill the view but don't want the image to go beyond the view's boundaries, we can clip it with the **clipped()** modifier.

```
struct ContentView: View {
    var body: some View {
        Image("Toronto")
            .resizable()
            .scaledToFill()
            .frame(width: 250, height: 100)
            .clipped()
    }
}
```

Listing 5-43: *Resizing and clipping the image to fill the view*

Figure 5-65: *Clipped image*

Often, the user interface must include a view with an image that adapts to the space available. An easy way to achieve this is to make the image resizable and set its mode to `fit`.

```
struct ContentView: View {
    var body: some View {
        Image("Toronto")
            .resizable()
            .scaledToFit()
    }
}
```

Listing 5-44: *Resizing image to fill the container*

When the size of the frame is not declared, the view works along with the content to set its final size. At first, the view takes all the space available in its container, but then it asks the image what size to take. Because the image mode was set to `fit`, the image allows the view to extend as much as it can but adjusts the view's height to its own height to preserve the original aspect ratio. The result is shown below.

Figure 5-66: *Flexible* `Image` *view*

Of course, we can also apply common modifiers to an `Image` view. Some modify the view, others the image. The following example adds a padding, round corners, and a shadow to our image.

```
struct ContentView: View {
    var body: some View {
        Image("Toronto")
            .resizable()
            .scaledToFit()
            .cornerRadius(25)
            .padding(20)
            .shadow(color: Color.black, radius: 5, x: 5, y: 5)
    }
}
```

Listing 5-45: *Applying style modifiers to an* Image *view*

Again, the order of the modifiers is important. In this example, we applied the **padding()** after the **cornerRadius()** to make sure the rounded corners are applied to the image, not the padding.

Figure 5-67: *Image view with common modifiers*

The **View** protocol also defines modifiers that are particularly useful with **Image** views. The following are the most frequently used.

blur(radius: CGFloat, **opaque:** Bool)—This modifier applies a blur effect to the view. The **radius** argument determines how diffuse the blur effect is, and the **opaque** argument determines whether the blur effect is going to be opaque or transparent.

colorMultiply(Color)—This modifier multiplies the view's colors with a specific color. As a result, the view's original colors tend toward the color defined by the argument.

saturation(Double)—This modifier increases or decreases the intensity of the colors.

contrast(Double)—This modifier applies contrast to the view.

opacity(Double)—This modifier defines the view's opacity. The argument takes values from 0.0 (fully transparent) to 1.0 (fully opaque).

scaleEffect(CGSize)—This modifier changes the horizontal and vertical scales of the view to the values specified by the argument. The modifier only affects the view's content.

The implementation of these modifiers is straightforward. The following example scales the image to half its size and makes it blurry.

```
struct ContentView: View {
    var body: some View {
        Image("Toronto")
            .resizable()
            .scaledToFit()
            .padding()
```

```
        .scaleEffect(CGSize(width: 0.5, height: 0.5))
        .blur(radius: 5)
   }
}
```

Listing 5-46: Applying visual effects to an `Image` *view*

The size of the view remains the same, but the size of the image is reduced by half with the `scaleEffect()` modifier.

Figure 5-68: Visual effects applied to an image

In addition to the modifiers available to specify the size of the view and scale the image, we can also adapt it to the font size selected by the user from Settings, as we did before with Dynamic fonts (see Listing 5-16). For this purpose, SwiftUI includes the following property wrapper.

@ScaledMetric(relativeTo: TextStyle**)**—This property wrapper scales a value according to the font size selected by the user from the Settings app. The **relativeTo** argument is an enumeration value that determines the dynamic font type of reference. The values available are **body**, **callout**, **caption**, **caption2**, **footnote**, **headline**, **largeTitle**, **subheadline**, **title**, **title2**, and **title3**. If the argument is ignored, the value is scaled relative to the style set by the system.

We will study property wrappers in Chapter 6. They create properties with predefined functionality that can store and process values. In this case, the **@ScaledMetric** property wrapper increments or decrements a base value according to the font size selected by the user from the Settings app. This is particularly useful with images. For instance, we can define a property with a value of 100 and use it to set the size of an **Image** view with the **frame()** modifier.

```
struct ContentView: View {
   @ScaledMetric var customSize: CGFloat = 100

   var body: some View {
      Image("Toronto")
         .resizable()
         .frame(width: customSize, height: customSize)
   }
}
```

Listing 5-47: Scaling an image to the selected font size

Because we use the **@ScaledMetric** property to define the size of the image, it changes when the user selects a different size from Settings. The figure below shows what we see when different sizes are selected (small on the left, large on the right).

Chapter 5 - SwiftUI Framework

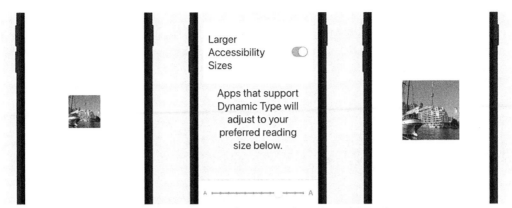

Figure 5-69: *Image adapting to the selected font size*

Do It Yourself: Update the `ContentView` view with the code in Listing 5-47. Run the application on the iPhone simulator. You should see the image with the size determined by the base value (100) and the dynamic font type set by the system. Press the Home button, open the Settings app, go to Accessibility / Display & Text Size / Large Text, activate Large Accessibility Sizes, and then change the size from the slider at the bottom (Figure 5-69, center). Open the app again. You should see the image changing size based on the selected value.

Basic) SF Symbols

Apple systems provide predefined images we can use in our applications. We have introduced emojis in Chapter 2 (see Figure 2-11). Emojis can be included in strings and displayed on the screen with a `Text` view, as any other character. Their purpose is to convey information or mood, so they don't scale well and should only be used to establish an emotional connection with the user or between users. To incorporate icons that represent functionality, such as a button to send an email, add an item to a list or share data, Apple recommends using symbols designed specifically for this purpose called *SF Symbols*. These symbols are scalable, come in different versions, and adapt to the current font, making it easy to integrate them with the rest of the interface.

There are plenty of symbols available to cover every need our application might have. To help us find the symbols we want, Apple provides a free application called SF Symbols that we can download from **developer.apple.com** (Develop/Downloads/Release/Applications). The app includes options to search for symbols by name or category.

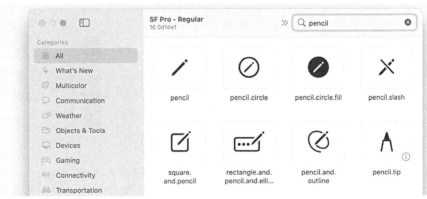

Figure 5-70: *SF Symbols app*

Symbols are loaded and displayed with an `Image` view, but we must implement the initializer `Image(systemName:)` with the name of the symbol, as in the following example.

```
struct ContentView: View {
   var body: some View {
      Image(systemName: "envelope")
   }
}
```

Listing 5-48: *Displaying SF symbols*

SF symbols were designed to work with text and therefore their size can be determined by a `Font` structure, and the style by the font's modifiers, as shown next.

```
struct ContentView: View {
   var body: some View {
      Image(systemName: "envelope")
         .font(Font.system(size: 100).weight(.semibold))
   }
}
```

Listing 5-49: *Styling a symbol*

In the example of Listing 5-49, we apply the `font()` modifier with the system font, a size of 100 points, and a weight of type **semibold**. Notice that we declare the modifiers all in one line, but we could have defined the `Font` in a constant and use that constant to apply it to the `Image` view, as in the following example.

```
struct ContentView: View {
   let myfont = Font.system(size: 100)

   var body: some View {
      Image(systemName: "envelope")
         .font(myfont.weight(.semibold))
   }
}
```

Listing 5-50: *Storing the font in a constant*

The code in Listing 5-50 initializes a `Font` structure with the system's font and a size of 100, and then modifies an `Image` view with this font and a weight of type **semibold**. This is the same as before, but makes our code easier to read.

No matter how our code is organized, the view always shows the symbol of an envelope on the screen.

Figure 5-71: *SF Symbol*

SF Symbols come in different versions. For instance, the symbol with the name "envelope" implemented in our example has a version with a circle around it, another with a badge, and more. These are called *Variants* and are specified after the symbol's name using dot notation, as in envelope.circle, or envelope.fill. All the variants of a symbol can be found in the SF Symbol application, but the framework also includes the following modifier to specify a variant.

symbolVariant(SymbolVariants**)**—This modifier assigns a variant to a symbol. The argument is a structure with the type properties **none**, **circle**, **square**, **rectangle**, **fill**, and **slash**.

The image is created as before, but now the modifier determines the symbol's variant.

```
struct ContentView: View {
    var body: some View {
        Image(systemName: "envelope")
            .font(Font.system(size: 100))
            .symbolVariant(.fill)
    }
}
```

Listing 5-51: Assigning a variant to a symbol

This is the same as creating the **Image** view with the "envelope.fill" string, but selecting the variant from a modifier allows us to modify the symbol and animate the changes according to changes in the state of the view, as we will see later.

Figure 5-72: A variant of an SF Symbol

SF Symbols are displayed in the color and size of the font, but some symbols can include up to three more colors, and all of them can be scaled up or down. SwiftUI includes the following modifiers for this purpose.

symbolRenderingMode(SymbolRenderingMode**)**—This modifier sets the symbol's rendering mode. The argument is a structure with the type properties **hierarchical**, **monochrome** (default), **multicolor**, and **palette**.

imageScale(Scale**)**—This modifier sets the symbol's scale. The size is determined from the size of the font and the scale specified by the attribute. The attribute is an enumeration with the values **small**, **medium**, and **large**.

The **symbolRenderingMode()** modifier can set four different color modes. By default, the **monochrome** mode is selected, which means that the symbol is displayed in only one color (the color of the font or the view), but there are others available. The **hierarchical** mode defines a set of colors from a base color, the **multicolor** mode shows the symbol with its original colors, and the **palette** mode shows the symbol with custom colors.

Not all the symbols are multicolor. We can find multicolor symbols by selecting the Multicolor category in the SF Symbol app. For instance, in the following example we show the mic.badge.plus, which has two colors.

```
struct ContentView: View {
    var body: some View {
        Image(systemName: "mic.badge.plus")
            .font(Font.system(size: 100))
            .symbolRenderingMode(.multicolor)
    }
}
```

Listing 5-52: Displaying multicolor symbols

Figure 5-73: Multicolor symbol

The microphone is displayed with the color by default (the font color or the foreground color assigned to the view), and the badge is green. These are the symbol's original colors, but we can change them by specifying the **hierarchical** or **palette** modes. The colors for these modes are specified by the **foregroundStyle()** modifier, as in the following example.

```
struct ContentView: View {
    var body: some View {
        Image(systemName: "mic.badge.plus")
            .font(Font.system(size: 100))
            .symbolRenderingMode(.palette)
            .foregroundStyle(.red, .blue)
    }
}
```

Listing 5-53: Displaying a multicolor symbol with custom colors

The colors are declared with the **foregroundStyle()** modifier separated by comma. In this example, the symbol requires two colors, one for the microphone and another for the badge, but some symbols may use more. The result is shown below.

Figure 5-74: Multicolor symbol with custom colors

Some SF Symbols can have variable colors to represent different states. For instance, some symbols include graphics resembling radio waves that change color to represent different signal levels. To implement these symbols, we must initialize the **Image** view with the **variableValue** argument. The value of this argument determines the variety of the symbol to be shown. The value required to jump from one state to another depends on the number of states the symbol can take. In the following example, we display a symbol with 5 states.

```
struct ContentView: View {
    var body: some View {
        Image(systemName: "dot.radiowaves.forward", variableValue: 0.8)
            .font(.largeTitle)
    }
}
```

Listing 5-54: Displaying a variable SF Symbol

The value of the **variableValue** argument must be below the threshold for each state. The symbol implemented in the view of Listing 5-54 have 5 states and therefore we just have to find a value that is below the threshold for the state we want to display. The following Figure shows possible values for this symbol and all the states it can take.

Chapter 5 - SwiftUI Framework

| 0.0 | 0.2 | 0.4 | 0.6 | 0.8 |

Figure 5-75: *Variable SF Symbol*

Although we can combine `Text` views with symbols to build the interface, as we will see later, SwiftUI includes a view called `Label` to show a text along with an image. This is specially useful with SF Symbols because they can automatically adapt to the size and style of the text. The structure includes the following initializers and modifier to create these views.

Label(String, **systemImage:** String)—This initializer creates a label with the text specified by the first attribute and the SF Symbol specified by the **systemImage** attribute.

Label(String, **image:** String)—This initializer creates a label with the text specified by the first attribute and the image specified by the **image** attribute.

labelStyle(LabelStyle)—This modifier configures the label. The argument is a structure that conforms to the **LabelStyle** protocol, which defines type properties to tell the label what to include. The properties available are **automatic** (default), **iconOnly**, **titleAndIcon**, and **titleOnly**.

A `Label` view determines the text and the image to be shown, but we can use the `font()` modifier to specify the characteristics of the font, as shown next.

```
struct ContentView: View {
    var body: some View {
        Label("Hello", systemImage: "envelope.circle")
            .font(.largeTitle)
            .labelStyle(.titleAndIcon)
            .imageScale(.large)
    }
}
```

Listing 5-55: *Displaying a text with an SF Symbol*

Notice that in this example we implement the `imageScale()` modifier to make the symbol slightly larger than the text. The result is shown below.

Figure 5-76: *Label with an SF Symbol*

Basic Event Modifiers

Besides the modifiers to change the styles and format of the views, SwiftUI includes modifiers to respond to events. These events can be produced by the user, such as when the user touches the screen with a finger, or by the system, such as when information is received from the network. There are multiple modifiers available to process events, some are generic, others more specific. For instance, the `View` protocol defines the following modifiers to perform a task when a view appears or disappears from the screen.

onAppear(perform: Closure)—This modifier executes the closure specified by the **perform** argument when the view appears on the screen.

onDisappear(perform: Closure)—This modifier executes the closure specified by the **perform** argument when the view disappears from the screen.

These modifiers are applied like any other, but unlike the rest, they are executed when the system detects the event to which they respond. For instance, in the following example we print a message on the console with the **onAppear()** modifier, but the text is not printed until the view appears on the screen.

```
struct ContentView: View {
    let fontSize: CGFloat = 100

    var body: some View {
        Image(systemName: "envelope.circle")
            .font(Font.system(size: fontSize))
            .onAppear(perform: {
                print("Current font size: \(self.fontSize)")
            })
    }
}
```

Listing 5-56: Performing a task when the view appears

The code in Listing 5-56 prints a message on the console with the value of a constant used to determine the size of the font. It is not a practical example, but it shows how to implement these modifiers. Besides the **onAppear()** and **onDisappear()** modifiers, SwiftUI includes others to process gestures, like the **onTapGesture()** modifier used to detect a tap on the view, and others even more specific, like the **onReceive()** modifier used to receive data emitted by a publisher, but all of them work in a similar way; they perform a task when the event is detected by the system. We will see more practical examples of the **onAppear()** modifier and work with other event modifiers in later chapters.

Medium Custom Modifiers

Interfaces with single views, like those we have created so far, are the exception. User interfaces are created from the combination of multiple views. This means that more often than not we will find ourselves applying the same modifiers over and over again. In cases like this, we can avoid repetition by implementing custom modifiers. Custom modifiers encapsulate multiple modifiers in a single structure that we can apply later to the views with the **modifier()** modifier. The structure must conform to the **ViewModifier** protocol and implement a method called **body** that receives a parameter of type **Content**. The parameter represents the views we want to modify and, therefore, it is to this parameter that we apply the actual modifiers, as shown next.

```
import SwiftUI

struct MyModifiers: ViewModifier {
    func body(content: Content) -> some View {
        content
            .font(Font.system(size: 100).weight(.semibold))
            .foregroundColor(Color.blue)
    }
}
```

```
struct ContentView: View {
   var body: some View {
      Image(systemName: "envelope.circle")
         .modifier(MyModifiers())
   }
}
```

Listing 5-57: Applying custom modifiers

In this example, we define a structure that conforms to the **ViewModifier** protocol and then apply the **font()** and **foregroundColor()** modifiers to the **content** parameter of the **body** method. This defines a custom modifier called **MyModifiers** that then we can apply to the views in our interface. The result is the same as applying the modifiers directly to the views, but it makes our code less repetitive.

Figure 5-77: Custom modifiers applied to a view

As any other structure, the **ViewModifier** structure can include properties, and those properties may get different values every time the modifier is applied. For instance, we can include a property to store a **CGFloat** value, so every time the custom modifier is applied, we can select the size to be assigned to the font.

```
struct MyModifiers: ViewModifier {
   var size: CGFloat

   init(size: CGFloat) {
      self.size = size
   }
   func body(content: Content) -> some View {
      content
         .font(Font.system(size: size).weight(.semibold))
         .foregroundColor(Color.blue)
   }
}
struct ContentView: View {
   var body: some View {
      Image(systemName: "envelope.circle")
         .modifier(MyModifiers(size: 50))
   }
}
```

Listing 5-58: Customizing a custom modifier

(Basic) **5.3 Layout**

The closure assigned to the **body** property must return only one view. We haven't had any issues so far because all our examples have returned only a **Text** view or an **Image** view, but a useful user interface requires the implementation of multiple views. Some work as containers, others display content, and there are several views designed to process user input. Therefore, to create the interface, we must be able to group multiple views in one single view and arrange them on the screen. The solution proposed by SwiftUI is to work with stacks.

Views can be arranged in three different ways: horizontally, vertically, or overlapping. SwiftUI defines the following views to create these stacks.

VStack(alignment: HorizontalAlignment, **spacing:** CGFloat?, **content:** Closure)—This view creates a vertical stack to arrange a group of views vertically. The **alignment** argument determines the horizontal alignment of the views. It is a structure with the type properties **center**, **leading**, and **trailing**. The **spacing** argument determines the space between the views, and the **content** argument is a closure that defines the list of views we want to show in the stack.

HStack(alignment: VerticalAlignment, **spacing:** CGFloat?, **content:** Closure) —This view creates a horizontal stack to arrange a group of views horizontally. The **alignment** argument determines the vertical alignment of the views. It is a structure with the type properties **bottom**, **center**, **firstTextBaseline**, **lastTextBaseline**, and **top**. The **spacing** argument determines the space between the views, and the **content** argument is a closure that defines the list of views we want to show in the stack.

ZStack(alignment: Alignment, **content:** Closure)—This view creates a stack that overlays a group of views. The **alignment** argument determines the horizontal and vertical alignment of the views. It is a structure with the type properties **bottom**, **bottomLeading**, **bottomTrailing**, **center**, **leading**, **top**, **topLeading**, **topTrailing**, and **trailing**. The **content** argument is a closure that defines the list of views we want to show in the stack.

Stacks are created with values by default. For instance, a **VStack** aligns its views to the center and with a standard space in between. If that's all we need, we just have to declare its content.

```
struct ContentView: View {
    var body: some View {
        VStack {
            Text("City")
            Text("New York")
        }
    }
}
```

Listing 5-59: Creating a vertical stack of views

The closure assigned to the **content** argument is a **Content** closure. **Content** closures are processed by a property wrapper called **@ViewBuilder** which job is to construct views from closures. This means that all we need to do to create the content of a stack is to list the views one after another, and the compiler takes care of creating the code to present them on the screen in that same order. (We will learn more about property wrappers in the next chapter.)

In the example of Listing 5-59, we included two **Text** views inside a **VStack** view. The **Text** views take the size of their content and are displayed one on top of the other, and the **VStack** view takes the width of its largest child and the height from the sum of the heights of its children.

City
New York

Figure 5-78: Vertical stack

By default, the views inside a **VStack** are aligned to the center, but we can change that with the **alignment** argument. In addition to **center**, the argument can take the values **leading** and **trailing**, which mean left and right when the device is configured with a left-to-right language like English.

```
struct ContentView: View {
   var body: some View {
      VStack(alignment: .leading) {
         Text("City")
         Text("New York")
      }
   }
}
```
Listing 5-60: Aligning views in a vertical stack

Another value defined by default is the space between the views. If we don't specify any value, the views are placed on top of each other with no space in between. There are multiple ways to include a space between the views. One is with the **padding()** modifier introduced before. But if the stack contains multiple views, we will have to assign the modifier to each one of them. An easier way to do this is to declare the **spacing** argument, as in the following example.

```
struct ContentView: View {
   var body: some View {
      VStack(alignment: .leading, spacing: 20) {
         Text("City")
         Text("New York")
      }
   }
}
```
Listing 5-61: Adding a space between the views

The space is added only between the views, not at the top or the bottom. The purpose is to separate the views, as shown below.

Figure 5-79: Vertical stack aligned to the left with a space of 20 points in between

The **HStack** view works in a similar way. The views are declared on a list, one after another, and the compiler takes care of creating the code to display them side by side.

```
struct ContentView: View {
   var body: some View {
      HStack {
         Image(systemName: "cloud")
            .font(.system(size: 80))
         Text("New York")
      }
   }
}
```
Listing 5-62: Creating a horizontal stack of views

By default, the views in a horizontal stack are aligned to the center and positioned with a standard space in between (usually 8 points).

Figure 5-80: *Horizontal stack aligned to the center*

An **HStack** view includes the same arguments as a **VStack** for alignment and spacing, but the **alignment** argument specifies the vertical alignment. This is useful when the stack is composed of views of different heights, as in our example. The height of the stack is determined by the height of its tallest view and the rest of the views are aligned according to the argument's value. Figure 5-81, below, shows all the possible vertical alignments. In this example, we reduced the width of the stack to force the **Text** view to display the text in two lines, which allows us to show how the **firstTextBaseline** and the **lastTextBaseline** alignments work.

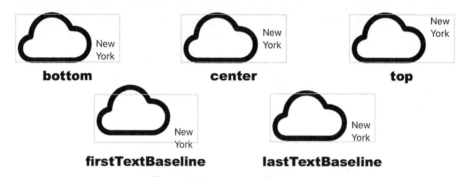

Figure 5-81: HStack *alignments*

Besides the vertical and horizontal stacks, SwiftUI also provides the **ZStack** view to overlay the views. The views appear on the screen in front of each other in the same order they are declared in the stack.

```
struct ContentView: View {
    var body: some View {
        ZStack(alignment: .center) {
            Image(systemName: "cloud")
                .font(.system(size: 80))
            Text("New York")
                .font(.body.bold())
                .foregroundColor(.gray)
        }
    }
}
```

Listing 5-63: *Creating a* ZStack

Figure 5-82: *Views in a* ZStack

Chapter 5 - SwiftUI Framework

If we ignore the **alignment** argument, the views are aligned to the center, but there are other alignments available. The values are `bottom`, `bottomLeading`, `bottomTrailing`, `center`, `leading`, `top`, `topLeading`, `topTrailing`, and `trailing`.

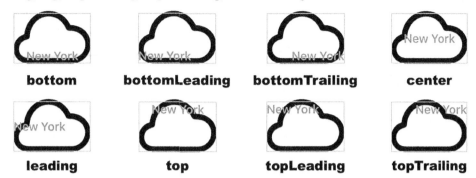

Figure 5-83: ZStack alignments

When views overlap, like those included in a **ZStack** view, the system determines the order in which they appear on the screen from the order in the code. The first view is drawn first, then the second view is drawn in front of it, and so on. The **View** protocol defines the following modifier to change this order.

zIndex(Double)—This modifier sets the order of the view in the Z axis (the axis perpendicular to the screen).

By default, all the views are assigned the index 0, which means they are all at the same level, and that is why the system draws the views according to the order in which they are declared in the code, but we can move a view to the back by assigning a negative Z index or to the front with a value greater than 0. When views have different indexes, they are drawn in the order determined by those values, starting from the view with the smallest index. In the following example, we include the same **Image** view and **Text** view used before, but because we set an index of -1 for the **Text** view, it is drawn in the back.

```
struct ContentView: View {
    var body: some View {
        ZStack {
            Image(systemName: "cloud")
                .font(.system(size: 80))
            Text("New York")
                .padding(8)
                .background(Color.yellow)
                .zIndex(-1)
        }
    }
}
```

Listing 5-64: Setting the Z index of a view

The **Text** view in Listing 5-64 includes a yellow background, so we can see its position in the Z axis. The **Image** view should be drawn first, and then the **Text** view should cover most of the image, but because we set an index of -1 for the **Text** view, it is drawn in the back.

Figure 5-84: Custom Z index

When we group views with a stack, we can apply modifiers to all the views at the same time by assigning the modifiers to the stack instead of the individual views. For instance, if we want to assign the same color to the **Text** view and the **Image** view of the previous example, we can apply the **foregroundColor()** modifier to the **ZStack** view.

```
struct ContentView: View {
    var body: some View {
        ZStack(alignment: .center) {
            Image(systemName: "cloud")
                .font(.system(size: 80))
            Text("New York")
                .font(.body.bold())
        }.foregroundColor(Color.red)
    }
}
```

Listing 5-65: Assigning modifiers to the stack and its content

Figure 5-85: Modifier applied to container

Stacks can be combined and nested as required by the interface. For instance, we can incorporate a **VStack** inside the previous **HStack** to include more text next to the image.

```
struct ContentView: View {
    var body: some View {
        HStack {
            Image(systemName: "cloud")
                .font(.system(size: 80))
            VStack(alignment: .leading) {
                Text("City")
                    .foregroundColor(.gray)
                Text("New York")
                    .font(.title)
            }
        }
    }
}
```

Listing 5-66: Nesting stacks

The code in Listing 5-66 defines a **Vstack** view inside an **HStack** view. The **VStack** includes two **Text** views aligned to the left and with different styles.

Figure 5-86: Nested stacks

Chapter 5 - SwiftUI Framework

IMPORTANT: When you decide to include a view in a stack, you can write the code yourself or get Xcode to do it for you by selecting the option from the context menu. We used this menu before to add modifiers to a `Text` view (Figure 5-23). If you press the Command key and click on the view, the context menu appears with the options to embed the view in a stack.

The alignment options available for `VStack` and `HStack` views align the views in the perpendicular axis. A vertical stack can align the views horizontally, and a horizontal stack can align the views vertically. To align the views on the same axis, we must add a flexible space. SwiftUI includes the `Spacer` view for this purpose.

Spacer(minLength: CGFloat)—This initializer creates a `Spacer` view that generates a flexible space. The **minLength** argument determines the minimum size in points the space can take. If the argument is not declared, the minimum length is 0.

A `Spacer` view can be implemented any time we need to add a flexible space. It provides a more customizable way to align the views or extend them to the sides of its container. For instance, in the following example we add a flexible space between the image and the `VStack` of our view to move the views to the left and right side of their container.

```
struct ContentView: View {
    var body: some View {
        HStack {
            Image(systemName: "cloud")
                .font(.system(size: 80))
            Spacer()
            VStack(alignment: .leading) {
                Text("City")
                    .foregroundColor(.gray)
                Text("New York")
                    .font(.title)
            }
        }
    }
}
```

Listing 5-67: Aligning the views with a flexible space

The system calculates the widths of the image and the stack, and then assigns the rest of the space available to the `Spacer` view in the middle.

Figure 5-87: Flexible space between views

A `Spacer` view can be positioned anywhere on the list, not only between views. This is useful when we want the views to be at the top or the bottom of the screen. For instance, we can embed the `HStack` of previous examples in a `VStack` and add a `Spacer` at the bottom to move our views to the top of the screen.

```
struct ContentView: View {
    var body: some View {
        VStack {
            HStack {
                Image(systemName: "cloud")
                    .font(.system(size: 80))
                VStack(alignment: .leading) {
                    Text("City")
                        .foregroundColor(.gray)
                    Text("New York")
                        .font(.title)
                }
                Spacer()
            }
            Spacer()
        }
    }
}
```

Listing 5-68: Aligning the views to the left and the top

In this example, we use two **Spacer** views, one at the end of the **HStack** to move the views to the left, and another at the end of the main **VStack** to move the **HStack** to the top. This **Spacer** view takes all the space available at the bottom, moving the rest of the views up.

Figure 5-88: Views at the top of the screen

(Basic) Safe Area

The system defines a layout guide called *Safe Area* where we can place the content of our interface. This is the area determined by the space remaining in the window after all the toolbars and special views are displayed by the system (including the notch at the top of modern iPhones). That's the reason why there is a space between the view of our previous example and the top of the screen (see Figure 5-88). The white bar at the top is the space occupied by the system's toolbar. Although it is recommended to always build the interface inside the safe area, the **View** protocol provides the following modifier to ignore it.

ignoresSafeArea(SafeAreaRegions, **edges:** Edge**)**—This modifier expands the view outside the safe area. The first argument determines the safe areas that are ignored. It is a structure with the type properties **all**, **container**, and **keyboard**. The **edges** argument is a value or a set of values that indicates the sides to be ignored. This is an enumeration with the values **all**, **bottom**, **leading**, **top**, and **trailing**.

There are two safe areas, one called **container** that determines the space available inside the window after all the navigation bars and toolbars are displayed, and another called **keyboard** that determines the remaining space after the virtual keyboard becomes visible.

Chapter 5 - SwiftUI Framework

Figure 5-89: Safe areas

For instance, if we want the interface of our previous example to always extend to the edges of the screen, we can apply the modifier to the **VStack** view with the value **all**.

```
struct ContentView: View {
    var body: some View {
        VStack {
            HStack {
                Image(systemName: "cloud")
                    .font(.system(size: 80))
                VStack(alignment: .leading) {
                    Text("City")
                        .foregroundColor(.gray)
                    Text("New York")
                        .font(.title)
                }
                Spacer()
            }
            Spacer()
        }.ignoresSafeArea(.all)
    }
}
```

Listing 5-69: Ignoring the safe area

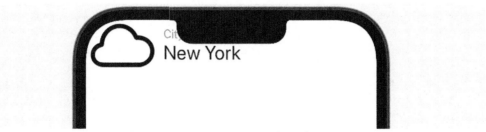

Figure 5-90: Views ignoring the safe area

In this example, we ignore all the safe areas and, therefore, our views extend to the edges of the screen, but we can ignore only the container safe area but not the keyboard, so when the virtual keyboard opens, it doesn't overlap the views.

```
struct ContentView: View {
    var body: some View {
        VStack {
            Spacer()
            HStack {
                Image(systemName: "cloud")
                    .font(.system(size: 80))
                VStack(alignment: .leading) {
                    Text("City")
                        .foregroundColor(.gray)
                    Text("New York")
                        .font(.title)
                }
                Spacer()
            }
        }.ignoresSafeArea(.container, edges: .bottom)
    }
}
```

Listing 5-70: Ignoring only the container safe area at the bottom

in this example, we move the `Spacer` view to the top of the vertical stack to push the content down. We ignore the safe area again, so the content is placed right at the bottom of the screen, but because we ignore only the `container` safe area at the bottom, if later we add an element that opens the keyboard, the views will move up to remain visible.

Figure 5-91: Views at the bottom of the screen

SwiftUI includes a modifier to expand the safe area. The modifier changes the safe area inset to include additional space.

safeAreaInset(edge: Axis, **alignment:** Alignment, **spacing:** CGFloat?, **content:** Closure)—This modifier expands the safe area with a custom view. The **edge** argument determines the side we want to modify. It is specified with the values `leading` and `trailing`, provided by the `HorizontalEdge` enumeration, or the values `bottom` and `top`, provided by the `VerticalEdge` enumeration. The **alignment** argument determines the alignment of the views inside the area. It is specified with the type properties `center`, `leading`, and `trailing`, provided by the `HorizontalAlignment` structure, or the type properties `bottom`, `center`, `firstTextBaseline`, `lastText-Baseline`, and `top`, provided by the `VerticalAlignment` structure. The **spacing** argument determines the space between the views inside the area. And finally, the **content** argument is a closure that returns the views to show inside the area.

This modifier may be used to make sure that important views at the edge of the screen are always visible, or to create our own navigation bars, as shown next.

```
struct ContentView: View {
    var body: some View {
        VStack {
            Spacer()
            HStack {
                Image(systemName: "cloud")
                    .font(.system(size: 80))
                VStack(alignment: .leading) {
                    Text("City")
                        .foregroundColor(.gray)
                    Text("New York")
                        .font(.title)
                }
                Spacer()
            }
        }
        .safeAreaInset(edge: .bottom, content: {
            HStack {
                Spacer()
                Text("Important")
                    .padding()
                Spacer()
            }.background(.yellow)
        })
    }
}
```

Listing 5-71: *Expanding the safe area*

In this example, we add an **HStack** view at the bottom of the safe area. This creates a yellow bar at the bottom of the screen with the text "Important", but because this view is part of the safe area, the rest of the content is shown on top.

Figure 5-92: *Views expanding the safe area*

Medium **Priorities**

Stacks divide the space equally among the views, but we must decide what to do when there is not enough room to show them all. By default, the system assigns a fixed size to images and reduces the size of **Text** views to make them fit, as shown next.

```
struct ContentView: View {
    var body: some View {
        HStack {
            Text("Manchester")
                .font(.title)
                .lineLimit(1)
            Image(systemName: "cloud")
                .font(.system(size: 80))
```

```
                Text("New York")
                    .font(.title)
                    .lineLimit(1)
            }
        }
    }
```

This example creates an **HStack** with three views: a text, an image, and another text. In an iPhone SE in portrait mode, where there is no room to display them all, the system preserves the image's original size but compresses the **Text** views to make them fit in the remaining space.

Figure 5-93: Priorities by default

Because the **Text** views are limited to only one line, the system truncates the texts. If what we want is to show one of the texts in full, we must assign a higher priority to it. The **View** protocol defines the following modifiers for this purpose.

layoutPriority(Double**)**—This modifier sets the view's priority. A higher priority determines that the view will get as much space as possible. The value by default is 0.

fixedSize(horizontal: Bool, **vertical:** Bool**)**—This modifier fixes the view to its ideal horizontal or vertical size. If no arguments are specified, the size is fixed on both dimensions.

All the views have a priority of 0 by default. If we want the system to reserve more space for a view, we must declare its priority higher than 0, as in the following example.

```
struct ContentView: View {
    var body: some View {
        HStack {
            Text("Manchester")
                .font(.title)
                .lineLimit(1)
            Image(systemName: "cloud")
                .font(.system(size: 80))
            Text("New York")
                .font(.title)
                .lineLimit(1)
                .layoutPriority(1)
        }
    }
}
```

The code in Listing 5-73 assigns a priority of 1 to the second **Text** view. Now the system calculates the space required by this view first and therefore the "New York" text is shown in full.

Figure 5-94: Custom priorities

Chapter 5 - SwiftUI Framework

When we assign a higher priority to a view and there is no space to show them all, the system lays out the views with lower priority first, gives them the minimum possible size, and then assigns the remaining space to the view with the higher priority. So, if there is still no room to show the entire view, its content is clipped. If what we want is to force the view to take the size of its content no matter what, we must apply the **fixedSize()** modifier.

```
struct ContentView: View {
    var body: some View {
        HStack {
            Text("Manchester")
                .font(.title)
                .lineLimit(1)
                .fixedSize()
            Image(systemName: "cloud")
                .font(.system(size: 80))
            Text("New York")
                .font(.title)
                .lineLimit(1)
                .layoutPriority(1)
        }
    }
}
```

Listing 5-74: Defining a view with a fixed size

This is the same code as before, but now we assign the **fixedSize()** modifier to the first **Text** view. In consequence, this view is going to adopt the size of its content and the "Manchester" text will be shown in full, regardless of the priority of the rest of the views.

Figure 5-95: View with a fixed size

(Medium) Alignment Guides

There are two possible alignments, horizontal and vertical. Horizontal stacks align the views vertically and vertical stacks align the views horizontally. This is because SwiftUI expects the views in the stack to be of different sizes and therefore it needs to know how they are going to be aligned in the perpendicular axis. Usually, this is enough to build a simple interface, but professional applications require more control. The **View** protocol defines the following modifiers to customize alignment.

alignmentGuide(Alignment, **computeValue:** Closure)—This modifier defines the values of the horizontal or vertical alignment. The first argument determines the type of alignment we want to customize. It is defined with the type properties **center**, **leading**, and **trailing** from the **HorizontalAlignment** structure, or the type properties **bottom**, **center**, **firstTextBaseline**, **lastTextBaseline**, and **top** from the **VerticalAlignment** structure. The **computeValue** argument is a closure that receives the current dimensions of the view and returns a **CGFloat** with the new value for the alignment.

The following example aligns three images of different sizes. They are all 100 points wide, but the signbus image is 200 points tall, the signplane image is 170 points tall, and the signphone image is 220 points tall. (The images are available on our website.)

```
struct ContentView: View {
    var body: some View {
        HStack(alignment: .center) {
            Image("signbus")
            Image("signplane")
            Image("signphone")
        }.border(Color.blue, width: 2)
    }
}
```

Listing 5-75: Aligning images to the center with standard values

A stack view determines a common point of alignment according to its alignment type and the dimensions of the views. For instance, if the alignment of a vertical stack is **center**, the stack gets the position of the **center** alignment of each view and from that value it calculates a common point of alignment (usually the point of alignment of its tallest view) and then repositions all the views to match that common point.

Figure 5-96: Images aligned to the center

Figure 5-96 shows our three images aligned to the center. In this example, we applied a blue border to the stack to make it easy to see the changes produced by the alignment and added a red line on top of the picture to visualize the common point of alignment chose by the stack.

 Do It Yourself: Download the signbus, signplane and signphone images from our website and add them to the Asset Catalog. Update the **ContentView** view with the code in Listing 5-75. You should see something similar to Figure 5-96.

The alignment values are determined by the stack's coordinates system, starting from the top-left corner. The value at the top is 0 and the value at the bottom of the view depends on the children's height. Every view has an alignment guide with values that determine their points of alignment. The value associated with the **top** alignment is 0, the value associated with the **bottom** alignment is equal to the view's height, and the value associated with the **center** alignment is the height divided by two (the formula is: **top** + (**bottom** - **top**) / 2).

The views return these alignment guides by default, but we can change them with the modifier introduced above. For instance, the wheels of the bus in our example are below the common point of alignment (see Figure 5-96, above). This image is 200 points tall, so the center alignment returned by the image is at 100 points, but the wheels are 18 points below.

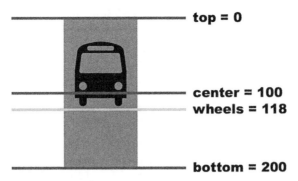

Figure 5-97: *Alignment guides for the bus*

As illustrated in Figure 5-97, the **center** alignment by default for the bus is 100 points (half its height), but the wheels are positioned at 118 points. If we want to center the image at this point, we must add 18 points to the image's natural center, as shown next.

```
struct ContentView: View {
    var body: some View {
        HStack(alignment: .center) {
            Image("signbus")
                .alignmentGuide(VerticalAlignment.center, computeValue:
{ dimension in
                    return dimension[VerticalAlignment.center] + 18
                })
            Image("signplane")
            Image("signphone")
        }.border(Color.blue, width: 2)
    }
}
```

Listing 5-76: *Aligning an image to the center with custom values*

The **alignmentGuide()** modifier requires two values. The first one is a value that represents the type of alignment we want to modify. In this case, we are aligning the views to the center, so we modify the **VerticalAlignment.center** type. The second value is a closure that must return the new value for this type of alignment. The closure receives a value of type **ViewDimensions**. This is a structure with two properties, **width** and **height**, to return the current width and height of the image, and also includes the definition of a subscript, which allows us to get the values for each alignment guide using square brackets and the alignment as the key. In the example of Listing 5-76, we get the current value of the **VerticalAlignment.center** key for the view, add 18 to it and return the result. From that moment on, the **center** alignment for this view will return 118 instead of 100, so the view is aligned 18 points higher.

Figure 5-98: *Bus aligned with custom values*

If we want to align all the images by the bottom of the graphic, we must modify the alignment guide for each **Image** view.

```
struct ContentView: View {
    var body: some View {
        HStack(alignment: .center) {
            Image("signbus")
                .alignmentGuide(VerticalAlignment.center) { dimension in
                    dimension[VerticalAlignment.center] + 18 }
            Image("signplane")
                .alignmentGuide(VerticalAlignment.center) { dimension in
                    dimension[VerticalAlignment.center] + 68 }
            Image("signphone")
                .alignmentGuide(VerticalAlignment.center) { dimension in
                    dimension[VerticalAlignment.center] + 89 }
        }.border(Color.blue, width: 2)
    }
}
```

Listing 5-77: Aligning all images to the center with custom values

The code in Listing 5-77 declares the closures as trailing closures and omits the **return** keyword to simplify the code, but the process is the same. The image of the bus is 200 points tall, its default center is at 100 points, but the base of the bus is at 118 points, so we add 18 points to the current center alignment (118 - 100). The image of the plane is 170 points tall, its default center is at 85 points, but the base of the plane is at 153 points, so we add 68 points to the current center alignment (153 - 85). And we do the same for the phone. The image is 220 points tall, its default center is at 110 points, but the base of the phone is at 199 points, so we add 89 points to the current center alignment (199 - 110). As a result, we get all the images aligned by the graphic's baseline.

Figure 5-99: Images aligned by the baselines

So far, we have modified the alignment guides of views that belong to the same stack. If our interface requires us to align views from different containers (stacks), we must define custom alignment types. Custom alignment types are defined as extensions of the alignment structures (**VerticalAlignment** and **HorizontalAlignment**). We worked with extensions before in Chapter 3. They add functionality to an existing data type (see Listing 3-180). In this case, we need an extension to add a custom alignment guide. For this purpose, the extension must include an enumeration that conforms to the **AlignmentID** protocol, which requires the implementation of a method called **defaultValue** to return the alignment's default value. The extension must also include a type property which sole purpose is to simplify the declaration of the alignment, as shown in the following example.

```
import SwiftUI

extension VerticalAlignment {
   enum BusAlignment: AlignmentID {
      static func defaultValue(in dimension: ViewDimensions) -> CGFloat {
         return dimension[VerticalAlignment.center]
      }
   }
   static let alignBus = VerticalAlignment(BusAlignment.self)
}
struct ContentView: View {
   var body: some View {
      HStack(alignment: .alignBus) {
         VStack {
            Image("signbus")
         }
         VStack(alignment: .leading) {
            Text("Transportation")
            Text("Bus")
               .font(.largeTitle)
         }
      }.border(Color.blue, width: 2)
   }
}
```

Listing 5-78: Defining custom alignment guides

This code defines an extension for the **VerticalAlignment** structure. We call the enumeration **BusAlignment** because we use it to align the image of the bus. Its default value was defined as the current value of the **center** alignment. After this, we define a type property called **alignBus** that returns an alignment of this type. Notice that the value provided to the **VerticalAlignment**'s initializer is a reference to the definition of the **BusAlignment** enumeration, not an instance of it (see Listing 3-143).

Our **ContentView** view includes two **VStack** views embedded in an **HStack** view, one for the image of the bus and another with two **Text** views. The custom **alignBus** alignment defined at the beginning is assigned to the **HStack**, and therefore the **VStack** views are aligned to the center.

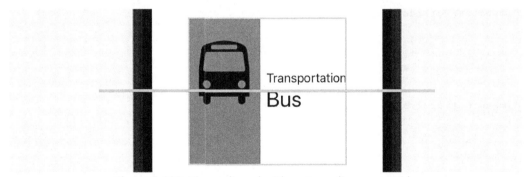

Figure 5-100: Views aligned with custom alignment guides

The red line drawn in front of the picture in Figure 5-100 shows the common point of alignment. The **HStack** calls the **defaultValue** method for each **VStack** view, gets in return the value of their current **center** alignment, and therefore it aligns the **VStack** views to the center.

Of course, we can change this alignment by modifying the alignment guides of the views. For instance, if we want to position the "Bus" text in line with the bus's window, we must move the

alignBus alignment for those views. The alignment for the bus image has to be at the center of the bus's window and the alignment for the text has to be at the center of the word.

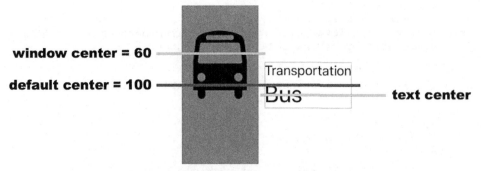

Figure 5-101: Alignments required for the views

The **center** alignment of the image of the bus is at the position 100, and the center of the bus's window is at the position 60, so to move the alignment point to the center of the window we must subtract 40 to this view's **center** alignment. For the text is simpler, we just have to return the value of the current **center** alignment, as in the following example.

```
import SwiftUI

extension VerticalAlignment {
   enum BusAlignment: AlignmentID {
      static func defaultValue(in dimension: ViewDimensions) -> CGFloat {
         return dimension[VerticalAlignment.center]
      }
   }
   static let alignBus = VerticalAlignment(BusAlignment.self)
}
struct ContentView: View {
   var body: some View {
      HStack(alignment: .alignBus) {
         VStack {
            Image("signbus")
               .alignmentGuide(.alignBus) { dimension in
dimension[VerticalAlignment.center] - 40 }
            }
            VStack(alignment: .leading) {
               Text("Transportation")
               Text("Bus")
                  .font(.largeTitle)
                  .alignmentGuide(.alignBus) { dimension in
dimension[VerticalAlignment.center] }
            }
      }.border(Color.blue, width: 2)
   }
}
```

Listing 5-79: Aligning views with custom alignment guides

The definition of the custom alignment is the same as before, but now we modify the values for each view we want to move with the **alignmentGuide()** modifier. The alignment for the image of the bus is moved 40 points up the center line, and the alignment for the **Text** view is moved to its center alignment, so we get the views right where we want them.

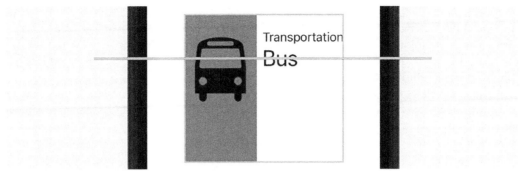

Figure 5-102: Views with a custom alignment

Groups

Stack views create a structure of type **TupleView** to organize their content. This structure can manage up to 10 views and therefore that's the maximum number of views a stack can contain. Although it is not common to find this issue in a professional application, if necessary, we can avoid it by using **Group** views.

Group(content: Closure)—This initializer creates a **Group** view that contains the views defined by the closure assigned to the argument.

The purpose of **Group** views is to group views together. We can use them to split large lists of views into groups of 10 or less to avoid the issue mentioned above, but also for other purposes, such as applying styles to several views at the same time, as in the following example.

```
struct ContentView: View {
    var body: some View {
        VStack {
            Group {
                Text("This is the list of")
                Text("Cities")
            }.foregroundColor(Color.gray)
            Group {
                Text("Manchester")
                Text("Viena")
            }.font(.largeTitle)
        }
    }
}
```

Listing 5-80: Arranging the views in groups

Each **Group** view defined in Listing 5-80 contains two **Text** views. To style these views, we apply modifiers to the **Group** views, not their content, so all the views within a group are affected by the same modifier.

Figure 5-103: Modifiers applied to groups of views

The closure assigned to the **body** property can only return one view, so the compiler is able to determine the data type of the view and process the value correctly. If we try to use an `if else` instruction to return different views depending on a condition, we will get an error. But we can use a **Group** view to solve this issue. The solution is to insert the conditional statement inside a **Group** view and return that view instead.

Usually, the views to show are selected depending on the current state. We will learn how to work with view states in the next chapter, but we can test it with a simple condition, as shown next.

```
struct ContentView: View {
    let valid = true

    var body: some View {
        Group {
            if valid {
                Image(systemName: "keyboard")
            } else {
                Text("The state is invalid")
            }
        }
    }
}
```

Listing 5-81: *Assigning different views to the* body *property*

This code defines a Boolean constant to select the view. If the constant is `true`, we show an **Image** view with an SF Symbol, otherwise, we show a **Text** view. Therefore, the view displayed on the screen is selected at run time, depending on the value of the **valid** constant, but because we embedded the views in a **Group** view, the compiler can identify the value returned and therefore the code is functional.

(Basic) Grids

We can embed one stack into another as many times as needed to achieve the design we are after, but SwiftUI defines an additional container view called **Grid** for this purpose. A **Grid** view can distribute static content in multiple rows and columns. The following is the view's initializer.

Grid(alignment: Alignment, **horizontalSpacing:** CGFloat, **verticalSpacing:** CGFloat, **content:** Closure)—This initializer creates a **Grid** view to define a grid-like layout. The **alignment** argument specifies the alignment of the content. It is a structure with the type properties `leading`, `center` (default), and `trailing`. The **horizontalSpacing** and **verticalSpacing** arguments define the space in points between cells. And the **content** argument provides the content for the grid.

The rows of the grid are defined by the `GridRow` structure.

GridRow(alignment: VerticalAlignment, **content:** Closure)—This initializer creates a row for a grid. The **alignment** argument specifies the vertical alignment of the content. It is a structure with the type properties `top`, `center`, `bottom`, `firstTextBaseline`, and `lastTextBaseline`. And the **content** argument provides the content for the row.

SwiftUI also includes the following modifiers to configure the rows.

gridCellColumns(Int**)**—This modifier specifies the number of columns the cell should occupy.

gridColumnAlignment(HorizontalAlignment**)**—This modifier overrides the horizontal alignment for a row. The argument is a structure with the type properties `leading`, `center`, and `trailing`.

gridCellUnsizedAxes(Axis**)**—This modifier returns a row that doesn't ask the grid for additional space in the axis specified by the argument. The argument is a structure with the type properties `horizontal` and `vertical`.

By default, the content of a grid is aligned to the center with a standard space between cells (usually 8 points). If that's what we want, all we need to do is to declare the grid's content. The rows are defined by `GridRow` structures and the columns are determined by the views inside these structures, as shown next.

```
struct ContentView: View {
    var body: some View {
        Grid {
            GridRow {
                Image(systemName: "message")
                    .frame(width: 100, height: 100)
                Image(systemName: "mic")
                    .frame(width: 100, height: 100)
            }.background(.red)
            GridRow {
                Image(systemName: "phone")
                    .frame(width: 100, height: 100)
                Image(systemName: "envelope")
                    .frame(width: 100, height: 100)
            }.background(.blue)
        }.font(.largeTitle)
    }
}
```

Listing 5-82: *Defining a grid layout*

This example creates a grid with two rows and two columns. The rows are defined by two `GridRow` structures and the columns by the views inside them. (In this case, two `Image` views per row.)

Figure 5-104: *Grid*

If we declare a different number of columns per row, the grid creates empty columns to fill the void. But we can also make a row occupy multiple columns with the `gridCellColumns()`, as in the following example.

```
struct ContentView: View {
    var body: some View {
        Grid(verticalSpacing: 5) {
```

```
        GridRow {
            Text("Send us a Message")
        }.gridCellColumns(2)
        GridRow {
            Image(systemName: "phone")
                .frame(width: 100, height: 100)
            Image(systemName: "envelope")
                .frame(width: 100, height: 100)
        }.background(.blue)
    }.font(.title2)
  }
}
```

Listing 5-83: Defining a multicolumn cell

In this example, the first row includes only one cell defined by a `Text` view, but because we apply the `gridCellColumns()` modifier with the value 2, the view occupies two columns.

Figure 5-105: Multicolumn cell

If what we want is for a cell to occupy two or more rows, we need to embed a grid within another grid, as shown next.

```
struct ContentView: View {
    var body: some View {
        Grid {
            GridRow {
                Image(systemName: "phone")
                    .frame(width: 100, height: 100)
                    .background(.blue)
                Grid(alignment: .leading) {
                    GridRow {
                        Text("My Name")
                    }
                    GridRow {
                        Text("My Number")
                    }
                }
            }
        }.font(.title2)
    }
}
```

Listing 5-84: Embedding a grid within another grid

In this example, the grid contains two columns, the one on the left with an image and the one on the right with another grid, which in turn contains two rows. Therefore, the two cells on the right share the same row with the cell on the left.

Figure 5-106: Multiple grids

(Basic) **Custom Views**

The code required to define the user interface can grow considerably as we build our application. When we reach a certain level of complexity, we must think about refactoring (reorganizing our code). The pattern proposed by SwiftUI involves breaking down the views into smaller pieces. For instance, we can define the second grid in our previous example as a separate view, so the code will be easier to read and maintain. One alternative is to extract the view. The option is available when we hold the Command key and click on the structure's name.

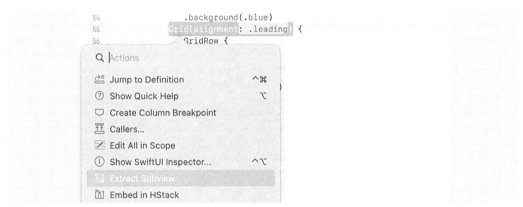

Figure 5-107: Extract Subview option

Once we select the Extract Subview option, a new view is created and placed at the bottom of the file. The view is assigned the name **ExtractedView**, but we can change it to one that better represents our view.

```
import SwiftUI

struct ContentView: View {
   var body: some View {
      Grid {
         GridRow {
            Image(systemName: "phone")
               .frame(width: 100, height: 100)
               .background(.blue)
            ExtractedView()
         }
      }.font(.title2)
   }
}
struct ExtractedView: View {
   var body: some View {
      Grid(alignment: .leading) {
```

```
            GridRow {
                Text("My Name")
            }
            GridRow {
                Text("My Number")
            }
        }
    }
}
```

Listing 5-85: Extracting views

The new view also conforms to the `View` protocol and implements the `body` property, as any other SwiftUI view. Once defined, we initialize it and the system takes care of creating the views and place them in the right location.

The views created with the Extract Subview option are defined in the same file, but in most cases it is better to move them to their own file. The option to create a new file is available from the File menu (File/New/File...) or by pressing Command + N. Xcode offers two templates to create Swift files, one for common Swift files, used to store Swift code, and another for SwiftUI views. We can find them in the iOS tab, under the names Swift File and SwiftUI View.

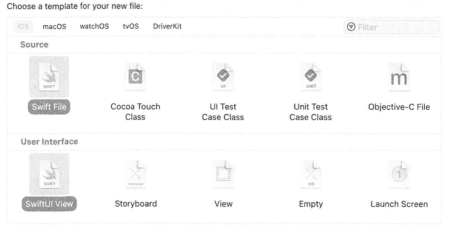

Figure 5-108: Swift files

Although they have different names, they are both Swift files and are created with the same extension (.swift). The only difference between the two is the code included by Xcode. A Swift file only includes an `import` statement for the `Foundation` framework, while a SwiftUI View file includes a `View` structure with a simple view inside and a `PreviewProvider` structure to create the preview on the canvas. The `View` structure takes the name assigned to the file. For instance, if we want to create a SwiftUI View file to store the `ExtractedView` structure from the previous example, we must call the file ExtractedView.swift, so Xcode creates the structures with the right name. (It is recommended to write the name in capital letters to match the structure's name.) Notice that if we store a view in a separate file, we must import the SwiftUI framework again or the SwiftUI views won't be recognized.

Medium Custom Layout

With stacks and grids we can organize our views as needed and create any structure we want, but there are times when the interface requires that unique touch that makes it special. For this purpose, SwiftUI includes custom layouts. Custom layouts allow us to specify the exact position of each view in a container. They are created with structures that conform to the `Layout` protocol. The following are the two methods required by the protocol.

sizeThatFits(proposal: ProposedViewSize, **subviews:** Subviews, **cache:** Cache)—This method is called on the layout structure when the system needs to know the size of the container view. The method must calculate the size and return a `CGSize` value with the container's width and height. The **proposal** argument is a structure that determines the proposed size for the container. The structure defines three type properties to return a proposal: `zero`, `infinity`, and `unspecified`. The **subviews** argument is a collection of structures that represent each view in the container. And the **cache** argument is a storage space to share the calculated values between methods.

placeSubviews(bounds: CGRect, **proposal:** ProposedViewSize, **subviews:** Subviews, **cache:** Cache)—This method is called on the layout structure when the system needs to know the position of each view inside the container. The **bounds** argument is the bounds of the container. The **proposal** argument is a structure that determines the proposed size for the container. The structure defines three type properties to return a proposal: `zero`, `infinity`, and `unspecified`. The **subviews** argument is a collection of structures that represent each view in the container. And the **cache** argument is a storage space to share the calculated values between methods.

The `sizeThatFits()` method receives a collection of `LayoutSubview` structures. This is a proxy between our code and the views we need to allocate inside the container. To provide information about the views, the `LayoutSubview` structure includes the following properties and methods.

spacing—This property returns a `ViewSpacing` structure with values that determine the space preferred by the view between itself and other views. The structure defines the `distance(to: ViewSpacing, along: Axis)` method to return a `CGFloat` value with the preferred spacing between two views.

priority—This property returns a `Double` value with the view's layout priority.

sizeThatFits(ProposedViewSize**)**—This method returns a `CGSize` value with the size of the view the structure represents. The argument is a structure that determines the proposed size we want to read. The structure defines three type properties to represent a proposal: `zero`, `infinity`, and `unspecified`.

dimensions(proposal: ProposedViewSize**)**—This method returns a `ViewDimensions` structure with the view's size and alignment guides. The **proposal** argument is a structure that determines the proposed size we want to read. The structure defines three type properties to represent a proposal: `zero`, `infinity`, and `unspecified`.

On the other hand, the `placeSubviews()` method is called in the layout structure when the system needs to know the position of each view within the container. This method receives similar values to allow us to calculate the right position for each view. To assign the position to the view, the `LayoutSubview` structure includes the following method.

place(at: CGPoint, **anchor:** UnitPoint, **proposal:** ProposedViewSize**)**—This method sets the position of the view. The **at** argument specifies the position in x and y coordinates. The **anchor** argument determines what point within the view is positioned at those coordinates. It is a structure returned by the type properties `bottom`, `bottomLeading`, `bottomTrailing`, `center`, `leading`, `top`, `topLeading` (default), `topTrailing`, `trailing`, and `zero`. And the **proposal** argument is the proposed size for which we want to set the position.

To define a custom layout, all we need to do is to define a structure that conforms to the `Layout` protocol and implement the protocol methods. In the `sizeThatFits()` method, we must use the size of each view to calculate the size of the container, and in the `placeSubviews()` method, we must calculate and assign the position of each view. The following example shows a possible implementation.

```
import SwiftUI

struct ContentView: View {
    var body: some View {
        MyLayout {
            Group {
                Text("First")
                    .padding(10)
                    .background(.red)
                    .cornerRadius(10)
                Text("Second")
                    .padding(10)
                    .background(.red)
                    .cornerRadius(10)
                Text("Third")
                    .padding(10)
                    .background(.red)
                    .cornerRadius(10)
            }.font(.title)
        }
    }
}
struct MyLayout: Layout {
    func sizeThatFits(proposal: ProposedViewSize, subviews: Subviews,
cache: inout ()) -> CGSize {
        var totalWidth: CGFloat = 0
        var totalHeight: CGFloat = 0

        for (index, view) in subviews.enumerated() {
            if index > 0 {
                totalHeight += 10
            }
            let viewSize = view.sizeThatFits(.unspecified)
            totalWidth += viewSize.width + CGFloat(30 * index)
            totalHeight += viewSize.height
        }
        return CGSize(width: totalWidth, height: totalHeight)
    }
    func placeSubviews(in bounds: CGRect, proposal: ProposedViewSize,
subviews: Subviews, cache: inout ()) {
        var posX: CGFloat = bounds.origin.x
        var posY: CGFloat = bounds.origin.y

        for (index, view) in subviews.enumerated() {
            if index > 0 {
                posY += 10
                posX += 30
            }
            view.place(at: CGPoint(x: posX, y: posY),
proposal: .unspecified)
            posY += view.sizeThatFits(.unspecified).height
        }
    }
}
```

Listing 5-86: Defining a custom layout

　　　　　　　　　　　　　　Chapter 5 - SwiftUI Framework

In this example, we define a layout structure called `MyLayout` and use it in the `ContentView` view to create the interface. The content of the layout structure must be embedded in a container view, such as a `Group` view or a `ForEach` view for dynamic lists. (We will learn how to implement the `ForEach` view in Chapter 7). In this case, we use a `Group` view to show three `Text` views, so the work of the layout structure is to determine the position of these three views.

We begin by calculating the size of the container from the `sizeThatFits()` method. For this purpose, we define two variables to store the width and height and then create a `for in` loop to get the size of each view and add it to the total. Because the views will be vertically separated by 10 points, we add this value to the `totalHeight` variable for the second and third views (when the view's index is greater than 0). Then, we get the view's size with the `sizeThatFits()` method and add the view's width and height to the total. To calculate the container's height, we add the height of each view, but for the width we add the width plus 30 points per view because we are going to displace each view 30 points to the right from the previous one. And finally, the total values are returned in a `CGSize` structure.

Notice that the `sizeThatFits()` method returns a proposed size. Views can take any size they want, but first they receive a proposal from the container, so we can calculate the size of the view according to the size proposed by the container. There are three types of proposals: `zero`, `infinity`, and `unspecified`. The `zero` proposal returns the minimum size the view can take (in our case, it is 20 by 20 points because of the padding), the `infinity` proposal returns the maximum size the view can take, and the `unspecified` proposal returns the view's ideal size (the size determined by the size of the content, padding, and border). In our example, we always returned the size we want for the `unspecified` proposal, but we can do it for each proposal by checking the value of the method's **proposal** argument.

In the `placeSubviews()` method, we must calculate the position of each view. The process is similar than before, we loop through the subviews collection and get the size of each view, but this time use it to calculate their positions. The position of the view is calculated from the container's position, returned by the **bounds** argument. To those values, we add the vertical and horizontal displacements for the second and third views, and assign the final values back to the views with the `place()` method. The result is shown below.

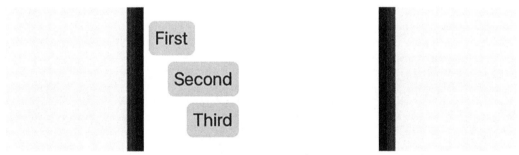

Figure 5-109: Custom layout

Although we can present different interfaces with conditional statements, this requires the system to recreate the views. SwiftUI includes the `AnyLayout` structure to create a wrapper that makes it easy to swap layouts without recreating the views. As we will see later, this allows us to implement complex features such as view identification and animations.

To show how we can switch layouts with the `AnyLayout` structure, we are going to use the custom layout defined in the previous example along with layouts provided by the system. SwiftUI includes the following structures to define horizontal and vertical layouts.

VStackLayout(alignment: HorizontalAlignment, **spacing:** CGFloat?)—This structure creates a layout that arranges a group of views vertically. The **alignment** argument determines the horizontal alignment of the views. It is a structure with the type properties `center`, `leading`, and `trailing`. And the **spacing** argument determines the space between the views.

HStackLayout(alignment: VerticalAlignment, **spacing:** CGFloat?)—This structure creates a layout that arranges a group of views horizontally. The **alignment** argument determines the vertical alignment of the views. It is a structure with the type properties **bottom**, **center**, **firstTextBaseline**, **lastTextBaseline**, and **top**. And the **spacing** argument determines the space between the views

These structures work like the **VStack** and **HStack** structures, but they conform to the **Layout** protocol and are therefore used to define the interface's layout. For instance, we can use a **VStackLayout** structure to replace our custom layout when the value of a state property changes. To switch between layouts, we need to assign them to a property, as shown next.

```
struct ContentView: View {
   @State private var selected: Bool = true

   var body: some View {
      let SelectedLayout = selected ? AnyLayout(MyLayout()) :
AnyLayout(VStackLayout(alignment: .leading))

      VStack(alignment: .leading) {
         Toggle(isOn: $selected, label: {
            Text(selected ? "Custom" : "Standard")
         }).padding(.bottom)
         SelectedLayout {
            Group {
               Text("First")
                  .padding(10)
                  .background(.red)
                  .cornerRadius(10)
               Text("Second")
                  .padding(10)
                  .background(.red)
                  .cornerRadius(10)
               Text("Third")
                  .padding(10)
                  .background(.red)
                  .cornerRadius(10)
            }
         }
         Spacer()
      }.padding()
      .font(.title)
   }
}
```

Listing 5-87: Selecting a layout

This code defines a **State** property of type **Bool** and adds a **Toggle** button to the interface to change the property's value. When the value of the property is **true**, we show the custom layout, otherwise, we show the views with a standard **VStackLayout** layout aligned to the left.

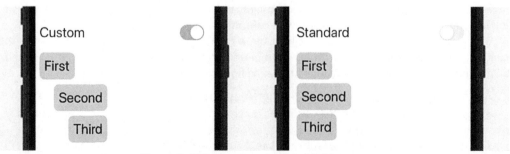

Figure 5-110: Custom and Standard layouts

Do It Yourself: Replace the code in your ContentView.swift file with the code in Listing 5-86. Remember to keep the `ContentView_Previews` structure at the bottom to be able to see the preview on the canvas. You should see the interface illustrated in Figure 5-109. Update the `ContentView` view with the code in Listing 5-87. You should now be able to swap layouts, as shown in Figure 5-110. We will learn how to define interfaces that adapt to the device and orientation in Chapter 8 and how to animate changes in Chapter 11.

(Medium) **Generic Views**

Views are of different data types, so if we want to pass different views around from a property or a method, we must wrap them in container views, such as the **Group** view introduced above. Although this is allowed, SwiftUI includes a structure called **AnyView** that we can use for that purpose.

AnyView(View**)**—This initializer creates an **AnyView** view to contain the views specified by the argument. The argument can be a single view or a hierarchy of views.

In the following example, we check a condition in a method and return an **AnyView** view with the content for the **body** property.

```
struct ContentView: View {
   var body: some View {
      getView()
   }
   func getView() -> AnyView {
      let valid = true
      var myView: AnyView!

      if valid {
         myView = AnyView(Image(systemName: "keyboard"))
      } else {
         myView = AnyView(Text("The state is invalid"))
      }
      return myView
   }
}
```

Listing 5-88: Wrapping views in an `AnyView` *view*

The **ContentView** structure in Listing 5-88 includes a method called **getView()** that returns a structure of type **AnyView**. This structure is defined according to the value of a Boolean property. If the value is **true**, we create an **Image** view, otherwise, we create a **Text** view, but both views are inside an **AnyView** view, so we always return the same type of view. When the content of the **body** property is processed, the method is called, and the view returned by the method is displayed on the screen.

The **AnyView** view is a wrapper we can use to pass different views around. The problem is that the views lose their identity. The system considers the views wrapped in an **AnyView** view to be the same, which affects performance. A better alternative is processing the views before they are returned by the method with the **@ViewBuilder** property wrapper. We introduced this property wrapper before. It is used to construct the views returned by **Content** closures (e.g., the closures assigned to the **body** property). The good news is that we can also apply it to our custom methods to be able to return different views without having to use a wrapper, as in the following example.

```
struct ContentView: View {
   var body: some View {
      getView()
   }
   @ViewBuilder
   func getView() -> some View {
      let valid = false

      if valid {
         Image(systemName: "keyboard")
      } else {
         Text("The state is invalid")
      }
   }
}
```

Listing 5-89: Constructing views with the `@ViewBuilder` *property wrapper*

The code in Listing 5-89 applies the **@ViewBuilder** property wrapper to the **getView()** method, so now we can use this method as a **Content** closure and produce any type of view we want without using a wrapper. (We will learn more about property wrappers in Chapter 6.)

When the views returned by a method are dynamically selected, as we did in the previous examples, we may not always be able to provide one. For cases like this, SwiftUI includes the **EmptyView** view.

EmptyView()—This initializer creates an **EmptyView** view with no content and no size.

The **EmptyView** view works like any other, but it doesn't provide any content and it has no size, so it doesn't affect the interface. The following example creates an empty view when a condition is not met.

```
struct ContentView: View {
   var body: some View {
      VStack {
         Text("View Title")
         getView()
      }
   }
   @ViewBuilder
   func getView() -> some View {
      let valid = false

      if valid {
         Image(systemName: "keyboard")
      } else {
         EmptyView()
      }
   }
}
```

Listing 5-90: Returning an empty view

(Basic) **5.4 Previews**

Xcode automatically builds the app and shows on the canvas a preview of the view we are currently working on. If we introduce large changes to the code, we must press the Resume button at top of the canvas to tell Xcode to resume the preview, but otherwise the process is automatic.

(Basic) Preview Modifiers

Every SwiftUI view includes a `PreviewProvider` structure to create the preview. The structure creates an instance of the view, so we can see on the canvas everything the user will see when running the app. This is useful enough, but by default we only get to see our interface in one device, and a specific configuration. To adapt the preview to our needs, the `View` protocol defines the following modifiers.

previewDevice(PreviewDevice**)**—This modifier determines the device used for the preview. The argument is a structure of type `PreviewDevice`. The structure includes an initializer that takes a string that represents the device we want to use. Some possible strings are "iPhone 13", "iPhone SE", "iPhone X", "iPad (9th generation)", "iPad Pro (9.7-inch)", "Apple TV", and "Mac".

previewDisplayName(String**)**—This modifier assigns a name to the preview. The argument is the string we want to display on the canvas, below the preview.

previewLayout(PreviewLayout**)**—This modifier defines the size of the preview. The argument is an enumeration of type `PreviewLayout` with three values: `device` (default), `fixed(width: CGFloat, height: CGFloat)`, and `sizeThatFits` (adapts the size to the size of the view).

previewInterfaceOrientation(InterfaceOrientation**)**—This modifier defines the orientation of the preview. The argument is a structure with the type properties `portrait`, `portraitUpsideDown`, `landscapeLeft`, and `landscapeRight`.

The preview is configured to work with the device selected in the scheme from the Xcode's toolbar (see Figure 5-9), but we can change it with the `previewDevice()` modifier.

```
struct ContentView_Previews: PreviewProvider {
    static var previews: some View {
        ContentView()
            .previewDevice(PreviewDevice(stringLiteral: "iPhone 13"))
    }
}
```

Listing 5-91: Configuring the preview

This example configures the preview to represent an iPhone 13, but we can include additional previews in the canvas for different devices by embedding the views in a **Group** view.

```
struct ContentView_Previews: PreviewProvider {
    static var previews: some View {
        Group {
            ContentView()
                .previewDevice(PreviewDevice(stringLiteral: "iPhone 13"))
                .previewDisplayName("iPhone 13")
            ContentView()
                .previewDevice(PreviewDevice(stringLiteral: "iPhone 13 Pro"))
                .previewDisplayName("iPhone 13 Pro")
        }
    }
}
```

Listing 5-92: Configuring the preview to represent multiple devices

This example also includes the `previewDisplayName()` modifier to define the label for the buttons displayed at the top of the canvas to select the device.

Do It Yourself: Update the `ContentView_Previews` structure in your ContentView.swift file with the code in Listing 5-92. Press the buttons at the top of the canvas to select a device. To see all the devices available, open the Terminal app and insert the command `xcrun simctl list devicetypes`.

Besides representing a device, a preview can have a free form. The `previewLayout()` modifier uses a value of the `PreviewLayout` enumeration to determine the preview's type. The value by default is **device**, which configures the preview to represent a device, but there are two more. The **fixed(width: CGFloat, height: CGFloat)** value specifies a fixed size, and the **sizeThatFits** value adapts the size of the preview to the size of the view. For instance, the following example applies the **sizeThatFits** value to the preview of the **ContentView** view created by the template.

```
struct ContentView_Previews: PreviewProvider {
    static var previews: some View {
        ContentView()
            .previewLayout(.sizeThatFits)
    }
}
```

Listing 5-93: Adapting the size of the preview to the size of the view

Figure 5-111: Preview of the size of the view

Medium | Environment

The environment is a data structure that belongs to the application and contains information about the application and the views. It is like an external storage space accessible from anywhere in our code. The values stored in the environment can be modified or more data can be added to it. Because of its characteristics, the environment is also used to provide access to the user's data, as we will see in the next chapter, or to access databases and files from anywhere in the application. But we can also modify its values to change the configuration of a view to simulate different conditions for previews, such as setting the light and dark appearances or the font type.

The environment stores the configuration for the views in properties, so changing the values of these properties affects how the views look or behave. The following is the modifier defined by the **View** protocol for this purpose.

environment(KeyPath, Value)—This modifier processes the view and returns a new one with the characteristics defined by the arguments. The first argument is a key path to the environment property we want to modify, and the second argument is the value we want to assign to that property.

Environment properties are defined in a structure called **EnvironmentValues**. Some of these properties are used to control the behavior of the application and the views, but others are useful when working with previews, as shown below.

colorScheme—This property sets or returns the interface appearance. It is an enumeration of type **ColorScheme** with the values **light** and **dark**.

dynamicTypeSize—This property sets or returns the size for dynamic content (It simulates the size set by the user from the Settings app). It is an enumeration with the values `large`, `medium`, `small`, `xLarge`, `xSmall`, `xxLarge`, and `xxxLarge`.

font—This property sets or returns the font by default. It is a value of type `Font`.

accessibilityEnabled—This property sets or returns a Boolean value that determines whether any accessibility service has been enabled on the device.

layoutDirection—This property sets or returns the layout's direction. It is an enumeration of type `LayoutDirection` with the values `leftToRight` and `rightToLeft`.

calendar—This property sets or returns the calendar used by the views to process dates. It is a value of type `Calendar`.

locale—This property sets or returns the locale used by the views to process local data, such as language, currency, etc. It is a value of type `Locale`.

timeZone—This property sets or returns the time zone used by the views to calculate dates and times. It is a value of type `TimeZone`.

The implementation is simple. We must apply the `environment()` modifier to the view with the key path of the property we want to modify and provide the new value. The key path is declared as always (see Chapter 3, Listing 3-32), but this time we can omit the data type because Swift can infer it, as in the following example.

```
struct ContentView: View {
   var body: some View {
      Text("Hello World")
         .foregroundColor(Color("MyColor"))
   }
}
struct ContentView_Previews: PreviewProvider {
   static var previews: some View {
      ContentView()
         .environment(\.colorScheme, .dark)
   }
}
```

Listing 5-94: Activating dark mode

In the code of Listing 5-94, we assign a dynamic color called MyColor to the `Text` view, and then set the appearance for the preview to dark. The example assumes that we have added a Color Set to the Asset Catalog called MyColor and assigned different colors for the modes Any/Dark, as we did before (see Figure 5-44). The `environment()` modifier assigns the value `dark` to the environment's `colorScheme` property, changing the view's appearance to dark, so the preview displays the text in the color we have selected for that appearance.

 Do It Yourself: Create a Color Set in the Asset Catalog with the name MyColor and assign different colors for the Any and Dark appearances, as we did in the example of Figure 5-44. Update the ContentView.swift file with the code in Listing 5-94. On the canvas, you should see the text in the color selected for the dark appearance. Remove the `environment()` modifier and resume the preview. Now, you should see the text in the color selected for Any.

If we need to compare configurations, we can group multiple views with a `Group` view and modify each one independently. The following example tests three different sizes for the text. The `dynamicTypeSize` property is where the environment stores the value that represents the size for the text selected by the user from Settings. By modifying this property, we can see what our interface looks like when the user selects different sizes of text.

```
struct ContentView: View {
   var body: some View {
      Text("Hello World")
   }
}
struct ContentView_Previews: PreviewProvider {
   static var previews: some View {
      Group {
         ContentView()
            .environment(\.dynamicTypeSize, .small)
            .previewDisplayName("Small")
         ContentView()
            .environment(\.dynamicTypeSize, .large)
            .previewDisplayName("Large")
         ContentView()
            .environment(\.dynamicTypeSize, .xxLarge)
            .previewDisplayName("XXLarge")
      }.previewLayout(PreviewLayout.sizeThatFits)
   }
}
```

Listing 5-95: *Generating multiple previews*

In this example, we also apply the `previewLayout()` modifier to adjust the views to the size of their content. Figure 5-112, below, shows the previews generated by this code.

Figure 5-112: *Multiple previews with different environment configurations*

 Do It Yourself: Replace the code in your ContentView.swift file with the code in Listing 5-95. Assign other values to the `dynamicTypeSize` property to see what the text looks like. We will see how to implement additional environment properties in practical situations in further chapters.

Chapter 6
Declarative User Interface

Basic **6.1 States**

In the previous chapter, we introduced SwiftUI's main feature, its declarative syntax. With SwiftUI we can declare the views the way we want them to appear on the screen and let the system take care of creating the code necessary to make it happen. But a declarative syntax is not just about organizing the views, it is also about how they are updated when the state of the app changes. For instance, we may have an interface like the one in Figure 6-1, below, with a `Text` view displaying a title, an input field for the user to insert a new title, and a button to replace the old title with the new one.

Figure 6-1: User Interface

The `Text` view with the original title represents the initial state of our interface. The state is updated with each character the user types in the input field (Figure 6-1, left), and when the button is pressed, the interface enters a new state in which the title inserted by the user has replaced the original title and the color of the text has changed (Figure 6-1, right).

Every time there is a change of state, the views must be updated to reflect it. In previous systems, this required the code to keep the data and the interface synchronized, but in a declarative syntax all we have to do is to declare what the configuration of the views should be in each state and the system takes care of generating all the code necessary to respond to those changes.

The possible states the interface can go through are determined by the information stored by the app. For instance, the characters inserted by the user in the input field and the color used in our example are values stored by the app. Every time these values change, the app is in a new state and therefore the interface is updated to reflect it. Establishing this dependency between the app's data and the interface demands a lot of code, but SwiftUI keeps it simple using property wrappers.

Advanced **Property Wrappers**

Property wrappers are a tool provided by the Swift language that allows us to encapsulate functionality in a property. They are like the computed properties introduced in Chapter 3 (see Listing 3-41), but applicable to multiple properties. As other Swift features, they were designed to simplify our code. For instance, we can define a property wrapper that limits the value of a property to a certain range. All the properties declared with it will only accept values between those limits.

A property wrapper is just a structure, but it must be preceded by the `@propertyWrapper` keyword and include a property with the name `wrappedValue` to process and store the value. The structure must also include an initializer for the `wrappedValue` property. The following is a Playground example that illustrates how to define a property wrapper that limits the value of a property to a minimum of 0 and a maximum of 255.

```
import Foundation
@propertyWrapper
struct ClampedValue {
   var storedValue: Int = 0
   var min: Int = 0
   var max: Int = 255

   var wrappedValue: Int {
      get {
         return storedValue
      }
      set {
         if newValue < min {
            storedValue = min
         } else if newValue > max {
            storedValue = max
         } else {
            storedValue = newValue
         }
      }
   }
   init(wrappedValue: Int) {
      self.wrappedValue = wrappedValue
   }
}
```

Listing 6-1: Defining a property wrapper

Listing 6-1 defines a property wrapper called **ClampedValue**. The structure contains three properties to store and control the value. The **storedValue** property stores the current value of the property, and the **min** and **max** properties determine the minimum and maximum values allowed for the properties defined with this property wrapper. There is also the required **wrappedValue** property, defined as a computed property with a getter and a setter. The getter returns the current value of the **storedValue** property, and the setter checks whether the new value is within the minimum and maximum allowed before storing it. If the new value exceeds a limit, the values of the **min** or **max** properties are assigned to the **storedValue** property instead.

The code in Listing 6-1 defines the property wrapper, but it doesn't define any property of this kind. Implementing a property wrapper is easy, we must declare the properties as we always do but preceded with the name of the property wrapper prefixed with the @ character.

```
struct Price {
   @ClampedValue var firstPrice: Int
   @ClampedValue var secondPrice: Int

   func printMessage() {
      print("First Price: \(firstPrice)")   // "First Price: 0"
      print("Second Price: \(secondPrice)")   // "Second Price: 255"
   }
}
var purchase = Price(firstPrice: -42, secondPrice: 350)
purchase.printMessage()
```

Listing 6-2: Using a property wrapper

The **Price** structure in Listing 6-2 includes two properties that use the **ClampedValue** property wrapper, **firstPrice** and **secondPrice**, and a method to print their values. The instances of the structure are initialized with the values -42 and 350. Both values exceed the limits established by the property wrapper, so the value stored for each property is the limit they exceeded (0 for **firstPrice** and 255 for **secondPrice**).

Do It Yourself: Create a new Playground file and replace the code in the template with the codes in Listings 6-1 and 6-2. Press play. You should see the messages " First Price: 0" and " Second Price: 255" printed on the console.

(Basic) **@State**

Property wrappers allow us to define properties that can perform tasks with the values assigned to them. SwiftUI implements property wrappers extensively to store values and report the changes to the views. The one designed to store the states of a single view is called **@State**. This property wrapper stores a value in a structure of type **State** and notifies the system when that value changes, so the views are automatically updated to reflect the change on the screen.

The **@State** property wrapper was designed to store the states of a single view, so we should declare the properties of this type as part of the view structure and as **private**, so the access is restricted to the structure in which they were declared.

```
struct ContentView: View {
   @State private var title: String = "Default Title"

   var body: some View {
      VStack {
         Text(title)
            .padding(10)
         Button(action: {
            title = "My New Title"
         }, label: {
            Text("Change Title")
         })
         Spacer()
      }.padding()
   }
}
```

Listing 6-3: Defining a state

The code in Listing 6-3 declares a **@State** property called **title** of type **String** and initializes it with the value "Default Title". In the **body** of the view, we show the value of this property with a **Text** view within a vertical stack. Below the text, we include a **Button** view. We will study **Button** views later, but for now all we need to know is that a **Button** view displays a label and performs an action when the label is tapped by the user. We defined the label as a **Text** view with the text "Change Title", so the user knows that it has to press that button to change the title, and in the closure assigned to the action we change the value of the **title** property to "My New Title".

The **title** property created with the **@State** property wrapper is used in two places, first in the **Text** view to show the current value to the user, and then in the action for the **Button** view to modify its value. In consequence, every time the button is pressed, the value of the **title** property changes, the **@State** property wrapper notifies the system, and the content of the **body** property is automatically refreshed to display the new value on the screen.

Figure 6-2: Initial state (left) and state after the button is pressed (right)

Do It Yourself: Create a new Multiplatform project. Update the `ContentView` view with the code in Listing 6-3. Make sure that Live Preview is activated on the canvas (Figure 5-18, number 1). Press the Change Title button to assign the string to the `Text` view. You should see something similar to Figure 6-2, right.

All this process works automatically. We don't have to assign the new value to the `Text` view or tell the view that a new value is available, it's all done by the `@State` property wrapper. And we can include all the `@State` properties we need to store every state of the interface. For instance, the following example adds a `@State` property of type `Bool` to our view to determine whether the user already inserted a new title or not and assign a different color to the text.

```
struct ContentView: View {
    @State private var title: String = "Default Title"
    @State private var titleActive: Bool = false

    var body: some View {
        VStack {
            Text(title)
                .padding(10)
                .foregroundColor(titleActive ? Color.red : Color.gray)
            Button(action: {
                title = "My New Title"
                titleActive = true
            }, label: { Text("Change Title") })
            Spacer()
        }.padding()
    }
}
```

Listing 6-4: Defining multiple states

The `titleActive` property stores a Boolean value that determines the color of the text, so we can check its value to assign the appropriate color. In this example, we use a ternary operator (see Listing 2-51). Using a ternary operator to set the state of the view is the recommended practice because it allows the system to determine all the possible states the view can respond to and produce a smooth transition from one state to another. if the value of `titleActive` is **true**, we assign the color red to the `foregroundColor()` modifier, otherwise, we assign the color gray.

In the button's action, besides assigning a new value to the `title` property, we now assign the value **true** to the `titleActive` property to change this state. The `titleActive` property informs the system that there is a new value available, the system refreshes the views, the ternary operator is evaluated again, and in consequence the color red is assigned to the text.

 IMPORTANT: There are two states in the example of Listing 6-4, and both change at the same time, but the system takes into consideration these situations and makes sure that the interface is updated only when necessary.

A `@State` property creates a dependency between itself and the view and therefore the view is updated every time its value changes. It is said that the view is *bound* to the property. The binding we have used so far is unidirectional. If the property is modified, the view is updated. But there are views which values are modified by the user and therefore they must be able to store the value back into the property without the code's intervention. For this purpose, SwiftUI allows us to define a bidirectional binding. Bidirectional bindings are declared by prefixing the name of the property with the **$** sign.

The views that usually require bidirectional binding are control views, such as those that create switches the user can turn on and off, or input fields to insert text. The following example implements a `TextField` view to illustrate this feature. A `TextField` view creates an input field. The values required by its initializer are a string with the text we want to show as placeholder and the binding property we are going to use to store the value inserted by the user. (We will learn more about **TextField** views and other control views later.)

```
struct ContentView: View {
    @State private var title: String = "Default Title"
    @State private var titleActive: Bool = false
    @State private var titleInput: String = ""

    var body: some View {
        VStack {
            Text(title)
                .padding(10)
                .foregroundColor(titleActive ? Color.red : Color.gray)
            TextField("Insert Title", text: $titleInput)
                .textFieldStyle(.roundedBorder)
            Button(action: {
                title = titleInput
                titleActive = true
                titleInput = ""
            }, label: { Text("Change Title") })
            Spacer()
        }.padding()
    }
}
```

Listing 6-5: *Defining bidirectional binding*

In this example, we add to the view the **@State** property we need to store the text inserted by the user, and then define a **TextField** view between the title and the button. The **TextField** view was initialized with the placeholder "Insert Title", and the new **titleInput** property was provided as the binding property for the view (**$titleInput**). This creates a permanent connection between the **TextField** view and the property, so every time the user types or removes a character in the input field, the new value is assigned to the property.

In the action for the **Button** view, we introduced two modifications. First, we assign the value of the **titleInput** property to the **title** property. This effectively updates the title of the view with the text inserted by the user. And finally, we assign an empty string to the **titleInput** property to clear the input field and leave it ready for the user to start typing again.

 Do It Yourself: Update the **ContentView** view with the code in Listing 6-5. Click on the text field and insert a text. Press the Change Title button. You should see something similar to Figure 6-1, right.

Basic **@Binding**

A **@State** property belongs to the structure in which it was declared and should only be accessed from the views assigned to the **body** property of that structure (that is why we declare them **private**), but, as we have seen in Chapter 5, when our views grow significantly, it is advisable to consolidate them into independent structures. The problem with organizing the views this way is that the additional structures lose the reference to the **@State** properties and therefore we are not able to read or modify their values anymore. Defining new **@State** properties inside these additional views is not a solution because all we are doing is to create new states. What we need is to create a bidirectional connection between the **@State** properties defined in one view and the code in the other. For this purpose, SwiftUI includes the **Binding** structure and the **@Binding** property wrapper.

The following view is the same as previous examples, but this time we move the **Text** view that displays the title to a custom view called **HeaderView** and define a **@Binding** property in this view to access one of the **@State** properties of the **ContentView** structure.

```
struct ContentView: View {
    @State private var title: String = "Default Title"
    @State private var titleInput: String = ""

    var body: some View {
        VStack {
            HeaderView(title: $title)
            TextField("Insert Title", text: $titleInput)
                .textFieldStyle(.roundedBorder)
            Button(action: {
                title = titleInput
                titleInput = ""
            }, label: { Text("Change Title") })
            Spacer()
        }.padding()
    }
}
struct HeaderView: View {
    @Binding var title: String

    var body: some View {
        Text(title)
            .padding(10)
    }
}
```

Listing 6-6: *Using* `@Binding` *properties*

In this example, the **VStack** view contains an input field and the button, as before, but the title is now managed by an instance of the new **HeaderView** structure defined at the bottom. In this view, we include the same **Text** view as before, but add a **@Binding** property to be able to access the **title** property defined in the **ContentView** structure.

A **@Binding** property always receives its value from a **@State** property, so we don't have to assign a default value to it, but the connection created between them is bidirectional, so we have to remember to prefix the **@State** property with the **$** sign to connect the **@Binding** property with it (**HeaderView(title: $title)**).

Because of the bidirectional binding created between the **@Binding** property and the **@State** property, every time the button is pressed, the changes are detected by the system, and the **body** property of the **HeaderView** structure is processed again to show the new values on the screen.

 Do It Yourself: Update the ContentView.swift file with the code in Listing 6-6. Remember to keep the **ContentView_Previews** structure at the bottom to be able to see the preview on the canvas. Insert a text in the text field, and press the Change Title button. Everything should work as before.

Medium **Binding Structures**

As we have already learned, property wrappers are defined as structures and therefore they contain their own properties. SwiftUI allows access to the underlying structure of a property wrapper by prefixing the property's name with an underscore (e.g., **_title**). Once we get the structure, we can access its properties. The structure that defines the **@State** property wrapper is called **State**. This is a generic structure and therefore it can process values of any type. The following are the properties defined by this structure to store the state's values.

wrappedValue—This property returns the value managed by the **@State** property.

projectedValue—This property returns a structure of type **Binding** that creates the bidirectional binding with the view.

Chapter 6 - Declarative User Interface

The **wrappedValue** property stores the value we assign to the **@State** property, like the "Default Title" string assigned to the **title** property in the last example. The **projectedValue** property stores a structure of type **Binding** that creates the bidirectional binding we need to store a value back to the property. If we read the **@State** property directly (e.g., **title**), the value returned is the one stored in the **wrappedValue** property, and if we prefix the property's name with a **$** sign (e.g., **$title**), we access the **Binding** structure stored in the **projectedValue** property. This is how SwiftUI proposes we work with **@State** properties, but in theory we can also access the properties directly, as in the following example.

```
struct ContentView: View {
   @State private var title: String = "Default Title"
   @State private var titleInput: String = ""

   var body: some View {
      VStack {
         Text(_title.wrappedValue)
            .padding(10)
         TextField("Insert Title", text: _titleInput.projectedValue)
            .textFieldStyle(.roundedBorder)
         Button(action: {
            _title.wrappedValue = _titleInput.wrappedValue
            _titleInput.wrappedValue = ""
         }, label: { Text("Change Title") })
         Spacer()
      }.padding()
   }
}
```

Listing 6-7: *Accessing the properties of a* State *structure*

This is the same example as before, but instead of using the SwiftUI shortcuts, we read the **wrappedValue** and **projectedValue** properties of the **State** structure directly. Of course, this is not necessary, but may be required sometimes to overcome SwiftUI's shortcomings. For instance, SwiftUI doesn't allow us to access and work with **@State** properties outside the closure assigned to the **body** property, but we can replace one **State** structure by another. For this purpose, the **State** structure includes the following initializers.

State(initialValue: Value)—This initializer creates a **State** property with the value specified by the **initialValue** argument.

State(wrappedValue: Value)—This initializer creates a **State** property with the wrapped value specified by the **wrappedValue** argument.

For example, if we want to assign an initial value to the input field of our previous example, we can add an initializer to the **ContentView** structure and use it to assign a new **State** structure to the property.

```
init() {
   _titleInput = State(initialValue: "Hello World")
}
```

Listing 6-8: *Initializing* @State *properties*

 Do It Yourself: Update the **ContentView** view with the code in Listing 6-7. Add the initializer in Listing 6-8 to the **ContentView** structure (below the **@State** properties). You should see the input field initialized with "Hello World".

IMPORTANT: Accessing the content of binding properties this way is only recommended when there are no other options. When possible, we should use the property wrappers provided by SwiftUI and initialize a **@State** property with the **onAppear()** modifier introduced in Chapter 5 (see Listing 5-54) or by storing the states in an observable object, as we will see later.

We can access the values of a **@Binding** property the same way we do with a **@State** property. If we just read the property, as we did in Listing 6-7, the value returned is the value stored in it, and if we prefix the name with a **$** sign, the value returned is the **Binding** structure the property wrapper uses to establish the bidirectional binding with the view. But if we prefix the name of the **@Binding** property with an underscore (e.g., **_title**), the value returned is not a **State** structure but another **Binding** structure. This is because a **@Binding** property wrapper is defined by a structure of type **Binding**. Of course, the structure also includes properties to access the values.

wrappedValue—This property returns the value managed by the **@Binding** property.

projectedValue—This property returns a structure of type **Binding** that creates the bidirectional binding with the view.

As we did with the **State** structure, we can access and work with the values stored in the **Binding** structure. For instance, the following example implements a separate view again to manage the title, as we did in Listing 6-6. This new **HeaderView** gets the value stored in the **Binding** structure from the **wrappedValue** property, counts the total number of characters in the string, and displays the result along with the title.

```
struct ContentView: View {
    @State private var title: String = "Default Title"
    @State private var titleInput: String = ""

    var body: some View {
        VStack {
            HeaderView(title: $title)
            TextField("Insert Title", text: $titleInput)
                .textFieldStyle(.roundedBorder)
            Button(action: {
                title = titleInput
                titleInput = ""
            }, label: { Text("Change Title") })
            Spacer()
        }.padding()
    }
}
struct HeaderView: View {
    @Binding var title: String
    let counter: Int

    init(title: Binding<String>) {
        _title = title

        let sentence = _title.wrappedValue
        counter = sentence.count
    }
    var body: some View {
        Text("\(title) (\(counter))")
            .padding(10)
    }
}
```

Listing 6-9: Accessing the values of a @Binding property

In the **HeaderView** view of Listing 6-9, we define a property called **counter** and initialize it with the number of characters in the string returned by the **wrappedValue** property. Because the **@Binding** property doesn't have an initial value, we must also initialize it with the value received from the **ContentView** view (**self._title = title**). Notice that the value received by the **HeaderView** structure is a **Binding** structure that can manage values of type **String**, so the data type for the argument must be declared as **Binding<String>**.

Once the values are initialized, we can display them in the view. The title now shows the text inserted by the user along with the number of characters in the string.

Hello (5)

Insert Title

Change Title

Figure 6-3: *Title defined with the values of the* @Binding *property*

Do It Yourself: Update the ContentView.swift file with the code in Listing 6-9. Insert a title. You should see the title with the number of characters on the right, as show in Figure 6-3.

The **@Binding** property of the **HeaderView** view is connected to the **@State** property of the **ContentView** view and therefore it receives its value from this property, but there are times when instances of structures like these are created independently and therefore, they require a binding value. To define this value, we can create the **Binding** structure ourselves. The structure includes the following initializer and type method.

Binding(get: Closure, **set:** Closure)—This initializer creates a **Binding** structure. The **get** argument is a closure that returns the current value, and the **set** argument is a closure that receives a new value for storage or processing.

constant(Value**)**—This type method creates a **Binding** structure with an immutable value. The argument is the value we want to assign to the structure.

There are many circumstances in which we may need a **Binding** value. For instance, if we want to create a preview of the **HeaderView**, we must provide a value for the **title** property. The following example illustrates how to create a new **Binding** structure to provide this value and how to define the preview for this view.

```
struct HeaderView_Previews: PreviewProvider {
    static var previews: some View {
        let constantValue = Binding<String>(
            get: { return "My Preview Title"},
            set: { value in
                print(value)
            })
        return HeaderView(title: constantValue)
    }
}
```

Listing 6-10: *Creating a* Binding *structure*

The code in Listing 6-10 instantiates a new **Binding** structure. The initializer works like a computed property. It includes a getter and a setter. The getter returns the current value and the setter receives the values assigned to the structure. In this example, we always return the same string and since we are not assigning new values to the structure, we just print the value on the console. The instance is assigned to the `constantValue` constant and then sent to the `HeaderView` structure, so the view has a value to show on the canvas.

There is not much use for the `Binding` structure of this example other than providing the value required by the `HeaderView` structure. In cases like this, we can simplify the code with the `constant()` method. This type method creates and returns a `Binding` structure with an immutable value, so we don't have to create the structure ourselves.

```
struct HeaderView_Previews: PreviewProvider {
    static var previews: some View {
        HeaderView(title: .constant("My Preview Title"))
    }
}
```

Listing 6-11: *Creating a* Binding *structure with an immutable value*

 Do It Yourself: Add the structure in Listing 6-11 to the ContentView.swift file. You should see an additional button at the top of the canvas to display the preview of the **HeaderView** view.

⟨Medium⟩ @Environment

Besides custom states, we can also respond to states set by the system in the environment. We have worked with the environment before to configure previews (see Environment in Chapter 5), but some of its properties, like **colorScheme** and **dynamicTypeSize**, represent states that can change while the app is running, so we can read their values and update the views accordingly. For this purpose, SwiftUI includes the **@Environment** property wrapper. This property wrapper works in a similar way to **@State** but it is designed to report to the system changes in the environment properties. The **@Environment** property wrapper is created with the **Environment** structure. The following is the structure's initializer.

Environment(KeyPath**)**—This initializer creates an **Environment** structure that provides access to an environment property. The argument is the key path of the property we want to access.

Because the initializer of the **Environment** structure receives an argument to specify the property's key path, connecting the property wrapper with the property we want to monitor is easy, as illustrated in the following example.

```
struct ContentView: View {
    @Environment(\.colorScheme) var mode

    var body: some View {
        Image(systemName: "trash")
            .font(Font.system(size: 100))
            .foregroundColor(mode == .dark ? Color.yellow : Color.blue)
            .symbolVariant(mode == .dark ? .fill : .circle)
    }
}
```

Listing 6-12: *Responding to updates in the states of the environment*

In Listing 6-12, we define a property called **mode** to create a binding between the view and the environment's **colorScheme** property, and then assign different values to the modifiers of a **Text** view depending on the current appearance (**dark** or **light**). When the user changes the appearance from Settings, the value of the **colorScheme** property in the environment changes, this changes the value of the **mode** property in our view, and the view is updated according to the new state. Notice that we check the value of the **mode** property in the modifiers with a ternary operator, as we did before, so SwiftUI can effectively process the changes. If the appearance is **light**, we display a blue trash can with a circle around it, otherwise, we display the can's **fill** variant in yellow.

Figure 6-4: *States in light and dark appearances*

Do It Yourself: Create a Multiplatform project. Update the **ContentView** view with the code in Listing 6-12. You should see the blue trash can (Figure 6-4, left). Press the Device Settings button at the bottom of the canvas and activate the Dark appearance option in the Color Scheme section (Figure 5-18, number 4). You should see the yellow trash can (Figure 6-4, right).

(Basic) 6.2 Model

Professional applications are composed of several views that represent all the screens the user can navigate through. These views need to access the same data and respond to the same changes in state to update the interface and stay synchronized. Therefore, the app must provide a unique source of data and the views must be able to read and modify it. This unique source of data is usually called *Model*.

The model is part of the basic organization of an application. In this paradigm, a group of structures or objects define the model (the app's data and states) and the views access the model to present the data on the screen and update it with the user's input.

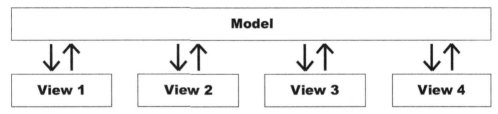

Figure 6-5: *App's model*

This organization cannot be created with **@State** properties. The **@State** property wrapper used in previous examples can only store values that control the states of a single view. What we need is to create an object that can be passed to the views and that will inform the system when its values change. SwiftUI defines the following protocol and property wrappers for this purpose.

ObservableObject—This protocol defines the tools required by an object to send a report to the system every time a value in the object changed.

@StateObject—This property wrapper listens to changes in an observable object and receives the new values.

@ObservedObject—This property wrapper listens to changes in the observable object stored in a **@StateObject** property and receives the new values.

@Published—This property wrapper turns any property into a publisher, which means that the changes on the property's values are going to be reported to the system. (This is the same as the **@State** property wrapper but for observable objects.)

To create the model and keep the view up to date, we must define a class that conforms to the **ObservableObject** protocol, define the properties we want to use to store the states with the **@Published** property wrapper, store an instance of this model with the **@StateObject** property wrapper, and then include a property defined with the **@ObservedObject** property wrapper inside every view we want to connect to this model.

Figure 6-6: *Implementation of an observable object*

The advantage of working with an observable object and **@Published** properties instead of **@State** properties is that the states can now be checked from all the views of our application (all the screens the user can navigate through). The **@StateObject** property contains a reference to the observable object, so we can modify its values, and the **@Published** properties inform the system when their values change, so the views, and therefore the entire interface, is synchronized with the data.

The following is an example of how to define this class. We call it **ApplicationData**, but it can take any name we want. The **ApplicationData** class conforms to the **ObservableObject** protocol and includes two **@Published** properties to store the data.

```
import SwiftUI

class ApplicationData: ObservableObject {
    @Published var title: String = "Default Title"
    @Published var titleInput: String = ""
}
```

Listing 6-13: *Storing our data in an observable object*

The purpose of this application is to store the title of a book. The **title** property stores the title, and the **titleInput** property is going to be used by the view to allow the user to insert a new one.

 IMPORTANT: The classes defined to store the data are a central part of our application and can be large, so it is a good idea to store them in a separate Swift file (see Figure 5-108). All you need to do is to open the File menu at the top of the screen, select the New/File options, and select the Swift File icon in the iOS panel. The file is added with the rest, and the data types defined inside are accessible from anywhere in the code.

Because the source of data (also called the *source of truth*) has to be unique, we cannot create one object for each view, we have to create only one object and then pass a reference to that object to all the views. Figure 6-7, below, illustrates this scheme. We store an instance of our model in a **@StateObject** property and then pass a reference to the initial view, which in turn passes that reference to the next view and so on.

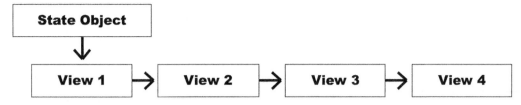

Figure 6-7: Observable object model

The first view to receive a reference to the model should be the view assigned as the root view of the window. In our examples, this is the **ContentView** view, which is instantiated in the **App** structure. So we create an instance of the **ApplicationData** class, store it in a **@StateObject** property, and send a reference to the **ContentView** structure, as shown next.

```
import SwiftUI
@main
struct TestApp: App {
    @StateObject private var appData = ApplicationData()

    var body: some Scene {
        WindowGroup {
            ContentView(appData: appData)
        }
    }
}
```

Listing 6-14: Initializing the observable object in the App structure

The instance of our model is stored in a **@StateObject** property. This ensures that the instance will never be recreated and it is the same for every view. Once the instance is created, we pass it to the initial view (**ContentView**). This view must include an **@ObservedObject** property to create a bidirectional binding with the **@StateObject** property and access the model, as shown next.

```
struct ContentView: View {
    @ObservedObject var appData: ApplicationData

    var body: some View {
        VStack(spacing: 8) {
            Text(appData.title)
                .padding(10)
            TextField("Insert Title", text: $appData.titleInput)
                .textFieldStyle(.roundedBorder)
            Button(action: {
                appData.title = appData.titleInput
            }, label: { Text("Save") })
            Spacer()
        }.padding()
    }
}
struct ContentView_Previews: PreviewProvider {
    static var previews: some View {
        ContentView(appData: ApplicationData())
    }
}
```

Listing 6-15: Working with the observable object from the views

This is very similar to what we have done before, but instead of reading and storing the values in **@State** properties, we do it in the **@Published** properties of our observable object. When we store a value in a **@Published** property, the property tells the system that new values are available, and the views are automatically updated. The difference of working with **@Published** properties in a model instead of **@State** properties is that if we add new views to the interface later (additional screens the user can navigate to), they will all have access to the same values and states.

There is another difference from previous examples we must consider. The **ApplicationData** object that represents our model is passed to the instance of the **ContentView** structure created for the application, but the **ContentView_Previews** structure creates a separate instance of the **ContentView** structure to show on the canvas, so we must provide an additional **ApplicationData** object to this structure, as we did in Listing 6-15 (**ContentView(appData: ApplicationData())**). Now, the preview on the canvas can also run the application.

Figure 6-8: *Interface updated with an observable object*

 Do It Yourself: Open the File menu at the top of the screen and click on the New/File options to create a new Swift file (Figure 5-108). Assign the name ApplicationData.swift to the file and replace the code defined by the template with the code in Listing 6-13. Update the code in your **App** structure with the code in Listing 6-14. Finally, update the **ContentView** view with the code in Listing 6-15. You should see something similar to Figure 6-8.

In the model of Listing 6-13, we define two properties, **title** to store the actual information and **titleInput** to receive input from the user. Other views added later to our application may need to access the **title** property to show its value to the user, but the **titleInput** property is only required by the view that contains the **TextField** view. This means that we are storing the private state of a view in the app's model. Although there is nothing wrong with this approach, it is recommended to use the model to store the app's data but manage the states of the views from the views themselves. There are different patterns we can implement to organize our application. One approach is to define **@State** properties for each view, as we did before, but a better alternative is to create additional observable objects. The following is the model we need for this example.

```
import SwiftUI

class ApplicationData: ObservableObject {
    @Published var title: String = "Default Title"
}
```

Listing 6-16: *Storing only the app's data in the model*

Our model now only stores the title of the book. To manage the states of the view and provide the binding properties for the **TextField** view, we can define an additional observable object for the **ContentView** view, as in the following example.

```
import SwiftUI

class ContentViewData: ObservableObject {
    @Published var titleInput: String = ""
}
```

```
struct ContentView: View {
   @ObservedObject var contentData = ContentViewData()
   @ObservedObject var appData: ApplicationData

   var body: some View {
      VStack(spacing: 8) {
         Text(appData.title)
            .padding(10)
         TextField("Insert Title", text: $contentData.titleInput)
            .textFieldStyle(.roundedBorder)
         Button(action: {
            appData.title = contentData.titleInput
         }, label: { Text("Save") })
         Spacer()
      }.padding()
   }
}
struct ContentView_Previews: PreviewProvider {
   static var previews: some View {
      ContentView(appData: ApplicationData())
   }
}
```

Listing 6-17: Defining an observable object for a view

Everything is the same as before, but we have defined an additional observable object for the **ContentView** view called **ContentViewData**, and now the characters inserted by the user are stored in the **@Published** property of this object (**titleInput**). When the user presses the Save button, we assign the value of this property to the **title** property to store the data in the model.

The advantage of using an observable object and **@Published** properties to manage the states of a view instead of **@State** properties is that it is easy to initialize the properties of the object dynamically. For instance, we can assign the current title stored in the model to the **titleInput** property as soon as the **ContentView** structure is initialized, so the user can see the previous value on the screen.

```
init(appData: ApplicationData) {
   self.appData = appData
   contentData.titleInput = self.appData.title
}
```

Listing 6-18: Initializing the view's observable object

The initializer passes the reference of the model to the **appData** property and then assigns the value of the model's **title** property to the **titleInput** property of the **contentData** object, so the **TextField** view shows the current value.

Figure 6-9: Text field initialized with the value in the model

Do It Yourself: Update the ApplicationData.swift file with the code in Listing 6-16 and the ContentView.swift file with the code in Listing 6-17. You should see something similar to Figure 6-8. Add the initializer of Listing 6-18 to the **ContentView** structure (below the **@ObservedObject** properties) and run the application again. You should see something like Figure 6-9.

Another way to initialize properties of an observable object or **@State** properties is with the **onAppear()** modifier. As we have seen before, this modifier executes a closure when the view appears on the screen. For instance, we can assign it to the **VStack** view of our **ContentView** view to initialize the **titleInput** property as soon as the view is shown on the screen.

```
.onAppear {
   contentData.titleInput = appData.title
}
```

Listing 6-19: Initializing the view's observable object when the views appear

 Do It Yourself: Remove the initializer introduced in Listing 6-18 from the **ContentView** structure. Add the **onAppear()** modifier of Listing 6-19 to the **VStack** view (below the **padding()** modifier). Run the application again. The result should be the same as before.

Medium **@EnvironmentObject**

Our application may have a view that presents a menu, another view that displays a list of items, and another one that shows information pertaining to the item selected by the user. All these views need to access the app's data and therefore all of them must contain a reference to the model. But passing this reference from one view to another until we reach the one that requires the values, as illustrated in Figure 6-7, can be cumbersome and error prone. A better alternative is to pass the reference of the model to the environment and then read it from the environment whenever we need it.

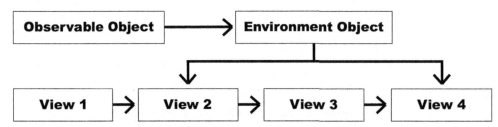

Figure 6-10: Accessing the model through the environment

As we already mentioned, the environment is a general-purpose container that stores information about the app and the views, but it can also store custom data, including references to observable objects. In the example of Figure 6-10, an instance of the observable object is added to the environment, and then accessed only by the views that require it (View 2 and View 4). To add the observable object to the environment, the **View** protocol includes the following modifier.

environmentObject(Object**)**—This modifier assigns an object to the environment. The argument is a reference to the object we want to share with the views.

And to access the object from the views, SwiftUI include the **@EnvironmentObject** property wrapper, which is defined by the following structure.

EnvironmentObject()—This initializer creates an `EnvironmentObject` structure that provides access to an environment object.

The `environmentObject()` modifier assigns an object to the environment of a view's hierarchy, so we must apply it to the initial view for all the views on the interface to have access to the model. The following code shows the modifications we must introduce to the `App` structure to create the `ApplicationData` object and add it to the environment of the `ContentView` view.

```
import SwiftUI

@main
struct TestApp: App {
   @StateObject private var appData = ApplicationData()

   var body: some Scene {
      WindowGroup {
         ContentView()
            .environmentObject(appData)
      }
   }
}
```

Listing 6-20: Assigning the observable object to the view's environment

Instead of passing the reference of the model to the `ContentView` view, as we did before (see Listing 6-14), we pass it to the view's environment. Now, to access the model from the views, we just have to get the reference from the environment with the `@EnvironmentObject` property wrapper, as shown next.

```
import SwiftUI

class ContentViewData: ObservableObject {
   @Published var titleInput: String = ""
}
struct ContentView: View {
   @ObservedObject var contentData = ContentViewData()
   @EnvironmentObject var appData: ApplicationData

   var body: some View {
      VStack(spacing: 8) {
         Text(appData.title)
            .padding(10)
         TextField("Insert Title", text: $contentData.titleInput)
            .textFieldStyle(.roundedBorder)
         Button(action: {
            appData.title = contentData.titleInput
         }, label: { Text("Save") })
         Spacer()
      }.padding()
      .onAppear(perform: {
         contentData.titleInput = appData.title
      })
   }
}
struct ContentView_Previews: PreviewProvider {
   static var previews: some View {
      ContentView()
         .environmentObject(ApplicationData())
   }
}
```

Listing 6-21: Getting a reference to the observable object from the environment

There are two changes in this code from the previous example. Instead of storing the reference of the model in an **@ObservedObject** property, we use an **@EnvironmentObject** property. The reference works the same way, but the **@EnvironmentObject** property automatically gets the reference from the environment, so we don't have to pass it to the views anymore. And second, an instance of our model was assigned to the environment of the **ContentView** view created for the preview. This is because this **ContentView** view does not belong to the hierarchy of the **ContentView** view created for the application, and therefore they work with different environments.

Do It Yourself: Update the **App** structure with the code in Listing 6-20, and the ContentView.swift file with the code in Listing 6-21. The application works as before, but now the values are taken from the observable object through the environment and therefore they are available to all the views that belong to the **ContentView**'s hierarchy. We will learn how to add more views to this hierarchy in Chapter 8.

IMPORTANT: The environment stores key/value pairs. These types of values are like dictionary values, they have a key and a value associated to that key. When we apply the **environmentObject()** modifier with an instance of our observable object, the environment stores an item with the **ApplicationData** key (the object's data type) and the object as the value. When an **@EnvironmentObject** property is defined, the property wrapper looks for an item which key is the property's data type and assigns its value to the property.

⟨ Medium ⟩ 6.3 View Model

Working with the values as they are provided by the model may cause some issues. Something we must consider is that views usually need to transform the values before presenting them to the user. But views in SwiftUI should only be responsible of defining the interface. In addition, multiple views may need to perform the same transformations on the data, but doing so from different views can be error prone. For instance, we may have an application that stores and displays the title and author of a book. If the model stores the title and the author in different properties, we would have to join the values in a single string every time they have to be shown to the user. But if this process is performed from multiple views, mistakes can be made. We may forget to join the strings and only show one value, or do it in the wrong order. To avoid mistakes, the string should not be created by the views but provided by the model, ready to use.

There are different patterns we can adopt to improve the organization of our application. The one recommended by Apple is called Model View View-Model (MVVM). In this pattern, there is a model with the basic information, a view-model that prepares that information for the views, and the views that present the information to the user.

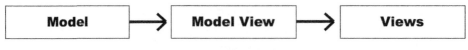

Figure 6-11: MVVM

To implement this pattern in our example, we need three elements: a structure with the basic information (the model), a structure that prepares that information to be presented by the views (the view model), and an observable object to keep the model and the views synchronized.

```
import SwiftUI
struct Book {
   var title: String
   var author: String
}
struct BookViewModel {
   var book: Book
   var header: String {
      return book.title + " " + book.author
   }
}
class ApplicationData: ObservableObject {
   @Published var userData: BookViewModel

   init() {
      userData = BookViewModel(book: Book(title: "Default Title", author:
"Unknown"))
   }
}
```

Listing 6-22: Defining an MVVM pattern

The code in Listing 6-22 replaces the model used in previous examples. First, we define a structure called **Book** with properties to store the title and the author of a book. Next, we define a structure called **BookViewModel** to prepare the information for the view. This structure contains two properties: the **book** property to store an instance of the **Book** structure and a computed property called **header** to return a string that combines the values of the book's **title** and **author** properties. Lastly, we define the observable object with a **@Published** property to store this data (a single book in this example).

Usually, the data is loaded from the web or a file, but in this case, we are working with temporary data, so we initialize the observable object with a new instance of the **BookViewModel** structure that contains an instance of the **Book** structure with values by default. Now, we can access the model from the views.

```
import SwiftUI
class ContentViewData: ObservableObject {
   @Published var titleInput: String = ""
   @Published var authorInput: String = ""
}
struct ContentView: View {
   @ObservedObject var contentData = ContentViewData()
   @EnvironmentObject var appData: ApplicationData

   var body: some View {
      VStack(spacing: 8) {
         Text(appData.userData.header)
            .padding(10)
         TextField("Insert Title", text: $contentData.titleInput)
            .textFieldStyle(.roundedBorder)
         TextField("Insert Author", text: $contentData.authorInput)
            .textFieldStyle(.roundedBorder)
         Button(action: {
            appData.userData.book.title = contentData.titleInput
            appData.userData.book.author = contentData.authorInput
         }, label: { Text("Save") })
         Spacer()
      }.padding()
   }
}
```

```
struct ContentView_Previews: PreviewProvider {
    static var previews: some View {
        ContentView().environmentObject(ApplicationData())
    }
}
```

Listing 6-23: Accessing the model in an MVVM pattern

This view now accesses the model through the observable object and the view model structure. To show the title and the author, we don't have to combine the values of the `title` and `author` properties, we just read the `header` property and the view model takes care of reading the values from the model and create the string for us. All the work of formatting and processing the values is performed in the view model, not the views.

To modify the values, we must follow the hierarchical chain. The title of the book is stored in the `title` property of the `Book` structure. This structure is available from the `book` property of the `BookViewModel` structure, which was assigned to the `userData` property of the `ApplicationData` object. So, to modify the title, we must write the `appData.userData.book.title` property, as we did in the action for the `Button` view.

The function of the model in this pattern doesn't change much. Instead of the observable object, the information is stored in the instance of the `Book` structure, but because that instance is assigned to the instance of the `BookViewModel` structure, which in turn is assigned to a `@Published` property of the observable object, every time a value in the model is modified, the `@Published` property reports the change to the system, the views are updated, and the new values are displayed on the screen.

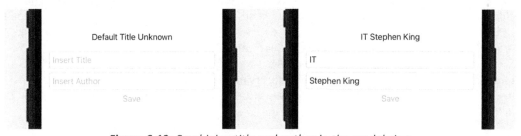

Figure 6-12: Combining title and author in the model view

 Do It Yourself: Update the ApplicationData.swift file with the code in Listing 6-22, and the ContentView.swift file with the code in Listing 6-23. If you start a new project instead, remember to inject an instance of the `ApplicationData` class into the environment, as we did in Listing 6-20. Run the application. Insert a title and an author, and press the Save button. You should see something like Figure 6-12.

 IMPORTANT: This is a basic example to illustrate how the MVVM pattern is organized, but in practical applications the observable object stores a collection of view models and it takes care of loading, adding, modifying and removing the elements of that collection. We will create applications that implement a more realistic MVVM pattern in further chapters.

(Basic) **6.4 Control Views**

Controls are visual tools the user interacts with to change the state of the interface, select options, or insert, modify or delete information. We have implemented some of them already, like the `Button` view and the `TextField` view used in previous examples. To define a useful interface, we need to learn more about these views and the rest of the control views provided by SwiftUI.

Button View

As we have already seen, the **Button** view creates a simple control that performs an action when pressed. The following are some of the structure's initializers.

Button(String, **action:** Closure)—This initializer creates a **Button** view. The first argument is a string that defines the button's label, and the **action** argument is a closure with the code to be executed when the button is pressed.

Button(**action:** Closure, **label:** Closure)—This initializer creates a **Button** view. The **action** argument is a closure with the code to be executed when the button is pressed, and the **label** argument is a closure that returns the views used to create the label.

Button(String, **role:** ButtonRole?, **action:** Closure)—This initializer creates a **Button** view. The first argument is a string that defines the button's label. The **role** argument is a structure with type properties to describe the purpose of the button. There are two properties available: **cancel** and **destructive**. And the **action** argument is a closure with the code to be executed when the button is pressed.

We have already implemented the second initializer to create our buttons, but if we only want to use a string for the label, we can simplify the code using the first initializer and a trailing closure for the action.

```
struct ContentView: View {
    @State private var colorActive: Bool = false

    var body: some View {
        VStack(spacing: 10) {
            Text("Default Title")
                .padding()
                .background(colorActive ? Color.green : Color.clear)
            Button("Change Color") {
                colorActive.toggle()
            }
            Spacer()
        }.padding()
    }
}
```

Listing 6-24: *Implementing* Button *views*

This example includes a **Text** view and a **Button** view in a **VStack**. The **Text** view displays always the same string with a background color defined by the **colorActive** property. If the value of this property is **true**, we assign the **green** color to the background, otherwise the color assigned is **clear** (transparent). When the button is pressed, we toggle the value of this property, the **body** property is evaluated again, and the text's background changes to the next color (for more information on the **toggle()** method, see Listing 3-55).

Figure 6-13: *Button view*

Do It Yourself: Create a Multiplatform project. Update the `ContentView` view with the code in Listing 6-24. Press the Change Color button. You should see the interfaces in Figure 6-13.

Of course, if we want to separate the views from the actions performed by the controls, we can move the statements to a function. For instance, we can add a function to the `ContentView` structure to toggle the value of the `colorActive` property and then call this function from the button's action. The application works the same way, but the code is better organized.

```
struct ContentView: View {
    @State private var colorActive: Bool = false

    var body: some View {
        VStack(spacing: 10) {
            Text("Default Title")
                .padding()
                .background(colorActive ? Color.green : Color.clear)
            Button("Change Color") {
                changeColor()
            }
            Spacer()
        }.padding()
    }
    func changeColor() {
        colorActive.toggle()
    }
}
```

Listing 6-25: *Using functions to organize the code*

If the only action performed by the button is to call a method, we can simplify the definition of the view by declaring the **action** argument and specifying the name of the method as the action to perform, as shown below.

```
Button("Change Color", action: changeColor)
```

Listing 6-26: *Referencing a method*

Declaring the name of a method with parentheses executes the method right away, but declaring only the name provides a reference to the method that the system can use later to execute it.

 Do It Yourself: Update the `ContentView` view with the code in Listing 6-25. Refresh the live preview if necessary. The application should work the same as before. Replace the **Button** view with the **Button** view in Listing 6-26. Refresh the live preview again and press the button to confirm the action is performed.

In previous examples, we used a ternary operator to select the value for the `background()` modifier depending on the value of the `colorActive` property. This is the recommended practice, so SwiftUI can identify the views and effectively manage the transition between one state to another, but we can also use **if else** statements to respond to changes. For instance, sometimes, controls like buttons are used to show or hide a view in the interface.

```
struct ContentView: View {
    @State private var showInfo = false

    var body: some View {
        VStack(spacing: 10) {
```

```
        Button("Show Information") {
            showInfo.toggle()
        }.padding()
        if showInfo {
            Text("This is the information")
        }
        Spacer()
        }
    }
}
```

Listing 6-27: Adding and removing views from the interface

The button in this example toggles the value of a **@State** property called **showInfo**. Below the button, we check the current value of the property. If the value is **true**, we show a **Text** view, otherwise, we do nothing. Therefore, when the button is pressed, the value of the **showInfo** property changes, the content of the **body** property is drawn again, and the **Text** view appears or disappears, depending on the current value of the property.

Figure 6-14: Dynamic interface

The **if else** statements can also be used to perform the button's action only when a condition is met, but we can also disable the button completely with the following modifier.

disabled(Bool**)**—This modifier determines whether the control responds to the user interaction or not.

The following example applies this modifier to disable the button after it is pressed, so the user can perform the action only once.

```
struct ContentView: View {
    @State private var color = Color.clear
    @State private var buttonDisabled = false

    var body: some View {
        VStack(spacing: 10) {
            Text("Default Title")
                .padding()
                .background(color)
            Button("Change Color") {
                color = Color.green
                buttonDisabled = true
            }
            .disabled(buttonDisabled)
            Spacer()
        }.padding()
    }
}
```

Listing 6-28: Disabling a button

This view includes two **@State** properties, one to keep track of the color, and another to know whether the button is enabled or not. When the button is pressed, the action assigns the value **true** to the **buttonDisabled** property and the button stops working, so the user can press it only once.

Figure 6-15: Button disabled

As we have seen before, the initializers for the `Button` view can include the **label** argument to define the label with any view we want. This argument is very flexible. It can include views like `Text` views and `Image` views. Images in buttons are displayed in the original rendering mode, which means they are showing in the original colors, but there is another mode available that creates a mask with the image and show it in the app's accent color or the foreground color assigned to the control. To select the rendering mode, the `Image` view includes the following modifier.

renderingMode(TemplateRenderingMode**)**—This modifier defines the rendering mode for an `Image` view. The argument is an enumeration with the values **original** and **template**.

The following example defines a button with an image and a text. The `renderingMode()` modifier is applied to the `Image` view to show the image as a template.

```
struct ContentView: View {
    @State private var expanded: Bool = false

    var body: some View {
        VStack(spacing: 10) {
            Text("Default Title")
                .frame(minWidth: 0, maxWidth: expanded ? .infinity : 150,
maxHeight: 50)
                .background(Color.yellow)
            Button(action: {
                expanded.toggle()
            }, label: {
                VStack {
                    Image(expanded ? "contract" : "expand")
                        .renderingMode(.template)
                    Text(expanded ? "Contract" : "Expand")
                }
            })
            Spacer()
        }.padding()
    }
}
```

Listing 6-29: Defining the label of a button with an `Image` view

The view in Listing 6-29 includes a `@State` property called **expanded** to control the width of the `Text` view. If the value of the property is **true**, we give the view an infinite width with the **infinity** value, otherwise, we make it 150 points wide. Every time the user presses the button, the value of the **expanded** property is toggled with the **toggle()** method and therefore the width of the `Text` view changes.

Figure 6-16: Button with template image

 Do It Yourself: Download the expand and contract images from our website and add them to the Asset Catalog. Update the **ContentView** view with the code in Listing 6-29 and press the Expand button. You should see the interfaces in Figure 6-16. Remove the **renderingMode()** modifier. You should see the images in their original colors.

We can also assign standard styles for the buttons with the following modifiers.

buttonStyle(ButtonStyle**)**—This modifier defines the style of the button. The argument is a structure that conforms to the **ButtonStyle** protocol.

controlSize(ControlSize**)**—This modifier defines the scale of the button. The argument is an enumeration with the values **large**, **mini**, **regular**, and **small**.

The SwiftUI framework includes the **PrimitiveButtonStyle** protocol to provide standard styles. For this purpose, the protocol defines the type properties **automatic**, **bordered**, **borderedProminent**, **borderless**, and **plain**. These styles fulfill different purposes. For instance, the **bordered** style creates a button with a gray background to represent secondary actions, and the **borderedProminent** style creates a button with the app's accent color to represent primary actions, such as the possibility to save or submit the data. For instance, the following view includes two buttons, one to cancel the process and another to send the information to a server.

```
struct ContentView: View {
   var body: some View {
      VStack(spacing: 10) {
         HStack {
            Button("Cancel") {
               print("Cancel Action")
            }.buttonStyle(.bordered)
            Spacer()
            Button("Send") {
               print("Send Information")
            }.buttonStyle(.borderedProminent)
         }
         Spacer()
      }.padding()
   }
}
```

Listing 6-30: Styling buttons

Prominent buttons should be used only to represent primary actions. In this example, the Cancel button is bordered, which tells the user that this is a secondary action, not important for the process, but the Send button is prominent, which means that an important operation is going to be performed when the button is pressed.

Figure 6-17: Buttons with standard styles

When the purpose of the button is to cancel a process, as in this case, or delete an item, we can assign that specific role to the button from the **Button** view's initializer. This allows the system to style the button according to the role and the device where the app is running. For instance, in mobile devices, a button with the **destructive** role is shown in red.

```
Button("Delete", role: .destructive) {
   print("Delete Action")
}.buttonStyle(.bordered)
```

Listing 6-31: Assigning a role

Figure 6-18: Destructive button

 Do It Yourself: Update the **ContentView** view with the code in Listing 6-30. You should see the button as illustrated in Figure 6-17. Replace the Cancel button with the **Button** view in Listing 6-31. Refresh the live preview. You should see the destructive button as illustrated in Figure 6-18.

These styles were designed to look good with SF Symbols. The advantage of using SF Symbols instead of our own images is that they are scaled to the size of the font assigned to the button. This, along with the possibility of scaling the button itself with the **controlSize()** modifier, allows us to create buttons of different sizes.

```
struct ContentView: View {
   var body: some View {
      VStack(spacing: 10) {
         Button(action: {
            print("Delete item")
         }, label: {
            HStack {
               Image(systemName: "mail")
                  .imageScale(.large)
               Text("Send")
            }
         })
         .buttonStyle(.borderedProminent)
         .font(.largeTitle)
         .controlSize(.large)
         Spacer()
      }.padding()
   }
}
```

Listing 6-32: Scaling buttons

Chapter 6 - Declarative User Interface

In this example, we implement the `imageScale()` modifier to scale the SF Symbol, the `font()` modifier to assign a large font to the button, and the `controlSize()` modifier to scale the button. The result is shown below.

Figure 6-19: *Button of custom size*

If we want to define a style that deviates from those provided by the system, we must create our own `ButtonStyle` structure. The protocol's only requirement is for the structure to implement the following method.

makeBody(configuration: Configuration)—This method defines and returns a view that replaces the body of the button. The **configuration** argument is a value of type `Configuration` that contains information about the button.

This method receives a value of type `Configuration`, a typealias of `ButtonStyle-Configuration`, which contains properties that return information about the button. The following are the properties available.

isPressed—This property returns a Boolean value that indicates whether the button was pressed or not.

label—This property returns the view or views that define the button's current label.

The following example defines a button that expands when pressed. The styles include a padding and a green border. To apply these styles, we must create a structure that conforms to the `ButtonStyle` protocol, implement the `makeBody()` method, and return from this method the view we want to assign to the body of the button.

The views that make up the body of the button are provided by the `label` property of the `Configuration` structure, so we can read and modify the value of this property to apply the new styles, as shown next.

```
import SwiftUI
struct MyStyle: ButtonStyle {
    func makeBody(configuration: MyStyle.Configuration) -> some View {
        let pressed = configuration.isPressed
        return configuration.label
            .padding()
            .border(Color.green, width: 5)
            .scaleEffect(pressed ? 1.2 : 1.0)
    }
}
struct ContentView: View {
    @State private var color = Color.gray

    var body: some View {
        VStack {
            Text("Default Title")
                .padding()
                .foregroundColor(color)
            Button("Change Color") {
                color = Color.green
            }.buttonStyle(MyStyle())
```

```
        Spacer()
    }.padding()
  }
}
```

Listing 6-33: Defining custom styles for the button

In Listing 6-33, we define a structure called **MyStyle** and implement the required **makeBody()** method. This method gets the current configuration of the button from the type properties and then proceeds to modify and return the label. First, we read the value of the **isPressed** property to know if the button was pressed or not, and then apply the new styles to the **label** property. This property returns a copy of the views that create the button's current label, and therefore by modifying its value we are effectively modifying the label. In this case, we apply a padding, a border, and then assign a scale depending on the value of the **isPressed** property. If the value is **true**, which means the button is being pressed, we assign a scale of 1.2 to expand it, but if the value is **false**, we bring the scale back to 1.

In the view, we create an instance of this structure and assign it to the **Button** view with the **buttonStyle()** modifier. The result is shown below.

Figure 6-20: Button with custom styles

 Do It Yourself: Update the ContentView.swift file with the code in Listing 6-33. Press the button. You should see the button expanding, as show in Figure 6-20, right. The button is automatically animated by SwiftUI. We will learn how to customize animations and create our own in Chapter 11.

(Basic) TextField View

The **TextField** view is another control we have introduced before. The view creates an input field the user can interact with to insert a value (a line of text). The following is one of the initializers included by the structure.

TextField(String, **text:** Binding, **axis:** Axis**)**—This initializer creates an input field. The first argument defines the field's placeholder, the **text** argument is the **Binding** property used to store the value inserted by the user, and the **axis** argument defines the axis in which the content will scroll when it exceeds the bounds of the view. It is an enumeration with the values **horizontal** and **vertical**.

The framework defines a few modifiers for **TextField** views. The following are the most frequently used.

textFieldStyle(TextFieldStyle**)**—This modifier defines the style of the text field. The argument is a structure that conforms to the **TextFieldStyle** protocol. The framework includes several structures to provide standard styles. These structures define the type properties **automatic**, **plain**, **roundedBorder**, and **squareBorder**.

autocorrectionDisabled(Bool**)**—This modifier enables or disables the system's autocorrection feature. By default, the value is **true** (disabled).

textInputAutocapitalization(TextInputAutocapitalization?**)**—This modifier defines the capitalization type used to format the text. The argument is a structure, which includes the type properties **characters**, **never**, **sentences** (default), and **words**.

keyboardType(UIKeyboardType**)**—This modifier defines the type of keyboard the system is going to open when the input field is selected. The argument is an enumeration with the values **default**, **asciiCapable**, **numbersAndPunctuation**, **URL**, **numberPad**, **phonePad**, **namePhonePad**, **emailAddress**, **decimalPad**, **twitter**, **webSearch**, **asciiCapableNumberPad**, and **alphabet**.

We have already seen how to include a simple **TextField** view to get input from the user, but we haven't applied any modifiers yet. The following example shows how to style the view and how to capitalize words.

```
struct ContentView: View {
    @State private var title: String = "Default Title"
    @State private var titleInput: String = ""

    var body: some View {
        VStack(spacing: 15) {
            Text(title)
                .lineLimit(1)
                .padding()
                .background(Color.yellow)
            TextField("Insert Title", text: $titleInput)
                .textFieldStyle(.roundedBorder)
                .textInputAutocapitalization(.words)
            Button("Save") {
                title = titleInput
                titleInput = ""
            }
            Spacer()
        }.padding()
    }
}
```

Listing 6-34: Configuring a text field

The style applied to the **TextField** view in Listing 6-34 is called **roundedBorder**. This adds a border to the input field that makes the area occupied by the view visible, as shown below.

Figure 6-21: Text field with a rounded border

 Do It Yourself: Update the **ContentView** view with the code in Listing 6-34. Insert a text in the input field and press the Save button. You should see something like Figure 6-21.

Besides a button, the user normally expects to be able to save the value by pressing the Done button on the keyboard. The framework includes the following modifiers for this purpose.

onSubmit(of: SubmitTriggers, Closure**)**—This modifier performs an action when a trigger is fired (e.g., the keyboard's Done/Return button is pressed). The **of** argument is a structure that determines the type of trigger to which the modifier responds. The structure includes the properties **search** and **text** (default). The second argument is the closure we want to execute.

submitLabel(SubmitLabel**)**—This modifier specifies the label to use for the Done button in the virtual keyboard. The argument is a structure with the type properties **continue**, **done**, **go**, **join**, **next**, **return**, **route**, **search**, and **send**.

submitScope(Bool**)**—This modifier determines whether the view will submit when is triggered.

The closure assigned to the **onSubmit()** modifier is executed when the focus is on the view (e.g., the user is editing the input field). If we apply it to a **TextField** view, the **of** argument can be omitted, as in the following example.

```
struct ContentView: View {
    @State private var title: String = "Default Title"
    @State private var titleInput: String = ""

    var body: some View {
        VStack(spacing: 15) {
            Text(title)
                .lineLimit(1)
                .padding()
                .background(Color.yellow)
            TextField("Insert Title", text: $titleInput)
                .textFieldStyle(.roundedBorder)
                .submitLabel(.continue)
                .onSubmit {
                    assignTitle()
                }
            HStack {
                Spacer()
                Button("Save") {
                    assignTitle()
                }
            }
            Spacer()
        }.padding()
    }
    func assignTitle() {
        title = titleInput
        titleInput = ""
    }
}
```

Listing 6-35: Responding to the Done button

The code in Listing 6-35 implements the **submitLabel()** modifier to change the title of the Done button to "Continue", and then adds a method to the structure called **assignTitle()** that performs the same action as before. The method is called from two places, the closure assigned to the **onSubmit()** modifier and the action of the **Button** view, so the operation is performed either when the button on the interface is pressed or when the keyboard's Done/Return button is pressed. The value inserted in the text field is always stored in the **title** property, regardless of the action the user decides to perform.

 Do It Yourself: Update the **ContentView** structure with the code in Listing 6-35 and run the app on the iPhone simulator. Click on the input field, insert a text, and press the Continue key on the keyboard. (To activate the virtual keyboard on the simulator, open the I/O menu, click on Keyboard, and select the option Toggle Software Keyboard.) The text should be assigned to the title, as before.

When a view that can take input or process feedback from the user is selected, it is said that the view is in focus. SwiftUI includes several tools to process this state. We can process a task when a view gains focus, know if the focus is on a view, or remove focus from a view. There are two property wrappers available for this purpose: **@FocusState** and **@FocusedBinding**. **@FocusState** stores a value that determines where the focus is at the moment, and **@FocusedBinding** is used to pass the state to other views. To manage the state, the framework includes the following modifiers.

focused(Binding, **equals:** Hashable)—This modifier stores the current state of the view in the **Binding** property. The first argument is a reference to the **@FocusState** property, and the equals argument is the Hashable value used to identify the view.

focusable(Bool)—This modifier determines if focus can be set on the view.

To track the states of the views, we need a **@FocusState** property of a Hashable data type that provides values we can use to identify the views. In the following example, the property is created with the values of an enumeration. We have defined two values, **name** and **surname**, to track the focus state of two input fields and change the background color when the user starts typing on them.

```
import SwiftUI
enum FocusName: Hashable {
    case name
    case surname
}
struct ContentView: View {
    @FocusState var focusName: FocusName?
    @State private var title: String = "Default Name"
    @State private var nameInput: String = ""
    @State private var surnameInput: String = ""

    var body: some View {
        VStack(spacing: 10) {
            Text(title)
                .lineLimit(1)
                .padding()
                .background(Color.yellow)
            TextField("Insert Name", text: $nameInput)
                .textFieldStyle(.roundedBorder)
                .padding(4)
                .background(focusName == .name ? Color(white: 0.9) : .white)
                .focused($focusName, equals: .name)
            TextField("Insert Surname", text: $surnameInput)
                .textFieldStyle(.roundedBorder)
                .padding(4)
                .background(focusName == .surname ? Color(white:
0.9) : .white)
                .focused($focusName, equals: .surname)
            HStack {
                Spacer()
                Button("Save") {
                    title = nameInput + " " + surnameInput
                }
            }
            Spacer()
        }.padding()
    }
}
```

Listing 6-36: Responding to changes in focus

The initial value of the `@FocusState` property is `nil`, which means no view is focused. When the user taps on a text field, the focus moves to that view and the value that identifies the view is assigned to the property. By comparing this value with the values in the enumeration, we know which `TextField` view is focused and can change the background color accordingly. Notice that the `roundedBorder` style adds a border and a white background to the text field, so only the background of the padding is visible in this example.

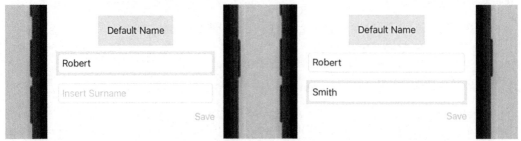

Figure 6-22: Focus

In mobile devices, the virtual keyboard opens when a view that can process the input gains focus (e.g., `TextField` view). The keyboard remains open as long as the focus is on a view that can process the input. This means that to close it, we must remove focus from the view. In SwiftUI this is achieved by assigning the value `nil` to the `@FocusState` property, as shown next.

```
Button("Save") {
    title = nameInput + " " + surnameInput
    focusName = nil
}
```

Listing 6-37: Closing the keyboard

The `Button` view in Listing 6-37 replaces the `Button` view of Listing 6-36. Now, every time the Save button is pressed, the values are processed and the keyboard is closed.

 Do It Yourself: Update the ContentView.swift file with the code in Listing 6-36 and run the application on the iPhone simulator. Click on an input field. You should see the background color changing to gray, as illustrated in Figure 6-22. Replace the `Button` view with the view in Listing 6-37. Run the application again. Insert values in both fields and press the Save button. The values should be assigned to the title and the virtual keyboard should be closed.

In previous examples, we didn't check whether the user inserted a value or not, but usually applications must prevent the user from saving invalid or empty values. There are different ways we can control this. One alternative is to check the values before storing them. We allow users to type whatever they want but only store the values accepted by the app.

```
Button("Save") {
    let tempName = nameInput.trimmingCharacters(in: .whitespaces)
    let tempSurname = surnameInput.trimmingCharacters(in: .whitespaces)

    if !tempName.isEmpty && !tempSurname.isEmpty {
        title = tempName + " " + tempSurname
        focusName = nil
    }
}
```

Listing 6-38: Checking the values before storing

In this example, we first trim the **nameInput** and **surnameInput** properties to remove spaces at the beginning and the end (see Strings in Chapter 4) and then check that the resulting values are not empty before assigning them to the **title** property. The Save button is still enabled, but the values are not stored until the user inserts a text in both fields.

 Do It Yourself: Update the **Button** view in the **ContentView** view with the code in Listing 6-38. You shouldn't be able to modify the title until you have inserted a name and a surname.

Another alternative is to disable the button with the **disabled()** modifier if the values inserted by the user are not what the application is expecting.

```
Button("Save") {
    let tempName = nameInput.trimmingCharacters(in: .whitespaces)
    let tempSurname = surnameInput.trimmingCharacters(in: .whitespaces)

    if !tempName.isEmpty && !tempSurname.isEmpty {
        title = tempName + " " + tempSurname
        focusName = nil
    }
}
.disabled(nameInput.isEmpty || surnameInput.isEmpty)
```
Listing 6-39: Disabling the button

In this example, we implement the **disabled()** modifier introduced before to disable the button until the user types a text in both fields. If one text field or both are empty, the button doesn't work.

 Do It Yourself: Update the **Button** view with the code in Listing 6-39. You shouldn't be able to press the Save button until you have inserted a name and a surname.

Besides checking whether the properties contain a valid value, we can also limit what the user can type on the fields. For instance, we could only accept numbers or a specific amount of characters. For this, we need to check whether the value inserted by the user is valid or not every time the state of the view changes. The framework includes the following modifier for this purpose.

onChange(of: Value, **perform:** Closure)—This modifier executes a closure when a state changes. The **of** argument is the value to check, and the **perform** argument is the closure we want to execute when the system reports a change in the value.

This modifier can only check one value, so we should apply it to every view we want to control. For instance, we can use it in the two **TextField** views of our example to limit the number of characters the user is allowed to type. If the user goes over the limit, we remove the extra characters and assign the result back to the property, as shown next.

```
TextField("Insert Name", text: $nameInput)
    .textFieldStyle(.roundedBorder)
    .padding(4)
    .background(focusName == .name ? Color(white: 0.9) : .white)
    .focused($focusName, equals: .name)
    .onChange(of: nameInput) { value in
        if value.count > 10 {
            nameInput = String(value.prefix(10))
        }
    }
```

```
TextField("Insert Surname", text: $surnameInput)
   .textFieldStyle(.roundedBorder)
   .padding(4)
   .background(focusName == .surname ? Color(white: 0.9) : .white)
   .focused($focusName, equals: .surname)
   .onChange(of: surnameInput) { value in
      if value.count > 15 {
         surnameInput = String(value.prefix(15))
      }
   }
}
```

Listing 6-40: *Controlling user's input*

In the code of Listing 6-40, we check for changes in the properties that store the state of the text fields. When the user types or removes a character, the value of the corresponding property changes, and the closure assigned to the `onChange()` modifier is executed. The closure receives the value of the property. Using this value, we can check whether the text inserted by the user is valid or not and respond accordingly. In this example, we count the number of characters in the string and if the value is longer than the limit, we subtract the beginning of the text with the `prefix()` method and assign the result back to the property, which updates the views and deletes the extra characters from the text field. As a result, when the number of characters exceeds the limit, the user cannot add more characters to the field.

 Do It Yourself: Update the `TextField` views in your project with the code in Listing 6-40. Run the application on the iPhone simulator. Insert a name and a surname. You shouldn't be able to add more than 10 characters for the name and 15 characters for the surname.

Of course, besides the number of characters we can set other conditions. The following example, creates a small application that only accepts integer numbers.

```
import SwiftUI
class ContentViewData: ObservableObject {
    @Published var title: String = "Default Name"
    @Published var numberInput: String = ""
    var currentNumber = ""
}
struct ContentView: View {
    @ObservedObject var contentData = ContentViewData()

    var body: some View {
        VStack(spacing: 10) {
            Text(contentData.title)
                .padding()
                .background(Color.yellow)
            TextField("Insert Number", text: $contentData.numberInput)
                .textFieldStyle(.roundedBorder)
                .padding(4)
                .keyboardType(.numbersAndPunctuation)
                .onChange(of: contentData.numberInput) { value in
                    if !value.isEmpty {
                        if Int(value) != nil {
                            contentData.currentNumber = contentData.numberInput
                        } else {
                            contentData.numberInput = contentData.currentNumber
                        }
                    } else {
                        contentData.currentNumber = ""
                    }
                }
```

```
            HStack {
                Spacer()
                Button("Save") {
                    contentData.title = contentData.numberInput
                    contentData.numberInput = ""
                }
            }
            Spacer()
        }.padding()
    }
}
```

Listing 6-41: Accepting only integer numbers

For this example, we need an additional property to store the last value inserted by the user, so if the new value is not valid, we restore the state back to the value stored in this property. To be able to update the value of this property every time the user inserts a character in the field, we must declare it in an external object. (The properties of a `View` structure cannot be modified, unless they are state properties.) In this case, we have decided to create an observable object and manage the values for the view from it, including the states (see Listing 6-17). We have the `title` property to store the title as before, the `numberInput` property to store the number inserted by the user, and the `currentNumber` property to store the last value.

As before, the view includes a `TextField` with the `onChange()` modifier. The difference is in how we check if the value is valid or not. We first check if the text field is empty or not. If empty, we clean the `currentNumber` property, otherwise, we check if the value is an integer with the `Int()` initializer. This initializer returns `nil` if the string cannot be converted into an `Int` value, so we compare the value returned by the initializer with `nil` and update the properties accordingly. If the value is an integer (different than `nil`), we update the `currentNumber` property with the number inserted by the user, otherwise, we assign the value of the `currentNumber` property to the `numberInput` property to update the text field with the last value inserted by the user and remove the invalid characters.

Notice that we have also implemented the `keyboardType()` modifier to show the appropriate keyboard for the input we are expecting from the user (in this case, numbers).

Do It Yourself: Create a Multiplatform project. Update the ContentView.swift file with the code in Listing 6-41. Run the application on the iPhone simulator. You should only be able to type numbers.

By default, a `TextField` view only displays one line of text, but we can allow the view to expand to include more with the `lineLimit()` modifier. (The same modifier implemented before to expand `Text` views.) Besides applying the modifier to set the number of lines we want, we also need to ask the view to scroll the content in the vertical axis, as shown next.

```
struct ContentView: View {
    @State private var text: String = ""

    var body: some View {
        TextField("Insert Text", text: $text, axis: .vertical)
            .textFieldStyle(.roundedBorder)
            .padding(20)
            .lineLimit(5)
    }
}
```

Listing 6-42: Defining a multiline text field

In this example, the `TextView` view expands until it reaches a height of 5 lines and then the text scrolls vertically to allow the user to keep typing. If we want to give the view a minimum and a maximum size, we can declare the modifier with a range, as in `lineLimit(3...5)`.

I'm selfish, impatient and a little insecure. I make mistakes, I am out of control and at times hard to handle. But if you can't handle me at my worst, then you sure as hell don't deserve me at my best.

Figure 6-23: *Multiline text field*

SecureField View

SwiftUI also includes a view to create a secure text field. The view replaces the characters inserted by the user with dots to hide sensitive information, such as passwords.

SecureField(String, **text:** Binding)—This initializer creates a secure input field. The first argument defines the text field's placeholder, and the **text** argument is the **Binding** property that stores the value inserted by the user.

The implementation is the same as with **TextField** views, and we can also apply some of the same modifiers, as shown next.

```
struct ContentView: View {
   @State private var pass: String = ""

   var body: some View {
      VStack(spacing: 15) {
         Text(pass)
            .padding()
         SecureField("Insert Password", text: $pass)
            .textFieldStyle(.roundedBorder)
         Spacer()
      }.padding()
   }
}
```

Listing 6-43: *Using a secure text field*

The **SecureField** view looks the same as the **TextField** view. The only difference is that the characters are hidden.

Figure 6-24: *Secure text field*

 Do It Yourself: Create a Multiplatform project. Update the **ContentView** view with the code in Listing 6-43. Insert characters in the input field. You should see the characters being replaced by black dots, as illustrated in Figure 6-24.

Chapter 6 - Declarative User Interface

TextEditor View

SwiftUI includes an additional view to allow the user to insert multiple lines of text called `TextEditor`. The following is the view's initializer.

TextEditor(text: Binding**)**—This initializer creates a text editor. The **text** argument is the **Binding** property that stores the text inserted by the user.

This view can take some of the modifiers we have already applied to `TextField` and `Text` views to format the text. For instance, we can tell the view how to align the text, the space we want between lines, and whether the view should correct the text inserted by the user.

```
struct ContentView: View {
   @State private var text: String = ""

   var body: some View {
      TextEditor(text: $text)
         .multilineTextAlignment(.leading)
         .lineSpacing(10)
         .disableAutocorrection(true)
         .padding(8)
   }
}
```

Listing 6-44: Implementing a text editor

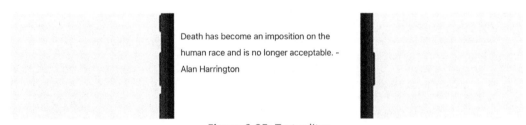

Death has become an imposition on the human race and is no longer acceptable. - Alan Harrington

Figure 6-25: Text editor

Basic **Toggle View**

The **Toggle** view creates a control to switch between two states. By default, it is displayed as a user-friendly toggle switch on mobile devices and as a checkbox on Macs. The view includes the following initializers.

Toggle(String, **isOn:** Binding**)**—This initializer creates a **Toggle** view. The first argument defines the control's label, and the **isOn** argument is the **Binding** property that stores the current state. The view also includes an initializer to define the label with the views returned by a closure (**Toggle(isOn: Binding, label: Closure)**).

The view requires a **Binding** property to store the current value. In the following example, we provide a **@State** property and use the value of this property to select the proper label.

```
struct ContentView: View {
   @State private var currentState: Bool = true

   var body: some View {
      VStack {
         Toggle(isOn: $currentState, label: {
            Text(currentState ? "On" : "Off")
         })
```

```
            Spacer()
        }.padding()
    }
}
```

Listing 6-45: Implementing a `Toggle`

The code in Listing 6-45 uses a ternary operator to check the value of the **currentState** property and display the corresponding text ("On" or "Off"). By default, we set the value of the property to **true**, so the switch is activated and the "On" label is displayed on the screen, but if we tap the switch, it is turned off, the view is updated, and the "Off" label is shown instead.

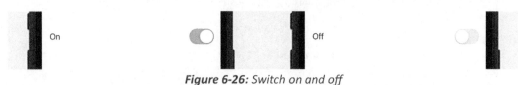

Figure 6-26: Switch on and off

 Do It Yourself: Create a new Multiplatform project. Update the **ContentView** view with the code in Listing 6-45. Click on the switch to turn it on and off. Use this project to test the following examples.

The closure assigned to the **label** argument can include a second view to define a subtitle, as in the following example.

```
struct ContentView: View {
    @State private var currentState: Bool = true

    var body: some View {
        VStack {
            Toggle(isOn: $currentState, label: {
                Text(currentState ? "On" : "Off")
                Text("Enable or Disable")
            })
            Spacer()
        }.padding()
    }
}
```

Listing 6-46: Including a subtitle

Figure 6-27: Switch with a title and subtitle

The **Toggle** view creates a horizontal stack to contain the label and the control with a flexible space in between, in consequence, the view occupies all the horizontal space available in its container and the label and the control are displaced to the sides. If we want to have absolute control on the position and size of the views, we can apply the **fixedSize()** modifier introduced before to reduce the view's size, or hide the label with the following modifier.

labelsHidden()—This modifier hides the labels assigned to controls.

This modifier works with several controls, but it is particularly useful with switches. The following example shows how to implement it to define a custom label for the control.

```
struct ContentView: View {
   @State private var currentState: Bool = true

   var body: some View {
      HStack {
         Toggle("", isOn: $currentState)
            .labelsHidden()
         Text(currentState ? "On" : "Off")
            .padding()
            .background(Color(currentState ? .yellow : .gray))
      }.padding()
   }
}
```

Listing 6-47: Defining a custom label for the `Toggle` *view*

The view is now of the size of the control and centered on the screen. The label is not shown anymore, so we declare it with an empty string, but include a **Text** view on the side to display the current value.

Figure 6-28: Custom size and label for the switch

Like **Button** views, **Toggle** views also implement a modifier to define the style of the control.

toggleStyle(ToggleStyle**)**—This modifier defines the style of the toggle. The argument is a structure that conforms to the **ToggleStyle** protocol. To create standard structures, the framework includes the properties **automatic**, **button**, **checkbox**, and **switch**.

The value by default is **automatic**, which means the style of the control is going to be selected by the system. If we want to always apply the same style, we can assign the values **switch** or **checkbox** (only available for Macs). These values are used to specify standard styles, but the framework also includes the value **button** to create a completely different type of control. When we assign this style to the view, the system shows a toggle button to represent the on and off states. When the button is in the on state, it is highlighted, otherwise it is shown as a standard button.

```
struct ContentView: View {
   @State private var currentState: Bool = true

   var body: some View {
      HStack {
         Toggle(isOn: $currentState, label: {
            Label("Send", systemImage: "mail")
         })
         .toggleStyle(.button)
      }.padding()
   }
}
```

Listing 6-48: Implementing a toggle button

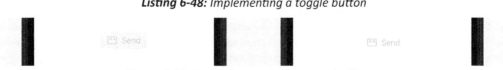

Figure 6-29: Toggle button in the on and off state

The styles offered by the framework are limited, but we can create our own. All we have to do is to define a structure that conforms to the **ToggleStyle** protocol. The protocol's requirement is for the structure to implement the following method.

makeBody(configuration: Configuration)—This method defines and returns a view that replaces the body of the toggle. The **configuration** argument is a value of type **Configuration** that contains information about the control.

This method receives a value of type **Configuration**, a typealias of **ToggleStyle-Configuration**, which contains the following properties to return information about the control.

isOn—This property returns a Boolean value that indicates if the toggle is on or off.

label—This property returns the view that defines the toggle's label.

The **isOn** property is a **Binding** property that creates a bidirectional binding with the view and therefore we can read and modify its value to activate or deactivate the control. In the following example, we create a **Toggle** view that looks like a checkbox. When the control is tapped, the graphic changes color indicating the current state (gray deactivated and green activated).

```
import SwiftUI
struct MyStyle: ToggleStyle {
    func makeBody(configuration: MyStyle.Configuration) -> some View {
        HStack(alignment: .center) {
            configuration.label
            Spacer()
            Image(systemName: "checkmark.rectangle.fill")
                .font(.largeTitle)
                .foregroundColor(configuration.isOn ? Color.green :
Color.gray)
                .onTapGesture {
                    configuration.$isOn.wrappedValue.toggle()
                }
        }
    }
}
struct ContentView: View {
    @State private var currentState: Bool = false

    var body: some View {
        VStack {
            HStack {
                Toggle("Enabled", isOn: $currentState)
                    .toggleStyle(MyStyle())
                }
                Spacer()
        }.padding()
    }
}
```

Listing 6-49: Defining a custom Toggle *view*

There are a few things we must consider before customizing a **Toggle** view. First, the **label** property of the **Configuration** structure contains a copy of the view that represents the control's current label, so if we want to keep this label, we must include the value of this property in the new content. Second, a **Toggle** view is designed with an **HStack** view and a **Spacer** view between the label and the control. If we want to stick to the standard design, we must preserve this arrangement. And third, we are responsible of responding to user interaction and update the state of the control, so we must check for a gesture and change the control's state by modifying the value of the **isOn** property when the gesture is performed by the user.

In the example of Listing 6-49, we define a structure called **MyStyle** and implement the required **makeBody()** method to provide the new design for the **Toggle** view. To preserve the standard design, we wrap the views with an **HStack** view and separate the label and the control with a **Spacer** view. We first read the value of the **label** property to include the current label, then declare the **Spacer** view, and finally define an **Image** view that presents an SF Symbol that looks like a checkbox. To turn this **Image** view into a control, we define its size with a **font()** modifier, apply the **foregroundColor()** modifier to change the color of the symbol depending on the current value of the **isOn** property, and finally, use the **onTapGesture()** modifier to detect when the user taps on the **Image** view. We will learn more about gesture modifiers in Chapter 12. For now, all we need to now is that this modifier executes a closure every time the view is tapped by the user. In this closure, we access the **Binding** value of the **isOn** property and toggle its value by applying the **toggle()** modifier to the Boolean value stored in its **wrappedValue** property. (In this case, the setter of the **Binding** value is private, so we access it from the **wrappedValue** property, as explained before in this chapter.) This modifies the current value of the property, which changes the state of the control, turning it on and off.

Figure 6-30: *Custom style for the* Toggle *view*

(Basic) Slider View

A **Slider** view creates a control that allows the user to select a value from a range of values. It is displayed as a horizontal bar with a knob that indicates the selected value. The structure includes the following initializer.

Slider(value: Binding, **in:** Range, **step:** Float, **onEditingChanged:** Closure)— This initializer creates a **Slider** view. The **value** argument is the **Binding** property we want to use to store the current value, the **in** argument is a range that specifies the minimum and maximum values the user can choose from, the **step** argument indicates the number by which the current value will be incremented or decremented, and the **onEditingChanged** argument is a closure that is executed when the user starts or finishes moving the slider.

To create a slider, we must provide at least a **@State** property to store the value and a range to determine the minimum and maximum values allowed.

```
struct ContentView: View {
   @State private var currentValue: Float = 5

   var body: some View {
      VStack {
         Text("Current Value: \
(currentValue.formatted(.number.precision(.fractionLength(0))))")
         Slider(value: $currentValue, in: 0...10, step: 1.0)
         Spacer()
      }.padding()
   }
}
```

Listing 6-50: *Creating a slider*

The code in Listing 6-50 creates a slider from the value 0 to 10 and displays the current value with a **Text** view. The **Slider** view takes values of type **Float** or **Double**, and therefore it allows us to select a floating-point value, but we can specify that we want the user to be able to select only integers by declaring the **step** argument with the value 1.0, as we did in this example. (Notice that we had to format the value for the **Text** view with the **formatted()** method introduced in Chapter 4 to display it as an integer.) Because the **currentValue** property was initialized with the number 5, the initial position of the knob is right in the middle.

Figure 6-31: Slider for integer values

The **Slider** view's initializer also includes the **onEditingChanged** argument, which takes a closure that receives a Boolean value to indicate whether the user started or finished moving the slider. We can use it to highlight the value that is been edited, as in the following example.

```
struct ContentView: View {
   @State private var currentValue: Float = 5
   @State private var textActive: Bool = false

   var body: some View {
      VStack {
         Text("Current Value: \
(currentValue.formatted(.number.precision(.fractionLength(0))))")
            .padding()
            .background(textActive ? Color.yellow : Color.clear)
         Slider(value: $currentValue, in: 0...10, step: 1.0,
onEditingChanged: { self.textActive = $0 })
         Spacer()
      }.padding()
   }
}
```

Listing 6-51: Responding to the slider state

The view in Listing 6-51 includes a new **@State** property called **textActive**. The closure assigned to the **onEditingChanged** argument assigns the value **true** to this property when the user begins moving the slider and the value **false** when the user let the knob go. The **background()** modifier of the **Text** view reads the value of this property to assign a different background color to the view depending on the current state. Because of this, the text that displays the slider's current value has a yellow background while the user is moving the slider, or no color otherwise.

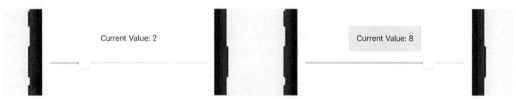

Figure 6-32: Slider states

Basic ProgressView View

SwiftUI includes the **ProgressView** view to create a progress bar. The view was designed to show the progress of a task over time.

ProgressView(String, value: Binding, **total:** Double)—This initializer creates a progress bar. The first argument specifies the label, the **value** argument indicates the current progress, and the **total** argument specifies the value that determines the completion of the process. (By default, the values go from 0.0 to 1.0).

The implementation of this view is straightforward. All we need is a property with the value that represents the current progress, as shown next.

```
struct ContentView: View {
    @State private var currentValue: Float = 5

    var body: some View {
        VStack {
            ProgressView(value: currentValue, total: 10)
            Spacer()
        }.padding()
    }
}
```

Listing 6-52: Showing progress

This **ProgressView** view goes from 0.0 to 10.0 and starts from the value 5 (the value assigned to the **currentValue** property by default), so the progress bar is set at the middle.

Figure 6-33: Progress bar

The **ProgressView** view was designed to show the progress of a task over time, such as the amount of data currently downloaded from a server or how far we are from finishing processing the data. We will learn how to perform some of these tasks later, but for now we can test it with a **Slider** view, as shown next.

```
struct ContentView: View {
    @State private var currentValue: Float = 5

    var body: some View {
        VStack {
            ProgressView(value: currentValue, total: 10)
            Slider(value: $currentValue, in: 0...10)
            Spacer()
        }.padding()
    }
}
```

Listing 6-53: Simulating progress

In this example, we set the same values for the **Slider** and the **ProgressView**. They go from 0 to 10, so every time we move the slider, the progress bar shows the same value.

Figure 6-34: Progress bar at work

The `ProgressView` structure includes the following modifier to define the style of the progress bar.

progressViewStyle(ProgressViewStyle**)**—This modifier specifies the style of a `ProgressView` view. The argument is a structure that conforms to the `ProgressView-Style` protocol. The framework defines the properties `automatic`, `circular`, and `linear` to create standard views.

The style by default is `automatic`, which means that the view is going to be shown as a linear progress bar, but we can specify the `circular` value to create an activity indicator. This is a spinning wheel that indicates that a task is in progress, but unlike progress bars, this type of indicator has no implicit limitations, so we don't need to specify any values, as shown next.

```
struct ContentView: View {
    @State private var currentValue: Float = 5

    var body: some View {
        VStack {
            ProgressView()
                .progressViewStyle(.circular)
            Spacer()
        }.padding()
    }
}
```

Listing 6-54: Showing an activity indicator

Figure 6-35: Activity indicator

(Basic) **Stepper View**

The `Stepper` view creates a control with two buttons to increment or decrement a value. The structure provides multiple initializers with several combinations of arguments for configuration. The following are the most frequently used.

Stepper(String, **value:** Binding, **in:** Range, **step:** Float, **onEditingChanged:** Closure**)**—This initializer creates a `Stepper` view. The first argument defines the label, the **value** argument is the `Binding` property we want to use to store the current value, the **in** argument is a range that determines the minimum and maximum values allowed, the **step** argument is a `Float` or a `Double` (depending on the `Binding` property) that determines the amount by which the value is going to be increased or decreased, and the **onEditingChanged** argument is a closure that is executed when the user begins and ends editing the value.

Stepper(String, **onIncrement:** Closure?, **onDecrement:** Closure?, **on-EditingChanged:** Closure**)**—This initializer creates a `Stepper` view. The first argument defines the label, the **onIncrement** argument is a closure that is executed when the user taps on the **+** button, the **onDecrement** argument is a closure that is executed when the user taps on the **-** button, and the **onEditingChanged** argument is a closure that is executed when the user begins and ends editing the value.

To implement a `Stepper` view, we need a `@State` property to store the current value and define the range of values we want the user to choose from.

Chapter 6 - Declarative User Interface

```
struct ContentView: View {
   @State private var currentValue: Float = 0

   var body: some View {
      VStack {
         Text("Current Value: \
(currentValue.formatted(.number.precision(.fractionLength(0))))")
         Stepper("Counter", value: $currentValue, in: 0...100)
         Spacer()
      }.padding()
   }
}
```

Listing 6-55: Creating a stepper

The **Stepper** view works with floating-point values of type **Float** or **Double**, so we format the value again to display only integers. The result is shown below.

Current Value: 0   Counter   − +   Counter   Current Value: 8   − +

Figure 6-36: Stepper

By default, the value is incremented or decremented by one unit, but we can change that with the **step** argument. The following example defines a **Stepper** view that increments or decrements the value by 5 units.

```
struct ContentView: View {
   @State private var currentValue: Double = 0

   var body: some View {
      VStack {
         Text("Current Value: \
(currentValue.formatted(.number.precision(.fractionLength(0))))")
         Stepper("Counter", value: $currentValue, in: 0...100, step: 5)
         Spacer()
      }.padding()
   }
}
```

Listing 6-56: Defining the steps of a stepper

Like the **Toggle** view, the **Stepper** view is implemented with a horizontal stack and a flexible space between the label and the control. If we want to provide our own label and define a custom position for the control, we need to apply the **labelsHidden()** modifier, as we did in Listing 6-47. The following example defines a custom label and creates the view with the **onIncrement** and **onDecrement** arguments to display an arrow on the screen that tells the user whether the last value was incremented or decremented.

```
struct ContentView: View {
   @State private var currentValue: Float = 0
   @State private var goingUp: Bool = true

   var body: some View {
      VStack {
         HStack {
            Text("Current Value: \
(currentValue.formatted(.number.precision(.fractionLength(0))))")
```

```
            Image(systemName: goingUp ? "arrow.up" : "arrow.down")
               .foregroundColor(goingUp ? Color.green : Color.red)
            Stepper("", onIncrement: {
               currentValue += 5
               goingUp = true
            }, onDecrement: {
               currentValue -= 5
               goingUp = false
            }).labelsHidden()
         }
         Spacer()
      }.padding()
   }
}
```

Listing 6-57: Modifying the interface when the value is incremented or decremented

In this example, we define two **@State** properties: **currentValue** to store the current value of the stepper, and a Boolean property called **goingUp** to indicate whether the last value was incremented or decremented. The views are included in an **HStack** to show them side by side. The first one is the same **Text** view used before to display the stepper's current value. After this view, we include an **Image** view that checks the **goingUp** property to show an SF Symbol of an arrow pointing up or down, depending on the property's value. The same property is used to determine the color of the arrows. Finally, we define the **Stepper** view with the **onIncrement** and **onDecrement** arguments. In the closures assigned to these arguments, we increment or decrement the value by 5 and change the value of the **goingUp** property to indicate whether the last value was incremented or decremented. As a result, the user can see a green arrow pointing up when the + button is pressed and a red arrow pointing down when the - button is pressed.

Figure 6-37: Custom stepper

Basic GroupBox View

SwiftUI includes a view called **GroupBox** to create a box around the views. The view is defined with a background color and round corners to visually group views and controls. The following is one of the view's initializers.

GroupBox(String, **content:** Closure**)**—This initializer creates a **GroupBox** view. The first argument defines the label to show at the top of the box, and the **content** argument is the closure that defines the views contained by the group.

The view is styled by default with a background color, so all we need to do is to implement it and provide the closure with all the views we want to include inside the box.

```
struct ContentView: View {
   @State private var setting1: Bool = true
   @State private var setting2: Bool = true
   @State private var setting3: Bool = true

   var body: some View {
      GroupBox("Settings") {
         VStack(spacing: 10) {
            Toggle("Autocorrection", isOn: $setting1)
            Toggle("Capitalization", isOn: $setting2)
```

```
            Toggle("Editable", isOn: $setting3)
        }
    }.padding()
    }
}
```

Listing 6-58: Defining a group of views

Figure 6-38: Group box

(Basic) **6.5 Adaptivity**

SwiftUI views can adapt to the space available. We can implement flexible views to expand the interface or align the views using alignment values, but in practice this is only useful when the proportions of the window remain the same. For example, the screen of an iPhone 13 in portrait mode is slightly taller than the screen of an older iPhone in the same orientation, but the proportions between width and height are similar. Adapting the interface to these variations only requires simple transformations, such as extending or contracting the views. Things change when we compare devices with very different screens, such as iPhones and iPads, or the same device in different orientations. The interface must be drastically modified to adapt to these disparate conditions. To know when to perform these changes, the system defines values that represent the relative size of the space in which the interface is being presented. The classification is based on the magnitude of the horizontal and vertical dimensions of the space available. The value is called *Regular* if the space is large enough to fit a regular interface, or *Compact* otherwise. These values make up a unit of measurement called *Size Classes*.

(Basic) **Size Classes**

Because of the rectangular shape of the screen, the interface is defined by two size classes, one for the horizontal and another for the vertical space. Every device is assigned different size classes, depending on the size of their screens and orientations, as illustrated below.

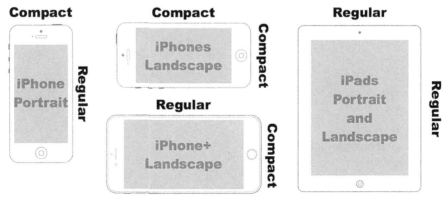

Figure 6-39: Size classes assigned to mobile devices

The illustration in Figure 6-39 represents the only four possible combinations of size classes, but they change according to the current layout. For instance, the horizontal size class changes from Regular to Compact if the screen is split in two on an iPad, or when an iPhone is rotated from landscape to portrait mode. But no matter what causes the change, we can detect it and adapt the interface accordingly. For this purpose, the environment includes the following values.

horizontalSizeClass—This value is a `UserInterfaceSizeClass` enumeration that represents the current horizontal size class of the space occupied by the view. The values available are **compact** and **regular**.

verticalSizeClass—This value is a `UserInterfaceSizeClass` enumeration that represents the current vertical size class of the space occupied by the view. The values available are **compact** and **regular**.

As explained before, we access these environment values with the **@Environment** property wrapper (see Listing 6-12). Once the **@Environment** properties are created, adapting the interface is a matter of organizing the views according to their values (**compact** or **regular**). For instance, in the following example we define the interface's content in two custom views, **HeaderView** and **BodyView**, and then display them in a vertical or horizontal stack depending on the current horizontal size class.

```
struct ContentView: View {
    @Environment(\.horizontalSizeClass) var horizontalClass

    var body: some View {
        Group {
            if horizontalClass == .compact {
                VStack(spacing: 0) {
                    HeaderView(isCompact: true)
                    BodyView()
                }
            } else {
                HStack(spacing: 0) {
                    HeaderView(isCompact: false)
                    BodyView()
                }
            }
        }.ignoresSafeArea()
    }
}
struct HeaderView: View {
    let isCompact: Bool

    var body: some View {
        Text("Food Menu")
            .frame(minWidth: 0, maxWidth: .infinity, minHeight: 0,
maxHeight: isCompact ? 150 : .infinity)
            .background(Color.yellow)
    }
}
struct BodyView: View {
    var body: some View {
        Text("Content Title")
            .frame(minWidth: 0, maxWidth: .infinity, minHeight: 0,
maxHeight: .infinity)
            .background(Color.gray)
    }
}
```

Listing 6-59: Detecting changes in the horizontal size class

Chapter 6 - Declarative User Interface

For didactic purposes we have defined all the views in the same file. In the `ContentView` view, we specify the basic layout of our app. The view creates two layouts according to the horizontal size class. If the size class is **compact**, which means that the interface is being presented in a small space, we create a `VStack` to show the views on top of each other, otherwise, we create an `HStack` to show them side by side.

Organizing the views on the screen is not enough to adapt the interface to the space available, sometimes we also must adapt their content. In this case, we do it by passing a value to the `HeaderView` to indicate whether the interface is been shown in a compact or a regular space, and then use this value inside the view to select the appropriate height.

The `HeaderView` and `BodyView` views are flexible, so the space available is distributed between the two, but we limit the height of the `HeaderView` view to 150 when it is presented in a vertical layout, so this view will only be 150 points tall in a vertical layout but extend from top to bottom in a horizontal layout.

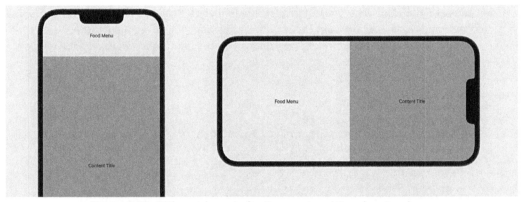

Figure 6-40: *Different layouts for Compact and Regular size classes*

 Do It Yourself: Create a Multiplatform project. Update the ContentView.swift file with the code in Listing 6-59. Select a large iPhone that presents the interface in two size classes, such as the iPhone 13 Pro Max. Rotate the preview. You should see the interfaces illustrated in Figure 6-40.

 IMPORTANT: Notice that `isCompact` is a normal property. We didn't have to use a `Binding` property in this case because every time the value of the `horizontal` property changes, the views are redrawn and the `isCompact` property is updated with the current value.

(Medium) GeometryReader View

Apple recommends to always adapt the interface according to the size classes, but there are times when this information is not enough. For instance, apps running fullscreen on iPads are always Regular and Regular (see Figure 6-39), but the difference between the width and height in portrait and landscape orientation is still significant. In cases like this, we must adapt the interface according to the size of the views, the window, or the screen. SwiftUI includes a view called `GeometryReader` that can help us on this task. The `GeometryReader` view takes the size of its container and sends this information to its children, so they can adapt to those values.

GeometryReader(content: Closure)—This initializer creates a `GeometryReader` view. The closure assigned to the **content** argument contains the views we want to measure. This closure receives a `GeometryProxy` value with the view's position and dimensions.

The **GeometryReader** view calculates its position and size and sends this information to the closure that defines the content. The values are stored in an instance of the **GeometryProxy** structure. This structure provides the following properties and method to get the values.

size—This property returns a **CGSize** value with the width and height of the **GeometryReader** view.

safeAreaInsets—This property returns an **EdgeInsets** value with the insets of the safe area.

frame(in: CoordinateSpace)—This method returns a **CGRect** value with the position and size of the **GeometryReader** view. The values are returned according to the coordinate space specified by the **in** argument. The argument is an enumeration with the values **global**, **local**, and **named(String)**.

The **GeometryReader** view works like a flexible view. It stretches to occupy all the space available and sends a **GeometryProxy** value with its position and size to the closure. Using these values, we can adapt the views or perform any change on the content we want, as shown below.

```
struct ContentView: View {
    var body: some View {
        GeometryReader { geometry in
            let isPortrait = geometry.size.height > geometry.size.width
            let message = isPortrait ? "Portrait" : "Landscape"

            HStack {
                Text(message)
            }.frame(minWidth: 0, maxWidth: .infinity, minHeight: 0,
maxHeight: .infinity, alignment: .center)
        }.ignoresSafeArea()
    }
}
```

Listing 6-60: Using a GeometryReader *to detect orientation*

In this example, we embed the whole interface inside a **GeometryReader** view, so the view expands to fill the screen. This means that the values produced by the view reflect the size of the screen, so we use them to determine whether the view is being shown in a portrait or landscape orientation. For this purpose, we get the values sent to the closure and compare the **height** and **width** properties of the **CGSize** structure returned by the **size** property. If the view's height is greater than the width, we are in portrait orientation, otherwise, the orientation is landscape.

Figure 6-41: Orientations

Chapter 6 - Declarative User Interface

Do It Yourself: Create a Multiplatform project. Update the `ContentView` view with the code in Listing 6-60. Run the application on the iPhone simulator. Rotate the screen. The text should change according to the orientation.

 IMPORTANT: With a `GeometryReader` view we can determine the orientation of the view, but this not always matches the device's orientation. For instance, the view may be shown inside an overlay on an iPad in landscape orientation, and the values will still indicate a portrait orientation. SwiftUI does not provide a way to determine the orientation of the device, but we can resort to the tools included in the UIKit framework for this purpose, as we will see in Chapter 14.

In the previous example, we select the content of a `Text` view depending on the view's orientation, but we can also adapt any other aspect of the content, including the views and sizes. For instance, we can set the size of an image.

```
struct ContentView: View {
    var body: some View {
        GeometryReader { geometry in
            HStack {
                Image("spot1")
                    .resizable()
                    .scaledToFit()
                    .frame(width: geometry.size.width / 2, height:
geometry.size.height / 4)
                    .background(Color.gray)
            }.frame(minWidth: 0, maxWidth: .infinity, minHeight: 0,
maxHeight: .infinity)
        }
    }
}
```

***Listing 6-61:** Adapting an* Image *view to the size of its container*

This code creates an **Image** view, but the view is embedded in a **GeometryReader** view, so we know the space available for it. In this example, we have decided to give the image a width that is half of the width of the container (**geometry.size.width / 2**) and a height that is a quarter of its height (**geometry.size.height / 4**). This determines the size of the **Image** view, but the aspect ratio of the image was set to **fit**, so the image is reduced even more to fit within the view's frame. (We gave the view a gray background to make the frame visible.)

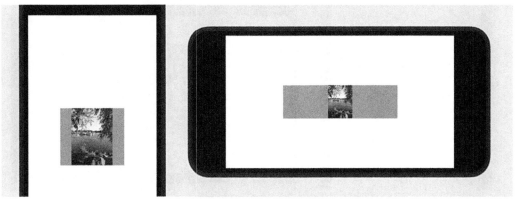

***Figure 6-42:** Image of relative size*

Do It Yourself: Update the `ContentView` view with the code in Listing 6-61. Download the spot1 image from our website and add it to the Asset Catalog. Run the application on the iPhone simulator. Rotate the screen. You should see the `Image` view adapting to the space available on the screen.

Besides the size, we can also get the position of the `GeometryReader` view. This information is returned by the `frame()` method of the `GeometryProxy` structure and the values depend on the selected coordinate space. A SwiftUI interface defines two types of coordinates spaces, one called `global` that represents the coordinates of the screen, and another called `local` that represents the coordinates of the view (every view has its own coordinate space). If we read the values considering the `local` coordinate space, the position is 0,0 (0 horizontal points and 0 vertical points), because the coordinate space of the `GeometryReader` view always starts at the position 0,0, but if we select the `global` coordinate space, the values returned by the method represent the position of the view relative to the screen. The following example implements this method to show how to work with these values.

```
struct ContentView: View {
    var body: some View {
        GeometryReader { geometry in
            let globalX = Int(geometry.frame(in: .global).origin.x)
            let globalY = Int(geometry.frame(in: .global).origin.y)
            Text("Position: \(globalX) / \(globalY)")
                .frame(minWidth: 0, maxWidth: .infinity, minHeight: 0,
maxHeight: .infinity)
        }.frame(width: 200, height: 250)
        .background(.gray)
    }
}
```

Listing 6-62: *Reading the position of the* GeometryReader *view*

This view includes a `Text` view embedded in a `GeometryReader` view. We made the `Text` view flexible to fill the container, and gave the `GeometryReader` view a fixed size of 200 by 250. Because of this, the views are positioned at the center of the screen, which means that the position of the `GeometryReader` view on the screen will be different in portrait and landscape orientation. Figure 6-43, below, shows what we see when we run this application on a small iPhone. In portrait, the `GeometryReader` view is 60 points from the left and 169 points from the top, but in landscape, the view is 184 points from the left and 35 points from the top.

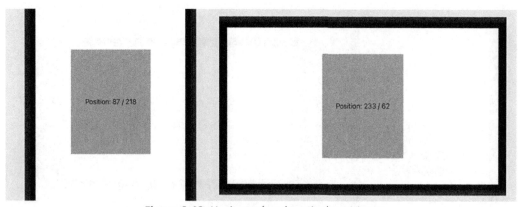

Figure 6-43: *Horizontal and vertical positions*

Do It Yourself: Update the `ContentView` view with the code in Listing 6-62. Run the application on the iPhone simulator. Rotate the screen. You should see the values of the x and y coordinates change because of the changes in the `GeometryReader` view's position relative to the screen.

The `GeometryReader` view is a flexible view and therefore it takes all the space available in its container. This means that we can use it to calculate the size and position of any view by presenting the `GeometryReader` view as a secondary view. Secondary views are those assigned to other views, like the ones assigned to the view's background. For instance, we can add a background to an image and embed the background view in a `GeometryReader` view to determine the size of the image.

```
struct ContentView: View {
    @State private var size: CGSize = .zero

    var body: some View {
        VStack {
            Image("spot1")
                .resizable()
                .scaledToFit()
                .background(
                    GeometryReader { geometry in
                        Color.clear
                            .onAppear {
                                size = geometry.size
                            }
                    })
            Text("\(Int(size.width)) x \(Int(size.height))")
        }.padding(100)
    }
}
```

Listing 6-63: *Reading the position and size of a view*

This example includes an **Image** view with a clear background (`Color.clear`). The `GeometryReader` view is used to embed the **Color** view. Views assigned to the background adopt the size of the original view. In this case, the `GeometryReader` view expands to occupy the space of the **Image** view and therefore its values reflect the image's position and size.

175 x 234

Figure 6-44: *View measured by a* GeometryReader *view*

 Do It Yourself: Update the `ContentView` view with the code in Listing 6-63. Run the application on the iPhone simulator. You should see the size of the **Image** view at the bottom, as shown in Figure 6-44.

 IMPORTANT: Notice that the `onAppear()` modifier is only called the first time the view appears on the screen. This means that the values are not updated when the device is rotated. To have access to these values at any time, we need to implement Preferences, as shown next.

The **GeometryReader** view sends the information down the hierarchy. Only the views within the **GeometryReader** view can read and use these values. If we need to send the values up the hierarchy, we must use Preferences.

Despite what the name suggests, Preferences are just named values that we can generate from a view and read from the rest of the views in the hierarchy. For instance, if we have a **Text** view inside a **VStack** view, the preference values generated by the **Text** view are accessible from the **VStack** view. The values are stored in what is called a Preference Key. This is a structure that conforms to the **PreferenceKey** protocol. The protocol has the following requirements.

Value—This property is an associated type that defines the data type of the values we are going to work with.

defaultValue—This property defines the value the Preference Key is going to have by default.

reduce(value: Value, **nextValue:** Closure**)**—This method adds a new value to the structure. The **value** argument is a reference to the values stored in the structure from previous calls, and the **nextValue** argument is a closure that returns the new value.

We must define a structure that conforms to the **PreferenceKey** protocol and then use it to pass the values from one view to another with the following modifiers.

preference(key: Type, **value:** Value**)**—This modifier sets a value for a specific preference key. The **key** argument is a reference to the key's data type, and the **value** argument is the value we want to assign to that key.

onPreferenceChange(Type, **perform:** Closure**)**—This modifier executes a closure when the value of a preference key changes. The first argument is a reference to the key's data type, and the **perform** argument is the closure to be executed when the value changes.

The process to pass a value from one view to another begins by defining a structure that conforms to the **PreferenceKey** protocol. Then, we must apply the **preference()** modifier to a view with the value we want to send. And finally, we must apply the **onPreferenceChange()** modifier to a view in the hierarchy (a parent view or a container of the previous view) to process the value. The following example illustrates how the process works. We implement a **GeometryReader** view to determine the size of an image, as we did in the previous example, but send the values to the rest of the views using a **PreferenceKey** structure.

```
import SwiftUI

struct BoxPreference: PreferenceKey {
   typealias Value = CGSize
   static var defaultValue: CGSize = .zero

   static func reduce(value: inout CGSize, nextValue: () -> CGSize) {
      value = nextValue()
   }
}
struct ContentView: View {
   @State private var size: CGSize = .zero

   var body: some View {
```

```
VStack {
    Image("spot1")
        .resizable()
        .scaledToFit()
        .background(
            GeometryReader { geometry in
                Color.clear
                    .preference(key: BoxPreference.self, value:
geometry.size)
            })
        Text("\(Int(size.width)) x \(Int(size.height))")
    }.padding()
    .onPreferenceChange(BoxPreference.self) { value in
        size = value
    }
    }
}
```

Listing 6-64: Setting and reading preferences

The first thing we do in Listing 6-64 is to define the structure to store the values. To conform to the **PreferenceKey** protocol, this structure must meet some requirements. First, we must define a typealias called **Value**. Because we are going to store the **CGSize** value returned by the **size** property of the **GeometryProxy** structure, we define **Value** as a typealias of **CGSize**. Next comes a type property called **defaultValue**. This property defines the value of the structure by default. Since we are working with a **CGSize** structure, we define it as a **CGSize** structure with its values set to 0 (**zero**). Finally, we implement the **reduce()** method. This method receives a reference to the values already stored in the structure and a closure that returns the new value. To store this new value, we must execute the closure and add the value returned to the values already stored in the structure. In this case, we are working only with one value (a **CGSize** structure), so we assign it directly to the property (**value = nextValue()**).

In the view, we embed an **Image** view with a **VStack** view and apply a **GeometryReader** view to the background, as done before, but this time we store the values in an instance of our **BoxPreference** structure with the **preference()** modifier. Now, this value is defined as a Preference and therefore we can read it from the views in the hierarchy with the **onPreferenceChange()** modifier. In this example, the modifier is applied to the **VStack** view. When a new value is received, we assign it to a **@State** property to update the view. As a result, the view always shows the size of the image on the screen, even when the device is rotated.

Figure 6-45: Interface updated with preferences

 Do It Yourself: Update the ContentView.swift file with the code in Listing 6-64. Run the application on the iPhone simulator. Rotate the screen. You should see the size of the image change according to the orientation.

IMPORTANT: In this example, we store a single **CGSize** value, but the **PreferenceKey** protocol was designed to manage values from multiple views and therefore they are usually stored in arrays. For more information on Preferences, visit our website and follow the links for this chapter.

(Basic) 7.1 Lists of Views

One of the main characteristics of computer systems is their ability to process sequential data. Due to their elementary structure, made up of sequences of switches on and off, computers excel at organizing information into lists of values, and this is the perfect format for displaying data to users. We can implement this type of organization with vertical and horizontal stacks, but SwiftUI provides additional tools to create dynamic lists of views and edit their content.

(Basic) ForEach View

The simplest tool provided by SwiftUI to create a list of views is the **ForEach** view. This view generates a loop that iterates through the values of a collection and creates a new view for each one of them. The structure includes the following initializer.

ForEach(Data, **id:** KeyPath, **content:** Closure**)**—This initializer creates a **ForEach** view. The first argument is the collection of values the loop is going to iterate through, the **id** argument is the key path to the unique identifier for each value, and the **content** argument is the closure that creates the views in each cycle.

A **ForEach** view needs two values: the collection from which is going to get the data to build the list of views, and a key path that determines the value used to identify the views. This is important because the system needs to identify the views to remove them or add new ones when the collection is updated. If the collection is made of standard Swift values like **Int** or **String**, assigning an identifier is easy. These data types conform to the **Hashable** protocol and therefore they have a hash value that identifies each instance (see Listing 3-177). To use this hash value as the identifier, we must specify the **\.self** key path, as in the following example.

```
struct ContentView: View {
    var body: some View {
        VStack {
            ForEach(1...5, id: \.self) { value in
                Text("Value: \(value)")
            }
            Spacer()
        }
    }
}
```

Listing 7-1: Creating a list of views dynamically

The **ForEach** view adds the content to its container, so we must declare it inside a container view like a **VStack** or an **HStack**, as we did in Listing 7-1. In this example, the loop is defined with a range of integers from 1 to 5, and the views are identified by the hash value (**\.self**). The **ForEach** view loops through the values in the range and sends them to the closure one by one. The closure receives each value and then creates a **Text** view with it to show it on the screen.

Value: 1
Value: 2
Value: 3
Value: 4
Value: 5

Figure 7-1: *List of views generated by a* ForEach *loop*

In this example, the values are presented on the screen with a **VStack** and the configuration by default (center alignment and a width determined by the widest view). Although we can use all the views at our disposal to present each value and apply any styles we want, there is a standard design that users immediately recognize in which the values are separated by a line. SwiftUI includes the following view to create this line.

Divider()—This initializer creates a **Divider** view. The view displays a line to separate content.

The **Divider** view is like any other view. If we want to position the line generated by this view below the value, we must embed the **Text** view and the **Divider** view in a **VStack**.

```
struct ContentView: View {
    let listCities: [String] = ["Paris", "Toronto", "Dublin"]

    var body: some View {
        VStack {
            ForEach(listCities, id: \.self) { value in
                VStack {
                    Text(value)
                    Divider()
                }
            }
            Spacer()
        }
    }
}
```

Listing 7-2: *Creating a list with a standard design*

The **ForEach** view in Listing 7-2 creates a list of views from an array of strings. The structure defines the array with the name of three cities and then implements the **ForEach** view to create the list. Notice that **String** values are hashable, so we can also identify them by the hash value with **\.self**.

Paris

Toronto

Dublin

Figure 7-2: *List of views with a standard design*

Values of primitive data types like integers and strings conform to the **Hashable** protocol and therefore we can use their hash value to identify the views, as we did in these examples. But when working with data stored by the user in our model, it is better to provide a unique identifier that is stored along with the data and therefore is always the same. For this purpose, SwiftUI offers the **identifiable** protocol. The protocol requires the structure to define a property called **id** to store a unique identifier for each instance, and this is how we prepare the values in our model to work with list of views. For example, the following model creates a structure to store information about a book, and another to work as the view model for our application that includes an **id** property with the unique identifier for each book.

```swift
import SwiftUI

struct Book: Hashable {
    var title: String
    var author: String
    var cover: String
    var year: Int
    var selected: Bool
}
struct BookViewModel: Identifiable, Hashable {
    let id = UUID()
    var book: Book

    var title: String {
        return book.title.capitalized
    }
    var author: String {
        return book.author.capitalized
    }
    var cover: String {
        return book.cover
    }
    var year: String {
        return String(book.year)
    }
    var selected: Bool {
        get {
            return book.selected
        }
        set {
            book.selected = newValue
        }
    }
}
class ApplicationData: ObservableObject {
    @Published var userData: [BookViewModel]

    init() {
        userData = [
            BookViewModel(book: Book(title: "Steve Jobs", author: "Walter Isaacson", cover: "book1", year: 2011, selected: false)),
            BookViewModel(book: Book(title: "HTML5 for Masterminds", author: "J.D Gauchat", cover: "book2", year: 2017, selected: false)),
            BookViewModel(book: Book(title: "The Road Ahead", author: "Bill Gates", cover: "book3", year: 1995, selected: false)),
            BookViewModel(book: Book(title: "The C Programming Language", author: "Brian W. Kernighan", cover: "book4", year: 1988, selected: false)),
            BookViewModel(book: Book(title: "Being Digital", author: "Nicholas Negroponte", cover: "book5", year: 1996, selected: false)),
            BookViewModel(book: Book(title: "Only the Paranoid Survive", author: "Andrew S. Grove", cover: "book6", year: 1999, selected: false)),
            BookViewModel(book: Book(title: "Accidental Empires", author: "Robert X. Cringely", cover: "book7", year: 1996, selected: false)),
            BookViewModel(book: Book(title: "Bobby Fischer Teaches Chess", author: "Bobby Fischer", cover: "book8", year: 1982, selected: false)),
```

```
        BookViewModel(book: Book(title: "New Guide to Science", author:
"Isaac Asimov", cover: "book9", year: 1993, selected: false)),
        BookViewModel(book: Book(title: "Christine", author: "Stephen
King", cover: "book10", year: 1983, selected: false)),
        BookViewModel(book: Book(title: "IT", author: "Stephen King",
cover: "book11", year: 1987, selected: false)),
        BookViewModel(book: Book(title: "Ending Aging", author: "Aubrey
de Grey", cover: "book12", year: 2007, selected: false))
      ]
   }
}
```

Listing 7-3: Defining a model to work with lists of views

The **Book** structure is the actual model. It includes properties to store the title of the book, the author, the name of the image for the cover, the year the book was published, and a Boolean property to indicate whether the book is currently selected or not. On the other hand, the **BookViewModel** structure defines the view-model. It includes a property to store all the information about the book (**book**), computed properties to prepare the information for the views, and the **id** property required by the protocol to store the value that identifies each book. In this case, we have decided to use a **UUID** value. This is a structure defined by the Foundation framework that guarantees that every time it is created it returns a unique value, so it is perfect to identify the books.

The observable object is defined with a property called **userData** to store an array of **BookViewModel** structures with the information of every book stored by the user. And finally, the array is initialized with a total of 12 books to test the application.

 IMPORTANT: The **Book** and **BookViewModel** structures also conform to the **Hashable** protocol. When a structure conforms to this protocol, the system creates a unique identifier that is used later to identify the instances of the structure within collections. Conformance to this protocol is required for navigation, as we will see in Chapter 8.

Once we have the model, we need to decide how are we going to access it from the views. For small applications, we can store it in a **@StateObject** property and pass it to the views one by one, as we did in Chapter 6 (see Listing 6-14), but as we will see in Chapter 8, professional applications are composed of multiple views, so a better approach is to assign the instance to the environment and then access it from the views with the **@EnvironmentObject** property wrapper, as we also did in Chapter 6 (see Listings 6-20 and 6-21). The following are the changes we need to introduce to the **App** structure to inject our model into the environment.

```
import SwiftUI

@main
struct TestApp: App {
   @StateObject var appData = ApplicationData()

   var body: some Scene {
      WindowGroup {
         ContentView()
            .environmentObject(appData)
      }
   }
}
```

Listing 7-4: Injecting the model into the environment

When the data conforms to the **identifiable** protocol, the system knows how to identify the items, so all we need to do is to declare the collection, and the list of views is automatically created from the values.

```
struct ContentView: View {
   @EnvironmentObject var appData: ApplicationData

   var body: some View {
      VStack {
         ForEach(appData.userData) { book in
            VStack {
               HStack(alignment: .top) {
                  Image(book.cover)
                     .resizable()
                     .scaledToFit()
                     .frame(width: 80, height: 100)
                  VStack(alignment: .leading, spacing: 2) {
                     Text(book.title).bold()
                     Text(book.author)
                     Text(book.year).font(.caption)
                  }.padding(.top, 5)
                  Spacer()
               }
               Divider()
            }
         }
         Spacer()
      }
   }
}
struct ContentView_Previews: PreviewProvider {
   static var previews: some View {
      ContentView().environmentObject(ApplicationData())
   }
}
```

Listing 7-5: Creating a list of views with data from the model

The **ForEach** view reads the array with all the books from the **userData** property of our observable object and sends the items one by one to the closure. The items are instances of the **BookViewModel** structure, each with the information of a book, so we read the structure's properties to show the information on the screen.

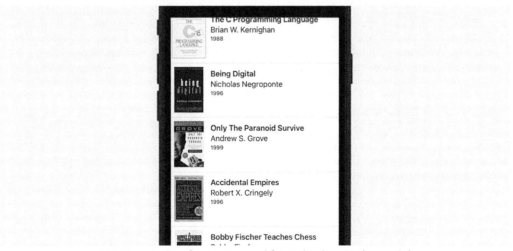

Figure 7-3: List of views created from the data in the model

Do It Yourself: Create a Multiplatform project. Download the book covers from our website and add them to the Asset Catalog. (You can use the Asset Catalog for development included by the template, as explained in Chapter 5.) Create a Swift file called ApplicationData.swift for the model in Listing 7-3. Update the `App` structure with the code in Listing 7-4. Update the `ContentView` view with the code in Listing 7-5. You should see a list of books, as illustrated in Figure 7-3.

(Basic) ScrollView View

The `ApplicationData` class defined in Listing 7-3 stores 12 books in the model for testing purposes. This generates a long list of books that extends beyond the screen boundaries and therefore the user is not be able to see it. For a list to effectively show all the content available in the model, it must be able to scroll. To convert a static list of views into a scrollable one, SwiftUI includes the `ScrollView` view. The following is the structure's initializer.

ScrollView(Axis, **showsIndicators:** Bool, **content:** Closure)—This initializer creates a container view the user can scroll. The first argument is an enumeration of type `Axis` that indicates the axis in which the views are going to scroll. The values available are `horizontal` and `vertical` (default). The **showsIndicators** argument is a Boolean value that determines if the view is going to display the scroll indicators or not. And the **content** argument is the closure that defines the scrollable content.

The `ScrollView` structure just creates a scrollable view, but the content is still generated by a vertical or a horizontal stack. SwiftUI defines the following views for this purpose.

LazyVStack(alignment: HorizontalAlignment, **spacing:** CGFloat?, **pinned-Views:** PinnedScrollableViews, **content:** Closures)—This initializer creates a lazy vertical stack. The **alignment** argument determines the horizontal alignment of the views. It is a structure with the type properties `center`, `leading`, and `trailing`. The **spacing** argument determines the space between the views. The **pinnedViews** argument is a structure that determines which views will be momentarily pinned to the bounds of the scroll view while the content is scrolling. The structure defines the type properties `sectionFooters` and `sectionHeaders`. And the **content** argument is the closure that defines the list of views we want to show in the stack.

LazyHStack(alignment: VerticalAlignment, **spacing:** CGFloat?, **pinned-Views:** PinnedScrollableViews, **content:** Closure)—This initializer creates a lazy horizontal stack. The arguments are the same as the lazy vertical stack, except for the **alignment** argument, which defines the vertical alignment of the views. It is a structure with the type properties `bottom`, `center`, `firstTextBaseline`, `lastTextBaseline`, and `top`.

Lazy stacks are similar to the normal stacks created by the `VStack` and `HStack` views, with the difference that the views in a lazy stack are created as needed. The system takes care of creating the views only before they are about to be rendered onscreen, consuming less resources and improving performance. Other than the use of lazy stacks, the list is defined as before, but embedded in a `ScrollView` view.

```
struct ContentView: View {
    @EnvironmentObject var appData: ApplicationData

    var body: some View {
        ScrollView {
            LazyVStack {
```

```
ForEach(appData.userData) { book in
   VStack {
      HStack(alignment: .top) {
         Image(book.cover)
            .resizable()
            .scaledToFit()
            .frame(width: 80, height: 100)
         VStack(alignment: .leading, spacing: 2) {
            Text(book.title).bold()
            Text(book.author)
            Text(book.year).font(.caption)
         }.padding(.top, 5)
         Spacer()
      }.padding([.leading, .trailing], 10)
      .padding([.top, .bottom], 5)
      Divider()
   }
  }
 }
}
```

Listing 7-6: *Making a list of views scrollable*

By default, the axis of the view is set to vertical, the indicators are shown, and the content adapts to the size of the view, so all we need to do in our example is to replace the **VStack** views implemented before with a **LazyVStack** and embed the list in a **SrollView** view. Now the user can scroll the list of books.

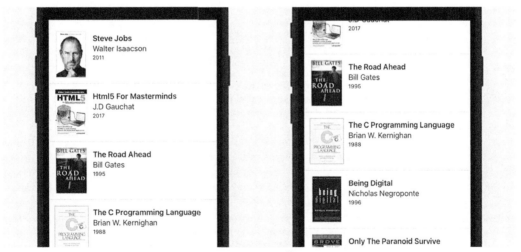

Figure 7-4: *Scroll view*

IMPORTANT: The lazy vertical stack is used to create each row on the list, but the views inside a row are organized with normal stacks. This is because we need the system to create the rows only when they are needed, but the views that define the content of each row are always required.

The **View** protocol also includes the following modifiers to dynamically perform changes in the configuration of the scroll view.

scrollIndicators(ScrollIndicatorVisibility, **axes:** Axis**)**—This modifier sets the visibility of the scroll indicators. The first argument is a structure with the type properties **automatic**, **hidden**, **never**, and **visible** to define the scroll indicators' visibility, and the **axes** argument defines the axis we want to affect. It is an enumeration with the values `vertical` and `horizontal`. (If the argument is ignored, the visibility is applied to both axes.)

scrollDismissesKeyboard(ScrollDismissesKeyboardMode**)**—This modifier determines the behavior of the keyboard when the drag gesture begins. The argument is a structure with the type properties `automatic`, `immediately`, `interactively`, and `never` (default).

The following example demonstrates how to implement both modifiers. We have added a `TextField` view on top of the `ScrollView` view to allow the user to insert a text, and applied the modifiers below. By default, once the keyboard is opened, it never closes, but applying the `scrollDismissesKeyboard()` modifier with the value `immediately` we get it to close as soon as the user stars scrolling the view.

```
struct ContentView: View {
    @EnvironmentObject var appData: ApplicationData
    @State private var title: String = ""

    var body: some View {
        VStack {
            TextField("Title", text: $title)
                .padding()
            ScrollView {
                LazyVStack {
                    ForEach(appData.userData) { book in
                        VStack {
                            HStack(alignment: .top) {
                                Image(book.cover)
                                    .resizable()
                                    .scaledToFit()
                                    .frame(width: 80, height: 100)
                                VStack(alignment: .leading, spacing: 2) {
                                    Text(book.title).bold()
                                    Text(book.author)
                                    Text(book.year).font(.caption)
                                }.padding(.top, 5)
                                Spacer()
                            }.padding([.leading, .trailing], 10)
                                .padding([.top, .bottom], 5)
                            Divider()
                        }
                    }
                }
            }
            .scrollIndicators(.never)
            .scrollDismissesKeyboard(.immediately)
        }
    }
}
```

Listing 7-7: Configuring the scroll view

Do It Yourself: Update the `ContentView` view with the example you want to try. After updating the view with the code in Listing 7-7, the keyboard will close as soon as you drag the view and the scroll indicators will not be visible.

The content of a `ScrollView` view has to be inside a vertical or a horizontal stack, depending on the axis. If we want to scroll the list of books horizontally, we must embed the `ForEach` view of our example in a `LazyHStack` view, as shown next.

```
struct ContentView: View {
   @EnvironmentObject var appData: ApplicationData

   var body: some View {
      ScrollView(.horizontal, showsIndicators: false) {
         LazyHStack(spacing: 0) {
            ForEach(appData.userData) { book in
               CellView(book: book)
            }
         }
      }
   }
}
struct CellView: View {
   let book: BookViewModel

   var body: some View {
      VStack {
         Image(book.cover)
            .resizable()
            .scaledToFit()
            .frame(width: 80, height: 100)
         Text(book.title)
            .font(.caption)
      }.padding(10)
         .frame(width: 100, height: 150)
   }
}
```

Listing 7-8: Scrolling the list of views horizontally

In this example, we tell the **ScrollView** view to create a horizontal view without indicators, and then place the views inside a **LazyHStack** to display the list horizontally.

Notice that we have also moved the code that creates the views for each item to a separate view called **CellView** (These views represent the cells or rows on the list). This is not required but is recommended because it improves the workflow and simplifies the code. The only thing we need to remember is that the view we use to build the row doesn't have access to the values processed by the main view, so we must pass the data this view needs to define its content. In this case, we pass a copy of the **BookViewModel** structure processed by the loop.

The application works the same way as before, but because of the changes we have introduced to the main view, the books are displayed side by side.

Figure 7-5: Horizontal scroll view

The user can scroll the list vertically or horizontally, depending on the view's orientation, but we can also do it from code. SwiftUI includes the following view for this purpose.

ScrollViewReader(content: Closure)—This initializer creates a container view to allow programmatic scrolling on a **ScrollView** view. The **content** argument is a closure with the **ScrollView** view we want to control.

The **ScrollViewReader** view creates a structure of type **ScrollViewProxy** with the information required to scroll the list of views to a specific row. For this purpose, the structure includes the following method.

scrollTo(Value, anchor: UnitPoint?)—This method scrolls the list of views to the view identified with the value specified by the first argument. The **anchor** argument determines the position of the view after the scrolling is over. It is a structure that we can create from the type properties **bottom, bottomLeading, bottomTrailing, center, leading, top, topLeading, topTrailing, trailing**, and **zero**.

The **scrollTo()** method scrolls the list to make the view with the specified identifier visible. The **ForEach** view automatically assigns an identifier to the views on the list (in our case, this is the **UUID** value assigned to the **id** property), but the **scrollTo()** method requires the identifier to be declared explicitly. The framework includes the following modifiers for this purpose.

id(Value)—This modifier assigns a new identifier to the view. The argument is the **Hashable** value we want to use to identify the view.

tag(Value)—This modifier assigns an identifier to the view. The argument is a **Hashable** value, usually defined with an integer.

To be able to scroll the **ScrollView** view programmatically, we must embed it in a **ScrollViewReader** view and use the proxy value provided by this view to call the **scrollTo()** method when necessary. And for this method to work, we need to identify the views with the **id()** or **tag()** modifiers. These modifiers work the same way in most circumstances, but for **ScrollView** views is recommended to identify the rows with the **id()** modifier, as in the following example.

```
struct ContentView: View {
    @EnvironmentObject var appData: ApplicationData

    var body: some View {
        ScrollViewReader { proxy in
            ScrollView(.horizontal, showsIndicators: false) {
                LazyHStack(spacing: 0) {
                    ForEach(appData.userData) { book in
                        CellView(book: book)
                            .id(book.id)
                    }
                    Button("< Go Back") {
                        if let firstIdentifier = appData.userData.first?.id {
                            proxy.scrollTo(firstIdentifier, anchor: .top)
                        }
                    }.padding()
                }
            }
        }
    }
}
```

Listing 7-9: Scrolling the list programmatically

This **ContentView** view replaces the same view from the previous example. It creates a horizontal scrollable list of books, but this time the **ScrollView** view is embedded in a **ScrollViewReader** view so we can control it from code. To be able to scroll to any row on the list, we assign the **id()** modifier to all the **CellView** views created by the loop and use the value of the book's **id** property as the view's identifier. Below the **ForEach** view, we include a **Button** view to let the user scroll the list to the beginning. For this purpose, we get the first item in the `userData` array, read the `id` property, and call the `scrollTo()` method on the proxy with this value. As a result, when the user scrolls the list to the end, a button appears, and if pressed, it scrolls the list back to the beginning.

Figure 7-6: Custom scroll

Do It Yourself: Update the `ContentView` view from the project created in the previous section with the code in Listing 7-8. You should see something like Figure 7-5. Update the `ContentView` view with the code in Listing 7-9. Scroll the list to the end. You should see the Go Back button, as illustrated in Figure 7-6. Press the button to scroll the list back to the beginning.

(Basic) Lazy Grids

Regardless of the stack view, horizontal or vertical, only one item is included per row or column. If we want to include more, we need to create a lazy grid. SwiftUI defines the following views for this purpose.

LazyVGrid(columns: [GridItem], **alignment:** HorizontalAlignment, **spacing:** CGFloat?, **pinnedViews:** PinnedScrollableViews, **content:** Closure)—This view creates a grid of views. The **columns** argument is an array of `GridItem` structures that determine how the items are arranged on the grid. The **alignment** argument determines how the items are aligned inside the container. It is a structure with the type properties `center`, `leading`, and `trailing`. The **spacing** argument determines the space between views. The **pinnedViews** argument is a structure that determines which views will be momentarily pinned to the bounds of the scroll view while the content is scrolling. And the **content** argument is the closure that provides the list of views.

LazyHGrid(rows: [GridItem], **alignment:** VerticalAlignment, **spacing:** CGFloat?, **pinnedViews:** PinnedScrollableViews, **content:** Closure)—This view is similar to the `LazyVGrid` view, but the items are arranged horizontally and the **alignment** argument determines the vertical alignment instead of the horizontal alignment. It is a structure with the type properties `bottom`, `center`, `firstText-Baseline`, `lastTextBaseline`, and `top`.

The `LazyVGrid` and `LazyHGrid` views create a grid of views arranged in rows and columns, but the size and quantity of views in a row or a column is determined by instances of the `GridItem` structure.

GridItem(Size, spacing: CGFloat?, **alignment:** Alignment?)—This structure defines the size, padding, and alignment of each item on the grid. The first argument is an enumeration that includes three associated values: `adaptive(minimum: CGFloat, maximum: CGFloat)`, `fixed(CGFloat)`, and `flexible(minimum: CGFloat, maximum: CGFloat)`. The **spacing** argument defines the space around the item. And the **alignment** argument defines the item's alignment. It is a structure with the type properties `bottom`, `bottomLeading`, `bottomTrailing`, `center`, `leading`, `top`, `topLeading`, `topTrailing`, and `trailing`.

With a `GridItem` structure we can determine the number of views we want to display per row or column, or if we want the grid to determine the number of items to show depending on the space available. For this purpose, the structure can take three different associated values. The `fixed()` and `flexible()` values define the fixed or flexible size of a single view, and the `adaptive()` value defines the flexible size of multiple views. For instance, if we want to create a vertical grid with a specific number of items per row and a fixed size, we must create an array of `GridItem` structures with the `fixed()` value. The number of instances of the `GridItem` structure included in the array determine the number of items per row, as shown next.

```
struct ContentView: View {
    @EnvironmentObject var appData: ApplicationData

    let guides = [
        GridItem(.fixed(75)),
        GridItem(.fixed(75)),
        GridItem(.fixed(75))
    ]
    var body: some View {
        ScrollView {
            LazyVGrid(columns: guides) {
                ForEach(appData.userData) { book in
                    Image(book.cover)
                        .resizable()
                        .scaledToFit()
                }
            }
        }.padding()
    }
}
```

Listing 7-10: *Creating a grid with a fixed number of items*

In this example, we define an array of three `GridItem` structures, all with a fixed size of 75 points, and use it to define a vertical grid of books. Because we use a fixed size, and include three instances of the structure, the `LazyVGrid` view creates a grid with three books per row, of a size of 75 points each, no matter the space available.

Figure 7-7: *Fixed grid*

In the previous example, the views are always 75 points wide. If what we want is to create three items per row but expand the items to occupy all the space available, we can turn the items flexible with the `flexible()` value, as shown next.

```
let guides = [
    GridItem(.flexible(minimum: 75), alignment: .top),
    GridItem(.flexible(minimum: 75), alignment: .top),
    GridItem(.flexible(minimum: 75), alignment: .top)
]
```

Listing 7-11: *Defining flexible items*

The **flexible()** value still represents one single item, so we still must include three **GridItem** structures in the array to include three items per row in our grid, but because we are not declaring a fixed size, the items expands to occupy all the space available in the container, as shown below. (Notice that we have also align the items to the top with the **alignment** argument.)

Figure 7-8: *Flexible grid*

The **flexible()** value represents a single item, so the number of items per row is always the same. If what we want is to display as many items as possible per row but keeping the same proportions and space between views, we can use the **adaptive()** value.

```
let guides = [
    GridItem(.adaptive(minimum: 75))
]
```

Listing 7-12: *Defining adaptive items*

The **adaptive()** value represents multiple items, so we only need to declare one. This item tells the grid to include as many items per row as possible but they must be at least 75 points wide. The **LazyVGrid** view calculates the number of items that fit inside a row according to the space available. If there is any space left, it expands the items to keep the same space in between.

Figure 7-9: *Adaptive grid*

 Do It Yourself: Update the **ContentView** view with the code in Listing 7-10. You can remove the **CellView** structure included in the previous example. You should see the grid of books illustrated in Figure 7-7. Update the **guides** array with the examples in Listings 7-11 and 7-12. Test different values to understand how the grid adapts and how the layout values work.

(Basic) **7.2 List View**

Presenting information in a scrollable list of rows and columns is a common requirement of any application. For this reason, SwiftUI includes an additional view to create lists of values called

List. Like a `LazyVStack` view, a `List` view creates a vertical list with a single column of items,, but the items are automatically separated by a line, and the view includes built-in functionality to select, add, or remove content. The following are some of the view's initializers.

List(Data, **rowContent:** Closure**)**—This initializer creates a list of views. The first argument is the collection of values to create the rows. These values must conform to the **identifiable** protocol and implement the **id** property to provide a unique identifier. The **rowContent** argument is a closure that defines the views used to create the rows.

List(Data, **id:** KeyPath, **rowContent:** Closure**)**—This initializer creates a list of views. The first argument is the collection of values to create the rows, the **id** argument is the key path to the unique identifier of each value, and the **rowContent** argument is a closure that defines the views used to create the rows.

List(Data, **selection:** Binding, **rowContent:** Closure**)**—This initializer creates a list of views. The first argument is the collection of values to create the rows, the **selection** argument is a **Binding** property that stores one or a set of identifiers to recognize the selected rows, and the **rowContent** argument is a closure that defines the views used to create the rows.

The syntax to implement a `List` view is the same we have used before for the `ForEach` view. The view requires a reference to the collection of data to be shown and a closure with the views that define the content of each row.

```
struct ContentView: View {
    @EnvironmentObject var appData: ApplicationData

    var body: some View {
        List(appData.userData) { book in
            CellBook(book: book)
        }
    }
}
struct CellBook: View {
    let book: BookViewModel

    var body: some View {
        HStack(alignment: .top) {
            Image(book.cover)
                .resizable()
                .scaledToFit()
                .frame(width: 80, height: 100)
            VStack(alignment: .leading, spacing: 2) {
                Text(book.title).bold()
                Text(book.author)
                Text(book.year).font(.caption)
                Spacer()
            }.padding(.top, 5)
            Spacer()
        }
    }
}
```

Listing 7-13: Creating a list of views with the `List` *view*

Like the `ForEach` view, the `List` view in Listing 7-13 reads the values in the model and creates the rows with the views defined by the closure. In this example, we use a custom view to create the rows called `CellBook`. This view includes an `HStack` with all the same views we used before to display the book's information.

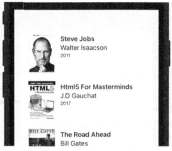

Figure 7-10: *List of rows created by a* `List` *view*

 Do It Yourself: Update the ContentView.swift file with the code in Listing 7-13. This example assumes that you have implemented the model of Listing 7-3 with all the testing data, and have injected the `ApplicationData` object into the environment, as we did in Listing 7-4. You should see a scrollable list of books, as illustrated in Figure 7-10.

In mobile devices, the list is shown with a style that generates a padding around the views and includes a background color. The `View` protocol defines the following modifier to customize the style.

listStyle(ListStyle**)**—This modifier assigns a style to the `List` view. The argument is a structure that conforms to the `ListStyle` protocol. SwiftUI defines multiple styling structures, and these structures include the type properties `automatic`, `plain`, `inset`, `grouped`, `insetGrouped`, and `sidebar` to apply standard styles.

The style set by default in mobile devices is called `insetGrouped`, but we can change it with the `listStyle()` modifier. The `plain` style displays the views with not background or padding, the `inset` style adds padding to the list, the `insetGrouped` style adds a background and a padding around the views, and the `sidebar` style adds a background to the whole list. The following example applies a plain styling to the list.

```
struct ContentView: View {
    @EnvironmentObject var appData: ApplicationData

    var body: some View {
        List(appData.userData) { book in
            CellBook(book: book)
        }.listStyle(.plain)
    }
}
```

Listing 7-14: *Creating a plain list*

The result is similar to what we achieved with the `ForEach` and `Divider` views before (see Listing 7-2), but now the list has an inset on the left side that gives it a distinctive look and is able to manage large number of items.

Figure 7-11: *Plain list*

The list styles provide a standard configuration. The **View** protocol includes the following modifiers for customization.

listRowBackground(View**)**—This modifier defines the background view for the row. The argument is a SwiftUI view, such as **Color**.

listRowInsets(EdgeInsets**)**—This modifier defines the insets for the rows (padding). The argument is an **EdgeInsets** structure. This structure includes the initializer **EdgeInsets(top: CGFloat, leading: CGFloat, bottom: CGFloat, trailing: CGFloat)** to define the top, leading, bottom, and trailing insets.

listRowSeparator(Visibility, **edges:** VerticalEdge**)**—This modifier configures the row separators. The first argument determines if the separators are visible or hidden. It is an enumeration with the values **automatic**, **hidden**, and **visible**. And the **edges** argument defines which separators are affected. It is a structure with the type properties **all**, **bottom**, and **top**.

listRowSeparatorTint(Color?, **edges:** VerticalEdge**)**—This modifier defines the separators' color. The first argument specifies the new color, and the **edges** argument determines which separator is affected. It is a structure with the type properties **all**, **bottom**, and **top**.

listItemTint(Color?**)**—This modifier defines a new tint color for the row. It overwrites the app's accent color (see Figure 5-45).

These modifiers are applied to the rows, but by modifying the rows we can change the style of the entire list. For instance, we can remove the padding assigned to the rows by the **plain** style with the **listRowInsets()** modifier.

```
struct ContentView: View {
    @EnvironmentObject var appData: ApplicationData

    var body: some View {
        List(appData.userData) { book in
            CellBook(book: book)
                .listRowInsets(EdgeInsets(top: 0, leading: 0, bottom: 10,
trailing: 0))
                .listRowBackground(Color(white: 0.95))
                .listRowSeparator(.hidden)
        }.listStyle(.plain)
    }
}
```

Listing 7-15: Customizing the rows

In this example, we remove the insets on the sides, but assign an inset of 10 points to the bottom of each row. To show how other modifiers work, we have also assigned a background color and removed the separators. The result is shown below.

Figure 7-12: Custom list

The `listRowBackground()` modifier applied in Listing 7-15 changes the background color of each row, so they all look the same. If we want to apply alternate backgrounds, we need to identify each row and then apply a color accordingly. For instance, we can use the index of the book in the `userData` array. This value is unique for every book stored in the array, so we can use it to know which view we are working with.

```
struct ContentView: View {
    @EnvironmentObject var appData: ApplicationData
    let colors = [.white, Color(white: 0.95)]

    var body: some View {
        List(appData.userData) { book in
            let index = appData.userData.firstIndex(where: { $0.id ==
book.id }) ?? 0

            CellBook(book: book)
                .listRowBackground(index % 2 == 0 ? colors[0] : colors[1])
                .listRowSeparator(.hidden)
        }.listStyle(.plain)
    }
}
```

Listing 7-16: Assigning alternate backgrounds

The view in Listing 7-16 defines a property called **colors** with the two colors we want to assign to the views (white and gray). In the closure assigned to the **List** view, we get the index of the book with the `firstIndex()` method. The method looks for an item in the array which **id** property has the same value than the **id** property of the current book, and returns the index of the item if found, or **nil** otherwise. To make sure that we always get a value, we use the nil-coalescing operator (`??`) to return the index 0 if no value is found. The `listRowBackground()` applies the remainder operator to the index value to select the color (see Chapter 2, Listing 2-49). If the value is even, the first color is assigned to the background (white), and if the index is odd, the second value is assigned instead (gray).

Figure 7-13: Alternate backgrounds

The **List** view was designed to work along with the **ForEach** view to mix static and dynamic content. The advantage is that we can create a list of rows with the data from the model and at the same time include other rows with static content to incorporate additional information or for styling purposes, as in the following example.

```
struct ContentView: View {
    @EnvironmentObject var appData: ApplicationData

    var body: some View {
        List {
            HStack {
                Image(systemName: "book.circle")
                    .font(.largeTitle)
```

```
            Spacer()
            Text("My Favorite Books")
                .font(.headline)
        }.frame(height: 50)
        ForEach(appData.userData) { book in
            CellBook(book: book)
        }
    }.listStyle(.plain)
    }
}
```

Listing 7-17: Mixing static and dynamic content in a list

A **List** view takes a list of views, one or more **ForEach** loops, or a combination of both, and includes every view in a row. In Listing 7-17, we create one static view with an SF Symbol and some text, and then a **ForEach** view to list the data in the model. The static content is shown along with the dynamic content and even scrolls with the rest of the rows, as shown below.

Figure 7-14: Static and dynamic content

(Basic) Sections

A list may be organized in sections. Sections help the user identify common values. SwiftUI includes the **Section** view to create these sections.

Section(content: Closure**)**—This initializer creates a **Section** view to group related content. The **content** argument is the closure that defines the rows for the section.

Section(content: Closure, **header:** View, **footer:** View**)**—This initializer creates a **Section** view to group related content. The **content** argument is the closure that defines the rows for the section, the **header** argument is a view or a group of views that define the section's header, and the **footer** argument is a view or a group of views that define the section's footer.

The text assigned to the section's header is displayed at the top of the section with a style that matches the style of the list, but we can make it more prominent with the following modifier.

headerProminence(Prominence**)**—This modifier defines the prominence of the section's title. The argument is an enumeration with the values **increased** and **standard**.

Although a section may contain no header or footer, for most situations it is better to provide a visual cue of where a section begins and ends. The following example creates two sections with a prominent header defined by a **Text** view.

```
struct ContentView: View {
    @EnvironmentObject var appData: ApplicationData

    var body: some View {
        List {
            Section(header: Text("Statistics")) {
                HStack {
                    Text("Total Books:")
                    Spacer()
                    Text(String(appData.userData.count))
                }
            }.headerProminence(.increased)
            Section(header: Text("My Books")) {
                ForEach(appData.userData) { book in
                    CellBook(book: book)
                }
            }.headerProminence(.increased)
        }
    }
}
```

Listing 7-18: Dividing the content into sections

This example creates two sections, one to show the total number of books in the model and another to list the books.

Figure 7-15: Sections with headers

 Do It Yourself: Update the `ContentView` view with the code in Listing 7-18. Try to expand the views in the headers with stacks and modifiers to see how they work.

If the style of the list is `plain` or `inset`, the sections show separators at the top and bottom. The `View` protocol includes the following modifiers to configure these lines.

listSectionSeparator(Visibility, **edges:** VerticalEdge)—This modifier configures the sections separators. The first argument determines if the separators are visible or hidden. It is an enumeration with the values `automatic`, `hidden`, and `visible`. And the **edges** argument defines which separators are affected. It is a structure with the type properties `all`, `bottom`, and `top`.

listSectionSeparatorTint(Color?, **edges:** VerticalEdge)—This modifier defines the separators' color. The first argument specifies the new color, and the **edges** argument determines which separator is affected. It is a structure with the type properties `all`, `bottom`, and `top`.

These modifiers work similarly to the same modifiers for rows. We can remove the top and bottom lines, or both, and change their colors. For instance, in the following view we remove the top line and change the color of the bottom line for the first section, and completely remove the lines for the second section.

```
struct ContentView: View {
    @EnvironmentObject var appData: ApplicationData

    var body: some View {
        List {
            Section(header: Text("Statistics")) {
                HStack {
                    Text("Total Books:")
                    Spacer()
                    Text(String(appData.userData.count))
                }
            }.listSectionSeparator(.hidden, edges: .top)
            .listSectionSeparatorTint(.blue)

            Section(header: Text("My Books")) {
                ForEach(appData.userData) { book in
                    CellBook(book: book)
                }
            }.listSectionSeparator(.hidden)
        }.listStyle(.plain)
    }
}
```

Listing 7-19: Configuring the section separators

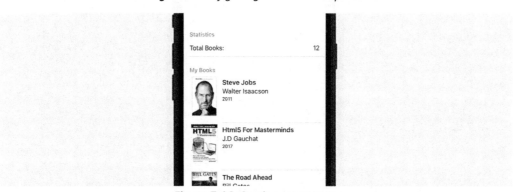

Figure 7-16: Section separators

 IMPORTANT: If you scroll down the list, you will see that the views go all to the top, behind the status bar. This is because `List` views were designed to work with the navigation bars provided by `NavigationStack` views. We will learn how to use these views and navigate between views in the next chapter.

By default, the height of headers and rows is determined by their content, but the environment includes two properties to modify those values.

defaultMinListHeaderHeight—This property defines the minimum height for the headers. It is a value of type `CGFloat`.

defaultMinListRowHeight—This property defines the minimum height for the rows. It is a value of type `CGFloat`.

To change the values of these properties, we must apply the `environment()` modifier to the `List` view (see Listing 5-94). These properties are useful when the content of the headers or the rows is variable. For instance, we can assign a minimum size to the rows of our previous example so the row in the first section is of the same height as the rows with the books.

```
struct ContentView: View {
   @EnvironmentObject var appData: ApplicationData

   var body: some View {
      List {
         Section(header: Text("Statistics")) {
            HStack {
               Text("Total Books:")
               Spacer()
               Text(String(appData.userData.count))
            }
         }
         Section(header: Text("My Books")) {
            ForEach(appData.userData) { book in
               CellBook(book: book)
            }
         }
      }.environment(\.defaultMinListRowHeight, 100)
   }
}
```

Listing 7-20: Configuring the list from the environment

Figure 7-17: Same height for all the rows

So far, we have used sections to group different types of content. The first section of our example contains information about the model and the second section contains the list of books. But sections also come in handy when we need to separate the content in groups, like movies in categories, or organize items alphabetically. For this purpose, we must prepare the data according to the organization we want to present to the user. An alternative is to define a computed property in the view that returns the list of books in alphabetical order.

```
struct ContentView: View {
   @EnvironmentObject var appData: ApplicationData

   var orderList: [(key: String, value: [BookViewModel])] {
      let listGroup: [String: [BookViewModel]] = Dictionary(grouping:
appData.userData, by: { value in
         let index = value.title.startIndex
         let initial = value.title[index]
         return String(initial)
      })
      return listGroup.sorted(by: { $0.key < $1.key })
   }
   var body: some View {
```

```
      List {
         ForEach(orderList, id: \.key) { sections in
            Section(header: Text(sections.key)) {
               ForEach(sections.value) { book in
                  CellBook(book: book)
               }
            }.headerProminence(.increased)
         }
      }
   }
}
```

Listing 7-21: Providing an ordered list of values

Before defining the **body** property, the view in Listing 7-21 defines a computed property that returns an array of tuples with the books organized by the title's first letter. First, the closure applies the **Dictionary(grouping:, by:)** initializer to create a dictionary from the values of the **userData** array (the list of books in the model). The way this initializer works is that for every value in the array, it executes a closure and then groups the results by the values returned by the closure (see Listing 3-122). In this example, we get the index of the first character in the book's title with the **startIndex** property. Then, we use that index to extract the first character. And finally, we turn it into a string and return it. This creates an array with tuples which first value is a letter of the alphabet and the second value is an array with all the books which titles begin with that letter (**[(key: String, value: [BookViewModel])]**). After this array is created, we sort the values alphabetically with the **sorted()** method and return it, so every time the views read the **orderList** property, they get an array of tuples with the books sorted alphabetically.

The values of the tuples were identified with the labels **key** and **value**, so we can use these labels to read them and create our list. In this example, we define a **List** view with two **ForEach** loops inside, one to create the sections for each letter and another to list the books inside the sections. The first **ForEach** loop reads the content of the **orderList** property and creates a section with the value identified by the **key** label (the letter). Inside the section, another **ForEach** loop iterates through the array identified with the **value** label to create the list of books. As a result, we get a list of books organized alphabetically into sections.

Figure 7-18: Alphabetical sections

Basic Edit Mode

List views also provide tools to work with the values on the list. The following are the modifiers available to remove and sort views.

onDelete(perform: Closure)—This modifier executes the closure specified by the **perform** argument when the user tries to remove a row. The closure receives an **IndexSet** value with integers representing the indexes of the rows the user wants to delete.

deleteDisabled(Bool**)**—This modifier enables or disables the possibility for the user to delete a row.

onMove(perform: Closure**)**—This modifier executes the closure specified by the **perform** argument when the user tries to move a row to a different position on the list. The closure receives an **IndexSet** value with integers representing the indexes of the rows the user is moving, and an integer representing the index where the rows should be moved.

moveDisabled(Bool**)**—This modifier enables or disables the possibility for the user to move a row.

These modifiers produce a value of type **IndexSet** that contains a set of integers representing the indexes of the values to be modified in the collection. To modify an array from these values, the Swift Standard Library defines the following methods.

remove(atOffsets: IndexSet**)**—This method removes the items in the array with the indexes provided by the **atOffsets** argument.

move(fromOffsets: IndexSet, **toOffset:** Int**)**—This method moves the items of the array in the indexes specified by the **fromOffsets** argument to the index determined by the **toOffset** argument.

The **onDelete()** and **onMove()** modifiers identify the items by the indexes in the array. The closure assigned to these modifiers receives a set with the indexes of the items to be deleted or moved, and all we need to do is to call the **remove()** or **move()** methods with these values.

There are different ways to allow the user to modify the list. For instance, if we apply the **onDelete()** modifier to the list, the system automatically activates a feature that lets the user drag the rows to the left to expose a Delete button. When this button is pressed, the closure assigned to the modifier is executed and we can proceed accordingly, as shown next.

```
struct ContentView: View {
    @EnvironmentObject var appData: ApplicationData

    var body: some View {
        List {
            ForEach(appData.userData) { book in
                CellBook(book: book)
            }.onDelete { indexes in
                appData.userData.remove(atOffsets: indexes)
            }
        }
    }
}
```

Listing 7-22: Deleting rows

Notice that the modifiers are implemented by the **ForEach** view, so we need to create the list with this view. In the example of Listing 7-22, we use the **onDelete()** modifier. The closure assigned to the modifier receives an **IndexSet** value with the index of the row to be deleted and calls the **remove()** method on the **userData** array to remove the item from the model. Now the user can delete the book by dragging the row to the left and pressing the Delete button.

Figure 7-19: Automatic delete feature

Do It Yourself: Update the `ContentView` view with the code in Listing 7-22. Drag a row to the left and press the Delete button, as shown in Figure 7-19. The row should be removed from the list.

Besides the possibility to drag a row to delete it, **List** views also include a set of tools that allow the user to select, remove, and move rows. The tools are displayed to the user when the list is in edit mode. The easiest way to activate this mode is with the **EditButton** view. This view creates a button that activates and deactivates the edit mode when pressed, as shown next.

```
struct ContentView: View {
    @EnvironmentObject var appData: ApplicationData

    var body: some View {
        VStack {
            EditButton()
            List {
                ForEach(appData.userData) { book in
                    CellBook(book: book)
                }.onDelete { indexes in
                    appData.userData.remove(atOffsets: indexes)
                }
            }.listStyle(.plain)
        }
    }
}
```

Listing 7-23: Activating the edit mode

The view in Listing 7-23 embeds the **List** view in a **VStack** view to add an **EditButton** at the top. When the button is pressed, the system activates the edit mode and the tools are shown according to the modifiers applied. For instance, in our example, we included the **onDelete()** modifier, so the view exposes buttons to let the user delete the row.

Figure 7-20: Edit button

The tool to move rows is included when the **onMove()** modifier is applied to the **ForEach** view, as in the following example.

```
struct ContentView: View {
    @EnvironmentObject var appData: ApplicationData

    var body: some View {
        VStack {
            EditButton()
            List {
                ForEach(appData.userData) { book in
                    CellBook(book: book)
                }.onDelete { indexes in
                    appData.userData.remove(atOffsets: indexes)
                }
                .onMove { source, destination in
                    appData.userData.move(fromOffsets: source, toOffset:
destination)
                }
            }.listStyle(.plain)
        }
    }
}
```

Listing 7-24: Moving rows

The system detects that we have implemented the **onMove()** modifier and automatically provides the tools for the user to move the rows and reorganize the list. After the user drops a row in a new position, the modifier sends the indexes of the rows and the new location to the closure, and here is where we have the chance to call the **move()** method to perform the change in the **userData** array, so the next time the list is redrawn, the rows remain in the position selected by the user.

Figure 7-21: Move buttons

 Do It Yourself: Update the **ContentView** view with the code in Listing 7-24. Press the Edit button. Use the tools to remove a row or move it to a different position. You should see the interfaces illustrated in Figures 7-20 and 7-21.

The edit mode also allows the user to select one or more rows. For single selection, the mode is enabled by default. All we need to do is to initialize the **List** view with the **selection** argument. The argument takes a **Binding** property to store the identifier of the selected row, which we can use later to process the item, as shown next.

```
struct ContentView: View {
    @EnvironmentObject var appData: ApplicationData
    @State private var selectedRow: BookViewModel.ID? = nil
```

```
var body: some View {
    VStack {
        HStack {
            Spacer()
            Button(action: {
                removeSelected()
            }, label: {
                Image(systemName: "trash")
            }).disabled(selectedRow == nil ? true : false)
        }.padding()

        List(selection: $selectedRow) {
            ForEach(appData.userData) { book in
                CellBook(book: book)
            }
        }.listStyle(.plain)
    }
}
func removeSelected() {
    if let index = appData.userData.firstIndex(where: { $0.id ==
selectedRow }) {
        appData.userData.remove(at: index)
        selectedRow = nil
    }
}
}
```

Listing 7-25: *Selecting a row*

When working with structures that conform to the **Identifier** protocol, the **List** view automatically identifies the views with the values assigned to the **id** property. In our example, these are the **UUID** values assigned to each book. When a row is selected, the **List** view assigns this identifier to the **@State** property, so we must declared that property with the same data type. But in this example we use a different approach. The **Identifier** protocol defines a typealias for the property's data type called **ID** (a typealias is an alternative name for a data type). By declaring a **@State** property of type **BookViewModel.ID** we make sure that the data type assigned to the property is the same assigned to the **id** property, no matter if later we replace this identifier with another one.

If the user selects an item, the **List** view assigns the value of the item's **id** property to the **selectedRow** property, so we can do whatever we want with it. In this case, we add a **Button** view at the top that calls a method to remove the selected book. The method gets the index of the selected item in the **userData** array, calls the **remove()** method to remove it, and assigns the value **nil** to the **selectedRow** property to cancel the selection. Notice that we have applied the **disabled()** modifier to the button to only enable it when a book has been selected.

Figure 7-22: *Single selection*

The **selection** argument supports the selection of one or more items, but for multiple selection to be enabled we must activate the edit mode, as we did before (unless a keyboard is present). To process multiple values, we can store the identifiers in an **IndexSet** structure and apply the same methods used above to move and remove rows. The **IndexSet** structure provides the following method for this purpose.

insert(Int)—This method adds the index specified by the argument to the set.

In the following example, we modify the **@State** property to take a **Set** of **UUID** values instead of just one (**Set<BookViewModel.ID>**), and create an **IndexSet** structure with the indexes of the selected rows to remove the values from the model.

```
struct ContentView: View {
    @EnvironmentObject var appData: ApplicationData
    @State private var selectedRows: Set<BookViewModel.ID> = []

    var body: some View {
        VStack {
            HStack {
                EditButton()
                Spacer()
                Button(action: {
                    removeSelected()
                }, label: {
                    Image(systemName: "trash")
                }).disabled(selectedRows.count == 0 ? true : false)
            }.padding()

            List(selection: $selectedRows) {
                ForEach(appData.userData) { book in
                    CellBook(book: book)
                }
            }.listStyle(.plain)
        }
    }
    func removeSelected() {
        var indexes = IndexSet()
        for item in selectedRows {
            if let index = appData.userData.firstIndex(where: { $0.id ==
item }) {
                indexes.insert(index)
            }
        }
        appData.userData.remove(atOffsets: indexes)
        selectedRows = []
    }
}
```

Listing 7-26: Selecting multiple rows

The view now includes two views at the top: the **EditButton** view to activate or deactivate the edit mode, and the trash can button to remove the books selected by the user. When the user activates the edit mode, checkboxes appear on the left to select the rows. If the user selects a row, the **List** view adds the value of the item's **id** property to the **selectedRows** property, so we can call our **removeSelected()** method again to remove the books. In this case, the method creates an empty **IndexSet** structure and then iterates through the values in the **selectedRows** property to find the index of each book and add it to the set. Once all the indexes are found, we call the **remove()** method on the **userData** array to erase the books, and then clean the **selectedRows** property to allow the user to start the process again.

Figure 7-23: Selected rows

 Do It Yourself: Update the **ContentView** view with the code in Listing 7-26. Press the Edit button. Select a row and click the button on the right. The row should be removed, as shown in Figure 7-23.

If we want to deactivate the edit mode after books are removed, or after any other action for that matter, we must control the mode programatically. The environment offers the following property for this purpose.

editMode—This property defines the state of the edit mode for the view. It is a **Binding** property of type **EditMode**, an enumeration with the values **active**, **inactive**, and **transient**. The enumeration also includes the **isEditing** property to return a Boolean value that indicates whether the view is in edit mode or not.

To manage the mode, we need a **@State** property with a Boolean value that stores the state of the edit mode (active or inactive), we must set the mode according to the value of this property with the **environment()** modifier, as we did before for other environment properties, and we also need to create a button to toggle this value and change the mode.

```
struct ContentView: View {
   @EnvironmentObject var appData: ApplicationData
   @State private var selectedRows: Set<BookViewModel.ID> = []
   @State private var editActive: Bool = false

   var body: some View {
      VStack {
         HStack {
            Button(editActive ? "Done" : "Edit") {
               editActive.toggle()
            }
            Spacer()
            Button(action: {
               removeSelected()
            }, label: {
               Image(systemName: "trash")
            }).disabled(selectedRows.count == 0 ? true : false)
         }.padding()

         List(selection: $selectedRows) {
            ForEach(appData.userData) { book in
               CellBook(book: book)
            }
         }.listStyle(.plain)
         .environment(\.editMode, .constant(editActive ?
EditMode.active : EditMode.inactive))
      }
   }
```

```
func removeSelected() {
    var indexes = IndexSet()
    for item in selectedRows {
        if let index = appData.userData.firstIndex(where: { $0.id ==
item }) {
            indexes.insert(index)
        }
    }
    appData.userData.remove(atOffsets: indexes)
    selectedRows = []
    editActive = false
    }
}
```

Listing 7-27: Customizing the edit mode

This code defines a **@State** property called **editActive** to keep track of the edit mode and replaces the **EditButton** view with a regular **Button** view. If the value of the property is **true**, it means that the mode is active, otherwise inactive, so we use it to select the mode, to deactivate it after the selected books are deleted, and to set the title for the button ("Done" if **true**, "Edit" if **false**). Notice that the environment's **editMode** property is a **Binding** property and therefore we had to use the **constant()** method to provide a **Binding** value of type **EditMode** (see Listing 6-11).

The result is the same as before, but the process is now customized and therefore we can change the edit mode from code anytime we want by assigning the value **true** or **false** to the **editActive** property.

 Do It Yourself: Update the **ContentView** view with the code in Listing 7-27. Press the Edit button. Select a row and click the Remove button. The row should be removed, as before, but now the edit mode is automatically deactivated.

The selection process can also be customized, but it requires us to keep track of the selected rows ourselves and detect the selection with the **onTapGesture()** modifier. We have implemented this modifier before to detect when an image was tapped by the user (see Listing 6-49). We will study gestures in Chapter 12, but for our purpose all we need to know is that the modifier executes a closure when the user taps the view. In our case, we need to apply it to every **CellBook** view to assign the value of the **id** property of the selected book to a **@State** property, as shown next.

```
struct ContentView: View {
    @EnvironmentObject var appData: ApplicationData
    @State private var selectedRow: BookViewModel.ID? = nil

    var body: some View {
        List {
            ForEach(appData.userData) { book in
                CellBook(selected: $selectedRow, book: book)
                    .background(.white)
                    .onTapGesture {
                        if selectedRow == book.id {
                            selectedRow = nil
                        } else {
                            selectedRow = book.id
                        }
                    }
            }
        }.listStyle(.plain)
    }
}
```

```
struct CellBook: View {
    @Binding var selected: BookViewModel.ID?
    let book: BookViewModel

    var body: some View {
        HStack(alignment: .top) {
            Image(book.cover)
                .resizable()
                .scaledToFit()
                .frame(width: 80, height: 100)
            VStack(alignment: .leading, spacing: 2) {
                Text(book.title).bold()
                Text(book.author)
                Text(book.year).font(.caption)
                Spacer()
            }.padding(.top, 5)
            Spacer()
            if selected == book.id {
                Image(systemName: "checkmark")
                    .foregroundColor(Color.green)
                    .frame(width: 25, height: 25)
            }
        }
    }
}
```

Listing 7-28: *Customizing the selection*

In this example, we allow the selection of one row at a time. If the user taps on a row, the **onTapGesture()** modifier checks whether the book's id was already stored in the **@State** property. If it was, it deselects the row by assigning the value **nil** to the property, otherwise, the value of the book's **id** property is assigned to the **@State** property to indicate that the row was selected. To show the selection to the user, we connect the **@State** property with a **@Binding** property in the **CellBook** view and then show an image if the value of this property is equal to the book's identifier. As a result, a checkmark is shown on the row when it is selected.

Figure 7-24: *Custom selection*

 Do It Yourself: Update the **ContentView** and **CellBook** views with the code in Listing 7-28. Click on a row. You should see the checkmark shown in Figure 7-24. Of course, you can add a button to perform a task on the selected item, like removing the selected book from the model, as we did before.

 IMPORTANT: Notice that we have applied the **background()** modifier to the **CellBook** view with a white color. The modifier generates a **Color** view that occupies the whole area, providing a surface for the **onTapGesture()** to detect the taps. This allows the user to select the row by tapping anywhere, not only on its content. SwiftUI also provides the **contentShape()** modifier for this purpose. We will learn more about it and gestures in Chapter 12.

Chapter 7 - Lists

The selection performed in the applications created by previous examples are stored in a `@State` property in the view. If for any reason the view is removed, the selection is removed with it. If we need to keep the selection active or access it from other views, we can store it in the model. The **Book** and **BookViewModel** structures in our model already include a **selected** property to store this value, so all we need to do is to modify the value of this property every time the user taps on a row, as shown next.

```
struct ContentView: View {
    @EnvironmentObject var appData: ApplicationData

    var body: some View {
        List {
            ForEach($appData.userData) { $book in
                CellBook(book: book)
                    .background(.white)
                    .onTapGesture {
                        book.selected.toggle()
                    }
            }
        }.listStyle(.plain)
    }
}
struct CellBook: View {
    let book: BookViewModel

    var body: some View {
        HStack(alignment: .top) {
            Image(book.cover)
                .resizable()
                .scaledToFit()
                .frame(width: 80, height: 100)
            VStack(alignment: .leading, spacing: 2) {
                Text(book.title).bold()
                Text(book.author)
                Text(book.year).font(.caption)
                Spacer()
            }.padding(.top, 5)
            Spacer()
            if book.selected {
                Image(systemName: "checkmark")
                    .foregroundColor(Color.green)
                    .frame(width: 25, height: 25)
            }
        }
    }
}
```

Listing 7-29: Storing the selection in the model

Although we can access and modify the **Book** structures in the model using the array index, the **List** and **ForEach** views can take a **Binding** value, which allows us to modify the model directly. In this example, we toggle the value of the **selected** property every time the user taps on a row. If the value is **true**, it becomes **false**, and vice versa. Notice that we modify the value of the **selected** property from the view-model. This is possible because we have declared a setter for this property that sets the value of the **Book** structure for us (see Listing 7-3).

The result is the same as before, but now we can select multiple books and each **Book** structure knows whether the book is currently selected or not.

The Delete button displayed by the list when the user swipes a row to the left is called *Swipe Action*. The swipe action that defines the Delete button is provided by the **List** view, but we can define our own with the following modifier.

swipeActions(edge: HorizontalEdge, **allowsFullSwipe:** Bool, **content:** Closure)—This modifier defines swipe actions for a row on a list. The **edge** argument determines the side of the row where the buttons are going to be placed (left or right). It is an enumeration with the values **leading** and **trailing**. The **allowsFullSwipe** argument determines whether the first action is executed if the user swipes the row all the way to the side. And the **content** argument is a closure that provides the **Button** views that represent the swipe actions.

By default, the swipe action is created on the trailing side and it allows to perform the first action with a full swipe, so if that configuration is good for our application, all we need to do is to define the closure with the **Button** views we want to include.

```
struct ContentView: View {
   @EnvironmentObject var appData: ApplicationData

   var body: some View {
      List {
         ForEach(appData.userData) { book in
            CellBook(book: book)
               .swipeActions {
                  Button(role: .destructive, action: {
                     removeBook(book: book)
                  }, label: {
                     Image(systemName: "trash")
                  })
               }
         }
      }.listStyle(.plain)
   }
   func removeBook(book: BookViewModel) {
      var indexes = IndexSet()
      if let index = appData.userData.firstIndex(where: { $0.id ==
book.id }) {
         indexes.insert(index)
      }
      appData.userData.remove(atOffsets: indexes)
   }
}
struct CellBook: View {
   let book: BookViewModel

   var body: some View {
      HStack(alignment: .top) {
         Image(book.cover)
            .resizable()
            .scaledToFit()
            .frame(width: 80, height: 100)
         VStack(alignment: .leading, spacing: 2) {
            Text(book.title).bold()
            Text(book.author)
            Text(book.year).font(.caption)
            Spacer()
         }.padding(.top, 5)
```

```
            Spacer()
        }
    }
}
```

Listing 7-30: Defining custom swipe actions

In this example, we include only one button. We assign the **destructive** role to the button, so it is shown in red, and create an **Image** view for the label with the SF Symbol of a trash can. If the user swipes the row and presses the button, the closure calls a method to remove the book from the model, as we did before.

Figure 7-25: Custom swipe action

 Do It Yourself: Update the ContentView.swift file with the code in Listing 7-30. Drag a row to the left, and press the trash can button. The row should be deleted. You will notice that the process of removing the row is not animated. We will learn how to create animations in Chapter 11.

(Basic) **Custom Buttons**

Besides the buttons generated by the system, we can include our own. Of course, when we use custom buttons to perform tasks on the list, there is no need to implement the methods defined for the edit mode. The following example illustrates how to include a remove button in each row.

```
struct ContentView: View {
    @EnvironmentObject var appData: ApplicationData

    var body: some View {
        List {
            ForEach(appData.userData) { book in
                CellBook(book: book)
            }
        }.listStyle(.plain)
    }
}
struct CellBook: View {
    @EnvironmentObject var appData: ApplicationData
    let book: BookViewModel

    var body: some View {
        HStack(alignment: .top) {
            Image(book.cover)
                .resizable()
                .scaledToFit()
                .frame(width: 80, height: 100)
            VStack(alignment: .leading, spacing: 2) {
                Text(book.title).bold()
                Text(book.author)
                Text(book.year).font(.caption)
```

```
            Spacer()
        }.padding(.top, 5)
        Spacer()

        Button(action: {
            removeBook(book: book)
        }, label: {
            Image(systemName: "trash")
                .foregroundColor(.red)
                .frame(width: 30, height: 30)
        }).padding(.top, 5)
        .buttonStyle(.plain)
    }
}
func removeBook(book: BookViewModel) {
    if let index = appData.userData.firstIndex(where: { $0.id ==
book.id }) {
        appData.userData.remove(at: index)
    }
}
}
```

Listing 7-31: Implementing a custom button to delete the rows

The buttons created by default by the **Button** view pass to the row the responsibility of responding to the user tapping the screen. To get the button to respond, we must define it as a plain button with the **plain** style. The action and the label are defined as always. In this example, we create a button on the right hand side of each row to delete it. The label is an SF Symbol of a trash can, and the action calls the **removeBook()** method implemented before.

Figure 7-26: Custom button to remove a row

(Basic) **Refreshable**

There is a useful feature, usually provided by modern applications, that allows users to refresh the data by scrolling down the list. When the user keeps scrolling down, a spinning wheel appears at the top of the screen to indicate that the system is refreshing the data. The **View** protocol includes the following modifier to add this feature to a **List** view.

refreshable(action: Closure)—This modifier adds a refreshable control to a list. The **action** argument is the closure to be executed when the user performs the action.

To add this feature to the list, we must implement the modifier on the **List** view and provide a closure with the task we want to perform, as in the following example.

Chapter 7 - Lists

```
struct ContentView: View {
    @EnvironmentObject var appData: ApplicationData

    var body: some View {
        List {
            ForEach(appData.userData) { book in
                CellBook(book: book)
            }
        }.listStyle(.plain)
        .refreshable {
            print("Loading values")
        }
    }
}
```

Listing 7-32: *Refreshing the list*

When the user scrolls down the list, the closure is executed to perform the task. In this example, we print a message on the console, but the task usually involves accessing a server or a database to download and process information. (We will learn how to perform these processes later.)

Figure 7-27: *Refresh control*

 Do It Yourself: Update the **ContentView** view with the code in Listing 7-32. Drag the list down. You should see a spinning wheel to indicate the list is refreshing its content. This example assumes that you are using the **CellBook** view defined in Listing 7-13.

 IMPORTANT: The task is performed asynchronously, which means that the statement in the closure are executed in the background, while the app keeps performing other tasks, such as refreshing the interface. We will learn more about concurrent and asynchronous tasks in Chapter 9.

(Medium) **Outline List**

In addition to the list of views we have created so far, SwiftUI also provide tools to create hierarchical lists. These are list of views in which some rows can expand or collapse to display or hide other rows. The main views, also called *parents*, work as containers for other views, called *children*, that the user can see by tapping on the top view's accessory. The **List** view provides the following initializer to create these lists.

List(Data, **children:** KeyPath, **rowContent:** Closure)—This initializer creates a hierarchical list. The first argument is the data used to create the views, the **children** argument is a key path to the property that contains the data to create the children views, and the **rowContent** argument is the closure with the views to create each row.

We don't need anything new to create these types of lists, all the functionality is provided by the `List` view, but the information in the model must be organized accordingly. For instance, the following model includes a structure to store all the items, but the structure includes a property with an array of instances of the same structure to store the items that are going to be shown when the parent item is expanded.

```
import SwiftUI

struct MainItems: Identifiable {
    var id = UUID()
    var name: String!
    var options: [MainItems]!
}
class ContentViewData: ObservableObject {
    @Published var items: [MainItems]

    init() {
        items = [
            MainItems(name: "Food", options: [
                MainItems(name: "Oatmeal", options: nil),
                MainItems(name: "Bagels", options: nil),
                MainItems(name: "Brownies", options: nil),
                MainItems(name: "Cheese", options: [
                    MainItems(name: "Roquefort", options: nil),
                    MainItems(name: "Mozzarella", options: nil),
                    MainItems(name: "Cheddar", options: nil)
                ]),
                MainItems(name: "Cookies", options: nil),
                MainItems(name: "Donuts", options: nil)
            ]),
            MainItems(name: "Beverages", options: [
                MainItems(name: "Coffee", options: nil),
                MainItems(name: "Juice", options: nil),
                MainItems(name: "Lemonade", options: nil)
            ])
        ]
    }
}
struct ContentView: View {
    @ObservedObject var contentData = ContentViewData()

    var body: some View {
        List(contentData.items, children: \.options) { item in
            Text(item.name)
        }
    }
}
```

Listing 7-33: Defining the model and the view to create a hierarchical list

The `MainItems` structure includes the `name` property to store the item's name, and the `options` property to store the children (also defined by `MainItems` structures). In this example, we define two parent items called "Food" and "Beverages", each with their own children assigned to the `options` property. There is one item called "Cheese" with three more children, creating an additional hierarchy. When the user taps on the "Food" or "Beverages" items, all the items stored in their `options` property are displayed, and the same happens whit the "Cheese" item.

Figure 7-28: Hierarchical list

The **List** view implements another view in the background called **OutlineGroup** to create the hierarchical list of views, but we can declare this view ourselves to create more complex hierarchies. The **OutlineGroup** view includes the following initializer.

OutlineGroup(Data, **children:** KeyPath, **content:** Closure**)**—This view creates a hierarchical list. The first argument is the data used to create the views, the **children** argument is a key path to the property that contains the data to create the children view, and the **content** argument is the closure with the views for each row.

For instance, we can include this view inside a **Section** view to divide the hierarchy in sections. We can even make the sections expandable with a **sidebar** style list, as shown next.

```
struct ContentView: View {
    @ObservedObject var contentData = ContentViewData()

    var body: some View {
        List {
            ForEach(contentData.items) { section in
                Section(header: Text(section.name)) {
                    OutlineGroup(section.options ?? [], children: \.options)
{ item in
                        Text(item.name)
                    }
                }
            }
        }.listStyle(.sidebar)
    }
}
```

Listing 7-34: Implementing an OutlineGroup *view*

In this example, we create the list with a **ForEach** view and the values of the **items** property. This property contains two items, "Food" and "Beverages", that we use to create the sections with a **Section** view. To display the content of the sections, we use an **OutlineGroup** view. This view takes the values in the **options** property of each item and creates an outline list. This creates a list with two sections and the children views inside, but because we declared the style for the list as **sidebar**, the sections include a disclosure accessory and become expandable.

Figure 7-29: Custom hierarchy

Do It Yourself: Create a Multiplatform project. Update the ContentView.swift file with the code in Listing 7-33. You should see the interface illustrated in Figure 7-28. Update the **ContentView** view with the code in Listing 7-34. Now you should see the interface illustrated in Figure 7-29.

Basic 7.3 Tables

List views were designed for the small screen of mobile devices like iPhones and Apple Watches. iPads and Macs have a larger screen and therefore more space to display content. If we only need one column of values, we can use a **List** view, as we have done so far, but to present more columns SwiftUI includes the **Table** view. The following is the view's initializer.

Table(Data, **selection:** Binding, **sortOrder:** Binding, **columns:** Closure**)**—This initializer creates a **Table** view with the configuration specified by the arguments. The first argument is the data used to fill the table, the **selection** argument is a **Binding** value with the identifiers of the selected rows, the **sortOrder** argument is a **Binding** value with the sort descriptors used to sort the values on the table, and the **columns** argument provides the views to create the columns.

The columns are defined by the **TableColumn** view. The following is the view's initializer.

TableColumn(String, **value:** KeyPath, **content:** Closure**)**—This initializer defines a column for a table. The first argument specifies the column's title, the **value** argument is a key path to the property that provides the values for the column, and the **content** argument defines the views to display by the column.

By default, the columns are flexible, which means that the width is determined by the number of columns in the table and the space available, but the **TableColumn** structure includes the following modifiers to specify a custom width.

width(CGFloat?**)**—This modifier defines a fixed width for the column.

width(min: CGFloat?, **ideal:** CGFloat?, **max:** CGFloat?**)**—This modifier defines a flexible column but with constraints.

As always, we need a model with some data to test the app. The following includes a structure with a few properties to provide the values for the columns, a **@Published** property to provide the values to the views, and some data for testing.

```
import SwiftUI

struct ConsumableItem: Identifiable {
    let id = UUID()
    var name: String
    var category: String
    var calories: Int
    var included: Bool
}
class ApplicationData: ObservableObject {
    @Published var listOfItems: [ConsumableItem]

    init() {
        listOfItems = [
            ConsumableItem(name: "Bagels", category: "Baked", calories: 250,
included: false),
            ConsumableItem(name: "Brownies", category: "Baked", calories:
466, included: false),
            ConsumableItem(name: "Butter", category: "Dairy", calories: 717,
included: false),
```

```
            ConsumableItem(name: "Cheese", category: "Dairy", calories: 402,
included: false),
            ConsumableItem(name: "Juice", category: "Beverages", calories:
23, included: false),
            ConsumableItem(name: "Lemonade", category: "Beverages",
calories: 40, included: false)
        ]
    }
}
```

Listing 7-35: Defining a model to test tables

The **Table** structure includes multiple initializers, each one with a different combination of arguments, so we can only implement those we need. Something similar happens with the **TableColumn** view. For instance, if the value presented by the column is a string, we can just specify the key path and the view takes cares of creating the **Text** view to show the value. If not, we must provide the closure to the **content** argument, format the value, and create the view we want to use to show it.

The following example shows a possible implementation. The **Table** view is defined only with the data source (the **listOfItems** property) and a closure to create the columns. Some columns use a key path to provide the values and the last one a closure with a **Text** view.

```
struct ContentView: View {
    @EnvironmentObject var appData: ApplicationData

    var body: some View {
        Table(appData.listOfItems) {
            TableColumn("Name", value: \.name)
            TableColumn("Category", value: \.category)
            TableColumn("Calories") { item in
                Text("\(item.calories)")
            }.width(100)
        }
    }
}
```

Listing 7-36: Creating a table with multiple columns

In this example, the first and second columns access the values of the **name** and **category** properties of the **ConsumableItem** structure with key paths, but we use a closure for the **calories** property because its value is an integer that we must convert into a string.

This example assigns a width of 100 points to the Calories column with the **width()** modifier and keeps the rest of the columns flexible. On iPads and Macs, the system creates the Calories column with a size of 100 points and distributes the rest of the space between the first two columns, while on iPhones only the first column is displayed.

Figure 7-30: Table in iPads and iPhones

Do It Yourself: Create a Multiplatform project. Create a Swift file called ApplicationData.swift for the model in Listing 7-35 and update the `ContentView` view with the code in Listing 7-36. Remember to inject an instance of the `ApplicationData` class into the environment and the preview, as we did in Listing 7-4. Run the application on the iPad simulator or the Mac (My Mac). You should see a table with three columns, as shown in Figure 7-30, left. Run the application again on the iPhone simulator. You should see only one column, as illustrated in Figure 7-30, right.

On iPads and Macs, tables include a feature that allows the user to sort the items by tapping or clicking on the column's title. For instance, if we tap on the header of the Name column in our example, the items will be sorted by name. The feature is added to the table when we include the **sortOrder** argument in the initializer. The argument takes a `Binding` property with an array of values that determine the properties which values we want to sort. Foundation defines the `KeyPathComparator` structure for this purpose.

KeyPathComparator(KeyPath, **order:** SortOrder**)**—This initializer defines a sort comparator for the property and in the order specified by the arguments. The first argument is the key path of the property whose values we want to sort, and the **order** argument determines if the items will be sorted in ascending or descending order. It is an enumeration with the values **forward** and **reverse**.

The `KeyPathComparator` structure determines the values sort, but we are responsible for sorting the values in the model. For this purpose, the Swift Standard Library includes the following method.

sorted(using: Comparator**)**—This method returns a collection with the items sorted according to the sort comparator provided by the **using** argument.

The following example defines an array of `KeyPathComparator` structures to sort the items in the model by name and calories, and implements a computed property to sort the values in place, so every time the model is updated, the view is recreated, and the values are sorted again.

```
struct ContentView: View {
    @EnvironmentObject var appData: ApplicationData
    @State private var sort = [KeyPathComparator(\ConsumableItem.name),
KeyPathComparator(\ConsumableItem.calories)]

    var sortedItems: [ConsumableItem] {
        let list = appData.listOfItems.sorted(using: sort)
        return list
    }
    var body: some View {
        Table(sortedItems, sortOrder: $sort) {
            TableColumn("Name", value: \.name)
            TableColumn("Category", value: \.category)
            TableColumn("Calories", value: \.calories) { item in
                Text("\(item.calories)")
            }.width(100)
        }
    }
}
```

Listing 7-37: Sorting the values by column

The `Table` view requires the sort comparators to be stored in a `Binding` property so it can select which one to use according to the action performed by the user. In this example, we define a @State property with two sort comparators to allow the user to sort the items by name and calories. Next, we define a computed property called `sortedItems` that sorts the items according to these sort comparators and returns the list of values for the view.

Notice that we have added a key path to the Calories column. The value is produced by the closure, but the key path is still required to tell the table which column to sort.

 Do It Yourself: Update the `ContentView` view with the code in Listing 7-37. Run the application on the iPad simulator or the Mac (My Mac). Click on the header of the Name and Calories columns. You should see the items sorted by name or calories, respectively.

Tables also allow the user to select one or multiple rows. The process is the same used before for `List` views. We must provide a @State property to store the identifiers of the items selected by the user and assign that property to the table. For single selection, everything works out of the box, but iPads without a keyboard require the edit mode to be enabled. In the following example, we include an `EditButton` view to allow the user to enable this mode and also a `Text` view below to show the names of the items selected by the user.

```
struct ContentView: View {
    @EnvironmentObject var appData: ApplicationData
    @State private var selectedItems: Set<ConsumableItem.ID> = []

    var body: some View {
        VStack {
            EditButton()
            Table(appData.listOfItems, selection: $selectedItems) {
                TableColumn("Name", value: \.name)
                TableColumn("Category", value: \.category)
                TableColumn("Calories") { item in
                    Text("\(item.calories)")
                }.width(100)
            }
            Text(listSelected())
                .padding()
        }
    }
    func listSelected() -> String {
        let list: [String] = selectedItems.map({ id in
            let item = appData.listOfItems.first(where: { $0.id == id })
            return item?.name ?? ""
        })
        return String(list.sorted().joined(separator: " "))
    }
}
```

Listing 7-38: Allowing the user to select items in a table

If we want to select just one item, we can tap on it, but selecting multiple items is only available if we have a keyboard or press the button created by the `EditButton` view. To show the names of the selected items, we created a method that maps the identifiers, gets the items from the `listOfItems` array, returns the value of the `name` property, and then sorts and joins the values to create a string with all the names.

In this example, we display the selected names on the screen, but of course we can add buttons to the interface to process the values as we need. A useful tool provided by tables for this purpose are context menus. With context menus, the user can right-click a selected row or rows and perform an action. SwiftUI includes the following modifier to create the menu.

contextMenu(forSelectionType: Type, **menu:** Closure)—This modifier assigns a context menu to an item or multiple items of a view. The **forSelectionType** argument specifies the data type of the values we want to associate with the menu, and the **menu** argument provides the options for the menu.

The closure assigned to the **menu** argument receives a copy of the set with the values selected by the user. By checking these values, we can configure the menu with options for when the user right-clicks on a single row, on multiple selected rows, or the table's empty area. All we need to do to configure the menu is to count how many items are in the array, as shown next.

```
struct ContentView: View {
    @EnvironmentObject var appData: ApplicationData
    @State private var selectedItems: Set<ConsumableItem.ID> = []

    var body: some View {
        Table(appData.listOfItems, selection: $selectedItems) {
            TableColumn("Name", value: \.name)
            TableColumn("Category", value: \.category)
            TableColumn("Calories") { item in
                Text("\(item.calories)")
            }.width(100)
        }
        .contextMenu(forSelectionType: ConsumableItem.ID.self, menu:
{ selected in
            if selected.count <= 0  {
                Button("Create New Item") {
                    let newItem = ConsumableItem(name: "Test", category:
"Test", calories: 0, included: false)
                    appData.listOfItems.append(newItem)
                }
            } else if selected.count == 1 {
                Button("Remove Item") {
                    appData.listOfItems.removeAll(where: { item in
                        item.id == selected.first
                    })
                }
            } else {
                Button("Remove Selected Items") {
                    appData.listOfItems.removeAll(where: { item in
                        selected.contains(item.id)
                    })
                }
            }
        })
    }
}
```

Listing 7-39: *Using a context menu to process a row*

If there are no items in the set, which means that the user right-clicked on an empty area of the table, we show a button to add a new item to the model. If there is one item, we offer a button to remove the value from the model, and if there are multiple items in the set, the option removes them all. The context menu is created by the same `contextMenu()` modifier, but it adapts based on where the user right-clicks (taps and holds on iPads).

 Do It Yourself: Update the `ContentView` view with the code in Listing 7-39. Run the application on the iPad simulator or the Mac (My Mac). Right click on a row (Click and hold on the iPad simulator). Select the "Remove Item" option. The item should be removed. Select two or more rows and repeat the process to remove them. Do the same but in the table's empty area below and select the option "Create New Item". You should see a new item with the name "Test" at the bottom of the list. In this example, we always add the same item with the name "Test". Later we will learn how to open additional views to allow the user to insert custom values.

In addition to **Text** views, tables can show other views, from images to control views. For instance, we can include a **Toggle** view, which is presented as a checkbox on the Mac, to allow the user to check or uncheck the items.

```
struct ContentView: View {
    @EnvironmentObject var appData: ApplicationData

    var body: some View {
        Table(appData.listOfItems) {
            TableColumn("Name", value: \.name)
            TableColumn("Category", value: \.category)
            TableColumn("Calories") { item in
                Text("\(item.calories)")
            }.width(100)
            TableColumn("Included") { item in
                Toggle("", isOn: itemBinding(id: item.id).included)
                    .labelsHidden()
            }.width(100)
        }
    }
    func itemBinding(id: UUID) -> Binding<ConsumableItem> {
        let index = appData.listOfItems.firstIndex(where: { $0.id ==
id }) ?? 0
        return $appData.listOfItems[index]
    }
}
```

Listing 7-40: Defining the content of a column with a Toggle *view*

The **Toggle** view needs a bidirectional **Binding** value to read and store the current value. The easiest way to provide this value is with a method. We call the method with the item's id, use this identifier to get the index of the item in the array, and return the item as a **Binding** value of type **ConsumableItem**. This creates the bidirectional connection between the **Toggle** view and the **ConsumableItem** structure, so every time the user clicks on the switch or the checkbox, the new value is stored directly into the item's **included** property.

Figure 7-31: Column of Toggle *views*

The **KeyPathComparator** structure implemented before to sort the values conforms to the **SortComparator** protocol. This protocol defines the tools required to sort the values. The sort comparator implemented by this structure can compare and sort values of common data types like **String** and **Int** values, but it cannot sort custom data types or special values like Booleans. For instance, if we want to sort the Included column from our previous example, we must define our own **SortComparator** structure and implement the following protocol requirements.

order—This property defines the order of the values. It is a **SortOrder** enumeration with the values **forward** and **reverse**.

compare(lhs: Value, **rhs:** Value)—This method compares two values at a time and must return an enumeration value of type **ComparisonResult** to determine the order. The values available are **orderedAscending**, **orderedDescending**, and **orderedSame**.

In addition, we need to define a typealias with the name **Compared** of the data type of the values we want to compare, as shown next.

```
struct CompareBool: SortComparator {
    typealias Compared = Bool
    var order: SortOrder = .forward

    func compare(_ lhs: Bool, _ rhs: Bool) -> ComparisonResult {
        if lhs && !rhs {
            return order
== .forward ? .orderedAscending : .orderedDescending
        } else if !lhs && rhs {
            return order
== .forward ? .orderedDescending : .orderedAscending
        } else {
            return .orderedSame
        }
    }
}
```

Listing 7-41: Defining a custom sort comparator

The **order** property determines the order of the values (ascending or descending). We provide an initial value, but the property is updated every time the user clicks on the column's header. In the **compare()** method, we compare the values received by the method and return a **ComparisonResult** value depending on the value of this property. We return **ordered-Ascending**, if the property is equal to **forward**, the first value is **true**, and the second value **false**. On the other hand, if the value of the **order** property is **reverse**, the value returned is **orderedDescending**. And we do the opposite if the values receive by the method are inverted (**false** for the first one, and **true** for the second one). This shows the On switches at the top and the Off switches at the bottom; or vice versa, depending on the order selected by the user.

Now that we have a comparator for Boolean values, we must apply it to the table. The **TableColumn** view includes the following initializer to apply a custom sort comparator.

TableColumn(String, **value:** KeyPath, **comparator:** StandardComparator, **content:** Closure)—This initializer defines a column for a table. The first argument specifies the column's title, the **value** argument is a key path to the property that provides the values for the column, the comparator is a custom **SortComparator** structure to sort the values, and the **content** argument defines the views to display by the column.

This initializer is applied as before. The only difference is that now we must include an instance of our **CompareBool** structure to tell the table how to sort the values.

```
struct ContentView: View {
    @EnvironmentObject var appData: ApplicationData
    @State private var sort = [KeyPathComparator(\ConsumableItem.name)]

    var sortedItems: [ConsumableItem] {
        let list = appData.listOfItems.sorted(using: sort)
        return list
    }
```

```
    var body: some View {
        Table(sortedItems, sortOrder: $sort) {
            TableColumn("Name", value: \.name)
            TableColumn("Category", value: \.category)
            TableColumn("Calories") { item in
                Text("\(item.calories)")
            }.width(100)
            TableColumn("Included", value: \.included, comparator:
CompareBool()) { item in
                Toggle("", isOn: itemBinding(id: item.id).included)
                    .labelsHidden()
            }.width(100)
        }
    }
    func itemBinding(id: UUID) -> Binding<ConsumableItem> {
        let index = appData.listOfItems.firstIndex(where: { $0.id ==
id }) ?? 0
        return $appData.listOfItems[index]
    }
}
```

Listing 7-42: Sorting Boolean values on a table

 Do It Yourself: Add the structure in Listing 7-41 to the ApplicationData.swift file. Update the `ContentView` view with the code in Listing 7-42. Run the application and turn some of the switches on. Click on the column's title. You should see the items sorted by the condition of the boxes: on or off.

(Basic) **7.4 Pickers**

SwiftUI also provides pickers to present lists of values. A picker can show the values in a graphic that simulates a wheel, on a list, or as a row of buttons, depending on the platform and the configuration. The framework includes two views for this purpose, one to create a general-purpose list, and another to generate a list of dates and times.

(Basic) **Picker View**

The `Picker` view creates a general-purpose picker to show a list of values. The structure includes the following initializer.

Picker(String, **selection:** Binding, **content:** Closure)—This initializer creates a `Picker` view with the label defined by the first argument. The **selection** argument is a `Binding` property that stores the value selected by the user, and the closure assigned to the **content** argument provides the list of views required to present the values.

A `Picker` view needs a `Binding` property to store the value currently selected by the user and a list of views to present the values available. The list of views can be created manually, one view per line, or dynamically with a `ForEach` view, as in the following example.

```
struct ContentView: View {
    @State private var selectedValue: String = "No Value"
    let listCities: [String] = ["Paris", "Toronto", "Dublin"]

    var body: some View {
        VStack {
            Text(selectedValue)
            Picker("Cities:", selection: $selectedValue) {
                ForEach(listCities, id: \.self) { value in
                    Text(value)
```

```
        }
      }
      Spacer()
    }.padding()
  }
}
```

Listing 7-43: Defining a picker

By default, the picker is shown with a style of type **menu**. This creates a drop down menu on the Mac, and a button that opens a context menu when tapped in mobile devices. The label is not included on mobile devices at the moment, so if we test the application on an iPhone or iPad simulator, only the content of the picker is shown on the screen.

Figure 7-32: Menu picker

The value of the **Binding** property is used to store the value selected by the user and also to initialize the picker. If the property contains a value, and the value is available in the model, the picker is shown with that value selected. There are several ways to provide this initial value. For instance, we can assign it to the **@State** property when the property is declared, or we can select it later when the views appear with the **onAppear()** modifier, as shown next.

```
struct ContentView: View {
  @State private var selectedValue: String = "No Value"
  let listCities: [String] = ["Paris", "Toronto", "Dublin"]

  var body: some View {
    VStack {
      Text(selectedValue)
      Picker("Cities:", selection: $selectedValue) {
        ForEach(listCities, id: \.self) { value in
          Text(value)
        }
      }
      Spacer()
    }.padding()
    .onAppear {
      selectedValue = listCities[1]
    }
  }
}
```

Listing 7-44: Selecting an initial value

In this example, we initialize the **selectedValue** property with the second value in the **listCities** array and therefore this is the initial value selected by the **Picker** view.

> **Do It Yourself:** Create a Multiplatform project. Update the **ContentView** view with the code in Listing 7-43. Press the button. You should see a context menu, as shown in Figure 7-32. Update the view with the code in Listing 7-44. Press the button again. You should see a context menu with the Toronto option already selected.

The picker identifies the items by their ids, and therefore the items on the list are identified with the same value shown to the user (in our example, the name of the cities). If this is not what we want, we can provide a unique identifier for each item with the `tag()` modifier. For instance, we can use the indexes of the array instead of the values. When the user selects a value, we can use the selected index to get the name of the city and display it on the screen. For this purpose, we can take advantage of the `indices` property provided by the Swift Standard Library to return a `Range` value with the indexes of a collection.

```
struct ContentView: View {
    @State private var selectedValue: Int = 0
    let listCities: [String] = ["Paris", "Toronto", "Dublin"]

    var body: some View {
        VStack {
            Text(listCities[selectedValue])
            Picker("Cities:", selection: $selectedValue) {
                ForEach(listCities.indices, id: \.self) { value in
                    Text(listCities[value])
                        .tag(value)
                }
            }
            Spacer()
        }.padding()
    }
}
```

Listing 7-45: Listing values by index

Because we are now working with the indexes of the array instead of the values, we define the `selectedValue` property of type `Int`. To get the index of each value, we define the `ForEach` view with the `Range` returned by the `indices` property of the `listCities` array, and then assign the index to each value with the `tag()` modifier. When a value is selected, the picker assigns the value of the `tag()` modifier to the `selectedValue` property, and therefore we can use this property to get the name of the city from the array.

 Do It Yourself: Update the `ContentView` view with the code in Listing 7-45. The application should work as before, but now the values processed by the picker are integers instead of strings.

The `Picker` view adopts a design according to the device and the conditions in which it is presented, but we can force the picker to adopt the design we want with the following modifier.

pickerStyle(Style**)**—This modifier sets the style of the picker. The argument is a structure that conforms to the `PickerStyle` protocol. The system defines a few structures with predefined styles. To declare these values, the structures include the type properties `automatic`, `menu`, `segmented`, and `wheel`.

The `automatic` style allows the picker to adapt the design to the device and conditions, and the `menu` style create a context menu, as we have seen in the previous examples. But there are two additional styles. The `wheel` style displays the values in a virtual wheel the user can rotate to make a pick, and the `segmented` style defines a unique picker where the values are turned into buttons. The latter is frequently used to allow the user to select a value from a limited set of options, as illustrated by the following example.

```
struct ContentView: View {
    @State private var selectedValue: String = "No Value"
    let listCities: [String] = ["Paris", "Toronto", "Dublin"]

    var body: some View {
        VStack {
            Text(selectedValue)
            Picker("Cities:", selection: $selectedValue) {
                ForEach(listCities, id: \.self) { value in
                    Text(value)
                }
            }.pickerStyle(.segmented)
            Spacer()
        }.padding()
    }
}
```

Listing 7-46: Implementing a segmented picker

The implementation is the same, but by applying a custom style we change the way the values are presented to the user. Below are the different pickers we see when the style is set to **wheel** or **segmented**.

Figure 7-33: Wheel and segmented pickers

 Do It Yourself: Update the **ContentView** view with the code in Listing 7-46. You should be able to click on the buttons to select a different city. Assign the **wheel** value to the **pickerStyle()** modifier. You should be able to drag a wheel up or down to select a value.

(Basic) **Date Pickers**

SwiftUI includes two picker views designed to simplify the creation of pickers that allow the user to select a date or a time: **DatePicker** for a single date and **MultiDatePicker** for multiple dates. The following are the most frequently used initializers.

DatePicker(String, **selection:** Binding, **in:** Range, **displayedComponents:** Components**)**—This initializer creates a **DatePicker** view with the label defined by the first argument. The **selection** argument is a **Binding** property of type **Date** that stores the date selected by the user, the **in** argument defines the range of dates the user can choose from, and the **displayComponents** argument is a structure of type **DatePickerComponents** that defines the type of values managed by the picker. The structure includes two type properties for this purpose: **date** and **hourAndMinute**.

MultiDatePicker(String, **selection:** Binding, **in:** Range**)**—This initializer creates a **MultiDatePicker** view with the label defined by the first argument. The **selection** argument is a **Binding** property to a set of **DateComponents** values with the dates selected by the user, and the **in** argument defines the range of dates the user can choose from.

To define a **DatePicker** view, we must provide a **@State** property to store the value selected by the user and tell the picker the type of values we want to show. If we want to allow the user to select dates, we must specify the **date** value for the **displayedComponents** argument, for times is the **time** value, but if we want the user to be able to select both, we must ignore the argument altogether, as we do in the following example.

```
struct ContentView: View {
   @State private var selectedDate: Date = Date()

   var body: some View {
      VStack {
         DatePicker("Date:", selection: $selectedDate)
         Spacer()
      }.padding()
   }
}
```

Listing 7-47: *Defining a* DatePicker *to select a date*

The **@State** property used to store the selected value was initialized with the current date (**Date()**) and therefore the picker shows this as the selected date and time, but we can initialize this value with any date we want. The picker is presented with the style by default, which in mobile devices shows buttons to open a calendar to select the date and a spinning wheel to select the time.

Figure 7-34: *Picker for dates*

 Do It Yourself: Update the **ContentView** view with the code in Listing 7-47. You should see the interface in Figure 7-34, left. Add the **displayComponents** argument to the **DatePicker** view initializer with the value **date** or **hourandminute** to allow users to select only dates or times. You can also include the **labelsHidden()** modifier to remove the label.

By default, the **DatePicker** view presents a list with all the dates from a distant date in the past to a distant date in the future. To limit the list of values the user can select from, we must provide a range of dates. The range can be closed (from one date to another), or open. The following example shows a list of dates from the current date to a distant date in the future using an open range.

```
struct ContentView: View {
   @State private var selectedDate: Date = Date()

   var body: some View {
      VStack {
         DatePicker("Date:", selection: $selectedDate, in: Date()...,
displayedComponents: .date)
```

```
            Spacer()
        }.padding()
    }
}
```

Listing 7-48: Limiting the `DatePicker` *to a range of values*

In this example, we limit the picker with the range `Date()...` and therefore the user is not allowed to select a date before the current date. A range `...Date()` does the opposite, it only allows the user to select a date from the past. But we can also provide specific dates by creating custom `Date` structures, as we did in Chapter 4 (see Listing 4-23).

A `DatePicker` view adopts a design according to the device and the conditions in which it is presented, but it includes the following modifier to specify the style we want.

datePickerStyle(Style**)**—This modifier sets the style of the picker. The argument is a structure that conforms to the **DatePickerStyle** protocol. To provide standard styles, the system defines a few structures with the type properties **automatic**, **compact**, **graphical**, and **wheel**.

By default, the **DatePicker** view is configured with the **compact** style, which shows a button the user must press to reveal a calendar to select a date or a spinning wheel to select a time. But we can also show the calendar right away with the **graphical** style, or a spinning wheel with the **wheel** style, as we do in the following example.

```
struct ContentView: View {
    @State private var selectedDate: Date = Date()

    var body: some View {
        VStack {
            Text("Date: \(selectedDate.formatted(.dateTime.day().month()))")
            DatePicker("Date:", selection: $selectedDate,
displayedComponents: .date)
                .labelsHidden()
                .datePickerStyle(.wheel)
            Spacer()
        }.padding()
    }
}
```

Listing 7-49: Presenting a picker with a spinning wheel

In addition to assigning the wheel style to the picker, the view in Listing 7-49 also includes a **Text** view to show the day and month selected by the user. The result is shown below.

Figure 7-35: Wheel picker

To allow the user to select multiple dates, we must create the picker with a **MultiDatePicker** view and a **Binding** property that stores a set of **DateComponents** values.

```
struct ContentView: View {
   @State private var selectedDates: Set<DateComponents> = []
   @State private var mydates: String = ""

   var body: some View {
      VStack {
         MultiDatePicker("Dates:", selection: $selectedDates)
         Spacer()
         Text(mydates)
      }.padding()
      .onChange(of: selectedDates) { values in
         let days = values.map({ value in String(value.day!) })
         mydates = days.joined(separator: ",")
      }
   }
}
```

Listing 7-50: Picking multiple dates

A **MultiDatePicker** view works like the **DatePicker** view, but the selected values are stored in an array. In this example, we apply the **onChange()** modifier to show the days selected by the user in a **Text** view at the bottom of the screen.

Figure 7-36: Multiple date picker

 Do It Yourself: Update the **ContentView** view with the code in Listing 7-50. Run the application on the iPhone simulator and select a few dates. You should see the days displayed at the bottom (Figure 7-36).

(Basic) **7.5 Forms**

Most applications include views with a list of options users can select to set the app's configuration, the style of the interface, or the type of information they want to see. We can create these screens with a list of controls in a **VStack**, as we have done before, but SwiftUI provides a view specifically designed for this purpose called **Form**.

(Basic) **Form View**

A **Form** view is a container that organizes the views in a list, like the **List** view, but adapts the controls to the device and the platform in which the app is running. Creating a form in SwiftUI is easy, we just have to include the controls one after another inside the **Form** view, as shown next.

```
struct ContentView: View {
   @State private var setActive: Bool = false
   @State private var setShowPictures: Bool = false
   @State private var setTotal: Int = 10

   var body: some View {
```

```
Form {
    Toggle("Active", isOn: $setActive)
    Toggle("Show Pictures", isOn: $setShowPictures)
    HStack {
        Text("Total")
        Spacer()
        Text(String(setTotal))
        Stepper("", value: $setTotal, in: 0...10)
            .labelsHidden()
    }
}
}
}
}
```

Listing 7-51: Defining a form

The **Form** view adds padding on the sides of the controls and present the list with a **grouped** style (see Listing 7-14).

Figure 7-37: Simple form

Most views allow us to specify a string that the **Form** view can use to create the label for the control, but in some cases, we may need to hide the label and specify our own, as we did for the **Stepper** view in the previous example. To create custom labels, SwiftUI includes the **LabeledContent** view. This view attaches a label to another view. The following is the most frequently used initializer.

LabeledContent(String, **content:** Closure**)**—This initializer attaches a label to a view. The first argument specifies the label and the **content** argument provides the views.

With this view, we can better organize our previous example and provide a custom label for the **Stepper** view.

```
struct ContentView: View {
    @State private var setActive: Bool = false
    @State private var setShowPictures: Bool = false
    @State private var setTotal: Int = 10

    var body: some View {
        Form {
            Toggle("Active", isOn: $setActive)
            Toggle("Show Pictures", isOn: $setShowPictures)
            LabeledContent("Total") {
                Text(String(setTotal))
                Stepper("", value: $setTotal, in: 0...10)
                    .labelsHidden()
            }
        }
    }
}
```

Listing 7-52: Defining a custom label

Chapter 7 - Lists

A **Form** view works like a **List** view, so we can separate the content in sections to provide a more standard design.

```
struct ContentView: View {
    @State private var setActive: Bool = false
    @State private var setShowPictures: Bool = false
    @State private var setTotal: Int = 10

    var body: some View {
        Form {
            Section(header: Text("Options"), footer: Text("Activate the
options you want to see")) {
                Toggle("Active", isOn: $setActive)
                Toggle("Show Pictures", isOn: $setShowPictures)
            }
            Section(header: Text("Values"), footer: Text("Insert the number
of items to display")) {
                LabeledContent("Total") {
                    Text(String(setTotal))
                    Stepper("", value: $setTotal, in: 0...10)
                        .labelsHidden()
                }
            }
        }
    }
}
```

Listing 7-53: Styling a form

Figure 7-38: Form with a standard design

 Do It Yourself: Create a Multiplatform project. Update the **ContentView** view with the code in Listing 7-53. You should see the interface in Figure 7-38. Add controls to the **Form** view and create more sections to see how they look like.

 IMPORTANT: In these examples, we have stored the values locally with **@State** properties. This means that the values inserted by the user are going to be available only for this view. To make them available to the rest of the app, we can store them in the model with **@Published** properties, or send them to other views, as we will see in the next chapter.

(Basic) **Disclosure Group**

Some forms are extensive and hard to read. SwiftUI includes the **DisclosureGroup** view to expand and collapse several controls together to make it easy for the user to insert the values and work with the form. This is similar to the **OutlineGroup** view implemented before to create hierarchical lists, but the **DisclosureGroup** view works with non hierarchical information, such as the one we find in a form. The structure includes the following initializer.

DisclosureGroup(String, **isExpanded:** Binding, **content:** Closure)—This initializer creates a `DisclosureGroup` view to hide or show content. The first argument is the view's label, the **isExpanded** argument is a `Binding` property of type `Bool` that determines whether the view is expanded or collapsed, and the **content** argument is the closure that provides the views we want to show or hide.

With this view, we can organize the two sections of our form in expandable lists.

```
struct ContentView: View {
    @State private var setActive: Bool = false
    @State private var setShowPictures: Bool = false
    @State private var setTotal: Int = 10

    var body: some View {
        Form {
            DisclosureGroup("Controls") {
                Toggle("Active", isOn: $setActive)
                Toggle("Show Pictures", isOn: $setShowPictures)
            }
            DisclosureGroup("Values") {
                HStack {
                    Text("Total")
                    Spacer()
                    Text(String(setTotal))
                    Stepper("", value: $setTotal, in: 0...10)
                        .labelsHidden()
                }
            }
        }
    }
}
```

Listing 7-54: Disclosing controls

When the views are collapsed, all we see is the view's label. If we tap on these labels or the disclosure indicator, the content is expanded and we can interact with the controls.

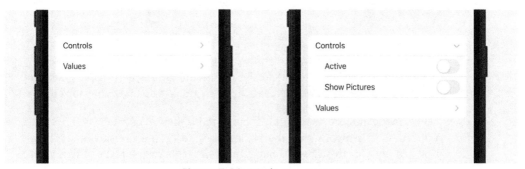

Figure 7-39: Disclosure groups

Basic 8.1 Multiple Views

The **ContentView** view we have been using in the examples of previous chapters defines the interface for the initial screen, but apps that only require one view and a simple interface are hard to find. Due to the size of the screen, apps for mobile devices require multiple views that replace one another in response to the user. Professional apps are made up of several views connected with each other in predetermined paths that users can follow to navigate throughout the content. Figure 8-1, below, illustrates how these views work together to expand the interface.

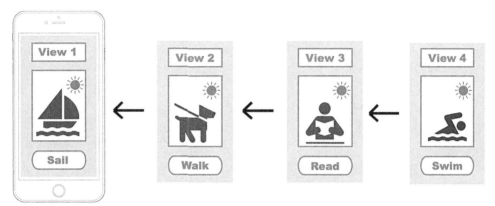

Figure 8-1: *Multiple views to expand the interface*

Basic Navigation Stack

The **ContentView** view included in the Multiplatform template represents the app's initial view, but we are responsible for creating the rest. The way these additional views are defined is always the same, we declare a structure that conforms to the **View** protocol and implement the **body** property, but there are different mechanisms to present them to the user. The one recommended by Apple creates a transition by moving the views from right to left, as illustrated in Figure 8-1. If the user wants to go back to the previous view, the current view is removed with a transition in the opposite direction. To create this navigation system, SwiftUI defines the **NavigationStack** view. The following is the structure's initializer.

NavigationStack(path: Binding, **root:** Closure)—This initializer creates a navigation stack to manage the views the user can navigate through. The **path** argument is the **Binding** property that stores the navigation path the user has followed, and the **root** argument is a closure that returns the root view (the first view presented by the navigation stack).

A **NavigationStack** view incorporates a navigation bar at the top of the interface to provide tools for navigation. The following are the modifiers available to configure this bar.

navigationTitle(Text**)**—This modifier defines the title to show in the navigation bar. There is also a version of this modifier that takes a **Binding** property to assign a title dynamically (**navigationTitle(Binding)**).

navigationBarTitleDisplayMode(TitleDisplayMode**)**—This modifier determines the display mode for the title. The argument is an enumeration with the values `automatic` (the same mode as the previous view), `inline` (adapts to the size of the bar), and `large` (expands the bar to show a large title).

navigationBarBackButtonHidden(Bool**)**—This modifier hides the Back button that is automatically generated by the `NavigationStack` view to navigate to previous views.

statusBarHidden(Bool**)**—This modifier hides the status bar for all the views in the navigation hierarchy.

A `NavigationStack` view creates a stack of views with the views opened by the user. Therefore, to start this navigation hierarchy we need to embed the content of our app's initial view in a `NavigationStack` view, as we do in the following example.

```
struct ContentView: View {
    @EnvironmentObject var appData: ApplicationData

    var body: some View {
        NavigationStack {
            List(appData.userData) { book in
                CellBook(book: book)
            }.navigationTitle(Text("Books"))
        }
    }
}
struct CellBook: View {
    let book: BookViewModel

    var body: some View {
        HStack(alignment: .top) {
            Image(book.cover)
                .resizable()
                .scaledToFit()
                .frame(width: 80, height: 100)
            VStack(alignment: .leading, spacing: 2) {
                Text(book.title).bold()
                Text(book.author)
                Text(book.year).font(.caption)
                Spacer()
            }.padding(.top, 5)
            Spacer()
        }
    }
}
struct ContentView_Previews: PreviewProvider {
    static var previews: some View {
        ContentView().environmentObject(ApplicationData())
    }
}
```

Listing 8-1: Initiating a navigation stack

This is the same application created in Chapter 7 to present a list of books, with the difference that now the list is embedded in a `NavigationStack` view and therefore the interface includes a navigation bar at the top with the title provided by the `navigationTitle()` modifier.

The size of the navigation bar created by the `NavigationStack` view depends on the title mode. By default, the mode is defined as `automatic` and therefore all the views in the navigation hierarchy show a large title, but if we scroll the list down, the size of the navigation bar and the title is automatically reduced to make room for the content.

Chapter 8 - Navigation

Figure 8-2: Navigation stack

 Do It Yourself: Create a Multiplatform project. For this application to work, you need to create a Swift file called ApplicationData.swift with the model in Chapter 7, Listing 7-3 and inject an instance of the **ApplicationData** class into the environment and the previews, as we did in Chapter 7, Listing 7-4. Update the **ContentView** view with the code in Listing 8-1. Download the book covers from our website and add them to the Asset Catalog. You should see an interface similar to Figure 8-2. Scroll the list down to see how the size of the navigation bar changes.

 IMPORTANT: Notice that the modifiers are applied to the content. For instance, the **navigationTitle()** modifier in our example is applied to the **List** view, not to the **NavigationStack** view. This is because the rest of the views added to the stack are not going to be embedded in a **NavigationStack** view. This view is only required for the initial view to start building the stack. This will become clear later.

By default, the navigation bar shows a large title, but we can change that behavior by assigning the **inline** mode instead. This is particularly useful when the list is implemented with a style that doesn't include any backgrounds or padding, as in the following example.

```
struct ContentView: View {
    @EnvironmentObject var appData: ApplicationData

    var body: some View {
        NavigationStack {
            List(appData.userData) { book in
                CellBook(book: book)
            }
            .listStyle(.plain)
            .navigationTitle(Text("Books"))
            .navigationBarTitleDisplayMode(.inline)
        }
    }
}
```

Listing 8-2: Setting the title mode

Now the title is shown in a standard size and with a predefined style, and all the views in the hierarchy will inherit this mode.

Figure 8-3: Inline mode

(Basic) Toolbar

Besides the title, the navigation bar can contain other elements, including images and buttons. SwiftUI provides the following modifiers to add items and configure the navigation bar and other toolbars.

toolbar(id: String, **content:** Closure)—This modifier adds elements to a toolbar or navigation bar. The **id** argument is an optional identifier used by the system to store the toolbar's last configuration, and the closure assigned to the **content** argument defines the views we want to include.

toolbar(Visibility, **for:** ToolbarPlacement)—This modifier shows or hides the bars. The first argument is an enumeration with the values **automatic**, **visible**, and **hidden**, and the **for** argument is a list of values representing the bars we want to modify, separated by comma. To specify the bars, the structure defines the type properties **automatic**, **bottomBar**, **navigationBar**, **tabBar**, and **windowToolbar**.

toolbarRole(ToolbarRole)—This modifier defines the purpose of the toolbar's content. The argument is a structure with the type properties **browser**, **editor**, **navigationStack**, and **automatic**.

Items can be added to the left or right side of the toolbar, and to different toolbars, including the navigation bar generated by the **NavigationStack** view, a toolbar at the bottom of the screen, and a toolbar on top of the keyboard. For this reason, SwiftUI includes the **ToolbarItem** view to define the items.

ToolbarItem(id: String, **placement:** ToolbarItemPlacement, **content:** Closure)—This view defines an item for a toolbar. The **id** argument is an optional identifier used by the system to store the item's configuration. The **placement** argument is a structure that determines the place and the toolbar where the item will be located. The structure includes type properties to define standard configurations for every system. The properties available are **automatic**, **bottomBar**, **cancellationAction**, **confirmationAction**, **destructiveAction**, **keyboard**, **navigation**, **navigationBarLeading**, **navigationBarTrailing**, **primaryAction**, **secondaryAction**, **principal**, and **status**. The closure assigned to the **content** argument defines the view we want to include in the toolbar.

As we already mentioned, the **toolbar()** modifier can add items to the navigation bar, to a toolbar at the bottom of the screen, or to a toolbar that appears at the top of the virtual keyboard. For instance, we can use it to add a button to the navigation bar of our example.

```
struct ContentView: View {
    @EnvironmentObject var appData: ApplicationData

    var body: some View {
        NavigationStack {
            List(appData.userData) { book in
                CellBook(book: book)
            }
            .navigationTitle(Text("Books"))
            .toolbar {
                ToolbarItem(placement: .navigationBarTrailing) {
                    Button(action: {
                        print("Delete Element")
                    }, label: { Image(systemName: "trash") })
                }
            }
        }
    }
}
```

Listing 8-3: *Adding a button to the navigation bar*

The modifier is applied to the views inside the **NavigationStack** view and then the items are defined inside the closure. In this case, we include one **ToolbarItem** view with the **navigationBarTrailing** placement to position the item on the right side of the navigation bar. The item is defined with a **Button** view and an SF Symbol. The result is shown below.

Figure 8-4: *Navigation bar button*

 Do It Yourself: Update the **ContentView** view with the code in Listing 8-3. Run the application on the iPhone simulator. Press the button in the navigation bar. You should see a message printed on the console.

The **ToolbarItem** view defines a single item. If we want to define multiple items at once, we can use a **ToolbarItemGroup** view.

ToolbarItemGroup(placement: ToolbarItemPlacement, **content:** Closure)—
This view defines multiple items for a toolbar. The **placement** argument is a structure that determines the place and the toolbar where the items will be located. The structure includes type properties to define standard configurations for every system. The properties available are **automatic**, **bottomBar**, **cancellationAction**, **confirmationAction**, **destructiveAction**, **keyboard**, **navigation**, **navigation-BarLeading**, **navigationBarTrailing**, **primaryAction**, **secondaryAction**, **principal**, and **status**. The closure assigned to the **content** argument defines the views we want to include.

The button in the previous example prints a message on the console, but of course we can perform more meaningful tasks. For instance, we can add buttons to the navigation bar to scroll the list of books to the top and the bottom, as shown next.

```
struct ContentView: View {
    @EnvironmentObject var appData: ApplicationData

    var body: some View {
        NavigationStack {
            ScrollViewReader { proxy in
                List(appData.userData) { book in
                    CellBook(book: book)
                        .id(book.id)
                }
                .navigationTitle(Text("Books"))
                .toolbar {
                    ToolbarItemGroup(placement: .navigationBarTrailing) {
                        Button(action: {
                            if let lastIndex = appData.userData.first?.id {
                                proxy.scrollTo(lastIndex, anchor: .bottom)
                            }
                        }, label: { Image(systemName: "arrow.up.doc") })
                        Button(action: {
                            if let lastIndex = appData.userData.last?.id {
                                proxy.scrollTo(lastIndex, anchor: .bottom)
                            }
                        }, label: { Image(systemName: "arrow.down.doc") })
                    }
                }
            }
        }
    }
}
```

Listing 8-4: Adding multiple buttons

To be able to scroll the list programmatically, we embed the `List` view in a `ScrollViewReader` view (see Chapter 7, Listing 7-9). Using a `ToolbarItemGroup` view, we include two buttons at the right side of the navigation bar. The first button gets the identifier of the first book in the `userData` array and scrolls the list to the beginning, and the second button gets the identifier of the last book in the array and scrolls the list to the end.

Figure 8-5: Group of buttons in the navigation bar

As we have already mentioned, in addition to the navigation bar, the buttons may be added to a toolbar at the bottom of the screen or on top of the keyboard. These toolbars are automatically incorporated into the interface when a button is assigned to them. For instance, to show a toolbar at the bottom of the screen, all we need to do is to define a `ToolbarItem` view with the `bottomBar` placement value, as shown next.

Chapter 8 - Navigation

```
struct ContentView: View {
    @EnvironmentObject var appData: ApplicationData

    var body: some View {
        NavigationStack {
            List(appData.userData) { book in
                CellBook(book: book)
            }
            .navigationTitle(Text("Books"))
            .toolbar(.hidden, for: .navigationBar)
            .toolbar {
                ToolbarItem(placement: .bottomBar) {
                    HStack {
                        Button("Show") {
                            print("Show Values")
                        }
                    }.frame(minWidth: 0, maxWidth: .infinity,
alignment: .trailing)
                }
            }
        }
    }
}
```

Listing 8-5: Adding buttons to the bottom toolbar

Buttons added to the bottom toolbar are displayed at the center. That's the reason why in our example we have defined the button inside an `HStack` view, so it could be placed on the right and share the bar with other buttons, if necessary. Notice that we have also implemented the other version of the `toolbar()` modifier to hide the navigation bar.

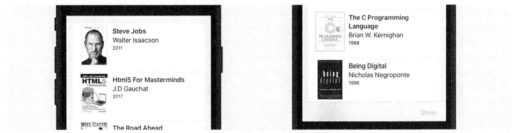

Figure 8-6: Bottom toolbar

Although we can position the buttons on the left or right side of the navigation bar with placement values like `navigationBarLeading` and `navigationBarTrailing`, the `ToolbarItemPlacement` structure also allows us to specify the intent of the buttons and let the system decide where and how to present them depending on the space available and the device. For instance, the structure returned by the `primaryAction` property usually places the buttons on the right, and the one returned by the `secondaryAction` property tells the system that the buttons are not essential for the operation of the application and therefore are placed inside a popup menu, as shown in the following example.

```
struct ContentView: View {
    @EnvironmentObject var appData: ApplicationData

    var body: some View {
        NavigationStack {
            List(appData.userData) { book in
                CellBook(book: book)
            }
            .navigationTitle(Text("Books"))
```

```
    .navigationBarTitleDisplayMode(.inline)
    .toolbar {
        ToolbarItemGroup(placement: .primaryAction) {
            Button(action: {
                print("Adding Book...")
            }, label: {
                Image(systemName: "plus.app")
            })
        }
        ToolbarItemGroup(placement: .secondaryAction) {
            Button(action: {
                print("Sorting Books...")
            }, label: {
                Label("Sort Books", systemImage: "arrow.up.arrow.down")
            })
        }
    }
    .toolbarRole(.editor)
}
}
}
```

Listing 8-6: Defining the buttons intent

The `toolbar()` modifier includes two `ToolbarItemGroup` items with one button each. The purpose of the button in the first group is to add books to the list, which is a primary function and therefore we declare it as a primary action, but the purpose of the button included in the second group is to sort the list and therefore we declare it as secondary. On an iPhone, the system places both buttons on the right, but includes the second button in a popup menu.

Figure 8-7: Primary and secondary buttons

The navigation bar is split in three areas: leading, center, and trailing. By default, the title is positioned at the center and the buttons on the sides, but we can change this behavior with the `toolbarRole()` modifier. This is specially useful on iPads and Mac computers, where larger screens and windows allow us to add more elements to the bar. For instance, if we declare the role as `editor` or `browser`, as we did in the example in Listing 8-6, on iPads the title is shown on the leading area and the secondary buttons at the center.

Figure 8-8: Secondary buttons on an iPad

There is a built-in tool that allows the user to add or remove buttons to the navigation bar when they are declared as secondary actions. To activate this feature, we must declare the identifiers for the `toolbar()` modifier and the items, as shown next.

```
struct ContentView: View {
   @EnvironmentObject var appData: ApplicationData

   var body: some View {
      NavigationStack {
         List(appData.userData) { book in
            CellBook(book: book)
         }
         .navigationTitle(Text("Books"))
         .toolbar(id: "mybar") {
            ToolbarItem(id: "sort", placement: .secondaryAction) {
               Button(action: {
                  print("Sorting Books...")
               }, label: {
                  Label("Sort Books", systemImage: "arrow.up.arrow.down")
               })
            }
            ToolbarItem(id: "settings", placement: .secondaryAction) {
               Button(action: {
                  print("Settings...")
               }, label: {
                  Label("Settings", systemImage: "gearshape")
               })
            }
         }
         .toolbarRole(.editor)
      }
   }
}
```

***Listing 8-7:** Customizing the bar*

In this example, we declare the bar with the "mybar" identifier and two buttons with the identifiers "sort" and "settings". The system uses these identifiers to store the last configuration and restore it the next time the app is launched. On iPhones the buttons are shown in a popup menu, as any other secondary action, but on iPads and Mac computers the system shows the buttons at the center and an additional button with an option to configure the bar.

***Figure 8-9:** Button to customize the toolbar*

When this option is selected, the system opens a windows were the user can drag and drop the buttons to configure the bar.

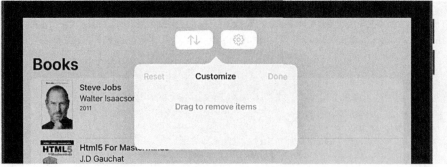

Figure 8-10: Toolbar customization

If we want to manually create a popup menu, instead of a button we need to add a `Menu` view to the toolbar. The following is the view's initializer.

Menu(String, **content:** Closure)—This initializer creates a menu with the title specified by the first argument. The closure assigned to the **content** argument provides the **Button** views that represent the options. The view also includes the `Menu(content: Closure, label: Closure)` initializer to declare the title with a view.

The `Menu` view works with any button, but it is usually implemented with toolbar buttons, as illustrated in the following example.

```
struct ContentView: View {
    @EnvironmentObject var appData: ApplicationData

    var body: some View {
        NavigationStack {
            List(appData.userData) { book in
                CellBook(book: book)
            }
            .navigationTitle(Text("Books"))
            .toolbar {
                Menu(content: {
                    Button("Option 1") { print("Option 1") }
                    Button("Option 2") { print("Option 2") }
                    Button("Option 3") { print("Option 3") }
                }, label: {
                    Image(systemName: "filemenu.and.selection")
                })
            }
        }
    }
}
```

Listing 8-8: Creating a popup menu

Our `Menu` view includes three buttons. In this case, we print messages on the console, but the buttons can perform any task we want. The view is represented by a button with an SF Symbol, and the menu opens when the button is pressed.

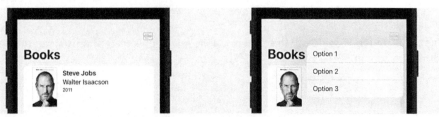

Figure 8-11: Custom popup menu

Chapter 8 - Navigation

Search

A `NavigationStack` view can include a search bar to allow the user to search for values in the model. The following is the modifier we need to apply to this view to enable that feature.

searchable(text: Binding, **tokens:** Binding, **suggestedTokens:** Binding, **placement:** SearchFieldPlacement, **prompt:** String, **token:** Closure)—This modifier adds and configures a search bar. The **text** argument stores the value inserted by the user. The **tokens** argument keeps track of the search tokens shown to the user. The **suggestedTokens** argument provides a list of tokens to suggest to the user. The **placement** argument specifies the place where the bar will be located. For this purpose, the structure includes the type properties `automatic`, `navigationBarDrawer`, `sidebar`, and `toolbar`, and the method `navigationBarDrawer(displayMode: NavigationBar-DrawerDisplayMode)` that can take the type properties `always` and `automatic` to always display or automatically hide the bar. The **prompt** argument specifies the bar's placeholder text. And the **token** argument provides the views to display the tokens.

This modifier comes in different versions, which allow us to implement only the arguments we need. For instance, to perform a search, all we need is a `Binding` property for the **text** argument to store the user's input. The rest of the arguments are only required if we want to provide additional functionality, as we will see in the examples below.

The `searchable()` modifier displays the search bar, but how the search is performed depends on the characteristics of our model. In a model that stores values in an array, as the one we are using in this chapter, the search can be performed by filtering the values with the `filter()` method. The following are the changes we need to introduce to the `ApplicationData` class in our model to filter books.

```
class ApplicationData: ObservableObject {
    var userData: [BookViewModel] {
        didSet {
            filterValues(search: "")
        }
    }
    @Published var filteredItems: [BookViewModel] = []

    func filterValues(search: String) {
        if search.isEmpty {
            filteredItems = userData.sorted(by: { $0.title < $1.title })
        } else {
            let list = userData.filter( { item in
                return item.title.localizedCaseInsensitiveContains(search)
            })
            filteredItems = list.sorted(by: { $0.title < $1.title })
        }
    }
    init() {
        userData = [
            BookViewModel(book: Book(title: "Steve Jobs", author: "Walter
Isaacson", cover: "book1", year: 2011, selected: false)),
            BookViewModel(book: Book(title: "HTML5 for Masterminds", author:
"J.D Gauchat", cover: "book2", year: 2017, selected: false)),
            BookViewModel(book: Book(title: "The Road Ahead", author: "Bill
Gates", cover: "book3", year: 1995, selected: false)),
            BookViewModel(book: Book(title: "The C Programming Language",
author: "Brian W. Kernighan", cover: "book4", year: 1988, selected:
false)),
            BookViewModel(book: Book(title: "Being Digital", author:
"Nicholas Negroponte", cover: "book5", year: 1996, selected: false)),
```

```
        BookViewModel(book: Book(title: "Only the Paranoid Survive",
author: "Andrew S. Grove", cover: "book6", year: 1999, selected: false)),
        BookViewModel(book: Book(title: "Accidental Empires", author:
"Robert X. Cringely", cover: "book7", year: 1996, selected: false)),
        BookViewModel(book: Book(title: "Bobby Fischer Teaches Chess",
author: "Bobby Fischer", cover: "book8", year: 1982, selected: false)),
        BookViewModel(book: Book(title: "New Guide to Science", author:
"Isaac Asimov", cover: "book9", year: 1993, selected: false)),
        BookViewModel(book: Book(title: "Christine", author: "Stephen
King", cover: "book10", year: 1983, selected: false)),
        BookViewModel(book: Book(title: "IT", author: "Stephen King",
cover: "book11", year: 1987, selected: false)),
        BookViewModel(book: Book(title: "Ending Aging", author: "Aubrey
de Grey", cover: "book12", year: 2007, selected: false))
      ]
      filterValues(search: "")
   }
}
```

Listing 8-9: Filtering the data in the model

In this model, we have turned the **userData** property into a normal property. This is because all we need from this property is to store the books available, but the data is provided to the views by a new **@Published** property called **filteredItems**. To feed this property with the books that match the search performed by the user, we define a method we will call every time the list needs an update (when a new search is performed or books are added or removed).

The **filterValues()** method receives a string with the value inserted by the user in the search bar. If the value is empty, we assign all the books in the **userData** property to the **filteredItems** property to show the full list on the screen, but if there is a value to search, we filter the books in the **userData** property with the **filter()** method. This method receives a value and must return **true** or **false** to determine if it is going to be included in the result. In this case, we return **true** only when the book's title contains the value inserted by the user. The resulting array is assigned to the **filteredItems** property to make it available to the views. Notice that in both cases, the arrays are sorted with the **sorted()** method, so the values are displayed in alphabetical order.

After the testing data is stored in the **userData** property, we call the **filterValues()** method with an empty array to initialize the list. Now we can use the **filteredItems** property to show the books, as we do next.

```
struct ContentView: View {
   @EnvironmentObject var appData: ApplicationData
   @State private var searchTerm: String = ""

   var body: some View {
      NavigationStack {
         List(appData.filteredItems) { book in
            CellBook(book: book)
         }.navigationTitle(Text("Books"))
      }
      .searchable(text: $searchTerm, prompt: Text("Insert title"))
      .onChange(of: searchTerm) { value in
         let search = value.trimmingCharacters(in: .whitespaces)
         appData.filterValues(search: search)
      }
   }
}
```

Listing 8-10: Displaying a search bar

This view includes a `@State` property to store the value inserted by the user, and two modifiers to manage the search. The `searchable()` modifier asks the system to display a search bar. For this example, we only need to provide two values, the `Binding` property to store the value (`searchTerm`) and a `Text` view with the placeholder text we want to show in the bar. This stores the value inserted by the user, but the search is performed by the `onChange()` modifier added below. This modifier executes a closure every time the value of the `searchTerm` property changes. In this closure, we trim the value to make sure there are no spaces at the beginning or the end, and then call the `filterValues()` method in the model. The method filters the values, assigns the result to the `filteredItems` property, and because we used this property to define the `List` view, only the books that match the search are shown on the screen.

Figure 8-12: Search bar

 Do It Yourself: Update the `ApplicationData` class with the code in Listing 8-9 and the `ContentView` view with the code in Listing 8-10. Run the application on the simulator or a device. Tap on the bar and perform a search. The list should only show the books which titles match what you type on the bar.

 IMPORTANT: In this example, we filter the items with a function in the model. This means that every time the filter changes or books are added, modified or removed, we must call the function again to update the views. This is why we declared the `didSet` method for the `userData` property, so every time a book is added or removed from this property, we call the `filterValues()` method to update the views. There are different programming patterns available. An alternative is to create a computed property inside the view to filter the items and use that property to provide the values for the list, as we did in the example of Listing 7-21. All you need to remember is that the views take the values from the `@Published` properties, so you always have to make sure that these properties are up-to-date.

By default, the search bar disappears when the user scrolls the list, but we can keep it permanently on the screen by defining the display mode. This is an additional argument included in the `searchable()` modifier called **placement**. This argument defines the location of the bar, which depends on the system and the organization of the interface, but it can also define the bar's display mode. The structure used to define this value includes the `navigationBar-Drawer()` method for this purpose. If we specify this method with the value `always`, as shown below, the bar is permanently displayed on the screen.

```
struct ContentView: View {
    @EnvironmentObject var appData: ApplicationData
    @State private var searchTerm: String = ""

    var body: some View {
        NavigationStack {
            List(appData.filteredItems) { book in
                CellBook(book: book)
```

```
        }
        .navigationTitle(Text("Books"))
    }
    .searchable(text: $searchTerm,
placement: .navigationBarDrawer(displayMode: .always), prompt:
Text("Insert title"))
        .onChange(of: searchTerm) { value in
            let search = value.trimmingCharacters(in: .whitespaces)
            appData.filterValues(search: search)
        }
    }
}
```

Listing 8-11: Keeping the search bar on the screen

The **searchable()** modifier automatically stores every character typed by the user into the **Binding** property. This means that the search is performed for each character typed or removed from the bar. If we want the user to decide when the search takes place, we can include the **onSubmit()** modifier. We have implemented this modifier before with **TextField** views to processing a value when the Return/Done key is pressed on the keyboard, but if we declare it with the **search** value, we can use it to perform a search, as shown below.

```
struct ContentView: View {
    @EnvironmentObject var appData: ApplicationData
    @State private var searchTerm: String = ""

    var body: some View {
        NavigationStack {
            List(appData.filteredItems) { book in
                CellBook(book: book)
            }
            .navigationTitle(Text("Books"))
        }
        .searchable(text: $searchTerm, prompt: Text("Insert title"))
        .onSubmit(of: .search) { performSearch() }
        .onChange(of: searchTerm) { value in
            if value.isEmpty {
                performSearch()
            }
        }
    }
    func performSearch() {
        let search = searchTerm.trimmingCharacters(in: .whitespaces)
        appData.filterValues(search: search)
    }
}
```

Listing 8-12: Performing the search when the Return/Done key is pressed

Because we need to perform the search from two different modifiers, we move the process to a new method called **performSearch()**. When the Return/Done key is pressed, the closure assigned to the **onSubmit()** modifier is executed and we call that method to trim the text and filter the books. The **performSearch()** method is also called from the **onChange()** modifier, but only when the search is empty. This is because we don't want to update the list every time the user types or removes a character, as we did before, but still need to do it when the user cancels the search. If the user presses the Cancel button, the system assigns an empty string to the **searchTerm** property, so we check this condition and update the list accordingly.

Another important feature is the possibility of showing a list of values to suggest to the user what to type. SwiftUI includes the following modifier to create this list.

searchSuggestions(Closure)—This modifier creates a list of values to suggest to the user. The argument provides the list of **Text** views we need to present the values.

The suggestions are provided with a list of **Text** views defined in a closure. If the views are created with the same model used to create the **List** view, only values that match the search are shown. The user can close the suggestion list by pressing the Return/Done key or by selecting one of the values. To allow selection, the framework includes the following modifier.

searchCompletion(String)—This modifier associates a search value with a view. The argument is the value we want the search bar to contain when the view is selected.

The **Text** views with the suggestions may be declared manually to create a static list, or with a **ForEach** loop to create a dynamic list. In our case, we want to show suggestions according to the value inserted by the user, so we must create a dynamic list with a **ForEach** loop.

```
struct ContentView: View {
    @EnvironmentObject var appData: ApplicationData
    @State private var searchTerm: String = ""

    var body: some View {
        NavigationStack {
            List(appData.filteredItems) { book in
                CellBook(book: book)
            }
            .navigationTitle(Text("Books"))
        }
        .searchable(text: $searchTerm, prompt: Text("Insert title"))
        .searchSuggestions({
            ForEach(appData.filteredItems) { item in
                Text("\(item.title) - \(item.author)")
                    .searchCompletion(item.title)
            }
        })
        .onChange(of: searchTerm) { value in
            let search = value.trimmingCharacters(in: .whitespaces)
            appData.filterValues(search: search)
        }
    }
}
```

Listing 8-13: Suggesting terms to the user

In this example, we applied the **searchable()** modifier, as before, but also included the **searchSuggestions()** modifier to display a list of suggested values. The closure assigned to this modifier creates a list of **Text** views with the values of the **filteredItems** property, so only the books that match the current search are included. To help the user identify the books, the **Text** view shows the book's title and author, but when the user selects a suggestion, only the title is assigned to the search bar by the **searchCompletion()** modifier.

Figure 8-13: Suggestions

The search bar includes two buttons, one to clear the bar and another to allow the user to cancel the search, but we can also do it programatically. The environment includes the following values to control the process.

isSearching—This is a Boolean value that determines if the user is currently performing a search or not.

dismissSearch—This property creates an action to cancel the search. It is a `DismissSearchAction` structure. The structure exposes a handler we can call to perform the action.

The `searchable()` modifier sends the information down the view hierarchy through the environment, so the system can determine where to show the search bar and when to display it. This means that the environment values are only available within the views in the hierarchy. Therefore, to be able to read them, we must embed the list of books in a custom view. In the following example, we call this view `SearchableView`.

```
struct ContentView: View {
   @EnvironmentObject var appData: ApplicationData
   @State private var searchTerm: String = ""

   var body: some View {
      NavigationStack {
         SearchableView()
            .navigationTitle(Text("Books"))
      }
      .searchable(text: $searchTerm, prompt: Text("Insert title"))
      .onChange(of: searchTerm) { value in
         let search = value.trimmingCharacters(in: .whitespaces)
         appData.filterValues(search: search)
      }
   }
}
struct SearchableView: View {
   @EnvironmentObject var appData: ApplicationData
   @Environment(\.isSearching) var isSearching
   @Environment(\.dismissSearch) var dismissSearch

   var body: some View {
      List {
         if isSearching {
            Button("Dismiss") {
               dismissSearch()
            }
         }
         ForEach(appData.filteredItems) { book in
            CellBook(book: book)
         }
      }
   }
}
```

Listing 8-14: *Cancelling the search programmatically*

The `SearchableView` view implements a `ForEach` view to generate the list of books, so we are able to include an additional row at the top with a button to dismiss the search. But to avoid interfering with the content, the button is only shown when the user is performing a search. For this purpose, we check whether a search is taking place with the `isSearching` value and cancel the search with the `dismissSearch` value when the Dismiss button is pressed. Notice that the `dismissSearch` value is a structure that exposes a closure that we can call as we do with any other closure or function. The result is shown below.

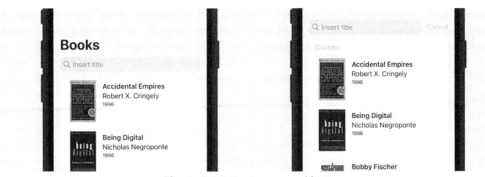

Figure 8-14: Custom cancel button

Another feature we can add to a search bar are scope buttons. These are buttons placed below the bar that allow the user to specify the scope of the search (e.g., search by title or by author). To incorporate these buttons, SwiftUI includes the following modifier.

searchScopes(Binding, **scopes:** Closure)—This modifier defines a list of search scopes. The first argument is a **Binding** property to store the currently selected scope, and the **scopes** argument provides the views to create the buttons.

This modifier needs two things: the values to represent the scopes and a **Binding** property to keep track of the scope selected by the user.

```
import SwiftUI
enum Scopes {
    case title, author
}
struct ContentView: View {
    @EnvironmentObject var appData: ApplicationData
    @State private var searchTerm: String = ""
    @State private var searchScope: Scopes = .title

    var body: some View {
        NavigationStack {
            List(appData.filteredItems) { book in
                CellBook(book: book)
            }.navigationTitle(Text("Books"))
        }
        .searchable(text: $searchTerm, prompt: Text("Insert title"))
        .searchScopes($searchScope, scopes: {
            Text("Title").tag(Scopes.title)
            Text("Author").tag(Scopes.author)
        })
        .onChange(of: searchTerm) { _ in performSearch() }
        .onChange(of: searchScope) { _ in performSearch() }
    }
    func performSearch() {
        let search = searchTerm.trimmingCharacters(in: .whitespaces)
        appData.filterValues(search: search, scope: searchScope)
    }
}
```

Listing 8-15: Adding scope buttons

In this example, we define the scopes with an enumeration and two values: **title** and **author**. The **@State** property is initialized with the **title** value, so the searches are first performed by title. The closure assigned to the **searchScopes()** modifier includes two **Text** views to create two scope buttons, one to select the **title** scope and another to select the

author scope. To perform the search in the current scope, we send the value of the **searchScope** property to the **filterValues()** method in the model. The method must now check the selected scope and search the value accordingly, as shown below.

```
func filterValues(search: String, scope: Scopes = .title) {
   if search.isEmpty {
      filteredItems = userData.sorted(by: { $0.title < $1.title })
   } else {
      let list = userData.filter( { item in
         let value = scope == .title ? item.title : item.author
         return value.localizedCaseInsensitiveContains(search)
      })
      filteredItems = list.sorted(by: { $0.title < $1.title })
   }
}
```

Listing 8-16: Searching by title and author

The search bar now includes two buttons below. If the user presses the Title button, we search by title, and if the user presses the Author button, we search by author.

Figure 8-15: Search scopes

Another feature we can incorporate to a search bar are search tokens. These are values that appear inside the bar to help the user perform complex search queries. For instance, if we want to allow the user to search books by author, we can create a token that shows the current selected author so the user knows the current search constraint and can also remove it.

As with scopes, we need a **Binding** property to store the current tokens and also provide a **Text** view to present the tokens on the screen, but because tokens must be created from values that conform to the **Identifiable** protocol, we need to define a custom data type, as shown next. (The data type must also conform to the **Equatable** protocol to be able to track changes with the **onChange()** modifier. See Chapter 3 for more information on these protocols).

```
import SwiftUI
struct Tokens: Identifiable, Equatable {
   let id = UUID()
   let name: String
}
struct ContentView: View {
   @EnvironmentObject var appData: ApplicationData
   @State private var searchTerm: String = ""
   @State private var searchTokens: [Tokens] = []

   var body: some View {
      NavigationStack {
         List(appData.filteredItems) { book in
            CellBook(book: book)
         }.navigationTitle(Text("Books"))
```

```
        .toolbar {
            let list = appData.userData.map { $0.author }
            let authors = Set(list).sorted()
            Menu(content: {
                ForEach(authors, id: \.self) { author in
                    Button(author) {
                        let token = Tokens(name: author)
                        searchTokens = [token]
                    }
                }
            }, label: {
                Image(systemName: "pencil.circle")
            })
        }
    }
    .searchable(text: $searchTerm, tokens: $searchTokens, token:
{ token in
        Text(token.name)
    })
    .onChange(of: searchTerm) { _ in performSearch() }
    .onChange(of: searchTokens) { _ in performSearch() }
    }
    func performSearch() {
        let search = searchTerm.trimmingCharacters(in: .whitespaces)
        appData.filterValues(search: search, author:
searchTokens.first?.name ?? "")
    }
}
```

Listing 8-17: Adding tokens

In this example, we define a structure called **Tokens** to create the tokens. The structure includes the required **id** property to identify the value and a **String** property to store the token's name. The **searchable()** modifier stores the tokens in an array, so we define the **@State** property as an array of **Tokens** structures. To create the tokens, we have added a **toolbar()** modifier with a **Menu** view. The menu's options are defined with the name of the authors available in the model. This creates a button in the navigation bar the user can press to select an author. Notice that to get the list of authors, we map the **userData** array, extract the author's name, turn the array into a **Set** to remove duplicates, and sort them in alphabetical order.

Once an author is selected, we create an instance of the **Tokens** structure with the author's name and assign it to the **searchTokens** property. This adds a token to the search bar, which tells the user that the search will be performed on the books written by that author. As always, we need to modify the **filterValues()** method in the model for this search to work.

```
func filterValues(search: String, author: String = "") {
    if search.isEmpty && author.isEmpty {
        filteredItems = userData.sorted(by: { $0.title < $1.title })
    } else {
        let list = userData.filter( { item in
            var valid = true
            if !author.isEmpty && author != item.author {
                valid = false
            }
            if valid && !search.isEmpty && !
item.title.localizedCaseInsensitiveContains(search) {
                valid = false
            }
            return valid
        })
```

```
        filteredItems = list.sorted(by: { $0.title < $1.title })
    }
}
```

Listing 8-18: Filtering books by author

In this new method, we must check if the user has selected an author and then filter the array by author and title. The easiest way to do it is to start with a valid condition (`valid = true`) and then invalidate it if something doesn't match. We first check if the user selected an author and compare it with the author of the book. If they don't match, the condition becomes invalid. Next, we do the same for the title, but only if the condition was not already invalidated by the author. As a result, when the user selects an author, a token with the author's name appears in the search bar and the search is only performed on the books written by that author.

Figure 8-16: Tokens

Basic ## Navigation Link

There is no stack of views if we only have one. To allow the user to open additional views, SwiftUI includes the **NavigationLink** view. This is a control view that creates a button the user can press to replace the current view with another. The following are the view's initializers.

NavigationLink(String, **destination:** View**)**—This initializer creates a button for navigation. The first argument is the text we want to assign to the button's label, and the **destination** argument is the view we want to open when the button is pressed. If we want to define a complex label for the button, we can use the initializer **NavigationLink-(destination: View, label: Closure)** instead.

NavigationLink(String, **value:** Value**)**—This initializer creates a button for dynamic navigation. The first argument is the text we want to assign to the button's label, and the **value** argument is a value that identifies the link. If we want to define a complex label for the button, we can use the initializer **NavigationLink(value: Value, label: Closure)** instead.

The **NavigationLink** view requires a view to open and a label the user can tap to perform the action. For instance, the following example adds a link to the navigation bar to open a view the user can use to change the app's settings.

```
struct ContentView: View {
    @EnvironmentObject var appData: ApplicationData

    var body: some View {
        NavigationStack {
            List(appData.userData) { book in
                CellBook(book: book)
            }.navigationTitle(Text("Books"))
            .toolbar {
                ToolbarItem(placement: .navigationBarTrailing) {
```

```
                    NavigationLink(destination: SettingsView(), label: {
                        Image(systemName: "gearshape")
                    })
                }
            }
        }
    }
}
```

Listing 8-19: Including a navigation link

Like the **Button** view, the **NavigationLink** view creates a button but with the purpose of replacing the current view with another one. In this case, we create the button with an SF Symbol image of a gear, and set the destination view to be a custom view we call **SettingsView**.

```
import SwiftUI
struct SettingsView: View {
    @State private var showPictures: Bool = true
    @State private var showYear: Bool = true

    var body: some View {
        Form {
            Toggle("Show Pictures", isOn: $showPictures)
            Toggle("Show Year", isOn: $showYear)
        }.navigationTitle("Settings")
    }
}
struct SettingsView_Previews: PreviewProvider {
    static var previews: some View {
        NavigationStack {
            SettingsView()
        }
    }
}
```

Listing 8-20: Defining a second view

Our **SettingsView** view includes two **@State** properties to store the values of the two **Toggle** views we use to create a form. Other than that, the view is the same as any other we have created before, but because it represents the interface for the whole screen, we should put it in a separate SwiftUI file (see Figure 5-108).

The **SettingsView** view is opened from the **ContentView** view and therefore it is part of its hierarchy, so we don't have to embed it in a **NavigationStack** view, but we still need to declare its title with the **navigationTitle()** modifier, as we did for the initial view.

When the user taps the button in the **ContentView** view, an instance of the **SettingsView** view is created and presented on the screen transitioning from right to left.

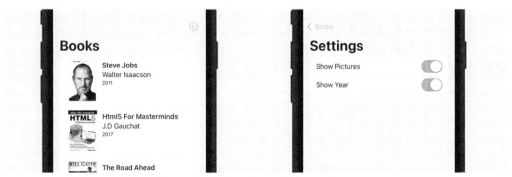

Figure 8-17: Interface with two views

Do It Yourself: This example assumes that you are implementing the model defined in Chapter 7, Listing 7-3 (We do not need to filter the items anymore, as we did in the previous section). Update the `ContentView` view with the code in Listing 8-19. Press Command + N or select the options New/File from the File menu at the top of the screen to create a new SwiftUI View file with the name SettingsView.swift (see Figure 5-108). Update this file with the code in Listing 8-20. Select the ContentView.swift file to activate the view on the canvas. Press the button on the navigation bar. You should see the `SettingsView` view appear on the screen, transitioning from right to left, as shown in Figure 8-17.

IMPORTANT: The views defined by the `SettingsView` structure of Listing 8-20 are not embedded in a `NavigationStack` view because the `SettingsView` view is opened from the `ContentView` view and therefore it is already part of a navigation hierarchy, but the instance of this view created for the preview is not part of that hierarchy and therefore if we want to see on the canvas what this view is going to look like when it is presented to the user, we must embed it in a `NavigationStack` view, as we did in Listing 8-20.

The view opened by a `NavigationLink` view includes a button in the navigation bar that the user can tap to go back to the previous view. This button is automatically generated by SwiftUI and it is part of the basic tools provided for navigation. Usually, it is displayed with the label "Back", but it changes according to the title of the previous view. If the title is short enough, it is assigned to the button's label, and that's why in our example it is called "Books" (see Figure 8-17, right). This helps the user identify the view that is going to appear on the screen if the button is pressed. But that is about all the configuration options we have for this button. If we need something different, we must remove the back button with the `navigationBarBackButton-Hidden()` modifier and create our own.

Custom back buttons must provide a way for the user to remove the view. An alternative is to modify the state of the presentation from the environment. For this purpose, the environment includes the following values.

dismiss—This property creates an action to dismiss the view. It is a `DismissAction` structure. The structure exposes a handler we can call to perform the action.

isPresented—This is a Boolean value that determines whether the view is being presented or not.

We have worked with values from the environment before (see Listing 6-12). All we have to do is to add an `@Environment` property to the view and then read or modify its values. The `dismiss` value is a structure that provides access to a closure with code to dismiss the view, so all we need to do to remove the `SettingsView` view is to define an `@Environment` property with this value and then execute the closure when a button is pressed, as shown next.

```
struct SettingsView: View {
    @Environment(\.dismiss) var dismiss
    @State private var showPictures: Bool = true
    @State private var showYear: Bool = true

    var body: some View {
        Form {
            Toggle("Show Pictures", isOn: $showPictures)
            Toggle("Show Year", isOn: $showYear)
        }.navigationTitle("Settings")
        .navigationBarBackButtonHidden(true)
        .toolbar {
            ToolbarItem(placement: .navigationBarLeading) {
                Button("Go Back") {
```

```
            dismiss()
          }
        }
      }
    }
}
```

Listing 8-21: Dismissing the view from the environment

As always, it is recommended to use the name of the environment value to define the property. In this example, we call it `dismiss`. To add a custom back button, we first remove the one provided by the system with the `navigationBarBackButtonHidden()` modifier, and then add a new button on the left side of the navigation bar (leading) with the `toolbar()` modifier. When the button is pressed, we execute the closure provided by the `DismissAction` structure in the `dismiss` property, and the view is removed.

Figure 8-18: Custom back button

 Do It Yourself: Update the `SettingsView` view with the code in Listing 8-21. Select the ContentView.swift file to open the view on the canvas. Press the button to open the `SettingsView` view and then press the Go Back button to close this view and show the list of books on the screen again.

In the previous example, we used an `Image` view to declare the label for the `NavigationLink` view, but we can use any view we want, including custom views. A common practice is to declare the rows of a list as the labels of a `NavigationLink` view, so when the user taps on a row, another view opens to show additional information.

```
struct ContentView: View {
   @EnvironmentObject var appData: ApplicationData

   var body: some View {
      NavigationStack {
         List(appData.userData) { book in
            NavigationLink(destination: {
               DetailView(book: book)
            }, label: {
               CellBook(book: book)
            })
         }.navigationTitle(Text("Books"))
      }
   }
}
```

Listing 8-22: Selecting rows with a navigation link

The view opened when a row is selected is usually called *Detail view* because its role is to show details about the selected item. In our example, we want to show additional information about the book selected by the user. For this purpose, the `NavigationLink` view opens a new view called `DetailView` and send to this view a copy of the `BookViewModel` structure that represents the book. The view receives this instance and displays the values on the screen.

```
import SwiftUI
struct DetailView: View {
   let book: BookViewModel

   var body: some View {
      VStack {
         Text(book.title)
            .font(.title)
         Text(book.author)
         Image(book.cover)
            .resizable()
            .scaledToFit()
      }.padding()
      .navigationTitle("Book")
      .navigationBarTitleDisplayMode(.inline)
   }
}
struct DetailView_Previews: PreviewProvider {
   static var previews: some View {
      NavigationStack {
         DetailView(book: ApplicationData().userData[0])
      }
   }
}
```

Listing 8-23: *Defining a Detail view*

When the user selects a row in the `ContentView` view, an instance of the `DetailView` view is created and presented on the screen transitioning from right to left, and the values of the book are shown to the user.

Figure 8-19: *Detail view*

 Do It Yourself: Update the `ContentView` view with the code in Listing 8-22. Create a new SwiftUI View file called DetailView.swift and update the code generated by the template with the code in Listing 8-23. Tap on a book. You should see the information of the book on the screen, as in Figure 8-19 (right).

Although this is a valid approach, we don't have much control over the navigation process. The system automatically includes back buttons that we can replace with custom buttons and the `dismiss` value, as we did in previous examples (see Listing 8-21), but these buttons only remove the current view. Professional applications allow the user to navigate through many views that comprise long navigation paths. Going back to previous views one by one becomes tedious and time consuming. To have more control over the navigation path, we can access the views through the `NavigationStack` view. This view can keep track of all the views opened by the user and can store references to those views in a `Binding` property, so by modifying the values stored in this property we can modify the path programmatically (add or remove views).

There are a few steps we need to follow to control the navigation path. First, we must create the navigation links with the `NavigationLink(String, value: Value)` initializer. This initializer identifies the link with the value provided by the **value** argument. Once the link is identified, we must add the following modifier to tell the system what to open.

navigationDestination(for: Type, **destination:** Closure)—This modifier specifies the destination view for a `NavigationLink` view. The **for** argument is the data type of the values used by the `NavigationLink` view to identify the link, and the **destination** argument creates an instance of the destination view to present it on the screen.

The `NavigationLink` view and the `navigationDestination()` modifier are connected by the data type of the value used by the view to identify the link. When the user taps on a `NavigationLink` view identified with a value, the `navigationDestination()` modifier associated to that data type creates a destination view and presents it on the screen. Once the destination view is presented on the screen, the `NavigationStack` view stores it in a navigation stack and the value assigned to the `NavigationLink` is added to a `Binding` property that we can modify later to control the navigation path. The values in this property are stored in a collection, but because they can be of different data types, SwiftUI provides the following structure to manage them.

NavigationPath()—This initializer creates a structure to store values associated with views in a navigation path. This initializer defines an empty path, but there are two more that create instances with predefined paths. We can create it from a collection of values or from a `CodableRepresentation` structure, which allows us to restore previous navigation paths when the app is launched.

The `NavigationPath` structure includes the following properties and methods to manage the values.

isEmpty—This property returns a Boolean value that indicates if the path is empty.

count—This property returns the number of values (views) in the path.

append(Value**)**—This method adds a value (a view) to the path.

removeLast(Int**)**—This method removes the last value from the path. The argument is the number of values (views) to remove. By default, only the last value is removed.

When we add a value to the `NavigationPath` structure, the view associated to that value is shown on the screen, and when we remove a value, the view is removed from the navigation path (and the screen if it is currently active). For this process to work, we need to define a `Binding` property with a `NavigationPath` structure (this could be a `@State` property inside the view or a `@Published` property in the model), initialize the `NavigationStack` view with a reference to this property, create the `NavigationLink` views with a value, and implement the `navigationDestination()` modifier to tell the system which view to open when a link is tapped by the user. The following example applies these changes to the `ContentView` view of our project.

```
struct ContentView: View {
    @EnvironmentObject var appData: ApplicationData
    @State private var path = NavigationPath()
```

```
    var body: some View {
        NavigationStack(path: $path) {
            List(appData.userData) { book in
                NavigationLink(value: book, label: {
                    CellBook(book: book)
                })
            }.navigationTitle(Text("Books"))
            .navigationDestination(for: BookViewModel.self, destination:
{ book in
                DetailView(path: $path, book: book)
            })
        }
    }
}
```

Listing 8-24: Defining custom navigation

As we already mentioned, the **NavigationLink** view and the **navigationDestination()** modifier are connected by the data type of the value that identifies the link. In our example, we use the **BookViewModel** structure. When the user taps on a **NavigationLink** view identified with an instance of the **BookViewModel** structure, the **navigationDestination()** modifier associated to this data type creates a **DetailView** view with that value, and the view is shown on the screen. Once the view is presented, the **NavigationStack** view appends the **NavigationLink** value to the **NavigationPath** structure assigned to the **stack** property. Now, the **NavigationPath** structure contains a value that represents the **DetailView** view and we can remove it to remove the view from the navigation path, as we do next.

```
struct DetailView: View {
    @Binding var path: NavigationPath
    let book: BookViewModel

    var body: some View {
        VStack {
            Text(book.title)
                .font(.title)
            Text(book.author)

            NavigationLink(value: "Picture View", label: {
                Image(book.cover)
                    .resizable()
                    .scaledToFit()
            })
        }.padding()
        .navigationTitle(Text("Book"))
        .navigationBarTitleDisplayMode(.inline)
        .navigationBarBackButtonHidden(true)
        .toolbar {
            ToolbarItem(placement: .navigationBarLeading) {
                Button("Go Back") {
                    path.removeLast()
                }
            }
        }
        .navigationDestination(for: String.self, destination: { _ in
            PictureView(path: $path, book: book)
        })
    }
}
struct DetailView_Previews: PreviewProvider {
    static var previews: some View {
        NavigationStack {
```

```
            DetailView(path: .constant(NavigationPath()), book:
ApplicationData().userData[0])
         }
      }
}
```

Listing 8-25: Adding and removing views from the path

The **DetailView** view receives a reference to the **stack** property, so we can add or remove values from the **NavigationPath** structure and in consequence add or remove views from the navigation path. For instance, in this example, we add a button to the navigation bar that calls the **removeLast()** method. This method removes the last value in the **NavigationPath** structure, which in our case is the **BookViewModel** structure that represents the **DetailView** view, so this view is removed from the screen when the button is pressed.

To add views to the path, we can include another **NavigationLink** view, as we did in the example of Listing 8-25. The label was declared as the **Image** view that shows the books cover, so when the user taps on the cover, a new view is presented on the screen. Notice that the value for the link was declared as a string, so the **navigationDestination()** modifier works with **String** values this time (**String.self**). When the user taps on the book's cover, the modifier opens the **PictureView** view, the **NavigationStack** view adds the view to the stack and the string to the **NavigationPath** structure. Now this structure contains two values: the **BookViewModel** structure that represents the **DetailView** view and the string "Picture View" that represents the **PictureView** view. Again, we pass the reference of the **stack** property to this view to be able to add or remove views from the path.

```
import SwiftUI

struct PictureView: View {
   @Binding var path: NavigationPath
   let book: BookViewModel

   var body: some View {
      VStack {
         Image(book.cover)
            .resizable()
            .scaledToFit()
         Spacer()
      }
      .navigationTitle(Text("Cover"))
      .navigationBarTitleDisplayMode(.inline)
      .navigationBarBackButtonHidden()
      .toolbar {
         ToolbarItem(placement: .navigationBarLeading) {
            Button("Go Back") {
               path.removeLast()
            }
         }
         ToolbarItem(placement: .navigationBarTrailing) {
            Button("Back to List") {
               path = NavigationPath()
            }
         }
      }
   }
}
struct PictureView_Previews: PreviewProvider {
   static var previews: some View {
      NavigationStack {
```

```
        PictureView(path: .constant(NavigationPath()), book:
ApplicationData().userData[0])
      }
    }
}
```

Listing 8-26: Going back to any view in the path

The `PictureView` view in Listing 8-26 includes two buttons in the navigation bar: one to go back to the previous view (the `DetailView` view) and another to go back to the initial view (the `ContentView` view). To go back to the previous view, we remove the last value in the `NavigationPath` structure with the `removeLast()` method, as we did before. The method removes the "Picture View" string and therefore the `PictureView` view is removed from the screen.

To go back to the initial view, we follow a different approach. As we mentioned, the values stored in the `NavigationPath` structure represent the views opened by the user. In our example, an empty `NavigationPath` structure represents the `ContentView` view (the initial view), the `BookViewModel` structure stored first represents the `DetailView` view, and the "Picture View" string stored second represents the `PictureView` view. Therefore, to go back to the initial view we can remove these two values with the `removeLast()` method (`removeLast(2)`), or just assign a new `NavigationPath` structure to the `stack` property with an empty path. The last approach is recommended and the one we follow in this example. This is to avoid making the mistake of removing more values than those available in the path. The result is shown below.

Figure 8-20: Custom navigation path

 Do It Yourself: Update the `ContentView` view with the code in Listing 8-24, and the `DetailView` view with the code in Listing 8-25. Create a new SwiftUI View file called PictureView.swift with the code in Listing 8-26. Select a book from the list and tap on the book's cover. You should see the `PictureView` view on the screen with an enlarged image of the cover. If you press the Go Back button, you should go back to the `DetailView` view, but if you press the Back to List button, the interface should transition back to the list of books.

Besides using a `NavigationLink` view, we can also add values directly to the `NavigationPath` structure with the `append()` method. For instance, the following `DetailView` view implements a `Button` view instead of the `NavigationLink` view to add the `PictureView` view to the path.

```
struct DetailView: View {
    @Binding var path: NavigationPath
    let book: BookViewModel

    var body: some View {
        VStack {
            Text(book.title)
```

```
            .font(.title)
        Text(book.author)

        Button(action: {
            path.append("Picture View")
        }, label: {
            Image(book.cover)
                .resizable()
                .scaledToFit()
        })
    }.padding()
    .navigationTitle(Text("Book"))
    .navigationBarTitleDisplayMode(.inline)
    .navigationBarBackButtonHidden(true)
    .toolbar {
        ToolbarItem(placement: .navigationBarLeading) {
            Button("Go Back") {
                path.removeLast()
            }
        }
    }
    .navigationDestination(for: String.self, destination: { _ in
        PictureView(path: $path, book: book)
    })
    }
}
```

Listing 8-27: Adding values to the path

The label for the button is again the book's cover. When the user taps on the cover, we call the `append()` method on the `NavigationPath` structure to add a string to the path, and this triggers the same process as before; the `navigationDestination()` modifier detects that a value of type `String` has been added to the path, the `NavigationStack` view adds the `PictureView` view to the stack, and the view is presented on the screen.

(Basic) 8.2 Modal Views

Besides navigation links, we can expand the interface with modal views. Modal views are normal views but are presented on top of the rest of the views on the screen.

(Basic) Sheets

Sheets are general-purpose modal views. On iPhones, they occupy the whole screen, and on iPads and Mac computers they are shown as a rectangular view at the center of the screen. The `View` protocol defines the following modifiers to present a sheet.

sheet(isPresented: Binding, **onDismiss:** Closure?, **content:** Closure)—This modifier displays a sheet. The **isPresented** argument is a `Binding` property of type `Bool` that determines whether the sheet has to be presented (`true`) or removed (`false`), the **onDismiss** argument is a closure that is executed when the sheet is removed, and the **content** argument is a closure that defines the view to be shown on the screen.

sheet(item: Binding, **onDismiss:** Closure?, **content:** Closure)—This modifier displays a sheet. The **item** argument is an optional `Binding` value that determines whether the sheet has to be presented or removed (`nil`), the **onDismiss** argument is a closure that is executed when the sheet is removed, and the **content** argument is a closure that defines the view to be shown on the screen. The closure receives the value stored in the `Binding` property.

These modifiers create a sheet that partially covers the interface. SwiftUI also includes the following modifiers to create a full-screen sheet.

fullScreenCover(isPresented: Binding, **onDismiss:** Closure, **content:** Closure)—This modifier displays a full-screen sheet. The **isPresented** argument is a **Binding** property of type **Bool** that determines whether the sheet has to be presented (**true**) or removed (**false**), the **onDismiss** argument is a closure that is executed when the sheet is removed, and the **content** argument is a closure that defines the view to be shown on the screen.

fullScreenCover(item: Binding, **onDismiss:** Closure, **content:** Closure)—This modifier displays a full-screen sheet. The **item** argument is an optional **Binding** value that determines whether the sheet has to be presented or removed (**nil**), the **onDismiss** argument is a closure that is executed when the sheet is removed, and the **content** argument is a closure that defines the view to be shown on the screen. The closure receives the value stored in the **Binding** property.

These modifiers work like the **NavigationLink** view. We provide a **Binding** property and the sheet is shown on the screen or removed depending on the value of this property. When there is a value or the value is **true**, the modifier opens a view on top of the current interface, and we can use this view for anything we want. A common practice is opening sheets to allow the user to add values to the model. For instance, we can open a sheet to allow the user to add a book to the list.

```
struct ContentView: View {
    @EnvironmentObject var appData: ApplicationData
    @State private var showSheet: Bool = false

    var body: some View {
        NavigationStack {
            List(appData.userData) { book in
                CellBook(book: book)
            }.navigationTitle(Text("Books"))
            .toolbar {
                ToolbarItem(placement: .navigationBarTrailing) {
                    Button(action: {
                        showSheet = true
                    }, label: { Image(systemName: "plus") })
                }
            }
            .sheet(isPresented: $showSheet) {
                AddBookView()
            }
        }
    }
}
```

Listing 8-28: Displaying a sheet

This view defines a **@State** property to control the state of the sheet and adds a **Button** view to the navigation bar that assigns the value **true** to this property to open the sheet when pressed. The sheet is managed by the **sheet()** modifier applied to the **List** view. The modifier is connected to the **showSheet** property, so when the value of this property is **true** a custom view called **AddBookView** is presented on the screen. This is the view we are using to allow the user to add new books. The view includes **TextField** views to insert the book's title, author and year, and a button to store the values in the model.

```swift
import SwiftUI

struct AddBookView: View {
    @EnvironmentObject var appData: ApplicationData
    @Environment(\.dismiss) var dismiss
    @State private var titleInput: String = ""
    @State private var authorInput: String = ""
    @State private var yearInput: String = ""

    var body: some View {
        VStack(alignment: .trailing, spacing: 10) {
            HStack {
                Spacer()
                Button("Close") {
                    dismiss()
                }.padding([.top, .bottom], 10)
            }
            TextField("Insert Title", text: $titleInput)
                .textFieldStyle(.roundedBorder)
            TextField("Insert Author", text: $authorInput)
                .textFieldStyle(.roundedBorder)
            TextField("Insert Year", text: $yearInput)
                .textFieldStyle(.roundedBorder)
                .keyboardType(.numbersAndPunctuation)
            Button("Save") {
                storeBook()
                dismiss()
            }.buttonStyle(.borderedProminent)
            Spacer()
        }.padding()
    }
    func storeBook() {
        let title = titleInput.trimmingCharacters(in: .whitespaces)
        let author = authorInput.trimmingCharacters(in: .whitespaces)
        if let year = Int(yearInput), !title.isEmpty && !author.isEmpty {
            let newBook = BookViewModel(book: Book(title: title, author:
author, cover: "nocover", year: year, selected: false))
            appData.userData.append(newBook)
        }
    }
}
struct AddBookView_Previews: PreviewProvider {
    static var previews: some View {
        NavigationStack {
            AddBookView().environmentObject(ApplicationData())
        }
    }
}
```

Listing 8-29: Defining the view for the sheet

There is nothing new in this view, all we do is take the input from the user, trim the values to remove additional space, check whether the values are valid, and store a new book in the model. For this purpose, we create a new **BookViewModel** structure with the values inserted by the user and add it to the **userData** array in the model. After the process is over, we perform the **dismiss** handler, the view is closed, and the new book appears at the end of the list.

Figure 8-21: Sheet to insert new values

Do It Yourself: Update the `ContentView` view from the previous example with the code in Listing 8-28. Create a new SwiftUI View file called AddBookView.swift for the code in Listing 8-29. Press the + button in the navigation bar. You should see a sheet with three input fields. Insert the values and press Save. The book should be added at the end of the list.

In this example, we have included a button to close the view, but there is a built-in feature that allows the user to remove the view by dragging it down with the finger. SwiftUI includes the following modifier to disable this tool.

interactiveDismissDisabled(Bool**)**—This modifier enables or disables the possibility of dragging down the view to close it (`true` disabled, `false` enabled).

There are also modifiers to configure the sheet. We can determine the height of the sheet and when multiple heights are available, we can determine if the indicator provided by the system is going to be shown or not.

presentationDetents(Set, **selection:** Binding**)**—This modifier determines the sheet's height. The first argument is a set of values that determine all the different sizes the sheet can take. The values are defined by a structure of type `PresentationDetent`. The structure includes the type properties `large` and `medium` to set predefined sizes, and the type methods `custom(Type)`, `fraction(CGFloat)`, and `height(CGFloat)` to set custom sizes. And the **selection** argument is a `Binding` property we can use to keep track of the current height.

presentationDragIndicator(Visibility**)**—This modifier shows or hides the indicator that is provided by the system to drag the sheet when there are multiple heights available. The argument is an enumeration with the values `automatic`, `visible`, and `hidden`.

We can apply this modifiers directly to the view presented by the sheet. For instance, the following example don't allow the user to drag down the sheet to close it.

```
.sheet(isPresented: $showSheet) {
   AddBookView()
      .interactiveDismissDisabled(true)
}
```

Listing 8-30: Disabling the interactive dismiss feature

To determine the sheet's height, we have different options available. By default, the height is set to `large`, which means that the view will take up as much space as possible. The value `medium` sets the height to around half the space available, but we can also specify a custom height. For instance, with the `height()` method, we can declare a height in points, and the `fraction()` method allows us to set a height proportional to that of the screen (values from 0.0 to 1.0). The following example shows how to set it to `medium`.

```
.sheet(isPresented: $showSheet) {
   AddBookView()
      .presentationDetents([.medium])
}
```

Listing 8-31: Assigning a predefined height

The sheet now occupies less space on the screen, but we can even reduce it further with the `height()` method, as shown next.

```
.sheet(isPresented: $showSheet) {
   AddBookView()
      .presentationDetents([.height(250)])
}
```

Listing 8-32: Assigning a custom height

 Do It Yourself: Replace the `sheet()` modifier in the `ContentView` view with the modifier you want to try. Press the + button to open the sheet. Try to assign multiple values to the first argument of the `presentationDetents()` modifier to see how the sheet adapts to different heights.

There is a second `sheet()` modifier designed to open a sheet for each of the values in the model. It is usually implemented to open a sheet for each row on a list. The modifier needs an optional `Binding` property of the same data type of the items in our model (the data type must conform to the `identifiable` protocol). If the property contains a value, a sheet is opened with that value, and when the value `nil` is assigned to the property, the sheet is closed.

In the following example, we implement this modifier to allow the user to edit the values of the books. When a row is selected, we assign a copy of the `BookViewModel` structure that represents the book to the state property, so the sheet is opened with this value, as shown next.

```
struct ContentView: View {
   @EnvironmentObject var appData: ApplicationData
   @State private var showSheet: Bool = false
   @State private var editItem: BookViewModel?

   var body: some View {
      NavigationStack {
         List(appData.userData) { book in
            CellBook(book: book)
               .background(.white)
               .onTapGesture {
                  editItem = book
               }
         }.navigationTitle(Text("Books"))
         .toolbar {
            ToolbarItem(placement: .navigationBarTrailing) {
               Button(action: {
                  showSheet = true
               }, label: { Image(systemName: "plus") })
            }
         }
         .sheet(isPresented: $showSheet) {
            AddBookView()
         }
         .sheet(item: $editItem) { item in
            AddBookView(book: item)
         }
```

```
        }
    }
}
```

Listing 8-33: Presenting a sheet for every value on the list

This view defines a **@State** property called **editItem** to store the **BookViewModel** value for the sheet. To allow the user to select a row, we add the **onTapGesture()** modifier to the **CellBook** view. We have implemented this modifier before to perform a task when the user taps a row (see Listing 7-28). In this case, we assign the row's **BookViewModel** structure to the **editItem** property. When this value changes, the sheet is opened with a second **sheet()** modifier added to the **List** view. The closure assigned to this modifier receives a copy of the **BookViewModel** structure, that we send to the **AddBookView** view so the user is able to edit the values.

The **AddBookView** view must be updated to be able to receive the book selected by the user and show the current values in the input fields. But we also must contemplate that the view might be opened by the user to insert a new book. The following are the modifications we need to introduce to the view for this purpose.

```
struct AddBookView: View {
    @EnvironmentObject var appData: ApplicationData
    @Environment(\.dismiss) var dismiss
    @State private var titleInput: String = ""
    @State private var authorInput: String = ""
    @State private var yearInput: String = ""
    var book: BookViewModel?

    var body: some View {
        VStack(alignment: .trailing, spacing: 10) {
            HStack {
                Text(book == nil ? "Add Book" : "Edit Book")
                    .font(.body.weight(.bold))
                Spacer()
                Button("Close") {
                    dismiss()
                }.padding([.top, .bottom], 10)
            }
            TextField("Insert Title", text: $titleInput)
                .textFieldStyle(.roundedBorder)
            TextField("Insert Author", text: $authorInput)
                .textFieldStyle(.roundedBorder)
            TextField("Insert Year", text: $yearInput)
                .textFieldStyle(.roundedBorder)
                .keyboardType(.numbersAndPunctuation)
            Button("Save") {
                storeBook()
                dismiss()
            }.buttonStyle(.borderedProminent)
            Spacer()
        }.padding()
        .onAppear {
            titleInput = book?.title ?? ""
            authorInput = book?.author ?? ""
            yearInput = book?.year ?? ""
        }
    }
    func storeBook() {
        let title = titleInput.trimmingCharacters(in: .whitespaces)
        let author = authorInput.trimmingCharacters(in: .whitespaces)
        if let year = Int(yearInput), !title.isEmpty && !author.isEmpty {
```

```
                if let index = appData.userData.firstIndex(where: { $0.id ==
book?.id }) {
                    let newBook = BookViewModel(book: Book(title: title, author:
author, cover: appData.userData[index].cover, year: year, selected:
false))
                    appData.userData[index] = newBook
                } else {
                    let newBook = BookViewModel(book: Book(title: title, author:
author, cover: "nocover", year: year, selected: false))
                    appData.userData.append(newBook)
                }
            }
        }
}
```

Listing 8-34: Editing a book

There are a few differences in this view from the one defined in Listing 8-29. First, we added an optional property called **book** to receive the book. If the user opens the view to add a new book, the value of this property will be **nil**, but if the view is opened by selecting a row, the property will contain the **BookViewModel** structure with the information about the selected book. By checking this value, we can perform tasks for each situation. For instance, at the top of the view, we added a **Text** view to display the texts "Add Book" or "Edit Book" depending on the value of this property. At the bottom, the **onAppear()** modifier was included to show the values of the book on the screen. If the **book** property contains a book, we assign the values to the input fields so the user knows which book is being edited.

The **storeBook()** method updates or adds the book to the model. We first get the index of the selected book with the **firstIndex()** method. If an index is returned, we create a new **BookViewModel** structure with the values inserted by the user and the current image, otherwise, we create the structure with an image by default and add it to the **userData** array.

Figure 8-22: Sheet to edit values

Do It Yourself: Update the **ContentView** view with the code in Listing 8-33 and the **AddBookView** view with the code in Listing 8-34. Select a row. You should see the values of the book on the screen. Edit a value and press Save. You should see the new value on the list.

(Basic) **Popovers**

Another type of views we can introduce to our interface are popovers. Popovers are presented like sheets on iPhones, but as small views on iPads and Mac computers. The **View** protocol defines the following modifier to present them.

popover(isPresented: Binding, **attachmentAnchor:** PopoverAttachment-Anchor, **arrowEdge:** Edge, **content:** Closure)—This modifier displays a popover. The **isPresented** argument is a **Binding** property of type **Bool** that determines whether the popover has to be displayed (**true**) or removed (**false**). The **attachmentAnchor**

argument is an enumeration of type **PopoverAttachmentAnchor** that includes the **point()** and **rect()** methods to determine the part of the view to which the popover should be anchored. The **arrowEdge** argument is an enumeration of type **Edge** that determines the side in which the popover's arrow should be placed. The values available are **bottom**, **leading**, **top**, and **trailing**. And the **content** argument is a closure that defines the view to be shown on the screen.

In iPhones, a popover is presented as a sheet, but on iPads they are presented as small views with a size determined by the view that defines the content. The position is determined by the view to which the modifier is applied and the location of the popover's arrow (top, left, right, or bottom). For instance, the following example shows a popover anchored to a **Button** view with a **top** arrow, so it appears below the button.

```
struct ContentView: View {
    @State private var showPopover: Bool = false

    var body: some View {
        VStack {
            Button("Show Popover") {
                showPopover = true
            }
            .popover(isPresented: $showPopover, arrowEdge: .top) {
                HelpView()
            }
            Spacer()
        }.font(.title)
    }
}
```

Listing 8-35: Showing a popover

The **popover()** modifier in Listing 8-35 has two arguments: the **isPresented** argument to control when the popover is shown, and the **arrowEdge** argument to determine the side where the arrow is placed and therefore the position of the view relative to the anchor view. When the value of the **showPopover** property is **true**, the modifier creates an instance of the **HelpView** view and shows it on the screen.

The **HelpView** view is the custom view we use to define the popover's content. From this view, we can also determine the size of the popover with a **frame()** modifier, as shown next.

```
import SwiftUI

struct HelpView: View {
    @Environment(\.dismiss) var dismiss

    var body: some View {
        VStack {
            HStack {
                Spacer()
                Button("X") {
                    dismiss()
                }.padding(.trailing, 16)
            }
            Text("Press this button when you need help")
                .font(.title)
                .padding()
        }.frame(width: 250, height: 250)
    }
}
```

Listing 8-36: Defining the content of the popover

The view can be removed by dragging it down with the finger on iPhones and by clicking outside the view on iPads, but we can also do it programmatically with the **dismiss** value, as in this example.

Show Popover

Press this button
when you need
help

Figure 8-23: *Popover on iPad*

 Do It Yourself: Create a Multiplatform project. Update the **ContentView** view with the code in Listing 8-35. Create a SwiftUI View file called HelpView.swift for the view in Listing 8-36. Run the application on the iPad simulator and press the Show Popover button. You should see the popover illustrated in Figure 8-23.

Basic   Alert Views

Alert views are predefined modal views that can display messages and receive input from the user. Their purpose is to deliver to the user important information that requires immediate attention. For example, an alert view may be used to ask confirmation from the user before deleting data from the model. The following is the most frequently used modifier provided by the framework to create these views.

alert(String, isPresented: Binding, **actions:** Closure, **message:** Closure)—This modifier presents an alert view. The first argument is the title, the **isPresented** argument is a **Binding** value of type **Bool** that determines whether the alert view has to be presented (**true**) or removed (**false**), the **actions** argument is a closure with **Button** views to create the buttons for the view, and the **message** argument is a closure with the view that provides the message.

The process to open these views is the same as with sheets. We have to define a **@State** property to manage the state of the view and then apply the **alert()** modifier.

```
struct ContentView: View {
   @State private var name: String = ""
   @State private var openAlert: Bool = false

   var body: some View {
      VStack(spacing: 10) {
         TextField("Insert your Name", text: $name)
            .textFieldStyle(.roundedBorder)
         HStack {
            Spacer()
            Button("Save") {
               openAlert = name.isEmpty
            }
         }
      }
      Spacer()
   }.padding()
```

```
   .alert("Error", isPresented: $openAlert, actions: {
      Button("Cancel", role: .cancel, action: {
         openAlert = false
      })
   }, message: { Text("Insert your name") })
   }
}
```

Listing 8-37: *Displaying an alert view*

The `@State` property for this view is called `openAlert`. The view includes a `TextField` view and a button. When the button is pressed, the code checks whether the user inserted a value. If not, the value `true` is assigned to the `openAlert` property to present the alert view. The view was defined with the title "Error", the message "Insert your name", and a `Button` view that allows the user to dismiss it. Notice that the button has been assigned a role that corresponds to the action performed (in this case, `cancel`) so that the system knows its purpose and can style it appropriately.

Figure 8-24: *Alert view*

 Do It Yourself: Create a Multiplatform project. Update the `ContentView` view with the code in Listing 8-37. Press the Save button. If you didn't insert anything in the text field, you should see the alert view illustrated in Figure 8-24.

In the example of Listing 8-37, we assign the value `false` to the `openAlert` property to remove the alert view when the Cancel button is pressed, but this is actually not necessary. After the action is performed, the view is automatically closed.

Our current view contains only one button, but we can include more. If there are two buttons, they are shown side by side, but three or more are displayed on a list, with the Cancel button at the end, as shown next.

```
.alert("Error", isPresented: $openAlert, actions: {
   Button("Cancel", role: .cancel, action: {})
   Button("Delete", role: .destructive, action: {
      name = ""
   })
   Button("Save Anyway", role: .none, action: {
      print("Save value")
   })
}, message: { Text("Insert your name") })
```

Listing 8-38: *Defining an Alert view with multiple buttons*

This modifier includes three buttons. A button to cancel the action and two more to perform other tasks. The Cancel button was defined first, but because the role is set to `cancel`, the system places it at the end of the list.

Chapter 8 - Navigation

Figure 8-25: Alert view with multiple buttons

Basic **Confirmation Dialog**

SwiftUI includes another type of alert views called *Confirmation Dialogs* (also known as Action Sheets). These views are usually presented when our application needs the user to make a decision and there is more than one option available. The following is the modifier we need to apply to create this view.

confirmationDialog(String, **isPresented:** Binding, **titleVisibility:** Visibility, **actions:** Closure, **message:** Closure)—This modifier creates a confirmation dialog. The first argument is the text for the title, the **isPresented** argument is a `Binding` value of type `Bool` that determines whether the view has to be presented (`true`) or removed (`false`), the **titleVisibility** argument is an enumeration with the values `automatic`, `hidden`, and `visible` that determines the visibility of the title, the **actions** argument defines the buttons to include in the view, and the **message** argument provides the text for the message.

There is not much difference between confirmation dialogs and alert views other than the design and location. For instance, in iPhones, a confirmation dialog is presented at the bottom of the screen. The following example creates a confirmation dialog with three buttons. The buttons don't perform any action but illustrate how to implement and work with these kinds of views.

```
struct ContentView: View {
    @State private var openDialog: Bool = false

    var body: some View {
        VStack(spacing: 10) {
            Button("Open Confirmation Dialog") {
                openDialog = true
            }
            Spacer()
        }.padding()
        .confirmationDialog("Email", isPresented: $openDialog, actions: {
            Button("Move to Inbox", role: .none, action: {})
            Button("Delete", role: .destructive, action: {})
            Button("Cancel", role: .cancel, action: {})
        }, message: {
            Text("What do you want to do with the message?")
        })
    }
}
```

Listing 8-39: Defining an action sheet

As always, we define a `@State` property to manage the view. When the value `true` is assigned to this property by the button, the `confirmationDialog()` modifier opens a view with three buttons. There is a standard button to perform a normal operation, a `destructive` button to delete data, and a `cancel` button to allow the user to dismiss the view.

Figure 8-26: Confirmation dialog

 Do It Yourself: Create a Multiplatform project. Update the `ContentView` view with the code in Listing 8-39. Run the application and press the Open Confirmation Dialog button to open the view.

(Basic) **8.3 Tab Views**

Another way to organize multiple views (screens), is with a `TabView` view. This view designates two areas on the screen, one for the views and a small one at the bottom for a tool bar with tabs the users can tap to select the view they want to open. Each tab is associated with only one view and therefore users can tap on them to move from one view to another.

Figure 8-27: `TabView` *with two views*

The `TabView` structure includes the following initializers.

TabView(content: Closure)—This initializer creates a `TabView` view with the views and tabs defined by the closure assigned to the **content** argument.

TabView(selection: Binding, **content:** Closure)—This initializer creates a `TabView` view. The **selection** argument is a `Binding` property that returns a value that identifies the view currently open, and the **content** argument is a closure with the list of views the tab view is going to include and their tabs.

The following is the modifier provided by the `View` protocol to define the tabs.

tabItem(Closure)—This modifier is used to configure the tab items (the buttons the user taps to select the views). The argument is a closure with a `Label` view that provides the title and the icon.

The content of a `TabView` view is defined inside the closure. The views are introduced in a list, one after another, and the `tabItem()` modifier is applied to each one of them to configure the tabs, as shown next.

```
struct ContentView: View {
    var body: some View {
        TabView {
            BooksView()
                .tabItem({
                    Label("Books", systemImage: "book.circle")
                })
            SettingsView()
                .tabItem({
                    Label("Settings", systemImage: "gear")
                })
        }
    }
}
```

Listing 8-40: Defining a `TabView`

This **TabView** view includes two views, **BooksView** and **SettingsView**. For the **BooksView** view, we define a tab with an SF Symbol called book.circle and the text "Books", and for the **SettingsView** view we include the SF Symbol called gear and the text "Settings".

Figure 8-28: Tabs

The **BooksView** and **SettingsView** views represent two different screens and therefore they should be stored in separate files. For this example, we are going to define two simple views with a text in the center. The following is the code for the **BooksView**, stored in the BooksView.swift file.

```
import SwiftUI

struct BooksView: View {
    var body: some View {
        Text("Books")
            .font(.largeTitle)
    }
}
```

Listing 8-41: Defining the `BooksView`

And for the **SettingsView** view, we must create a file called SettingsView.swift and include the following code.

```
import SwiftUI

struct SettingsView: View {
    var body: some View {
        Text("Settings")
            .font(.largeTitle)
    }
}
```

Listing 8-42: Defining the `SettingsView`

These are simple views but illustrate how a `TabView` view works. When the app is launched, the first view on the list is shown on the screen and then the user can open the rest from the tabs at the bottom.

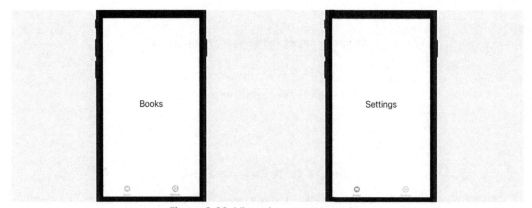

Figure 8-29: *Views in a* TabView *view*

 Do It Yourself: Create a Multiplatform project. Update the `ContentView` view with the code in Listing 8-40. Create two SwiftUI View files called BooksView.swift and SettingsView.swift for the views in Listings 8-41 and 8-42, respectively. You should see the screen illustrated in Figure 8-29. Click on the tabs to switch between the views.

We can include all the views we want in a `TabView` view. If there is no room in the tool bar to display all the tabs, the system adds a tab called *More* that allows the user to select the tabs that are not visible.

Figure 8-30: *More tabs*

The `View` protocol includes the following modifier to add a badge to the tabs.

badge(Value**)**—This modifier generates a badge with the value provided by the argument. The argument can be an integer, a string, or a `Text` view.

In `TabView` views, the `badge()` modifier is applied to the view which tab we want to use to show the badge. For instance, we can apply it to the Settings view to show how many issues require the user's attention.

```
struct ContentView: View {
    var body: some View {
        TabView {
            BooksView()
                .tabItem({
                    Label("Books", systemImage: "book.circle")
                })
            SettingsView()
                .tabItem({
                    Label("Settings", systemImage: "gear")
                })
```

```
                .badge(12)
            }
        }
    }
}
```

Listing 8-43: Displaying a badge in a tab

In this case, the badge is created with the number 12, so it will always show that value, but badges are usually defined with values from properties or counters used to alert the user of important issues that need attention.

Figure 8-31: Badge

The user can tap the tabs at the bottom of the screen to open a view, but we can also do it from code. The **TabView** view can use a **Binding** property to store a value that determines which view is currently opened. By modifying the value of this property, we can open a view programmatically. For this to work, we must assign the **Binding** property to the **selection** argument of the **TabView** initializer and identify each view with the **tag()** modifier.

```
struct ContentView: View {
    @State private var selectedView: Int = 1

    var body: some View {
        TabView(selection: $selectedView) {
            BooksView()
                .tabItem({
                    Label("Books", systemImage: "book.circle")
                }).tag(0)
            SettingsView()
                .tabItem({
                    Label("Settings", systemImage: "gear")
                }).tag(1)
        }
    }
}
```

Listing 8-44: Selecting the initial view

Every time a new value is assigned to the **@State** property, the view with that identifier is shown on the screen. This also means that we can determine the view to show by default by initializing the property with the view's identifier. In our example, we assign the value 1 to the property, so the Settings view is shown first.

A **TabView** view is no different from a **NavigationStack** view other than the way the views are presented to the user, so we can integrate it with a model and define each screen as we did before. For instance, we can define a view to show a list of books, and another view to configure the list, as shown in Figure 8-27. The following example updates previous models to store the app's configuration and show how tabs can work together.

```
class ApplicationData: ObservableObject {
    @Published var userData: [BookViewModel]
    @Published var showPictures: Bool = true
    @Published var showYear: Bool = true
```

```
init() {
    userData = [
        BookViewModel(book: Book(title: "Steve Jobs", author: "Walter
Isaacson", cover: "book1", year: 2011, selected: false)),
        BookViewModel(book: Book(title: "HTML5 for Masterminds", author:
"J.D Gauchat", cover: "book2", year: 2017, selected: false)),
        BookViewModel(book: Book(title: "The Road Ahead", author: "Bill
Gates", cover: "book3", year: 1995, selected: false)),
        BookViewModel(book: Book(title: "The C Programming Language",
author: "Brian W. Kernighan", cover: "book4", year: 1988, selected:
false)),
        BookViewModel(book: Book(title: "Being Digital", author:
"Nicholas Negroponte", cover: "book5", year: 1996, selected: false)),
        BookViewModel(book: Book(title: "Only the Paranoid Survive",
author: "Andrew S. Grove", cover: "book6", year: 1999, selected: false)),
        BookViewModel(book: Book(title: "Accidental Empires", author:
"Robert X. Cringely", cover: "book7", year: 1996, selected: false)),
        BookViewModel(book: Book(title: "Bobby Fischer Teaches Chess",
author: "Bobby Fischer", cover: "book8", year: 1982, selected: false)),
        BookViewModel(book: Book(title: "New Guide to Science", author:
"Isaac Asimov", cover: "book9", year: 1993, selected: false)),
        BookViewModel(book: Book(title: "Christine", author: "Stephen
King", cover: "book10", year: 1983, selected: false)),
        BookViewModel(book: Book(title: "IT", author: "Stephen King",
cover: "book11", year: 1987, selected: false)),
        BookViewModel(book: Book(title: "Ending Aging", author: "Aubrey
de Grey", cover: "book12", year: 2007, selected: false))
    ]
}
}
```

Listing 8-45: *Updating the model*

This new `ApplicationData` class includes two additional `@Published` properties to store Boolean values that users can change from the Settings tab. The values determine whether the list of books should show the books' covers and year of publication, so we must use them in the `BooksView` view to configure the rows, as shown below.

```
import SwiftUI

struct BooksView: View {
    @EnvironmentObject var appData: ApplicationData

    var body: some View {
        List(appData.userData) { book in
            CellBook(book: book)
        }
    }
}
struct CellBook: View {
    @EnvironmentObject var appData: ApplicationData
    let book: BookViewModel

    var body: some View {
        HStack(alignment: .top) {
            if appData.showPictures {
                Image(book.cover)
                    .resizable()
                    .scaledToFit()
                    .frame(width: 80, height: 100)
            }
            VStack(alignment: .leading, spacing: 2) {
                Text(book.title).bold()
                Text(book.author)
```

```
            if appData.showYear {
                Text(book.year).font(.caption)
            }
            Spacer()
        }.padding(.top, 5)
        Spacer()
        }
    }
}
struct BooksView_Previews: PreviewProvider {
    static var previews: some View {
        BooksView()
            .environmentObject(ApplicationData())
    }
}
```

Listing 8-46: Designing the rows according to the app's configuration

The list is created from the values in the **userData** array, as always, but the rows are now designed according to the app's configuration. If the value of the **showPictures** property is **true**, we show the book's cover, and if the value of the **showYear** property is **true**, we show the year of publication.

To allow the user to set these values, we must provide a form in the **SettingsView** view.

```
import SwiftUI
struct SettingsView: View {
    @EnvironmentObject var appData: ApplicationData

    var body: some View {
        Form {
            Section(header: Text("Settings"), footer: Text("Select what you
want to see")) {
                Toggle("Show Pictures", isOn: $appData.showPictures)
                Toggle("Show Year", isOn: $appData.showYear)
            }
        }
    }
}
struct SettingsView_Previews: PreviewProvider {
    static var previews: some View {
        SettingsView()
            .environmentObject(ApplicationData())
    }
}
```

Listing 8-47: Configuring the app

This view includes two **Toggle** views to set the values in the model. Now the user can decide what to show on the list. For instance, if both switches are off, the list only includes the books' titles and authors.

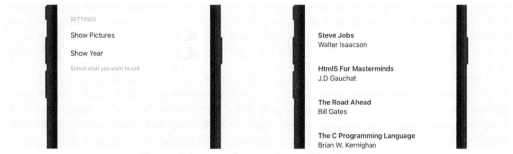

Figure 8-32: Interface configured by the user

Do It Yourself: This example implements the model defined in Chapter 7, Listing 7-3, and the `ContentView` view defined in Listing 8-40. Create a new Swift file called ApplicationData.swift for the model in Listing 7-3 and update the `ApplicationData` class with the code in Listing 8-45. Remember to inject the `ApplicationData` object into the environment for the app and the previews (Chapter 7, Listing 7-4). Download the books covers from our website and add them to the Asset Catalog. Update the BooksView.swift file with the code in Listing 8-46 and the SettingsView.swift file with the code in Listing 8-47. Select the Settings tab and turn off the switches. You should see the books on the list without the cover and year of publication, as illustrated in Figure 8-32, right.

In SwiftUI, a `TabView` view can present two configurations. The user can select the views from the tabs at the bottom of the screen or by dragging the views to the sides, like turning the pages of a book. To select the configuration we want, the `TabView` structure includes the following modifiers.

tabViewStyle(TabViewStyle**)**—This modifier defines the appearance of a `TabView` view. The argument is a structure that conforms to the `TabViewStyle` structure. The framework defines the structures `DefaultTabViewStyle` and `PageTabViewStyle` to provide standard configurations, which in turn include the type properties `automatic` and `page` to apply them to the view.

indexViewStyle(IndexViewStyle**)**—This modifier defines the appearance of the indicators at the bottom of the view that help the user identify the current page. The argument is a `PageIndexViewStyle` structure with the type method `page-(backgroundDisplayMode: BackgroundDisplayMode)` to specify the style. The method takes a structure of type `BackgroundDisplayMode`. This structure includes the type properties `always`, `automatic`, `interactive`, and `never`.

The `page` style is usually implemented when we need to provide easy access to visual content, such as images. For instance, we can use it to allow the user to navigate through the books covers by swiping the images to one side or the other.

```
struct ContentView: View {
   @EnvironmentObject var appData: ApplicationData

   var body: some View {
      TabView {
         ForEach(appData.userData) { book in
            Image(book.cover)
               .resizable()
               .scaledToFit()
         }
      }.tabViewStyle(.page)
       .indexViewStyle(.page(backgroundDisplayMode: .always))
   }
}
```

Listing 8-48: Configuring the `TabView` *to show content in pages*

This view creates a `TabView` view with a list of `Image` views, one for each book, but because we declare the `tabViewStyle()` modifier with the value `page`, instead of showing the tabs at the bottom, the view allows the user to swipe the images to the left or the right. Notice that we've also implemented the `indexViewStyle()` modifier with the value `always` to include a page indicator. The results is shown below.

Figure 8-33: Pages

 Do It Yourself: Update the `ContentView` view with the code in Listing 8-48. You should be able to swipe the covers to the left to unveil the next one, as shown in Figure 8-33.

(Basic) # 8.4 Universal Interface

Working with one view per screen is enough for small devices, like iPhones and the Apple Watch, but iPads and Macs require a more elaborated design. SwiftUI offers a container view called `NavigationSplitView` to present two or three views on the screen at the same time. The advantage of using this container view is not only that we can get multiple views to share the screen, but also that it adapts to small screens or windows, so we can use it to create universal interfaces that work seamlessly on iPhones, iPads and Macs.

NavigationSplitView(columnVisibility: Binding, **sidebar:** Closure, **content:** Closure, **detail:** Closure)—This initializer creates a container view to present two or three views on the screen simultaneously. The **columnVisibility** argument is a `Binding` property that determines the visibility of the columns. This value is determined by a `NavigationSplitViewVisibility` structure, which includes the type properties `automatic`, `all`, `doubleColumn`, and `detailOnly`. And the **sidebar**, **content**, and **detail** arguments return the views we want to present in each column. If we only want to present two columns, we must omit the **content** argument.

The columns are called Sidebar, Content, and Detail, and they are interconnected. A `NavigationLink` view in the Sidebar column updates the content of the Content column, and a `NavigationLink` view in the Content column updates the content of the Detail column.

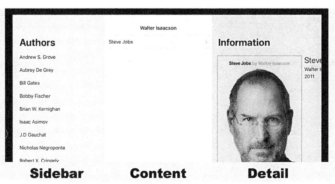

Sidebar   **Content**   **Detail**

Figure 8-34: iPad app configured with three columns

The Sidebar and Content columns are removable, and are presented on the screen depending on the number of columns and the space available. By default, on iPads in landscape mode, only one of the removable columns is shown. In a two-column design, the `NavigationSplitView` view displays the sidebar column, while in a three-column design the content column is shown instead. In iPads on portrait mode and large iPhones in landscape mode, only the Detail column is displayed, and a button is provided in the navigation bar to open the removable columns. iPhones in portrait mode present a different configuration; the columns are displayed as in a `NavigationStack` view; they replace one another and buttons are included to navigate back.

Figure 8-35: `NavigationSplitView` view *in iPhones in portrait mode*

The purpose of the `NavigationSplitView` view is to allow the user to select an item in the columns on the left and show the result in the column on the right. For instance, if we show a list of books on the left, when the user taps on a book, the information about it is shown in the column on the right. But if the app runs in a small screen or window, such as an iPhone in portrait orientation, the views are presented one by one, as if they were inside a `NavigationStack` view, as shown in Figure 8-35.

To keep track of the selected items, the `NavigationSplitView` view works with `List` selection (see Edit Mode in Chapter 7). We need a `@State` property to keep track of the item selected on the left column, pass a reference of this property to the views, and create the rows on the `List` view with a `NavigationLink` view and the same type of value we use for the selection, so the selection is updated every time the user selects a row.

A `NavigationSplitView` view may contain two or three columns. A two columns design is very common. The interface is simple. We define the `NavigationSplitView` view and assign the view we want to show on the left to the **sidebar** argument and the one we want to show on the right to the **detail** argument.

```
struct ContentView: View {
    @State private var selectedBook: BookViewModel?
    @State private var visibility: NavigationSplitViewVisibility
= .automatic

    var body: some View {
        NavigationSplitView(columnVisibility: $visibility, sidebar: {
            BooksView(selectedBook: $selectedBook)
        }, detail: {
            if let book = selectedBook {
                DetailView(book: book)
            } else {
                PlaceholderView()
            }
        })
    }
}
struct ContentView_Previews: PreviewProvider {
    static var previews: some View {
        ContentView().environmentObject(ApplicationData())
    }
}
```

Listing 8-49: *Defining a two-column split view*

This example includes a @**State** property called **selectedBook** to store the book selected by the user, another for the **NavigationSplitView** view to store the columns' visibility state, and the view itself with two columns. The column on the left (Sidebar) opens the **BooksView** view with a list of books, and the column on the right (Detail) opens the **DetailView** view with information about the selected book, or a placeholder view if no book was selected yet.

When a book is selected, the **BookViewModel** structure that represents the book is assigned to the **selectedBook** property, the content of the **ContentView** view is recreated, and a new **DetailView** view opens on the right column to present the book on the screen.

To know when a new row has been selected, we pass a reference of the **selectedBook** property to the **BooksView** view. Therefore, every time the user selects a book in the **BooksView** view, the value is stored in the **selectedBook** property, and the interface is updated. For the selection to work, the **BooksView** view must include a **List** view connected to the **selectedBook** property and also create the rows with a **NavigationLink** view identified with a value that matches the value stored in that property, as shown next.

```
struct BooksView: View {
    @EnvironmentObject var appData: ApplicationData
    @Binding var selectedBook: BookViewModel?

    var body: some View {
        List(appData.userData, selection: $selectedBook) { book in
            NavigationLink(value: book, label: {
                Text(book.title)
            })
        }
        .listStyle(.sidebar)
        .navigationTitle("Books")
    }
}
struct BooksView_Previews: PreviewProvider {
    static var previews: some View {
        BooksView(selectedBook: .constant(nil))
            .environmentObject(ApplicationData())
    }
}
```

Listing 8-50: Defining the view for the left column

When a **NavigationLink** is selected, the value is assigned to the **selectedBook** property and the selection is performed on the interface. Notice that we have assigned the **sidebar** style to the list to reproduce the interface in Figure 8-34.

No functionality is required for the **PlaceholderView** view. This view only opens on some devices to have something to show before the user selects a book and replaces it with a **DetailView** view, so we only need it to display a message.

```
struct PlaceholderView: View {
    var body: some View {
        VStack {
            Text("Select a Book")
            Spacer()
        }.padding(50)
    }
}
```

Listing 8-51: Defining a placeholder view for the right column

The **PlaceholderView** view is displayed on the right column until the user selects a book, in which case it is replaced with a **DetailView** view. The **DetailView** view is similar to the one we have created before for an iPhone application, but now we must consider that it may be shown on devices with very different characteristics, such as an iPhone in portrait orientation or an iPad in landscape. For this types of applications, Apple recommends adapting the interface according to the size classes (see Chapter 6). For instance, if the horizontal size class is compact, we can display the values on a list, as we did before, otherwise, we can take advantage of the larger screen and present the values side by side.

Selecting the right view for the device and the space available is quite simple in SwiftUI. All we need to do is to get the view's horizontal size class from the environment and display one view or the other, as we do in the following example.

```
import SwiftUI

struct DetailView: View {
    @Environment(\.horizontalSizeClass) var horizontal
    let book: BookViewModel

    var body: some View {
        Group {
            if horizontal == .regular {
                DetailLarge(book: book)
            } else {
                DetailSmall(book: book)
            }
        }.padding()
        .navigationTitle(Text("Information"))
    }
}
struct DetailLarge: View {
    let book: BookViewModel

    var body: some View {
        HStack {
            VStack {
                Image(book.cover)
                    .resizable()
                    .scaledToFit()
                    .frame(maxWidth: 300)
                Spacer()
            }
            VStack(alignment: .leading, spacing: 4) {
                Text(book.title)
                    .font(.title)
                Text(book.author)
                Text(book.year)
                Spacer()
            }.frame(minWidth: 0, maxWidth: .infinity, alignment: .leading)
            Spacer()
        }
    }
}
struct DetailSmall: View {
    let book: BookViewModel

    var body: some View {
        VStack {
            Text(book.title)
                .font(.title)
            Text(book.author)
            Text(book.year)
                .font(.caption)
```

```
            Image(book.cover)
                .resizable()
                .scaledToFit()
                .frame(maxWidth: 300)
        }.multilineTextAlignment(.center)
    }
}
struct DetailView_Previews: PreviewProvider {
    static var previews: some View {
        DetailView(book: ApplicationData().userData[1])
    }
}
```

Listing 8-52: Defining a Multiplatform Detail view

The views can be declared in the same file or in separate files, depending on their complexity. In this example, we have declared two additional views in the same file, the `DetailLarge` view to define the interface for a regular size class, and the `DetailSmall` view for the interface of a compact size class. When the `DetailView` is loaded, we check the value of the `horizontalSizeClass` property in the environment and load the corresponding view. As a result, the `DetailView` view shows the book's information next to the cover on iPads and on top of the cover on iPhones.

Figure 8-36: Different design for iPhones and iPads

 Do It Yourself: Create a Multiplatform project. Create a Swift file called ApplicationData.swift for the model in Chapter 7, Listing 7-3. Update the ContentView.swift file with the code in Listing 8-49. Create a new SwiftUI View file called BooksView.swift for the code in Listing 8-50, another called PlaceholderView.swift for the code in Listing 8-51, and another called DetailView.swift for the code in Listing 8-52. Download the covers from our website and add them to the Asset Catalog. Remember to inject the `ApplicationData` object into the environment for the app and the previews (Chapter 7, Listing 7-4). Run the application on the iPad simulator in landscape mode and select a book. You should see the interface illustrated in Figure 8-36, left. Repeat the process on the iPhone simulator. You should see the interface on the right.

When our app is launched on a device with a large screen, the interface is presented in two columns. The column on the left shows the list of books, and the column on the right shows the `PlaceholderView` view with a message to indicate to the user what to do. This view is replaced by the `DetailView` view when a book is selected from the list. Depending on the characteristics of our application, sometimes it might be better to show an item by default. For instance, we can show the `DetailView` view instead of the `PlaceholderView` view when there are books available in the model, as shown next.

```
struct ContentView: View {
   @EnvironmentObject var appData: ApplicationData
   @State private var selectedBook: BookViewModel?
   @State private var visibility: NavigationSplitViewVisibility
= .automatic

   var body: some View {
      NavigationSplitView(columnVisibility: $visibility, sidebar: {
         BooksView(selectedBook: $selectedBook)
      }, detail: {
         if let book = selectedBook {
            DetailView(book: book)
         } else {
            PlaceholderView()
         }
      })
      .onAppear {
         if let book = appData.userData.first {
            selectedBook = book
         }
      }
   }
}
```

Listing 8-53: Showing an item by default

Although we could get a book from the model and show the `DetailView` view with it, it is better to assign that book to the `selectedBook` property instead. This way, the item is also selected in the `List` view on the left. In our example, we use the `onAppear()` modifier for this purpose. On iPhones in portrait, the application works as before, but on iPads in landscape, the first row is selected and the book is shown on the screen.

 Do It Yourself: Update the `ContentView` view with the code in Listing 8-53. Run the application on the iPad simulator in landscape mode. You should see on the screen the first book found in the `userData` array.

The view on the right is just one view, but we can allow the user to navigate to other views by embedding the `DetailView` view in a `NavigationStack` view. To control the navigation, we need to add a `NavigationPath` property, as shown next.

```
struct ContentView: View {
   @State private var selectedBook: BookViewModel?
   @State private var path = NavigationPath()
   @State private var visibility: NavigationSplitViewVisibility
= .automatic

   var body: some View {
      NavigationSplitView(columnVisibility: $visibility, sidebar: {
         BooksView(selectedBook: $selectedBook)
      }, detail: {
         NavigationStack(path: $path) {
            if let book = selectedBook {
               DetailView(path: $path, book: book)
            } else {
               PlaceholderView()
            }
         }
      })
      .onChange(of: selectedBook) { _ in
         path = NavigationPath()
      }
```

```
      }
}
```

Listing 8-54: *Enabling navigation in the right column*

The procedure is the same used before to control the navigation path. We declare the NavigationPath property and then use it to initialize the NavigationStack view, but because we are enabling navigation for the right column, we need to pass a reference of the path to the DetailView view. Notice that to make sure the navigation path always begins with the DetailView view, we clear the NavigationPath structure when a book is selected (when the value of the selectedBook property changes).

When this application is launched, the DetailView view becomes the initial view of the navigation stack, so the rest of the navigation is managed from this view. We can, for instance, allow the user to tap on the cover to expand it, as we did in previous examples.

```
struct DetailView: View {
    @Environment(\.horizontalSizeClass) var horizontal
    @Binding var path: NavigationPath
    let book: BookViewModel

    var body: some View {
        Group {
            if horizontal == .regular {
                DetailLarge(path: $path, book: book)
            } else {
                DetailSmall(path: $path, book: book)
            }
        }.padding()
        .navigationTitle(Text("Information"))
        .navigationDestination(for: String.self, destination: { _ in
            PictureView(book: book)
        })
    }
}
struct DetailLarge: View {
    @Binding var path: NavigationPath
    let book: BookViewModel

    var body: some View {
        HStack {
            VStack {
                Button(action: {
                    path.append("Picture View")
                }, label: {
                    Image(book.cover)
                        .resizable()
                        .scaledToFit()
                        .frame(maxWidth: 300)
                })
                Spacer()
            }
            VStack(alignment: .leading, spacing: 4) {
                Text(book.title)
                    .font(.title)
                Text(book.author)
                Text(book.year)
                Spacer()
            }.frame(minWidth: 0, maxWidth: .infinity, alignment: .leading)
            Spacer()
        }
    }
}
```

```
struct DetailSmall: View {
    @Binding var path: NavigationPath
    let book: BookViewModel

    var body: some View {
        VStack {
            Text(book.title)
                .font(.title)
            Text(book.author)
            Text(book.year)
                .font(.caption)
            Button(action: {
                path.append("Picture View")
            }, label: {
                Image(book.cover)
                    .resizable()
                    .scaledToFit()
                    .frame(maxWidth: 300)
            })
        }.multilineTextAlignment(.center)
    }
}
struct DetailView_Previews: PreviewProvider {
    static var previews: some View {
        DetailView(path: .constant(NavigationPath()), book:
ApplicationData().userData[1])
    }
}
```

Listing 8-55: Creating a navigation path for the right column

This **DetailView** view receives a reference to the **path** property to add or remove views from the navigation stack. We pass this reference to the subviews and then embed the book's cover in a **Button** view to append a value to the path. We use a **Button** view instead of a **NavigationLink** view because there is no **List** view in this interface to control selection, but the result is the same. When the user presses the button, the **append()** method adds a string to the **path** property, the **navigationDestination()** modifier detects that a **String** value has been added to the path, and the **NavigationStack** view opens the **PictureView** view to show the expanded cover on the screen.

The **PictureView** view is similar to previous examples, but this time we must adapt the interface to the space available (the size class).

```
struct PictureView: View {
    @Environment(\.horizontalSizeClass) var horizontal
    let book: BookViewModel

    var body: some View {
        VStack {
            if horizontal == .regular {
                Image(book.cover)
                    .resizable()
                    .scaledToFit()
                    .padding([.top, .bottom], 20)
                    .padding([.leading, .trailing], 50)
            } else {
                Image(book.cover)
                    .resizable()
                    .scaledToFit()
            }
            Spacer()
        }.navigationBarTitleDisplayMode(.inline)
```

```
        }
}
struct PictureView_Previews: PreviewProvider {
    static var previews: some View {
        NavigationStack {
            PictureView(book: ApplicationData().userData[0])
        }
    }
}
```

Listing 8-56: Expanding the cover in a Multiplatform application

 Do It Yourself: Update the `ContentView` view with the code in Listing 8-54 and the DetailView.swift file with the code in Listing 8-55. Create a SwiftUI View file called PictureView.swift for the view in Listing 8-56. Run the application on the iPad simulator in landscape orientation, select a book, and tap on the cover. You should see the `PictureView` view on the right column transitioning from right to left. Select another book. You should see the `DetailView` view again in the right column. Try removing the `onChange()` modifier in the `ContentView` view and repeat the process. You should see that the cover in the `PictureView` view changes, but the interface does not transition back to the `DetailView` view because the path was not cleared.

We can also add navigation to the left column (Sidebar). The problem is that the `NavigationSplitView` view is configured by default to always open navigation links on the Detail column. In a two-column layout, the `NavigationLink` views in the left column will always open the destination view in the right column, but we can change this behavior with the following modifier.

isDetailLink(Bool**)**—This modifier determines whether the link will open in the Detail column or not (`true` or `false`).

If we apply this modifier with the value `false` to a `NavigationLink` view in the left column, the view will open in the same column. For instance, we can embed the `BooksView` view in a `NavigationStack` view and add a button to the navigation bar to allow the user to configure the list of books.

```
struct ContentView: View {
    @State private var selectedBook: BookViewModel?
    @State private var path = NavigationPath()
    @State private var visibility: NavigationSplitViewVisibility
= .automatic

    var body: some View {
        NavigationSplitView(columnVisibility: $visibility, sidebar: {
            NavigationStack {
                BooksView(selectedBook: $selectedBook)
            }
        }, detail: {
            NavigationStack(path: $path) {
                if let book = selectedBook {
                    DetailView(path: $path, book: book)
                } else {
                    PlaceholderView()
                }
            }
        })
        .onChange(of: selectedBook) { _ in
```

```
                path = NavigationPath()
            }
        }
    }
}
```

Listing 8-57: Adding navigation to the left column

The button in the toolbar is added with a `NavigationLink` associated to a value. In this case, we use a string and open a view called `SettingsView` when the button is pressed.

```
struct BooksView: View {
    @EnvironmentObject var appData: ApplicationData
    @Binding var selectedBook: BookViewModel?

    var body: some View {
        List(appData.userData, selection: $selectedBook) { book in
            NavigationLink(value: book, label: {
                Text(book.title)
            })
        }
        .listStyle(.sidebar)
        .navigationTitle("Books")
        .toolbar {
            ToolbarItem(placement: .navigationBarTrailing) {
                NavigationLink(value: "Settings View", label: {
                    Image(systemName: "gear")
                })
                .isDetailLink(false)
            }
        }
        .navigationDestination(for: String.self, destination: { _ in
            SettingsView()
        })
    }
}
```

Listing 8-58: Opening a view on the left column

The `BooksView` view now includes an item in the navigation bar defined by a `NavigationLink` view and an SF Symbol that opens a view to configure the application, but because we applied the `isDetailLink()` modifier with the value `false`, the `SettingsView` view opens in the same column, as shown below.

Figure 8-37: Link opens the view in the left column

Do It Yourself: Update the `ContentView` view with the code in Listing 8-57 and the `BooksView` view with the code in Listing 8-58. Create a SwiftUI View file called SettingsView.swift with a single `Text` view. Run the application on the iPad simulator. Press the Settings button in the navigation bar. You should see the `SettingsView` view open in the left column.

Chapter 8 - Navigation

(Basic) Three-Columns Layout

A `NavigationSplitView` view can present up to three columns. So far, we have been using the two-column layout, but we can add one more by including the **content** argument in the `NavigationSplitView`'s initializer.

In a three-column layout, the links in the Sidebar column update the content in the Content column, and the links in the Content column update the content in the Detail column. Therefore, we have two columns on the left to select information and a column on the right to show it. This process is not automatic, we need to prepare the data in the model to feed the views. For instance, if we want to show a list of authors in the first column, and the books that belong to the selected author in the second column, as we do in the example in Figure 8-34, the model must provide the list of values in that order.

How we organize and store the data in our model depends on the characteristics or the application. For our example, we are going to store the list of books in an array and implement a method that extracts the names of the authors from it.

```
class ApplicationData: ObservableObject {
   var userData: [BookViewModel] = [] {
      didSet {
         updateAuthors()
      }
   }
   @Published var listAuthors: [String] = []

   func updateAuthors() {
      var list: [String] = []
      for name in userData.map({ $0.author }) {
         if !list.contains(name) {
            list.append(name)
         }
      }
      listAuthors = list.sorted(by: { $0 < $1 })
   }
   init() {
      userData = [
         BookViewModel(book: Book(title: "Steve Jobs", author: "Walter
Isaacson", cover: "book1", year: 2011, selected: false)),
         BookViewModel(book: Book(title: "HTML5 for Masterminds", author:
"J.D Gauchat", cover: "book2", year: 2017, selected: false)),
         BookViewModel(book: Book(title: "The Road Ahead", author: "Bill
Gates", cover: "book3", year: 1995, selected: false)),
         BookViewModel(book: Book(title: "The C Programming Language",
author: "Brian W. Kernighan", cover: "book4", year: 1988, selected:
false)),
         BookViewModel(book: Book(title: "Being Digital", author:
"Nicholas Negroponte", cover: "book5", year: 1996, selected: false)),
         BookViewModel(book: Book(title: "Only the Paranoid Survive",
author: "Andrew S. Grove", cover: "book6", year: 1999, selected: false)),
         BookViewModel(book: Book(title: "Accidental Empires", author:
"Robert X. Cringely", cover: "book7", year: 1996, selected: false)),
         BookViewModel(book: Book(title: "Bobby Fischer Teaches Chess",
author: "Bobby Fischer", cover: "book8", year: 1982, selected: false)),
         BookViewModel(book: Book(title: "New Guide to Science", author:
"Isaac Asimov", cover: "book9", year: 1993, selected: false)),
         BookViewModel(book: Book(title: "Christine", author: "Stephen
King", cover: "book10", year: 1983, selected: false)),
         BookViewModel(book: Book(title: "IT", author: "Stephen King",
cover: "book11", year: 1987, selected: false)),
         BookViewModel(book: Book(title: "Ending Aging", author: "Aubrey
de Grey", cover: "book12", year: 2007, selected: false)) ]
```

```
        updateAuthors()
    }
}
```

Listing 8-59: Providing the list of authors

This new **ApplicationData** class defines the **userData** property as a normal property to store the books, and includes a new **@Published** property called **listAuthors** to store the names of the authors. To get the authors from the data, we have created a method called **updateAuthors()**. The method gets the names of the authors with the **map()** method and assigns it to the **listAuthors** property in alphabetical order. Notice that before adding the name, we check if it already exists to avoid duplicates (**!list.contains(name)**).

The **updateAuthors()** method should be called every time the values in the **userData** property change to keep the views up to date. In our example, we call it after the property is initialized with testing values, and also with a property observer applied to the **userData** property, so the authors are updated every time a book is added or removed from the model.

Now that we have the values for the first column, it is time to define the three-column layout in the **ContentView** view.

```
struct ContentView: View {
    @State private var selectedAuthor: String?
    @State private var selectedBook: BookViewModel?
    @State private var visibility: NavigationSplitViewVisibility
= .automatic

    var body: some View {
        NavigationSplitView(columnVisibility: $visibility, sidebar: {
            AuthorsView(selectedAuthor: $selectedAuthor)
        }, content: {
            BooksView(selectedBook: $selectedBook, selectedAuthor:
selectedAuthor)
        }, detail: {
            if let book = selectedBook {
                DetailView(book: book)
            } else {
                PlaceholderView()
            }
        })
    }
}
```

Listing 8-60: Defining a three-column layout

Because we now have two columns with list of values the user can choose from, we need two properties to store the selection. We call them **selectedAuthor** and **selectedBook**. The view in the first column, called **AuthorsView**, presents the list of authors available, so we pass a reference to the **selectedAuthor** property to capture the user's selection. On the other hand, the view in the second column, called **BooksView**, presents the list of books that belong to the selected author, so we need to pass a reference to the **selectedBook** property to control selection and also the value of the **selectedAuthor** property to filter the books by author.

The **AuthorsView** view must create a list of authors and allow the user to select one. The code is similar to previous examples.

```
struct AuthorsView: View {
    @EnvironmentObject var appData: ApplicationData
    @Binding var selectedAuthor: String?

    var body: some View {
```

```
        List(appData.listAuthors, id: \.self, selection: $selectedAuthor) {
author in
            NavigationLink(value: author, label: {
                Text(author)
            })
        }
        .listStyle(.sidebar)
        .navigationTitle("Authors")
    }
}
struct AuthorsView_Previews: PreviewProvider {
    static var previews: some View {
        AuthorsView(selectedAuthor: .constant(nil))
            .environmentObject(ApplicationData())
    }
}
```

Listing 8-61: Showing the authors

The **BooksView** view is also similar to previous examples, but now we only need to display the list of books that belong to the author selected by the user. To filter the values, we define a computed property called **listBooks** and use it to feed the **List** view.

```
struct BooksView: View {
    @EnvironmentObject var appData: ApplicationData
    @Binding var selectedBook: BookViewModel?
    let selectedAuthor: String?

    var listBooks: [BookViewModel] {
        let list = appData.userData.filter({ item in
            return item.author == selectedAuthor
        })
        return list.sorted(by: { $0.title < $1.title })
    }
    var body: some View {
        List(listBooks, selection: $selectedBook) { book in
            NavigationLink(value: book, label: {
                Text(book.title)
            })
        }.listStyle(.grouped)
        .navigationBarTitleDisplayMode(.inline)
        .navigationTitle(selectedAuthor ?? "Undefined")
    }
}
struct BooksView_Previews: PreviewProvider {
    static var previews: some View {
        BooksView(selectedBook: .constant(nil), selectedAuthor: nil)
            .environmentObject(ApplicationData())
    }
}
```

Listing 8-62: Showing the books

The **listBooks** property gets the author's books and returns them in alphabetical order. The view is the same as before. We create a **List** view with these values and embed the rows in a **NavigationLink** view to update the **selectedBook** property when a book is selected.

 Do It Yourself: Update the **ApplicationData** class in the ApplicationData.swift file with the code in Listing 8-59. Update the **ContentView** view with the code in Listing 8-60. Create a new SwiftUI View file called AuthorsView.swift and update the view with the code in Listing 8-61.

Update the `BooksView` view with the code in Listing 8-62. The `PlaceholderView` view and the `DetailView` view used in this example are the same defined for previous examples (see Listings 8-51 and 8-52). Run the application on the iPad simulator in landscape orientation. You should see the three columns on the screen, as shown in Figure 8-34.

Basic Configuration

The width of the columns, which columns will be visible, and how they are going to be presented on the screen, is determined by the space available, but we can suggest a specific configuration and the system will try to comply when possible. One of the things we can do is to suggest the number of columns we want to be visible by modifying the value of the Binding property assigned to the **columnVisibility** argument. We can ask the system to show all the columns (`all`), only the Content and Detail (`doubleColumn`), and only the Detail column (`detailOnly`). For example, we can hide the column on the left when an item is selected.

```
struct ContentView: View {
   @State private var selectedAuthor: String?
   @State private var selectedBook: BookViewModel?
   @State private var visibility: NavigationSplitViewVisibility
= .automatic

   var body: some View {
      NavigationSplitView(columnVisibility: $visibility, sidebar: {
         AuthorsView(selectedAuthor: $selectedAuthor)
      }, content: {
         BooksView(selectedBook: $selectedBook, selectedAuthor:
selectedAuthor)
      }, detail: {
         if let book = selectedBook {
            DetailView(book: book)
         } else {
            PlaceholderView()
         }
      })
      .onChange(of: selectedBook) { _ in
         visibility = .detailOnly
      }
   }
}
```

Listing 8-63: *Hiding columns programmatically*

This example applies the `onChange()` modifier to change the value of the `visibility` property to `detailOnly` when a book is selected. This closes the columns on the left and expands the column on the right to take up all the space available.

In a three-column design, the Detail column is blurred and displaced to the right when the columns on the left become visible. The `NavigationSplitView` view implements the following modifiers to configure this behavior and define the columns' width.

navigationSplitViewStyle(NavigationSplitViewStyle**)**—This modifier defines how the Detail column is displayed when other columns are present. The argument is a structure that conforms to the `NavigationSplitViewStyle` protocol. The protocol defines the type properties `automatic` (default), `balanced` (the size of the Detail column is reduced to make room for the rest of the columns), and `prominentDetail` (the size of the Detail column is maintain and the rest of the columns are overlaid on top).

navigationSplitViewColumnWidth(CGFloat**)**—This modifier defines a fixed width for the column.

navigationSplitViewColumnWidth(min: CGFloat?, **ideal:** CGFloat, **max:** CGFloat?**)**—This modifier defines a flexible column but with constraints.

The style is applied to the `NavigationSplitView` view, but the width is applied to the columns. In the following example, we set the width for the Sidebar and Content columns to 200 points, and apply the `prominentDetail` style to the view, so the columns on the left open over the Detail column but take up only a portion of the screen.

```
struct ContentView: View {
    @State private var selectedAuthor: String?
    @State private var selectedBook: BookViewModel?
    @State private var visibility: NavigationSplitViewVisibility
= .automatic

    var body: some View {
        NavigationSplitView(columnVisibility: $visibility, sidebar: {
            AuthorsView(selectedAuthor: $selectedAuthor)
                .navigationSplitViewColumnWidth(200)
        }, content: {
            BooksView(selectedBook: $selectedBook, selectedAuthor:
selectedAuthor)
                .navigationSplitViewColumnWidth(200)
        }, detail: {
            if let book = selectedBook {
                DetailView(book: book)
            } else {
                PlaceholderView()
            }
        })
        .navigationSplitViewStyle(.prominentDetail)
    }
}
```

***Listing 8-64:** Configuring the columns*

Chapter 9
Concurrency

Basic **9.1 Asynchronous and Concurrent Tasks**

Apple systems can take advantage of the large number of cores in modern processors to execute multiple pieces of code simultaneously, increasing the amount of work the application can perform at any given time. For example, we may have a code that downloads a file from the Internet and another code that shows the progress on the screen. In cases like this, we cannot wait for one code to finish to execute the other; we need the two pieces of code to run simultaneously.

To be able to process code in parallel, the system groups units of code in tasks. In Swift, tasks can be implemented with asynchronous and concurrent programming. Asynchronous programming is a programming pattern in which the code waits for a process to finish before completing the task. This allows the system to share computing resources among many processes. While waiting, the system can use the resources to perform other tasks. On the other hand, concurrent programming implements code that can take advantage of multiple core processors to execute tasks simultaneously.

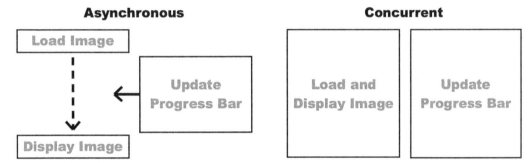

Figure 9-1: *Asynchronous and concurrent programming*

Because multiple applications can run at the same time, the system doesn't allocate a specific number of cores per application. What it does is to create execution threads, assign the tasks to these threads, and then decide which threads are going to be executed by which core depending on the available resources. In the example of Figure 9-1, left, there is an asynchronous task that loads an image from the Web and then displays it on the screen. While waiting for the server to respond, the thread is free to perform other tasks, so the system may use it to execute a different task that updates the progress bar. On the right, the tasks were created as concurrent tasks and therefore they are executed simultaneously in different threads.

Basic **Tasks**

Asynchronous and concurrent code is defined by tasks. The Swift Standard Library includes the **Task** structure to create and manage these tasks. The following is the structure's initializer.

Task(priority: TaskPriority?, **operation:** Closure)—This initializer creates and runs a new task. The **priority** argument is a structure that helps the system decide when to execute the task. The structure includes type properties to defined standard priorities. The currently available are **background**, **high**, **low**, **medium**, **userInitiated**, and **utility**. The **operation** argument is a closure with the statements to be executed by the task.

The **Task** structure includes the following properties to cancel a task.

isCancelled—This property returns a Boolean value that indicates if the task was cancelled.

cancel()—This method cancels the task.

There are also a few type properties and methods available to get information from the current task or create tasks that perform specific processes. The following are the most frequently used.

currentPriority—This property returns the priority of the current task. It is a **TaskPriority** structure with the properties **background**, **high**, **low**, **medium**, **userInitiated**, and **utility**.

isCancelled—This property returns a Boolean value that indicates whether the current task was cancelled.

sleep(nanoseconds: UInt64)—This method suspends the current task the time specified by the **nanoseconds** argument.

Although we can create **Task** structures anywhere in our code to initiate an asynchronous task, SwiftUI includes the following modifier to do it when the view appears. The task is perform as soon as the view appears and it is automatically canceled when the view disappears.

task(priority: TaskPriority, Closure)—This modifier executes the task specified by the second argument when the view appears. The **priority** argument is a structure that helps the system decide when to execute the task. The values available are **background**, **high**, **low**, **medium**, **userInitiated**, and **utility**.

task(id: Value, priority: TaskPriority, Closure)—This modifier executes the task specified by the third argument when the view appears. The **id** argument is a value used to identify the task. Every time this value changes, the task is restarted. And the **priority** argument is a structure that helps the system decide when to execute the task. The values available are **background**, **high**, **low**, **medium**, **userInitiated**, and **utility**.

(Basic) Async and Await

Asynchronous and concurrent tasks are defined in Swift with the **async** and **await** keywords. For instance, to create an asynchronous task, we mark a method with **async** and then wait for that method to complete with **await**. This means that an asynchronous method can only be called with the **await** keyword from inside another asynchronous method, which creates an indefinite cycle. To start the cycle, we can initiate the asynchronous task when the view appears with the **task()** modifier, as shown next.

```
struct ContentView: View {
   var body: some View {
      VStack {
         Text("Hello, world!")
            .padding()
      }
      .task(priority: .background) {
         let imageName = await loadImage(name: "image1")
         print(imageName)
      }
   }
}
```

```
    func loadImage(name: String) async -> String {
        try? await Task.sleep(nanoseconds: 3 * 1000000000)
        return "Name: \(name)"
    }
}
```

Listing 9-1: Initiating an asynchronous task

The task in this example is created with a **background** priority, which means that it is not going to have priority over other parallel tasks. In the closure, we call the **loadImage()** method and then print on the console the value returned. This is a method we define to simulate the process of downloading an image form the Web. We will learn how to download data and connect to the Web later, but for now we use the **sleep()** method to pause the task for 3 seconds and pretend that the image is downloading (the method takes a value in nanoseconds). Once this pause is over, the method returns a string with the file's name. To define the method as asynchronous, we add the **async** keyword after the parameters, and then call it with the **await** keyword to indicate that the task must wait for this process to be over.

The **task()** modifier creates the task and adds it to the thread. When the view is loaded, the closure assigned to the modifier is executed. In the closure, we call the **loadImage()** method and wait for its completion. The method pauses for 3 seconds and then returns a string. After this, the task continues executing the statements, and a message is printed on the console.

 Do It Yourself: Create a Multiplatform project. Update the **ContentView** structure with the code in Listing 9-1. Run the application on the simulator. You should see a message appear on the console after 3 seconds.

A task can perform multiple asynchronous processes. For instance, in the following example we call the **loadImage()** method three times to download three images.

```
struct ContentView: View {
    var body: some View {
        VStack {
            Text("Hello, world!")
                .padding()
        }.task(priority: .background) {
            let imageName1 = await loadImage(name: "image1")
            let imageName2 = await loadImage(name: "image2")
            let imageName3 = await loadImage(name: "image3")
            print("\(imageName1), \(imageName2), and \(imageName3)")
        }
    }
    func loadImage(name: String) async -> String {
        try? await Task.sleep(nanoseconds: 3 * 1000000000)
        return "Name: \(name)"
    }
}
```

Listing 9-2: Running multiple asynchronous processes

The processes are executed one by one, in sequential order. The task waits for a process to be over before executing the next. In this case, the whole task is going to take 9 seconds to finish (3 seconds per process).

 Do It Yourself: Update the **ContentView** structure with the code in Listing 9-2. Run the application on the simulator. You should see a message appear on the console after 9 seconds (3 seconds per process).

The `task()` modifier is useful when all we need is to run an asynchronous task after the views are loaded, but most of the time tasks are not dependent on the views' life cycle and must be created explicitly with the `Task` initializer. For instance, we can reproduce the previous example with the `onAppear()` method and a `Task` structure.

```
struct ContentView: View {
    var body: some View {
        VStack {
            Text("Hello, world!")
                .padding()
        }
        .onAppear {
            Task(priority: .background) {
                let imageName1 = await loadImage(name: "image1")
                let imageName2 = await loadImage(name: "image2")
                let imageName3 = await loadImage(name: "image3")
                print("\(imageName1), \(imageName2), and \(imageName3)")
            }
        }
    }
    func loadImage(name: String) async -> String {
        try? await Task.sleep(nanoseconds: 3 * 1000000000)
        return "Name: \(name)"
    }
}
```

Listing 9-3: *Defining a task explicitly*

This view performs the same three processes as before, but now the task is defined explicitly, which gives us more control over it. For instance, now we can assign the task to a variable and then call the `cancel()` method to cancel it.

The `cancel()` method cancels the task, but the processes are not automatically cancelled; we must detect whether the task has been cancelled with the `isCancelled` property and stop the process ourselves, as shown next.

```
struct ContentView: View {
    var body: some View {
        VStack {
            Text("Hello, world!")
                .padding()
        }
        .onAppear {
            let myTask = Task(priority: .background) {
                let imageName = await loadImage(name: "image1")
                print(imageName)
            }
            Timer.scheduledTimer(withTimeInterval: 2.0, repeats: false)
{ (timer) in
                print("The time is up")
                myTask.cancel()
            }
        }
    }
    func loadImage(name: String) async -> String {
        try? await Task.sleep(nanoseconds: 3 * 1000000000)
        if !Task.isCancelled {
            return "Name: \(name)"
        } else {
            return "Task Cancelled"
```

```
            }
        }
    }
```

Listing 9-4: Cancelling a task

This example assigns the previous task to a constant and then creates a timer to call the `cancel()` method on the task 2 seconds later. In the `loadImage()` method, we read the `isCancelled` property and respond accordingly. If the task was cancelled, we return the "Task Cancelled" message, otherwise, the name is returned as before. Notice that in this case we are working inside a process executed by the task, so we use the type property instead of the instance property (we read the `isCancelled` property from the data type, not the instance). This property returns **true** or **false** depending on the state of the current task. As a result, the task is cancelled before it is completed.

Tasks can receive and return values. The **Task** structure includes the **value** property to provide access to the value returned by the task. Of course, we also need to wait for the task to complete before reading this value, as shown next.

```
struct ContentView: View {
    var body: some View {
        VStack {
            Text("Hello, world!")
                .padding()
        }
        .onAppear {
            Task(priority: .background) {
                let imageName = await loadImage(name: "image1")
                print(imageName)
            }
        }
    }
    func loadImage(name: String) async -> String {
        let result = Task(priority: .background) { () -> String in
            let imageData = await getMetadata()
            return "Name: \(name) Size: \(imageData)"
        }
        let message = await result.value
        return message
    }
    func getMetadata() async -> Int {
        try? await Task.sleep(nanoseconds: 3 * 1000000000)
        return 50000
    }
}
```

Listing 9-5: Reading a value returned by a task

Because we need to wait for the task to finish before using the value, we have defined a second task. The process starts as always, with a task that calls the `loadImage()` method, but now we create a second task that returns a string. This task executes another asynchronous method that waits for 3 seconds and returns the number 50000. After this process is over, the task creates a string with the name and the number and returns it. We then get the string from the **value** property, and return it to the original task, which prints it on the console.

So far, we have worked with asynchronous methods, but we can also define asynchronous properties. All we need to do is to define the getter with the **async** keyword, as shown next.

```
struct ContentView: View {
   var thumbnail: String {
      get async {
         try? await Task.sleep(nanoseconds: 3 * 1000000000)
         return "mythumbnail"
      }
   }
   var body: some View {
      VStack {
         Text("Hello, world!")
            .padding()
      }
      .onAppear {
         Task(priority: .background) {
            let imageName = await thumbnail
            print(imageName)
         }
      }
   }
}
```

Listing 9-6: Defining asynchronous properties

This time, instead of calling a method, the task reads a property. The property suspends the tasks for 3 seconds and returns a string. Again, we are suspending the task for didactic purposes, but we can perform any demanding task we want in this property, such as downloading an image from the Web or processing data.

(Basic) **Errors**

Asynchronous tasks are not always successful, so we must be prepared to process the errors returned. If we are creating our own tasks, we can define the errors with an enumeration that conforms to the **Error** protocol, as explain in Chapter 3 (see Listing 3-189). The following example defines a structure with two errors, one to return when no metadata is found on the server (**noData**), and another for when the image is not available (**noImage**).

```
import SwiftUI
enum MyErrors: Error {
   case noData, noImage
}
struct ContentView: View {
   var body: some View {
      VStack {
         Text("Hello, world!")
            .padding()
      }
      .onAppear {
         Task(priority: .background) {
            do {
               let imageName = try await loadImage(name: "image1")
               print(imageName)
            } catch MyErrors.noData {
               print("Error: No Data Available")
            } catch MyErrors.noImage {
               print("Error: No Image Available")
            }
         }
      }
   }
}
```

Chapter 9 - Concurrency

```
func loadImage(name: String) async throws -> String {
    try? await Task.sleep(nanoseconds: 3 * 1000000000)

    let error = true
    if error {
        throw MyErrors.noImage
    }
    return "Name: \(name)"
}
}
```

Listing 9-7: Responding to errors

The **loadImage()** method in this example always throws a **noImage** error to test the code. The task checks for errors with a **do catch** statement and prints a message on the console to report the result. Notice that when an asynchronous function can throw errors, we must declare the **throws** keyword after **async**.

(Basic) **Concurrency**

Asynchronous tasks are useful when we want to free resources for the system to perform other tasks, like updating the interface, but when we want to run two tasks simultaneously, we need concurrency. For this purpose, the Swift Standard Library defines the **async let** statement. To turn an asynchronous task into multiple concurrent tasks, all we need to do is to declare the processes with the **async let** statement, as shown next.

```
struct ContentView: View {
    var body: some View {
        VStack {
            Text("Hello, world!")
                .padding()
        }
        .onAppear {
            let currentTime = Date()

            Task(priority: .background) {
                async let imageName1 = loadImage(name: "image1")
                async let imageName2 = loadImage(name: "image2")
                async let imageName3 = loadImage(name: "image3")

                let listNames = await "\(imageName1), \(imageName2), and \
(imageName3)"
                print(listNames)
                print("Total Time: \(Date().timeIntervalSince(currentTime))")
            }
        }
    }
    func loadImage(name: String) async -> String {
        try? await Task.sleep(nanoseconds: 3 * 1000000000)
        return "Name: \(name)"
    }
}
```

Listing 9-8: Defining a concurrent task

Every time a process is declared with the **async let** statement the system creates a new concurrent task that runs in parallel with the rest of the tasks. In the example of Listing 9-8, we create three concurrent tasks (**imageName1**, **imageName2**, and **imageName3**). The process is the same as before, they call the **loadImage()** method, the method pauses the task for 3 seconds, and returns a string. But because this time the processes run in parallel, the time they take to complete is around 3 seconds (not 9 seconds, as previous examples).

Do It Yourself: Update the `ContentView` structure with the code in Listing 9-8. Run the application on the simulator. After a few seconds, you should see a message on the console with the time that took for the processes to be over.

(Medium) ## Actors

When working with concurrent tasks, we could run into a problem called *Data Race*. A data race happens when two or more tasks running in parallel try to access the same data. For instance, they try to modify the value of a property at the same time. This could lead to errors or serious bugs. To solve this issue, the Swift Standard Library includes Actors.

Actors are data types that isolate parallel tasks from one another, so when a task is modifying the values of an actor, other tasks are forced to wait. Actors are reference types and are defined like classes, but instead of the **class** keyword, they are declared with the **actor** keyword. Another important difference with classes is that the properties and methods must be accessed asynchronously (we must wait with the **await** keyword). This ensures that the code can wait until the actor is free to respond (no other task is accessing the actor).

The following example illustrates how actors work. The code declares an actor with a property and a method, creates an instance, and then calls the method from multiple tasks.

```
import SwiftUI
actor ItemData {
    var counter: Int = 0

    func incrementCount() -> String {
        counter += 1
        return "Value: \(counter)"
    }
}
struct ContentView: View {
    var item: ItemData = ItemData()

    var body: some View {
        Button("Start Process") {
            Timer.scheduledTimer(withTimeInterval: 0.1, repeats: true)
{ (timer) in
                Task(priority: .background) {
                    async let operation = item.incrementCount()
                    print(await operation)
                }
            }
            Timer.scheduledTimer(withTimeInterval: 0.2, repeats: true)
{ (timer) in
                Task(priority: .high) {
                    async let operation = item.incrementCount()
                    print(await operation)
                }
            }
        }
    }
}
```

Listing 9-9: Defining an actor

The interface includes a button to start two timers that repeat indefinitely, one every 0.1 seconds and another every 0.2 seconds. The timers perform a task with a concurrent operation that calls the `incrementCount()` method in the Actor. This means that different tasks in different threads will be calling the method, and eventually they will do it at the same time, creating a data race. If we declare `ItemData` as a class, we will have errors, unexpected behavior, or even crashes, but because we declared this data type as an actor, the code works correctly. Every time a task calls the `incrementCount()` method, the actor takes control and makes sure that the tasks have access to the method one at a time.

 Do It Yourself: Update the ContentView.swift file with the code in Listing 9-9. Run the application on the iPhone simulator and press the button. You should see the values produced by the `incrementCount()` method printed on the console. Stop the application. Declare the actor as a class (replace the **actor** keyword by the **class** keyword). Now the application will produce an error when the method is called by multiple tasks at the same time.

 IMPORTANT: By default, Xcode doesn't show the errors on the console. To detect problems with asynchronous operations, you must activate the Thread Sanitizer. Click on the Scheme button on the Xcode's toolbar (Figure 5-4, number 2). Select the Edit Scheme option from the menu (Figure 5-8). On the new window, select the Run option and open the Diagnostics tab. Check the box to enable the Thread Sanitizer. Declare the actor as a class, run the app again on the iPhone simulator, and press the button. After a few successful attempts, you should see an access race error on the console.

As we mentioned, the actor isolates the properties and methods from the rest of the code and other threads. This means that we can only access an actor asynchronously (we must wait for the actor to allow access), but in some circumstances, this isolation is not required. In these cases, we can revert the condition of isolation with the following keyword.

nonisolated—This keyword breaks the isolation of a property or a method.

Non-isolated properties and methods may be necessary to conform to protocols and can also simplify our code when all we need is to access immutable values in the actor. For instance, in the following example we add a constant to the `ItemData` actor called maximum and a method that prints its value. Because the value of the constant never changes, we can declare the method non-isolated and call it without waiting for the actor to give us access to it.

```
import SwiftUI
actor ItemData {
   var counter: Int = 0
   let maximum: Int = 50

   func incrementCount() -> String {
      counter += 1
      return "Value: \(counter)"
   }
   nonisolated func maximumValue() -> String {
      return "Maximum Value: \(maximum)"
   }
}
struct ContentView: View {
   var item: ItemData = ItemData()

   var body: some View {
      Button("Start Process") {
         let value = item.maximumValue()
         print(value)
      }
   }
}
```

Listing 9-10: Defining a non-isolated method

In these examples, we have worked with values defined by the actor, but usually values are also sent to the actor for processing. Sending values to a method in the actor is dangerous. Because an actor's job is to make sure that two or more asynchronous tasks don't modify values simultaneously, not every values is safe. Value types, including custom structures and primitive data types like `Int` and `String`, are thread safe because they are copied. When we call a method in the actor with one of these values, the system creates a copy and sends that copy to the method, so the original value is not modified. But objects are reference types and therefore only a reference to the object is sent to the actor, which means that the object may be modified from elsewhere in the code, potentially creating a data race. To ensure that the values we want to sent to a method are safe, the Swift Standard Library defines the following protocol and attribute.

Sendable—This protocol tells the system that the values created from the data type can be safely shared between asynchronous threads.

@Sendable—This attribute indicates to the system that a method or a closure can be safely shared between asynchronous threads.

The `Sendable` protocol doesn't do anything other than telling the compiler that the data type is thread safe. When a data type conforms to this protocol, the compiler shows errors if it includes unsafe values. For instance, although structures are safe, we can make them conform to this protocol to make sure we don't add any unsafe properties later. Classes are also safe if they only include immutable values, but subclasses may not be safe, so we have to mark the class with the `final` keyword to make sure that nobody can create a subclass from it, as shown next.

```
import SwiftUI
final class Product: Sendable {
   let name: String

   init(name: String) {
      self.name = name
   }
}
actor ItemData {
   var stock: Int = 100

   func sellProduct(product: Product, quantity: Int) {
      stock = stock - quantity
      print("Stock: \(stock) \(product.name)")
   }
}
struct ContentView: View {
   var item: ItemData = ItemData()

   var body: some View {
      Button("Start Process") {
         Task(priority: .background) {
            let product = Product(name: "Lamp")
            await item.sellProduct(product: product, quantity: 5)
         }
      }
   }
}
```

Listing 9-11: Defining a non-isolated method

This example defines a class called `Product` that is final (no subclasses can be created from it) and includes an immutable property (`let`). Also, the property is of type `String`, a sendable data type by default. This means that objects created from this class are thread safe and can be sent to an actor.

IMPORTANT: Classes with mutable values (`var`) can also be sendable, but we are responsible of making sure that they cannot produce a data race. The topic is beyond the scope of this book. For more information, visit our website and follow the links for this chapter.

If we really need to include unsafe values and we know for sure that they are not going to be modified from different threads, we can tell the compiler not to check for errors with the following attribute.

@unchecked—This attribute asks the compiler not to check whether the data type conforms to the `Sendable` protocol or not.

This is useful when we need to work with unsafe data types, or to send to an actor a value produced by an old framework. For instance, in the following example we turn the `Product` class into a structure and use the `name` property to store an `NSString` value. The `NSString` data type is not sendable and therefore the `Product` structure does not conform to the requirements of the `Sendable` protocol, but because we know that the value is not going to be modified anywhere else, we ask the compiler not to worry about it with the `@unchecked` attribute, and Xcode doesn't show any warnings or errors.

```
struct Product: @unchecked Sendable {
    let name: NSString
}
```

Listing 9-12: *Asking the compiler not to check conformity to the* Sendable *protocol*

IMPORTANT: The `@unchecked` attribute is usually implemented to wrap an unsafe value before sending it to the Main Actor. We will learn how to work with the Main Actor next and implement the attribute in practical situations later.

(Basic) Main Actor

As we already mentioned, tasks are assigned to execution threads and then the system distributes these threads among the multiple cores of a processor to perform the tasks as fast and smoothly as possible. A thread can manage multiple tasks, and multiple threads may be created for our application. Besides the threads initialized to process asynchronous and concurrent tasks, the system always creates a thread, called *Main Thread*, to start the application and run non-asynchronous code, including the code that creates and updates the interface. This means that if we try to modify the interface from an asynchronous or concurrent task, we may cause a data race or a serious bug. To avoid these conflicts, the Swift Standard Library defines the Main Actor. The Main Actor is an actor created by the system that makes sure that every task that wants to interact with the main thread or modify the elements of the interface waits for other tasks to finish.

Swift provides two easy ways to make sure that our code runs on the Main Actor (the main thread): the `@MainActor` modifier and the `run()` method. With the `@MainActor` modifier we can mark an entire method to run on the main thread, while the `run()` method executes a closure in the main thread. For instance, in the following example we mark the `loadImage()` method with `@MainActor` to make sure that the code inside the method is executed in the main thread and we are able to modify the value of a `Text` view with no issues.

```
struct ContentView: View {
    @State private var myText: String = "Hello, world!"

    var body: some View {
        VStack {
            Text(myText)
                .padding()
        }
        .onAppear {
            Task(priority: .background) {
                await loadImage(name: "image1")
            }
        }
    }
    @MainActor func loadImage(name: String) async {
        myText = name
    }
}
```

Listing 9-13: Executing a method in the Main Actor

This code creates an asynchronous task as before, but now the method is marked with **@MainActor**, so the code is executed in the main thread and we can safely update the **myText** property and the interface.

Most of the time, only part of our code deals with the interface, but the rest can be executed in the current thread. For cases like this, we can implement the **run()** method. This is a type method defined by the **MainActor** structure (the structure used to create the Main Actor). The method takes a closure with the statements we need to execute in the main thread.

```
struct ContentView: View {
    @State private var myText: String = "Hello, world!"

    var body: some View {
        VStack {
            Text(myText)
                .padding()
        }
        .onAppear {
            Task(priority: .background) {
                await loadImage(name: "image1")
            }
        }
    }
    func loadImage(name: String) async {
        await MainActor.run {
            myText = name
        }
        print(name)
    }
}
```

Listing 9-14: Executing code in the Main Actor

The **loadImage()** method now includes a statement at the end to print the string on the console, but only the statement that assigns the new value to the **myText** property needs to run in the main thread, so we execute it within the **run()** method. Notice that this method is marked with **await**. The **await** keyword is necessary because the method may have to wait for the main thread to be free to execute the statements.

The **run()** method can also return a value. This is useful when we need to report the result of a complex operation. All we need to remember is to declare the type of value returned by the closure, as shown next.

```
func loadImage(name: String) async {
    let result: String = await MainActor.run {
        myText = name
        return "Name: \(name)"
    }
    print(result)
}
```

Listing 9-15: Returning a value from the Main Actor

(Medium) ## Asynchronous Sequences

Sometimes, information is returned as a sequence of values, but the values may not be available all at once. In cases like this, we can create an asynchronous sequence. This sequence is like an array, but the values are returned asynchronously, so we must wait for each value to be ready.

The Swift Standard Library includes two protocols to create asynchronous sequences: the **AsyncSequence** protocol to define the sequence and the **AsyncIteratorProtocol** protocol to define the code that iterates through the sequence to return the values. The **AsyncSequence** protocol requires the data type to include a typealias with the name **Element** that represents the data type returned by the sequence, and the following method.

makeAsyncIterator()—This method returns the instance of the iterator in charge of producing the values. The value returned is an instance of a data type that conforms to the **AsyncIteratorProtocol** protocol.

On the other hand, the **AsyncIteratorProtocol** protocol only requires the data type to implement the following method.

next()—This method returns the next element on the list. The method is called over and over again until the value returned is **nil**, which indicates the end of the sequence.

To create an asynchronous sequence, we must define two data types, one that conforms to the **AsyncSequence** to describe the data type of the values returned by the sequence and initialize the iterator, and another that conforms to the **AsyncIteratorProtocol** protocol to produce the values. In the following example, we define an asynchronous sequence that processes an array of strings one by one and returns a sequence of **String** values.

```
import SwiftUI

struct ImageIterator : AsyncIteratorProtocol {
    let imageList: [String]
    var current = 0

    mutating func next() async -> String? {
        guard current < imageList.count else {
            return nil
        }
        try? await Task.sleep(nanoseconds: 3 * 1000000000)

        let image = imageList[current]
        current += 1
        return image
    }
}
```

```
struct ImageLoader : AsyncSequence {
   typealias Element = String
   let imageList: [String]

   func makeAsyncIterator() -> ImageIterator {
      return AsyncIterator(imageList: imageList)
   }
}
struct ContentView: View {
   let list = ["image1", "image2", "image3"]

   var body: some View {
      VStack {
         Text("Hello World!")
            .padding()
      }
      .onAppear {
         Task(priority: .background) {
            let loader = ImageLoader(imageList: list)
            for await image in loader {
               print(image)
            }
         }
      }
   }
}
```

Listing 9-16: Defining an asynchronous sequence

The code in Listing 9-16 simulates the process of asynchronously downloading images from the Web. The iterator with the **next()** method is defined first. In this method, we read the strings from the **list** array and update a counter to know when we have reached the end (the value of the counter is equal or greater than the number of elements in the array).

The asynchronous sequence is defined next by the **ImageLoader** structure. The structure includes a typealias called **Element** to indicate that the sequence returns **String** values, and the **makeAsyncIterator()** method to initialize the iterator.

Everything is ready to read the values in the sequence, so we start a task, create an instance of the **ImageLoader** sequence, and then iterate through the elements with a **for in** loop. Notice that the **for in** loop requires the **await** keyword to wait for each element of the sequence. The loop runs until the value returned by the iterator is **nil**.

 Do It Yourself: Update the ContentView.swift file with the code in Listing 9-16. Run the application on the simulator. You should see the values in the **list** array printed on the console every 3 seconds.

(Medium) **Task Group**

A task group is a container for dynamically generated tasks. Once the group is created, we can add and manage tasks from code as required by the application. The Swift Standard Library defines the following global methods to create a group.

withTaskGroup(of: Type, **returning:** Type, **body:** Closure)—This method creates a task group. The **of** argument defines the data type returned by the tasks, the **returning** argument defines the data type returned by the group, and the **body** argument is the closure where the tasks are defined. If no values are returned, the arguments may be ignored.

withThrowingTaskGroup(of: Type, **returning:** Type, **body:** Closure)—This method creates a task group that can throw errors. The **of** argument defines the data type returned by the tasks, the **returning** argument defines the data type returned by the group, and the **body** argument is the closure where the tasks are defined. If no values are returned, the arguments may be ignored.

The group is defined by an instance of the `TaskGroup` structure, which includes properties and methods to manage the tasks in the group. The following are the most frequently used.

isCancelled—This property returns a Boolean value that indicates whether the group was cancelled.

isEmpty—This property returns a Boolean value that indicates whether the group has any remaining tasks.

addTask(priority: TaskPriority?, **operation:** Closure)—This method adds a task to the group. The **priority** argument is a structure that helps the system decide when to execute the task. The structure includes type properties to defined standard priorities. The currently available are `background`, `high`, `low`, `medium`, `userInitiated`, and `utility`. And the **operation** argument is a closure with the statements to be executed by the task.

cancelAll()—This method cancels all the tasks in the group.

A task group is an asynchronous sequence of tasks. This sequence is generic, which means that the tasks and the group can return any types of values. This is the reason why the methods to create a task group have two arguments to specify the data types returned by the tasks and the group.

The two methods available to create a task group are the same. The one we implement depends on whether we want to throw errors or not. These methods create a `TaskGroup` structure that works with the data types specified by the arguments and send the instance to the closure. Using this value inside the closure, we can add to the group all the tasks we want, as shown next.

```
struct ContentView: View {
    var body: some View {
        VStack {
            Text("Hello World!")
                .padding()
        }
        .onAppear {
            Task(priority: .background) {
                await withTaskGroup(of: String.self) { group in
                    group.addTask(priority: .background) {
                        let imageName = await self.loadImage(name: "image1")
                        return imageName
                    }
                    group.addTask(priority: .background) {
                        let imageName = await self.loadImage(name: "image2")
                        return imageName
                    }
                    group.addTask(priority: .background) {
                        let imageName = await self.loadImage(name: "image3")
                        return imageName
                    }
                    for await result in group {
                        print(result)
                    }
                }
            }
        }
    }
}
```

```
                }
            }
        }
    }
    func loadImage(name: String) async -> String {
        try? await Task.sleep(nanoseconds: 3 * 1000000000)
        return "Name: \(name)"
    }
}
```

Listing 9-17: Defining a task group

In this example, we create a task group that doesn't throw errors. The group doesn't return a value either, but the tasks return a string, so we declare the **of** argument of the **withTaskGroup()** method with a reference to the **String** data type (**String.self**). The tasks are added to the group one after another. Each task performs the same process as before. They call the **loadImage()** method asynchronously and get a string in return.

Because a task group is an asynchronous sequence of tasks, we can iterate though the values with a **for in** loop, as we did for the asynchronous sequence created in the previous section of this chapter. Every time a task is completed, the group returns the value produced by the task until no tasks remain, in which case the value **nil** is returned to finish the loop.

 IMPORTANT: Task Groups store the tasks in sequence. You can remove, filter, or even check whether a group contains a specific task. The topic is beyond the scope of this book. For more information, visit our website and follow the links for this chapter.

(Basic) Asynchronous Images

Although we can perform any type of asynchronous or concurrent task we need with these tools, SwiftUI offers the **AsyncImage** view to simplify our work when working with images. This view takes care of downloading an image from a server and displaying the image on the screen when it is ready. The following are the view's most frequently used initializers.

AsyncImage(url: URL, **scale:** CGFloat)—This view downloads an image from a server and displays it on the screen. The **url** argument is a **URL** structure with the image's url, and the **scale** argument is the scale we want to assign to the image (1 by default).

AsyncImage(url: URL, **scale:** CGFloat, **content:** Closure, **placeholder:** Closure)—This view downloads an image from a server and displays it on the screen. The **url** argument is a **URL** structure with the image's url, the **scale** argument is the scale we want to assign to the image (1 by default), the **content** argument is a closure to process the image, and the **placeholder** argument is a closure that returns a view to show in place of the image while we wait for the image to download.

The location of the image is determined by a **URL** structure. These structures are used to store the address of remote and local documents, files, and resources. The following are the initializers we need to create URLs to access documents or resources on the web.

URL(string: String)—This initializer creates a **URL** structure with the URL specified by the **string** argument.

URL(string: String, **relativeTo:** URL?)—This initializer creates a **URL** structure with the URL specified by the arguments. The URL is created by adding the value of the **string** argument to the value of the **relativeTo** argument.

URL(dataRepresentation: Data, **relativeTo:** URL?, **isAbsolute:** Bool)—This initializer creates a **URL** structure with the URL specified by the arguments. The URL is created by adding the value of the **dataRepresentation** argument to the value of the **relativeTo** argument. The **isAbsolute** argument is a Boolean value that determines if the URL is absolute or not (it includes all the information required to access the resource).

There are two types of URL: secure and non-secure. Non-secure URLs are identified with the http protocol (Hypertext Transfer Protocol) and secure URLs are identified with the https protocol (Hypertext Transfer Protocol Secure). Secure URLs are allowed by default, but if we need to open non-secure URLs we must configure our app to circumvent a security system called ATS (App Transport Security) implemented by Apple devices.

The option to configure the App Transport Security system is called "App Transport Security Settings", and it is added to the app's configuration from the Info panel. We have introduced this panel before (see Figure 5-13) and use it to add custom fonts (see Figure 5-34). As explained before, new options are added from the + button on the right side of the items.

Key		Type	Value
Bundle name		String	$(PRODUCT_NAME)
Bundle identifier		String	$(PRODUCT_BUNDLE_IDENTIFIER)
InfoDictionary version		String	6.0
> Supported interface orientations (iPho...		Array	(3 items)

Figure 9-2: Button to add configuration options

After we click on the + button (circled in Figure 9-2), a new empty text field is added below the option. If we start typing, a drop down menu shows the options available and we can select it from the list.

Key		Type	Value
Bundle name		String	$(PRODUCT_NAME)
App Transport Security Settings		Dictionary	(0 items)
Bundle identifier		String	$(PRODUCT_BUNDLE_IDENTIFIER)
InfoDictionary version		String	6.0
> Supported interface orientations (iPho...		Array	(3 items)

Figure 9-3: App Transport Security option

The App Transport Security Settings option is just a container. To configure the option we must add subitems. To add a subitem, we must click on the arrow on the left (circled in Figure 9-3), and then press the + button again. The option to allow the app to open non-secure URLs is called "Allow Arbitrary Loads".

Key		Type	Value
Bundle name		String	$(PRODUCT_NAME)
∨ App Transport Security Settings		Dictionary	(1 item)
Allow Arbitrary Loads		Boolean	YES
Bundle identifier		String	$(PRODUCT_BUNDLE_IDENTIFIER)

Figure 9-4: App Transport Security configured to allow non-secure URLs

The Allow Arbitrary Loads key takes a Boolean value specified with the strings YES and NO (or 1 and 0, respectively). Setting this key to YES (1) allows any URL to be opened. If what we want is to allow only specific domains, we must use the Exception Domains key and add to the key additional items with the domains we want to include. These items in turn require at least three more items with the keys **NSIncludesSubdomains** (Boolean), **NSTemporaryException-AllowsInsecureHTTPLoads** (Boolean), and **NSTemporaryExceptionMinimumTLSVersion**

(String). For example, the following configuration allows documents from the formasterminds.com domain to be opened.

Key		Type	Value
Bundle name	↕	String	$(PRODUCT_NAME)
˅ App Transport Security Settings	↕	Dictionary	(1 item)
˅ Exception Domains	↕	Dictionary	(1 item)
formasterminds.com	⊕⊖	Dictionary ↕	(3 items)
NSIncludesSubdomains		Boolean	1
NSTemporaryExceptionAllowsInsec…		Boolean	1
NSTemporaryExceptionMinimumTL…		String	TLSv1.1

Figure 9-5: App Transport Security configured to allow URLs from formasterminds.com

Configuring the App Transport Security system may be necessary or not, depending on the type of URLs we want our users to be able to access. Secure URLs are allowed by default, but if we want to allow our users to access non-secure URLs, we must add the options to the app configuration, as shown above. For instance, the following example loads an image from the non-secure version of our website.

```
struct ContentView: View {
    let website = URL(string: "http://www.formasterminds.com/images/
coveruikit4big.png")

    var body: some View {
        VStack {
            AsyncImage(url: website)
        }.padding()
    }
}
```

Listing 9-18: Loading an image asynchronously

All the `AsyncImage` view needs to download and display an image is a URL. In this example, we store a URL in a constant and then implement the view to load the image. Although the image is effectively loaded and displayed, the `AsyncImage` view doesn't allow any configuration, so the image is shown in its original size.

Figure 9-6: Image loaded asynchronously

If we want to configure the image, we must provide a closure for the **content** argument. This closure receives an `Image` view that we can configure with view modifiers, as before.

　　　　　　　　　　　Chapter 9 - Concurrency

```
struct ContentView: View {
    let website = URL(string: "http://www.formasterminds.com/images/
coveruikit4big.png")

    var body: some View {
        VStack {
            AsyncImage(url: website, content: { image in
                image
                    .resizable()
                    .scaledToFit()
            }, placeholder: {
                Image("nopicture")
            })
            Spacer()
        }.padding()
    }
}
```

Listing 9-19: *Configuring the image after it is downloaded*

When we provide the **content** argument, the `AsyncImage` view relegates the job of displaying the image to the `Image` view received by the closure, so we can configure this view as before. In this example, we resize the image with the `resizable()` modifier and scale it to fit within the view with the `scaledToFit()` modifier. Notice that we have also defined the **placeholder** argument to show a temporary image while the final image is downloading.

Figure 9-7: *Image configuration*

Do It Yourself: Create a Multiplatform project. Download the nopicture image from our website and add it to the Asset Catalog. Update the `ContentView` view with the code in Listing 9-19. Click on the item at the top of the Navigator Area to open the app's configuration panels (Figure 5-4, number 6). Open the info panel and follow the steps explained in Figures 10-2, 10-3, and 10-4 to add the Allow Arbitrary Loads option with the value YES. After a few seconds, you should see the cover of the UIKit for Masterminds book replacing the nopicture image.

⟨ Basic ⟩ 10.1 User Preferences

Up to this point, we stored all the data in arrays created in the model, and the values were hard-coded, meaning they were always the same every time the user launched the app. Any changes applied to the model were only preserved while the app was running but erased as soon as the app was closed. To preserve the values and all the changes introduced by the user, we need to store the data permanently on the device. Apple includes several systems for storing data. They all work with files but can take various forms, from simple text files to databases (indexed data).

⟨ Basic ⟩ App Storage

The simplest storage system available on Apple devices is called *Users Defaults*. This system was designed to store user preferences, which may include values set by the user to determine how the app should work or values set by the app to restore previous states. These values are stored in a system-managed database and therefore continue to exist after the application is closed and for as long as the user or the application decides to keep them. SwiftUI includes the following property wrapper to store and retrieve User Defaults values.

@AppStorage(String**)**—This property wrapper stores or retrieves a value from User Defaults. The argument is a string with the key of the value we want to access.

The User Defaults system can store any amount of data we want, but it is recommended to use it to store short strings and small values. Its main purpose is to store the app's settings. For instance, we can use it to allow the user to store a limit on the number of items managed by the application, and then set that limit back every time the app is executed.

To create this application, all we need is to define a property with the `@AppStorage` property wrapper and then use it as we do with a state property.

```
struct ContentView: View {
    @AppStorage("counter") var mycounter: Double = 0

    var body: some View {
        HStack {
            Stepper("", value: $mycounter)
                .labelsHidden()
            Text("\
(mycounter.formatted(.number.precision(.fractionLength(0))))")
                .font(.title)
        }
    }
}
```

Listing 10-1: Storing and reading values from User Defaults

This view defines an `@AppStorage` property with the "counter" key and the name `mycounter`, and includes a `Stepper` and a `Text` view to let the user select a value and show the current value on the screen.

An `@AppStorage` property is used as any other state property before, but now the value is stored in the User Defaults system. In consequence, when the app is closed and opened again, the `mycounter` property gets the value from User Defaults, and the latest value stored by the user is shown on the screen.

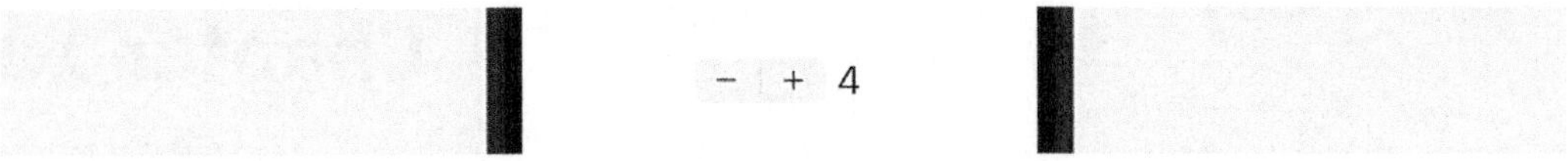

Figure 10-1: Interface to store settings

Do It Yourself: Create a Multiplatform project. Update the `ContentView` view with the code in Listing 10-1. Run the application on the iPhone simulator. Press the buttons on the stepper to change the value. Wait for a few seconds. Stop the execution of the app from the Stop button in Xcode. Run the application again. The value displayed on the screen should be the last one you selected.

IMPORTANT: The `@AppStorage` property wrapper can only store simple values like strings and numbers, but you can also store other values, including custom data types, by converting them into `Data` structures, as we will see later.

As we already mentioned, we can also store values generated by the application. For example, we can add a value to User Defaults to check how long it's been since the last time the app was launched. The process to read and store the value is the same, but this time we need to store a date. The `@AppStorage` property wrapper doesn't take `Date` structures, but we can store a `TimeInterval` value from a reference date, and then create the `Date` structure from this value.

```
struct ContentView: View {
   @AppStorage("interval") var interval =
Date.timeIntervalSinceReferenceDate
   @State private var message: String = ""

   var body: some View {
      HStack {
         Text("\(message)")
            .lineLimit(nil)
      }.onAppear {
         let calendar = Calendar.current
         let lastDate = Date(timeIntervalSinceReferenceDate: interval)
         let components =
calendar.dateComponents([.year, .month, .day, .hour, .minute, .second],
from: lastDate, to: Date())
         message = "You haven't use this app in \(components.year!)
years, \(components.month!) months, \(components.day!) days, \
(components.hour!) hours, \(components.minute!) minutes, \
(components.second!) seconds"
         interval = Date.timeIntervalSinceReferenceDate
      }
   }
}
```

Listing 10-2: Storing app settings in User Defaults

This view creates a property of type `TimeInterval` called `interval` with the number of seconds from a reference date (January 1st, 2001). When the view appears, the `onAppear()` modifier turns this value into a `Date` structure, extracts the components of the date, creates a string with these values, and assigns it to a state property to show it on the screen. At the end, we update the `interval` property with the current interval to be able to calculate the time again when the app is relaunched.

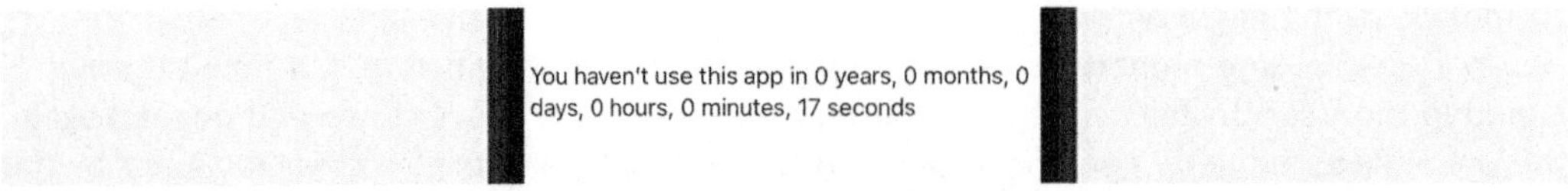

You haven't use this app in 0 years, 0 months, 0 days, 0 hours, 0 minutes, 17 seconds

Figure 10-2: Displaying app settings

Do It Yourself: Update the `ContentView` view with the code in Listing 10-2. Run the application on the iPhone simulator. The first time, you should see all the date components with the value 0. Stop the app from Xcode and run it again. You should see how long it has been since the last time the app was launched.

The previous examples were designed for didactic purposes. User Defaults is frequently used to store the app's settings, and users are provided a separate view where they can change these values and configure the app to their liking. In the following example, we are going to follow this approach to allow the user to configure the rows of a `List` view that presents a list of books. By modifying the values from the Settings view, the user can define the corners of the book's cover and hide the cover and the year.

Figure 10-3: Settings view

The model for this project needs the usual **Book** and **BookViewModel** structures implemented in Chapter 7, Listing 7-3, and the observable object must include the **@Published** property to store the books, and also the **@AppStorage** properties to store the app's settings.

```
class ApplicationData: ObservableObject {
    @Published var userData: [BookViewModel]
    @AppStorage("cornerSize") var cornerSize: Double = 0
    @AppStorage("showYear") var showYear: Bool = true
    @AppStorage("showCover") var showCover: Bool = true

    init() {
        userData = [
            BookViewModel(book: Book(title: "Steve Jobs", author: "Walter
Isaacson", cover: "book1", year: 2011, selected: false)),
            BookViewModel(book: Book(title: "HTML5 for Masterminds", author:
"J.D Gauchat", cover: "book2", year: 2017, selected: false)),
            BookViewModel(book: Book(title: "The Road Ahead", author: "Bill
Gates", cover: "book3", year: 1995, selected: false)),
            BookViewModel(book: Book(title: "The C Programming Language",
author: "Brian W. Kernighan", cover: "book4", year: 1988, selected:
false)),
            BookViewModel(book: Book(title: "Being Digital", author:
"Nicholas Negroponte", cover: "book5", year: 1996, selected: false)),
            BookViewModel(book: Book(title: "Only the Paranoid Survive",
author: "Andrew S. Grove", cover: "book6", year: 1999, selected: false)),
            BookViewModel(book: Book(title: "Accidental Empires", author:
"Robert X. Cringely", cover: "book7", year: 1996, selected: false)),
            BookViewModel(book: Book(title: "Bobby Fischer Teaches Chess",
author: "Bobby Fischer", cover: "book8", year: 1982, selected: false)),
            BookViewModel(book: Book(title: "New Guide to Science", author:
"Isaac Asimov", cover: "book9", year: 1993, selected: false)),
            BookViewModel(book: Book(title: "Christine", author: "Stephen
King", cover: "book10", year: 1983, selected: false)),
```

```
        BookViewModel(book: Book(title: "IT", author: "Stephen King",
cover: "book11", year: 1987, selected: false)),
        BookViewModel(book: Book(title: "Ending Aging", author: "Aubrey
de Grey", cover: "book12", year: 2007, selected: false)) ]
   }
}
```

Listing 10-3: Managing the app's settings from the model

In addition to our usual **userData** property, we have defined three **@AppStorage** properties. The **cornerSize** property stores a **Double** value that determines the corner radius of the book's cover, and the **showYear** and **showCover** properties store Boolean values that indicate whether the year and the cover should be shown or hidden.

Now, we can use these properties to configure the list of books. The following view includes a **List** view to display the books embedded in a **NavigationStack** view.

```
struct ContentView: View {
    @EnvironmentObject var appData: ApplicationData

    var body: some View {
        NavigationStack {
            List(appData.userData) { book in
                VStack {
                    HStack(alignment: .top) {
                        if appData.showCover {
                            Image(book.cover)
                                .resizable()
                                .scaledToFit()
                                .cornerRadius(appData.cornerSize)
                                .frame(width: 80, height: 100)
                        }
                        VStack(alignment: .leading, spacing: 2) {
                            Text(book.title).bold()
                            Text(book.author)
                            if appData.showYear {
                                Text(book.year).font(.caption)
                            }
                        }.padding(.top, 5)
                        Spacer()
                    }.padding([.leading, .trailing], 10)
                    .padding([.top, .bottom], 5)
                }
            }
            .navigationBarTitle("Books")
            .toolbar {
                ToolbarItem(placement: .navigationBarTrailing) {
                    NavigationLink("Settings", destination: {
                        SettingsView()
                    })
                }
            }
        }
    }
}
```

Listing 10-4: Adapting the interface to the app's settings

Each row on the list is configured according to the values in User Defaults. The **Image** view is only displayed when the value of the **showCover** property is **true**, the corner radius of the book's cover is determined by the value stored in the **cornerSize** property, and the year is shown depending on the value of the **showYear** property.

The navigation bar of the **ContentView** view includes a button on the right to open a view called **SettingsView**. This is the view where we allow the user to change the configuration.

```
struct SettingsView: View {
    @EnvironmentObject var appData: ApplicationData

    var body: some View {
        Form {
            Section {
                HStack(alignment: .top) {
                    Text("Corner Radius")
                        .padding(.top, 6)
                    VStack {
                        Slider(value: $appData.cornerSize, in: 0...30)
                        Image("nocover")
                            .resizable()
                            .scaledToFit()
                            .cornerRadius(appData.cornerSize)
                            .frame(width: 80, height: 100)
                    }
                }
            }
            Section {
                List {
                    Toggle("Show Picture", isOn: $appData.showCover)
                    Toggle("Show Year", isOn: $appData.showYear)
                }
            }
        }
        .navigationBarTitle("Settings")
    }
}
```

Listing 10-5: *Modifying the app's settings*

This view includes a **Slider** view to assign a value between 0 and 30 to the **cornerSize** property, and two **Toggle** views to toggle the values of the **showCover** and **showYear** properties. When the user modifies any of these values, the values in User Defaults are updated, and the views are redrawn, as shown in Figure 10-3, above.

 Do It Yourself: Download the book covers from our website and add them to the Asset Catalog. Create a Swift file called ApplicationData.swift for the model in Chapter 7, Listing 7-3. Update the **ApplicationData** class with the code in Listing 10-3 and the **ContentView** view with the code in Listing 10-4. Create a SwiftUI View file called SettingsView.swift for the view in Listing 10-5. Remember to inject the **ApplicationData** object into the environment for the app and the previews (Chapter 7, Listing 7-4). Run the application on the iPhone simulator. You should see the interface in Figure 10-3, left. Press the Settings button. In the Settings view, change the corner radius and turn the switches off (Figure 10-3, center). Press the Back button to see the changes on the interface (Figure 10-3, right).

Basic 10.2 Files

The User Defaults system is meant to be used to store single values for configuration. For large amounts of data, we must create our own files. To manage files and directories, the Foundation framework defines a class called **FileManager**. One object of this class is assigned to the app and from that instance we can create, delete, copy, and move files and directories in the storage space reserved for our application. The class offers the following type property to get a reference to this object.

default—This type property returns a reference to the app's `FileManager` object.

The `FileManager` class offers multiple properties and methods to manage files and directories. The following are the most frequently used.

urls(for: SearchPathDirectory, **in:** SearchPathDomainMask**)**—This method returns an array with the locations of a directory. The **for** argument is an enumeration with values that represent common system directories. The most frequently used are `documentDirectory` to represent the Documents directory, and `application-SupportDirectory` to reference the Application Support directory. And the **in** argument is an enumeration with values that determine the domain in which the files are located. The most frequently used is `userDomainMask` to represent the user's home directory.

createDirectory(at: URL, **withIntermediateDirectories:** Bool, **attributes:** Dictionary?**)**—This method creates a new directory. The **at** argument specifies the location of the directory, including its name, the **withIntermediateDirectories** argument indicates whether intermediate directories will also be created or not, and the **attributes** argument is a dictionary with values that determine the directory's arguments (e.g., ownership). The value `nil` sets the arguments by default, which are usually enough.

createFile(atPath: String, **contents:** Data?, **attributes:** Dictionary?**)**—This method creates a file. The **atPath** argument specifies the location of the file, including its name and extension, the **contents** argument represents the content of the file, and the **attributes** argument is a dictionary with values that determine the file's arguments (e.g., ownership). The value `nil` sets the arguments by default, which are usually enough.

contents(atPath: String**)**—This method returns the contents of the file at the path specified by the **atPath** argument. The value returned is an optional of type `Data`.

contentsOfDirectory(atPath: String**)**—This method returns an array with the paths of the files and directories inside the directory indicated by the **atPath** argument.

copyItem(atPath: String, **toPath:** String**)**—This method copies the file or directory at the path specified by the **at** argument to the path specified by the **to** argument.

moveItem(atPath: String, **toPath:** String**)**—This method moves the file or directory at the path specified by the **at** argument to the path specified by the **to** argument.

removeItem(atPath: String**)**—This method removes the file or directory at the path indicated by the **atPath** argument.

fileExists(atPath: String**)**—This method returns a Boolean value that determines if the file or the directory at the path specified by the **atPath** argument exists.

attributesOfItem(atPath: String**)**—This method returns a dictionary with the arguments of the file or directory at the location indicated by the **atPath** argument. The `FileManager` class includes constants to define the arguments, including `creationDate`, `modificationDate`, `size`, and `type`, among others.

Basic URLs and Paths

As in any other operating system, files are organized in directories (folders). There is a basic directory called *root*, which can contain other files and directories in a tree-like structure. To establish a route to reference a file, Apple systems adopt a conventional syntax that separates each component with a forward slash (/), starting with a single slash to indicate the root directory (e.g., /Pictures/Travels/Hawaii.png). This is called *path*, and it is used to access any file in the system. Paths are a simple way to access files but are not enough to identify the location of a file in the storage system. This is because in practice files are usually not stored in a single storage space, but in several units or even in remote servers. Following a long path to find a file also takes time and consumes resources. For these reasons, locations are always identified by URLs (Uniform Resource Locator). We have introduced URLs in Chapter 9 and use them to asynchronously downloading images from a server. They are created from the **URL** structure provided by the Foundation framework and can be used for multiple purposes, including referencing remote and local resources. The following are some of the initializers, properties and methods included by this structure to work with local files and directories.

URL(fileURLWithPath: String**)**—This initializer returns a **URL** object referencing a local file or directory. The **fileURLWithPath** argument is a string with the file's path.

URL(fileURLWithPath: String, **relativeTo:** URL**)**—This initializer returns a **URL** object referencing a local file or directory. The **fileURLWithPath** argument is a string with the file's path, and the **relativeTo** argument is a **URL** object referencing the base URL.

path—This property returns the path of a URL. It is a conditional of type **String**.

pathComponents—This property returns an array of **String** values that represent the components of a path extracted from a URL (the strings between forward slashes).

lastPathComponent—This property returns a string with the last component of a path extracted from a URL. It is usually used to get the file's name and extension.

pathExtension—This property returns a string with the extension of the path extracted from a URL. It is used to get the file's extension.

appendingPathComponent(String**)**—This method returns a new **URL** structure with the URL of the original object plus the component specified by the argument.

 IMPORTANT: The **FileManager** class includes methods to work with both paths and URLs. For example, there are two versions of the **createDirectory()** method, one to create the directory from a path and another from a URL. The methods that work with paths take care of converting the path into a URL and are usually easier to implement. For a complete list, visit our website and follow the links for this chapter.

(Basic) **Files and Directories**

Apple's operating systems allow users to create and access any files and directories they want, but applications are restricted to their own storage space to ensure that they do not interfere with each other. This means that we can only access the files and directories that belong to our application.

When the application is installed on the device, the system creates a group of standard directories that we can use to store our files. The most useful are the Documents directory, where we can store the user's files, and the Application Support directory, for files our app needs to create during run time that are not directly generated by the user. The location of these directories is not guaranteed, so we always must ask the system for the current URL that points to the directory or file we want to access. To get the location of common directories like Documents, the **FileManager** class includes the **urls()** method. This method requires two arguments. The first argument is an enumeration with values that represent different directories. There are several values available, including **documentDirectory** to reference the Documents directory and **applicationSupportDirectory** to reference the Application Support directory. The second argument is another enumeration with values that indicate the domain where the directory is located. The system organizes directories and files in separate domains depending on their intended usage. The domain where our app's files are stored is the User Domain, identified with the constant **userDomainMask**. In consequence, to get the URL of any of the directories generated for our app and create files to store the user's data, we must get a reference to the **FileManager** object and then call the **urls()** method with the values that represent the location we want to use.

Although we can read and create files from anywhere in the code, it is recommended to manage all our files from the model. The following is a simple model with an observable object to illustrate how to access the directories available for the application and how to create a file.

```
import SwiftUI
class ApplicationData: ObservableObject {
    func saveFile(name: String) {
        let manager = FileManager.default
        let documents = manager.urls(for: .documentDirectory,
in: .userDomainMask)
        let docURL = documents.first!

        let newFileURL = docURL.appendingPathComponent(name)
        let path = newFileURL.path
        manager.createFile(atPath: path, contents: nil, attributes: nil)
    }
}
```

Listing 10-6: *Accessing directories and creating files*

This model defines a method called **saveFile()** to create a file with the name specified by the argument. The method gets a reference to the **FileManager** object assigned to the application and then calls the **urls()** method on the manager to get the URL of the Documents directory. The **urls()** method returns an array of optional **URL** structures with all the possible locations of the directory. In the case of the Documents directory, the right value is always the first item in the array. Once we have this URL, we add the name of our file to it with the **appendingPathComponent()** method. This method adds a string to the end of the URL and takes care of including the necessary forward slashes to ensure that it is valid. Because we are working with paths, we get the URL's path from the **path** property and finally call the **createFile()** method to create the file. (If the file already exists, the method updates its content.)

The model is ready, now we must create the view. The idea is to create a simple project that later we can expand to add more functionality. Therefore, we are going to need a simple view to present the files and open a sheet to let the user add a new one, as shown below.

Figure 10-4: *Interface to create files*

The following is the code for the initial view.

```
struct ContentView: View {
    @EnvironmentObject var appData: ApplicationData
    @State private var openSheet: Bool = false

    var body: some View {
        NavigationStack {
            VStack {
                Text("No Files")
```

```
            Spacer()
        }.padding()
        .navigationBarTitle("Files")
        .toolbar {
            ToolbarItem(placement: .navigationBarTrailing) {
                Button("Add File") {
                    openSheet = true
                }
            }
        }
        .sheet(isPresented: $openSheet) {
            AddFileView()
        }
        }
    }
}
```

Listing 10-7: Opening a sheet to add files to the model

For the moment, the view only displays a message on the screen, but it provides a button in the navigation bar to open a sheet with a view called **AddFileView** that allows the user to create new files.

```
struct AddFileView: View {
    @EnvironmentObject var appData: ApplicationData
    @Environment(\.dismiss) var dismiss
    @State private var nameInput: String = ""

    var body: some View {
        VStack {
            HStack {
                Text("Name:")
                TextField("Insert File Name", text: $nameInput)
                    .textFieldStyle(.roundedBorder)
                    .autocapitalization(.none)
                    .disableAutocorrection(true)
            }.padding(.top, 25)
            HStack {
                Spacer()
                Button("Create") {
                    var fileName =
nameInput.trimmingCharacters(in: .whitespaces)
                    if !fileName.isEmpty {
                        fileName += ".txt"
                        appData.saveFile(name: fileName)
                        dismiss()
                    }
                }
            }
            Spacer()
        }.padding()
    }
}
```

Listing 10-8: Creating new files

This view includes a **TextField** view for the user to insert the name of the file and a **Button** view to create it. When the button is pressed, we trim the string to remove white spaces at the beginning and the end, add the ".txt" string to the name (adding an extension is not necessary), and then call the **saveFile()** method in the model to create the file. After this, the Documents directory designated to our app will contain an empty file with the name inserted by the user and the txt extension.

Do It Yourself: Create a Multiplatform project. Create a Swift file called ApplicationData.swift for the model in Listing 10-6. Update the **ContentView** view with the code in Listing 10-7. Create a SwiftUI View file called AddFileView.swift for the view in Listing 10-8. Remember to inject the **ApplicationData** object into the environment for the app and the previews (Chapter 7, Listing 7-4). Run the application on the iPhone simulator and press the Add File button. Insert the name of the file and press the Create button. The file is created, and the sheet is closed.

At the moment, the initial view only shows the message "No Files", but the purpose of this application is to allow the user to create multiple files and show them on the screen. For this purpose, the **FileManager** class includes methods to list the content of a directory. For instance, we can use the **contentsOfDirectory()** method to get an array of strings with the names of the files and directories in a specific path, store them in an array, and then present them on the screen with a **List** view. For this purpose, we need a model to store the names of the files along with an id, as we did for books in previous models, and a **@Published** property to provide the list to the views. The following is the new model for this project.

```
import SwiftUI

struct File: Identifiable {
    let id: UUID = UUID()
    var name: String
}
class ApplicationData: ObservableObject {
    @Published var listOfFiles: [File] = []

    var manager: FileManager
    var docURL: URL

    init() {
        manager = FileManager.default
        let documents = manager.urls(for: .documentDirectory,
in: .userDomainMask)
        docURL = documents.first!

        if let list = try? manager.contentsOfDirectory(atPath: docURL.path) {
            for name in list {
                let newFile = File(name: name)
                listOfFiles.append(newFile)
            }
        }
    }
    func saveFile(name: String) {
        let newFileURL = docURL.appendingPathComponent(name)
        let path = newFileURL.path
        manager.createFile(atPath: path, contents: nil, attributes: nil)
        if !listOfFiles.contains(where: { $0.name == name}) {
            listOfFiles.append(File(name: name))
        }
    }
}
```

Listing 10-9: Managing the app's files

The first structure, called **File**, provides the model. It conforms to the **Identifiable** protocol and includes the corresponding **id** property to identify each value, and a property called **name** to store the file's name. Next, we define a property to store a reference to the **FileManager** object assigned to the application and another to store the URL of the Documents directory. In the initializer, we get a reference to the **FileManager** object with the **default** property and assign it to the **manager** property. Then, we get the URL of the Documents directory with the **urls()** method and assigns it to the **docURL** property. After the properties are initialized, we get the list of files in the directory with the **contentsOfDirectory()** method. This method returns an array of strings with the name of the files, so we create a loop, initialize an instance of the **File** structure with each name, and add them to the **listOfFiles** array. Notice that the method throws errors, so we use the **try?** keyword to handle them and only store the name of the files if the value returned is not **nil**.

The **saveFile()** method is the same as before, but after creating a new file we now check if the name of the file already exists in the **listOfFiles** property and only add an instance of the **File** structure to the array if there isn't already a file with that name.

After the **ApplicationData** structure is initialized, the **listOfFiles** property contains the names of all the files in the directory, so we can show them to the user.

```
struct ContentView: View {
    @EnvironmentObject var appData: ApplicationData
    @State private var openSheet: Bool = false

    var body: some View {
        NavigationStack {
            VStack {
                List {
                    ForEach(appData.listOfFiles) { file in
                        Text(file.name)
                    }
                }.listStyle(.plain)
            }.padding()
            .navigationBarTitle("Files")
            .toolbar {
                ToolbarItem(placement: .navigationBarTrailing) {
                    Button("Add File") {
                        openSheet = true
                    }
                }
            }
            .sheet(isPresented: $openSheet) {
                AddFileView()
            }
        }
    }
}
```

Listing 10-10: *Listing the files created by the user*

The **List** view includes a **ForEach** view that lists the values of the **listOfFiles** property. Each row includes the name of a file, as shown below.

Figure 10-5: *List of files*

Do It Yourself: Update the ApplicationData.swift file with the code in Listing 10-9 and the **ContentView** view with the code in Listing 10-10. Run the application on the iPhone simulator. Press the Add File button to add a file. Insert the name of the file and press the Create button. You should see on the screen the list of all the files you have created, as shown in Figure 10-5, right.

The same way we create a file, we can create a directory. The method to create a directory is called **createDirectory()**. The method takes three values: the path of the new directory (including its name), a Boolean value that indicates if we want to create all the directories included in the path that do not exist (in case the path includes directories we have not created yet), and the directory's arguments. This method throws an error if it cannot complete the task, so we must handle the error with the **try** keyword. Using this method, we can expand our project to store files in two directories called *original* and *archived*. The original folder will contain the files created by the user, and the archived folder will contain the files the user decides to archive. The following is the model we need for this application.

```swift
class ApplicationData: ObservableObject {
    @Published var listOfFiles: [Int:[File]] = [:]
    @Published var currentDirectory: Int

    var manager: FileManager
    var docURL: URL
    let directories = ["original", "archived"]

    init() {
        listOfFiles = [0: [], 1: []]
        currentDirectory = 0
        manager = FileManager.default
        docURL = manager.urls(for: .documentDirectory,
in: .userDomainMask).first!

        for (index, directory) in directories.enumerated() {
            let newDirectoryURL = docURL.appendingPathComponent(directory)
            let path = newDirectoryURL.path
            do {
                try manager.createDirectory(atPath: path,
withIntermediateDirectories: false, attributes: nil)
            } catch {
                print("The directory already exists")
            }
            if let list = try? manager.contentsOfDirectory(atPath: path) {
                for name in list {
                    let newFile = File(name: name)
                    listOfFiles[index]?.append(newFile)
                }
            }
        }
    }
    func saveFile(name: String) {
        let newFileURL = docURL.appendingPathComponent("\(directories[0])/\
(name)")
        let path = newFileURL.path
        manager.createFile(atPath: path, contents: nil, attributes: nil)

        if let exists = listOfFiles[0]?.contains(where: { $0.name ==
name }) {
            if !exists {
                let newFile = File(name: name)
                listOfFiles[0]?.append(newFile)
            }
        }
```

```
        }
    }
```

Listing 10-11: Working with custom directories

This model stores two lists of files, one for the original directory and another for the archive directory. For this purpose, we turned the **listOfFiles** property from an array into a dictionary. The items in the dictionary are identified with an integer and their values are arrays of strings. The item with the 0 key is going to contain an array with the names of the files in the original directory, and the item with the 1 key is going to contain an array with the names of the files in the archived directory. To know which directory the user is currently working on, we define a new **@Published** property called **currentDirectory**, and to store the names of the directories, we define an array called **directories** with two strings: "original" and "archived".

In the structure's initializer, we initialize the **listOfFiles** dictionary with two items, 0 and 1, and empty arrays. We also assign the value 0 to the **currentDirectory** property to select the original directory by default, and then initialize the rest of the properties. Finally, we load the files for each directory with a **for in** loop; first the original (0) and then the archived (1).

The **saveFile()** method stores the files as always, but the path now includes the name of the original directory, so the new files are always stored in that folder. We also have to contemplate the directory when we check whether the file already exists or not (**listOfFiles[0]?.contains(where: { $0.name == name })**).

The view must provide a way for the user to switch between one directory and another. (Although at this time the application doesn't provide a way to assign files to the archived directory.) For this example, we have decided to use a segmented picker with two buttons.

```
struct ContentView: View {
    @EnvironmentObject var appData: ApplicationData
    @State private var openSheet: Bool = false

    var body: some View {
        NavigationStack {
            VStack {
                Picker("", selection: $appData.currentDirectory) {
                    ForEach(0..<appData.directories.count, id: \.self) { index in
                        Text(appData.directories[index])
                            .tag(index)
                    }
                }.padding([.leading, .trailing], 8)
                .pickerStyle(.segmented)
                List {
                    ForEach(appData.listOfFiles[appData.currentDirectory] ??
[]) { file in
                        Text(file.name)
                    }
                }.listStyle(.plain)
            }
            .navigationBarTitle("Files")
            .toolbar {
                ToolbarItem(placement: .navigationBarTrailing) {
                    Button("Add File") {
                        openSheet = true
                    }.disabled(appData.currentDirectory != 0 ? true : false)
                }
            }
            .sheet(isPresented: $openSheet) {
                AddFileView()
            }
        }
    }
```

```
    }
}
```

Listing 10-12: *Listing files from two directories*

The **ContentView** view in Listing 10-12 includes a **Picker** view with the values in the **directories** property ("original" and "archived"). When the user selects one or the other, the value of the **currentDirectory** changes, and this tells our model which directory the user is currently working on. To create the list of files, we read again the value of this property. If the value is 0, we list the files of the original directory, but if the value is 1, we list the files of the archived directory.

One thing we must contemplate when working with dictionaries, is that they return an optional. Therefore, the **ForEach** view won't work unless we provide an alternative value. In this case, we use the nil-coalescing operator (**??**) to create the list with an empty array if the value of the **currentDirectory** property does not exist in the dictionary (it is different than 0 or 1).

Because we want the user to be able to add new files only to the original directory, we applied the **disabled()** modifier to the Add File button in the navigation bar. If the user is working on the archived directory, the button is disabled, as shown below.

Figure 10-6: *Files from two directories*

 Do It Yourself: Update the **ApplicationData** class with the code in Listing 10-11 and the **ContentView** view with the code in Listing 10-12. Remove the application from the simulator to erase the files created with the previous example. Run the app again. Create new files. Press the tab buttons to switch between directories.

Now, we can allow the user to archive files and delete them. For this, we need to move files from the original directory to the archived directory and remove them from storage. The **FileManager** class includes the **moveItem()** and **removeItem()** methods for this purpose. The following are the methods we need to add to our model to be able to move and remove files from the view.

```
func deleteFile(name: String) {
   let fileURL = docURL.appendingPathComponent("\
(directories[currentDirectory])/\(name)")
   do {
      try manager.removeItem(atPath: fileURL.path)
      listOfFiles[currentDirectory]?.removeAll(where: { $0.name ==
name} )
   } catch {
      print("File was not removed")
   }
}
func moveToArchived(name: String) {
   let origin = docURL.appendingPathComponent("\(directories[0])/\
(name)")
```

```
        let destination = docURL.appendingPathComponent("\(directories[1])/\
(name)")
        if !manager.fileExists(atPath: destination.path) {
            do {
                try manager.moveItem(atPath: origin.path, toPath:
destination.path)
                listOfFiles[0]?.removeAll(where: { $0.name == name} )
                listOfFiles[1]?.append(File(name: name))
            } catch {
                print("File was not moved")
            }
        }
    }
}
```

Listing 10-13: Moving and deleting files

The first method is called **deleteFile()** and it receives the name of the file to remove. Because the user can only delete files from the directory in which is currently working, we use the value of the **currentDirectory** property to define the file's URL. With this URL, we call the **removeItem()** method on the **FileManager** object to delete the file. If the operation is successful, we also remove the name of the file from the array corresponding to the current directory with the **removeAll(where:)** method, so the file is removed from the array and the screen.

The next method is called **moveToArchived()**. The purpose of this method is to move the file selected by the user from the original directory to the archived directory. For this purpose, we define two URLs, one to indicate the current location of the file (**\(directories[0])/\ (name)**) and another to indicate where the file is going to be created and with what name (**\ (directories[1])/\(name)**). Before doing anything, we check if the file already exists at the destination with the **fileExists()** method. If the file doesn't exist, we use those two URLs to call the **moveItem()** method on the **FileManager** object and move it. If the operation is successful, we still must update the information in the model. First, we remove the file from the array of the original directory (0) with the **removeAll(where:)** method. This removes all the strings in the array that are equal to the name of the file we are moving. And second, we add the file to the array corresponding to the archived directory, so the name appears on the right folder.

The view now needs to provide the tools for the user to move and remove each file. For this example, we have decided to generate the rows with a custom view and include two buttons per row, one to move the file to the archived folder and another to delete it.

```
struct ContentView: View {
    @EnvironmentObject var appData: ApplicationData
    @State private var openSheet: Bool = false

    var body: some View {
        NavigationStack {
            VStack {
                Picker("", selection: $appData.currentDirectory) {
                    ForEach(0..<appData.directories.count, id: \.self) { index
in
                        Text(appData.directories[index]).tag(index)
                    }
                }.pickerStyle(.segmented)
                List {
                    ForEach(appData.listOfFiles[appData.currentDirectory] ??
[]) { file in
                        RowFile(file: file)
                    }
                }.listStyle(.plain)
            }
            .navigationBarTitle("Files")
```

```
            .toolbar {
               ToolbarItem(placement: .navigationBarTrailing) {
                  Button("Add File") {
                     openSheet = true
                  }.disabled(appData.currentDirectory != 0 ? true : false)
               }
            }
            .sheet(isPresented: $openSheet) {
               AddFileView()
            }
         }
      }
   }
}
struct RowFile: View {
   @EnvironmentObject var appData: ApplicationData
   let file: File

   var body: some View {
      HStack {
         Text(file.name)
         Spacer()
         if appData.currentDirectory == 0 {
            Button(action: {
               appData.moveToArchived(name: file.name)
            }, label: {
               Image(systemName: "folder")
                  .font(.body)
                  .foregroundColor(Color.green)
            }).buttonStyle(.plain)
         }
         Button(action: {
            appData.deleteFile(name: file.name)
         }, label: {
            Image(systemName: "trash")
               .font(.body)
               .foregroundColor(Color.red)
         }).buttonStyle(.plain)
      }
   }
}
```

Listing 10-14: Adding tools to move and delete files

Nothing changes in the view, except that instead of showing the name of the file with a **Text** view, we now create a **RowFile** view to include the buttons. The buttons are created with SF Symbols, one that represents a folder and another that represents a trash can. The button with the image of a folder calls the **moveToArchived()** method in the model to move the file to the archived directory, but it is only displayed when the current directory is original (**currentDirectory == 0**). On the other hand, the button with the image of a trash can is displayed in both directories and calls the **deleteFile()** method in the model to delete the file. Notice that we declare the styles for the buttons as **plain**. This makes the buttons responsive when they are inserted in a row (the buttons have precedence over the selection of the row).

Figure 10-7: Buttons to move and delete a file

Do It Yourself: Add the methods in Listing 10-13 to the `ApplicationData` class. Update the ContentView.swift file with the code in Listing 10-14. Run the application on the iPhone simulator. Press the Add File button to add some files and then tap the folder icon on one of the rows. The file should be moved to the archived folder. Press the trash can icon to remove a file.

<u>Medium</u> **File Attributes**

Some applications need to know more than the name of the file. The **FileManager** class offers the **attributesOfItem()** method to get the file's attributes, such as the date the file was created or its size. The method returns a dictionary with predefined keys to identify each value. There are several constants available we can use as keys. The most frequently used are **creationDate** (the date the file was created), **modificationDate** (last time it was modified), **size**, and **type**. The following method shows how to read these keys to get the attributes of the file selected by the user.

```
func getDetails(file: UUID) -> (String, String, String, String) {
    var values = ("", "", "", "")
    if let file = listOfFiles[currentDirectory]?.first(where: { $0.id ==
file }) {
        let fileURL = docURL.appendingPathComponent("\
(directories[currentDirectory])/\(file.name)")
        let filePath = fileURL.path

        if manager.fileExists(atPath: filePath) {
            if let attributes = try? manager.attributesOfItem(atPath:
filePath) {
                let type = attributes[.type] as! FileAttributeType
                let size = attributes[.size] as! Int
                let date = attributes[.creationDate] as! Date
                if type != FileAttributeType.typeDirectory {
                    values.0 = file.name
                    values.1 = fileURL.pathExtension
                    values.2 = String(size)
                    values.3 = date.formatted(date: .abbreviated,
time: .omitted)
                }
            }
        }
    }
    return values
}
```

Listing 10-15: Reading the file's attributes

The **getDetails()** method receives a **UUID** value to identify the file the user wants to read. From this value, the method gets the name of the file and builds the path. Once we get the path to the file, we are able to call the **attributesOfItem()** method to read its attributes. The method returns the values in a dictionary, but they are of type **Any**, so we must cast them to the right types. For instance, the **type** value must be converted into a **FileAttributeType** structure, the **size** into an **Int**, and the **creationDate** into a **Date** structure. The **File-AttributeType** structure determines the resource's type. The structure includes properties to represent different types of resources. The most frequently used are **typeRegular** to represent files and **typeDirectory** to represent directories. By reading these properties, we can determine if the item is a file or a directory. This is useful when our application allows the user to create folders. If the item is a file, we assign the attributes to a tuple and return it.

To show the file's attributes to the user, we have decided to create an additional view that opens when the user taps on a file on the list. We call it **FileDetailsView**.

```
struct FileDetailsView: View {
    @EnvironmentObject var appData: ApplicationData
    let file: UUID

    var body: some View {
        let values = appData.getDetails(file: file)
        return VStack {
            HStack {
                Text("Name:")
                    .frame(width: 80, alignment: .trailing)
                Text(values.0)
                    .frame(minWidth: 0, maxWidth: .infinity,
alignment: .leading)
            }
            HStack {
                Text("Extension:")
                    .frame(width: 80, alignment: .trailing)
                Text(values.1)
                    .frame(minWidth: 0, maxWidth: .infinity,
alignment: .leading)
            }
            HStack {
                Text("Size:")
                    .frame(width: 80, alignment: .trailing)
                Text(values.2)
                    .frame(minWidth: 0, maxWidth: .infinity,
alignment: .leading)
            }
            HStack {
                Text("Date:")
                    .frame(width: 80, alignment: .trailing)
                Text(values.3)
                    .frame(minWidth: 0, maxWidth: .infinity,
alignment: .leading)
            }
            Spacer()
        }.padding()
        .navigationBarTitle("Details")
    }
}
struct FileDetailsView_Previews: PreviewProvider {
    static var previews: some View {
        FileDetailsView(file: UUID())
            .environmentObject(ApplicationData())
    }
}
```

Listing 10-16: Showing the file's attributes

This view receives the file's id from the list and then calls the **getDetails()** method in the model with that value. The tuple returned is assigned to the **values** constant, and finally the constant is used to show the attributes to the user (**values.0** is the name, **values.1** is the extension, **values.2** is the size, and **values.3** is the date).

Of course, to open this view we must embed each row in a **NavigationLink** view that creates an instance of the **FilesDetailsView** structure with the file's id. The following are the modifications we must introduce to the **List** view in the **ContentView** view for this purpose.

```
List {
    ForEach(appData.listOfFiles[appData.currentDirectory] ?? []) { file in
        NavigationLink(destination: {
            FileDetailsView(file: file.id)
```

```
        } , label: {
          RowFile(file: file)
        })
      }
    }
}.listStyle(.plain)
```

Listing 10-17: Opening the details view

Notice that we send the value of the **id** property to the **FileDetailsView** view to work with the file's id, not its name. The result is shown below.

Figure 10-8: Details view with the file's attributes

 Do It Yourself: Add the method in Listing 10-15 to the **ApplicationData** class. Create a SwiftUI View file called FileDetailsView.swift for the view in Listing 10-16. Update the **List** view in the **ContentView** view with the code of Listing 10-17. Run the application on the iPhone simulator. Tap on a file. You should see the attributes of that file on the screen, as shown in Figure 10-8.

Basic File Content

Storage systems, like hard drives and solid-state drives, store information the only way a computer knows, as a series of ones and zeros. Therefore, the information we want to store in files has to be converted into a stream of Bytes that can be later turned back into the original values. For this purpose, the Foundation framework includes the **Data** structure.

Although we can work directly with a **Data** structure, most frameworks provided by Apple include tools to convert our data into **Data** structures. For instance, to work with images, the UIKit framework includes the **UIImage** class. This class can convert an image into data, and create an image from data, strings, or other images. Once we have this value, we can turn it into an **Image** view with the **Image(uiImage: UIImage)** initializer introduced before. The following are some of the initializers provided by the class.

UIImage(named: String)—This initializer creates an object that contains the image from the file specified by the **named** argument. The argument is a string with the name of the file or the image set in the Asset Catalog.

UIImage(data: Data, **scale:** CGFloat)—This initializer creates an object that contains an image generated from the data provided by the **data** argument and with an associated scale specified by the **scale** argument. If the last argument is ignored, the image is assigned a scale of 1.

UIImage(contentsOfFile: String)—This initializer creates an object that contains the image stored in the file indicated by the **contentsOfFile** argument. The argument is a string with a path that determines the location of the file.

UIImage(cgImage: CGImage, **scale:** CGFloat, **orientation:** Orientation)—This initializer creates an object that contains an image generated from a **CGImage** object and with a scale and orientation defined by the arguments. The `CGImage` class is defined by the Core Graphics framework to store a low-level representation of an image, and the **orientation** argument is an enumeration with the values **up**, **down**, **left**, **right**, **upMirrored**, **downMirrored**, **leftMirrored**, and **rightMirrored**.

The `UIImage` class includes properties and methods to get information about the image and process it. The following are the most frequently used.

size—This property returns a `CGSize` value with the size of the image.

scale—This property returns a `CGFloat` value with the scale of the image.

imageOrientation—This property returns a value that identifies the image's orientation. It is an enumeration called **Orientation**. The values available are **up**, **down**, **left**, **right**, **upMirrored**, **downMirrored**, **leftMirrored**, and **rightMirrored**.

cgImage—This property returns the image in the Core Graphic format. It is of type `CGImage`, a Core Graphic data type.

To convert an image into data, the `UIImage` class includes the following methods.

pngData()—This method converts the image into raw data in the PNG format and returns a `Data` structure with it.

jpegData(compressionQuality: CGFloat)—This method converts the image into raw data in the JPEG format and returns a `Data` structure with it. The **compressionQuality** argument is a value between 0.0 and 1.0 to determine the level of compression.

The process to load an image from file is simple. Once we get the data with the `contents()` method provided by the `FileManager` class, we convert it into an image with the `UIImage(data:)` initializer. On the contrary, storing an image in a file requires a few more steps. The image must be loaded with a `UIImage` object, then the object must be converted into a `Data` structure with the `pngData()` or `jpegData()` methods, and finally stored in a file with the `createFile()` method of the `FileManager` object implemented before. This method creates a file if it doesn't exist or updates its content otherwise, so we can use it to store different images. In the following example, we implement it to store the image selected by the user. If the user selects another image later, we just replace the old image in the file with the new one. As always, most of the process is performed by the model, as shown next.

```
import SwiftUI
class ApplicationData: ObservableObject {
    @Published var imageInFile: UIImage?
    var manager: FileManager
    var docURL: URL
    let listPictures = ["spot1", "spot2", "spot3"]

    init() {
        manager = FileManager.default
        docURL = manager.urls(for: .documentDirectory,
in: .userDomainMask).first!

        let fileURL = docURL.appendingPathComponent("imagedata.dat")
        let filePath = fileURL.path
        if manager.fileExists(atPath: filePath) {
            if let content = manager.contents(atPath: filePath) {
                imageInFile = UIImage(data: content)
            }
        }
    }
}
```

```
func saveFile(namePicture: String) {
    let image = UIImage(named: namePicture)
    if let imageData = image?.pngData() {
        let fileURL = docURL.appendingPathComponent("imagedata.dat")
        let filePath = fileURL.path
        if manager.createFile(atPath: filePath, contents: imageData,
attributes: nil) {
            imageInFile = image
        }
    }
}
}
```

Listing 10-18: Loading and saving an image

This model includes a **@Published** property called **imageInFile** to store the image loaded from file and a method to store a new one. The initializer defines the **manager** and **docURL** properties, as always, and then it checks if there is a file called imagedata.dat (the name and extension could be anything we want). If the file exists, we get its content with the **contents()** method of the **FileManager** object. This method returns a **Data** structure with the data to reconstruct the image, so we create a **UIImage** object with it and assign it to the **imageInFile** property to update the views.

The model also includes an array with the names of three images: spot1, spot2, and spot3. These are the images we are going to allow the user to select to store in the file. When the user selects one of these images, the **saveFile()** method in the model is called. In this method, we create a new **UIImage** object with the image selected by the user and then convert it into a **Data** structure with the **pngData()** method. If the method is successful, we use the **createFile()** method of the **FileManager** object to create the file or update it with the new image if already exists. Notice that the **Data** structure created from the image is assigned to the **contents** argument to provide the content to store in the file. If the file is successfully created or updated, we assign the **UIImage** object to the **imageInFile** property to update the views.

The views are simple. The initial view displays the image stored in the **imageInFile** property (the current image in the file), and it allows the user to open a sheet to select another one.

```
struct ContentView: View {
    @EnvironmentObject var appData: ApplicationData
    @State private var openSheet: Bool = false

    var body: some View {
        VStack {
            Image(uiImage: appData.imageInFile ?? UIImage(named:
"nopicture")!)
                .resizable()
                .scaledToFill()
                .frame(minWidth: 0, maxWidth: .infinity, minHeight: 0,
maxHeight: .infinity)
                .onTapGesture {
                    openSheet = true
                }
        }.edgesIgnoringSafeArea(.all)
        .sheet(isPresented: $openSheet) {
            SelectPictureView()
        }
    }
}
```

Listing 10-19: Showing the image in the file

The **Image** view in Listing 10-19 is created from the **UIImage** value stored in the **imageInFile** property (the image stored in the file). Notice that the **UIImage** initializer always returns an optional, so we must provide an alternative image in case the file can't be loaded, or it doesn't exist. For this purpose, we use the nil-coalescing operator (**??**) to load the image nopicture from the Asset Catalog.

The **Image** view includes the **onTapGesture()** modifier to open a sheet when the image is tapped by the user. In the view opened by the sheet, we are going to show to the user three images to select from. We call this view **SelectPictureView**.

```
struct SelectPictureView: View {
   @EnvironmentObject var appData: ApplicationData
   @Environment(\.dismiss) var dismiss

   var body: some View {
      VStack {
         ScrollView(.horizontal, showsIndicators: true) {
            HStack(spacing: 15) {
               ForEach(appData.listPictures, id: \.self) { name in
                  ZStack(alignment: .bottom) {
                     Image(name)
                        .resizable()
                        .scaledToFit()
                        .frame(width: 160)
                     Button(action: {
                        appData.saveFile(namePicture: name)
                        dismiss()
                     }, label: {
                        Text("Select Picture")
                           .foregroundColor(Color.white)
                     }).buttonStyle(.borderedProminent)
                        .offset(x: 0, y: -15)
                  }
               }
            }
         }.padding(.top, 25)
         Spacer()
      }.padding()
   }
}
```

Listing 10-20: Displaying a list of images for the user to select

The images are inside a horizontal **ScrollView** view and are embedded in a **ZStack** to be able to display a button on top that the user can tap to select the image. When the button is pressed, we call the **saveFile()** method in the model with the name of the selected image and that image is stored in the file. The result is shown below.

Figure 10-9: Interface to select and store an image

Do It Yourself: Create a Multiplatform project. Download the nopicture, spot1, spot2, and spot3 images from our website and add them to the Asset Catalog. Create a Swift file called ApplicationData.swift for the model in Listing 10-18. Update the **ContentView** view with the code in Listing 10-19. Create a SwiftUI View file called SelectPictureView.swift for the view in Listing 10-20. Remember to inject the **ApplicationData** object into the environment for the app and the previews (Listing 7-4). Run the application on the iPhone simulator. You should see the image nopicture on the screen. Tap on the image and select another one from the list. Stop the application from Xcode and run it again. You should see the selected image on the screen, as shown in Figure 10-9.

The size of photographs taken by the camera or images loaded from the Photo Library are often too large for processing and storage. Storing these images in files and databases can consume too much storage space and memory. The **UIImage** class includes the following methods to optimize an image and reduce its size.

preparingThumbnail(of: CGSize**)**—This method returns a new image created from the original and with a size determined by the **of** argument.

prepareThumbnail(of: CGSize, **completionHandler:** Closure**)**—This method creates a new image from the original and calls a closure with the result. The **of** argument determines the size of the image. The closure receives a **UIImage** object with the result.

preparingForDisplay()—This method decompresses the original image and returns a new one ready to be shown on the screen.

prepareForDisplay(completionHandler: Closure**)**—This method decompress the original image and calls a closure when the process is over. The closure receives a **UIImage** object with the result.

The process of preparing an image for display is often only necessary in high-performance applications, but reducing the size of an image is a very common requirement. For example, we can modify our example to store a thumbnail instead of the full image.

```
func saveFile(namePicture: String) {
    guard let image = UIImage(named: namePicture) else {
        return
    }
    guard let thumbnail = image.preparingThumbnail(of: CGSize(width: 100,
height: 100)) else {
        return
    }
    if let imageData = thumbnail.pngData() {
        let fileURL = docURL.appendingPathComponent("imagedata.dat")
        let filePath = fileURL.path
        if manager.createFile(atPath: filePath, contents: imageData,
attributes: nil) {
            imageInFile = thumbnail
        }
    }
}
```

Listing 10-21: Reducing the size of an image

The process performed by the **saveFile()** method is the same, but before we convert the image to data and store it in the file, we reduce its size to 100 points, minimizing the use of memory and storage space.

Figure 10-10: Image reduced

Do It Yourself: Update the `saveFile()` method in the `ApplicationData` class with the code in Listing 10-21. To see the image at its current size, remove the `resizable()` and `scaledToFill()` modifiers in the `ContentView` view.

IMPORTANT: The `UIImage` class also defines two asynchronous methods to prepare an image: `byPreparingForDisplay()` and `byPreparingThumbnail(ofSize: CGSize)`. The advantage of using asynchronous methods is that the system can perform other tasks while the image is being processed.

Besides the `UIImage` class, there are other classes and structures available in Apple's frameworks that can turn values into a `Data` structure for storage. For instance, the `String` structure includes a method that turns a string into data an also an initializer that can get back the string from a `Data` structure.

String(data: Data, encoding: Encoding)—This initializer creates a `String` value with the text in the `Data` structure provided by the **data** argument. The **encoding** argument is a structure that determines the type of encoding used to generate the string. The encoding usually depends on the language the text was written in. The most frequently used are the structures returned by the properties `utf8` and `ascii`.

data(using: Encoding, allowLossyConversion: Bool)—This method returns a `Data` structure containing the string from a `String` value. The **using** argument is a structure that determines the type of encoding used to generate the string. The encoding usually depends on the language the text was written in. The most frequently used are the structures returned by the properties `utf8` and `ascii`. The **allowLossyConversion** argument determines the precision of the conversion.

The `String` structure also includes a convenient method to turn a string into data and store it in a file, all at once.

write(to: URL, atomically: Bool, encoding: Encoding)—This method converts a string into a `Data` structure and stores it in the file located at the URL specified by the **to** argument. The **atomically** argument determines if we want the data to be stored in an auxiliary file first to ensure that the original file is not corrupted (recommended). And the **encoding** argument is a structure that determines the type of encoding used to generate the string. The encoding usually depends on the language the text was written in. The most frequently used are the structures returned by the properties `utf8` and `ascii`.

To store text in a file and read it back, we must follow the same procedure used for images. We must convert the string to data and then the data back to a string. The following example shows how to do this with the text inserted by the user in a `TextEditor` view. The difference from previous examples is that these types of applications usually store the text as the user types or deletes a character, which means that we must save the file each time a new value is assigned to the `@Published` property. For this purpose, we can use property observers, as we do in the following model.

```
import SwiftUI

class ApplicationData: ObservableObject {
   @Published var textInFile: String = "" {
      didSet {
         if let textData = textInFile.data(using: .utf8,
allowLossyConversion: true) {
            let fileURL = docURL.appendingPathComponent("textdata.dat")
            let filePath = fileURL.path
            manager.createFile(atPath: filePath, contents: textData,
attributes: nil)
         }
      }
   }
   var manager: FileManager
   var docURL: URL

   init() {
      manager = FileManager.default
      docURL = manager.urls(for: .documentDirectory,
in: .userDomainMask).first!
      let fileURL = docURL.appendingPathComponent("textdata.dat")
      let filePath = fileURL.path
      if manager.fileExists(atPath: filePath) {
         if let content = manager.contents(atPath: filePath) {
            if let text = String(data: content, encoding: .utf8) {
               textInFile = text
            }
         }
      }
   }
}
```

Listing 10-22: Storing text in a file

As we have seen in Chapter 3, property observers are methods that are executed when a value is assigned to the property (see Chapter 3, Listing 3-45). In this example, we have implemented the **didSet()** method to the **textInFile** property to store the value of the property in a file every time a new one is assigned to it. In the method, we convert the string into a **Data** structure with the **data()** method and then store the data in the file with the **createFile()** method of the **FileManager** object, as we did before for images.

The model's initializer is also similar. We first look for a file with the name textdata.dat. If the file exists, we get its content with the **contents()** method, convert the data into a string with the **String(data:)** initializer, and assign the result to the **textInFile** property to update the views.

The view for this example must include the **TextEditor** view to show the text currently stored in the file and allow the user to change it.

```
struct ContentView: View {
   @EnvironmentObject var appData: ApplicationData
   @State private var inputText: String = ""

   var body: some View {
      GroupBox("Editor") {
         TextEditor(text: $appData.textInFile)
            .cornerRadius(10)
      }.padding()
   }
}
```

Listing 10-23: Editing the text stored in a file

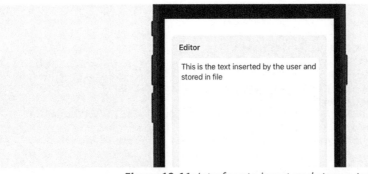

Figure 10-11: Interface to insert and store a text

 Do It Yourself: Create a Multiplatform project. Create a Swift file called ApplicationData.swift for the model in Listing 10-22. Update the `ContentView` view with the code in Listing 10-23. Remember to inject the `ApplicationData` object into the environment for the app and the previews (Chapter 7, Listing 7-4). Run the application on the iPhone simulator. Type a text. Stop the application from Xcode and run it again. You should see the same text on the screen.

(Medium) Bundle

In previous examples, we have worked with files created by the user, but sometimes we need to access files added to our project during development. The problem is the app's files, code, and resources are not stored in a single directory; they are encapsulated in a bundle. Bundles are directories assigned to each application by the system. They create a hierarchical structure to organize all the app's files and resources.

To create and manage bundles, Foundation includes the `Bundle` class. The class offers properties and methods to work with bundles and get their location, including a type property that returns a reference to the bundle created by default for our application.

main—This type property returns a reference to the app's bundle.

bundleURL—This property returns a `URL` structure with the bundle's URL.

bundlePath—This property returns a string with the bundle's path.

Because we are not able to determine the location of our app's files and resources during development, every time we want to access these files from code, we must get their URLs from the `Bundle` object. The class provides the following methods for this purpose.

url(forResource: String?, **withExtension:** String?**)**—This method returns a `URL` structure with the URL of a file or directory inside the bundle. The first argument specifies the name of the file or directory we are looking for, and the **withExtension** argument specifies the extension.

path(forResource: String?, **ofType:** String?**)**—This method returns the path of a file or directory inside the bundle. The first argument specifies the name of the file or directory we are looking for, and the **ofType** argument specifies the extension.

We frequently have to use the `Bundle` object in professional applications to access files that are required for some services, like databases, for example, but we can also take advantage of this object to load files with initial data or to restore the app's initial state. The following example illustrates how this process works by loading a single file with some content. The app loads a text file called quote.txt from the bundle as soon as the application is launched. The file must be added to the project during development by dragging it from Finder to the Navigator Area.

```
import SwiftUI
class ApplicationData: ObservableObject {
   @Published var textInFile: String = ""

   init() {
      let manager = FileManager.default
      let bundle = Bundle.main
      if let path = bundle.path(forResource: "quote", ofType: "txt") {
         if let data = manager.contents(atPath: path) {
            if let message = String(data: data, encoding: .utf8) {
               textInFile = message
            }
         }
      } else {
         textInFile = "File Not Found"
      }
   }
}
```

Listing 10-24: *Loading a file from the bundle*

The model's initializer in Listing 10-24 gets a reference to the app's bundle and then finds the path for the quote.txt file with the **path()** method. After we get the path, we can read the file as we did before. As always, the value is stored in the **@Published** property to update the views.

```
struct ContentView: View {
   @EnvironmentObject var appData: ApplicationData

   var body: some View {
      VStack {
         Text(appData.textInFile)
            .lineLimit(nil)
            .padding(15)
            .frame(minWidth: 0, maxWidth: .infinity)
            .background(Color(white: 0.8))
         Spacer()
      }.padding()
   }
}
```

Listing 10-25: *Displaying the text stored in a file in the bundle*

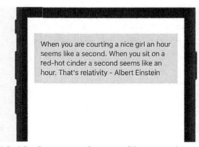

Figure 10-12: *Content of a text file stored in the bundle*

 Do It Yourself: Create a Multiplatform project. Create a Swift file called ApplicationData.swift for the model in Listing 10-24. Update the **ContentView** view with the code in Listing 10-25. Download the quote.txt file from our website or create your own and add it to the project. Remember to inject the **ApplicationData** object into the environment for the app and the previews (Chapter 7, Listing 7-4). Run the application on the iPhone simulator. You should see the text loaded from the file on the screen, as shown in Figure 10-12.

Documents

The **FileManager** class provides the tools we need to create and store files in the storage space designated by the system for our application, but sometimes users need to share that information with other applications. For this purpose, Apple systems allow users to create and share documents. Documents are containers that can process and store a specific type of information in a file. They can be stored on the device and shared with other apps, sent to servers, or stored in iCloud to make them available to other devices.

Enabling apps to create, edit, and share documents is so important these days that SwiftUI includes tools to create a Document app (an application with the sole purpose of managing documents). The system includes a predefined interface where users can manage all the documents available in their accounts and create new ones.

Figure 10-13: Document app

To create a Scene for these types of applications, the SwiftUI framework includes the **DocumentGroup** structure.

DocumentGroup(newDocument: Closure, **editor:** Closure)—This initializer creates a **DocumentGroup** structure that defines a Scene with all the tools required to open, create, edit, and save documents. The **newDocument** argument is a closure that returns a document model to create the documents, and the **editor** argument is a closure that provides the view used to edit the document's content.

The documents are created from a document model. This is a structure or a class that defines the type of data managed by the document and how the information is converted to and from a format the app can process. The model is defined from a structure that conforms to the **FileDocument** protocol, or a class that conforms to the **ReferenceFileDocument** protocol. What to use depends on the requirements of our application, but both protocols define similar properties and methods for configuration. For instance, the following are the requirements of the **FileDocument** protocol.

readableContentTypes—This property returns an array of **UTType** structures to indicate the type of values managed by the document.

init(configuration: ReadConfiguration)—This initializer is used by the Document app to get the document's data when the user wants to read it. The **configuration** argument is a structure with information about the document. The structure includes the **file** property to return a **FileWrapper** structure, which in turn includes properties to return information about the document. The most frequently used are **filename** and **preferredFilename** to return the file's name and extension, **fileAttributes** to return the file's attributes, and **regularFileContents** to return the file's content.

fileWrapper(configuration: WriteConfiguration)—This method is called by the Document app to get the content we want to include in the document. The configuration argument is a structure with information about the current document. The structure includes the `existingFile` property to return a `FileWrapper` structure with this information or the value `nil` if the document was not saved yet. The method must return a `FileWrapper` structure with the content we want to save.

The document's content is managed by an instance of the `FileWrapper` structure. The following is the structure's initializer.

FileWrapper(regularFileWithContents: Data)—This initializer creates a file wrapper for a document with the data provided by the argument.

To allow the user to work with documents, we need to define the document model with the tools introduced above. This could be a structure or a class, depending on what we need for our application. The following example shows how to define a document model with a structure that conforms to the `FileDocument` protocol.

```swift
import SwiftUI
import UniformTypeIdentifiers
struct TextDocument: FileDocument {
   static var readableContentTypes: [UTType] = [.plainText]

   var documentText: String
   init() {
      documentText = ""
   }
   init(configuration: ReadConfiguration) throws {
      if let data = configuration.file.regularFileContents {
         if let text = String(data: data, encoding: .utf8) {
            documentText = text
         } else {
            throw CocoaError(.fileReadCorruptFile)
         }
      } else {
         throw CocoaError(.fileReadCorruptFile)
      }
   }
   func fileWrapper(configuration: WriteConfiguration) throws ->
FileWrapper {
      let data = documentText.data(using: .utf8)
      let wrapper = FileWrapper(regularFileWithContents: data!)
      return wrapper
   }
}
```

Listing 10-26: Defining a document model

One of the things defined by the document model is the type of data the document can handle. This is determined by the `UTType` structure. This structure provides a universal identifier that every application can recognize. Although we can define our own, as we will see in further chapters, the structure provides type properties to represent the most common types, including `png`, `gif`, `jpeg`, `pdf`, `mp3`, `avi`, `json`, `image`, `text`, and `plainText`. In this example, we assign the `plainText` type to the `readableContentTypes` property to configure the document to store plain text. (Notice that to use the `UTType` data type, we had to import the `UniformType-Identifiers` framework where the structure is defined.)

To store the document's content, we define a `String` property called `documentText` and use the structure's initializer to initialize it with an empty string. Every document created from this model, will be empty by default.

The document model requires an initializer to read the document's content, and a method to write it. The initializer is used to recreate the model when the user selects the document. The system reads the document's file and provides the data with a `FileWrapper` object that we can read from the `regularFileContents` property. So we read this property, turn the data into a string with the `String` initializer, and assign it to the `documentText` property. To write the content of this property back to the document, we implement the `fileWrapper()` method. In this case, all we need to do is to turn the value of the `documentText` property into a `Data` structure, create a `FileWrapper` object with it, and return it.

 IMPORTANT: Notice that if the process of reading the document fails, we must return an error. The Foundation framework defines a class called `CocoaError` to return common error codes. The class includes an initializer to create an object from a `Code` structure, and several type properties to return `Code` values. The most frequently used for reading files are `fileReadCorruptFile`, `fileReadNoSuchFile`, and `fileReadUnknown`.

Now that the document model is ready, we can create the Scene with the **DocumentGroup** structure. The **DocumentGroup** structure's initializer requires an instance of our document model and a closure with the view we want to use to edit the documents. This closure receives a `FileDocumentConfiguration` structure with a reference to the document and its properties. The structure includes the following properties to return these values.

document—This is a `Binding` property with a reference to the document.

fileURL—This property returns a `URL` structure with the file's URL.

isEditable—This property returns a Boolean value that indicates whether the user is allowed to edit the document or not.

The **DocumentGroup** structure creates a Scene to process documents and therefore it replaces the **WindowGroup** structure used before in the **App** structure to define the app's windows and the initial view. The following is a possible implementation.

```
import SwiftUI

@main
struct TestApp: App {
   var body: some Scene {
      DocumentGroup(newDocument: TextDocument(), editor: { config in
         ContentView(document: config.$document)
      })
   }
}
```

Listing 10-27: Creating a Document app

This **App** structure creates an app to manage documents. We initialize the **DocumentGroup** structure with an instance of our **TextDocument** structure to tell the app how to create the documents, and a closure that returns a **ContentView** view to provide a view to edit them. Notice that we take the `Binding` property from the `FileDocumentConfiguration` structure received by the closure and pass it to the view, so the view can access the document and edit its content. For the view to receive this value, it must contain a `Binding` property, as shown next.

```
struct ContentView: View {
   @Binding var document: TextDocument

   var body: some View {
      GroupBox("Editor") {
         TextEditor(text: $document.documentText)
            .cornerRadius(10)
      }.padding()
```

Chapter 10 - Storage

```
        .navigationBarTitleDisplayMode(.inline)
    }
}
struct ContentView_Previews: PreviewProvider {
    static var previews: some View {
        ContentView(document: .constant(TextDocument()))
    }
}
```

Listing 10-28: Editing the document

This application is similar to the previous one (see Listing 10-23), but instead of storing the text in a file, we store it in a document. A Document app allows the user to store and share documents on the device, iCloud, or a server. The provided user interface includes two tabs, one with the recent files, and another where we can select the location where we want to store the document and an option to create a new one, as shown below. When we press the + button, the app creates a new document and opens the `ContentView` view to allow the user to edit its content.

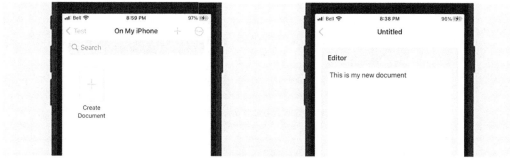

Figure 10-14: Custom Document app

 Do It Yourself: Create a Multiplatform project. Create a Swift file called TextDocument.swift for the structure in Listing 10-26. Update the **App** structure with the code in Listing 10-27 and the `ContentView` view with the code in Listing 10-28. Run the application on the iPhone simulator. Select the Browse tab. You should see the + button to add a document (Figure 10-14, left). Press the button. You should see the document editor (Figure 10-14, right).

The **DocumentGroup** structure provides an interface with all the tools the user needs to create, modify, and remove documents, but sometimes all we need is to allow the user to export or import documents from our own custom interface. For this purpose, SwiftUI includes the following modifiers.

fileExporter(isPresented: Binding, **document:** FileDocument, **contentType:** UTType, **defaultFilename:** String, **onCompletion:** Closure)—This modifier presents an interface to allow the user to save a document on the device, iCloud, or a remote location. The **isPresented** argument is a `Binding` property of type `Bool` that indicates whether the interface is shown or hidden. The **document** argument is the document model we want to use to create the document. The **contentType** argument determines the type of content the document is going to handle. The **defaultFilename** argument is the name we want to assign to the document. And finally, the **onCompletion** argument is the closure to execute when the process is over. The closure receives a `Result` value with the document's URL and an `Error` value to report errors.

fileImporter(isPresented: Binding, **allowedContentTypes:** [UTType], **onCompletion:** Closure)—This modifier presents an interface to allow the user to open a document. The **isPresented** argument is a `Binding` property of type `Bool` that indicates whether the interface is shown or hidden. The **allowedContentTypes** argument determines the type of document we want to allow the user to open. And the **onCompletion** argument is the closure to execute when the process is over. The closure receives a `Result` value with the document's URL and an `Error` value to report errors.

fileMover(isPresented: Binding, **file:** URL, **onCompletion:** Closure)—This modifier presents an interface to allow the user to move a document. The **isPresented** argument is a `Binding` property of type `Bool` that indicates whether the interface is shown or hidden. The **file** argument is the URL of the document we want to move. And the **onCompletion** argument is the closure to execute when the process is over. The closure receives a `Result` value with the document's URL and an `Error` value.

These modifiers open an interface when a Boolean state changes. For instance, the `fileExporter()` modifier opens an interface to allow the user to export and share a file when the value `true` is assigned to the state property. The modifier creates a document from a document model, as before, but from our own application, as shown next.

```
struct ContentView: View {
    @State private var document = TextDocument()
    @State private var openExport: Bool = false

    var body: some View {
        NavigationStack {
            GroupBox("Editor") {
                TextEditor(text: $document.documentText)
                    .cornerRadius(10)
            }.padding()
            .navigationTitle("Document")
            .navigationBarTitleDisplayMode(.inline)
            .toolbar {
                ToolbarItem(placement: .navigationBarTrailing) {
                    Button(action: {
                        openExport = true
                    }, label: {
                        Image(systemName: "square.and.arrow.up")
                    })
                }
            }
        }
        .fileExporter(isPresented: $openExport, document: document,
contentType: .plainText, defaultFilename: "My Message", onCompletion:
{ result in
            print("Document exported")
        })
    }
}
```

Listing 10-29: Exporting a document

To create the document, we need an instance of the document model. In this example, we create a `@State` property called `document` and initialize it with an instance of the same `TextDocument` structure used in the previous example. The view includes a `TextEditor` view to allow the user to edit the document's content. And to export it, we provide a button in the navigation bar. When the button is pressed, we assign the value `true` to a state property and the `fileExporter()` modifier opens the interface. Notice that the modifier is applied to the `NavigationStack` view, but this is just to keep the code organized. The modifier can be applied to any view we want. Now, we can insert a text and export it as a document from our application without having to create the Scene with the `DocumentGroup` structure.

Chapter 10 - Storage

Figure 10-15: Export a document

Do It Yourself: Create a Multiplatform project. Create a Swift file called TextDocument.swift for the document model in Listing 10-26. Update the `ContentView` view with the code in Listing 10-29. Run the application on a device. Type some text. Press the Export button to export the text as a document, as shown in Figure 10-15.

The same way we can create a document with the text inserted by the user and export it, we can import a document, read it, and show the text to the user by implementing the `fileImporter()` modifier. The only difference is that instead of working with a document, we must work directly with the file associated to the document.

The `fileImporter()` modifier returns a `URL` structure with the location of the file. To read the file at this URL and extract the data, the `Data` structure includes the following initializer.

Data(contentsOf: URL)—This initializer creates a `Data` structure with the content of the file at the location specified by the **contentsOf** argument.

Because the files we access with this modifier are not stored in our app's storage space but in the file system, they are protected and inaccessible by default. To grant access to these files for our application, the `URL` structure includes the following methods.

startAccessingSecurityScopedResource()—This method grants access to the resource referenced by the `URL` structure. The method returns a Boolean value to report whether access was granted or not.

stopAccessingSecurityScopedResource()—This method revokes the access granted to the application to the resource referenced by the `URL` structure.

The implementation of the `fileImporter()` modifier is very similar to the `fileExporter()` modifier. We apply it to a view and define a Boolean state to indicate when we want to open the interface. In the following example, we include an additional button in the navigation bar. When the button is pressed, we assign the value `true` to the `@State` property to open the interface, then read the document selected by the user, and assign the text to the `TextEditor` view to show it on the screen.

```
struct ContentView: View {
    @State private var document = TextDocument()
    @State private var openExport: Bool = false
    @State private var openImport: Bool = false

    var body: some View {
        NavigationStack {
            GroupBox("Editor") {
                TextEditor(text: $document.documentText)
                    .cornerRadius(10)
            }.padding()
            .navigationTitle("Document")
```

```
                .navigationBarTitleDisplayMode(.inline)
                .toolbar {
                    ToolbarItem(placement: .navigationBarLeading) {
                        Button(action: {
                            openImport = true
                        }, label: {
                            Image(systemName: "square.and.arrow.down")
                        })
                    }
                    ToolbarItem(placement: .navigationBarTrailing) {
                        Button(action: {
                            openExport = true
                        }, label: {
                            Image(systemName: "square.and.arrow.up")
                        })
                    }
                }
        }
        .fileExporter(isPresented: $openExport, document: document,
contentType: .plainText, defaultFilename: "My Message", onCompletion:
{ result in
            print("Document exported")
        })
        .fileImporter(isPresented: $openImport, allowedContentTypes:
[.plainText], onCompletion: { result in
            if let fileURL = try? result.get() {
                if fileURL.startAccessingSecurityScopedResource() {
                    if let data = try? Data(contentsOf: fileURL) {
                        if let text = String(data: data, encoding: .utf8) {
                            document.documentText = text
                        }
                    }
                    fileURL.stopAccessingSecurityScopedResource()
                }
            }
        })
    }
}
```

Listing 10-30: Importing a document

The `fileImporter()` modifier imports the document and calls the closure assigned to the **onCompletion** argument to report the result. This closure receives a `Result` value that we can read to get the file's URL (see Chapter 3, Listing 3-195). In this example, we use the `get()` method to get the URL and then read the file with the `Data(contentsOf:)` initializer. The data is converted into a string and assigned to the document, so the text is shown on the screen.

Figure 10-16: Interface to import a document

Do It Yourself: Update the `ContentView` view with the code in Listing 10-30. Run the application again on your device. Press the Import button and select the document created before. You should see the content of the document on the screen.

These examples illustrate how to import and export documents from external sources (the device or a server), but all we do is to create a document from the text inserted by the user and replace that text with the content of the document the user decides to import. This is not how normal applications work. Usually, the application allows the user to generate content, store it in files, and provides the tools to export those files to other applications or devices if necessary. For instance, we can implement the same application we have developed before to create and show a list of files (see Figure 10-5), but this time incorporate tools to allow the user to edit and export the files.

Figure 10-17: *Application to create and export files*

Because we are going to manage the document from the data model, we can apply the `fileExporter()` modifier to the `ContentView` in the `App` structure.

```
import SwiftUI
@main
struct TestApp: App {
   @StateObject var appData = ApplicationData()

   var body: some Scene {
      WindowGroup {
         ContentView()
            .environmentObject(appData)
            .fileExporter(isPresented: $appData.openExporter, document:
appData.document, contentType: .plainText, defaultFilename:
appData.selectedFile.name, onCompletion: { result in
               print("Document saved")
            })
      }
   }
}
```

Listing 10-31: *Exporting multiple documents*

This modifier works like before, but now the property that determines when to open the interface is a `@Published` property in the model. The application is going to allow the user to create files, edit their content, and export them, so the model needs a few more properties and methods, as shown next.

```
import SwiftUI

struct File: Identifiable {
   let id: UUID = UUID()
   var name: String
}
struct FileContent {
   var name: String
   var content: String
}
```

```
class ApplicationData: ObservableObject {
    @Published var listOfFiles: [File] = []
    @Published var selectedFile: FileContent
    @Published var openExporter: Bool = false
    var manager: FileManager
    var docURL: URL
    var document: TextDocument

    init() {
        manager = FileManager.default
        let documents = manager.urls(for: .documentDirectory,
in: .userDomainMask)
        docURL = documents.first!
        document = TextDocument()
        selectedFile = FileContent(name: "", content: "")
        if let list = try? manager.contentsOfDirectory(atPath: docURL.path) {
            for name in list {
                let newFile = File(name: name)
                listOfFiles.append(newFile)
            }
        }
    }
    func saveFile(name: String) {
        let newFileURL = docURL.appendingPathComponent(name)
        let path = newFileURL.path
        manager.createFile(atPath: path, contents: nil, attributes: nil)
        if !listOfFiles.contains(where: { $0.name == name}) {
            listOfFiles.append(File(name: name))
        }
    }
    func saveContent() {
        if let data = selectedFile.content.data(using: .utf8,
allowLossyConversion: true) {
            let path = docURL.appendingPathComponent(selectedFile.name).path
            manager.createFile(atPath: path, contents: data, attributes:
nil)
        }
    }
    func exportDocument(file: File) {
        let content = getDocumentContent(file: file)
        selectedFile = FileContent(name: file.name, content: content)
        document.documentText = content
        openExporter = true
    }
    func getDocumentContent(file: File) -> String {
        selectedFile.name = file.name
        let path = docURL.appendingPathComponent(file.name).path
        if manager.fileExists(atPath: path) {
            if let data = manager.contents(atPath: path) {
                if let content = String(data: data, encoding: .utf8) {
                    return content
                }
            }
        }
        return ""
    }
}
```

Listing 10-32: Managing files and documents from the model

We have defined two structures to store the data: one called `File` to store the files and another called `FileContent` to manage the content of the selected file. To know which file was selected by the user, we define another `@Published` property called `selectedFile`. The document is stored in a normal property called `document`. When the model is initialized, we defined all the values as before, assign an instance of the `TextDocument` structure to this property, and initialize the `selectedFile` property with an empty `FileContent` structure (no name and no content).

The views are going to offer buttons to add new files to the list, to save the text, and one on each row to export the file as a document, but all the work is managed by the methods in the model. We have the `saveFile()` method to add a new file to the list, the `saveContent()` method to save the text inserted by the user, the `exportDocument()` method to export a file as a document, and the `getDocumentContent()` method to read the content of the selected file when the user decides to open or export it.

The following is the main view. In this view, we show the list of files created by the user and provide a button to add more.

```
struct ContentView: View {
    @EnvironmentObject var appData: ApplicationData
    @State private var openSheet: Bool = false

    var body: some View {
        NavigationStack {
            VStack {
                List {
                    ForEach(appData.listOfFiles) { file in
                        NavigationLink(destination: {
                            EditFileView(file: file)
                        } , label: {
                            HStack {
                                Text(file.name)
                                Spacer()
                                Button(action: {
                                    appData.exportDocument(file: file)
                                }, label: {
                                    Image(systemName: "square.and.arrow.up")
                                }).buttonStyle(.plain)
                            }
                        })
                    }
                }.listStyle(.plain)
            }.padding()
            .navigationBarTitle("Files")
            .navigationBarTitleDisplayMode(.inline)
            .toolbar {
                ToolbarItem(placement: .navigationBarTrailing) {
                    Button("Add File") {
                        openSheet = true
                    }
                }
            }
            .sheet(isPresented: $openSheet) {
                AddFileView()
            }
        }
    }
}
```

Listing 10-33: *Exporting files from the list*

This view includes a button in the navigation bar to open a sheet with the `AddFileView` view used in previous examples to create new files (see Listing 10-8).

The list of files is built with a `NavigationLink` view that includes the file's name and a button to call the `exportDocument()` method in the model to export the file as a document. When a row is selected, the `NavigationLink` view opens a new view called `EditFileView()` to allow the user to edit the file's content.

```
struct EditFileView: View {
    @EnvironmentObject var appData: ApplicationData
    @Environment(\.dismiss) var dismiss
    let file: File

    var body: some View {
        GroupBox(file.name) {
            TextEditor(text: $appData.selectedFile.content)
                .cornerRadius(10)
        }.navigationTitle("Editor")
        .toolbar {
            ToolbarItem(placement: .navigationBarTrailing) {
                Button("Save") {
                    appData.saveContent()
                    dismiss()
                }
            }
        }
        .onAppear {
            let content = appData.getDocumentContent(file: file)
            appData.selectedFile.content = content
        }
    }
}
struct EditFileView_Previews: PreviewProvider {
    static var previews: some View {
        EditFileView(file: File(name: ""))
            .environmentObject(ApplicationData())
    }
}
```

Listing 10-34: Editing a file

This view receives a copy of the **File** structure representing the selected file and includes a **TextEditor** view to allow the user to edit the file's content. But this is actually managed by an instance of the **FileContent** structure stored in the **selectedFile** property, so we implement the **onAppear()** method to get the content of the file and assign the current text to the structure's **content** property. Now the **TextEditor** view displays the content of the file and allows the user to edit it. To save the changes, the navigation bar includes a Save button that calls the **saveContent()** method in the model. This method converts the text into data and stores it in the file.

The application is finally ready. The user can create new files, edit their content, and export them, as shown in Figure 10-17.

 Do It Yourself: Update the **App** structure with the code in Listing 10-31. Create a Swift file called ApplicationData.swift for the model in Listing 10-32. Update the **ContentView** view with the code in Listing 10-33. Create a SwiftUI View file called EditFileView.swift file for the view in Listing 10-34. You will also need a SwiftUI file called AddFileView.swift for the view in Listing 10-8. Run the application on the iPhone simulator. Press the Add File button to add a new file. Select the file and write some text. Press the Save button to save it. Press the Export button on the file's row. You should be able to create a document with the file's content.

Basic 10.3 Archiving

The methods we have just implemented to store data in files are enough for simple models but present some limitations. We can only work with single values and with classes that already provide a way to turn their content into data. Professional applications rely on more elaborated models that include collection of values and custom data types. To give us more flexibility, Foundation offers the **NSCoder** class. This class can encode and decode values to **Data** structures for storage purposes in a process called *Archiving*.

An **NSCoder** object not only encodes an object but also the objects it is connected to, preserving the connections and the hierarchy. For example, we may have two objects with properties that reference the other object. Object 1 references Object 2 and Object 2 references Object 1. With archiving, both objects are encoded, stored, and then decoded and connected again when we need them, conforming a structure called *Object Graph*.

(Basic) Encoding and Decoding

The **NSCoder** class provides all the methods necessary to encode and decode the values of an object, but all the work is done by instances of two **NSCoder** subclasses called **NSKeyedArchiver** and **NSKeyedUnarchiver**. The **NSKeyedArchiver** class calls the **encode()** method on the objects to encode their values and stores the data in a **Data** structure or a file. On the other hand, the **NSKeyedUnarchiver** class initializes the objects with the protocol's initializer and returns the original values.

The **NSKeyedArchiver** class offers the following type method to encode an Object Graph and store it in a **Data** structure.

archivedData(withRootObject: Any, **requiringSecureCoding:** Bool)—This type method encodes the Object Graph of the object specified by the **withRootObject** argument and stores it in a **Data** structure. The **requiringSecureCoding** argument is a Boolean value that determines whether the data will be secured or not.

And the **NSKeyedUnarchiver** class offers the following type method to decode an Object Graph from a **Data** structure.

unarchivedObject(ofClass: Class, **from:** Data)—This type method decodes the data specified by the **from** argument and returns the original Object Graph. The **ofClass** argument determines the data type of the decoded object.

Implementing these methods, we can generate **Data** structures for processing, or we can just store and retrieve the data from a file. In the following example, we encode and decode a string to a **Data** structure and use **FileManager** methods to create and read the file.

```
struct ContentView: View {
    @State private var myquote: String = "Undefined"

    var body: some View {
        VStack {
            Text(myquote)
                .padding()
            Spacer()
        }
        .onAppear {
            let manager = FileManager.default
            let documents = manager.urls(for: .documentDirectory,
in: .userDomainMask)
            let docURL = documents.first!

            let fileURL = docURL.appendingPathComponent("quotes.dat")
            let filePath = fileURL.path
            if manager.fileExists(atPath: filePath) {
                if let content = manager.contents(atPath: filePath) {
                    if let result = try? NSKeyedUnarchiver.unarchivedObject
(ofClass: NSString.self, from: content) as String? {
```

```
                myquote = result
            }
        }
    } else {
        let quote = "Fiction is the truth inside the lie"
        if let fileData = try? NSKeyedArchiver.archivedData
(withRootObject: quote, requiringSecureCoding: false) {
            manager.createFile(atPath: filePath, contents: fileData,
attributes: nil)
        }
    }
    }
    }
}
```

Listing 10-35: Encoding and decoding data

When the view defined in Listing 10-35 appears on the screen, the `onAppear()` modifier encodes a single string and stores it in a file called quotes.dat. As we did in previous examples, we first check if the file exists with the `fileExists()` method and then proceed accordingly. If the file does not exist, we convert the string to a `Data` value with the `archivedData()` method and create a file with it, but if the file already exists, we read its content with the `contents()` method and decode the data with the `unarchivedObject()` method to get back the string.

The `unarchivedObject()` method can only work with data types that conform to a protocol called `NSSecureCoding`. That is the reason why we had to specify the `NSString` class as the value of the `ofClass` argument and convert it at the end to a `String` structure with the `as` operator. (The `NSString` class conforms to the `NSSecureCoding` protocol but the `String` structure does not.)

 Do It Yourself: Create a Multiplatform project. Update the `ContentView` view with the code in Listing 10-35. Run the application on the iPhone simulator. The first time, the file is created and the string "Undefined" is shown on the screen. Stop and run the application again. Now the file created before is loaded and you should see the quote on the screen.

The methods of the `NSKeyedArchiver` and `NSKeyedUnarchiver` classes work with Property List values (`NSNumber`, `NSString`, `NSDate`, `NSArray`, `NSDictionary`, `NSData`, and the equivalents in Swift). In the previous example, we were able to to use an `NSString` value because we wanted to store a simple string, but if we want to archive our own data types, we must convert them to Property List values. Foundation offers two classes for this purpose, `PropertyListEncoder` and `PropertyListDecoder`, which include the following methods to encode and decode values.

encode(Value**)**—This method of the `PropertyListEncoder` class encodes a value into a Property List value.

decode(Type, **from:** Data**)**—This method of the `PropertyListDecoder` class decodes a Property List value into a value of the type specified by the first argument. The **from** argument is a `Data` structure with the data to be decoded.

Another requirement for custom structures is that they implement the initializers and methods defined in a protocol called `NSCoding`. These initializers and methods tell the system how to encode and decode the data for storage or distribution. Fortunately, the Swift Standard Library defines a protocol called `Codable` that turns a structure into an encodable and decodable data type. All we need to do is to get our structure to conform to this protocol and the compiler takes care of adding all the methods required to encode and decode the values. The following example recreates a model used in previous examples to store information about a book, but now it implements these tools to store the data on file.

```
import SwiftUI
struct Book: Codable {
   var title: String
   var author: String
   var year: Int
   var cover: String?
}
struct BookViewModel: Identifiable {
   let id: UUID = UUID()
   var book: Book

   var title: String {
      return book.title.capitalized
   }
   var author: String {
      return book.author.capitalized
   }
   var year: String {
      return String(book.year)
   }
   var cover: UIImage {
      if let imageName = book.cover {
         let manager = FileManager.default
         let docURL = manager.urls(for: .documentDirectory,
in: .userDomainMask).first!
         let imageURL = docURL.appendingPathComponent(imageName)
         let path = imageURL.path
         if let coverImage = UIImage(contentsOfFile: path) {
            return coverImage
         }
      }
      return UIImage(named: "nopicture")!
   }
}
class ApplicationData: ObservableObject {
   @Published var bookInFile: BookViewModel
   var manager: FileManager
   var docURL: URL

   init() {
      manager = FileManager.default
      let documents = manager.urls(for: .documentDirectory,
in: .userDomainMask)
      docURL = documents.first!
      bookInFile = BookViewModel(book: Book(title: "", author: "", year:
0, cover: nil))

      let fileURL = docURL.appendingPathComponent("userdata.dat")
      let path = fileURL.path
      if manager.fileExists(atPath: path) {
         if let content = manager.contents(atPath: path) {
            let decoder = PropertyListDecoder()
            if let book = try? decoder.decode(Book.self, from: content) {
               bookInFile.book = book
            }
         }
      }
   }
   func saveBook(book: Book) {
      let fileURL = docURL.appendingPathComponent("userdata.dat")
      let path = fileURL.path
      let encoder = PropertyListEncoder()
      if let data = try? encoder.encode(book) {
```

```
              if manager.createFile(atPath: path, contents: data, attributes:
nil) {
                bookInFile = BookViewModel(book: book)
            }
        }
    }
    func storeCover() -> String? {
        let placeholder = UIImage(named: "bookcover")
        let imageName = "bookcover.dat"
        if let imageData = placeholder?.pngData() {
            let fileURL = docURL.appendingPathComponent(imageName)
            let path = fileURL.path
            if manager.createFile(atPath: path, contents: imageData,
attributes: nil) {
                return imageName
            }
        }
        return nil
    }
}
```

Listing 10-36: Encoding and decoding a custom structure

As in previous examples, the **Book** structure is our data model, but now it conforms to the **Codable** protocol, so we can encode it into a **Data** structure and store it in a file. The structure includes properties to store the title, author, cover, and year of publication.

The observable object includes a **@Published** property to store the book, an initializer that reads the values from a file, a method to store new values, and a method to store the book's cover. The initializer reads the file, creates an instance of the **PropertyListDecoder** class, and calls the **decode()** method on it to decode the data into a **Book** structure (**Book.self**). If successful, the structure is assigned to the **book** property of the **BookViewModel** structure stored in the **bookInFile** property to make the values available for the view. The **saveFiles()** method performs the opposite process. It creates an instance of the **PropertyListEncoder** class and calls the **encode()** method on it with the instance of the **Book** structure created by the user to convert the values into data and store it in the file.

When storing data in files or databases, it is recommended to store the images in separate files. This is the job of the **storeCover()** method. This method is called before the **saveFile()** method to store the book's cover in a file and return the file's name to include it in the data model with the rest of the values. In this example we always use the same image and the same file for the book's cover, but in a real application the image is usually taken from the device's Photo library or the camera, and each image is stored in different files. (We will see how to name these files in the next project and how to access the Photo library and the camera in Chapter 18.)

As always, all the work is done by the model. Therefore, all the view needs to do is to read the values from the view model, show them on the screen, and provide the user the possibility to modify them.

```
struct ContentView: View {
    @EnvironmentObject var appData: ApplicationData
    @State private var openSheet: Bool = false

    var body: some View {
        NavigationStack {
            VStack(alignment: .leading) {
                Text("Title: \(appData.bookInFile.title)")
                Text("Author: \(appData.bookInFile.author)")
                Text("Year: \(appData.bookInFile.year)")
                Image(uiImage: appData.bookInFile.cover)
                    .resizable()
```

```
                   .scaledToFit()
            }.padding()
            .frame(minWidth: 0, maxWidth: .infinity)
            .navigationBarTitle("Book")
            .toolbar {
               ToolbarItem(placement: .navigationBarTrailing) {
                  Button(action: {
                     openSheet = true
                  }, label: {
                     Image(systemName: "plus")
                  })
               }
            }
            .sheet(isPresented: $openSheet) {
               InsertBookView()
            }
         }
      }
   }
}
```

Listing 10-37: Showing the values stored in the file

This view opens a sheet with an instance of the **InsertBookView** view when a button in the navigation bar is pressed. The view allows the user to modify the book's values.

```
struct InsertBookView: View {
   @EnvironmentObject var appData: ApplicationData
   @Environment(\.dismiss) var dismiss
   @State private var inputTitle: String = ""
   @State private var inputAuthor: String = ""
   @State private var inputYear: String = ""

   var body: some View {
      VStack {
         HStack {
            Text("Title:")
            TextField("Insert Title", text: $inputTitle)
               .textFieldStyle(.roundedBorder)
         }
         HStack {
            Text("Author:")
            TextField("Insert Author", text: $inputAuthor)
               .textFieldStyle(.roundedBorder)
         }
         HStack {
            Text("Year:")
            TextField("Insert Year", text: $inputYear)
               .textFieldStyle(.roundedBorder)
         }
         HStack {
            Spacer()
            Button("Save") {
               let newTitle =
inputTitle.trimmingCharacters(in: .whitespaces)
               let newAuthor =
inputAuthor.trimmingCharacters(in: .whitespaces)
               let newYear = Int(inputYear)
               if !newTitle.isEmpty && !newAuthor.isEmpty && newYear !=
nil {
                  let coverName = appData.storeCover()
                  appData.saveBook(book: Book(title: newTitle, author:
newAuthor, year: newYear!, cover: coverName))
                  dismiss()
```

```
                }
            }
        }
        Spacer()
    }.padding()
  }
}
```

Listing 10-38: Allowing the user to insert new values

The `InsertBookView` view includes three `TextField` views to let the user insert the book's title, author, and year (the cover is always the same). The view stores the values inserted by the user in `@State` properties. When the user presses the Save button to save the book, we check the values in these properties. If they are all valid, we call the `storeCover()` method in the model to create a file with the cover, create a new instance of the `Book` structure with all these values, and call the `saveFile()` method to store the structure in the file.

Figure 10-18: Interface to store a custom value in a file

Do It Yourself: Create a Multiplatform project. Download the nopicture and the bookcover images from our website and add them to the Asset Catalog. Create the ApplicationData.swift file for the model in Listing 10-36. Update the **ContentView** view with the code in Listing 10-37. Create a SwiftUI View file called InsertBookView.swift for the view in Listing 10-38. Remember to inject the **ApplicationData** object into the environment for the app and the previews (Chapter 7, Listing 7-4). Run the application on the iPhone simulator. Press the + button in the navigation bar and insert new values. Stop the application and run it again. You should see the same values on the screen.

The previous model stores the values of one book. If new values are inserted, a new **Book** structure is instantiated with those values and stored in the same file, replacing the previous one. This example illustrates how custom data types, like the **Book** structure, are encoded and stored in files, but most of the time we need to work with collections of values. For this purpose, all we have to do is to encode an array of structures instead of a single one. The following are the modifications required in our observable object to store multiple books.

```
class ApplicationData: ObservableObject {
    @Published var userData: [BookViewModel] = []
    var manager: FileManager
    var docURL: URL

    init() {
        manager = FileManager.default
        let documents = manager.urls(for: .documentDirectory,
in: .userDomainMask)
        docURL = documents.first!

        let fileURL = docURL.appendingPathComponent("userdata.dat")
```

```
            let path = fileURL.path
            if manager.fileExists(atPath: path) {
                if let content = manager.contents(atPath: path) {
                    let decoder = PropertyListDecoder()
                    if let list = try? decoder.decode([Book].self, from: content) {
                        userData = list.map({ value in
                            return BookViewModel(book: value)
                        })
                    }
                }
            }
        }
        func saveBook(book: Book) {
            userData.append(BookViewModel(book: book))
            saveModel()
        }
        func saveModel() {
            let list = userData.map({ value in
                return value.book
            })
            let fileURL = docURL.appendingPathComponent("userdata.dat")
            let path = fileURL.path
            let encoder = PropertyListEncoder()
            if let data = try? encoder.encode(list) {
                manager.createFile(atPath: path, contents: data, attributes:
nil)
            }
        }
        func storeCover() -> String? {
            let placeholder = UIImage(named: "bookcover")
            let imageName = "image-\(UUID()).dat"
            if let imageData = placeholder?.pngData() {
                let fileURL = docURL.appendingPathComponent(imageName)
                let path = fileURL.path
                if manager.createFile(atPath: path, contents: imageData,
attributes: nil) {
                    return imageName
                }
            }
            return nil
        }
    }
```

Listing 10-39: Storing multiple books

Every time the values in the model are modified, either because a book is added or removed, or the information of a book is updated, we must update the data in the file. For this purpose, we define a method called **saveModel()**. This method prepares the data and stores it in a file called userdata.dat. In this example, we store in the file instances of the data model (the **Book** structure), but the observable object stores an array of **BookViewModel** structures. These are instances of the view model used to prepare the values for the view. To convert this array into an array of **Book** structures, the method extracts the values with the **map()** method. This method processes the items in the array and returns the instance of the **Book** structure inside each **BookViewModel** structure, creating the list of **Book** structures we need to store in the file.

In this example, we only let the user add books. The books can't be erased or modified. This is why there is only one method to edit the information called **addBook()**. This method receives an instance of the **Book** structure with the values inserted by the user, adds it to the array in the **userData** property, and calls the **saveModel()** method to store all the values in the file again, so the file always contains the latest information.

The initializer performs the opposite process of the **saveModel()** method. It reads the content of the file, decodes the data with the **decode()** method into an array of **Book** structures

([`Book`].`self`), and then converts the `Book` structures into `BookViewModel` structures with the `map()` method before assigning them to the `userData` property to make the values available for the views.

Another change introduced in this observable object is the name assigned to the files for the covers in the `storeCover()` method. We are still using the same image for every book (bookcover), but because the user can now store multiple books, we define the file's name with a `UUID` value to make every name unique.

The view must create a list with all the books in the `userData` property and provide a button for the user to insert new ones.

```
struct ContentView: View {
    @EnvironmentObject var appData: ApplicationData
    @State private var openSheet: Bool = false

    var body: some View {
        NavigationStack {
            List {
                ForEach(appData.userData) { book in
                    RowBook(book: book)
                }
            }
            .navigationBarTitle("Books")
            .toolbar {
                ToolbarItem(placement: .navigationBarTrailing) {
                    Button(action: {
                        openSheet = true
                    }, label: {
                        Image(systemName: "plus")
                    })
                }
            }
            .sheet(isPresented: $openSheet) {
                InsertBookView()
            }
        }
    }
}
struct RowBook: View {
    let book: BookViewModel

    var body: some View {
        HStack(alignment: .top) {
            Image(uiImage: book.cover)
                .resizable()
                .scaledToFit()
                .frame(width: 80, height: 100)
                .cornerRadius(10)
            VStack(alignment: .leading, spacing: 2) {
                Text(book.title)
                    .bold()
                Text(book.author)
                Text(book.year)
                    .font(.caption)
                Spacer()
            }.padding(.top, 5)
            Spacer()
        }.padding(.top, 10)
    }
}
```

Listing 10-40: Showing all the values stored in the file

This view shows the list of the books stored in the file with a **List** view. The navigation bar includes a button to open the **InsertBookView** view defined before to let the user add new books. Therefore, the application works like before, but now instead of one the user can insert and store multiple books.

Figure 10-19: *Interface to store multiple values in a file*

 Do It Yourself: Update the observable object in your model (the **ApplicationData** class) with the code in Listing 10-39 and the ContentView.swift file with the code in Listing 10-40. Run the application on the iPhone simulator. Press the + button to add a book and press the Save button to save it. Stop and run the application again. You should see all the books on the screen.

(Medium) **JSON**

Another way to encode and decode custom data types is with JSON (JavaScript Object Notation). This format was created to transmit information on the web, but the fact that it is a very simple format to read and process, made it suitable to store data for applications. Apple systems adopted JSON long time ago to store and retrieve information. Foundation includes the **JSONDecoder** class to decode JSON data into Swift structures and the **JSONEncoder** class to encode Swift structures into JSON data. The classes define their respective methods to decode and encode the values.

decode(Type, **from:** Data**)**—This method returns a value of the type specified by the first argument with the information provided by the **from** argument. The **from** argument is a **Data** structure that contains the JSON data we want to decode.

encode(Value**)**—This method returns a JSON representation of the data provided by the argument.

A JSON file is just a text file that stores the data in a specific syntax. The syntax includes the values of an object or a structure as key/value pairs separated by a colon, like dictionaries. The name of the property becomes the key for the value, and each object or structure is enclosed in braces. The following example shows how a JSON file looks like if we store one instance of our **Book** structure.

```
{
    "author": "Stephen King",
    "title": "The Shining",
    "year": 1977,
    "cover": "bookcover.dat"
}
```

Listing 10-41: *JSON file*

As always, the objects or structures we want to encode must conform to the **Codable** protocol and the data must be encoded and decoded before it is stored or read. Therefore, adapting our app to work with JSON is simple. We just have to replace the Property List encoders and decoders with JSON's. For instance, the following example works exactly like the one before, but now the data is stored in JSON format.

```
class ApplicationData: ObservableObject {
    @Published var userData: [BookViewModel] = []
    var manager: FileManager
    var docURL: URL

    init() {
        manager = FileManager.default
        let documents = manager.urls(for: .documentDirectory,
in: .userDomainMask)
        docURL = documents.first!

        let fileURL = docURL.appendingPathComponent("userdata.dat")
        let path = fileURL.path
        if manager.fileExists(atPath: path) {
            if let content = manager.contents(atPath: path) {
                let decoder = JSONDecoder()
                if let list = try? decoder.decode([Book].self, from: content) {
                    userData = list.map({ value in
                        return BookViewModel(book: value)
                    })
                }
            }
        }
    }
    func saveBook(book: Book) {
        userData.append(BookViewModel(book: book))
        saveModel()
    }
    func saveModel() {
        let list = userData.map({ value in
            return value.book
        })
        let fileURL = docURL.appendingPathComponent("userdata.dat")
        let path = fileURL.path
        let encoder = JSONEncoder()
        if let data = try? encoder.encode(list) {
            manager.createFile(atPath: path, contents: data, attributes:
nil)
        }
    }
    func storeCover() -> String? {
        let placeholder = UIImage(named: "bookcover")
        let imageName = "image-\(UUID()).dat"
        if let imageData = placeholder?.pngData() {
            let fileURL = docURL.appendingPathComponent(imageName)
            let path = fileURL.path
            if manager.createFile(atPath: path, contents: imageData,
attributes: nil) {
                return imageName
            }
        }
        return nil
    }
}
```

Listing 10-42: Encoding and decoding the data with JSON

Do It Yourself: Update the observable object in the model (the `ApplicationData` class) with the code in Listing 10-42. Remove the application on the simulator to erase previous files and run it again. The list should be empty. Press the + button to add a book and save it. Stop and run the application again. You should see the book on the screen.

Of course, JSON can format nested structures and objects. For instance, we may have a **Book** structure with a property that stores another structure with information about the publisher.

```
struct Publisher: Codable {
    let name: String
    let date: Date
}
struct Book: Codable {
    let title: String
    let author: String
    let publisher: Publisher
}
```

Listing 10-43: Defining nested structures

If we store an instance of this **Book** structure in JSON format, it may look as follows.

```
{
    "title": "The Shining",
    "author": "Stephen King",
    "publisher": {
        "name": "Random House",
        "date": 598999514.87258303
    }
}
```

Listing 10-44: Nested data in JSON

Notice that the date in JSON doesn't look like a date. This is because **Date** values contain the difference in seconds from a specific date in the past to the date they represent. To convert these values into values of type **Date**, we must declare what kind of format the decoder has to use. For this purpose, the **JSONDecoder** class includes the following property.

dateDecodingStrategy—This property defines the strategy the decoder follows to decode a date. It is an enumeration of type **DateDecodingStrategy** with the values **millisecondsSince1970**, **secondsSince1970**, **deferredToDate**, and **iso8601**. The enumeration also includes the methods **formatted()** and **custom()** to define custom formats.

Dates in JSON are shared in different formats, but when working with **Date** values, we just have to declare the **deferredToDate** formatting and the decoder will have enough information to decode the value back into a **Date** structure.

The following is a simple model that illustrates how to read and process these values. The observable object in this model loads a JSON file from the bundle with the code introduced in Listing 10-44 and decodes it into the structures introduced in Listing 10-43.

```
import SwiftUI

struct Publisher: Codable {
    let name: String
    let date: Date
}
```

```
struct Book: Codable {
   let title: String?
   let author: String?
   let publisher: Publisher?
}
struct BookViewModel {
   var book: Book

   var title: String {
      return book.title?.capitalized ?? "Undefined"
   }
   var author: String {
      return book.author?.capitalized ?? "Undefined"
   }
   var publisher: String {
      return book.publisher?.name.capitalized ?? "Undefined"
   }
   var date: String {
      if let date = book.publisher?.date {
         let format = date.formatted(date: .abbreviated, time: .omitted)
         return format
      } else {
         return "Undefined"
      }
   }
}
class ApplicationData: ObservableObject {
   @Published var bookInFile: BookViewModel

   init() {
      bookInFile = BookViewModel(book: Book(title: nil, author: nil,
publisher: nil))

      let manager = FileManager.default
      let bundle = Bundle.main
      if let path = bundle.path(forResource: "template", ofType: "json") {
         if let data = manager.contents(atPath: path) {
            let decoder = JSONDecoder()
            decoder.dateDecodingStrategy = .deferredToDate
            if let book = try? decoder.decode(Book.self, from: data) {
               bookInFile.book = book
            }
         }
      }
   }
}
```

Listing 10-45: Reading values in a nested structure

Besides the **Publisher** and **Book** structures introduced before, this model also includes the
BookViewModel structure to prepare the values for the view, and the observable object to load
the data. The initializer looks for a file called template.json. The code assumes that the file has a
structure like the example in Listing 10-44. If found, the content of the file is loaded with the
contents() method of the **FileManager** object, decoded with a **JSONDecoder** object, and
the **Book** structure resulting from this process is assigned to the **bookInFile** property to make
it available for the view. The following is the view we need to show these values on the screen.

```
struct ContentView: View {
   @EnvironmentObject var appData: ApplicationData

   var body: some View {
      VStack(alignment: .leading) {
         Text(appData.bookInFile.title)
         Text(appData.bookInFile.author)
```

```
            Text(appData.bookInFile.publisher)
            Text(appData.bookInFile.date)
            Spacer()
        }.padding()
    }
}
```

Listing 10-46: *Showing the values of a nested structure*

Figure 10-20, below, shows what we see if the project includes a file called template.json in the bundle with the JSON code of Listing 10-44.

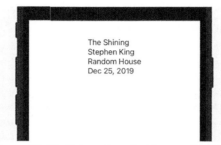

The Shining
Stephen King
Random House
Dec 25, 2019

Figure 10-20: *Values decoded from a JSON file*

Do It Yourself: Create a Multiplatform project. Create a text file called template.json with the code in Listing 10-44 and drag it into the Navigation Area (the file is available on our website). Create the ApplicationData.swift file for the model in Listing 10-45. Update the **ContentView** view with the code in Listing 10-46. Remember to inject the **ApplicationData** object into the environment for the app and the previews (Chapter 7, Listing 7-4). Run the application on the iPhone simulator. You should see all the values in the file printed on the screen.

Basic 10.4 Core Data

With archiving, we can store not only objects but also their connections. This organization is called *Object Graph*. Archiving is a good tool to store an Object Graph on file but presents some limitations. The Object Graph stored this way is difficult to expand or modified. The entire graph must be stored in the file again after the smallest change, and it is not easy to control the connections between objects to determine exactly which objects will be stored. The solution is called *Core Data*. Core Data is an Object Graph manager that defines and manages its own objects and connections and stores them in a database. We can determine the composition of the objects and their relationships. The system takes care of encoding and decoding the objects, preserving consistency and maximizing efficiency.

Basic Data Model

The structure of the Core Data's Object Graph is defined with a data model. This has nothing to do with the data model of the MVC pattern implemented in previous examples. A Core Data model is the definition of the type of objects the graph is going to contain (called *Entities*) and their connections (called *Relationships*).

A model can be created from code, but Xcode offers a practical editor to define the structure of the graph. The model is stored in a file and then the file is compiled and included in the Core Data system created for our application. Xcode offers a template to create this file.

Choose a template for your new file:

Figure 10-21: *Option to create a Core Data model in the iOS panel*

The file may be created with any name we want but it must have the extension xcdatamodel. Once created, it is included in our project along with the rest of the files. Clicking on it reveals the Xcode editor in the Editor Area.

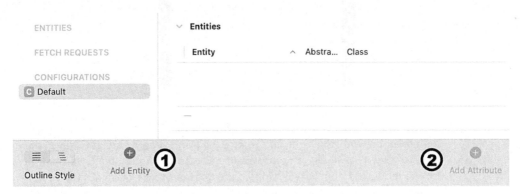

Figure 10-22: *Model editor*

The model contains three main components: Entities, Attributes, and Relationships. Entities are the objects, Attributes are the objects' properties, and Relationships are the connections between objects. The first step is to add Entities to the model. Entities are created from the Add Entity button at the bottom of the editor (Figure 10-22, number 1). When we press this button, Xcode creates an entity with the generic name "Entity".

Figure 10-23: *New Entities*

We can change the name of the newly created entity by double-clicking the item (Figure 10-23, number 1) or editing the field in the Data Model Inspector panel (Figure 10-23, number 2).

An entity defines the objects that are going to be part of the Object Graph, so the next step is to declare the type of values those objects are going to manage. For this purpose, entities include Attributes. To add an attribute, we must select the entity and press the + button under the Attributes area (Figure 10-23, number 3) or press the Add Attribute button at the bottom of the editor (Figure 10-22, number 2). The attribute is added with the generic name "attribute" and the data type Undefined. Again, we can change the name of the attribute by double-clicking on it or from the Data Model Inspector panel (Figure 10-23, number 2). For our example, we call the entity *Books* and the first attribute *title* (Figure 10-24, number 1).

Figure 10-24: *New Attributes*

 IMPORTANT: The name of entities must start with an upper-case letter and the names of attributes and relationships with a lower-case letter. This is mandatory and Xcode will show you an error if the names are invalid.

Every attribute must be associated with a data type for the objects to know what kind of values they can manage (Figure 10-24, number 2). Clicking on the attribute's type, we can open a menu to select the right data type. The most frequently used are Integer 16, Integer 32, Integer 64, Double, Float, String, Boolean, Date, and Binary Data. The Integer 16, 32, or 64 options are for `Int16`, `Int32`, and `Int64` values, Double and Float are for `Double` and `Float` values, String is for `String` values, Boolean is for `Bool` values, Date is for `Date` values, and Binary Data is for `Data` values.

An entity may contain as many attributes as our objects need. For example, we may add a few more attributes to complement the information required for books.

Attribute	Type	
cover	Binary Data	↕
thumbnail	Binary Data	↕
title	String	↕
year	Integer 32	↕

Figure 10-25: *Multiple Attributes*

In this example, we have added an attribute called *year* to store the year in which the book was published, and two attributes of type Binary Data to store images (the book's cover and thumbnail). The data types used by these attributes are analog to Swift data types. The title attribute takes a `String` value, the year attribute stores a value of type `Int32`, and the images are stored as `Data` structures.

Most values don't require much consideration, but images are made of big chunks of data. Storing large amounts of data in a Persistent Store can affect the system's performance and slow down essential processes like searching for values or migrating the model. One alternative is to store the images in separate files, but as we have seen in previous examples, this can get cumbersome. Fortunately, Core Data can perform the process for us. All we need to do is to store the image as Binary Data and select the option Allows External Storage, available in the Data Model inspector panel inside the Utilities Area, as shown below. After the option is selected, the images assigned to that attribute are stored in separate files managed by the system.

Figure 10-26: *Option to store images outside the Persistent Store*

We could have also included another attribute for the author's name, but here is when we need to think about the structure of the Object Graph and how the information will be stored. If we include a String type attribute for the author's name inside the Books entity, every time the user inserts a new book it will have to type the name of the author. This is error prone, time consuming, and when several books of the same author are available, it is impossible to make sure that all share the same exact name (for example, one book could have the author's middle name and others just the first one). Without the certainty of having the exact same name, we can never incorporate features in our app such as ordering the books by author or getting the list of books written by a particular author. Things get worse when, along with the name, we also decide to store other information about the author, like his or her date of birth or their nationality. A proper organization of this information demands separate objects and therefore we must create new entities to represent them.

Additional entities are added to the model in the same way as we did with the first one. Figure 10-27, below, shows our model with a new entity called *Authors* containing an attribute called *name*.

Figure 10-27: *Multiple Entities*

Entities are blueprints that we use to define the characteristics of the objects we want to store in the database. For instance, when we want to store a new book in our example, we create a new object based on the Books entity. That object will have four properties corresponding to the values of its title, year, cover, and thumbnail. The same happens when we want to store information of an author. We create a new object based on the Authors entity and assign the name of the author to its name property. At the end, we will have two objects in the database, one for the book and another for the author. But if we want to retrieve these objects later, we need a way to know which Books object is related to which Authors object. To create this connection, the Core Data model includes Relationships.

A relationship is a property in one object containing a reference to another object. Relationships can have a reference to only one object or a set of objects. For example, in the Books entity, we can create a relationship that contains a reference to only one object of the Authors entity, because there can only be one author per book (for this example we are assuming that our app is storing books written only by one author). On the contrary, in the Authors entity, we need to establish a relationship that contains references to multiple Books objects, because an author may have written several books. Core Data calls these relationships according to the number of objects they may reference. The names are *To-One* and *To-Many*, and they are created pressing the **+** button in the Relationships area below the Attributes area. Figure 10-28, below, shows a relationship called *author* we have created for the Books entity of our example.

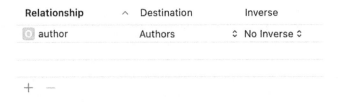

Figure 10-28: *Relationship for the Books entity*

A relationship only needs two values: its name (the name of the property) and the destination (the type of objects it is referencing), but it requires some parameters to be set. We must tell the model if the relationship is going to be optional, define its type (To-One or To-Many), and determine what should happen to the destination object if the source object is deleted (the Delete Rule). All these options are available in the Data Model Inspector panel when the relationship is selected, as shown below.

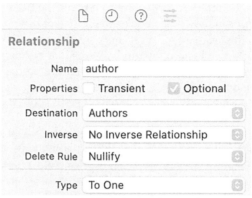

Figure 10-29: *Relationship settings*

By default, the relationship is set as Optional, which means that the source may be connected to a destination object or not (a book can have an author or not), the Type of the relationship is set to To-One (a book can only have one author), and the Delete Rule is set to Nullify. The following are all the values available for this rule.

- **Deny:** If there is at least one object at the destination, the source is not deleted (if there is an Authors object assigned to the Books object, the book is not deleted).
- **Nullify:** The connections between objects are removed, but the objects at the destination are not deleted (if a Books object is deleted, the Authors object associated with that book loses the connection but is not deleted).
- **Cascade:** The objects at the destination are deleted when the source is deleted (the Authors object is deleted if one of its books is deleted).
- **No Action:** The objects at the destination are not deleted or modified (the connections are preserved, even when the source object does not exist anymore).

To find the right rule for a relationship, we must think in terms of the information we are dealing with. Is it right to delete the author if one of its books is deleted? In our case, the answer is simple. An author can have more than one book, so we cannot delete the author when we delete a book because there could be other books that are connected to that same author. Therefore, the Nullify rule set by default is the right one for this relationship. But this could change when we create the opposite relationship, connecting the Authors entity to the Books entity. We need this second relationship to search for books that belong to an author. Figure 10-30 shows a relationship called *books* that we have created for the Authors entity.

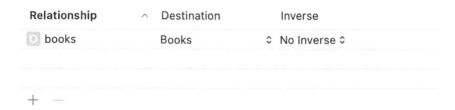

Figure 10-30: *Relationship for the Authors entity*

IMPORTANT: Relationships must always be bidirectional. If we set a relationship from entity A to entity B, we must set the opposite relationship from entity B to A. Core Data offers another type of relationship called *Fetched Properties* to connect entities in only one direction. You can add a Fetched Property from the area below the Relationships area in the model's editor.

The new relationship added in Figure 10-30 is in the Authors entity, so every Authors object will have a property called **books** that we can use to retrieve the Books objects associated to the author. Because one author can have many books, the setting of this relationship is going to differ from the previous one. In this case, we must set the Type of the relationship as To-Many (to many books) and modify the Delete Rule according to how we want our application to respond when an author is deleted. If we don't want to keep books that are not connected to an author, we should select the Cascade option, so when an author is deleted all his or her books are deleted too. But if we don't mind having books with no author, then the option should be kept as Nullify.

 IMPORTANT: The Delete Rules are a way to ensure that the objects remaining in the Object Graph are those that our application and the user need. But we can always set the rule to Nullify and take care of deleting all the objects ourselves.

There is a third value for the relationship called *Inverse*. Once we set the relationships on both sides, it is highly recommendable to set this value. It just tells the model what the name of the opposite relationship is. Core Data needs this to ensure the consistency of the Object Graph. Figure 10-32 shows the final setup for both relationships.

Relationship for the Books entity

Relationship	∧	Destination	Inverse
◉ author		Authors	⇕ books ⇕

Relationship for the Authors entity

Relationship	∧	Destination	Inverse
◉ books		Books	⇕ authors ⇕

Figure 10-31: Inverse Relationships

 Do It Yourself: Create a Multiplatform project. Open the File menu and select the File option to create a new file. Move to the Core Data section and select the option Data Model from the iOS panel (Figure 10-21). Save the file with the name "books". Click on the file to open the editor (Figure 10-22). Press the Add Entity button to create two entities with the names Authors and Books. Create the attributes for these entities as illustrated in Figures 10-25 and 10-27. Create the relationships for both entities as shown in Figure 10-31. Set the books relationship as To-Many and keep the rest of the values by default.

(Basic) **Core Data Stack**

The creation of the model is just the first step in the definition of the Core Data system. Once we have all the entities along with their attributes and relationships set up, we must initialize Core Data. Core Data is created from a group of objects that are in charge of all the processes required to manage the data, from the organization of the Object Graph to the storage of the graph in a database. There is an object that manages the model, an object that stores the data on file, and an object that intermediates between this Persistent Store and our own code. The scheme is called *Stack*. Figure 10-32 illustrates a common Core Data stack.

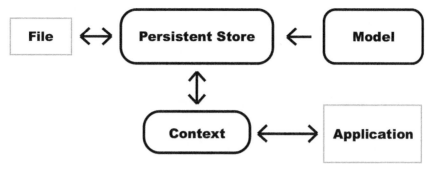

Figure 10-32: Core Data stack

The code in our application interacts with the Context to manage the objects it needs to access, the Context asks the Persistent Store to read or add new objects to the graph, and the Persistent Store processes the Object Graph according to the model and saves it in a file.

The Core Data framework offers classes to create objects that represent every part of the stack. The **NSManagedObjectModel** class manages the model, the **NSPersistentStore** class manages a Persistent Store, the **NSPersistentStoreCoordinator** class is used to manage all the Persistent Stores available (a Core Data stack can have multiple Persistent Stores), and the **NSManagedObjectContext** creates and manages the context that intermediates between our app and the store. Although we can instantiate these objects and create the stack ourselves, the framework offers the **NSPersistentContainer** class that takes care of everything for us. The class includes the following initializer and properties to access each object of the stack.

NSPersistentContainer(name: String**)**—This initializer creates an **NSPersistent-Container** object that defines a Core Data stack. The **name** argument is a string representing the name of the container. This value must match the name of the Core Data model (the file's name, without the extension).

managedObjectModel—This property sets or returns an **NSManagedObjectModel** object that represents the Core Data model.

persistentStoreCoordinator—This property sets or returns the **NSPersistent-StoreCoordinator** object that manages all the Persistent Stores available.

viewContext—This property sets or returns the **NSManagedObjectContext** object in charge of the stack's context that we use to access and modify the Object Graph.

The **NSPersistentContainer** object automatically resolves conflicts for us, but we must configure the context to determine how those conflicts are going to be solved. The **NSManaged-ObjectContext** class includes the following properties for this purpose.

automaticallyMergesChangesFromParent—This property sets or returns a Boolean value that determines whether the context automatically merges the changes in the Persistent Store and the context.

mergePolicy—This property sets or returns an object that decides the policy that the context is going to use to merge the changes in the Persistent Store and the context. The Core Data framework defines global variables to set standard policies. The **NSErrorMergePolicy** variable returns an error if the objects are different, the **NSMergeByPropertyStoreTrumpMergePolicy** variable replaces changes in memory by the external changes, the **NSMergeByPropertyObjectTrumpMergePolicy** replaces the external changes by the changes in memory, the **NSOverwriteMergePolicy** variable replaces the values in the Persistent Store by the current changes, and the **NSRollbackMergePolicy** uses the version of the objects in the Persistent Store.

To create the Core Data stack, we must initialize a new **NSPersistentContainer** object and then load the Persistent Stores (one by default). Because the stores may take time to load, the class offers a specific method for this purpose.

loadPersistentStores(completionHandler: Closure)—This method loads the Persistent Stores and executes a closure when the process is over. The closure receives two arguments, an **NSPersistentStoreDescription** object with the configuration of the stack, and an optional **Error** value to report errors.

All the communication between our app and the data in the Persistent Store is done through the context. The context is created by the container from the **NSManagedObjectContext** class. This class includes properties and methods to manage the context and the objects in the Persistent Store. The following are the most frequently used.

hasChanges—This property returns a Boolean value that indicates if the context has changes that must be saved to the Persistent Store.

save()—This method saves the changes to the Persistent Store.

reset()—This method resets the context to a basic state. All the objects and modifications our app introduced to the context are ignored.

fetch(NSFetchRequest**)**—This method returns an array with the objects requested by the **NSFetchRequest** object.

delete(NSManagedObject**)**—This method deletes an object from the Persistent Store.

count(for: NSFetchRequest**)**—This method returns the number of objects found in the Persistent Store by the request. The **for** argument specifies the request we want to perform.

When working with Core Data, the Core Data's Persistent Store becomes our app's data model. Therefore, we can define a specific class to initialize the Core Data stack, or just do it from our model, as in the following example.

```
import SwiftUI
import CoreData

class ApplicationData: ObservableObject {
    let container: NSPersistentContainer

    init() {
        container = NSPersistentContainer(name: "books")
        container.viewContext.automaticallyMergesChangesFromParent = true
        container.loadPersistentStores(completionHandler:
{ storeDescription, error in
            if let error = error as NSError? {
                fatalError("Unresolved error \(error), \(error.userInfo)")
            }
        })
    }
}
```

Listing 10-47: Initializing the Core Data stack from the model

The **ApplicationData** class in this example defines a property called **container** to store a reference to the Persistent Store. When the object is initialized, we create an instance of the **NSPersistentContainer** class with the name of the Core Data model (in our example, we called it "books") and configure it to merge the changes between the context and the Persistent Store (this is the configuration recommended by Apple). The object creates the stack but does not load the Persistent Stores, we have to do it ourselves with the **loadPersistentStores()** method. After completion, this method executes a closure with two values: a reference to the Persistent Store just created, and an **Error** value to report errors. Errors are infrequent, but if one occurs, we should warn the user. For instance, we can modify a state property to open an Alert View to report the situation. In this example, we just call the **fatalError()** function to stop the execution of the app.

Once we have the container, we must get the context from it and share it with the views, so they can add, fetch, or remove objects from the Persistent Store. The environment offers the **managedObjectContext** property for this purpose. The following are the modifications we must introduced to the **App** structure to inject a reference to the context into the environment.

```
import SwiftUI
@main
struct TestApp: App {
   @StateObject var appData = ApplicationData()

   var body: some Scene {
      WindowGroup {
         ContentView()
            .environmentObject(appData)
            .environment(\.managedObjectContext,
appData.container.viewContext)
      }
   }
}
```

Listing 10-48: Injecting the context into the environment

The model is initialized and injected into the environment as before. To provide direct access to the Core Data context, we get a reference from the **viewContext** property of the **NSPersistentContainer** object and then assign it to the environment's **managedObject-Context** property with the **environment()** modifier. From now on, the views can access the Core Data context from the environment to fetch, add, modify or remove objects from the Persistent Store.

 Do It Yourself: Create a Swift file called ApplicationData.swift for the model in Listing 10-47 and update the **App** structure with the code in Listing 10-48. Replace the value of the **name** argument in the **NSPersistentContainer** initializer with the name of your model's file (in our example, it is called "books"). At this moment, the app doesn't do anything other than creating the stack. We will see how to read and store data next.

(Basic) **Managed Objects**

Core Data does not store our custom objects; it defines a class called **NSManagedObject** for this purpose. Every time we want to store information in the database, we must create an **NSManagedObject** object, associate that object to an Entity, and store the data the entity allows. For example, if we create an object associated to the Books entity, we are only allowed to store five values that corresponds to the Entity's attributes and relationship (title, year, cover, thumbnail, and author). The class includes the following initializer and methods to create and manage the objects.

NSManagedObject(context: NSManagedObjectContext**)**—This initializer creates a new instance of the **NSManagedObject** class, or a subclass of it, and adds it to the context specified by the **context** argument.

fetchRequest()—This type method generates a fetch request for an entity. A fetch request is a request we use to fetch objects of a particular entity from the Persistent Store.

entity()—This type method returns a reference to the entity from which the managed object was created. It is an object of type **NSEntityDescription** with a description of the entity.

To simplify our work, the system allows us to define subclasses of the **NSManagedObject** class that correspond to the entities in our model. (Instead of creating instances of the **NSManagedObject** class, we create instances of the **Books** and **Authors** classes.) Because this is common practice, Xcode automatically creates the subclasses for us. All we need to do is to associate each Entity with a subclass from the Data Model Inspector panel.

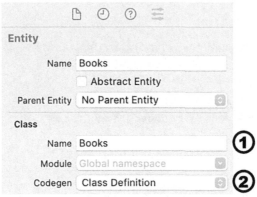

Figure 10-33: *Entity's subclass*

To ask Xcode to create the subclasses for us, we must select the entities one by one, select the Class Definition value for the Codegen option (Figure 10-33, number 2), and make sure that the name of the subclass is specified in the Name field (Figure 10-33, number 1). Once the options are set, the classes are automatically created. For example, when we set these options for the entities in our model, Xcode creates a subclass of **NSManagedObject** called **Books** with the properties **title**, **year**, **cover**, **thumbnail**, and **author**, and a subclass called **Authors** with the properties **name** and **books**. From now on, all we need to do to store a book in the Persistent Store is to create an instance of the **Books** class using the **NSManagedObject** initializer.

Do It Yourself: By default, Xcode configures the Entities and creates the subclasses for us, but you can do it yourself from the editor. Select the Books or the Authors entity, open the Data Model Inspector panel on the right, and make sure that the value of the Codegen option is set to Class Definition and the name of the Entity is assigned to the Name field, as shown in Figure 10-33.

IMPORTANT: The subclasses of the **NSManagedObject** class created to represent each entity in our model are not visible in Xcode. They are created internally and automatically modified every time entities or attributes are added or removed from the model. If you decide not to use these subclasses, you can select the value Manual/None from the Codegen option and work directly with **NSManagedObject** objects or define your own subclasses.

(Basic) **Fetch Request**

To store an object in the Persistent Store, we must create an **NSManagedObject** object (or an instance of our subclasses), add it to the context, and then save the context. The process to get the objects back from the Persistent Store is the opposite. Instead of moving the changes from the context to the Persistent Store, we must fetch the objects from the Persistent Store and move them into the context. Once the objects are in the context, we can read their properties, modify the values or delete them. Core Data defines the **NSFetchRequest** class to fetch objects from the Persistent Store. The class includes the following properties for configuration.

predicate—This property sets or returns the predicate used to filter the objects fetched by the request. It is a value of type **NSPredicate**; a Foundation class used to establish logical conditions to filter objects.

sortDescriptors—This property sets or returns an array of sort descriptors that determine how the objects fetched by the request should be ordered. It is an array of values of type **NSSortDescriptor**; a Foundation class used to sort the objects according to the value of a property in ascending or descending order.

fetchLimit—This property sets or returns the maximum number of objects that the request should return. It takes a value of type **Int**.

propertiesToFetch—This property sets or returns an array of values that determine the properties we want to get (by default, all the properties of the **NSManagedObject** objects are returned). The properties of an entity (attributes) are represented by objects of the **NSPropertyDescription** class, or subclasses of it.

Every time we need to get data from the Persistent Store, we must create an **NSFetch-Request** object to determine what type of objects we want. To simplify our work, SwiftUI includes the **@FetchRequest** property wrapper. With this property wrapper, we can create a request or apply our own **NSFetchRequest** object. The property wrapper takes care of performing the request and updating the views with the values returned. It is created from a structure of type **FetchRequest**. The following are some of the structure's initializers.

FetchRequest(sortDescriptors: [SortDescriptor], predicate: NSPredicate?, animation: Animation?)—This initializer creates a fetch request with the configuration determined by the arguments and produces a **FetchedResults** structure that manages and delivers the objects to the view. The **sortDescriptors** argument is an array of **SortDescriptor** structures that determine the order of the objects, the **predicate** argument is an **NSPredicate** object that filters the objects, and the **animation** argument determines how the changes are going to be animated.

FetchRequest(fetchRequest: NSFetchRequest, animation: Animation?)—This initializer creates a fetch request with the **NSFetchRequest** object provided by the **fetchRequest** argument and produces a **FetchedResults** structure that manages and delivers the objects to the view. The **animation** argument determines how the changes are going to be animated.

A fetch request loads all the objects available in the Persistent Store. This is not a problem when the number of objects is not significant. But a Persistent Store can manage thousands of objects, which can consume resources that the app and the system need to run. Therefore, instead of the fetch request, the **@FetchRequest** property wrapper produces a value of type **FetchedResults**. This is a structure that takes care of loading into the context only the objects that are required by the view at any given moment. We will learn more about it later.

(Basic) Asynchronous Access

Reading and writing information on a database is a delicate process. The database may be accessed by different parts of the application and from different threads, which can cause errors or even data corruption. To make sure the data is accurate and safe, we must access the database from the same thread assigned to the Core Data context. For this purpose, the **NSManagedObjectContext** class includes the following asynchronous method.

perform(schedule: ScheduledTaskType, Closure**)**—This asynchronous method performs a closure in the thread assigned to the Core Data context. The **schedule** argument determines how the closure is going to be executed. It is an enumeration with the values **immediate** (the closure runs asynchronously), and **enqueued** (the closure runs concurrently). If the argument is ignored, the closure is executed asynchronously.

(Basic) Core Data Application

It is time to see how all these tools work together to store and retrieve data from a Persistent Store. We are going to use a project like the one created before for archiving. The purpose of the application is to show the list of books stored in the Persistent Store and add new ones.

Figure 10-34: *Interface to work with Core Data*

The initial view lists all the books available in the Persistent Store and includes a button to open a second view to create new objects with the values provided by the user.

```
import SwiftUI
import CoreData
struct ContentView: View {
   @FetchRequest(sortDescriptors: [], predicate: nil,
animation: .default) private var listOfBooks: FetchedResults<Books>

   var body: some View {
      NavigationStack {
         List {
            ForEach(listOfBooks) { book in
              RowBook(book: book)
            }
         }
         .navigationBarTitle("Books")
         .toolbar {
            ToolbarItem(placement: .navigationBarTrailing) {
               NavigationLink(destination: InsertBookView(), label: {
                  Image(systemName: "plus")
               })
            }
         }
      }
   }
}
struct RowBook: View {
   let book: Books

   var imageCover: UIImage {
      if let data = book.thumbnail, let image = UIImage(data: data) {
         return image
```

```
        } else {
            return UIImage(named: "nopicture")!
        }
    }
    var body: some View {
        HStack(alignment: .top) {
            Image(uiImage: imageCover)
                .resizable()
                .scaledToFit()
                .frame(width: 80, height: 100)
                .cornerRadius(10)
            VStack(alignment: .leading, spacing: 2) {
                Text(book.title ?? "Undefined")
                    .bold()
                Text(book.author?.name ?? "Undefined")
                    .foregroundColor(book.author != nil ? .black : .gray)
                Text(String(book.year))
                    .font(.caption)
                Spacer()
            }.padding(.top, 5)
            Spacer()
        }.padding(.top, 5)
    }
}
```

Listing 10-49: *Fetching objects from the Persistent Store*

To have access to Core Data from the view, we must import the framework with the **import** keyword, as we did in this example. After this, we are ready to fetch and store objects from the Persistent Store, and the first step is to get the list of objects already inserted by the user. To this end, the **ContentView** view defines a **@FetchRequest** property. This property creates a fetch request to fetch objects of the Books entity in no specific order (the **sortDescriptor** argument was declared with an empty array). Notice that the property wrapper produces a structure of type **FetchedResults** and this structure is generic. The data type specified for the structure is the one that determines the type of objects to fetch. In our case it is **Books** objects (**FetchedResults<Books>**).

Once the **@FetchRequest** property is ready, we can provide it to a **List** view to show the objects on the screen. The **ForEach** view in our example goes through this list and creates a **RowBook** view for each object to show the values. Reading these values is easy. The attributes of an entity are turned into properties of the **NSManagedObject** (the **Books** object in our example), and they are available as any other property. The only thing we must consider is that some of these properties return optional values. For instance, the **title** property returns an optional string. To show this value, we use a nil-coalescing operator (**??**). If there is a value in the property, we display it, otherwise, we show the string "Undefined". The **author** property is a little bit different. This property doesn't represent an attribute but a relationship. The value we need is actually the name of the author, which is returned by the **name** property inside the **Authors** object (**book.author?.name**). If this property contains a value, we show it, otherwise, we show the text "Undefined" again.

The image is more complicated. The value returned by the **thumbnail** property is a **Data** structure that we must convert to an **UIImage** object before creating the **Image** view with it. There are different ways to perform this process. In this example, we have decided to do it with a computed property called **imageCover**. When the view reads this property, we check if there is a value in the object's **thumbnail** property, create an **UIImage** object with it, and return it. On the other hand, if the **thumbnail** property is empty, or there was a problem converting the data into an image, we return a **UIImage** object with the image nopicture from the Asset Catalog.

Now, it is time to let the user create new **Books** objects. The **ContentView** view includes a **NavigationLink** in the navigation bar that opens the **InsertBookView** view for this purpose.

```
import SwiftUI
import CoreData

struct InsertBookView: View {
    @Environment(\.managedObjectContext) var dbContext
    @Environment(\.dismiss) var dismiss
    @State private var inputTitle: String = ""
    @State private var inputYear: String = ""

    var body: some View {
        VStack(spacing: 12) {
            HStack {
                Text("Title:")
                TextField("Insert Title", text: $inputTitle)
                    .textFieldStyle(.roundedBorder)
            }
            HStack {
                Text("Year:")
                TextField("Insert Year", text: $inputYear)
                    .textFieldStyle(.roundedBorder)
            }
            HStack {
                Text("Author:")
                Text("Undefined")
                    .foregroundColor(.gray)
            }.frame(minWidth: 0, maxWidth: .infinity, alignment: .leading)
            Spacer()
        }.padding()
        .navigationBarTitle("Add Book")
        .toolbar {
            ToolbarItem(placement: .navigationBarTrailing) {
                Button("Save") {
                    let newTitle =
inputTitle.trimmingCharacters(in: .whitespaces)
                    let newYear = Int32(inputYear)
                    if !newTitle.isEmpty && newYear != nil {
                        Task(priority: .high) {
                            await storeBook(title: newTitle, year: newYear!)
                        }
                    }
                }
            }
        }
    }
    func storeBook(title: String, year: Int32) async {
        await dbContext.perform {
            let newBook = Books(context: dbContext)
            newBook.title = title
            newBook.year = year
            newBook.author = nil
            newBook.cover = UIImage(named: "bookcover")?.pngData()
            newBook.thumbnail = UIImage(named: "bookthumbnail")?.pngData()
            do {
                try dbContext.save()
                dismiss()
            } catch {
                print("Error saving record")
            }
        }
    }
}
```

Listing 10-50: Adding new objects to the Persistent Store

All the interaction between our code and the Persistent Store is done through the context. When we want to access the objects already stored, add new ones, remove them, or modify any of their values, we have to do it in the context and then move those changes from the context to the Persistent Store. The **@FetchRequest** property wrapper automatically gets a reference of the context from the environment (this is the reference we injected into the context in the **App** structure of Listing 10-48), but when working directly with Core Data, we must get the reference from the environment with the **@Environment** property wrapper and the **managedObjectContext** key. In this example, we called this property **dbContext**.

The view includes two **TextField** views to let the user insert the title of the book and the year of publication, and a button in the navigation bar to save the values. When the button is pressed, the code checks if the values are valid and then calls an asynchronous method to create and store a new object in the Persistent Store. We moved the code to an asynchronous method so that we can implement the **perform()** method provided by the context and thus ensure that the process is performed in a safe thread, which is recommended every time we are adding, removing, or modifying an object.

The process to add a new book begins with the creation of the new object with the **Books()** initializer. This not only creates a new object of type **Books** but it also adds it to the context specified by the argument (**dbContext**). The next step is to assign the values to the object's properties. We assign the value of the first input field to the **title** property, the value of the second input field to the **year** property, the images bookcover and bookthumbnail to the **cover** and **thumbnail** properties, respectively (we assign standard images to every book for now), and the **nil** value to the **author** property (we still don't have an **Authors** object to associate with this book).

The **Books()** initializer inserts the new object into the context, but this change is not permanent. If we close the app after the values are assigned to the properties, the object is lost. To persist the changes, we must save the context with the **save()** method. This should be done every time we finish a process that modifies the context. The method takes the information in the context and updates the Persistent Store with it, so everything is stored permanently in the file.

 Do It Yourself: This example assumes that you have followed the previous steps to create a project, prepare a model with the Books and Authors entities, define the Core Data stack, and inject the context into the environment in the **App** structure (Listing 10-48). Download the bookcover, bookthumbnail, and nopicture images from our website and add them to the Asset Catalog. Update the ContentView.swift file with the code in Listing 10-49. Create a SwiftUI View file called InsertBookView.swift for the view in Listing 10-50. Run the application on the iPhone simulator. (Later we will learn how to generate the previews and run the application in the canvas.) Press the + button and insert a book. You should see the interface illustrated in Figure 10-34.

There are no view models in Core Data. The objects stored in the Persistent Store (**Books** and **Authors** in our example), represent the application's data model. They store the values and return them as they are. But the views need the values to be formatted or casted before showing them on the screen. For instance, in the **RowBook** view in Listing 10-49, we had to process the value of the **thumbnail** property with a computed property to turn it into an **UIImage** view. We also had to use the nil-coalescing operator to show a string if there was no value in the **title** and **author** properties. And we even had to cast the value of the **year** property to a string with the **String()** initializer. All this work should not be done by the view, it should be done by a view model. To create a view model for the Core Data objects, we can extend the classes defined by the system (see Extensions in Chapter 3). For example, we can create an extension of the **Books** class to provide computed properties that always return **String** values for the views to display, and process the images in the **thumbnail** and **cover** properties, so we don't have to do it inside the view.

```
import SwiftUI

extension Books {
   var showTitle: String {
      return title ?? "Undefined"
   }
   var showYear: String {
      return String(year)
   }
   var showAuthor: String {
      return author?.name ?? "Undefined"
   }
   var showCover: UIImage {
      if let data = cover, let image = UIImage(data: data) {
         return image
      } else {
         return UIImage(named: "nopicture")!
      }
   }
   var showThumbnail: UIImage {
      if let data = thumbnail, let image = UIImage(data: data) {
         return image
      } else {
         return UIImage(named: "nopicture")!
      }
   }
}
extension Authors {
   var showName: String {
      return name ?? "Undefined"
   }
}
```

Listing 10-51: Defining a view model for the Core Data objects

Extensions have access to the properties defined by the data type. This means that we can access those properties, process their values, and return something else. The example in Listing 10-51 defines an extension for the **Books** class and an extension for the **Authors** class. The extensions include computed properties that format the values in the original properties and return a value for the views to display. In the extension of the **Books** class, we also include a property that returns a string with the name of the author, so the views don't have to read this value from the **Authors** object anymore, they can do it directly from the **Books** object.

```
struct RowBook: View {
   let book: Books

   var body: some View {
      HStack(alignment: .top) {
         Image(uiImage: book.showThumbnail)
            .resizable()
            .scaledToFit()
            .frame(width: 80, height: 100)
            .cornerRadius(10)
         VStack(alignment: .leading, spacing: 2) {
            Text(book.showTitle)
               .bold()
            Text(book.showAuthor)
            Text(book.showYear)
               .font(.caption)
            Spacer()
         }.padding(.top, 5)
```

```
            Spacer()
        }.padding(.top, 10)
    }
}
```

Listing 10-52: Using the values from the view model

The view has been greatly simplified. There is no formatting or processing. All it has to do now is to read the values from the view model and show them to the user.

 Do It Yourself: Create a Swift file called Extensions.swift for the code in Listing 10-51. Update the **RowBook** view in the ContentView.swift file with the code in Listing 10-52. Run the application on the iPhone simulator. (We will learn how to do it on the canvas next.) You should see the interface in Figure 10-34.

Authors objects are generated and stored the same way as **Books** objects. This demands our application to provide new views where the user can select and add more objects. For our example, we have decided to expand our interface with a view that lists the authors already inserted by the user and another view to insert new ones.

Figure 10-35: Interface to list and add authors

The view on the left in Figure 10-35 is the **InsertBookView** view introduced before to insert new books. This view now shows three input options, an input field to insert the title of the book, another to insert the year, and the Select Author button to select the author. This button is a **NavigationLink** view that opens a view to list all the authors available (Figure 10-35, center). In turn, this view includes a + button in the navigation bar to open a view that includes an input field to insert the name of an author (Figure 10-35, right). The first step we need to take to create this interface is to add the Select Author button to the **InsertBookView** view, as shown below.

```
struct InsertBookView: View {
   @Environment(\.managedObjectContext) var dbContext
   @Environment(\.dismiss) var dismiss
   @State private var selectedAuthor: Authors? = nil
   @State private var inputTitle: String = ""
   @State private var inputYear: String = ""

   var body: some View {
      VStack(spacing: 12) {
         HStack {
            Text("Title:")
            TextField("Insert Title", text: $inputTitle)
               .textFieldStyle(.roundedBorder)
         }
         HStack {
            Text("Year:")
            TextField("Insert Year", text: $inputYear)
               .textFieldStyle(.roundedBorder)
         }
         HStack(alignment: .top) {
```

```
                    Text("Author:")
                    VStack(alignment: .leading, spacing: 8) {
                        Text(selectedAuthor?.name ?? "Undefined")
                            .foregroundColor(selectedAuthor != nil ? Color.black :
Color.gray)
                        NavigationLink(destination: AuthorsView(selected:
$selectedAuthor), label: {
                            Text("Select Author")
                        })
                    }
                }.frame(minWidth: 0, maxWidth: .infinity, alignment: .leading)
                Spacer()
            }.padding()
            .navigationBarTitle("Add Book")
            .toolbar {
                ToolbarItem(placement: .navigationBarTrailing) {
                    Button("Save") {
                        let newTitle =
inputTitle.trimmingCharacters(in: .whitespaces)
                        let newYear = Int32(inputYear)
                        if !newTitle.isEmpty && newYear != nil {
                            Task(priority: .high) {
                                await storeBook(title: newTitle, year: newYear!)
                            }
                        }
                    }
                }
            }
        }
        func storeBook(title: String, year: Int32) async {
            await dbContext.perform {
                let newBook = Books(context: dbContext)
                newBook.title = title
                newBook.year = year
                newBook.author = selectedAuthor
                newBook.cover = UIImage(named: "bookcover")?.pngData()
                newBook.thumbnail = UIImage(named: "bookthumbnail")?.pngData()
                do {
                    try dbContext.save()
                    dismiss()
                } catch {
                    print("Error saving record")
                }
            }
        }
    }
}
```

Listing 10-53: Selecting the author

Every time an author is selected or created, we must get its **Authors** object and send it back to the **InsertBookView** view to assign it to the book. To store this value, the view includes a **@State** property called **selectedAuthor**. If the property contains an **Authors** object, we show the value of its **name** property to the user, otherwise, we show the text "Undefined". Below the name, we include a **NavigationLink** button to open a view called **AuthorsView** to let the user select an author. This view must list the authors and provide a button to add more.

```
import SwiftUI

struct AuthorsView: View {
    @FetchRequest(sortDescriptors: [], predicate: nil,
animation: .default) private var listOfAuthors: FetchedResults<Authors>
    @Environment(\.dismiss) var dismiss
```

```
    @Binding var selected: Authors?
    var body: some View {
        List {
            ForEach(listOfAuthors) { author in
                HStack {
                    Text(author.showName)
                }
                .frame(minWidth: 0, maxWidth: .infinity, minHeight: 0,
maxHeight: .infinity, alignment: .leading)
                .background(.white)
                .onTapGesture {
                    selected = author
                    dismiss()
                }
            }
        }
        .navigationBarTitle("Authors")
        .toolbar {
            ToolbarItem(placement: .navigationBarTrailing) {
                NavigationLink(destination: InsertAuthorView(), label: {
                    Image(systemName: "plus")
                })
            }
        }
    }
}
struct AuthorsView_Previews: PreviewProvider {
    static var previews: some View {
        AuthorsView(selected: .constant(nil))
    }
}
```

Listing 10-54: Listing all the authors available

This view lists the authors already inserted by the user. The **@FetchRequest** property is called **listOfAuthors** and it is defined to work with **Authors** objects, but other than that, the rest of the code is the same we used to list books. The only significant difference is that the rows now include the **onTapGesture()** modifier to let the user select an author. When the user taps on the name of an author, we assign the **Authors** object to a **@Binding** property called **selected** and close the view. Because the **selected** property is connected to the **selectedAuthor** property defined in the **InsertBookView** view, the name of the author selected by the user will be shown on the screen.

If there are no authors in the Persistent Store yet, or the author the user is looking for is not on the list, the user can press a button in the navigation bar that opens the **InsertAuthorView** view to insert a new author.

```
import SwiftUI
import CoreData
struct InsertAuthorView: View {
    @Environment(\.managedObjectContext) var dbContext
    @Environment(\.dismiss) var dismiss
    @State private var inputName: String = ""

    var body: some View {
        VStack {
            HStack {
                Text("Name:")
                TextField("Insert Name", text: $inputName)
                    .textFieldStyle(.roundedBorder)
            }
```

```
            HStack {
                Spacer()
                Button("Save") {
                    let newName =
inputName.trimmingCharacters(in: .whitespaces)
                    if !newName.isEmpty {
                        Task(priority: .high) {
                            await storeAuthor(name: newName)
                        }
                    }
                }
            }
            Spacer()
        }.padding()
        .navigationBarTitle("Add Author")
    }
    func storeAuthor(name: String) async {
        await dbContext.perform {
            let newAuthor = Authors(context: dbContext)
            newAuthor.name = name
            do {
                try dbContext.save()
                dismiss()
            } catch {
                print("Error saving record")
            }
        }
    }
}
```

Listing 10-55: Inserting new authors

This is a simple view. It includes one **TextField** view to insert the name of the author and a button to save it. When the button is pressed, we follow the same procedure as before. The **Authors** object is initialized and stored in the context, the name inserted by the user is assigned to the object's **name** property, and the context is saved to make the changes permanent.

With these additions, our basic app is complete. When we pressed the Select Author button, the app opens a view with all the authors available (Figure 10-35, center). If there are no authors yet or the author we want is not on the list, we can press the + button to insert a new one (Figure 10-35, right). Every time we select an author from the list, the app goes back to the view with the book's information and shows the name of the selected author on the screen (Figure 10-35, left). The **Authors** object that represents the author is assigned to the book's **author** property and therefore the name of the author is now shown on the list of books.

 Do It Yourself: Update the **InsertBookView** view with the code in Listing 10-53. Create a SwiftUI View file called AuthorsView.swift for the view in Listing 10-54 and another called InsertAuthorView.swift for the code in Listing 10-55. Run the application on the iPhone simulator. Press the + button to insert a new book. Press the Select Author button. Press the + button to add an author. After adding the author, tap on it to select it. You should see the name of the author on the screen.

Basic **Previews**

So far, we have run the application on the iPhone simulator or a device. This is because Apple recommends to create the Persistent Store for previews in memory, so all the objects added for testing are removed as soon as the preview is over. Therefore, if we want to develop the interface on the canvas, we need to define two Persistent Stores, one for the application and another for the previews. In the following example, we achieve this with a type property. The model works as before, but if we read this property, we get an `ApplicationData` class that creates a Persistent Store in memory. To know what kind of Persistent Store to create, we add a Boolean parameter to the `ApplicationData` initializer called `preview`. If the value of this parameter is `false`, the Persistent Store is created as always, otherwise, it is created in memory.

```
import SwiftUI
import CoreData

class ApplicationData: ObservableObject {
   let container: NSPersistentContainer

   static var preview: ApplicationData = {
      let model = ApplicationData(preview: true)
      return model
   }()
   init(preview: Bool = false) {
      container = NSPersistentContainer(name: "books")
      if preview {
         container.persistentStoreDescriptions.first!.url =
URL(fileURLWithPath: "/dev/null")
      }
      container.loadPersistentStores(completionHandler:
{ (storeDescription, error) in
         if let error = error as NSError? {
            fatalError("Unresolved error \(error), \(error.userInfo)")
         }
      })
   }
}
```

Listing 10-56: Creating a Persistent Store for previews

This model creates the Persistent Store as before, but it also includes a type property called `preview` to create a Persistent Store in memory for the previews. The closure assigned to this property initializes the `ApplicationData` object with the value `true`. The initializer checks this value and assigns a `URL` structure with a null URL to the `url` property of the `NSPersistent-StoreDescription` object returned by the `persistentStoreDescriptions` property of the `NSPersistentContainer` class. The `NSPersistentStoreDescription` object is used by Core Data to create and load the Persistent Store, so when we assign a URL with the "/dev/null" path to this object, the Persistent Store is created in memory.

Now that we have a type property to create the Persistent Store for previews, we can use it in the `PreviewProvider` structures. All we need to do is to inject it into the environment as we did in the `App` structure, but this time we access the `viewContext` property of the `NSPersistentContainer` object returned by the `ApplicationData` object created by the `preview` property, as shown next.

```
struct ContentView_Previews: PreviewProvider {
   static var previews: some View {
      ContentView()
         .environment(\.managedObjectContext,
ApplicationData.preview.container.viewContext)
   }
}
```

Listing 10-57: Accessing the Core Data context from the preview

 Do It Yourself: Update the `ApplicationData` class with the code in Listing 10-56. Update `PreviewProvider` structure in the ContentView.swift file with the code in Listing 10-57. Use the same `environment()` modifier to inject the context in the preview of every view we have created so far. Select the `ContentView` view. You should be able to add new books and see the list of books on the canvas.

Basic Sort Descriptors

Objects returned from a request are usually in the order they were created, but this is not guaranteed. Foundation defines two data types to sort objects, the `NSSortDescriptor` class to define `NSFetchRequest` objects, and the `SortDescriptor` structure, designed to work with the `@FetchRequest` property wrapper. The most useful in SwiftUI applications is the `SortDescriptor` structure. From these structure, we can specify an order according to the values of a property. The structure includes the following initializer.

SortDescriptor(KeyPath, **comparator:** StandardComparator, **order:** SortOrder)—This initializer creates a `SortDescriptor` structure that sorts the objects according to the value of the property specified by the first argument. This argument is the key path of the property we want to use to sort the objects. The **comparator** argument determines how to compare the values. It is a structure with the type properties `lexical`, `localized`, and `localizedStandard` (default). And the **order** argument determines if the objects will be sorted in ascending or descending order. It is an enumeration with the values `forward` and `reverse`.

The `@FetchRequest` property wrapper includes the **sortDescriptors** argument to define the order of the objects in the request. Therefore, all we have to do to sort the objects is to create at least one `SortDescriptor` structure and assign it to this argument. The following example sorts the **Books** objects by title in ascending order.

```
struct ContentView: View {
   @FetchRequest(sortDescriptors: [SortDescriptor(\Books.title,
order: .forward)], predicate: nil, animation: .default) var listOfBooks:
FetchedResults<Books>

   var body: some View {
      NavigationStack {
         List {
            ForEach(listOfBooks) { book in
               RowBook(book: book)
            }
         }
         .navigationBarTitle("Books")
         .toolbar {
            ToolbarItem(placement: .navigationBarTrailing) {
               NavigationLink(destination: InsertBookView(), label: {
                  Image(systemName: "plus")
               })
            }
         }
      }
   }
}
```

Listing 10-58: Sorting the books by title

The **sortDescriptors** argument takes an array of `SortDescriptor` structures, so we can specify multiple conditions to sort the list. The final order is established according to the location of the `SortDescriptor` structures in the array. For example, we can sort the books by author first and then by year.

```
@FetchRequest(sortDescriptors: [SortDescriptor(\Books.author?.name,
order: .forward), SortDescriptor(\.year, order: .forward)], predicate:
nil, animation: .default) var listOfBooks: FetchedResults<Books>
```

Listing 10-59: *Sorting books by author and year*

The values are sorted according to a comparator. The **String** structure defines the **StandardComparator** structure to create them. The structure includes type properties to create instances for common comparators. The currently available are **lexical**, **localizedStandard** (default), and **localized**. The structure returned by the **lexical** property sorts the values alphabetically. For instance, if we have an array with the values 1, 2, and 10, the order will be 1, 10, 2 (the value 10 begins with 1, which comes before 2). This also applies to letters. Uppercase letters come before lowercase letters, so words beginning with a lowercase letter will be moved to the end of the list. The structure returned by the **localizedStandard** property sorts the values numerically (1, 2, 10), which also applies to letters (words beginning with uppercase letters will be sorted along with lowercase letters). And finally, the structure returned by the **localized** property sorts the values alphabetically as the **lexical** structure, but uppercase and lowercase letters are sorted together, as the **localizedStandard** structure.

By default, the values are sorted with the **localizedStandard** structure. The following example shows how to apply a **lexical** structure instead.

```
@FetchRequest(sortDescriptors: [SortDescriptor(\Books.title,
comparator: .lexical, order: .forward)], predicate: nil,
animation: .default) var listOfBooks: FetchedResults<Books>
```

Listing 10-60: *Sorting with a lexical comparator*

 Do It Yourself: Update the **ContentView** view with the code in Listing 10-58 and try any of the **@FetchRequest** properties defined above to see how sort descriptors work. Change the value of the **order** argument to see how the order changes in each case (**forward** and **reverse**).

If later we need to change the order of the objects, we can assign new **SortDescriptor** structures to the **FetchedResults** structure created by the **@FetchRequest** property wrapper. For this purpose, the structure includes the **sortDescriptors** property. In the following example, we add a button to the navigation bar that opens a menu with three options to sort the values.

```
struct ContentView: View {
   @FetchRequest(sortDescriptors: [SortDescriptor(\Books.title,
order: .forward)], predicate: nil, animation: .default) var listOfBooks:
FetchedResults<Books>

   var body: some View {
      NavigationStack {
         List {
            ForEach(listOfBooks) { book in
               RowBook(book: book)
            }
         }
         .navigationBarTitle("Books")
         .toolbar {
            ToolbarItem(placement: .navigationBarLeading) {
               Menu("Sort") {
                  Button("Sort by Title", action: {
                     let sort = SortDescriptor(\Books.title,
order: .forward)
```

```
                    listOfBooks.sortDescriptors = [sort]
                })
                Button("Sort by Author", action: {
                    let sort = SortDescriptor(\Books.author?.name,
order: .forward)
                    listOfBooks.sortDescriptors = [sort]
                })
                Button("Sort by Year", action: {
                    let sort = SortDescriptor(\Books.year,
order: .forward)
                    listOfBooks.sortDescriptors = [sort]
                })
            }
        }
        ToolbarItem(placement: .navigationBarTrailing) {
            NavigationLink(destination: InsertBookView(), label: {
                Image(systemName: "plus")
            })
        }
    }
}
}
```

Listing 10-61: Modifying the sorting criteria

The button is created by a `Menu` view, and the menu includes three `Button` views for each option. When a button is pressed, we create a `SortDescriptor` structure with the configuration we want and then assign it to the `sortDescriptors` property of the `FetchedResults` structure. The first button sorts the books by title (the configuration by default), the second button sorts the books by author, and the third button by year.

Figure 10-36: Different sorting criteria

(Basic) Predicates

The requests performed in previous examples are getting all the objects associated to a particular entity and the values of all their properties. The Foundation framework defines a class called `NSPredicate` to filter collections of objects. For instance, using this class we could get only the books that were published in the year 1983 or the authors which names start with "Stephen". The class defines the following initializer to create a predicate with all the conditions we need.

NSPredicate(format: String, **argumentArray:** [Any]?**)**—This initializer creates an `NSPredicate` object with the conditions set by the **format** argument. The **argumentArray** argument is an optional array of values that replace placeholders in the string assigned to the **format** argument. The **argumentArray** argument may be ignored or replaced by a list of values separated by commas.

To filter values in a request, we must create the **NSPredicate** object and assign it to the **predicate** argument of the **@FetchRequest** property wrapper. The following example assigns an **NSPredicate** object to the request in the **ContentView** view to search for the books that have the value 1983 assigned to their **year** property.

```
struct ContentView: View {
    @FetchRequest(sortDescriptors: [], predicate: NSPredicate(format:
"year = 1983")) var listOfBooks: FetchedResults<Books>

    var body: some View {
        NavigationStack {
            List {
                ForEach(listOfBooks) { book in
                    RowBook(book: book)
                }
            }
            .navigationBarTitle("Books")
            .toolbar {
                ToolbarItem(placement: .navigationBarTrailing) {
                    NavigationLink(destination: InsertBookView(), label: {
                        Image(systemName: "plus")
                    })
                }
            }
        }
    }
}
```

Listing 10-62: Filtering books by year

If we want to search for a value in a relationship, we must concatenate the properties with dot notation, as we did before to read the **name** property in the **Authors** object. For example, the following request searches for books written by Stephen King.

```
@FetchRequest(sortDescriptors: [], predicate: NSPredicate(format:
"author.name = 'Stephen King'")) var listOfBooks: FetchedResults<Books>
```

Listing 10-63: Filtering books by author

 Do It Yourself: Update the **ContentView** view with the code in Listing 10-62 and try the **@FetchRequest** property defined in Listing 10-63 to see how predicates work. Add books with different authors and years to test the filters.

Of course, these are predefined conditions, but we can allow the user to provide the values used to filter the objects. To achieve this, we need to replace the current predicate with a new one configured with the values inserted by the user.

To dynamically assign a new predicate to the request, the **FetchedResults** structure includes the **nspredicate** property. In the following example, we show how to search books by year by assigning a new predicate to this property every time the user inserts a 4 digits number in the search field.

```
struct ContentView: View {
    @FetchRequest(sortDescriptors: [], predicate: nil,
animation: .default) var listOfBooks: FetchedResults<Books>
    @State private var search: String = ""

    var body: some View {
        NavigationStack {
            List {
```

```
            ForEach(listOfBooks) { book in
                RowBook(book: book)
            }
        }
        .navigationBarTitle("Books")
        .toolbar {
            ToolbarItem(placement: .navigationBarTrailing) {
                NavigationLink(destination: InsertBookView(), label: {
                    Image(systemName: "plus")
                })
            }
        }
        .searchable(text: $search, prompt: Text("Insert year"))
        .onChange(of: search) { value in
            if value.count == 4 {
                if let year = Int32(value) {
                    listOfBooks.nsPredicate = NSPredicate(format: "year =
%@", NSNumber(value: year))
                }
            } else {
                listOfBooks.nsPredicate = nil
            }
        }
    }
  }
}
```

Listing 10-64: *Assigning new predicates to search for values inserted by the user*

To add a search bar, we implement the `searchable()` modifier (see Listing 8-10), and to perform the search, we implement the `onChange()` modifier. This modifier checks the value of a state property called `search`. If the value of this property changes, the modifier executes a closure where we replace the current predicate with a new one. When the value inserted by the user is a number, we filter books by year, otherwise, we assign a `nil` value to the `nsPredicate` property to show all the books available. (Notice that the `NSPredicate` initializer only takes Property List values, so we must cast the `Int32` value into an `NSNumber`.)

Figure 10-37: *Searching*

 Do It Yourself: Update the `ContentView` view with the code in Listing 10-64. Run the application on the iPhone simulator. Insert some books and then insert a year in the input field. Only the books published that year should be shown on the list, as illustrated in Figure 10-37.

 IMPORTANT: The placeholder `%@` is replaced by the value specified in the arguments between quotes. If you need to add the value to the predicate without the quotes, you must use the placeholder `%K` instead (called *Dynamic Key*). This is also useful to insert key paths into the format string.

Predicates use comparison and logical operators like those offered by Swift. For example, we can compare values with the operators = (==), !=, >, <, >= and <=, and also concatenate conditions with the characters && (or the word **AND**), || (or the word **OR**) and ! (or the word **NOT**). Predicates also include keywords for a more meticulous search. The following are the most frequently used.

BEGINSWITH—The condition determined by this keyword is true when the expression on the left begins with the expression on the right.

CONTAINS—The condition determined by this keyword is true when the expression on the left contains the expression on the right.

ENDSWITH—The condition determined by this keyword is true when the expression on the left ends with the expression on the right.

LIKE—The condition determined by this keyword is true when the expression on the left is equal to the expression on the right.

IN—The condition determined by this keyword is true when the expression on the left is equal to any of the values included in the expression on the right. The values are provided as an array between parentheses.

TRUEPREDICATE—This condition always produces a true predicate, which means that all the objects are returned from the request. There is also a **FALSEPREDICATE** condition that always produces a false predicate and therefore the request returns no objects.

These keywords may be accompanied by the characters **c** or **d** between square brackets to specify a case and diacritic insensitive search. For example, we may search for books which authors' names begin with the characters inserted by the user, but without considering uppercase or lowercase letters (**[c]**).

```
.searchable(text: $search, prompt: Text("Insert Name"))
.onChange(of: search) { value in
   if !value.isEmpty {
      listOfBooks.nsPredicate = NSPredicate(format: "author.name
BEGINSWITH[c] %@", value)
   } else {
      listOfBooks.nsPredicate = nil
   }
}
```

Listing 10-65: Filtering values with predicate keywords

Another useful keyword is CONTAINS, used to search for a value within a string. For instance, we can check if the characters inserted by the user can be found in the title of a book.

```
.searchable(text: $search, prompt: Text("Insert Title"))
.onChange(of: search) { value in
   if !value.isEmpty {
      listOfBooks.nsPredicate = NSPredicate(format: "title CONTAINS[dc]
%@", value)
   } else {
      listOfBooks.nsPredicate = nil
   }
}
```

Listing 10-66: Searching for characters in a string

The predicate in Listing 10-66 implements the **dc** modifiers to make the search case insensitive and ignore diacritic characters (the small marks used in some languages to change the pronunciation of a letter). For example, we can search for the term "éry" (with a stress in the letter e) and the request will return books which title contains the characters "ery" (e.g., "Misery").

 Do It Yourself: Update the **searchable()** and **onChange()** modifiers in your project with the example you want to try. Run the application on the iPhone simulator and perform a search to see how predicate keywords work.

Another situation where we may have to dynamically create the predicate is when we don't have the values we need to filter the objects until the view is loaded. For instance, our application may include an option to list books by author. In this case, we don't know which author the user is going select until the view is opened, so we must create the predicate dynamically.

For our example, we are going to embed the rows in a **NavigationLink** view, so when a row is selected a new view opens to list the books that belong to the selected author.

```
List {
    ForEach(listOfBooks) { book in
        NavigationLink(destination: AuthorBooksView(selectedAuthor:
book.author), label: {
            RowBook(book: book)
        })
    }
}
```

Listing 10-67: Selecting an author

Now, when a book is selected, the app opens the **AuthorBooksView** view with a reference to the **Authors** object that represents the author of the book. In this view, we use that reference to create a new fetch request as soon as the view appears on the screen.

```
import SwiftUI

struct AuthorBooksView: View {
    @FetchRequest(sortDescriptors: [], predicate: NSPredicate(format:
"FALSEPREDICATE")) var listOfBooks: FetchedResults<Books>
    var selectedAuthor: Authors?

    init(selectedAuthor: Authors?) {
        self.selectedAuthor = selectedAuthor
        if selectedAuthor != nil {
            _listOfBooks = FetchRequest(sortDescriptors:
[SortDescriptor(\Books.title, order: .forward)], predicate:
NSPredicate(format: "author = %@", selectedAuthor!), animation: .default)
        }
    }
    var body: some View {
        List {
            ForEach(listOfBooks) { book in
                Text(book.title ?? "Undefined")
            }
        }
        .navigationBarTitle(selectedAuthor?.name ?? "Undefined")
    }
}
```

```
struct AuthorBooksView_Previews: PreviewProvider {
    static var previews: some View {
        AuthorBooksView(selectedAuthor: nil)
            .environment(\.managedObjectContext,
ApplicationData.preview.container.viewContext)
    }
}
```

Listing 10-68: Listing books by author

This view receives a reference to the **Authors** object that represents the author selected by the user, but we cannot use this value in the **@FetchRequest** property wrapper because the property is not available until the whole structure is initialized. We must define a basic request with a false predicate (nothing is loaded at first) and then assign a new **FetchRequest** structure to the property wrapper from the initializer with the predicate we need to only get the books published by the selected author.

As explained in Chapter 6 (see Listing 6-7), to access the underlining structure of the property wrapper, we must precede the property name with an underscore (_listOfBooks). In this example, we initialize the **selectedAuthor** property, and then assign a new **FetchRequest** structure to the property wrapper with a predicate that filters the books by the author assigned to that property. The result is shown below.

Figure 10-38: Dynamic fetch request

 Do It Yourself: Update the **List** view in the **ContentView** view with the code in Listing 10-67. Create a SwiftUI View file called AuthorBooksView.swift for the view in Listing 10-68. Run the application on the iPhone simulator. Select a book. You should see the titles of all the books published by the selected author on the screen.

Basic) **Modifying Objects**

Modifying an object in the Persistent Store is easy. All we need to do is pass the object to a view that allows the user to modify the object's values. For this example, we are going to modify the navigation link introduced in the previous example to open a view with input fields that allow the user to update the selected book.

```
List {
    ForEach(listOfBooks) { book in
        NavigationLink(destination: ModifyBookView(book: book), label: {
            RowBook(book: book)
                .id(UUID())
        })
    }
}
```

Listing 10-69: Selecting the book to modify

In this example, we apply the `id()` modifier to the `RowBook` view. We have introduced this modifier before; it assigns a unique identifier to each view. In this case, we use a new `UUID` value, which means that every time the view is recreated, the identifier will be different. This makes the system believe that this is a different view and therefore it updates the content, showing on the screen the new values inserted by the user.

The `NavigationLink` view opens a view called `ModifyBookView` to allow the user to modify the values of the selected book. The following is our implementation of this view.

```swift
import SwiftUI
import CoreData
struct ModifyBookView: View {
    @Environment(\.managedObjectContext) var dbContext
    @Environment(\.dismiss) var dismiss
    @State private var selectedAuthor: Authors? = nil
    @State private var inputTitle: String = ""
    @State private var inputYear: String = ""
    @State private var valuesLoaded: Bool = false
    let book: Books?

    var body: some View {
        VStack(spacing: 12) {
            HStack {
                Text("Title:")
                TextField("Insert Title", text: $inputTitle)
                    .textFieldStyle(.roundedBorder)
            }
            HStack {
                Text("Year:")
                TextField("Insert Year", text: $inputYear)
                    .textFieldStyle(.roundedBorder)
            }
            HStack(alignment: .top) {
                Text("Author:")
                VStack(alignment: .leading, spacing: 8) {
                    Text(selectedAuthor?.name ?? "Undefined")
                        .foregroundColor(selectedAuthor != nil ? Color.black :
Color.gray)
                    NavigationLink(destination: AuthorsView(selected:
$selectedAuthor), label: {
                        Text("Select Author")
                    })
                }
            }.frame(minWidth: 0, maxWidth: .infinity, alignment: .leading)
            Spacer()
        }.padding()
        .navigationBarTitle("Modify Book")
        .toolbar {
            ToolbarItem(placement: .navigationBarTrailing) {
                Button("Save") {
                    let newTitle =
inputTitle.trimmingCharacters(in: .whitespaces)
                    let newYear = Int32(inputYear)
                    if !newTitle.isEmpty && newYear != nil {
                        Task(priority: .high) {
                            await saveBook(title: newTitle, year: newYear!)
                        }
                    }
                }
            }
        }
        .onAppear {
            if !valuesLoaded {
```

Chapter 10 - Storage

```
                selectedAuthor = book?.author
                inputTitle = book?.title ?? ""
                inputYear = book?.showYear ?? ""
                valuesLoaded = true
            }
        }
    }
    func saveBook(title: String, year: Int32) async {
        await dbContext.perform {
            book?.title = title
            book?.year = year
            book?.author = selectedAuthor
            do {
                try dbContext.save()
                dismiss()
            } catch {
                print("Error saving record")
            }
        }
    }
}
struct ModifyBookView_Previews: PreviewProvider {
    static var previews: some View {
        ModifyBookView(book: nil)
            .environment(\.managedObjectContext,
ApplicationData.preview.container.viewContext)
    }
}
```

Listing 10-70: Modifying the values of an object in the Persistent Store

This view defines a constant called **book** to receive the **Books** object that represents the book selected by the user. Because the user needs to see the book to be able to modify it, we implement the **onAppear()** modifier to initialize state properties with the book's values. Notice that there is an additional property called **valuesLoaded** that we check to only load the values when the property is **false**. This is to make sure that the values are only loaded when the user selected a book from the **ContentView** view, but not when a new author has been selected from the **AuthorsView** view.

The view includes two **TextField** views for the user to be able to modify the title and the year, and the same Select Author button included before to open the **AuthorsView** view to select an author. When the Save button is pressed, the values inserted by the user are assigned to the object's properties and the context is saved.

In this case, we do not create a new **Books** object, we just modify the properties of the **Books** object received by the view. The result is shown below.

Figure 10-39: Interface to modify objects

Do It Yourself: Update the **List** view in the **ContentView** view with the code in Listing 10-69. Create a SwiftUI View file called ModifyBookView.swift for the view in Listing 10-70. Run the application on the iPhone simulator. Tap on a book to select it. Change the title and press Save. You should see the changes on the list.

Basic Deleting Objects

Deleting objects in the Persistent Store is no different than any other values in the model. As we did in the example in Listing 7-22, we must apply the **onDelete()** modifier to the **ForEach** view and remove from the model the objects in the indexes received by the closure.

```
struct ContentView: View {
   @Environment(\.managedObjectContext) var dbContext
   @FetchRequest(sortDescriptors: [], predicate: nil,
animation: .default) var listOfBooks: FetchedResults<Books>
   var body: some View {
      NavigationStack {
         List {
            ForEach(listOfBooks) { book in
               RowBook(book: book)
            }
            .onDelete(perform: { indexes in
               Task(priority: .high) {
                  await deleteBook(indexes: indexes)
               }
            })
         }
         .navigationBarTitle("Books")
         .toolbar {
            ToolbarItem(placement: .navigationBarTrailing) {
               NavigationLink(destination: InsertBookView(), label: {
                  Image(systemName: "plus")
               })
            }
         }
      }
   }
   func deleteBook(indexes: IndexSet) async {
      await dbContext.perform {
         for index in indexes {
            dbContext.delete(listOfBooks[index])
         }
         do {
            try dbContext.save()
         } catch {
            print("Error deleting objects")
         }
      }
   }
}
```

Listing 10-71: Deleting objects

In our example, the objects retrieved from the Persistent Store are stored in the **listOfBooks** property. The indexes received by the closure in the **onDelete()** modifier are the indexes of the objects the user wants to delete from this collection. Therefore, to remove the objects selected by the user, we iterate through the indexes of all the objects to be removed with a **for in** loop, get the objects from the **listOfBooks** collection using the indexes, and remove them from the context with the **delete()** method. Once the objects are removed from the context, the **listOfBooks** property is automatically updated and the changes are reflected on the screen. The last step is to save the context with the **save()** method to persist the changes in the Persistent Store, as we did before. (Notice that in this example we had to get a direct reference to the context from the environment with the **@Environment** property wrapper to be able to call the **delete()** method on it.)

Do It Yourself: Update the `ContentView` view with the code in Listing 10-71. Run the application on the iPhone simulator. Drag a book to the left. You should see the Delete button. Press the button to remove the book. In this example, we have implemented the code to remove the object in the view, but you can move it to a method or an observable object, as we did in the example in Listing 7-22, and also implement the `EditButton()` view or some of the tools introduced in Chapter 7 to provide more options to the user.

(Medium) Custom Fetch Requests

So far, we have let the `@FetchRequest` property wrapper create the request for us, but there are situations in which we must create our own requests to process the values in the Persistent Store. Because a request has to be associated to an entity, subclasses of the `NSManagedObject` class, like `Books` and `Authors`, include the `fetchRequest()` method. This method returns an `NSFetchRequest` object with a fetch request associated to the entity represented by the class. To perform this request, the context includes the `fetch()` method.

Next, we create a request when the view appears and when an object is removed to count the number of books in the Persistent Store and show the value at the top of the list.

```
struct ContentView: View {
    @Environment(\.managedObjectContext) var dbContext
    @FetchRequest(sortDescriptors: [SortDescriptor(\Books.title,
order: .forward)], predicate: nil, animation: .default) var listOfBooks:
FetchedResults<Books>
    @State private var totalBooks: Int = 0

    var body: some View {
        NavigationStack {
            List {
                HStack {
                    Text("Total Books")
                    Spacer()
                    Text("\(totalBooks)")
                        .bold()
                }.foregroundColor(Color.green)

                ForEach(listOfBooks) { book in
                    NavigationLink(destination: ModifyBookView(book: book),
label: {
                        RowBook(book: book)
                            .id(UUID())
                    })
                }
                .onDelete(perform: { indexes in
                    for index in indexes {
                        dbContext.delete(listOfBooks[index])
                        countBooks()
                    }
                    do {
                        try dbContext.save()
                    } catch {
                        print("Error deleting objects")
                    }
                })
            }
            .navigationBarTitle("Books")
            .toolbar {
                ToolbarItem(placement: .navigationBarTrailing) {
                    NavigationLink(destination: InsertBookView(), label: {
                        Image(systemName: "plus")
```

```
            })
          }
        }
        .onAppear {
           countBooks()
        }
      }
    }
    func countBooks() {
        let request: NSFetchRequest<Books> = Books.fetchRequest()
        if let list = try? self.dbContext.fetch(request) {
           totalBooks = list.count
        }
    }
}
```

Listing 10-72: Counting the books available

To store the number of books, this view defines a `@State` property called `totalBooks`, and to show the value, it includes an `HStack` view with two `Text` views on top of the list. The request is created by a method called `countBooks()`. The method is executed when the view appears and when an object is removed. It creates a request for the `Books` entity, and then executes the request in the context with the `fetch()` method. If there are no errors, this method returns an array with all the objects that match the request. In this case, we didn't define any predicate, so the array contains all the `Books` objects in the Persistent Store. Finally, we count the objects with the `count` property and assign the value to the `totalBooks` property to show it to the user.

Figure 10-40: Total number of books in the Persistent Store

Do It Yourself: Update the `ContentView` view with the code in Listing 10-72. Run the application on the iPhone simulator. You should see the total number of books on the screen. Slide a row to the left and press the Delete button. You should see the number on the screen go down by one unit.

Although this is a legitimate way to count objects in the Persistent Store, it loads all the objects into memory and therefore it consumes too many resources. To avoid this issue, the `NSManagedObjectContext` class includes the `count()` method. This method returns an integer with the number of objects we would get if we call the `fetch()` method with the same request. The method does not fetch the objects, so we can call it without being afraid of consuming too much memory. The following example improves the `countBooks()` method using the `count()` method.

```
func countBooks() {
   let request: NSFetchRequest<Books> = Books.fetchRequest()
   if let count = try? self.dbContext.count(for: request) {
      totalBooks = count
   }
}
```

Listing 10-73: Counting objects with the `count()` method

Chapter 10 - Storage

Do It Yourself: Update the `countBooks()` method from the previous example with the code in Listing 10-73. The method counts the `Books` objects as before, but without consuming resources.

If what we want is to get the number of objects associated to a To-Many relationship, we just have to count the number of items returned by the property that represents the relationship. For example, we can count the number of books of every author and show it along with the name.

```
struct AuthorsView: View {
    @FetchRequest(sortDescriptors: [], predicate: nil,
animation: .default) private var listOfAuthors: FetchedResults<Authors>
    @Environment(\.dismiss) var dismiss
    @Binding var selected: Authors?

    var body: some View {
        List {
            ForEach(listOfAuthors) { author in
                HStack {
                    Text(author.showName)
                    Spacer()
                    Text(String(author.books?.count ?? 0))
                }
                .frame(minWidth: 0, maxWidth: .infinity, minHeight: 0,
maxHeight: .infinity, alignment: .leading)
                .background(.white)
                .onTapGesture {
                    selected = author
                    dismiss()
                }
            }
        }
        .navigationBarTitle("Authors")
        .toolbar {
            ToolbarItem(placement: .navigationBarTrailing) {
                NavigationLink(destination: InsertAuthorView(), label: {
                    Image(systemName: "plus")
                })
            }
        }
    }
}
```

Listing 10-74: Counting the books of each author

This view includes a `Text` view that shows the total number of books next to the author's name. To get this value, we count the number of items in the `books` property or show the value 0 if the property is equal to `nil` (no books have been assigned to the author).

 Do It Yourself: Update the `AuthorsView` view with the code in Listing 10-74. Run the application on the iPhone simulator. Select a book and press the Select Author button. You should see the list of authors available and the number of books assigned to each author on the right.

Another handy application of custom requests and the `count()` method is to check for duplicates. Storing duplicated values is something every application should avoid. For example, if we insert an author that already exists, two `Authors` objects with the same name will be stored in the Persistent Store. To avoid this situation, we can use a request with a predicate that looks for authors of the same name before creating a new object. The following example modifies the `InsertAuthorView` view to check if the author inserted by the user already exists in the Persistent Store.

```
import SwiftUI
import CoreData

struct InsertAuthorView: View {
    @Environment(\.managedObjectContext) var dbContext
    @Environment(\.dismiss) var dismiss
    @State private var inputName: String = ""

    var body: some View {
        VStack {
            HStack {
                Text("Name:")
                TextField("Insert Name", text: $inputName)
                    .textFieldStyle(.roundedBorder)
            }
            HStack {
                Spacer()
                Button("Save") {
                    let newName =
inputName.trimmingCharacters(in: .whitespaces)
                    if !newName.isEmpty {
                        Task(priority: .high) {
                            await storeAuthor(name: newName)
                        }
                    }
                    dismiss()
                }
            }
            Spacer()
        }.padding()
        .navigationBarTitle("Add Author")
    }
    func storeAuthor(name: String) async {
        await dbContext.perform {
            let request: NSFetchRequest<Authors> = Authors.fetchRequest()
            request.predicate = NSPredicate(format: "name = %@", name)
            if let total = try? self.dbContext.count(for: request), total ==
0 {
                let newAuthor = Authors(context: dbContext)
                newAuthor.name = name
                do {
                    try dbContext.save()
                } catch {
                    print("Error saving record")
                }
            }
        }
    }
}
```

Listing 10-75: Checking for duplicates

The code in Listing 10-75 creates a request for the Authors entity and uses the value inserted in the **TextField** view to create a predicate. The predicate looks for objects with the name equal to the value of the **newName** constant. Using this request, we call the **count()** method in the context to get the total amount of objects that match the conditions. If the value returned is 0, we know that there are no authors in the Persistent Store with that name and we can proceed.

 Do It Yourself: Update the **InsertAuthorView** view with the code in Listing 10-75. Run the application on the iPhone simulator. Select a book, press the Select Author button, and press the Add Author button. You should only be able to insert a new author if there is no other author with the same name.

Sections

The information in the Persistent Store can be presented in sections. For instance, we can create a section for every author, each of which contains the author's books. To create these sections, SwiftUI includes the `@SectionedFetchRequest` property wrapper. The main difference between this property wrapper and the `@FetchRequest` property wrapper is the addition of an argument to specify the section identifier.

SectionedFetchRequest(sectionIdentifier: KeyPath, **sortDescriptors:** [SortDescriptor], **predicate:** NSPredicate?, **animation:** Animation?**)**—This initializer creates a request with the configuration determined by the arguments and produces a `SectionedFetchResults` structure that manages and delivers the objects to the view. The **sectionIdentifier** argument is a key path to the property that the request is going to use to create the sections, the **sortDescriptors** argument is an array of `SortDescriptor` structures that determine the order of the objects, the **predicate** argument is an `NSPredicate` object that filters the objects, and the **animation** argument determines how the changes are going to be animated.

SectionedFetchRequest(fetchRequest: NSFetchRequest, **sectionIdentifier:** KeyPath, **animation:** Animation?**)**—This initializer creates a request with the `NSFetchRequest` object provided by the **fetchRequest** argument and produces a `SectionedFetchResults` structure that manages and delivers the objects to the view. The **sectionIdentifier** argument is a key path to the property that the request is going to use to create the sections, and the **animation** argument determines how the changes are going to be animated.

The `@SectionedFetchRequest` property wrapper produces a value of type `Sectioned-FetchResults`. This is a generic structure that works with two data types: the data type of the property used to identify the sections and the data type of the objects we are fetching.

The sections are created from the `Section` structure, defined by the `SectionedFetch-Results` structure. The structure includes the following properties to describe the section.

id—This property returns the value used to identify the section.

startIndex—This property returns an integer value that represents the index of the first item in the section.

endIndex—This property returns an integer value that represents the index that comes after the index of the last item in the section.

The following example shows how to define the `@SectionedFetchRequest` property wrapper to create a section for each author.

```
struct ContentView: View {
   @SectionedFetchRequest(sectionIdentifier: \Books.author?.name,
sortDescriptors: [SortDescriptor(\Books.author?.name, order: .forward)],
predicate: nil, animation: .default) private var sectionBooks:
SectionedFetchResults<String?, Books>

   var body: some View {
      NavigationStack {
         List {
            ForEach(sectionBooks) { section in
               Section(header: Text(section.id ?? "Undefined")) {
                  ForEach(section) { book in
                     NavigationLink(destination: ModifyBookView(book:
book), label: {
```

```
                RowBook(book: book)
                    .id(UUID())
                })
            }
        }
    }
}
.navigationBarTitle("Books")
.toolbar {
    ToolbarItem(placement: .navigationBarTrailing) {
        NavigationLink(destination: InsertBookView(), label: {
            Image(systemName: "plus")
        })
    }
}
```

Listing 10-76: *Fetching objects for sections*

In this example, we use the **name** property of the Authors entity to identify the sections, so we get one section per author. Because a book may not have an associated author, the **author** property of the **Books** object may return **nil**, and therefore the value used to identify the section is an optional **String**. That's the reason why we declare the **SectionedFetchResults** data types as **<String?, Books>**.

The sections are created as before (see Chapter 7, Listing 7-21). We need to define a **ForEach** loop for the sections, and then another **ForEach** loop to list the objects in each section. The sections are identified with a **Section** view, and the section's label is created with a **Text** view from the value returned by the **id** property. (In our example, this is the author's name.)

Figure 10-41: *Sections*

 Do It Yourself: Update the **ContentView** view with the code in Listing 10-76. Run the application on the iPhone simulator. You should see the books organized by author into sections, as shown in Figure 10-41.

If we want to create the sections based on a different value, we must add it to the Core Data model. For instance, to organize the books alphabetically into sections, one section per letter, we need to add an attribute to the Books entity to store the title's first letter.

Attribute	∧	Type	
Ⓞ cover		Binary Data	⌄
Ⓢ firstLetter		String	⌄
Ⓞ thumbnail		Binary Data	⌄
Ⓢ title		String	⌄
Ⓝ year		Integer 32	⌄

Figure 10-42: *Attribute to create alphabetical sections*

In this example, we have added an attribute called firstLetter to the Books entity. When a book is added or modified, we must get the first letter of the book's title and store it in this property. The following are the changes we need to introduce to the `storeBook()` method in the `InsertBookView` view.

```
func storeBook(title: String, year: Int32) async {
  await dbContext.perform {
      let newBook = Books(context: dbContext)
      newBook.title = title
      newBook.year = year
      newBook.author = selectedAuthor
      newBook.cover = UIImage(named: "bookcover")?.pngData()
      newBook.thumbnail = UIImage(named: "bookthumbnail")?.pngData()

      var letter = String(title.first!).uppercased()
      if Int(letter) != nil {
         letter = "#"
      }
      newBook.firstLetter = letter

      do {
         try dbContext.save()
         dismiss()
      } catch {
         print("Error saving record")
      }
   }
}
```

Listing 10-77: Storing the first letter of the book's title

When the user presses the Save button to save the book, we read the `first` property to get the letter in the string and make sure that is an uppercase letter. If the letter is a number, we replace it with a # character. (All books which titles begin with a number will be listed in a unique section identified with the # character.) Finally, the letter is stored in the `firstLetter` property and the book is saved.

We must perform the same process when a book is modified. The following are the changes we need to introduce to the `saveBook()` method in the `ModifyBookView` view.

```
func saveBook(title: String, year: Int32) async {
   await dbContext.perform {
      book?.title = title
      book?.year = year
      book?.author = selectedAuthor

      var letter = String(title.first!).uppercased()
      if Int(letter) != nil {
         letter = "#"
      }
      book?.firstLetter = letter

      do {
         try dbContext.save()
         dismiss()
      } catch {
         print("Error saving record")
      }
   }
}
```

Listing 10-78: Modifying the book's first letter

Now that every book knows the letter it belongs to, we can list them in alphabetical sections. The following is the new **@SectionedFetchRequest** property wrapper we need for the **ContentView** view.

```
@SectionedFetchRequest(sectionIdentifier: \Books.firstLetter,
sortDescriptors: [SortDescriptor(\Books.title, order: .forward)],
predicate: nil, animation: .default) private var sectionBooks:
SectionedFetchResults<String?, Books>
```

Listing 10-79: *Sorting the books by letter*

Now, the section identifier is the value of the **firstLetter** property and the books are sorted by title.

Figure 10-43: *Books in alphabetical sections*

 Do It Yourself: Update the **storeBook()** method in the **InsertBookView** view with the code in Listing 10-77, the **saveBook()** method in the **ModifyBookView** view with the code in Listing 10-78, and the **@SectionedFetchRequest** property wrapper in the **ContentView** view with the code in Listing 10-79. Uninstall the app to remove the books. Run the application again on the iPhone simulator. Add a few books. You should see the books organized in alphabetical sections, as shown in Figure 10-43.

Medium | To-Many Relationships

The previous examples assumed that there was only one author per book, but sometimes multiple authors collaborate to write a book. To assign multiple **Authors** objects to a book, we must turn the author relationship of the Books entity into a To-Many relationship, as shown below.

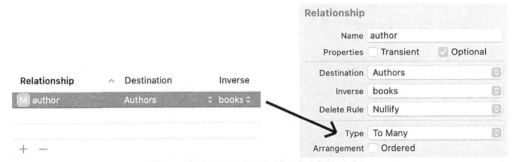

Figure 10-44: *Many-To-Many relationship*

Now, both relationships are of type To-Many, which means that we can assign multiple books to an author and multiple authors to a book. This introduces a problem. Before, every time we wanted to assign an author to a book, we just had to create a new **Authors** object and assign it to the book's **author** property. Core Data took care of adding the book to the **books** property of the **Authors** object, along with the rest of the books associated to that author. But we cannot do that anymore when both relationships are To-Many. In that case, we must read and write the values ourselves.

The values of a To-Many relationship are stored in an **NSSet** object. This is a class defined by the Foundation framework to store sets of values. To read the values in an **NSSet**, we can cast it as a Swift set, but to turn a Swift set or an array into an **NSSet** object, we must implement the following initializers.

NSSet(set: Set**)**—This initializer creates an **NSSet** object with the set provided by the attribute.

NSSet(array: Array**)**—This initializer creates an **NSSet** object with the array provided by the attribute.

In our application, the first place we need to read these values is in the view model (the Extensions.swift file). We must create a property that returns a string with the list of authors separated by comma.

```
import SwiftUI
extension Books {
    var showTitle: String {
        return title ?? "Undefined"
    }
    var showYear: String {
        return String(year)
    }
    var showAuthors: String {
        var authors: String!
        if let list = author as? Set<Authors> {
            let listNames = list.map({ $0.name ?? "Undefined" })
            if !listNames.isEmpty {
                authors = listNames.joined(separator: ", ")
            }
        }
        return authors ?? "Undefined"
    }
    var showCover: UIImage {
        if let data = cover, let image = UIImage(data: data) {
            return image
        } else {
            return UIImage(named: "nopicture")!
        }
    }
    var showThumbnail: UIImage {
        if let data = thumbnail, let image = UIImage(data: data) {
            return image
        } else {
            return UIImage(named: "nopicture")!
        }
    }
}
extension Authors {
    var showName: String {
        return name ?? "Undefined"
    }
```

```
}
```

The **showAuthors** property in this view model replaces the **showAuthor** property implemented before. To create the list of names, we cast the value of the **author** property to a **Set<Authors>** value. This creates a Swift set with **Authors** objects representing all the authors assigned to the book, so we can map the values into an array of strings and call the **joined()** method to create a single string with the names separated by comma.

Now, we can show all the authors of a book on the list by reading the **showAuthors** property.

```swift
struct ContentView: View {
    @FetchRequest(sortDescriptors: [SortDescriptor(\Books.title,
order: .forward)], predicate: nil, animation: .default) var listOfBooks:
FetchedResults<Books>

    var body: some View {
        NavigationStack {
            List {
                ForEach(listOfBooks) { book in
                    NavigationLink(destination: ModifyBookView(book: book),
label: {
                        RowBook(book: book)
                            .id(UUID())
                    })
                }
            }
            .navigationBarTitle("Books")
            .toolbar {
                ToolbarItem(placement: .navigationBarTrailing) {
                    NavigationLink(destination: InsertBookView(), label: {
                        Image(systemName: "plus")
                    })
                }
            }
        }
    }
}
struct RowBook: View {
    let book: Books

    var body: some View {
        HStack(alignment: .top) {
            Image(uiImage: book.showThumbnail)
                .resizable()
                .scaledToFit()
                .frame(width: 80, height: 100)
                .cornerRadius(10)
            VStack(alignment: .leading, spacing: 2) {
                Text(book.showTitle)
                    .bold()
                Text(book.showAuthors)
                    .lineLimit(2)
                Text(book.showYear)
                    .font(.caption)
                Spacer()
            }.padding(.top, 5)
            Spacer()
        }
    }
}
```

Listing 10-81: Showing the list of authors

The next step is to allow the users to associate multiple authors with a book. The following are the changes we must introduce to the `InsertBookView` view to allow the user to select multiple authors when a new book is added.

```swift
struct InsertBookView: View {
    @Environment(\.managedObjectContext) var dbContext
    @Environment(\.dismiss) var dismiss
    @State private var selectedAuthors: [Authors] = []
    @State private var inputTitle: String = ""
    @State private var inputYear: String = ""

    var showAuthors: String {
        var authors = "Undefined"
        if !selectedAuthors.isEmpty {
            let listNames = selectedAuthors.map({ $0.name ?? "Undefined" })
            if !listNames.isEmpty {
                authors = listNames.joined(separator: ", ")
            }
        }
        return authors
    }
    var body: some View {
        VStack(spacing: 12) {
            HStack {
                Text("Title:")
                TextField("Insert Title", text: $inputTitle)
                    .textFieldStyle(.roundedBorder)
            }
            HStack {
                Text("Year:")
                TextField("Insert Year", text: $inputYear)
                    .textFieldStyle(.roundedBorder)
            }
            HStack(alignment: .top) {
                Text("Authors:")
                VStack(alignment: .leading, spacing: 8) {
                    Text(showAuthors)
                        .foregroundColor(selectedAuthors.count > 0 ?
Color.black : Color.gray)
                    NavigationLink(destination: AuthorsView(selected:
$selectedAuthors), label: {
                        Text("Select Authors")
                    })
                }
            }.frame(minWidth: 0, maxWidth: .infinity, alignment: .leading)
            Spacer()
        }.padding()
        .navigationBarTitle("Add Book")
        .toolbar {
            ToolbarItem(placement: .navigationBarTrailing) {
                Button("Save") {
                    let newTitle =
inputTitle.trimmingCharacters(in: .whitespaces)
                    let newYear = Int32(inputYear)
                    if !newTitle.isEmpty && newYear != nil {
                        Task(priority: .high) {
                            await storeBook(title: newTitle, year: newYear!)
                        }
                    }
                }
            }
        }
    }
```

```
func storeBook(title: String, year: Int32) async {
    await dbContext.perform {
        let newBook = Books(context: dbContext)
        newBook.title = title
        newBook.year = year
        newBook.author = NSSet(array: selectedAuthors)
        newBook.cover = UIImage(named: "bookcover")?.pngData()
        newBook.thumbnail = UIImage(named: "bookthumbnail")?.pngData()

        var letter = String(title.first!).uppercased()
        if Int(letter) != nil {
            letter = "#"
        }
        newBook.firstLetter = letter

        do {
            try dbContext.save()
            dismiss()
        } catch {
            print("Error saving record")
        }
    }
}
```

Listing 10-82: Assigning multiple authors to a book

The values are now stored in an array, so we always know which ones were selected by the user. To show the list of authors, we define a computed property called **showAuthors** that follows the same process performed by the view model; it maps the **Authors** objects and returns a string with the names separated by comma. The view includes a **Text** view that reads this property and shows the names on the screen.

When the user decides to save the book, we perform the inverse procedure. The values in the **selectedAuthors** array are stored in an **NSSet** object and assigned to the **author** property.

To allow the user to select the authors when a book is modified, we must also apply these changes to the **ModifyBookView** view, as shown next.

```
struct ModifyBookView: View {
    @Environment(\.managedObjectContext) var dbContext
    @Environment(\.dismiss) var dismiss
    @State private var selectedAuthors: [Authors] = []
    @State private var inputTitle: String = ""
    @State private var inputYear: String = ""
    @State private var valuesLoaded: Bool = false
    let book: Books?

    var showAuthors: String {
        var authors = "Undefined"
        if !selectedAuthors.isEmpty {
            let listNames = selectedAuthors.map({ $0.name ?? "Undefined" })
            if !listNames.isEmpty {
                authors = listNames.joined(separator: ", ")
            }
        }
        return authors
    }
    var body: some View {
        VStack(spacing: 12) {
            HStack {
                Text("Title:")
                TextField("Insert Title", text: $inputTitle)
                    .textFieldStyle(.roundedBorder)
            }
```

```
                HStack {
                    Text("Year:")
                    TextField("Insert Year", text: $inputYear)
                        .textFieldStyle(.roundedBorder)
                }
                HStack(alignment: .top) {
                    Text("Author:")
                    VStack(alignment: .leading, spacing: 8) {
                        Text(showAuthors)
                            .foregroundColor(selectedAuthors.count > 0 ?
Color.black : Color.gray)
                        NavigationLink(destination: AuthorsView(selected:
$selectedAuthors), label: {
                            Text("Select Authors")
                        })
                    }
                }.frame(minWidth: 0, maxWidth: .infinity, alignment: .leading)
                Spacer()
            }.padding()
            .navigationBarTitle("Modify Book")
            .toolbar {
                ToolbarItem(placement: .navigationBarTrailing) {
                    Button("Save") {
                        let newTitle =
inputTitle.trimmingCharacters(in: .whitespaces)
                        let newYear = Int32(inputYear)
                        if !newTitle.isEmpty && newYear != nil {
                            Task(priority: .high) {
                                await saveBook(title: newTitle, year: newYear!)
                            }
                        }
                    }
                }
            }
            .onAppear {
                if let list = book?.author as? Set<Authors>, !valuesLoaded {
                    selectedAuthors = Array(list)
                    inputTitle = book?.title ?? ""
                    inputYear = book?.showYear ?? ""
                    valuesLoaded = true
                }
            }
        }
    func saveBook(title: String, year: Int32) async {
        await dbContext.perform {
            book?.title = title
            book?.year = year
            book?.author = NSSet(array: selectedAuthors)
            var letter = String(title.first!).uppercased()
            if Int(letter) != nil {
                letter = "#"
            }
            book?.firstLetter = letter
            do {
                try dbContext.save()
                dismiss()
            } catch {
                print("Error saving record")
            }
        }
    }
}
```

Listing 10-83: Modifying the authors of a book

This view is very similar to the `InsertBookView` view, the only difference is a new Boolean `@State` property called `changesAdded` that we use to know if the user is coming from the `ContentView` view or the `AuthorsView` view. If the user opened this view from the `ContentView` view, we need to load the list of authors from the Persistent Store and assign them to the `selectedAuthors` property when the view appears. Otherwise, the content of the `selectedAuthors` property is determined by the authors selected by the user in the `AuthorsView` view. Next are the changes we need to introduce to this view.

```
struct AuthorsView: View {
    @FetchRequest(sortDescriptors: [], predicate: nil,
animation: .default) private var listOfAuthors: FetchedResults<Authors>
    @Environment(\.dismiss) var dismiss
    @Binding var selected: [Authors]

    var body: some View {
        List {
            ForEach(listOfAuthors) { author in
                HStack {
                    Text(author.showName)
                    if selected.contains(where: { $0.name == author.name }) {
                        Image(systemName: "checkmark")
                            .foregroundColor(Color.blue)
                            .frame(width: 25, height: 25)
                    }
                }
                .frame(minWidth: 0, maxWidth: .infinity, minHeight: 0,
maxHeight: .infinity, alignment: .leading)
                .background(.white)
                .onTapGesture {
                    if selected.contains(where: { $0.name == author.name }) {
                        if let index = selected.firstIndex(of: author) {
                            selected.remove(at: index)
                        }
                    } else {
                        selected.append(author)
                    }
                    dismiss()
                }
            }
        }
        .navigationBarTitle("Authors")
        .toolbar {
            ToolbarItem(placement: .navigationBarTrailing) {
                NavigationLink(destination: InsertAuthorView(), label: {
                    Image(systemName: "plus")
                })
            }
        }
    }
}
struct AuthorsView_Previews: PreviewProvider {
    static var previews: some View {
        AuthorsView(selected: .constant([]))
            .environment(\.managedObjectContext,
ApplicationData.preview.container.viewContext)
    }
}
```

Listing 10-84: Selecting multiple authors

As always, this view displays all available authors. To show which one has been previously selected, we add an `Image` view with a checkmark to the row of the authors that are already in the **selectedAuthors** array. Then, when a row is tapped by the user, we check whether the author was previously selected or not. If it was selected, we remove it from the **selectedAuthors** array, otherwise, we add it to it. This makes sure that the array only contains the authors currently selected by the user.

 Do It Yourself: Open the Core Data model. Select the Books entity and change the Type of the author relationship to To-Many (Figure 10-44). Update the Extensions.swift file with the code in Listing 10-80, the **ContentView** view with the code in Listing 10-81, the **InsertBookView** with the code in Listing 10-82, the **ModifyBookView** view with the code in Listing 10-83, and the **AuthorsView** view with the code in Listing 10-84. Run the application on the iPhone simulator. Press the + button to add a new book. Press the Select Authors button to select an author. You should be able to add as many authors as you want.

The To-Many to To-Many relationships also change the way we search for values. For instance, we cannot search for a book by author as we did before because now a book may be associated to many authors. Instead, we must tell the predicate to search for the value inside the set of authors. For this purpose, predicates can include the following keywords.

ANY—This keyword returns true when the condition is true for some of the values in the set.

ALL—This keyword returns true when the condition is true for all the values in the set.

NONE—This keyword returns true when the condition is false for all the values in the set.

We have introduced predicate keywords earlier in this chapter. They are included in the format string to determine the way the predicate filters the data. For our example, we can add the ANY keyword in front of the comparison to get the books associated with at least one author with a specific name, as shown next.

```
.onAppear {
    let request: NSFetchRequest<Books> = Books.fetchRequest()
    request.predicate = NSPredicate(format: "ANY author.name == %@",
"Stephen King")
    if let list = try? dbContext.fetch(request) {
        for book in list {
            print(book.title!)
        }
    }
}
```

Listing 10-85: Fetching books by author

This example defines an **onAppear()** modifier that we can add to a view in the **ContentView** view. It creates a request that finds all the books associated with an author named "Stephen King". The predicate reads all the **Authors** objects in the relationship and returns the book when one of the names matches the string.

 Do It Yourself: Add the modifier of Listing 10-85 to the **List** view in the **ContentView** view. You also need to get access to the Core Data context with the **@Environment** property wrapper (**@Environment(\.managedObject-Context) var dbContext**). Run the application on the iPhone simulator and insert a few books with the author Stephen King. You should see the names of the books associated with that author printed on the console.

The example we have been working on so far turns the **NSSet** object returned by the author relationship into an array of **Authors** objects and then adds or removes authors from this array, but if we need to add or remove values directly from the **NSSet** object, we must turn it into an **NSMutableSet** object. This class creates a mutable set and therefore it allows us to add or remove values from it. To create an **NSMutableSet** object from an **NSSet** object, the **NSManagedObject** class includes the following method.

mutableSetValue(forKey: String)—This method reads the **NSSet** object of the relationship indicated by the **forKey** attribute and returns an **NSMutableSet** with the values.

The **NSMutableSet** class includes the following methods to add and remove items in the set.

add(Any)—This method adds the object specified by the argument to the set.

remove(Any)—This method removes the object specified by the argument from the set.

The following example shows a possible implementation of these methods. We get the object representing the author with the name "Stephen King" and then remove that author from every book.

```
.onAppear {
    let request: NSFetchRequest<Authors> = Authors.fetchRequest()
    request.predicate = NSPredicate(format: "name == %@", "Stephen King")
    if let list = try? dbContext.fetch(request), list.count > 0 {
        let author = list[0]

        Task(priority: .high) {
            await dbContext.perform {
                for book in listOfBooks {
                    let authorSet = book.mutableSetValue(forKey: "author")
                    authorSet.remove(author)
                    book.author = authorSet
                }
                try? dbContext.save()
            }
        }
    }
}
```

Listing 10-86: Systematically removing authors from books

This example updates the **onAppear()** modifier defined before to modify the **Books** objects in the Persistent Store as soon as the view is loaded. First, we perform a request to get the **Authors** object with the name "Stephen King". Then, we use a **for in** loop to modify the books loaded by the **@FetchRequest** property wrapper. In the loop, we turn the **NSSet** object returned by the author relationship into an **NSMutableSet** object, remove from the set the **Authors** object fetched before with the **remove()** method, and assign the result back to the author relationship, effectively removing that author from every book.

 Do It Yourself: Update the **onAppear()** modifier with the code in Listing 10-86. Run the application on the iPhone simulator. The author Stephen King should be removed from every book.

(Basic) **11.1 Shapes**

All the views we have used so far are containers or present predefined content on the screen, but SwiftUI also includes graphic views to create custom controls or to use for decoration. These views work like those introduced before and can take advantage of most of the modifiers we have seen so far, but are specifically designed to draw custom graphics on the screen.

(Basic) **Common Shapes**

SwiftUI allows us to create predefined or custom shapes. The following are the views available to create standard shapes.

Rectangle()—This initializer creates a `Rectangle` view. The size of the rectangle is determined by the view's frame.

RoundedRectangle(cornerRadius: CGFloat, style: RoundedCornerStyle)— This initializer creates a `RoundedRectangle` view. The `cornerRadius` argument determines the radius of the curvature of the corners, and the `style` argument is an enumeration of type `RoundedCornerStyle` that determines the type of curvature to use. The values available are `circular` and `continuous`. The view also includes the following initializer to define the radius with a `CGSize` value: `RoundedRectangle (cornerSize: CGSize, style: RoundedCornerStyle)`.

Circle()—This initializer creates a `Circle` view. The diameter of the circle is determined by the view's frame.

Ellipse()—This initializer creates an `Ellipse` view. The size of the ellipse is determined by the width and height of the view's frame.

Capsule(style: RoundedCornerStyle)—This initializer creates a `Capsule` view. The `style` argument is an enumeration that determines the type of curvature to apply to the corners. The values available are `circular` and `continuous`.

As with many other views, if no size is specified, graphic views take the size of their container, but we can declare a specific size with the `frame()` modifier. The following example shows all the standard shapes available. We included the views in a horizontal `ScrollView` to allow the list to scroll.

```
struct ContentView: View {
   var body: some View {
      VStack {
         ScrollView(.horizontal, showsIndicators: true) {
            HStack {
               Rectangle()
                  .frame(width: 100, height: 100)
               RoundedRectangle(cornerRadius: 25, style: .continuous)
                  .frame(width: 100, height: 100)
               Circle()
                  .frame(width: 100, height: 100)
               Ellipse()
                  .frame(width: 100, height: 50)
```

```
            Capsule()
                .frame(width: 100, height: 50)
            }.padding()
        }
        Spacer()
    }
  }
}
```

Listing 11-1: Drawing standard shapes

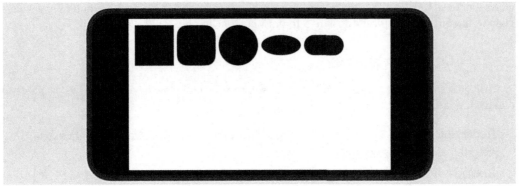

Figure 11-1: Standard shapes

 Do It Yourself: Create a Multiplatform project. Update the **ContentView** view with the code in Listing 11-1. If you don't see all the shapes on the screen, scroll the views to the left. Use this project to test the rest of the examples in this chapter.

By default, the views are rendered with a color depending on the appearance mode (black for light and white for dark), but we can change the filling and stroke of the shapes with the following modifiers.

fill(View)—This modifier fills the shape with the view specified by the argument. The argument is a view that represents a color, a gradient or an image.

stroke(View, **lineWidth:** CGFloat)—This modifier defines the shape's border. The first argument is a view that represents a color, a gradient, or an image, and the **lineWidth** argument defines the border's width.

stroke(View, **style:** StrokeStyle)—This modifier defines the shape's border. The first argument is a view that represents a color, a gradient or an image, and the **style** argument is a structure of type **StrokeStyle** that defines the border's width, cap, join, miter limit, dash, and dash phase.

strokeBorder(View, **lineWidth:** CGFloat)—This modifier defines the shape's inner border. The first argument is a view that represents a color, a gradient, or an image, and the **lineWidth** argument defines the border's width.

strokeBorder(View, **style:** StrokeStyle)—This modifier defines the shape's inner border. The first argument is a view that represents a color, a gradient or an image, and the **style** argument is a structure of type **StrokeStyle** that defines the border's width, cap, join, miter limit, dash, and dash phase.

There are two aspects we can change with these modifiers, the filling of the shape and its border. The filling is defined by the **fill()** modifier and a view that represents the content, like a **Color** view.

```
struct ContentView: View {
    var body: some View {
        RoundedRectangle(cornerRadius: 25)
            .fill(Color.red)
            .frame(width: 100, height: 100)
    }
}
```

Listing 11-2: Filling a shape with a color

Notice that the `fill()` modifier is implemented by the **RoundedRectangle** view, but the `frame()` modifier returns a different view, therefore all the modifiers defined for shapes, like `fill()`, must be applied before common modifiers like `frame()`. In this example, we use these modifiers to create a red rectangle with rounded corners.

Figure 11-2: Rectangle

Adding a border requires a similar process, but there are two types of modifiers and they produce a slightly different result. The **stroke()** modifier expands the border outward and inward, while the **strokeBorder()** modifier generates an inner border.

```
struct ContentView: View {
    var body: some View {
        HStack {
            RoundedRectangle(cornerRadius: 25)
                .stroke(Color.red, lineWidth: 20)
                .frame(width: 100, height: 100)
                .padding()
            RoundedRectangle(cornerRadius: 25)
                .strokeBorder(Color.red, lineWidth: 20)
                .frame(width: 100, height: 100)
                .padding()
        }
    }
}
```

Listing 11-3: Defining a border

This view includes two **RoundedRectangle** views with a border of 20 points, but because we use different modifiers, the borders are different. Half of the border for the first rectangle is drawn outside the shape, while the other half is drawn within the view's frame, but the border for the second rectangle is contained inside the frame.

Figure 11-3: Rectangles with different strokes

These two modifiers can also take a **StrokeStyle** structure to fine-tune the border. The structure provides the following initializer.

StrokeStyle(lineWidth: CGFloat, **lineCap:** CGLineCap, **lineJoin:** CGLineJoin, **miterLimit:** CGFloat, **dash:** [CGFloat], **dashPhase:** CGFloat)—This initializer creates a **StrokeStyle** structure to configure a stroke. The **lineWidth** argument determines the width. The **lineCap** argument determines the style of the end of the lines. It is an enumeration with the values **butt** (squared end), **round** (rounded end), and **square** (squared end). The **lineJoin** argument sets the style of the joint of two connected lines. It is an enumeration with the values **miter** (sharp end), **round** (rounded end), and **bevel** (squared end). The **miterLimit** argument determines how long the lines extend when the **lineJoin** argument is set to **miter**. The **dash** argument determines the length of the segments for a dashed stroke. And the **dashPhase** argument determines where the dashed line begins.

The following example creates a **RoundedRectangle** view with the stroke configured as a dashed line with a width of 15 points and rounded caps.

```
struct ContentView: View {
   let lineStyle = StrokeStyle(lineWidth: 15, lineCap: .round,
lineJoin: .round, miterLimit: 0, dash: [20], dashPhase: 0)

   var body: some View {
      RoundedRectangle(cornerRadius: 25)
         .stroke(Color.red, style: lineStyle)
         .frame(width: 100, height: 100)
   }
}
```

Listing 11-4: Defining a custom border

Figure 11-4: Rectangle with a custom stroke

Shapes are views and therefore they can be combined with other SwiftUI views and controls. For instance, the following example assigns a **Capsule** shape as the background of a button.

```
struct ContentView: View {
   @State private var setActive: Bool = true

   var body: some View {
      VStack {
         Button(action: {
            setActive.toggle()
         }, label: {
            Text(setActive ? "Active" : "Inactive")
               .font(.title)
               .foregroundColor(Color.white)
               .padding(.horizontal, 30)
               .padding(.vertical, 10)
         })
```

Chapter 11 - Graphics and Animations

```
        .background(
            Capsule()
                .fill(setActive ? Color.green : Color.red)
            )
        Spacer()
    }.padding()
  }
}
```

In fact, there is a version of the **background()** modifier specifically designed for shapes.

background(Color, **in:** Shape**)**—This modifier assigns a shape to the background of a view. The first argument specifies the color, and the **in** argument the shape.

Using this modifier, we can declare the background of the button in the previous example with a single line of code.

```
.background(setActive ? Color.green : Color.red, in: Capsule())
```

The button toggles the value of a **@State** property. If the value is **true**, we show the label "Active" and assign a green capsule to the button's background, otherwise, we display the label "Inactive" and turn the capsule red.

Figure 11-5: Graphic button

(Basic) **Gradients**

The filling and border of a shape can also be defined with gradients. SwiftUI includes four structures designed to present gradients: **LinearGradient**, **RadialGradient**, **Angular-Gradient**, and **EllipticalGradient**. These structures conform to the **ShapeStyle** protocol, which defines the following methods to create customized instances.

linearGradient(Gradient, **startPoint:** UnitPoint, **endPoint:** UnitPoint**)**—This method returns a linear gradient. The **gradient** argument is the gradient of colors to be used, and the **startPoint** and **endPoint** arguments determine the points inside the shape where the gradient starts and ends.

radialGradient(Gradient, **center:** UnitPoint, **startRadius:** CGFloat, **endRadius:** CGFloat**)**—This method returns a circular gradient. The **gradient** argument is the gradient of colors to be used. The **center** argument determines the position of the center of the circle, and the **startRadius** and **endRadius** arguments determine where the gradient starts and ends.

ellipticalGradient(Gradient, **center:** UnitPoint, **startRadiusFraction:** CGFloat, **endRadiusFraction:** CGFloat**)**—This method returns a radial gradient with the shape of an ellipse. The **gradient** argument is the gradient of colors to be used. The **center** argument determines the center of the ellipse, and the **startRadiusFraction** and **endRadiusFraction** argument determine the radius of the ellipse.

angularGradient(Gradient, **center:** UnitPoint, **startAngle:** Angle, **endAngle:** Angle**)**—This method returns an angular gradient. The **gradient** argument is the gradient of colors to be used. The **center** argument determines the center of the shape, the **startAngle** argument determines the angle at the beginning of the gradient and the **endAngle** determines the angle at the end.

conicGradient(Gradient, **center:** UnitPoint, **angle:** Angle**)**—This method returns a conic gradient. The **gradient** argument is the gradient of colors to be used. The **center** argument determines the position of the tip of the cone, and the **angle** argument determines the angle where the gradient begins.

These methods return an instance of one of the gradient structures introduced before, but the gradient of colors is defined by the `Gradient` structure.

Gradient(colors: [Color]**)**—This initializer creates a gradient with the colors specified by the argument. The **colors** argument is an array of `Color` views.

Gradient(stops: [Gradient.Stop]**)**—This initializer creates a gradient with the colors specified by the argument. The **stops** argument is an array of `Stop` structures that determine the colors and when they stop.

Another value required to present a gradient is the `UnitPoint` structure. This is like the `CGPoint` structure but specifically designed to work with graphic structures.

UnitPoint(x: CGFloat, **y:** CGFloat**)**—This initializer creates a `UnitPoint` structure. The **x** and **y** arguments determine the x and y coordinates of the point. For gradients, these arguments are defined with values from 0.0 to 1.0.

The `UnitPoint` structure also includes the type properties `bottom`, `bottomLeading`, `bottomTrailing`, `center`, `leading`, `top`, `topLeading`, `topTrailing`, `trailing`, and `zero` to define common points. For example, we can apply a linear gradient with the values `bottom` and `top` to draw the gradient from the bottom to the top of the shape.

```
struct ContentView: View {
   let gradient = Gradient(colors: [Color.red, Color.green])

   var body: some View {
      RoundedRectangle(cornerRadius: 25)
         .fill(.linearGradient(gradient, startPoint: .bottom,
endPoint: .top))
         .frame(width: 100, height: 100)
   }
}
```

Listing 11-7: Defining a linear gradient

The code in Listing 11-7 defines a gradient with two colors, red and green, and then applies the gradient to a `RoundedRectangle` view with the structure returned by the `linearGradient()` method. Because we declare the value `bottom` as the starting point and the value `top` as the ending point, the colors are displayed from bottom to top in the order declared by the `Gradient` structure.

Figure 11-6: Linear gradient

Chapter 11 - Graphics and Animations

When a gradient is created without specifying color stops, the colors are evenly distributed throughout the area occupied by the gradient. If we want to customize the distribution, we must define the colors for the gradient with **Stop** structures.

Stop(color: Color, **location:** CGFloat)—This initializer creates a color with a stop value. The **color** argument determines the color, and the **location** argument determines the position in the gradient where the color begins (it's a value from 0.0 to 1.0).

The following example reproduces the previous gradient, but this time the green color begins at the position 0.4 (40% of the area occupied by the gradient).

```
struct ContentView: View {
    let gradient = Gradient(stops: [
        Gradient.Stop(color: Color.red, location: 0.0),
        Gradient.Stop(color: Color.green, location: 0.4)
    ])
    var body: some View {
        RoundedRectangle(cornerRadius: 25)
            .fill(.linearGradient(gradient, startPoint: .bottom,
endPoint: .top))
            .frame(width: 100, height: 100)
    }
}
```

Listing 11-8: *Defining a linear gradient with custom stops*

Figure 11-7: *Linear gradient with custom stops*

Besides the linear gradient, we can also create gradients with different shapes. For instance, radial and elliptical gradients are created with circular layers drawn from the center of a circle outwards, as shown next.

```
struct ContentView: View {
    let gradient = Gradient(colors: [Color.red, Color.white])

    var body: some View {
        RoundedRectangle(cornerRadius: 25)
            .fill(.radialGradient(gradient, center: .center, startRadius: 0,
endRadius: 120))
            .frame(width: 100, height: 100)
    }
}
```

Listing 11-9: *Defining a circular gradient*

This example illustrates how to create a radial gradient. The values required are the **Gradient** structure, the center of the circle, and the location within the shape where the gradient begins and ends. These values determine where the gradient begins and ends, but only the part of the gradient that falls within the shape is drawn. In our example, the **endRadius** argument was declared as 120, but because the size of the shape is 100 by 100, only part of the gradient is visible.

Figure 11-8: Circular gradient

Another type of gradients we can use for our shapes are the angular or conic gradients. These gradients draw the colors around a circle, which makes it look like a cone seen from the top. The values required depend on the type of cone we want to define. For a simple cone, all we need is the `Gradient` structure, the center of the circle, and the angle where the gradient begins.

```
struct ContentView: View {
   let gradient = Gradient(colors: [Color.red, Color.white])
   var body: some View {
      RoundedRectangle(cornerRadius: 25)
         .fill(.conicGradient(gradient, center: .center,
angle: .degrees(180)))
         .frame(width: 100, height: 100)
   }
}
```

Listing 11-10: Defining a conic gradient

The angles for the gradient are declared with an instance of the **Angle** structure. This structure includes two type methods to defined the value in degrees or radians: **degrees(Double)** and **radians(Double)**. In the example of Listing 11-10, we declare the beginning of the gradient at an angle of 180 degrees, which is the opposite side of the default starting point.

Figure 11-9: Conic gradient

(Basic) **Effects**

The **ShapeStyle** protocol that defines the type methods to create gradient structures implemented in the previous section also defines multiple properties and methods to apply other effects to a view. The following are the most frequently used.

shadow(ShadowStyle)—This method applies a shadow to the view. The argument is a structure with two type methods to create drop and inner shadows: **drop(color: Color, radius: CGFloat, x: CGFloat, y: CGFloat)** and **inner(color: Color, radius: CGFloat, x: CGFloat, y: CGFloat)**.

opacity(Double)—This method assigns to the view the level of opacity specified by the argument. The argument takes values from 0.0 (fully transparent) to 1.0 (fully opaque).

Chapter 11 - Graphics and Animations

blendMode(BlendMode)—This method sets a blend mode that determines how the view is going to blend with the background and other views. The argument is an enumeration with the values `normal`, `darken`, `multiply`, `colorBurn`, `plusDarker`, `lighten`, `screen`, `colorDodge`, `plusLighter`, `overlay`, `softLight`, `hardLight`, `difference`, `exclusion`, `hue`, `saturation`, `color`, `luminosity`, `sourceAtop`, `destinationOver`, and `destinationOut`.

Many modifiers can take a structure that conforms to the `ShapeStyle` protocol to assign a style to a view. When working with shapes, these styles work better with the `foregroundStyle()` modifier. For instance, if we want to apply a shadow to our rectangular shape, we can use this modifier for the shadow and define the fill color with the `foregroundColor()` modifier, as we do in the following example.

```
struct ContentView: View {
    var body: some View {
        RoundedRectangle(cornerRadius: 25)
            .foregroundStyle(.shadow(.drop(color: .black, radius: 3, x: 4,
y: 4)))
            .foregroundColor(.red)
            .frame(width: 100, height: 100)
    }
}
```

Listing 11-11: Adding a shadow to a view

Figure 11-10: Shadow

(Basic) **Patterns**

Besides colors and gradients, we can also use images to fill a shape. SwiftUI includes the `ImagePaint` structure for this purpose. The structure includes the following type method to create a customized instance.

image(Image, **sourceRect:** CGRect, **scale:** CGFloat)—This method returns an `ImagePaint` structure with the image and configuration specified by the arguments. The first argument provides the `Image` view with the image we want to use, the **sourceRect** argument determines the part of the image to be drawn (by default, the entire image), and the **scale** argument defines the scale of the image (by default, the original scale).

By default, the `ImagePaint` structure uses the whole image in the original scale, so most of the time specifying the image is enough for the system to create the pattern.

```
struct ContentView: View {
    var body: some View {
        Rectangle()
            .fill(.image(Image("pattern")))
            .frame(width: 100, height: 100)
    }
}
```

Listing 11-12: Filling a shape with an image

The image repeats indefinitely to fill the entire shape. In this example, we define a square of 100 by 100 points and then paint it with an image of a size of 25 by 25 points. Because the image is smaller than the shape, it is drawn multiple times to cover the area.

Figure 11-11: *Pattern*

11.2 Paths

The shapes we have implemented so far are defined by paths. A path is a set of instructions that determine the outline of a 2D shape. In addition to the paths defined by the standard shapes introduced before, we can create our own. For this purpose, SwiftUI includes the **Path** view.

Path View

The **Path** view is designed to create a view that contains a custom path. The following are some of the initializers.

Path()—This initializer creates an empty **Path** view. The path is created by applying modifiers to this instance.

Path(Closure)—This initializer creates an empty **Path** view. The argument is a closure to define the path. The closure receives a reference to the **Path** structure that we can use to create the path.

The path is created with a combination of lines and curves. The strokes move from one point to another in the view's coordinates, as if following the movement of a pencil. The **Path** structure defines a set of modifiers to determine the position of the pencil and generate the path. The following are the most frequently used.

move(to: CGPoint)—This modifier moves the pencil to the coordinates determined by the **to** argument.

addLine(to: CGPoint)—This modifier adds a straight line to the path, from the pencil's current position to the coordinates indicated by the **to** argument.

addLines([CGPoint])—This modifier adds multiple straight lines to the path. The lines are added in sequence according to the order of the points in the array.

addArc(center: CGPoint, radius: CGFloat, startAngle: Angle, endAngle: Angle, clockwise: Bool)—This modifier adds an arc to the path. The **center** argument specifies the coordinates of the center of the circle formed by the arc, the **radius** argument is the length of the circle's radius, the **startAngle** and **endAngle** arguments are the angles in which the arc starts and ends, and the **clockwise** argument determines the orientation in which the arc is calculated (**true** clockwise and **false** counterclockwise).

addArc(tangent1End: CGPoint, tangent2End: CGPoint, radius: CGFloat)—This modifier adds an arc to the path using tangent points. The **tangent1End** argument defines the coordinates of the end of the first tangent line, the **tangent2End** argument defines the coordinates of the end of the second tangent line, and the **radius** argument determines the length of the circle's radius.

addCurve(to: CGPoint, control1: CGPoint, control2: CGPoint)—This modifier adds a cubic Bezier curve to the path with two control points. The **to** argument defines the coordinates of the ending point, and the **control1** and **control2** arguments define the coordinates of the first and second control points, respectively.

addQuadCurve(to: CGPoint, control: CGPoint)—This modifier adds a quadratic Bezier curve to the path with a control point. The **to** argument defines the coordinates of the ending point, and the **control** argument defines the coordinates of the control point.

addEllipse(in: CGRect)—This modifier adds an ellipse to the path. The **in** argument determines the area of the ellipse. If the rectangle is a square, the ellipse becomes a circle.

addRect(CGRect)—This modifier adds the rectangle defined by the argument to the path. There is a version of this modifier that takes an array of `CGRect` values to add multiple rectangles at a time (`addRects([CGRect])`).

addRoundedRect(in: CGRect, cornerSize: CGSize, style: RoundedCorner-Style)—This modifier adds a rounded rectangle to the path. The in argument determines the dimensions of the rectangle, the **cornerRadius** argument determines the radius of the curvature of the corners, and the **style** argument is an enumeration with the values `circular` and `continuous`.

A custom path works the same way as a predefined path. If we don't specify the filling or the stroke, the path is drawn with a color that depends on the appearance mode (black for light and white for dark), but we can change that with the `fill()` and `stroke()` modifiers, as we did before for standard shapes. If we paint the path with the `fill()` modifier, the path is automatically closed, but if we do it with the `stroke()` modifier, it remains open. To close the path and make sure all the lines are joined, the `Path` structure includes the following modifier.

closeSubpath()—This modifier closes the current path. If the path is not a closed path, the modifier adds a line between the end and the beginning of the path to close it.

To create a path, we must apply the modifiers in order, following the line of an imaginary pencil. The following example creates a path with the shape of a triangle.

```
struct ContentView: View {
    var body: some View {
        Path { path in
            path.move(to: CGPoint(x: 100, y: 150))
            path.addLine(to: CGPoint(x: 200, y: 150))
            path.addLine(to: CGPoint(x: 100, y: 250))
            path.closeSubpath()
        }.stroke(Color.blue, lineWidth: 5)
    }
}
```

Listing 11-13: Defining a custom path

By default, the pencil's initial position is at the coordinates 0, 0 (top-left corner of the view). If we want our graphic to start from a different position, we must apply the **move()** modifier first. In Listing 11-13, we move the pencil to the coordinates 100, 150 before adding the first line. Subsequent lines are generated from the current position of the pencil to the coordinates indicated by the modifier. For instance, after setting the initial point in our example, we create a line from that point to the point 200, 150. Therefore, the next line starts at that point and ends at 100, 250. Notice that we only created two lines. The line that goes from the point 100, 250 to the point 100, 150 is generated automatically by the `closeSubpath()` modifier to close the path. If we want to create an open path, we can ignore this modifier.

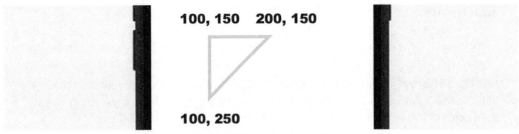

Figure 11-12: *Custom path*

Combining different modifiers, we can create complex paths. The following path is defined with two lines and an arc.

```
struct ContentView: View {
   var body: some View {
      Path { path in
         path.move(to: CGPoint(x: 100, y: 150))
         path.addLine(to: CGPoint(x: 200, y: 150))
         path.addArc(center: CGPoint(x: 200, y: 170), radius: 20,
startAngle: .degrees(270), endAngle: .degrees(90), clockwise: false)
         path.addLine(to: CGPoint(x: 100, y: 190))
      }.stroke(Color.blue, lineWidth: 5)
   }
}
```

Listing 11-14: *Combining lines and arcs*

Because arcs are calculated from the coordinates of the center of the circle and its radius, we must consider these two values to connect the arc with the previous line. If the initial coordinates of the arc do not coincide with the current position of the pencil, a line is created between these two points to connect the path. Figure 11-13, below, shows the path we get with the example of Listing 11-14 and what we see if we move up the center of the arc by 10 points (y: 160).

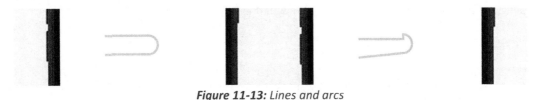

Figure 11-13: *Lines and arcs*

The **addRect()** and **addEllipse()** modifiers allow us to add rectangles and circles to the path. The modifiers add the shapes to the current path, but they move the pencil to the position indicated by the **CGRect** value, so they are considered independent shapes.

```
struct ContentView: View {
   var body: some View {
      Path { path in
         path.move(to: CGPoint(x: 100, y: 150))
         path.addLine(to: CGPoint(x: 200, y: 150))
         path.addEllipse(in: CGRect(x: 200, y: 140, width: 20, height:
20))
      }.stroke(Color.blue, lineWidth: 5)
   }
}
```

Listing 11-15: *Combining lines and ellipses*

Chapter 11 - Graphics and Animations

In this case, no line is generated between the current position of the pencil and the ellipse if they are not connected. Figure 11-14, below, shows the path we get with the example of Listing 11-15 and what we will see if we move the area of the circle 10 points to the right (x: 210).

Figure 11-14: Lines and ellipses

In addition to **addArc()** and **addEllipse()**, we have two more modifiers to draw curves. The **addQuadCurve()** modifier generates a quadratic Bezier curve, and the **addCurve()** modifier generates a cubic Bezier curve. The difference between these modifiers is that the first one has only one point of control and the second has two, thus creating different types of curves.

```
struct ContentView: View {
    var body: some View {
        Path { path in
            path.move(to: CGPoint(x: 50, y: 50))
            path.addQuadCurve(to: CGPoint(x: 50, y: 200), control:
CGPoint(x: 100, y: 125))
            path.move(to: CGPoint(x: 250, y: 50))
            path.addCurve(to: CGPoint(x: 250, y: 200), control1: CGPoint(x:
200, y: 125), control2: CGPoint(x: 300, y: 125))
        }.stroke(Color.blue, lineWidth: 5)
    }
}
```

Listing 11-16: Creating complex curves

To create a quadratic curve, we move the pencil to the point 50, 50, finish the curve at the point 50, 200, and set the control point at the position 100, 125.

The cubic curve generated by the **addCurve()** modifier is more complicated. There are two control points for this curve, the first one at the position 200, 125, and the second one at the position 300, 125. These points shape the curve, as shown below.

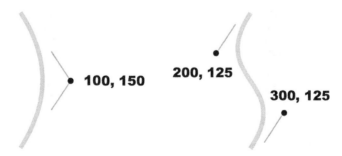

Figure 11-15: Complex curves

The paths we have created so far use fixed values. This means that the shape is always going to be of the same size, no matter the size of the view. To adapt the path to the size of the view, we must calculate how much space is available with the **GeometryReader** view (see Chapter 6).

```
struct ContentView: View {
    var body: some View {
        GeometryReader { geometry in
            Path { path in
```

```
        let width = geometry.size.width / 2
        let height = width
        let posX = (geometry.size.width - width) / 2
        let posY = (geometry.size.height - height) / 2

        path.move(to: CGPoint(x: posX, y: posY))
        path.addLine(to: CGPoint(x: posX + width, y: posY))
        path.addLine(to: CGPoint(x: posX, y: posY + height))
        path.closeSubpath()
      }.stroke(Color.blue, lineWidth: 5)
    }
  }
}
```

Listing 11-17: Adapting the size of the path to the size of the container

The code in Listing 11-17 draws a triangle that is always half the width of its container. For this purpose, we first calculate the triangle's width dividing the width of the geometry by 2. Then, we assign this value to the **height** constant to set the height equal to the width. After the dimensions are calculated, we determine the position of the initial point. Because we want to center the triangle in the container, we get the remaining space by subtracting the triangle's width from the width of the geometry and then divide the result by 2 to get the initial point. We do the same for the vertical position and store the values in the **posX** and **posY** constants. With these values, we can finally draw the path. The **move()** modifier moves the pencil to the initial position determined by **posX** and **posY**. Next, the **addLine()** modifier draws a line from this point to the point located at the right end of the triangle (**posX + width**). The next **addLine()** modifier draws a line from this point to the point at the bottom left of the triangle (**posY + height**). And finally, the **closeSubpath()** modifier draws the vertical line to close the path.

Because we calculate all the coordinates of the path from the values of the geometry, the triangle adapts to the size of its container and is always half the container's size and centered in the view, no matter the device or the size of the screen.

Figure 11-16: Path of relative size

(Medium) **Custom Shapes**

The common shapes introduced at the beginning of this chapter are structures that conform to the **Shape** protocol. A structure that conforms to this protocol defines its own path, which is created the same way as the path for a **Path** view, but the advantage of working with **Shape** structures instead of **Path** views is that a **Shape** structure receives a **CGRect** value with the dimensions of the view in which the shape is going to be drawn, so the shapes always adapts to the size of the container (we do not need to calculate its size with a **GeometryReader** view).

The protocol requires the structure to implement the following method to define the path of the shape.

Chapter 11 - Graphics and Animations

path(in: CGRect)—This method receives a **CGRect** value with the dimensions of the view and must return a **Path** view with the path we want to assign to the shape.

Creating a custom shape is easy. We must define a structure that conforms to the **Shape** protocol, implement the **path()** method, and create and return a **Path** view. The following example defines a shape structure called **Triangle** that draws a triangle.

```
import SwiftUI
struct Triangle: Shape {
    func path(in rect: CGRect) -> Path {
        var path = Path()
        let width = rect.width
        let height = rect.height
        let posX = rect.origin.x
        let posY = rect.origin.y

        path.move(to: CGPoint(x: posX, y: posY))
        path.addLine(to: CGPoint(x: posX + width, y: posY))
        path.addLine(to: CGPoint(x: posX, y: posY + height))
        path.closeSubpath()

        return path
    }
}
```

Listing 11-18: Creating a custom shape view

The path is the same as previous examples, but now we take the values from the **CGRect** structure received by the method to calculate the size of the shape. In this case, we extend the triangle from left to right and top to bottom to cover the whole view. (The size of the triangle matches the view's width and height, which is the recommended approach for custom shapes.)

Once the **Shape** view is defined, we can implement it in our interface as any other view. To illustrate how this works, we can instantiate multiple **Triangle** views of different sizes within a horizontal **ScrollView**.

```
struct ContentView: View {
    var body: some View {
        VStack {
            ScrollView(.horizontal, showsIndicators: true) {
                HStack {
                    Triangle()
                        .fill(Color.blue)
                        .frame(width: 120, height: 50)
                    Triangle()
                        .fill(Color.green)
                        .frame(width: 120, height: 100)
                    Triangle()
                        .fill(Color.yellow)
                        .frame(width: 120, height: 80)
                    Triangle()
                        .fill(Color.red)
                        .frame(width: 50, height: 50)
                }
            }.padding()
            Spacer()
        }
    }
}
```

Listing 11-19: Implementing custom shape views

When a **Triangle** view is created, the **path()** method is called with the dimensions of the view and the triangle is drawn according to those values. Therefore, if we define **Triangle** views of different sizes, we get triangles of different sizes and shapes on the screen.

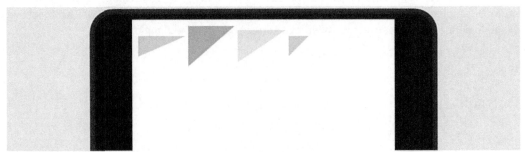

Figure 11-17: *Custom shape views*

Do It Yourself: Create a Swift file called Triangle.swift for the code in Listing 11-18. Update the **ContentView** view with the code in Listing 11-19. If you don't see all the triangles, scroll the view or rotate the device (Figure 11-17).

(Medium) 11.3 Transformations

There are multiple tools provided by SwiftUI to change physical aspects of a view or a **Shape** view, like the orientation, perspective, or the position of the content. The following are some of the modifiers available for this purpose.

offset(CGSize**)**—This modifier displaces the content of the view to the horizontal and vertical distance defined by the argument.

rotationEffect(Angle**)**—This modifier rotates the content of the view to the angle determined by the argument.

rotation3DEffect(Angle, Tuple**)**—This modifier rotates the content of the view in 3D. The first argument declares the angle in degrees or radians, and the second argument is a tuple with three values to represent the axes, as in **(x: Double, y: Double, z: Double)**. Values different than 0 rotate the image in that axis.

clipShape(Shape**)**—This modifier clips the view with the shape specified by the argument.

These modifiers affect the content of the view. For instance, if we apply an offset to an **Image** view, the image inside the view is displaced the distance determined by the modifier, but the view's frame is not affected.

```
struct ContentView: View {
   var body: some View {
      Image("spot1")
         .resizable()
         .scaledToFit()
         .frame(width: 150, height: 200)
         .offset(CGSize(width: 75, height: 0))
   }
}
```

Listing 11-20: *Displacing an image*

The code in Listing 11-20 displaces the image 75 points to the right (half the width of the **Image** view).

Chapter 11 - Graphics and Animations

Figure 11-18: Image displaced to the right

The rotation modifiers work in a similar way. They rotate the content of the view in 2D or 3D. The most interesting is the **rotation3DEffect()** which can rotate the content on any axis.

```
struct ContentView: View {
    var body: some View {
        Image("spot1")
            .resizable()
            .scaledToFit()
            .frame(width: 150, height: 200)
            .scaleEffect(CGSize(width: 0.9, height: 0.9))
            .rotation3DEffect(.degrees(30), axis: (x: 0, y: 1, z: 0))
    }
}
```

Listing 11-21: Rotating the image

The **rotation3DEffect()** modifier requires a tuple with values that determine the axes in which the content will be rotated. A value of 0 indicates no rotation and a value different than 0 indicates the direction of the rotation, negative to one side and positive to the other.

Figure 11-19: Image rotated in the y axis

Another transformation we can perform is clipping the view with the **clipShape()** modifier. This modifier superposes the view with a shape and only preserves the parts of the view covered by the shape. This is particularly useful with images. For instance, we can clip our image with a **Circle** shape to create a nice thumbnail.

```
struct ContentView: View {
    var body: some View {
        Image("spot1")
            .resizable()
            .scaledToFit()
            .frame(width: 150, height: 200)
            .clipShape(Circle())
```

```
        }
    }
```

Listing 11-22: Clipping the image

Figure 11-20: Image clipped with a `Circle` *shape*

SwiftUI also includes modifiers specifically designed to work and transform **Shape** views. The following are the most frequently used.

rotation(Angle, **anchor:** UnitPoint**)**—This modifier rotates the shape to the angle specified by the first argument. The **anchor** argument determines the point around which the shape will rotate. The point is specified with values between 0.0 and 1.0.

scale(CGFloat, **anchor:** UnitPoint**)**—This modifier changes the scale of the shape. The first argument determines the new scale (1.0 by default), and the **anchor** argument determines the point from which the shape is scaled. There is an additional modifier to change the scale independently for the x and y axes: **scale(x: CGFloat, y: CGFloat, anchor: UnitPoint)**.

trim(from: CGFloat, **to:** CGFloat**)**—This modifier trims the shape from the point determined by the **from** argument to the point determined by the **to** argument.

These modifiers are implemented by **Shape** views and therefore they must be applied before other modifiers, as in the following example.

```
struct ContentView: View {
    var body: some View {
        RoundedRectangle(cornerRadius: 20)
            .rotation(.degrees(45))
            .fill(Color.red)
            .frame(width: 100, height: 100)
    }
}
```

Listing 11-23: Rotating a shape

Again, the transformation modifiers affect the content of the view, in this case the shape, but the view itself remains the same. In the example of Listing 11-23, we create a **RoundedRectangle** view and rotate it 45 degrees.

Figure 11-21: Rotation

The **scale()** modifier is not only used to resize the shape but also to achieve cool effects. For instance, we can contract or expand shapes by declaring different values for the horizontal and vertical scales, or create a mirror image by declaring a negative value. The following example implements this trick to invert the coordinate system and draw an inverted shape.

```
struct ContentView: View {
    var body: some View {
        HStack {
            Triangle()
                .fill(Color.blue)
                .frame(width: 100, height: 100)
            Triangle()
                .scale(x: -1, y: 1)
                .fill(Color.blue)
                .frame(width: 100, height: 100)
        }
    }
}
```

Listing 11-24: *Inverting a shape with the* scale() *modifier*

This example implements the **Triangle** view defined in Listing 11-18. The first instance is displayed with a regular scale, but the second instance is transformed with the **scale()** modifier and a horizontal scale of -1, which inverts the coordinate system, creating a mirror image.

Figure 11-22: *Mirror shapes*

 Do It Yourself: Update the **ContentView** view with the code in Listing 11-24. To test this example, you also need the Triangle.swift file we created before with the **Triangle** view defined in Listing 11-18. You should see the shapes in Figure 11-22 on the canvas.

As we already mentioned, paths are drawn from one point to another, as if they were following the movement of a pencil. We can remove part of the process with the **trim()** modifier. This modifier determines what part of the path is drawn with values from 0.0 to 1.0, where 0.0 represents the beginning of the path and 1.0 the end.

```
struct ContentView: View {
    var body: some View {
        HStack {
            Triangle()
                .trim(from: 0, to: 0.70)
                .stroke(Color.blue, lineWidth: 10)
                .frame(width: 100, height: 100)
        }
    }
}
```

Listing 11-25: *Trimming a path*

This example creates a **Triangle** view, but trims the path at the point 0.70, which represent the 70% of the drawing. This allows the system to draw the first and second lines in full, but the process is interrupted, and therefore the triangle is never finished.

Figure 11-23: Incomplete shape

11.4 Canvas

With standard and custom shapes, we can add as many graphics to the interface as needed, but performance drops when too many views are required. To overcome these limitations, SwiftUI includes the **Canvas** view. A view specifically designed for dynamic 2D drawing.

Canvas(opaque: Bool, **colorMode:** ColorRenderingMode, **renders-Asynchronously:** Bool, **renderer:** Closure)—This initializer creates a **Canvas** view. The **opaque** argument determines whether the canvas is opaque (**true**) or transparent (**false**). The **colorMode** argument defines the color space used to draw the graphics. It is an enumeration with the values **extendedLinear**, **linear**, and **nonLinear**. The **rendersAsynchronously** argument determines whether the drawing is going to be made synchronously or asynchronously. And the **renderer** argument provides the graphics to be drawn. The closure receives two values, a **GraphicsContext** structure that represents the graphic context where all the drawing is performed, and a **CGSize** value with the canvas' width and height.

The closure assigned to the **Canvas** view provides an instance of the **GraphicsContext** structure that represents the drawing context. All the drawing is performed in this context from methods provided by the structure. The following are some of the methods available to draw images.

draw(Image, **at:** CGPoint, **anchor:** UnitPoint)—This method draws the image specified by the first argument. The **at** argument determines the image's position in the context, and the **anchor** argument determines the image's origin.

draw(Image, **in:** CGRect, **style:** FillStyle)—This method draws the image specified by the first argument in the area specified by the **in** argument. The **style** argument determines the style of the image. It is a structure with the initializer **FillStyle-(eoFill: Bool, antialiased: Bool)**.

The following are some of the methods available to draw text.

draw(Text, **at:** CGPoint, **anchor:** UnitPoint)—This method draws the text specified by the first argument. The **at** argument determines the position in the context, and the **anchor** argument determines the text's origin.

draw(Text, **in:** CGRect)—This method draws the text specified by the first argument within the area specified by the **in** argument. If there is not enough space in the area, the text is truncated.

Chapter 11 - Graphics and Animations

And the following are the methods available to draw paths.

stroke(Path, **with:** Shading, **lineWidth:** CGFloat**)**—This method draws the path specified by the first argument. The **with** argument specifies the color or pattern used to stroke the path, and the **lineWidth** argument determines the width.

stroke(Path, **with:** Shading, **style:** StrokeStyle**)**—This method draws the path specified by the first argument. The **with** argument specifies the color or pattern used to stroke the path, and the **style** argument determines the style (see Listing 11-4).

fill(Path, **with:** Shading, **style:** FillStyle**)**—This method draws the path specified by the first arguments and fills the shape. The **with** argument specifies the color or pattern used to fill the shape, and the **style** argument determines the style. It is a structure with the initializer `FillStyle(eoFill: Bool, antialiased: Bool)`.

Paths are drawn with the colors and patterns specified by a `Shading` structure. The structure includes the following type methods to produced customized styles.

color(Color**)**—This method returns a color. The argument is the `Color` view with the color we want to assign to the path.

color(red: Double, **green:** Double, **blue:** Double, **opacity:** Double**)**—This method returns a color. The **red**, **green**, and **blue** arguments determine the levels of red, green, and blue with values from 0.0 (no color) to 1.0 (full color).

color(white: Double, **opacity:** Double**)**—This method returns a color. The **white** argument determines the level of white with a value from 0.0 to 1.0 (black to white), and the **opacity** argument determines the level of opacity with a value from 0.0 (transparent) to 1.0 (opaque). The opacity may be ignored.

linearGradient(Gradient, **startPoint:** CGPoint, **endPoint:** CGPoint**)**—This method returns a linear gradient. The first argument is the gradient of colors to be used, and the **startPoint** and **endPoint** arguments determine the points inside the shape where the gradient starts and ends.

radialGradient(Gradient, **center:** CGPoint, **startRadius:** CGFloat, **endRadius:** CGFloat**)**—This method returns a circular gradient. The first argument is the gradient of colors to be used. The **center** argument determines the position of the center of the circle, and the **startRadius** and **endRadius** arguments determine where the gradient starts and ends.

conicGradient(Gradient, **center:** CGPoint, **angle:** Angle**)**—This method returns a conic gradient. The first argument is the gradient of colors to be used. The **center** argument determines the position of the tip of the cone, and the **angle** argument determines the angle where the gradient begins.

tiledImage(Image, **origin:** CGPoint, **sourceRect:** CGRect, **scale:** CGFloat**)**— This method draws the image specified by the first argument over and over again to cover the shape. The **origin** argument determines the point in the shape where the initial image is placed. The **sourceRect** argument determines the region of the original image we want to draw. And the **scale** argument defines the scale of the image.

By default, the canvas is non-opaque (the value `false` is assigned to the **opaque** argument), the color mode is set to `nonLinear`, and the rendering is performed synchronously. If that configuration is good enough for our application, all we need is to declare the closure to render the graphics.

```
struct ContentView: View {
   var body: some View {
      Canvas { context, size in
         let imageFrame = CGRect(origin: .zero, size: size)
         context.draw(Image("spot1"), in: imageFrame)
      }.ignoresSafeArea()
   }
}
```

Listing 11-26: *Drawing an image on the canvas*

This example creates a **Canvas** view of the size of the screen. (Notice the **ignoresSafeArea()** modifier at the end.) The **draw()** method takes a **CGRect** value and draws the image on that area. In this case, we have decided to use the whole canvas, so we define a **CGRect** value with the origin 0,0 and the size of the canvas, but we can provide a specific size. For instance, the image we use in this example is 644 pixels wide by 864 pixels tall. From these values, we can define the **CGRect** necessary to present the image in a smaller size.

```
struct ContentView: View {
   var body: some View {
      Canvas { context, size in
         let imageSize = CGSize(width: 161, height: 216)
         let posX = (size.width - imageSize.width) / 2
         let posY = posX

         let imageFrame = CGRect(x: posX, y: posY, width:
imageSize.width, height: imageSize.height)
         context.draw(Image("spot1"), in: imageFrame)
      }.ignoresSafeArea()
   }
}
```

Listing 11-27: *Drawing an image on the canvas*

In this example, we define an area a quarter the size of the original image and divide the remaining horizontal space by 2 to determine its position. As a result, the image is centered on the canvas.

Figure 11-24: *Image of a custom size*

Of course, we can also draw shapes, including standard and custom shapes and paths. For instance, we can combine our image with some graphic and text.

```
struct ContentView: View {
   var body: some View {
      Canvas { context, size in
         let imageFrame = CGRect(x: 60, y: 75, width: 215, height: 288)
         context.draw(Image("spot1"), in: imageFrame)

         let circleFrame = CGRect(x: 20, y: 50, width: 60, height: 60)
         context.fill(Circle().path(in: circleFrame),
with: .color(.yellow))

         let rectFrame = CGRect(x: 50, y: 60, width: 250, height: 40)
         context.fill(RoundedRectangle(cornerRadius: 25).path(in:
rectFrame), with: .color(.yellow))

         let textPos = CGPoint(x: 80, y: 80)
         context.draw(Text("My Picture").font(.title.bold()), at:
textPos, anchor: .leading)
      }.ignoresSafeArea()
   }
}
```

Listing 11-28: *Drawing shapes and text*

In this example, we create a banner on top of the image with a circle, a rounded rectangle, and a text. The result is shown below.

Figure 11-25: *Shapes and text on the canvas*

The **GraphicsContext** structure also includes methods to perform transformations on the canvas. The following are the most frequently used.

scaleBy(x: CGFloat, **y:** CGFloat)—This method determines the horizontal and vertical scale of the canvas. By default, the scale is 1.0.

rotate(by: Angle)—This method rotates the canvas the angle specified by the **by** argument.

translateBy(x: CGFloat, **y:** CGFloat)—This method moves the point of origin of the canvas to the position determined by the **x** and **y** arguments.

These methods work like those implemented before for shapes, but they only affect the matrix the context uses to calculate the position and size of the graphics. For instance, if we call the **rotate()** method on the context, the graphics already on the canvas are unchanged, only the graphics drawn afterwards are rotated. For an example, we can draw two copies of the same image on the canvas. The first one is drawn on the standard canvas and the second one is drawn after the canvas is rotated 20 degrees.

```
struct ContentView: View {
   var body: some View {
      Canvas { context, size in
         let imageFrame = CGRect(x: 60, y: 75, width: 161, height: 216)
         context.draw(Image("spot1"), in: imageFrame)
         context.rotate(by: .degrees(20))
         context.draw(Image("spot1"), in: imageFrame)
      }.ignoresSafeArea()
   }
}
```

Listing 11-29: *Rotating the canvas*

As illustrated by the picture below, only the image that has been drawn after the `rotate()` method was applied to the context is affected by the rotation, the previous image remains the same. This is because the transformation methods affect the matrix by which the context calculates how to draw the graphics, not the canvas itself.

Figure 11-26: *Rotation*

The rotation is performed around the canvas' origin, which by default is at the coordinates 0, 0 (top-left corner). If, for example, we want to rotate a graphic around its center, we must first move the origin to that position with the `translateBy()` method, as shown next.

```
struct ContentView: View {
   var body: some View {
      Canvas { context, size in
         context.translateBy(x: size.width/2, y: size.height/2)
         context.rotate(by: .degrees(45))

         let width = 161
         let height = 216
         let imageFrame = CGRect(x: -width/2, y: -height/2, width: width,
height: height)
         context.draw(Image("spot1"), in: imageFrame)
      }.ignoresSafeArea()
   }
}
```

Listing 11-30: *Rotating an image*

The code in Listing 11-30 translates the origin to the center of the canvas, rotates the canvas 45 degrees, and then calculates the position and size of the image. In this example, we are showing the image at a quarter of its original size, as before, but the position is estimated in relation to the new origin. Because the image's origin is at the position 0, 0 (top-left corner) and we want to rotate the image around its center, we must specify values that place the center of the image at the origin of the canvas, and that means using negative values. The horizontal

Chapter 11 - Graphics and Animations

position is at minus half the width of the image (-85), and the vertical position at minus half the height (-108), so the center of the image coincides with the origin of the canvas.

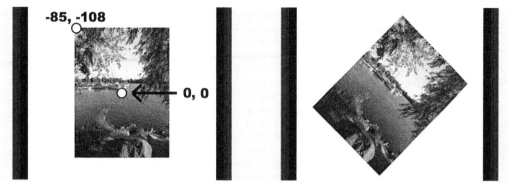

Figure 11-27: Custom rotation

Transformations are cumulative. This means that the transformations performed on the canvas are applied over the previous transformations. For instance, if we rotate the canvas 45 degrees, and then rotate it another 45 degrees, the final rotation will be 90 degrees.

```
struct ContentView: View {
   var body: some View {
      Canvas { context, size in
         let imageFrame = CGRect(x: 0, y: 0, width: 100, height: 100)
         context.translateBy(x: size.width/2, y: size.height/2)
         for _ in 0..<10 {
            context.rotate(by: .degrees(36))
            context.draw(Image("spot1"), in: imageFrame)
         }
      }.ignoresSafeArea()
   }
}
```

Listing 11-31: Performing multiple transformations

In this code, we create a loop with 10 cycles (from 0 to 9). Each cycle rotates the context 36 degrees and then draws an image. Because the rotations are cumulative, the rotation of each image adds to the previous rotation, forming a complete circle.

Figure 11-28: Multiple rotations

Drawing the same image several times affects performance. The system must prepare the image every time it is about to be drawn. If we need to improve performance, we can prepare the image beforehand with the following method.

resolve(Image**)**—This method returns an image that is configured according to the current context.

This method can also prepare **Text** views and **Shading** values, but it is particularly useful with images. The following is the previous example, but the image is resolved before drawing.

```
struct ContentView: View {
   var body: some View {
      Canvas { context, size in
         let imageReady = context.resolve(Image("spot1"))
         let imageFrame = CGRect(x: 0, y: 0, width: 100, height: 100)
         context.translateBy(x: size.width/2, y: size.height/2)
         for _ in 0..<10 {
            context.rotate(by: .degrees(36))
            context.draw(imageReady, in: imageFrame)
         }
      }.ignoresSafeArea()
   }
}
```

Listing 11-32: Preparing images

The **GraphicsContext** structure also includes the following method to create a clipping mask that determines what part of the canvas is available for drawing.

clip(to: Path**)**—This method creates a clipping mask. Only the parts of the graphics inside the mask are drawn.

The following code applies a clipping mask with the shape of a circle to the canvas of the previous example, so only the parts of the images that fall inside the circle are drawn.

```
struct ContentView: View {
   var body: some View {
      Canvas { context, size in
         let imageFrame = CGRect(x: 0, y: 0, width: 100, height: 100)
         context.translateBy(x: size.width/2, y: size.height/2)

         let clipFrame = CGRect(x: -100, y: -100, width: 200, height: 200)
         context.clip(to: Circle().path(in: clipFrame))
         for _ in 0..<10 {
            context.rotate(by: .degrees(36))
            context.draw(Image("spot1"), in: imageFrame)
         }
      }.ignoresSafeArea()
   }
}
```

Listing 11-33: Clipping the canvas

Figure 11-29: Clipping mask

　　　　　　　　　Chapter 11 - Graphics and Animations

In the previous examples, we keep modifying the context on top of prior modifications. If we want to work with multiple configurations, we can create and work on copies of the graphic context. The following example rotates an image in a copy of the context but then draws additional graphics in the original context with a standard configuration.

```
struct ContentView: View {
    var body: some View {
        Canvas { context, size in
            var copyContext = context
            copyContext.translateBy(x: size.width/2, y: size.height/2)
            copyContext.rotate(by: .degrees(45))
            let imageFrame = CGRect(x: -85, y: -108, width: 161, height: 216)
            copyContext.draw(Image("spot1"), in: imageFrame)

            let center = size.width/2
            let rectFrame = CGRect(x: center - 125, y: 160, width: 250,
height: 40)
            context.fill(RoundedRectangle(cornerRadius: 25).path(in:
rectFrame), with: .color(.yellow))

            let textPos = CGPoint(x: center, y: 180)
            context.draw(Text("My Picture").font(.title.bold()), at:
textPos, anchor: .center)
        }.ignoresSafeArea()
    }
}
```

Listing 11-34: *Working with different configurations*

Figure 11-30: *Multiple configurations*

The **GraphicsContext** structure also allows us to filter the graphics. With filters, we can add effects and configure multiple aspects of the graphics, such as brightness, contrast, blurriness, and more. The structure includes the following method to apply a filter.

addFilter(Filter**)**—This method applies a filter to the context. The argument defines the type of filter and its configuration. The structure includes multiple type methods to define standard filters. The most frequently used are **brightness(Double)**, **contrast (Double)**, **saturation(Double)**, **colorInvert(Double)**, **colorMultiply (Color)**, **hueRotation(Angle)**, **grayscale(Double)**, **blur(radius: CGFloat)**, and **shadow(color: Color, radius: CGFloat, x: CGFloat, y: CGFloat, blendMode: BlendMode, options: ShadowOptions)**.

Applying a filter is straightforward. We call the **addFilter()** method on the context for every effect we want to apply and all the graphics drawn afterward will be affected. For instance, the following example tints an image red and makes it blurry.

```
struct ContentView: View {
    var body: some View {
        Canvas { context, size in
            context.addFilter(.colorMultiply(Color.red))
            context.addFilter(.blur(radius: 5))

            let margin = (size.width - 161) / 2
            let imageFrame = CGRect(x: margin, y: margin, width: 161,
height: 216)
            context.draw(Image("spot1"), in: imageFrame)
        }.ignoresSafeArea()
    }
}
```

Listing 11-35: *Applying filters to the graphics*

Figure 11-31: *Filters*

Basic **11.5 Charts**

In addition to the tools provided by SwiftUI to create and display graphics on the screen, there is also a framework called *Swift Charts* that we can use to produce a graphical representation of the user's data. The following is the structure provided by the framework to create a chart.

Chart(Data, **content:** Closure)—This initializer creates a view to display a chart. The first argument is the data we want to represent by the chart, and the **content** argument is the closure that returns the views required to create the chart.

There are several predefined charts available. We can create a bar chart, line chart, point chart, and more. The graphics used to create these charts are called *Marks*. The following are the views included in the framework to create these marks.

BarMark(x: PlottableValue, **y:** PlottableValue)—This initializer creates a mark that represents the data with a bar. The **x** and **y** arguments represent the position and size of the bar in the chart's coordinates.

LineMark(x: PlottableValue, **y:** PlottableValue)—This initializer creates a mark that represents the data with lines between points. The **x** and **y** arguments represent the position of the point that is going to be used to connect the lines.

PointMark(x: PlottableValue, **y:** PlottableValue)—This initializer creates a mark that represents the data with a point. The **x** and **y** arguments represent the position of the point in the chart's coordinates.

Chapter 11 - Graphics and Animations

RectangleMark(x: PlottableValue, **y:** PlottableValue, **width:** Mark-Dimension, **height:** MarkDimension)—This initializer creates a mark that represents the data with a rectangle. The **x** and **y** arguments represent the position of the rectangle, and the **width** and **height** arguments determine the size.

AreaMark(x: PlottableValue, **y:** PlottableValue)—This initializer creates a mark that represents the data by filling the area below or between the points. The **x** and **y** arguments represent the position of the points used to calculate the area.

The positions in the chart's coordinate system are determined by an instance of the **PlottableValue** structure. The structure includes the following type methods to return these values.

value(String, Value**)**—This type method creates a value for a mark that represents quantitative data. The first argument is a custom string to describe the value, and the second argument is the value itself.

value(String, Date, **unit:** Component, **calendar:** Calendar?**)**—This type method creates a value for a mark that represents dates. The first argument is a custom string to describe the value. The second argument specifies the date we are representing. The **unit** argument determines the component of the date we want to use to represent the data. And **calendar** is an optional argument we can use to specify the calendar that should be used to determine the date.

A chart can take quantitative values, like integers, nominal values, like strings, and temporal values, like dates. Therefore, we can usually create charts from our app's data without any changes. For instance, we can use a model from previous examples that includes food items and their calorie content.

```
import SwiftUI

struct Consumables: Identifiable {
   let id = UUID()
   var name: String
   var category: String
   var calories: Int
}
class ApplicationData: ObservableObject {
   @Published var listOfItems: [Consumables]

   init() {
      listOfItems = [
         Consumables(name: "Bagels", category: "Baked", calories: 250),
         Consumables(name: "Brownies", category: "Baked", calories: 466),
         Consumables(name: "Butter", category: "Dairy", calories: 717),
         Consumables(name: "Cheese", category: "Dairy", calories: 402),
         Consumables(name: "Cookies", category: "Baked", calories: 502),
         Consumables(name: "Donuts", category: "Baked", calories: 452),
         Consumables(name: "Granola", category: "Baked", calories: 471)
      ]
   }
}
```

Listing 11-36: Providing the data for a chart

The syntax of the **Chart** view is similar to the **List** view. We can provide the data in the view's initializer or use a **ForEach** loop and then build the views with the value received by the closure, as shown next.

```
import SwiftUI
import Charts

struct ContentView: View {
    @EnvironmentObject var appData: ApplicationData

    var body: some View {
        VStack {
            Chart(appData.listOfItems) { item in
                BarMark(x: .value("Name", item.name), y: .value("Calories",
item.calories))
            }.frame(height: 300)
            .padding()
            Spacer()
        }
    }
}
struct ContentView_Previews: PreviewProvider {
    static var previews: some View {
        ContentView().environmentObject(ApplicationData())
    }
}
```

Listing 11-37: *Visualizing data with a bar chart*

Charts is a separate framework, so we need to import it with an **import** statement. Once we have access to the framework's views, we can create a chart. The **Chart** view generates a loop with the data in the model. In each cycle, the closure assigned to the **content** argument receives a value and creates the view to represent it. In this example, we use a **BarMark** view to display the values with bars. The value of the **name** property is assigned to the **x** axis and the number of calories to the **y** axis. This creates vertical bars, with the names of the food below the bars, and the calories on the side. But we can easily invert the axes by switching the values. (The calories are assigned to the **x** axis and the name to the **y** axis). The result of both configurations is shown below.

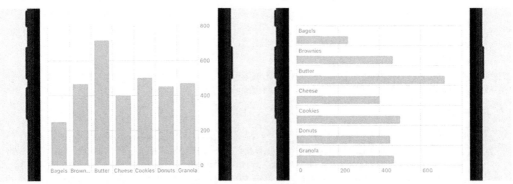

Figure 11-32: *Bar Charts*

If we want to create a different type of chart, all we need to do is to replace the **BarMark** view by the view we want. For instance, we can represent the same data with lines.

```
struct ContentView: View {
    @EnvironmentObject var appData: ApplicationData

    var body: some View {
        VStack {
            Chart(appData.listOfItems) { item in
                LineMark(x: .value("Name", item.name), y: .value("Calories",
item.calories))
```

```
            }.frame(height: 300)
            .padding()
            Spacer()
        }
    }
}
```

Listing 11-38: Visualizing data with a line chart

This chart generates a line between the points in the plot area determined by the positions assigned to the names in the **x** axis and the calories in the **y** axis. If we only want to show the point, we can implement the **PointMark** view to create the graphics. The **RectangleMark** view represents the values with rectangles, and the **AreaMark** view fills the area below or between the points.

Figure 11-33: Line, Point, Rectangle, and Area charts

 Do It Yourself: Create a Multiplatform project. Create a Swift file called ApplicationData.swift for the model in Listing 11-36. Update the ContentView.swift file with the code in Listing 11-37 and run the application. You should see a bar chart, as in Figure 11-32, left. Assign the value of the **calories** property to the **x** axis and the value of the **name** property to the **y** axis. Run the application again. You should see a chart with horizontal bars, as in Figure 11-32, right. Update the **ContentView** view with the code in Listing 11-38. Run the application again. You should see a line chart, as in Figure 11-33, left. Replace the **LineMark** view with the **PointMark**, **RectangleMark**, and **AreaMark** views. You should see on the screen the rest of the charts illustrated in Figure 11-33.

The scale used to represent the values is automatically calculated by the **Chart** view based on the data. In our example, the system defines a scale between 0 and 800 because the number of calories in our model are estimated by the hundreds and go over 700. If we remove the item named "Butter", the scale is now determined from 0 to 600 because there are no longer any values greater than 700. If we don't want the scale to adapt to the data, we can implement the following modifiers to configure the axis.

chartXScale(domain: Domain, **range:** Range, **type:** ScaleType?)—This modifier defines the scale for the **x** axis. The **domain** argument specifies the possible values with a range for quantitative values and an array for nominal values. The **range** argument defines the positions corresponding to the scale values in the plot area. And the **type** value is a structure that determines the type of scale to use. The structure includes the type properties **category**, **date**, **linear**, and **log**.

chartYScale(domain: Domain, **range:** Range, **type:** ScaleType?)—This modifier defines the scale for the **y** axis. The **domain** argument specifies the possible values with a range for quantitative values and an array for nominal values. The **range** argument defines the positions corresponding to the scale values in the plot area. And the **type** value is a structure that determines the type of scale to use. The structure includes the type properties **category**, **date**, **linear**, and **log**.

For example, if we know that all the food stored in our model have a maximum of 1000 calories, we can set a permanent scale between 0 and 1000.

```
struct ContentView: View {
   @EnvironmentObject var appData: ApplicationData

   var body: some View {
      VStack {
         Chart(appData.listOfItems) { item in
            BarMark(x: .value("Name", item.name), y: .value("Calories",
item.calories))
         }
         .chartYScale(domain: 0...1000)
         .frame(height: 300)
         .padding()
         Spacer()
      }
   }
}
```

Listing 11-39: Defining a custom scale for the y axis

In addition to the graphics that represent the data, the framework defines views to add other graphics, text, and overlays on top of the chart. The most frequently used is the `RuleMark` view, used to draw a line on the plot area. The following are the view's initializers.

RuleMark(x: PlottableValue, **yStart:** PlottableValue, **yEnd:** PlottableValue)— This initializer creates a view that represents data with a single line. The **x** argument determines the position of the line in the **x** axis, and the **yStart** and **yEnd** arguments determine the position where the line begins and ends in the **y** axis.

RuleMark(xStart: PlottableValue, **xEnd:** PlottableValue, **y:** PlottableValue)— This initializer creates a view that represents data with a single line. The **xStart** and **xEnd** arguments determine the position where the line begins and ends in the **x** axis, and the **y** argument determines the position of the line in the **y** axis.

The framework also includes modifiers to configure the view.

lineStyle(StrokeStyle)—This modifier defines the style of the line with a `Stroke-Style` structure.

annotation(position: AnnotationPosition, **alignment:** Alignment, **spacing:** CGFloat?, **content:** Closure)—This modifier adds an annotation to the line. The **position** argument specifies the position of the annotation in the plot area. It is a structure with the type properties `automatic`, `bottom`, `bottomLeading`, `bottomTrailing`, `leading`, `overlay`, `top`, `topLeading`, `topTrailing`, and `trailing`. The alignment argument aligns the annotation in relation to the line. It is a structure with the type properties `leading`, `center`, and `trailing`. The **spacing** argument defines the space between the line and the annotation. And the **content** argument provides the views to create the annotation.

The line generated by the `RuleMark` view belongs to the chart but it is independent of the rest of the graphics, so we should create the chart with a `ForEach` view and define the line on top or below the loop, as shown next.

```
struct ContentView: View {
   @EnvironmentObject var appData: ApplicationData
```

```
    var body: some View {
        VStack {
            Chart {
                ForEach(appData.listOfItems) { item in
                    BarMark(x: .value("Name", item.name),
y: .value("Calories", item.calories))
                        .foregroundStyle(.cyan)
                }
                RuleMark(y: .value("Average", averageCalories()))
                    .foregroundStyle(.black)
                    .lineStyle(StrokeStyle(lineWidth: 5))
                    .annotation(position: .bottom, alignment: .leading) {
                        Text("Average Calories")
                    }
            }.frame(height: 300)
            .padding()
            Spacer()
        }
    }
    func averageCalories() -> Int {
        let total = appData.listOfItems.reduce(0, { $0 + $1.calories })
        return total / appData.listOfItems.count
    }
}
```

Listing 11-40: *Drawing a line in the plot area*

In this example, the **Chart** view creates the chart, but the marks are generated by a **ForEach** loop. Below these loop, we define a **RuleMark** view to draw a horizontal line over the chart. (To draw the line below the chart, we must declare the **RuleMark** view on top of the **ForEach** view.) To calculate the line's vertical position, we define a method called **averageCalories()** that returns the average number of calories of all the items in the model. We also configure the line with a thickness of 5 points and an annotation at the bottom that reads "Average Calories".

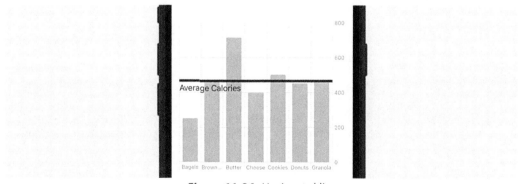

Figure 11-34: *Horizontal line*

In the previous example, we implemented the **foregroundStyle()** modifier to change the color of the bars, but this applies the same color to all the bars in the chart. To configure the chart according to values or categories, the framework includes the following modifier.

foregroundStyle(by: PlottableValue**)**—This modifier assigns different foreground styles to the marks based on a value. The **by** argument specifies the value to consider when assigning the styles.

The implementation is simple. We apply this modifier with a value that differentiates the marks, such as a category, and the chart takes care of assigning different styles to each one of them.

```
struct ContentView: View {
   @EnvironmentObject var appData: ApplicationData

   var body: some View {
      VStack {
         Chart(appData.listOfItems) { item in
            BarMark(x: .value("Name", item.name), y: .value("Calories",
item.calories))
               .foregroundStyle(by: .value("Category", item.category))
         }.frame(height: 300)
         .padding()
         Spacer()
      }
   }
}
```

Listing 11-41: Assigning different styles based on a category

The **foregroundStyle()** modifier applied in this example differentiates the bars by the value of the **category** property. The chart checks the values available and assigns different styles to each one of them. As a result, the bars associated to the Baked category are blue and those associated to the Dairy category are green (colors are assigned by the system). Notice that the chart also creates labels at the bottom to inform the user which categories the colors represent.

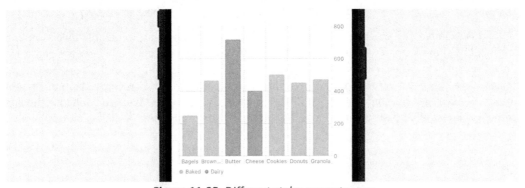

Figure 11-35: Different styles per category

There are also modifiers to configure the chart. The following are the most frequently used.

symbol(by: PlottableValue)—This modifier assigns different symbols to the points in a chart based on a value. The **by** argument specifies the value to consider when assigning the symbols.

symbolSize(CGFloat)—This modifier sets the size of the symbols that represent the points in the chart. The argument specifies the size of the area occupied by the symbol.

interpolationMethod(InterpolationMethod)—This modifier determines the style used to join the points when the chart contains lines or area marks. The argument is a structure with the type properties **cardinal**, **catmullRom**, **linear**, **monotone**, **stepCenter**, **stepEnd**, and **stepStart**.

chartForegroundStyleScale(Dictionary)—This modifiers assigns specific foreground styles to a scale of values. The argument is a dictionary with items that map the values to the styles.

Some of these modifiers are useful when using multiple marks to represent the values. For instance, if we want to use lines and points, we can specify a larger size for the symbols that represent the points to make them more visible.

```
struct ContentView: View {
   @EnvironmentObject var appData: ApplicationData

   var body: some View {
      VStack {
         Chart(appData.listOfItems) { item in
            LineMark(x: .value("Name", item.name), y: .value("Calories",
item.calories))
               .interpolationMethod(.catmullRom)
            PointMark(x: .value("Name", item.name), y: .value("Calories",
item.calories))
               .foregroundStyle(by: .value("Category", item.category))
               .symbol(by: .value("Category", item.category))
               .symbolSize(200)
         }.frame(height: 300)
         .padding()
         Spacer()
      }
   }
}
```

Listing 11-42: *Representing the values with different types of marks*

In this example, we apply an interpolation of type `catmullRom` to the `LineMark` view to smooth the lines. For the points, we apply a different color for each category with the `foregroundStyle()` modifier, as we did in the previous example for the bars, we also assign a different symbol to each category with the `symbol()` modifier, and finally enlarge the symbols with the `symbolSize()` modifier.

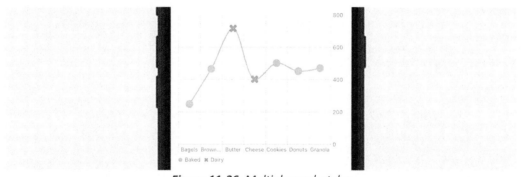

Figure 11-36: *Multiple mark styles*

Charts can also represent multiple series of values. The process is similar but we may have to organize the data in the model according to what we want to achieve. The following example shows a possible implementation. In this model, we have a structure to store the date and the amount of items sold (**Sales**), and another to store the sales per item (**Products**). To test the application, we initialize it with two products, Bagels and Brownies, and a week of sales each.

```
import SwiftUI

struct Sales: Identifiable {
   let id = UUID()
   var date: Date
   var amount: Int
}
struct Products: Identifiable {
   let id = UUID()
   var name: String
   var sales: [Sales]
}
```

```
class ApplicationData: ObservableObject {
   @Published var sales: [Products]

   init() {
      let salesBagels = [
         Sales(date: Date(timeInterval: -86400 * 7, since: Date()),
amount: 10),
         Sales(date: Date(timeInterval: -86400 * 6, since: Date()),
amount: 12),
         Sales(date: Date(timeInterval: -86400 * 5, since: Date()),
amount: 8),
         Sales(date: Date(timeInterval: -86400 * 4, since: Date()),
amount: 13),
         Sales(date: Date(timeInterval: -86400 * 3, since: Date()),
amount: 9),
         Sales(date: Date(timeInterval: -86400 * 2, since: Date()),
amount: 7),
         Sales(date: Date(timeInterval: -86400 * 1, since: Date()),
amount: 8) ]
      let salesBrownies = [
         Sales(date: Date(timeInterval: -86400 * 7, since: Date()),
amount: 3),
         Sales(date: Date(timeInterval: -86400 * 6, since: Date()),
amount: 5),
         Sales(date: Date(timeInterval: -86400 * 5, since: Date()),
amount: 2),
         Sales(date: Date(timeInterval: -86400 * 4, since: Date()),
amount: 8),
         Sales(date: Date(timeInterval: -86400 * 3, since: Date()),
amount: 6),
         Sales(date: Date(timeInterval: -86400 * 2, since: Date()),
amount: 5),
         Sales(date: Date(timeInterval: -86400 * 1, since: Date()),
amount: 9) ]
      sales = [ Products(name: "Bagels", sales: salesBagels),
Products(name: "Brownies", sales: salesBrownies) ]
   }
}
```

Listing 11-43: Representing the values with different types of marks

To create the chart, we must iterate through the items and then through the sales for each item, so we need two **ForEach** loops.

```
struct ContentView: View {
   @EnvironmentObject var appData: ApplicationData

   var body: some View {
      VStack {
         Chart {
            ForEach(appData.sales) { product in
               ForEach(product.sales) { sale in
                  LineMark(x: .value("Date", sale.date, unit: .day),
y: .value("Sales", sale.amount))
               }.foregroundStyle(by: .value("Products", product.name))
            }
         }.frame(height: 300)
         .padding()
         Spacer()
      }
   }
}
```

Listing 11-44: Visualizing two series of values

Chapter 11 - Graphics and Animations

This example creates a line chart. The first **ForEach** loop gets the products from the **sales** property in the model and then reads the **sales** property of each product to visualize the sales. Because we are using dates to define the **x** axis, we implement the **value()** method that allows us to specify the date and the unit we want to use to represent the value (**day**). As a result, we get two line charts, one for Bagels and another for Brownies.

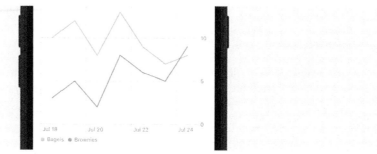

Figure 11-37: *Multiple series of values*

In a line chart, the series of values are independent, but bar and area charts add the marks on top of each other to display the total per value, as shown in the following example.

```
struct ContentView: View {
   @EnvironmentObject var appData: ApplicationData

   var body: some View {
      VStack {
         Chart {
            ForEach(appData.sales) { product in
               ForEach(product.sales) { sale in
                  BarMark(x: .value("Date", sale.date, unit: .day),
y: .value("Sales", sale.amount))
               }.foregroundStyle(by: .value("Products", product.name))
            }
         }
         .chartForegroundStyleScale(["Bagels": .red, "Brownies": .orange ])
         .frame(height: 300)
         .padding()
         Spacer()
      }
   }
}
```

Listing 11-45: *Visualizing two series of values with a bar chart*

In this chart, we replace the **LineMark** view with a **BarMark** view, but we also implement the **chartForegroundStyleScale()** modifier to assign custom colors to the bars. The modifier takes a dictionary. The keys are the values used by the **foregroundStyle()** modifier to identify each series of values, and the values are the styles we want to assign to the bars. (In this case, the color red for Bagels and orange for Brownies).

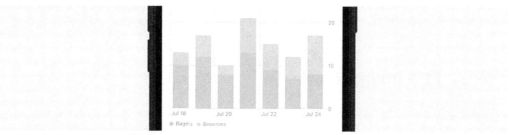

Figure 11-38: *Bar chart with two series of values*

By default, the bars are added up to show the total, but the framework offers the following modifier to customize the position.

position(by: PlottableValue, **axis:** Axis?, **span:** MarkDimension**)**—This modifier assigns a position for the bars. The **by** argument determines the value used to identify the bars. The **axis** argument specifies the axis used to position the bars. It is an enumeration with the values **horizontal** and **vertical**. And the **span** argument determines the space available for the bars. It is a structure with the type methods **fixed(CGFloat)**, **inset(CGFloat)**, and **ratio(CGFloat)**.

In the following example, we specify a different position for each product and separate the bars with a space by default.

```
struct ContentView: View {
    @EnvironmentObject var appData: ApplicationData

    var body: some View {
        VStack {
            Chart {
                ForEach(appData.sales) { product in
                    ForEach(product.sales) { sale in
                        BarMark(x: .value("Date", sale.date, unit: .day),
y: .value("Sales", sale.amount))
                        }.foregroundStyle(by: .value("Products", product.name))
                        .position(by: .value("Product", product.name))
                    }
            }.frame(height: 300)
            .padding()
            Spacer()
        }
    }
}
```

Listing 11-46: *Defining the positions of the bars*

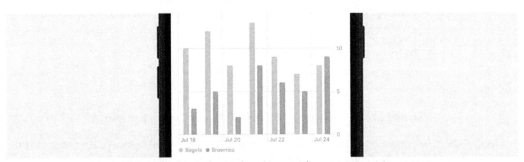

Figure 11-39: *Independent bars with custom positions*

 IMPORTANT: The Swift Charts framework includes additional tools to customize the charts and achieve any layout we need. There are also initializers for the marks that we can use to provide maximum and minimum values to limit the graphics. The topic is beyond the scope of this book. For more information, visit our website and follow the links for this chapter.

(Basic) **11.6 Image Renderer**

All the graphics and charts we have defined in previous examples are created on the spot. If we want to recreate a graphic or a complex view, we have to draw each line and circle again. But sometimes we may need to reuse a graphic or store it in a file or database. For cases like this, we can convert the view to an image. SwiftUI includes the `ImageRenderer` class for this purpose.

ImageRenderer(content: View)—This initializer creates an image from the view specified by the **content** argument.

The image is produced by the `ImageRenderer` object and then returned by its properties. There are three properties available: `uiImage` returns a `UIImage` object (UIKit), `cgImage` returns a `CGImage` object (Core Graphics), and `nsImage` returns an `NSImage` object (Appkit).

To turn a view into an image, we need to store the view in a property so we can use that property to reference the view from the `ImageRenderer`'s initializer. For instance, the following example defines a separate view called `NewPictureView` with an `Image` view that presents a circular image. The view is stored in a property called `newPicture` that we use to display it on the screen and then convert it to a `UIImage` object.

```
struct ContentView: View {
    @State private var pattern: UIImage?
    let newPicture = NewPictureView()

    var body: some View {
        VStack {
            newPicture
            Button("Export Image") {
                let renderer = ImageRenderer(content: newPicture)
                if let img = renderer.uiImage {
                    pattern = img.preparingThumbnail(of: CGSize(width: 25,
height: 25))
                }
            }
            if let pattern {
                Rectangle()
                    .fill(.image(Image(uiImage: pattern)))
                    .frame(width: 200, height: 200)
            }
            Spacer()
        }
    }
}
struct NewPictureView: View {
    var body: some View {
        Image("spot1")
            .resizable()
            .scaledToFit()
            .frame(width: 150, height: 200)
            .clipShape(Circle())
    }
}
```

Listing 11-47: Creating an image from a view

The interface includes a button. When the button is pressed, we create the `ImageRenderer` object from the view in the `newPicture` property and read the `uiImage` property to get the `UIImage` object with the new image. Once we have this object, we can process it as any other. In this example, we reduce its size to 25 by 25 points with the `preparingThumbnail()` method and assign it as the pattern of a `Rectangle` view, but we could have save it in a file or a database. The result is shown below.

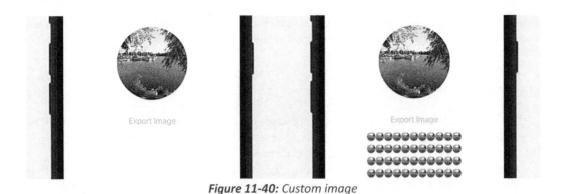

Figure 11-40: *Custom image*

 Do It Yourself: Create a Multiplatform project. Update the ContentView.swift file with the code in Listing 11-47. Download the spot1 image from our website and add it to the Asset Catalog. Press the Export Image button. You should see the rectangle filled with a pattern created from the new image (Figure 11-40).

(Basic) 11.7 Animations

SwiftUI views can be animated. The process is easy to implement. We set the new state, declare the type of animation we want, and SwiftUI takes care of producing the animation to move from the old state to the new one. For instance, if a state changes the opacity of the view, SwiftUI calculates the values between the initial and the new opacity, and then recreates the view for each of those values to produce every frame of the animation. To animate a state, SwiftUI includes the following function.

withAnimation(Animation, Closure**)**—This function performs an animation and returns the result. The first argument defines the type of animation to use. If ignored, the animation is defined as **default**. The second argument defines the closure that performs the changes we want to animate.

This function applies the animation to the states, but the animation is determined by an instance of the **Animation** structure. The structure provides properties and methods to create and configure the animation, including the following type properties to define standard animations.

default—This type property returns the animation defined by the system by default.

easeIn—This type property returns an animation that is slow at the beginning and faster at the end.

easeInOut—This type property returns an animation that is slow at the beginning and the end.

easeOut—This type property returns an animation that is fast at the beginning and slow at the end.

linear—This type property returns an animation that is always performed at the same speed.

The **withAnimation()** function asks the system to perform an animation if a state changes. For instance, in the following example, we change the scale of a **Rectangle** view from 1 to 2 when a button is pressed, but because the change is performed inside the closure assigned to the **withAnimation()** function, it is animated.

```
struct ContentView: View {
    @State private var boxScale: CGFloat = 1

    var body: some View {
        VStack {
            HStack {
                Rectangle()
                    .fill(Color.blue)
                    .frame(width: 50, height: 50)
                    .scaleEffect(boxScale)
            }.frame(width: 250, height: 120)
            Button("Animate") {
                withAnimation(.default) {
                    boxScale = 2
                }
            }
        }.padding()
    }
}
```

Listing 11-48: Animating a view

This view defines a **@State** property of type **CGFloat** with the value 1, uses this value to define the scale of a **Rectangle** view with the **scaleEffect()** modifier, and provides a button to modify it. When the button is pressed, we assign the value 2 to the property, expanding the view, but because the assignment is done within an animation closure, the change is animated.

Figure 11-41: Animation by default

The animation in this example is of type **default**, which on most systems is set as an **easeInOut** animation, but we can specify a different type if we think it will look better on our interface. The following example applies a **linear** animation instead.

```
Button("Animate") {
    withAnimation(.linear) {
        boxScale = 2
    }
}
```

Listing 11-49: Applying a linear animation

Do It Yourself: Create a Multiplatform project. Update the **ContentView** view with the code in Listing 11-48. Press the Animate button. You should see the blue square grow, as shown in Figure 11-41. Specify another type of animation, as we did in Listing 11-49, to see the difference between one type and another.

The animations created by type properties like **default** and **linear** are configured with values by default, but the **Animation** structure offers methods to customize the animation.

delay(Double**)**—This method sets the seconds the animator waits before starting the animation.

repeatCount(Int, **autoreverses:** Bool**)**—This method sets the number of times the animator performs an animation. The first argument determines the number of animations to be performed, and the **autoreverses** argument determines if the process of going back to the initial state is going to be animated as well (**true** by default).

repeatForever(autoreverses: Bool**)**—This method determines if the animator is going to perform the animation indefinitely. The **autoreverses** argument determines if the process of going back to the initial state is going to be animated as well (**true** by default).

speed(Double**)**—This method sets the speed of the animation (1 by default).

These methods are applied to the **Animation** structure, similar to how modifiers are applied to views. We create the **Animation** structure, call the methods to configure the animation, and then apply it to the state with the **withAnimation()** method, as in the following example.

```
Button("Animate") {
    let animation = Animation.easeInOut
        .delay(1)
        .speed(2)
        .repeatCount(3)
    withAnimation(animation) {
        boxScale = 2
    }
}
```

Listing 11-50: Configuring the animation

This animation is delayed by 1 second, reproduced at twice the normal speed, and repeated 3 times. Notice that by default, the **repeatCount()** method defines the auto-reverse option to **true**. This means that the view is going to animate back to its initial state. But because we specified 3 cycles, the animation is going forward and backward a total of 3 times (forward, backward, and forward again).

 Do It Yourself: Update the **Button** view in the **ContentView** view with the code in Listing 11-50. Press the Animate button. You should see the square animate two times forward and one time backward.

Up to now, we have applied standard animations, but the **Animation** structure also includes type methods to create custom animations.

easeIn(duration: Double**)**—This type method creates an **easeIn** animation with the duration determined by the argument.

easeInOut(duration: Double**)**—This type method creates an **easeInOut** animation with the duration determined by the argument.

easeOut(duration: Double**)**—This type method creates an **easeOut** animation with the duration determined by the argument.

linear(duration: Double**)**—This type method creates a **linear** animation with the duration determined by the argument.

spring(response: Double, **dampingFraction:** Double, **blendDuration:** Double**)**—This type method creates a spring animation. The **response** argument determines the duration of one animation period, the **dampingFraction** argument determines the amount of oscillation, and the **blendDuration** argument determines the time it takes for the animation to stop and the next animation to begin.

interactiveSpring(response: Double, **dampingFraction:** Double, **blend-Duration:** Double**)**—This type method creates a spring animation that can interact with the user. The **response** argument determines the duration of one animation period, the dampingFraction argument determines the amount of oscillation, and the **blendDuration** argument determines the time it takes for the animation to stop and the next animation to begin.

interpolatingSpring(mass: Double, **stiffness:** Double, **damping:** Double, **initialVelocity:** Double)—This type method creates a spring animation that combines the values with previous animations. The **mass** argument determines the mass we want to assign to the view, the **stiffness** argument determines the stiffness of the spring, the **damping** argument determines the amount of oscillation, and the **initialVelocity** determines the animation's initial velocity.

timingCurve(Double, Double, Double, Double, **duration:** Double)—This type method creates an animation with a custom timing curve. The four initial arguments determine the coordinates of the control points of a cubic Bezier curve, and the **duration** argument determines the duration of the animation.

These custom animations are created like the standard animations, and they can even take the same methods for configuration. For instance, we can create a customized spring animation (an animation that bounces the view back and forth) and set its speed and cycle.

```
Button("Animate") {
   let animation = Animation.interpolatingSpring(mass: 0.15, stiffness:
0.8, damping: 0.5, initialVelocity: 5)
      .speed(5)
      .repeatForever()
   withAnimation(animation) {
      boxScale = 2
   }
}
```

Listing 11-51: Defining a custom animation

 Do It Yourself: Update the **Button** view in the **ContentView** view with the code in Listing 11-51. Press the Animate button. You should see the square bounce indefinitely. Try different values for the **interpolatingSpring()** animation and implement other types of animations to see how they work.

The **withAnimation()** function can animate multiple states at a time. The system takes care of combining the animations, as shown in the following example.

```
struct ContentView: View {
   @State private var boxScale: CGFloat = 1
   @State private var roundCorners: Bool = false

   var body: some View {
      VStack {
         HStack {
            Rectangle()
               .fill(Color.blue)
               .frame(width: 50, height: 50)
               .cornerRadius(roundCorners ? 15 : 0)
               .scaleEffect(boxScale)
         }.frame(width: 250, height: 120)
         Button("Animate") {
            withAnimation(.easeInOut(duration: 2)) {
               boxScale = 2
               roundCorners = true
            }
         }
      }.padding()
```

```
        }
    }
```

Listing 11-52: Animating multiple states at a time

This example defines two **@State** properties, one to control the scale of the box and another to change the radius of the corners. When the button is pressed, we change the values of these two properties, and both changes are animated.

 Do It Yourself: Update the **ContentView** view with the code in Listing 11-52. Press the Animate button. You should see the square grow and the corners become round, all happening at the same time.

In the last example, we applied the same animation to both values (**easeInOut**), but SwiftUI allows us to perform as many animations as we need. All we have to do is to implement the **withAnimation()** function for each value we want to animate with the type of animation we want to use. For instance, the **Button** view in the following example performs two types of animations. We animate the **roundCorners** state with an **easeOut** animation, and the **boxScale** state with a **linear** animation. The effect is similar than before, but now each state is controlled by a different type of animation.

```
Button("Animate") {
    withAnimation(.easeOut) {
        roundCorners = true
    }
    withAnimation(.linear) {
        boxScale = 2
    }
}
```

Listing 11-53: Applying a different animation to each state

Medium Animating Custom Shapes

The system knows how to animate the views because they conform to a protocol included in SwiftUI called **Animatable**. The protocol defines a computed property called **animatableData** that provides the data required to create the frames for the animation. Every time we animate a view, the system gets the value from this property, increases or decreases it by a small amount, redraws the view, and repeats the process until the value matches the new one. For instance, the view returned by the **opacity()** modifier includes an **animatableData** property that provides the view's opacity value, so the system can gradually increase or decrease this value and redraw the view each time with a different opacity to make it look like it's being animated.

Most SwiftUI views include the **animatableData** property and therefore the system knows how to animate them, but if we want to animate a path in a custom **Shape** view, we must do it ourself. We need to make the structure conform to the **Animatable** protocol and implement the **animatableData** property to tell the system what is the value that it has to modify to get all the frames for the animation.

The **Shape** protocol already inherits from the **Animatable** protocol, so all we need to do is to implement the **animatableData** property to provide the value to animate. This value has to be something we can use to draw the path. For instance, if we want to animate a circle, we can provide its radius. If the animation goes from a radius of 0 to a radius of 10, the view will be able to draw the intermediate values required to create the animation (1, 2, 3, etc.). If the value we use to create the path is not animatable, we must turn it into something that can be animated. For instance, in the following example, we use a Boolean **@State** property to determine whether the graphic of a mouth should be smiling or not, but we turn this value into the number 0 or 1, so the system can generate values in between to animate the path (0.1, 0.2, 0.3, etc.).

```
struct ContentView: View {
    @State private var smiling: Bool = true

    var body: some View {
        VStack {
            Face(smile: smiling ? 1 : 0)
                .stroke(Color.blue, lineWidth: 5)
                .frame(width: 100, height: 120)
            Button("Change") {
                withAnimation(.default) {
                    smiling.toggle()
                }
            }
        }
    }
}
```

Listing 11-54: Instantiating a view with a value that can be animated

If the **smiling** property is **true**, we send the value 1 to the view, otherwise, we send the value 0. This means that the system can create an animation by instantiating this view with values from 0 to 1. The view takes this value and draws a mouth with the curve defined by an **addCurve()** method.

```
import SwiftUI

struct Face: Shape {
    var smile: CGFloat
    var animatableData: CGFloat {
        get { return smile }
        set {
            self.smile = newValue
        }
    }
    func path(in rect: CGRect) -> Path {
        let width = rect.width
        let smileClamp = min(max(smile, 0), 1)
        let section = rect.height / 5
        let smilePos = section + (section * 3 * smileClamp)

        var path = Path()
        path.addEllipse(in: CGRect(x: width/10*2 - 10, y: rect.minY + 10,
width: 20, height: 20))
        path.addEllipse(in: CGRect(x: width/10*8 - 10, y: rect.minY + 10,
width: 20, height: 20))

        path.move(to: CGPoint(x: width/10*2, y: rect.midY))
        path.addCurve(to: CGPoint(x: width/10*8, y: rect.midY), control1:
CGPoint(x: width / 4, y: smilePos), control2: CGPoint(x: width / 4 * 3,
y: smilePos))
        return path
    }
}
```

Listing 11-55: Defining an animatable path

The only difference with previous **Shape** structures is that now we have an **animatableData** property that provides the system with the value to animate. The system accesses this property, gets the value of the **smile** property from it, increases or decreases this value by a small amount, sends the result back to the **animatableData** property, and the path is redrawn with this new value.

Because the values received by the **Face** view are between 0 and 1, we must convert them to a range we can use to draw the mouth. First, we make sure that the value is between 0 and 1 with the **min()** and **max()** functions. After that, we calculate the position of the bottom of the mouth according to this value. If the value is close to 0, the bottom of the mouth will be close to the top of the view, and if the value is close to 1, it will be close to the bottom of the view, so we can get a mouth that is smiling or not.

Figure 11-42: Animated path

 Do It Yourself: Update the **ContentView** view with the code in Listing 11-54. Create a new Swift file called Face.swift for the structure of Listing 11-55. Press the Change button. You should see the curves illustrated in Figure 11-42.

(Medium) Canvas Animations

The content of a **Canvas** view can also be animated. The process requires to redraw the canvas over and over again. For this purpose, SwiftUI includes the following view.

TimelineView(Schedule, **content:** Closure)—This initializer creates a view that redraws its content according to a schedule. The first argument specifies the schedule the view must follow, and the **content** argument is a closure with the views we want to redraw at each point in time. The closure receives a **Context** structure, which includes the **date** property with the schedule date that triggered the update, and the **cadence** property with the rate at which the views are updated.

The schedule is defined by a structure that conforms to the **TimelineSchedule** protocol. SwiftUI defines several structures to create built-in schedules, which includes the following type properties and methods.

explicit(Dates)—This type method creates a schedule from the **Date** values specified by the argument. The argument is an array of **Date** values with the dates and times we want to schedule the task.

periodic(from: Date, **by:** TimeInterval)—This type method creates a schedule from the dates specified by the arguments. The **from** argument determines when the process begins, and the **by** argument determines the intervals at which the task is performed.

everyMinute—This type property creates a schedule that performs the task every minute.

animation—This type property creates a schedule that performs the task over and over again to produce an animation.

animation(minimumInterval: Double?, **paused:** Bool)—This type method creates a schedule to produce an animation that can be paused. The **minimumInterval** argument specifies the interval at which the animation should be performed (the value **nil** sets the interval by default), and the **paused** argument determines if the animation should be running or paused.

The `TimelineView` view can be used for any task that requires updating the interface after a period of time. This may involve anything from single strings to complex graphics. When the interface needs simple updates, we can use a periodic or explicit schedule, as shown next.

```
struct ContentView: View {
    var body: some View {
        TimelineView(.periodic(from: Date(), by: 2)) { time in
            let calendar = Calendar.current
            let components = calendar.dateComponents([.second], from:
time.date)
            HStack {
                Text("Time: \(components.second ?? 0)")
                    .font(.largeTitle.bold())
            }
        }
    }
}
```

Listing 11-56: *Updating the interface*

In this example, the `TimelineView` view begins drawing the views from the current date and does it again every two seconds. In the closure, we use the value produced by the view to get the date when the drawing is performed, extract the seconds, and show the number on the screen.

The `TimelineView` view works with any content, but it is particularly useful with the `Canvas` view. SwiftUI even defines a specific schedule structure to create animations with a canvas that can be obtained from the `animation` property or the `animation()` method. There is a caveat, though. The system doesn't know what we want to animate on the canvas, so we must take care of everything, including the frequency of the animation, the positions of the graphics, and more. The following example illustrates how to create a simple animation that repositions a circle on the screen after a few fractions of a second.

```
class ContentViewData {
    var posX: CGFloat = 0
    var posY: CGFloat = 0
    var lastTime: Double = 0
    var maxTime: Double = 0.2
}
struct ContentView: View {
    let contentData = ContentViewData()

    var body: some View {
        TimelineView(.animation) { time in
            let interval = time.date.timeIntervalSinceReferenceDate
            let delta = interval - contentData.lastTime

            Canvas { context, size in
                if delta > contentData.maxTime {
                    contentData.posX = CGFloat.random(in: 0..<size.width - 20)
                    contentData.posY = CGFloat.random(in: 0..<size.height - 20)
                    contentData.lastTime = interval
                }
                let circleFrame = CGRect(x: contentData.posX, y:
contentData.posY, width: 20, height: 20)
                context.fill(Circle().path(in: circleFrame),
with: .color(.red))
            }.ignoresSafeArea()
        }
    }
}
```

Listing 11-57: *Animating the canvas*

Notice that we have defined a class to store the position of the circle and the required values to control the frequency of the animation. This is a simple class that we need to store and update the values. The class doesn't conform to the **ObservableObject** protocol in this case because we don't need to store any state, but the values could have also been stored in an observable object or the model if necessary.

The timing is controlled from the date produced by the **TimelineView** view. From this value, we get the current date, extract the seconds with the **timeIntervalSinceReferenceDate** property, check how many seconds has passed since the last iteration, and update the position of the circle if the difference is greater than the maximum time set by the **maxTime** property. Notice that after the position of the circle is determined, we assign the current date in seconds to the **lastTime** property to know when the last iteration happened, so the graphics are only updated every 0.2 seconds.

 Do It Yourself: Update the ContentView.swift file with the code in Listing 11-57. You should see a red circle appearing in different locations on the screen every 0.2 seconds. Repeat the process for the following example.

The previous example shows how to update the graphics on the canvas, but it doesn't create any animation. To animate a graphic on the canvas, we must drawn every single frame. This means calculating the position of each graphic at every step of the animation. To demonstrate how this works, we are going to animate a single circle at the center of the screen. The animation is produced by controlling the circle's radius.

```
import SwiftUI

class ContentViewData {
    var radius: CGFloat = 0
    var step: CGFloat = 5
    var lastTime: Double = 0
    var maxTime: Double = 0.02
}
struct ContentView: View {
    let contentData = ContentViewData()

    var body: some View {
        TimelineView(.animation) { time in
            let interval = time.date.timeIntervalSinceReferenceDate
            let delta = interval - contentData.lastTime

            Canvas { context, size in
                if delta > contentData.maxTime {
                    calculateRadius()
                    contentData.lastTime = interval
                }
                let rad = contentData.radius
                let circleFrame = CGRect(x: size.width/2 - rad, y:
size.height/2 - rad, width: rad * 2, height: rad * 2)
                context.fill(Circle().path(in: circleFrame),
with: .color(.red))
            }.ignoresSafeArea()
        }
    }
    func calculateRadius() {
        contentData.radius = contentData.radius + contentData.step
        if contentData.step < 0 && contentData.radius < 0 {
            contentData.radius = 0
            contentData.step = 5
        }
        if contentData.step > 0 && contentData.radius > 150 {
            contentData.radius = 150
            contentData.step = -5
```

Chapter 11 - Graphics and Animations

```
      }
    }
  }
}
```

Listing 11-58: Creating a real animation

The process of controlling the frequency of the animation is the same as before, but we have defined a function to calculate the radius. If the radius is small, we add 5 points to expand the circle, otherwise we begin the opposite animation by reducing the radius by -5 points. To know whether the circle is expanding or contracting, we store the difference in an additional property called **step**. When the value of this property is negative, it means that the circle is contracting, otherwise it is expanding.

(Medium) **Transitions**

As we have seen before, we can add or remove views from the interface depending on a state (see Chapter 6, Listing 6-27). The process by which the view appears or disappears from the screen is called *Transition*. By default, the system doesn't use any transition, it just displays or removes the view, but we can assign a specific transition to a view with the following modifier.

transition(AnyTransition**)**—This modifier assigns the transition specified by the argument to the view.

SwiftUI defines standard transitions. The following are the type properties provided by the **AnyTransition** structure to create them.

opacity—This type property returns a transition that inserts or removes a view by modifying its opacity.

scale—This type property returns a transition that inserts or removes a view by modifying its scale.

slide—This type property returns a transition that inserts or removes a view by sliding it from or to the sides.

identity—This type property returns a transition that inserts or removes a view without any effect. This is the transition by default.

The **AnyTransition** structure defines the type of transition, but for the transition to be applied, we must define the type of animation used to produce it. The **AnyTransition** structure provides the following method for this purpose.

animation(Animation**)**—This method applies the animation defined by the argument to the transition.

The **animation()** method is called on the instance of the **AnyTransition** structure, so we have to define the transition and then call this method to determine the animation we are going to apply to it. In the following example, we show and hide a **Text** view with a transition of type **scale** and an animation of type **default**.

```
struct ContentView: View {
   @State private var showInfo = false

   var body: some View {
      VStack {
         Button("Show Information") {
            showInfo.toggle()
         }.padding()
```

```
        if showInfo {
            Text("This is the information")
                .transition(.scale.animation(.default))
        }
        Spacer()
    }
  }
}
```

Listing 11-59: Adding and removing a view with a transition

The button in this view toggles the value of the **showInfo** property. When the value is **true**, a **Text** view is added to the interface, otherwise, the view is removed, but because of the **scale** transition, the view expands until it reaches its natural size when the value of the property is **true**, and contracts until it disappears from the screen when it is **false**.

 Do It Yourself: Create a Multiplatform project. Update the **ContentView** view with the code in Listing 11-59. Run the application on the iPhone simulator. Press the Show Information button. You should see the **Text** view appear or disappear from the screen every time the button is pressed. Replace the **scale** transition by the **opacity** and **slide** types to see how they work.

In the previous example, we use a standard animation (**default**). In this case, the code is easy to read, but it can become cumbersome when we apply our own animations or combine custom transitions with custom animations. To improve readability and organize the code, it is better to define the transition externally. There are different ways to do it, but what is considered best practice is to declare an extension of the **AnyTransition** structure and define our custom transition as if it belonged to the structure itself. In the following example, we extend the **AnyTransition** structure to define a custom transition called **mytransition**.

```
struct ContentView: View {
    @State private var showInfo = false

    var body: some View {
        VStack {
            Button("Show Information") {
                showInfo.toggle()
            }.padding()
            if showInfo {
                Text("This is the information")
                    .transition(.mytransition)
            }
            Spacer()
        }
    }
}
extension AnyTransition {
    static var mytransition: AnyTransition {
        let animation = Animation.easeInOut(duration: 2)
        let transition = AnyTransition.scale
            .animation(animation)
        return transition
    }
}
```

Listing 11-60: Extending the AnyTransition *structure*

The code in Listing 11-60 defines an extension of the **AnyTransition** structure with a type property called **mytransition**. This is a computed property that creates and returns a custom transition. Of course, we can define any transition with any animation we want, the only requirement is that the property returns a structure of type **AnyTransition**, so we can use it to specify the transition for a view. In this example, we create a custom **easeInOut** animation with a duration of 2 seconds and apply it to a standard transition of type **scale**.

Because we declare our custom transition as an extension of the **AnyTransition** structure, we can assign it to the view as we do with any standard transition already defined by the structure.

 Do It Yourself: Update the ContentView.swift file with the code in Listing 11-60. Run the application on the iPhone simulator. Press the Show Information button. You should see the **Text** view appear with a **scale** transition, but the animation should last 2 seconds.

The transitions we have implemented so far are symmetric; they are the same when the view is added to the interface and when the view is removed. To create an asymmetric transition, the **AnyTransition** structure includes the following type method.

asymmetric(insertion: AnyTransition, **removal:** AnyTransition)—This type method defines an asymmetric transition. The **insertion** argument specifies the transition to use when the view is inserted, and the **removal** argument specifies the transition to use when the view is removed.

For example, we can fade-in the view by modifying the opacity when it is added to the interface, and then remove it by reducing the scale.

```
extension AnyTransition {
    static var mytransition: AnyTransition {
        let animation = Animation.easeInOut(duration: 2)
        let transition = AnyTransition.asymmetric(insertion: .opacity,
removal: .scale)
            .animation(animation)
        return transition
    }
}
```

Listing 11-61: Defining an asymmetric transition

 Do It Yourself: Update the **AnyTransition** extension from the previous example with the code in Listing 11-61. Run the application on the iPhone simulator. Press the Show Information button. You should see the text fade-in and then shrink when the button is pressed again.

In addition to defining one transition for the insertion and another for the removal, we can combine two transitions with the following method.

combined(with: AnyTransition)—This method combines the transition with the transition specified by the **with** argument.

The following example combines a type **scale** transition with a type **opacity** transition. The text fades in and out and also scales while it appears and disappears from the screen.

```
extension AnyTransition {
    static var mytransition: AnyTransition {
        let animation = Animation.easeInOut(duration: 2)
        let transition = AnyTransition.scale.combined(with: .opacity)
            .animation(animation)
```

```
        return transition
    }
}
```

Listing 11-62: Combining transitions

 Do It Yourself: Update the **AnyTransition** extension from the previous example with the code in Listing 11-62. Run the application on the iPhone simulator. Press the Show Information button. You should see the text fade in as it expands until it reaches the final size and position.

The **AnyTransition** structure also includes the following type methods to create custom transitions.

move(edge: Edge)—This type method defines a transition that moves the view in and out of the interface from the side defined by the argument. The **edge** argument is an enumeration of type **Edge** with the values **bottom**, **leading**, **top**, and **trailing**.

offset(x: CGFloat, **y:** CGFloat)—This type method defines a transition that moves the view in and out of the interface by the space determined by the arguments. The **x** and **y** arguments specify the offset of the view from the center of the frame.

scale(scale: CGFloat, **anchor:** UnitPoint)—This type method defines a transition that scales the view. The **scale** argument determines the initial scale for the transition, and the **anchor** argument determines the point from which the view is going to be scaled.

Custom transitions require an explicit animation. This means that instead of animating the transition itself, we must animate the change of the state with the **withAnimation()** function.

```
struct ContentView: View {
    @State private var showInfo = false

    var body: some View {
        VStack {
            Button("Show Information") {
                withAnimation {
                    showInfo.toggle()
                }
            }.padding()
            if showInfo {
                Text("This is the information")
                    .transition(.move(edge: .leading))
            }
            Spacer()
        }
    }
}
```

Listing 11-63: Customizing the transition

This example creates a transition that moves the view in and out of the interface from the left side of the screen. Notice that this transition reproduces the **slide** transition, but in this case the view always uses the same side of the screen.

 Do It Yourself: Update the **ContentView** view with the code in Listing 11-63. Run the application on the iPhone simulator. Press the Show Information button. You should see the text slide from the left side of the screen and then slide back to the same side when the button is pressed again. Replace the **move()** method by the **offset()** or **scale()** methods to see how they work.

Chapter 11 - Graphics and Animations

Of course, multiple views can transition at the same time, and because the interface is updated all at once, the animations are coordinated. For instance, we can use the same **showInfo** property to show and hide two **Text** views.

```
struct ContentView: View {
   @State private var showInfo = false

   var body: some View {
      VStack {
         Button("Show Information") {
            showInfo.toggle()
         }.padding()
         HStack {
            if !showInfo {
               Text("Left")
                  .transition(.scale.animation(.default))
            }
            Spacer()
            if showInfo {
               Text("Right")
                  .transition(.scale.animation(.default))
            }
         }.padding()
         Spacer()
      }
   }
}
```

Listing 11-64: Coordinating transitions

As always, the **showInfo** property is initialized with the value **false**. This means that the **Text** view with the string "Left" is shown on the left hand side of the screen. But when the button is pressed, the value of the **showInfo** property is toggled and the **Text** view with the string "Right" is shown instead. Both transitions are animated with a **scale** effect, so they shrink or expand to appear or disappear from the screen.

The transitions in this example look coordinated, but the strings are displayed by two different **Text** views and therefore each animation is independent. If we want to transition from one view to another with a single animation, we must declare both views to be the same. SwiftUI includes the following modifier for this purpose.

matchedGeometryEffect(id: Value, **in:** Namespace.ID, **properties:** MatchedGeometryProperties, **anchor:** UnitPoint, **isSource:** Bool)—This modifier includes a view in an animation group for synchronization. The **id** argument is a hashable value that identifies the associated views. The **in** argument is the namespace that groups the animations together. The **properties** argument is a structure that indicates the types of properties we want to synchronize. The type properties available to create these structures are **frame** (default), **position**, and **size**. The **anchor** argument determines the position shared by the views (**center** by default). And the **isSource** argument determines if the view should be used as the source of geometry for the rest of the views (**true** by default).

This modifier can be used to group and associate multiple views. To associate the views, we need to provide a common identifier, usually a string, but to create an animation group, we need to define a namespace. SwiftUI includes the **@Namespace** property wrapper for this purpose. All we need to do is to define a **@Namespace** property and then apply the **matchedGeometry-Effect()** modifier to each view with this value, as shown next.

```
struct ContentView: View {
    @Namespace private var myAnimations
    @State private var showInfo = false

    var body: some View {
        VStack {
            Button("Show Information") {
                withAnimation(.easeInOut) {
                    showInfo.toggle()
                }
            }.padding()
            HStack {
                if !showInfo {
                    Text("Left")
                        .matchedGeometryEffect(id: "TextAnimation", in:
myAnimations)
                }
                Spacer()
                if showInfo {
                    Text("Right")
                        .matchedGeometryEffect(id: "TextAnimation", in:
myAnimations)
                }
            }.padding()
            Spacer()
        }
    }
}
```

Listing 11-65: *Coordinating views*

This example includes the same views as before. There is a **Text** view that appears on the left and another on the right, but because we apply the **matchedGeometryEffect()** modifier to both of them with the same identifier and assign them to the same namespace, they are animated as one view. In this case, when the value of the **showInfo** property changes, the views move from left to right and right to left, and also the text gradually changes from "Left" to "Right", and vice versa. Notice that for the transition to be animated, we had to animate the state change with the **withAnimation()** function.

 Do It Yourself: Update the **ContentView** view with the code in Listing 11-65. Run the application on the iPhone simulator. Press the Show Information button. You should see the text slide from the left side of the screen to the right, and the text gradually change from "Left" to "Right".

12.1 Gesture Recognizers

Gestures are actions performed by the user on the screen, such as tapping, swiping, or pinching. These gestures are difficult to detect because the only thing the screen returns is the position of the fingers. That is why Apple offers gesture recognizers. A gesture recognizer performs all the calculations necessary to recognize a gesture, so instead of processing multiple events and values, we just wait for the notifications sent by the system when complex gestures are detected and respond accordingly.

Basic **Gesture Modifiers**

The most common gesture used in a mobile device is a tap gesture, which is detected when the user touches the screen with a finger. Because of how common it is to work with this gesture, SwiftUI defines two convenient modifiers to process it.

onTapGesture(count: Int, **perform:** Closure)—This modifier recognizes a single or multiple taps. The **count** argument determines how many taps are required for the gesture to be recognized (1 by default), and the **perform** argument is the closure to be executed when the gesture is detected. The closure receives a `CGPoint` value with the location of the tap in the view coordinates.

onLongPressGesture(minimumDuration: Double, **maximumDistance:** CGFloat, **perform:** Closure, **onPressingChanged:** Closure)—This modifier recognizes a long press gesture (the user keeps pressing the screen with a finger). The **minimumDuration** argument is the time in seconds the user must press the screen with the finger until the gesture is recognized. The **maximumDistance** argument is the distance in points the user can move the finger from the original position before the gesture is no longer recognized. The **perform** argument is the closure to be executed when the gesture is confirmed. And finally, the **onPressingChanged** argument is the closure to be executed when the user begins and ends pressing the view. The closure receives a Boolean value to indicate whether the user is pressing or not.

We worked with the `onTapGesture()` modifier multiple times before to recognize a tap and perform an action (see Listings 7-28). Something we didn't do in previous examples is get the position of the finger where the tap is made. This is a value of type `CGPoint` received by the closure with the x and y coordinates of the tap within the view. In the following example, we open a sheet when an image is tapped, and show how to access this value.

```
struct ContentView: View {
   @State private var expand: Bool = false

   var body: some View {
      Image("spot1")
         .resizable()
         .scaledToFit()
         .frame(width: 160, height: 200)
         .onTapGesture { location in
            expand = true
            print("Location: \(location)")
         }
```

```
            .sheet(isPresented: $expand) {
                ShowImage()
            }
        }
    }
}
```

Listing 12-1: Detecting a tap gesture on an image

The code in Listing 12-1 defines an **Image** view of a size of 160 by 200 points. The **onTapGesture()** modifier is applied to the view to detect the tap, and the **sheet()** modifier to present a sheet. The following is the **ShowImage** view opened by the sheet.

```
import SwiftUI

struct ShowImage: View {
    var body: some View {
        Image("spot1")
            .resizable()
            .scaledToFill()
            .edgesIgnoringSafeArea(.all)
    }
}
```

Listing 12-2: Expanding the image

This view creates an **Image** view and expands it to fill the sheet, including the safe area. As a result, the interface presents a small image on the screen, and when the user taps on it, it opens a sheet to show it in full size.

Figure 12-1: Image responding to the tap gesture

 Do It Yourself: Create a Multiplatform project. Download the spot1 image from our website and add it to the Asset Catalog. Update the **ContentView** view with the code in Listing 12-1. Create a SwiftUI View file called ShowImage.swift and update the view with the code in Listing 12-2. Run the app on the iPhone simulator. You should see the interface illustrated in Figure 12-1 (left). Tap on the image. A sheet opens with a full size image (Figure 12-1, right) and the location of the tap is printed on the console.

The long press gesture is similar to the tap gesture, but the system waits a moment before confirming the gesture and performing the task. With the **onLongPressGesture()** modifier, we can set the waiting time and also perform a task while the user is pressing and waiting for the gesture to complete, as in the following example.

```
struct ContentView: View {
   @State private var expand: Bool = false
   @State private var pressing: Bool = false

   var body: some View {
      Image("spot1")
         .resizable()
         .scaledToFit()
         .frame(width: 160, height: 200)
         .opacity(pressing ? 0 : 1)
         .onLongPressGesture(minimumDuration: 1, maximumDistance: 10,
            perform: {
               expand = true
            }, onPressingChanged: { value in
               withAnimation(.easeInOut(duration: 1.5)) {
                  pressing = value
               }
            })
         .sheet(isPresented: $expand) {
            ShowImage()
         }
   }
}
```

Listing 12-3: Detecting a long press gesture

This is the same example as before but now we apply a long press gesture to the **Image** view, so the user must hold the finger in position for a moment to open the sheet. In this case, we set the waiting time to 1 second and the maximum distance to 10 points, so the user cannot move the finger more than 10 points away from the initial position or the gesture is invalidated.

The closure performed while the view is being pressed modifies a **@State** property called **pressing** that we use to set the view's opacity. When the user puts the finger on the view, the value received by the closure is **true**, so the value 0 is assigned to the **opacity()** modifier, and when the user moves the finger away, lifts the finger, or the gesture ends, the closure receives the value **false** and therefore the value 1 is assigned to the view's opacity. The process is animated with an **easeInOut** animation that lasts 1.5 seconds. Because the animation is longer than the waiting time for the gesture, the sheet is opened before the image completely disappears, which provides the necessary feedback for the user to know that it must wait for the process to finish.

 Do It Yourself: Update the **ContentView** view with the code in Listing 12-3. Press and hold the finger on the image (long click). You should see the image fading-out and the sheet opening after 1 second.

Basic Hit Testing

Because views may sometimes overlap and some may have implemented their own gestures, the system must decide whether a view should process a gesture or pass it to other views. The process of finding the view the user wants to interact with and decide whether it should respond to the gesture or not is called *Hit Testing*. The **View** protocol defines the following modifiers to control this process.

allowsHitTesting(Bool)—This modifier determines whether the detection of hits is enabled on the view or not.

contentShape(Shape, eoFill: Bool)—This modifier defines the shape of the hitting area. The first argument is a shape view that determines the area the user can interact with, and the **eoFill** argument determines the algorithm to use to detect the hit.

The `allowsHitTesting()` modifier can be used to disable a gesture. For instance, we can enable or disable the tap gesture on the `Image` view of the previous example.

```
struct ContentView: View {
    @State private var expand: Bool = false
    @State private var allowExpansion: Bool = false

    var body: some View {
        VStack(spacing: 20) {
            Image("spot1")
                .resizable()
                .scaledToFit()
                .frame(width: 160, height: 200)
                .onTapGesture {
                    expand = true
                }
                .allowsHitTesting(allowExpansion)
                .sheet(isPresented: $expand) {
                    ShowImage()
                }
            Toggle("", isOn: $allowExpansion)
                .labelsHidden()
        }
    }
}
```

Listing 12-4: Disabling the tap gesture

The view in Listing 12-4 adds a **Toggle** view below the image to control the value of a **@State** property. We use this property to determine if hit testing is allowed on the **Image** view. The initial value of the property is set to **false**, so the user is not able to tap on the image to open the sheet, but when the switch is turned on, the value **true** is assigned to the property and therefore the gesture is recognized by the **Image** view.

 Do It Yourself: Update the **ContentView** view with the code in Listing 12-4. Run the application on the simulator. Tap on the image. Nothing should happen. Turn on the switch below the image. Now, the image should open the sheet when you tap on it.

The **contentShape()** modifier also plays an important role in recognizing a gesture. If we apply a gesture recognizer to an **Image** view or a **Text** view, the gesture is recognized when the user touches any part of the area occupied by the view. But this is not always the case. Container views, like **VStack** and **HStack**, only recognize the gesture when it is performed on the area occupied by their content. To make sure that every part of the view can recognize a gesture, we must force the content to occupy the entire area. We came across this issue before (see Listing 7-28). In those examples, we had to define a background with a **Color** view to provide a surface for the tap gesture to be recognized. This was enough for our purpose, but it generates content that may not be required by the interface. A better solution is to apply the **contentShape()** modifier. This modifier allows us to define the hit surface for the gesture without adding any real content to the view.

In the following example, we recreate the views we used in previous projects to create the rows of a list, but this time, instead of using a **Color** view to respond to the tap gesture, we define the row's content with a **Rectangle** view and the **contentShape()** modifier. This allows the user to tap anywhere on the row to select it.

```
struct ContentView: View {
    @State private var selected: Bool = false
```

```
var body: some View {
    VStack {
        HStack(alignment: .top) {
            Image("spot1")
                .resizable()
                .scaledToFit()
                .frame(width: 80, height: 100)
                .border(selected ? Color.yellow : Color.clear, width: 5)
            VStack(alignment: .leading, spacing: 2) {
                Text("Balmy Beach").bold()
                Text("Toronto")
                Text("2020").font(.caption)
                Spacer()
            }
            Spacer()
        }.frame(height: 100)
        .padding(5)
        .border(.gray, width: 1)
        .contentShape(Rectangle())
        .onTapGesture {
            selected.toggle()
        }
        Spacer()
    }
}
```

Listing 12-5: Defining the shape of the content

The view in Listing 12-5 displays a row with information about a location. If the user taps anywhere on the row, the gesture recognizer toggles the value of a **@State** property called **selected**, which we use to define the color for the picture's border. The value **true** makes the border yellow (selected) and the value **false** makes it transparent (deselected).

Figure 12-2: Responsive row

(Basic) **12.2 Gesture Structures**

The gestures processed by the **onTapGesture()** and **onLongPressGesture()** modifiers are defined by structures that conform to the **Gesture** protocol. The following are the most frequently used.

TapGesture(count: Int**)**—This initializer creates a gesture recognizer to detect a tap gesture. The **count** argument determines the number of taps required for the gesture to be recognized.

LongPressGesture(minimumDuration: Double, **maximumDistance:** CGFloat**)**—This initializer creates a gesture recognizer to detect a long-press gesture. The **minimumDuration** argument is the time in seconds the user must press the screen with the finger until the gesture is recognized. The **maximumDistance** argument is the distance in points the user can move the finger from the original position before the gesture is no longer recognized.

MagnificationGesture(minimumScaleDelta: CGFloat)—This initializer creates a gesture recognizer to detect a magnification gesture. The **minimumScaleDelta** argument is the minimum increment or decrement on the scale required for the gesture to be recognized.

RotationGesture(minimumAngleDelta: Angle)—This initializer creates a gesture recognizer to detect a rotation gesture. The **minimumAngleDelta** argument is the minimum increment or decrement on the angle of the view required for the gesture to be recognized.

These initializers configure the gestures recognizers, but to respond to the different states of the gestures, the structures implement the following methods.

onChanged(Closure)—This method executes a closure when the state of the gesture changes. The closure receives a value with information about the state of the gesture.

onEnded(Closure)—This method executes a closure when the gesture ends. The closure receives a value with information about the state of the gesture.

updating(GestureState, **body:** Closure)—This method executes a closure when the state of the gesture is updated, either because its value changed or the gesture was cancelled. The first argument is a **Binding** property that stores the gesture's state values, and the **body** argument is the closure to be executed every time the state is updated. The closure receives a value with information about the state of the gesture, a reference to the **Binding** property, and a value of type **Transaction** that contains information about the animation.

Because of the frequency at which the **updating()** method is called, we can't use a normal **@State** property to keep track of the state of the gesture. Any attempt to modify a state from inside the updating closure will return an error. Therefore, SwiftUI defines a specific property wrapper to work with this method.

@GestureState—This property wrapper stores the state of a gesture and resets its value to its initial value when the gesture ends.

Once we have the instance of the gesture recognizer properly configured, we must apply it to the view. The **View** protocol defines the following modifiers for this purpose.

gesture(Gesture)—This modifier assigns a gesture recognizer to the view with a lower priority than the gesture recognizers already applied to the view.

highPriorityGesture(Gesture)—This modifier assigns a gesture recognizer to the view with a higher priority than the gesture recognizers already applied to the view.

simultaneousGesture(Gesture)—This modifier assigns a gesture recognizer to the view that is processed along with the gesture recognizers already applied to the view.

The process is simple. We must instantiate a **Gesture** structure to define the gesture recognizer, apply the **onChanged()**, **onEnded()** or **updating()** methods to the structure depending on what we want to do during the process, and assign that instance to the view with a modifier, like **gesture()**. What methods to apply depends on the gesture and what we want to achieve, and the values received by these methods also depend on the type of gesture recognizer we are using. So there are multiple options available, as we will see next.

Basic Tap Gesture

Due to the simplicity of the tap gesture, there is not much difference between applying the **onTapGesture()** modifier or implementing the **TapGesture** structure. The structure can also define the number of taps required for the gesture to be recognized, and since there are no changes to report over time, it only uses the **onEnded()** method to perform a task when the gesture is detected. The following example reproduces the previous project, but this time we define the gesture recognizer with a **TapGesture** structure.

```
struct ContentView: View {
   @State private var expand: Bool = false

   var body: some View {
      Image("spot1")
         .resizable()
         .scaledToFit()
         .frame(width: 160, height: 200)
         .gesture(
            TapGesture(count: 1)
               .onEnded {
                  expand = true
               }
         )
         .sheet(isPresented: $expand) {
            ShowImage()
         }
   }
}
```

Listing 12-6: Defining a TapGesture *recognizer*

The **TapGesture** structure defines the gesture recognizer, but to attach it to a view we must apply the **gesture()** modifier. The result is the same as before. When the image is tapped, the closure assigned to the **onEnded()** method is executed, and the value **true** is assigned to the **expand** property to open the sheet. Notice that the **onEnded()** method is a method of the **TapGesture** structure and therefore it is called on the instance of this structure, not on the view.

Do It Yourself: For this example, you need the **ShowImage** view defined in Listing 12-2. Update the **ContentView** view with the code in Listing 12-6. You should see a small image on the screen. Tap the image to open the sheet.

(Basic) **Long Press Gesture**

Like the **TapGesture** structure, the **LongPressGesture** structure creates a simple gesture recognizer, but in this case there is some activity while the gesture is performed, so in addition to the **onEnded()** method, we can also implement the **updating()** method if we want to perform a task while the view is being pressed.

There are a few things we must considered when implementing the **updating()** method. First, as mentioned before, this method requires a **@GestureState** property instead of a **@State** property. A **@GestureState** property stores the current state but it also resets itself to its initial value when the gesture ends, so the initial value assigned to this property is the value we want the property to always have as default. Second, we need to update the state ourselves from the closure assigned to the method, but not directly, we must do it from the reference received by the method (usually called **state**). And third, because the change is not performed directly on the state property, it can't be animated. To animate the process, we must assigned the **Animation** structure to the **animation** property of the **Transaction** structure produced by the gesture, as shown next.

```
struct ContentView: View {
   @GestureState private var pressing: Bool = false
   @State private var expand: Bool = false
```

```
    var body: some View {
        Image("spot1")
            .resizable()
            .scaledToFit()
            .frame(width: 160, height: 200)
            .opacity(pressing ? 0 : 1)
            .gesture(LongPressGesture(minimumDuration: 1)
                .updating($pressing) { value, state, transaction in
                    state = value
                    transaction.animation = Animation.easeInOut(duration: 1.5)
                }
                .onEnded { value in
                    expand = true
                }
            )
            .sheet(isPresented: $expand) {
                ShowImage()
            }
    }
}
```

Listing 12-7: Defining a LongPressGesture *recognizer*

This is the same application created with the **onLongPressGesture()** modifier (see Listing 12-3). When the user touches the image for a second, the opacity changes and when the time is up the sheet opens. The values are also processed the same way as before, but instead of working with the **@State** property directly, we assign the new value received by the closure to a reference of the **pressing** property. In this case, we identify the value and the reference with the names **value** and **state**, but these names are arbitrary. Once the new value is assigned to **state**, the value of the **pressing** property changes and the opacity is modified accordingly. After a second, the **onEnded()** method is executed, and the value **true** is assigned to the **expand** property to open the sheet.

Although we can work with the values produced by the **updating()** method directly, as we did in Listing 12-7, this method was designed to process the state through an enumeration. Instead of assigning the value received by the method directly to the **@GestureState** property, we assign an enumeration value to this property and then get the state from the enumeration, as in the following example.

```
import SwiftUI

enum PressingState {
    case active
    case inactive

    var isActive: Bool {
        switch self {
        case .active:
            return true
        case .inactive:
            return false
        }
    }
}
struct ContentView: View {
    @GestureState private var pressingState = PressingState.inactive
    @State private var expand: Bool = false

    var body: some View {
        Image("spot1")
            .resizable()
            .scaledToFit()
            .frame(width: 160, height: 200)
```

Chapter 12 -Gestures

```
         .opacity(pressingState.isActive ? 0 : 1)
         .gesture(LongPressGesture(minimumDuration: 1)
            .updating($pressingState) { value, state, transaction in
               state = value ? .active : .inactive
               transaction.animation = Animation.easeInOut(duration: 1.5)
            }
            .onEnded { value in
               expand = true
            }
         )
         .sheet(isPresented: $expand) {
            ShowImage()
         }
      }
   }
}
```

Listing 12-8: Controlling the states of a gesture with an enumeration

This example works like before, but now we use an enumeration to keep track of the state of the gesture. The enumeration is called **PressingState** and it includes two cases, **active** and **inactive**, and a computed property that returns a Boolean value according to the current value of the instance (**true** for **active** and **false** for **inactive**). Now, instead of defining a **@GestureState** property of type **Bool** to store the value received by the **updating()** method, we can define a property of type **PressingState** and store an enumeration value. We call this property **pressingState** and assign it to the **updating()** method. When the method is called, we assign the value **active** or **inactive** to this property depending on the value received by the method. When it is time to read the state in the **opacity()** modifier, instead of reading the **@GestureState** property directly, we get the Boolean value from the **isActive** computed property defined by the enumeration. If the current value of the **pressingState** property is **active**, the **isActive** property returns **true** and the opacity is set to 0, otherwise the value returned is **false** and the opacity is set to 1.

The result is the same as before, but using enumeration values becomes necessary when working with more complex gestures or when multiple gestures are combined.

Basic Magnification Gesture

The magnification gesture is often called the *Pinch Gesture* because it is the gesture that is detected when the user spreads two fingers apart or brings them together as if pinching the screen. This gesture is mostly implemented to let the user zoom an image in and out.

The value sent to the **updating()**, **onChanged()** and **onEnded()** methods is a **CGFloat** that represents a multiple of the scale that we must multiply by the current scale to get the final scale of the picture, as in the following example.

```
struct ContentView: View {
   @GestureState private var magnification: CGFloat = 1
   @State private var zoom: CGFloat = 1

   var body: some View {
      Image("spot1")
         .resizable()
         .scaledToFit()
         .frame(width: 160, height: 200)
         .scaleEffect(zoom * magnification)

         .gesture(MagnificationGesture()
            .updating($magnification) { value, state, transaction in
               state = value
            }
            .onEnded { value in
```

```
            zoom = zoom * value
        }
    )
  }
}
```

Listing 12-9: Defining a `MagnificationGesture` *recognizer*

The code in Listing 12-9 defines two states, one to keep track of the magnification and another to store the final value. The idea is to allow the user to zoom in and out multiple times. While the gesture is performed, the magnification value is stored in the **magnification** property, but the value of the **zoom** property is only modified when the gesture is over, so the next time the user tries to zoom the picture, the new scale is calculated from the last one.

To set the scale of the image to the one selected by the user, we apply the **scaleEffect()** modifier to the **Image** view and calculate the new scale by multiplying the value of the **zoom** property (the last scale set by the user) by the value of the **magnification** property (the multiple generated by the gesture). As a result, the image is zoomed in and out following the movement of the fingers.

 Do It Yourself: Create a Multiplatform project. Download the spot1 image from our website and add it to the Asset Catalog. Update the **ContentView** view with the code in Listing 12-9. Run the application on a device. Pinch the view with two fingers to zoom in or out. If you run the application on the simulator, press the option key on your keyboard to activate the gesture.

The example in Listing 12-9 allows the users to zoom the image in and out as far as they want, but most of the time we must limit the scale of the view to values that make sense for the interface and the purpose of our application. To establish these limits, the scale must be controlled in two places: when it is applied to the view with the **scaleEffect()** modifier, and when the gesture ends and the final scale is assigned to the **zoom** property.

```
struct ContentView: View {
    @GestureState private var magnification: CGFloat = 1
    @State private var zoom: CGFloat = 1

    var body: some View {
        Image("spot1")
            .resizable()
            .scaledToFit()
            .frame(width: 160, height: 200)
            .scaleEffect(getCurrentZoom(magnification: magnification))
            .gesture(MagnificationGesture()
                .updating($magnification) { value, state, transaction in
                    state = value
                }
                .onEnded { value in
                    zoom = getCurrentZoom(magnification: value)
                }
            )
    }
    func getCurrentZoom(magnification: CGFloat) -> CGFloat {
        let minZoom: CGFloat = 1
        let maxZoom: CGFloat = 2

        var current = zoom * magnification
        current = max(min(current, maxZoom), minZoom)
        return current
    }
}
```

Listing 12-10: Determining a minimum and a maximum scale

Chapter 12 -Gestures

This example limits the scale of the view to a minimum of 1 and a maximum of 2. Because there are a few operations we must perform to limit the scale to these values, we move the process to a method called **getCurrentZoom()** and call it every time necessary. The method defines two constants with the minimum and maximum values for the scale, then calculates the current scale by multiplying the values of the **zoom** property by the magnification, and limits the result to a minimum of 1 and a maximum of 2 with the **max()** and **min()** functions. The **min()** function compares the scale with the maximum scale allowed and returns the smallest value (if the value is greater than 2, it returns 2), and then the **max()** function compares the result with the minimum scale allowed and returns the largest value (if the value is less than 1, it returns 1). The method is called by the **scaleEffect()** modifier to set the scale for the view, and by the **onEnded()** method to set the final scale. Consequently, the user can zoom the image in and out, but up to a maximum of 2 and a minimum of 1.

 Do It Yourself: Update the **ContentView** structure with the code in Listing 12-10 and run the application. You should be able to scale the view to the limits set by the **minZoom** and **maxZoom** constants.

(Basic) Rotation Gesture

The rotation gesture is recognized when the user touches the screen with two fingers and performs a circular motion. It is often used to rotate an image. As with previous gestures, if we want to let the user perform the gesture multiple times, we must keep track of two states, one for the current rotation and another for the last rotation. The value produced by the gesture is a structure of type **Angle**. We worked with this structure before. It includes two type methods, one to create an instance with a value in degrees (**degrees(Double)**) and another to do it with a value in radians (**radians(Double)**), but in our example we are going to rotate an image to follow the fingers, and for that we just need to add the current angle to the delta angle produced by the gesture.

```
struct ContentView: View {
   @GestureState private var rotationAngle: Angle = Angle.zero
   @State private var rotation: Angle = Angle.zero

   var body: some View {
      Image("spot1")
         .resizable()
         .scaledToFit()
         .frame(width: 160, height: 200)
         .rotationEffect(rotation + rotationAngle)

         .gesture(RotationGesture()
            .updating($rotationAngle) { value, state, transaction in
               state = value
            }
            .onEnded { value in
               rotation = rotation + value
            }
         )
   }
}
```

Listing 12-11: Defining a RotationGesture *recognizer*

This example applies the **rotationEffect()** modifier to rotate the view. The angle is calculated by adding the values of the two state properties. We also add the current rotation to the previous one when the gesture ends to preserve the current state in case the user wants to rotate the image again from that angle.

Figure 12-3: Image rotated by the user

 Do It Yourself: Update the `ContentView` view with the code in Listing 12-11 and run the application. You should be able to rotate the view with your fingers, as shown in Figure 12-3.

(Basic) **Drag and Drop Gesture**

Drag and drop is an operation we can perform to move an element from one app to another or between sections of the same app. This tool is useful on devices that can share the screen with two or more windows, like iPads and Mac computers. In Mac computers, the process is simple. We open two or more windows at the same time and use the mouse to drag an element from one window to the other. On iPads, we must split the screen in two. iPads include an icon with three dots at the top that we can tap to share the screen with other applications.

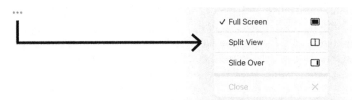

Figure 12-4: Tool to split the screen on iPads

When we tap on the three dots, the system shows a menu with three options (Figure 12-4, right). The Full Screen option assigns the entire screen to the app, the Split View option splits the screen in two to show the current app on the left and another app on the right, and the Slide Over option moves the app to an overlay window that is displayed on top of other apps. If we select the second or third options, the screen will be shared by two apps, so we can drag and drop elements between them.

To allow the user to drag and drop elements from and into our app, we must tell the system which views can be dragged or accept a drop. SwiftUI includes the following modifiers for this purpose.

draggable(Transferable, **preview:** Closure**)**—This modifier designates the view as the source of a drag and drop operation. The first argument is a value that conforms to the **Transferable** protocol and represents the data that will be transferred in the process. The **preview** argument provides the view to show to the user while the drag gesture is performed.

dropDestination(for: Type, **action:** Closure**)**—This modifier designates the view as the destination of a drag and drop operation. The **for** argument is a reference to the data type of the values we want to view to be able to receive, and the **action** argument provides a closure to process the data transferred by the gesture.

The drag and drop gestures are performed on the views, but the data to be transferred is determined from code. This doesn't mean that we can send any value we want, the data must be presented in a way apps can recognize. For this purpose, the framework defines the **Transferable** protocol. This protocol prepares the data to be sent and processes the data received in a drag and drop operation. Although we can conform to this protocol from our custom data types to transfer any value we want, some Swift data types and SwiftUI views do it by default. For instance, if we want to let the user drag an image from our app to another app, we can use the **Image** view.

```
struct ContentView: View {
   var body: some View {
      VStack {
         Image("husky")
            .resizable()
            .scaledToFit()
            .frame(width: 300, height: 400)
            .draggable(Image("husky"))
         Spacer()
      }
   }
}
```

Listing 12-12: *Allowing the user to drag an image*

This is a simple app with an **Image** view to show the picture of a husky, but because we applied the **draggable()** modifier, the user can drag the image to another app. To tell the system what data to share between applications, we provide the modifier with another **Image** view with the same picture. And because the **Image** view conforms to the **Transferable** protocol, the system knows how to share the data and external applications know how to process it. Figure 12-5, below, shows the app running on an iPad and sharing the screen with the Photo Library. If we drag the husky to an album on the right, the picture is added to the album.

Figure 12-5: *Drag and drop operation between apps*

 Do It Yourself: Create a Multiplatform project. Download the husky image from our website and add it to the Asset Catalog. Update the **ContentView** view with the code in Listing 12-12. Run the application on the iPad simulator. Tap the three dots at the top of the screen and select the Split View option (Figure 12-4). Open the Photo Library. You should see something like Figure 12-5. Open an album in the Photo Library and drag and drop the husky inside. The husky image should be added to the album.

The system creates an image from the view that is being dragged and use it to show a preview to the user, but we can assign an additional view to the **draggable()** modifier to provide a custom preview. For instance, the following example shows an SF Symbol instead.

```
struct ContentView: View {
   var body: some View {
      VStack {
         Image("husky")
            .resizable()
            .scaledToFit()
            .frame(width: 300, height: 400)
            .draggable(Image("husky"), preview: {
               Image(systemName: "scope")
                  .font(.system(size: 50))
            })
         Spacer()
      }
   }
}
```

Listing 12-13: *Providing a custom preview for the gesture*

Figure 12-6: *Custom preview*

In order for the user to be able to drop elements into our app, we must provide a view capable of receiving this data. To turn a view into a possible destination for a drag and drop operation, we must apply the **dropDestination()** modifier. The modifier takes a data type that determines the type of data the view can receive and a closure to process it. As before, the type must conform to the **Transferable** protocol. For instance, we can use an **Image** view.

```
struct ContentView: View {
   @State private var picture: Image = Image("nopicture")

   var body: some View {
      VStack {
         picture
            .resizable()
            .scaledToFit()
            .frame(minWidth: 0, maxWidth: .infinity)
            .frame(height: 400)
            .dropDestination(for: Image.self, action: { elements,
location in
               if let image = elements.first {
                  picture = image
                  return true
               }
```

```
                    return false
                })
            Spacer()
        }
    }
}
```

Listing 12-14: *Dropping images into an* `Image` *view*

The closure assigned to the **action** argument receives two values: an array with a list of the elements dropped by the user, and a **CGPoint** structure with the position within the view where the elements were dropped. Because in this example we process the data as **Image** types, the user can only drop images and the values are automatically turned into **Image** views, so we can assign it directly to a **@State** property and show it on the screen. Notice that the closure must return a Boolean value to indicate the result of the operation. If we are able to get the values and process them, we must return **true**, otherwise **false**.

Figure 12-7: *Dropping an image into our app*

 Do It Yourself: Update the **ContentView** view with the code in Listing 12-14. Download the nopicture image from our website and add it to the Asset Catalog. Run the application on the iPad simulator and split the screen to share it with the Photo Library. Drag the image of the husky back to the app. The nopicture image should be replaced by the husky. Drag and drop a different image. You should see that the gesture doesn't work anymore. We will see how to fix this issue next.

At the time of writing, the **Image** structure can only process PNG images. This is why, if we drag any other image than the husky, it won't be transferred to our app (The rest of the images provided by the simulator are in JPG format). To provide more alternatives to the user, instead of converting the image directly into an **Image** view, we can store it in a **Data** structure and convert the data later into a **UIImage** object.

Converting the data into an image is easy. Once we tell the **dropDestination()** modifier to only receive **Data** values, the data received is stored in a **Data** structure that we can turn into a **UIImage** object and use it create the **Image** view, as shown next.

```
struct ContentView: View {
    @State private var picture: Image = Image("nopicture")
    @State private var didEnter: Bool = false

    var body: some View {
        VStack {
            picture
                .resizable()
                .scaledToFit()
```

```
                .frame(minWidth: 0, maxWidth: .infinity)
                .frame(height: 400)
                .overlay(didEnter ? Color.green.opacity(0.2) : Color.clear)
                .dropDestination(for: Data.self, action: {elements, location in
                    if let data = elements.first, let image = UIImage(data:
data) {
                        picture = Image(uiImage: image)
                        return true
                    }
                    return false
                }, isTargeted: { value in
                    didEnter = value
                })
            Spacer()
        }
    }
}
```

Listing 12-15: Processing the image as data

In this example, we define a new **@State** property called **didEnter**. This property is used by the **dropDestination()** modifier to report to the application when the element dragged by the user enters or leaves the area occupied by the view, so we can use it to provide feedback. If the image is inside the view, we show a green overlay, otherwise the color is clear.

Figure 12-8: Data processing in a drag and drop operation

 Do It Yourself: Update the **ContentView** view with the code in Listing 12-15. Run the application on the iPad simulator and split the screen as before. You should now be able to drag any image you want from the Photo Library to the app, and the drop area should turn green when the finger is over it, as shown in Figure 12-8.

So far, we have use an **Image** view and a **Data** structure to transfer the data. These data types conform to the **Transferable** protocol and therefore we can use them to transfer data in a drag and drop operation without any additional work. But custom data types, including structures and classes, can be used as well. All we need to do is to make them conform to the **Transferable** protocol, which only requirement is the implementation of the following type property.

transferRepresentation—This type property returns a structure that represents the data to be transferred.

The property must return a structure that conforms to a protocol called **Transfer-Representation**. The framework defines multiple structures to create these representations. The most frequently used are **CodableRepresentation** to send and receive encodable and decodable data, `DataRepresentation` for raw data, `FileRepresentation` for files, and `ProxyRepresentation` to use predefined representations. The following are some of the initializers available.

CodableRepresentation(for: Type, **contentType:** UTType)—This initializer creates a structure that represents data that can be encoded and decoded. The **for** argument is a reference to the data type itself, and the **contentType** argument determines the type of values the user is allowed to drag and drop.

DataRepresentation(contentType: UTType, **exporting:** Closure, **importing:** Closure)—This initializer creates a structure that represents raw data. The **contentType** argument determines the type of values the user is allowed to drag and drop, the **exporting** argument provides the data to send when the view is dragged, and the **importing** argument creates an instance of the data type with the data dropped by the user. The structure also includes two more initializers to only import or export data: `DataRepresentation(importedContentType: UTType, importing: Closure)` and `DataRepresentation(exportedContentType: UTType, exporting: Closure)`.

FileRepresentation(contentType: UTType, **shouldAttemptToOpenInPlace:** Bool, **exporting:** Closure, **importing:** Closure)—This initializer creates a structure that represents files. The **contentType** argument determines the types of files the user is allowed to drag and drop, the **shouldAttemptToOpenInPlace** argument indicates if the receiver can access the original file, the **exporting** argument provides the file to be sent in a drag operation, and the **importing** argument creates the file from the information received from a drop operation. The structure also includes two more initializers to only import or export files: `FileRepresentation(importedContentType: UTType, shouldAttemptToOpenInPlace: Bool, importing: Closure)` and `FileRepresentation(exportedContentType: UTType, shouldAllowToOpenInPlace: Bool, exporting: Closure)`.

ProxyRepresentation(exporting: Closure, **importing:** Closure)—This initializer creates a structure that uses an existent transfer representation that is suitable for the type. The **exporting** argument provides a reference to the transfer representation used when an element is dragged, and the **importing** argument provides a reference to the transfer representation used when an element is dropped. The structure also includes two more initializers to only import or export data: `ProxyRepresentation(importing: Closure)` and `ProxyRepresentation(exporting: Closure)`.

The purpose of these structures is to prepare the data to be sent and process the data received in a drag and drop operation. Therefore, the structure we use to represent the data depends on what we want to transfer. The `CodableRepresentation` structure is used to represent encodable and decodable data, the `DataRepresentation` is used to represent raw data, like images, the `FileRepresentation` structure represents files, and the `ProxyRepresentation` structure is used to implement predefined representations.

No matter what structure we use, the values are transferred as generic data. To let applications know how to process that data, we must declare the content type with a `UTType` structure. We have introduced this structure before (see Chapter 10). As we will see later, we can define our own types, but we can also use the standard types provided by the framework. In the following example, we use the **png** type to send a PNG image when the view is dragged.

```
import SwiftUI
struct ImageRepresentation: Transferable {
   let name: String
```

```
    let image: UIImage

    static var transferRepresentation: some TransferRepresentation {
        DataRepresentation(exportedContentType: .png, exporting: { value in
            return value.image.pngData()!
        })
    }
}
struct ContentView: View {
    @State private var picture: UIImage = UIImage(named: "nopicture")!

    var body: some View {
        VStack {
            Image(uiImage: picture)
                .resizable()
                .scaledToFit()
                .draggable(ImageRepresentation(name: "My Picture", image:
picture))
                .dropDestination(for: Data.self, action: { elements, location
in
                    if let data = elements.first, let image = UIImage(data:
data) {
                        picture = image
                        return true
                    }
                    return false
                })
            Spacer()
        }
    }
}
```

Listing 12-16: Dragging custom values

Our data type is a structure called **ImageRepresentation** with two properties: **name** and **image**. For this application, we only want to transfer the image, so we get the structure to conform to the **Transferable** protocol, implement the **transferRepresentation** property, and define a **DataRepresentation** structure that gets the data from the image and returns it.

Although we are transferring data representing an image, we use our own custom data type to process it. When the user drags the view, the **draggable()** modifier creates an instance of the **ImageRepresentation** structure and the structure is sent to the closure assigned to the **DataRepresentation** structure, so we can get the **UIImage** object in the **image** property, turn it into data with the **pngData()** method, and return it. The external application receives this data, recognizes it as a PNG image thanks to the **UTType** structure, and processes it as such.

Notice that we have also applied the **dropDestination()** modifier, as we did in previous examples, so the user can drag and drop images back and forward between the application and external apps.

 Do It Yourself: Update the ContentView.swift file with the code in Listing 12-16. Run the application on the iPad simulator. Split the screen. Open the Photo Library. You should be able to drag and drop images back and forward between the Photo Library and your app.

In the last example, we use a **DataRepresentation** structure to prepare the data to be sent in a drag operation (exporting), but use a **Data** type to received any image dropped by the user. This is because we don't have control over the data other apps send to us. But we can send and receive custom data types as long as the app knows how to process it. For instance, if we want to allow the user to drag and drop elements within our app, we are in control of the whole process and therefore we can transfer any custom data type we want. The only requirement is for the data to be encoded. When data is sent, it must be encoded, and when data is received it must be decoded. This is easy to achieve with the **Codable** protocol and the **CodableRepresentation** structure, but because we are using custom data types, we need to define a custom **UTType** as well. The following is the structure's initializer.

UTType(exportedAs: String, **conformingTo:** UTType?)—This initializer creates a custom **UTType** identified by the string assigned to the **exportedAs** argument. The **conformingTo** argument is a predefined **UTType** that the custom type uses as reference.

The **UTType** requires an identifier that we must create from settings. We need to go to the project's settings (Figure 5-4, number 6), open the Info panel, expand the Exported Type Identifiers section, press the + button, and insert the values.

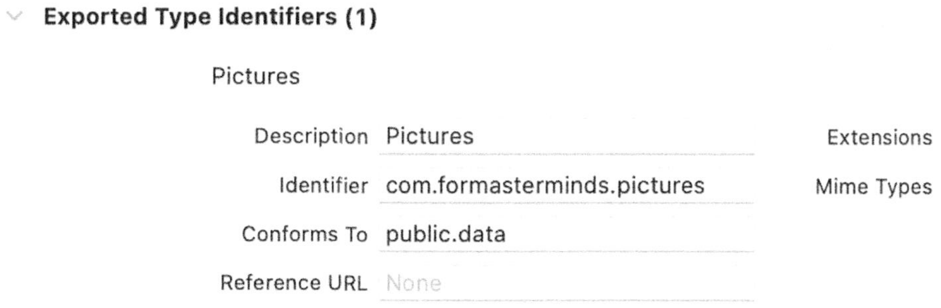

∨ **Exported Type Identifiers (1)**

Pictures

		Extensions
Description	Pictures	
Identifier	com.formasterminds.pictures	Mime Types
Conforms To	public.data	
Reference URL	None	

Figure 12-9: Custom content type

The values we need are the Description, the Identifier, and the Conforms To. The Description is just a text to describe the type, the Identifier must be unique and therefore it is recommendable to declare it with an inverted domain, as we did in our example, and the Conforms to option is a predefined **UTType** that closely matches what our type is going to represent. In this case, we use the public.data type, so the system knows we are transferring raw data.

Once we have the custom content type, we need to extend the **UTType** structure to include a type property that represents it. In the following example, we create a custom structure to manage the data (an image and an identifier), and extend the **UTType** structure with a property called **product** to store our custom type.

```
import SwiftUI
import UniformTypeIdentifiers
struct PictureRepresentation: Identifiable, Codable, Transferable {
   var id = UUID()
   var image: Data

   static var transferRepresentation: some TransferRepresentation {
      CodableRepresentation(for: PictureRepresentation.self, contentType:
.product)
   }
}
extension UTType {
   static var product = UTType(exportedAs: "com.formasterminds.pictures")
}
class ApplicationData: ObservableObject {
   @Published var listPictures: [PictureRepresentation]

   init() {
      listPictures = [
         PictureRepresentation(image: UIImage(named:
"spot1")!.pngData()!),
         PictureRepresentation(image: UIImage(named:
"spot2")!.pngData()!),
```

```
            PictureRepresentation(image: UIImage(named:
"spot3")!.pngData()!)
        ]
    }
}
```

Listing 12-17: Using a custom content type

After we define the **PictureRepresentation** structure to contain the data and extend the **UTType** to add our content type, we initialize the model with three instances containing the images spot1, spot2, and spot3. The purpose of this application is to allow the user to drag these pictures from the top of the screen to a larger view at the bottom. After a picture is dropped, we want to erase it from the list, and that's why, along with the image, we include an identifier.

For the interface, we need a **ForEach** loop to list all the images available at the top and another **Image** view at the bottom where the user can drop them.

```
struct ContentView: View {
    @EnvironmentObject var appData: ApplicationData
    @State private var currentPicture: UIImage = UIImage(named:
"nopicture")!

    var body: some View {
        VStack {
            HStack(spacing: 10) {
                ForEach(appData.listPictures) { picture in
                    Image(uiImage: UIImage(data: picture.image) ??
UIImage(named: "nopicture")!)
                        .resizable()
                        .frame(width: 80, height: 100)
                        .draggable(picture)
                }
            }.frame(height: 120)
            Image(uiImage: currentPicture)
                .resizable()
                .scaledToFit()
                .padding(10)
                .dropDestination(for: PictureRepresentation.self, action:
{ elements, location in
                    if let picture = elements.first {
                        currentPicture = UIImage(data: picture.image) ??
UIImage(named: "nopicture")!
                        appData.listPictures.removeAll(where: { $0.id ==
picture.id })

                        return true
                    }
                    return false
                })
        }
    }
}
struct ContentView_Previews: PreviewProvider {
    static var previews: some View {
        ContentView().environmentObject(ApplicationData())
    }
}
```

Listing 12-18: Dragging and dropping custom values

The **draggable()** and **dropDestination()** modifiers work with the **Picture-Representation** structure to transfer the data. When the user drags an image, the structure encodes the data, including the identifier and the image, and when the user drops the image into the target view, the data is decoded, an instance of the `PictureRepresentation` structure is created, and we can process the values. In this case, we assign the image to the `Image` view and then remove the original picture from the list. The result is shown below.

Figure 12-10: *Drag and drop with custom data*

Do It Yourself: Create a Swift file called ApplicationData.swift for the model in Listing 12-17. Update the `ContentView` view with the code in Listing 12-18. Download the spot1, spot2 and spot3 images from our website and add them to the Asset Catalog. Go to the project's settings (Figure 5-4, number 6), open the Info panel, expand the Exported Type Identifiers section, press the + button, and insert the values, as shown in Figure 12-9. Run the application on the iPhone simulator. Drag an image and drop it over the nopicture image. The original image should be removed, as shown in Figure 12-10 (right).

(Basic) 13.1 Map View

Often, users need to visualize their location or the places they want to go on a map to position themselves in the world. For these kinds of applications, Apple offers the MapKit framework. The framework includes all the tools necessary to create and configure maps, including the **Map** view to add the map to the interface.

Map(coordinateRegion: Binding, **interactionModes:** MapInteraction-Modes, **showsUserLocation:** Bool, **userTrackingMode:** Binding, **annotationItems:** Items, **annotationContent:** Closure)—This initializer creates a map with the configuration defined by the arguments. The **coordinateRegion** argument is a **Binding** property with an **MKCoordinateRegion** structure to determine the map's visible region. The **interactionModes** argument is a structure that determines the user interactions allowed. The structure includes the type properties **all**, **pan**, and **zoom**. The **showsUserLocation** argument determines if the map shows the user's current location. The **userTrackingMode** argument is a **Binding** property of type **MapUserTrackingMode** that determines if the map will be updated when the user's location changes. It is an enumeration with the values **follow** and **none**. The **annotationItems** argument is a collection of identifiable structures that represent the locations of the annotations to show on the map. And finally, the **annotationContent** argument provides the views used to present the annotations.

The region of the map to show on the screen is determined by an **MKCoordinateRegion** structure. The structure includes the following initializer.

MKCoordinateRegion(center: CLLocationCoordinate2D, **latitudinalMeters:** CLLocationDistance, **longitudinalMeters:** CLLocationDistance)—This initializer creates an **MKCoordinateRegion** structure with the values determined by the arguments. The **center** argument specifies the region's coordinates, and the **latitudinal-Meters** and **longitudinalMeters** arguments determine the vertical and horizontal size of the region in meters (**CLLocationDistance** is a typealias of **Double**).

The latitude and longitude of a location are determined by a **CLLocationCoordinate2D** structure. The structure includes the following initializer.

CLLocationCoordinate2D(latitude: CLLocationDegrees, **longitude:** CLLocationDegrees)—This initializer creates an **CLLocationCoordinate2D** structure with the values determined by the arguments. The **latitude** argument is a typealias of **Double** that determines the location's latitude, and the **longitude** argument is a typealias of **Double** that determines the location's longitude.

The first step is to define all these values to tell the **Map** view what region of the map to show. Because these values may change and more may be required later, it is better to manage the map from an observable object or the model, as we do in the following example.

```
import SwiftUI
import MapKit
```

```
class ApplicationData: ObservableObject {
   @Published var region: MKCoordinateRegion

   init() {
      let coordinates = CLLocationCoordinate2D(latitude:
40.7637825011971, longitude: -73.9731328627541)
      region = MKCoordinateRegion(center: coordinates, latitudinalMeters:
1000, longitudinalMeters: 1000)
   }
}
```

Listing 13-1: Configuring the map from the model

The code in this model defines a **CLLocationCoordinate2D** structure with the coordinates of the Apple Store in New York City, creates an **MKCoordinateRegion** structure that defines a region of a 1000 meters around that location, and assigns it to a **@Published** property that we are going to use to configure the map. Notice that we need to import the MapKit framework to have access to some of these structures.

To present a map, we must import the MapKit framework again and include the **Map** view configured with the values from the model.

```
import SwiftUI
import MapKit

struct ContentView: View {
   @EnvironmentObject var appData: ApplicationData

   var body: some View {
      Map(coordinateRegion: $appData.region)
         .ignoresSafeArea()
   }
}
struct ContentView_Previews: PreviewProvider {
   static var previews: some View {
      ContentView().environmentObject(ApplicationData())
   }
}
```

Listing 13-2: Displaying a map

The **Map** view shows the map in the region determined by the **MKCoordinateRegion** structure assigned to the **region** property. In this case, that's the area around the Apple store in New York City.

Figure 13-1: Map showing a specific region of New York City

The latitude and longitude values in the **region** property are updated every time the user drags the map to a different area, as shown in the following example.

Chapter 13 -Map Kit

```
struct ContentView: View {
    @EnvironmentObject var appData: ApplicationData

    var body: some View {
        VStack {
            Map(coordinateRegion: $appData.region)
                .ignoresSafeArea()
            HStack {
                Text(String(appData.region.center.latitude))
                Text(String(appData.region.center.longitude))
            }.padding(10)
            .font(.caption)
        }
    }
}
```

Listing 13-3: Showing the current latitude and longitude

When the user scrolls the map to a different area, the center of the region changes, and because we initialized the **Map** view with a bidirectional binding, those values are assigned back to the **region** property, and therefore we can read them, process them, or show them to the user, as in this example.

Figure 13-2: Current latitude and longitude

 Do It Yourself: Create a Multiplatform project. Create a Swift file called ApplicationData.swift for the model in Listing 13-1. Update the **ContentView** view with the code in Listing 13-3. Remember to inject the **ApplicationData** object into the environment for the app and the previews (Chapter 7, Listing 7-4). Run the application on the iPhone simulator. You should see the area around the Apple Store in New York City. Drag the map to a different area. You should see the latitude and longitude at the bottom of the screen changing to reflect the location of the visible region.

By default, the **Map** view allows the user to zoom and pan the map, but the view's initializer can include the **interactionModes** argument to enable only zooming or panning. For instance, we can disable panning to not allow the user to change the region.

```
struct ContentView: View {
    @EnvironmentObject var appData: ApplicationData

    var body: some View {
        Map(coordinateRegion: $appData.region, interactionModes: .zoom)
            .ignoresSafeArea()
    }
}
```

Listing 13-4: Disabling panning

The previous examples set the visible area around the Apple Store. Because this is a relevant location, the map shows an icon with the name of the store, but this is not always the case. Most locations do not show any reference at all, and the user has to guess where the exact location actually is. To add graphics to the map and mark locations, we use annotations.

Annotations provide additional information of a particular location. SwiftUI defines two views to create them: the `MapMarker` view to create annotations with standard views, and the `MapAnnotation` view to create annotations with custom views.

MapMarker(coordinate: CLLocationCoordinate2D, **tint:** Color)—This initializer creates an annotation with a view shaped as a balloon to mark a location. The **coordinate** argument is a `CLLocationCoordinate2D` structure with the annotation's latitude and longitude, and the **tint** argument determines the color of the balloon.

MapAnnotation(coordinate: CLLocationCoordinate2D, **anchorPoint:** CGPoint, **content:** Closure)—This initializer creates an annotation with custom views. The **coordinate** argument is a `CLLocationCoordinate2D` structure with the annotation's latitude and longitude, the **anchorPoint** argument indicates the area of the views that are going to be displayed over the exact location, and the **content** argument is the closure that provides the views to present the annotation.

Again, the first step is to provide the data required to configure the map and show the annotations. For the annotations, we need a structure that conforms to the `Identifiable` protocol and includes at least a `CLLocationCoordinate2D` property with the annotation's location. In the following example, we call this structure `PlaceAnnotation`.

```
import SwiftUI
import MapKit

struct PlaceAnnotation: Identifiable {
   let id = UUID()
   var selected: Bool = false
   var name: String
   var location: CLLocationCoordinate2D

   init(name: String, location: CLLocationCoordinate2D) {
      self.name = name
      self.location = location
   }
}
class ApplicationData: ObservableObject {
   @Published var region: MKCoordinateRegion
   @Published var annotations: [PlaceAnnotation] = []

   init() {
      let coordinates = CLLocationCoordinate2D(latitude:
40.7637825011971, longitude: -73.9731328627541)
      region = MKCoordinateRegion(center: coordinates, latitudinalMeters:
1000, longitudinalMeters: 1000)

      let location = CLLocationCoordinate2D(latitude: 40.7637825011971,
longitude: -73.9731328627541)
      annotations.append(PlaceAnnotation(name: "Apple Store", location:
location))
   }
}
```

Listing 13-5: Defining an annotation

The `PlaceAnnotation` structure includes the required `id` property to identify the instance, and three more properties to define the annotation. The `selected` property indicates if the annotation was tapped by the user, the `name` property stores the annotation's title, and the `location` property stores the annotation's latitude and longitude.

The model now includes a second `@Published` property to store all the annotations to show on the map, so all we need to do is to add instances of the `PlaceAnnotation` structure to this array and use this information to display the annotations on the map. The `Map` view's initializer includes two arguments for this purpose. The **annotationItems** argument specifies the array with the values to create the annotations, and the **annotationContent** argument defines the views to show each annotation on the screen.

To display the annotations on the screen, we can use standard or custom views. For instance, in the following example we show the annotations with a `MapMarker` view, which creates a standard view with the shape of a balloon.

```
struct ContentView: View {
   @EnvironmentObject var appData: ApplicationData

   var body: some View {
      Map(coordinateRegion: $appData.region, annotationItems:
appData.annotations, annotationContent: { place in
         MapMarker(coordinate: place.location, tint: .red)
      })
      .ignoresSafeArea()
   }
}
```

Listing 13-6: Displaying the annotations

The `Map` view in this example reads the array of `PlaceAnnotation` structures in the `annotations` property and calls the closure assigned to the **annotationContent** argument to create a `MapMarker` view to represent each annotation.

For testing, we included a single annotation in the model of Listing 13-5 with the location of the Apple store, so the map shows a ballon to mark that place.

Figure 13-3: Annotation on the map

 Do It Yourself: Update the ApplicationData.swift file with the code in Listing 13-5 and the `ContentView` view with the code in Listing 13-6. Run the application on the iPhone simulator. You should see a pin indicating the location of the Apple store, as shown in Figure 13-3.

The `MapMarker` view creates a standard view with a predefined design, but we can use any views we want to represent the annotations. All we need to do is to provide the views with a `MapAnnotation` view instead.

```
struct ContentView: View {
    @EnvironmentObject var appData: ApplicationData

    var body: some View {
        Map(coordinateRegion: $appData.region, annotationItems:
appData.annotations, annotationContent: { place in
            MapAnnotation(coordinate: place.location) {
                Circle()
                    .fill(Color.blue)
                    .frame(width: 40, height: 40)
            }
        }).ignoresSafeArea()
    }
}
```

Listing 13-7: *Presenting the annotation with custom views*

The `MapAnnotation` view in Listing 13-7 includes a 40 pixels by 40 pixels circle painted in blue. The result is shown below.

Figure 13-4: *Custom view for annotations*

Of course, we can design the annotation with any view we want, including images and text. The following example embeds an `Image` and a `Text` view in a `VStack` to show an icon at the top and the annotation's name below.

```
struct ContentView: View {
    @EnvironmentObject var appData: ApplicationData

    var body: some View {
        Map(coordinateRegion: $appData.region, annotationItems:
appData.annotations, annotationContent: { place in
            MapAnnotation(coordinate: place.location) {
                VStack(spacing: 0) {
                    Image("iconmap")
                        .resizable()
                        .frame(width: 40, height: 40)
                    Text(place.name)
                        .font(.caption)
                }
            }
        }).ignoresSafeArea()
    }
}
```

Listing 13-8: *Presenting the annotation with images and text*

Figure 13-5: *Custom image for annotations*

Do It Yourself: Download the iconmap image from our website and add it to the Asset Catalog. Update the `ContentView` view with the code in Listing 13-8. Run the application on the iPhone simulator. You should see something like Figure 13-5.

The `Map` view doesn't provide any tools to allow the user to select an annotation, but we can apply the `onTapGesture()` modifier to the views to allow the user to select them. The trick is to use the `selected` property we have included in the `PlaceAnnotation` structure. When the value of this property is `true`, which means that the annotation was selected, we can represent the selection on the interface by modifying the views. For instance, we can expand the image of the selected annotation, as we do in the following example.

```
struct ContentView: View {
   @EnvironmentObject var appData: ApplicationData

   var body: some View {
      Map(coordinateRegion: $appData.region, annotationItems:
appData.annotations, annotationContent: { place in
         MapAnnotation(coordinate: place.location) {
            VStack(spacing: 0) {
               Image("iconmap")
                  .resizable()
                  .frame(width: place.selected ? 60 : 40, height:
place.selected ? 60 : 40)
               Text(place.name)
                  .font(.caption)
            }
            .onTapGesture {
               for (index, item) in appData.annotations.enumerated() {
                  if item.id == place.id {
                     appData.annotations[index].selected.toggle()
                  } else {
                     appData.annotations[index].selected = false
                  }
               }
            }
         }
      }).ignoresSafeArea()
   }
}
```

Listing 13-9: *Selecting annotations*

The **MapAnnotation** view in this example includes a **VStack** with the same **Image** and **Text** views used before, but now the width and height for the **frame()** modifier applied to the **Image** view depend on the value of the annotation's **selected** property. If the value is **true**, the image will be 60x60 pixels, otherwise, the size assigned to the image is 40x40 pixels, as before.

When the user taps on an annotation to select it, we must assign the value **true** to its **selected** property, and also assign the value **false** to the rest of the annotations to deselect them. For this purpose, we define a **for in** loop. The loop implements the **enumerated()** method to get the item but also its index. If the item's identifier is equal to the identifier of the annotation selected by the user, we toggle the value (if the annotation is deselected, we select it, otherwise we deselect it), but if the item represent any of the annotations that were not tapped by the user, we assign the value **false** to make sure they are all deselected.

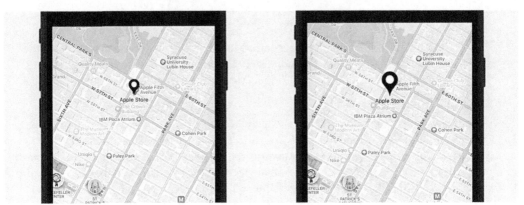

Figure 13-6: Selected and deselected annotation

Do It Yourself: Update the **ContentView** view with the code in Listing 13-9. Run the application on the iPhone simulator. Tap on the annotation. You should see the image expanding to a size of 60x60 points, as shown in Figure 13-6.

(Basic) **Local Search**

The MapKit framework incorporates a service to translate addresses into locations and find places of interest. The service is called *Local Search* and can take a freeform query string and return an array with the results. The query is created from the **Request** class included in the **MKLocalSearch** class. The following are some of the properties defined by the **Request** class to define the query.

naturalLanguageQuery—This property sets or returns a string with the term or address we want to search.

region—This property sets or returns an **MKCoordinateRegion** structure that determines the region in which the search is performed.

To perform a search, the **MKLocalSearch** class includes the following initializer and method.

MKLocalSearch(request: MKLocalSearchRequest**)**—This initializer creates an **MKLocalSearch** object to perform a search request.

start()—This asynchronous method performs a search and returns an **MKLocalSearchResponse** object with the results.

The search returns an **MKLocalSearchResponse** object that contains the following properties.

mapItems—This property returns an array of **MKMapItem** objects that represent the results produced by the search.

boundingRegion—This property returns an **MKCoordinateRegion** structure that determines the region occupied by the results produced by the search.

The Local Search service was designed to find all the places that match the query. The framework defines the **MKMapItem** class to represent a place. The following are some of the properties included by this class to return the data from the place.

name—This property sets or returns a string with the place's name.

phoneNumber—This property sets or returns a string with the place's phone number.

url—This property sets or returns a **URL** value with the URL of the place's website.

placemark—This property sets or returns an **MKPlacemark** object with additional information about the place. The **MKPlacemark** class inherits from the **CLPlacemark** class, which includes the **location** property. This property stores a value of type **CLLocation**, which in turn includes the **coordinate** property we can use to retrieve the **CLLocationCoordinate2D** structure with the place's latitude and longitude.

There are different ways an app can perform a search and display the results. As an example, we are going to search for places associated with the word "Pizza" as soon as the view is loaded.

```
struct ContentView: View {
    @EnvironmentObject var appData: ApplicationData

    var body: some View {
        Map(coordinateRegion: $appData.region, annotationItems:
appData.annotations, annotationContent: { place in
            MapAnnotation(coordinate: place.location) {
                VStack(spacing: 0) {
                    Image("iconmap")
                        .resizable()
                        .frame(width: 40, height: 40)
                    Text(place.name)
                        .font(.caption)
                        .padding(3)
                        .background(RoundedRectangle(cornerRadius:
4).foregroundStyle(.thickMaterial))
                }
            }
        }).ignoresSafeArea()
        .task(priority: .background) {
            await setAnnotations()
        }
    }
    func setAnnotations() async {
        let request = MKLocalSearch.Request()
        request.naturalLanguageQuery = "Pizza"
        request.region = appData.region

        let search = MKLocalSearch(request: request)
        if let results = try? await search.start() {
            let items = results.mapItems

            await MainActor.run {
                appData.annotations = []
                for item in items {
                    if let location = item.placemark.location?.coordinate {
```

```
              let place = PlaceAnnotation(name: item.name ??
"Undefined", location: location)
              appData.annotations.append(place)
          }
        }
      }
    }
  }
}
```

Listing 13-10: Searching for pizza places

The code in Listing 13-10 defines the **setAnnotations()** method to search for places associated with the term "Pizza" and adds an annotation to the model for each location found. When the view is loaded, the **task()** modifier asynchronously calls this method to start the process. The method creates a request with the query "Pizza" and the region defined in the model to find places of interest around the current location. The request is then used to create the **MKLocalSearch** object and the search is initiated by calling the **start()** method. This method is asynchronous, so we must wait for the results. Once the results are back from Apple servers, we remove the current annotations and create a loop to read all the places found and store them in the model.

Figure 13-7: Places found by the Local Search system

 Do It Yourself: Update the **ContentView** view with the code in Listing 13-10. Run the application on the iPhone simulator. You should see the pizzerias around the Apple store in New York City.

Basic User Location

Devices can detect the user's location, and the **Map** view's initializer includes the **showsUserLocation** argument to show it on the map, but first we must ask the user for permission. There are two types of authorization. We can ask permission to get updates only while the app is active (the app is being used by the user at the time), or all the time (even when the app moves to the background). The Core Location framework defines the **CLLocationManager** class to manage locations and get authorization from the user. The following are some of the properties and methods included in this class for this purpose.

authorizationStatus—This property returns the current authorization status. The value is an enumeration of type **CLAuthorizationStatus** with the values **notDetermined**, **restricted**, **denied**, **authorizedAlways**, and **authorizedWhen-InUse**.

requestWhenInUseAuthorization()—This method asks for authorization to get the location while the app is in use.

requestAlwaysAuthorization()—This method asks for authorization to get the location when the app is active or in the background.

For these methods to work, we must add an option to the app's configuration to explain to the users why we need to access their location. The option is called "Privacy - Location When In Use Usage Description", and it is added from the Info panel, as we did for other options in Chapter 5 (see Figure 5-34).

Key		Type	Value
Bundle name	◇	String	$(PRODUCT_NAME)
Privacy - Location When In Use Usage Description	◇	String	We need to access your location to show it on the map
Bundle identifier	◇	String	$(PRODUCT_BUNDLE_IDENTIFIER)
InfoDictionary version	◇	String	6.0
Bundle version	◇	String	$(CURRENT_PROJECT_VERSION)

Figure 13-8: Privacy - Location When In Use Usage Description option

After authorization is granted, we may request a one-time report of the user's location or ask the manager to track the user and report the changes. For this purpose, the **CLLocationManager** class includes the following property and methods.

location—This property returns a **CLLocation** object with information about the user's location.

requestLocation()—This method requests a one time-delivery of the user's location.

startUpdatingLocation()—This method asks the manager to generate a report every time the user's location changes.

stopUpdatingLocation()—This method asks the manager to stop reporting changes in the user's location.

Every time the **CLLocationManager** object needs to report the user's location, it calls methods on a delegate object. The framework defines the **CLLocationManagerDelegate** protocol to create this delegate. The following are some of the methods included in the protocol.

locationManagerDidChangeAuthorization(CLLocationManager**)**—This method is called on the delegate when the authorization status changes (the user grants or denies access to his or her location).

locationManager(CLLocationManager, **didFailWithError:** Error**)**—This method is called on the delegate when the manager fails to obtain the user's location.

locationManager(CLLocationManager, **didUpdateLocations:** [CLLocation]**)** —This method is called on the delegate when new locations are found.

The **CLLocationManager** class includes the **delegate** property to assign this delegate object and a few more properties for configuration. The following is the most frequently used.

desiredAccuracy—This property sets or returns a value of type **Double** with the accuracy of the location in meters.

The first thing we need to do is to define the delegate object for the location manager. As always, it could be any object we want, but it is recommended to use the model. There is only one caveat. The **CLLocationManagerDelegate** protocol inherits from **NSObjectProtocol**, a protocol defined in Objective-C, so our delegate object needs to inherit from the **NSObject** class.

This also requires us to override the `NSObject`'s initializer and call the initializer on the superclass, as shown below.

```
import SwiftUI
import MapKit

class ApplicationData: NSObject, ObservableObject,
CLLocationManagerDelegate {
    @Published var region: MKCoordinateRegion = MKCoordinateRegion()
    let manager = CLLocationManager()

    override init() {
        super.init()
        manager.delegate = self
        manager.desiredAccuracy = 100
    }
    func locationManager(_ manager: CLLocationManager, didUpdateLocations
locations: [CLLocation]) {
        if let coordinates = locations.first?.coordinate {
            region = MKCoordinateRegion(center: coordinates,
latitudinalMeters: 1000, longitudinalMeters: 1000)
        }
    }
    func locationManager(_ manager: CLLocationManager, didFailWithError
error: Error) {
        print("Error")
    }
}
```

Listing 13-11: *Conforming to the* `CLLocationManagerDelegate` *protocol*

In addition to the requirements of the **NSObject** class, there are a few more steps we must follow in our model for the system to work properly. For starters, we need to get the model to conform to the **CLLocationManagerDelegate** protocol and implement at least two methods. We need the **locationManager(CLLocationManager, didUpdateLocations:)** method to read the locations detected by the system, and the **locationManager(CLLocation-Manager, didFailWithError:)** method to respond to errors. (If this method is not implemented, the app crashes when the location cannot be determined or an error is found.) We also need to store the **CLLocationManager** object in a property to make sure it remains in memory for as long as we need it, and configure the manager when the model is initialized. For our example, we assign the model as the delegate and then set the desired accuracy to 100 meters. This makes sure that the system returns a location in a timely manner.

Notice that the **region** property is initialized with an empty **MKCoordinateRegion()** object, so we can show the map while we wait for a location. When the delegate method is called to report a new location, we get the **CLLocationCoordinate2D** structure with the user's location from the first value in the array (the method can receive multiple consecutive locations), use it to generate the new **MKCoordinateRegion** structure, and assign it to the **region** property to update the map.

There are also a few requirements for the view. We must initialize the **Map** view with the **showsUserLocation** argument and the value **true** to get the map to show an annotation on the user's location, ask the user for authorization with the **requestWhenInUseAuthorization()** method as soon as the view is shown on the screen, and request a location with the **requestLocation()** method when a button is pressed.

```
struct ContentView: View {
    @EnvironmentObject var appData: ApplicationData

    var body: some View {
```

```
    VStack {
        Button("My Location") {
            appData.manager.requestLocation()
        }.padding()
        Map(coordinateRegion: $appData.region, showsUserLocation: true)
            .ignoresSafeArea()
    }
    .onAppear {
        appData.manager.requestWhenInUseAuthorization()
    }
  }
}
```

Listing 13-12: Requesting authorization and showing the user's location

The view now includes a button on top of the map to start the process. When the button is pressed, the `requestLocation()` method is called, the manager gets the user's location, calls the protocol method to report it to the delegate object, the method updates the value of the `region` property with the new coordinates, and the `Map` view zooms in to that region and displays a blue circle on the place.

Figure 13-9: User's location on the map

 Do It Yourself: Update the model with the code in Listing 13-11 and the `ContentView` view with the code in Listing 13-12. Add the "Privacy - Location When In Use Usage Description" option to the app's configuration, as explain in Chapter 5 (see Figure 5-34). Run the application on the iPhone simulator. If you want to see your current location, you must run the app on a real device. Authorize the app to access your location. Press the My Location button. You should see a blue circle over your location on the map.

In the previous example, we requested authorization with the `requestWhenInUse-Authorization()` method. This presents an Alert View that includes two options: Allow Once and Allow While Using App. If the user allows the app only once, every time the app is launched, it will ask for permission again, which could be frustrating. To improve the user's experience, SwiftUI includes the `LocationButton` view.

LocationButton(Title, action: Closure)—This view creates a button to prompt the user for a one-time access to his or her location. The first argument is a predefined title determined by a `Title` structure. To define these values, the structure includes the type properties **currentLocation** ("Current Location"), **sendCurrentLocation** ("Send Current Location"), **sendMyCurrentLocation** ("Send My Current Location"), **shareCurrentLocation** ("Share Current Location"), and **shareMyCurrentLocation** ("Share My Current Location"). And the **action** argument is a closure to execute whatever code we need when the button is pressed.

By implementing this button instead of our custom button, we don't have to ask the user for permission anymore, and the process the user has to follow to grant permission is simplified.

```
import SwiftUI
import MapKit
import CoreLocationUI

struct ContentView: View {
    @EnvironmentObject var appData: ApplicationData

    var body: some View {
        VStack {
            LocationButton(.currentLocation) {
                appData.manager.requestLocation()
            }.padding()
            Map(coordinateRegion: $appData.region, showsUserLocation: true)
                .ignoresSafeArea()
        }
    }
}
```

Listing 13-13: *Implementing the user location button*

Notice that the `LocationButton` view is defined in the CoreLocationUI framework, so we must import this framework for the view to become available. The rest of the code works like the previous example. If the user grants permission, we call the `requestLocation()` method, the manager calls the protocol method on the delegate object with the new location, and the map shows it on the screen.

Figure 13-10: *User location button*

 Do It Yourself: Update the `ContentView` view with the code in Listing 13-13. Run the application on the iPhone simulator. If you want to see your current location, you must run the app on a real device. Press the Location button. You should see a window asking for authorization. Authorize the app. You should see a circle over your location on the map.

Chapter 14
Notifications

14.1 Notification Center

Besides the techniques we have seen so far to transfer data between different parts of an application, such as sending values from one view to another or providing a common model from which every view can get the information it needs, we can also send notifications to report changes across the application. Foundation includes the **NotificationCenter** class from which the system creates an object that serves as a Notification Center for the whole application. We send notifications (messages) to this object and then listen to those notifications from anywhere in the code. The class includes the following type property to get a reference to this object.

default—This type property returns the **NotificationCenter** object assigned to the application by default.

The Notification Center is like a bulletin board; we can post a notification and then read it from anywhere in the code. The **NotificationCenter** class defines the following methods to post and read notifications.

post(name: Name, **object:** Any?, **userInfo:** Dictionary**)**—This method posts a notification to the Notification Center. The **name** argument determines the name of the notification, the **object** argument is a reference to the object that sent the notification, and the **userInfo** argument is a dictionary with the information we want to send with the notification.

notifications(named: Name, **object:** AnyObject?**)**—This method returns a **Notifications** object with an asynchronous sequence that contains all the notifications posted to the Notification Center. The **named** argument is the name of the notification we want to read, and the **object** argument is a reference to the object that sent the notification (set to **nil** if we want to read notifications posted by any object).

Notifications are created from the **Notification** class. The **post()** method automatically creates a **Notification** object to represent the notification we want to post, but we can also do it ourselves from the **Notification** class initializer.

Notification(name: Name, **object:** Any?, **userInfo:** Dictionary**)**—This initializer creates a **Notification** object with the information defined by the arguments. The **name** argument determines the name of the notification, the **object** argument is a reference to the object that is sending the notification, and the **userInfo** argument is a dictionary with the information we want to send with the notification.

The class includes the following properties to read the values of the notification.

name—This property returns the name of the notification.

object—This property returns a reference to the object that posted the notification.

userInfo—This property returns the dictionary attached to the notification.

The name of the notification is created from a structure included in the **Notification** class called **Name**. The structure provides the following initializer to define custom names.

Name(String**)**—This initializer creates a structure that represents the notification's name. The argument is a string with the name we want to assign to the notification.

Notifications are used for multiple purposes. We can post a notification after a long process is over to tell the system that it is time to update the interface, we can communicate views with each other, or we can keep a view up-to-date by posting notifications from the model with information we receive from the Internet, to name a few. In the following example, we post a notification every time a new value is inserted by the user. For didactic purposes, we are going to use a simple interface with two views, one to allow the user to insert the title of a book and another to show the number of books already stored in the model.

Figure 14-1: *Interface to test notifications*

The model must store the values inserted by the user, as always, but also read the notifications to update the main view.

```
import SwiftUI
class ApplicationData: ObservableObject {
    @Published var total: Int = 0
    var titles: [String] = []

    init() {
        Task(priority: .background) {
            await readNotifications()
        }
    }
    func readNotifications() async {
        let center = NotificationCenter.default
        let name = Notification.Name("Update Data")

        for await _ in center.notifications(named: name, object: nil) {
            await MainActor.run {
                total = titles.count
            }
        }
    }
}
```

Listing 14-1: *Listening to notifications from the model*

This model defines a **@Published** property of type **Int** to update the view with the total number of titles inserted by the user, and a normal property called **titles** to store the values.

The Notification Center creates an asynchronous sequence with all the notifications received (see Asynchronous Sequences in Chapter 9). The sequence is managed by a **Notifications** object that we can get from the **notifications()** method. To read this sequence, we create an asynchronous **for in** loop with this object.

Because we must wait for the notifications to arrive, we mark the **for in** loop with the **await** keyword and put it inside an asynchronous method. Every time a notification is received, the loop performs a cycle, we get the total number of titles stored in the **titles** array, and assign it to the label. Notice that we call the **run()** method on the Main Actor to make sure that the statement that interacts with the label runs in the main thread.

The initial view shows the value of the **total** property on the screen and includes a button in the navigation bar to open a second view that allows the user to insert new values.

Chapter 14 - Notifications

```
struct ContentView: View {
   @EnvironmentObject var appData: ApplicationData

   var body: some View {
      NavigationStack {
         VStack {
            HStack {
               Text("Total Books:")
               Text("\(appData.total)")
                  .font(.largeTitle)
            }
            Spacer()
         }.padding()
         .navigationTitle("Books")
         .toolbar {
            ToolbarItem(placement: .navigationBarTrailing) {
               NavigationLink("Add Book", destination: {
                  AddBook()
               })
            }
         }
      }
   }
}
```

Listing 14-2: *Listening to notifications*

The values in the model are added from the **AddBook** view opened by the button in the navigation bar. The view includes a **TextField** view for the user to insert a new value and a button to save it. When the button is pressed, we store the value in the model and send a notification to let the rest of the application know that a new value is available.

```
struct AddBook: View {
   @EnvironmentObject var appData: ApplicationData
   @Environment(\.dismiss) var dismiss
   @State private var titleInput: String = ""

   var body: some View {
      VStack {
         HStack {
            Text("Title")
            TextField("Insert title", text: $titleInput)
               .textFieldStyle(.roundedBorder)
         }
         HStack {
            Spacer()
            Button("Save") {
               let title =
titleInput.trimmingCharacters(in: .whitespaces)
               if !title.isEmpty {
                  addValue(title: title)
                  dismiss()
               }
            }
         }
         Spacer()
      }.padding()
      .navigationBarTitle("Add Book")
   }
   func addValue(title: String) {
      appData.titles.append(title)

      let center = NotificationCenter.default
```

```
      let name = Notification.Name("Update Data")
      center.post(name: name, object: nil, userInfo: nil)
   }
}
```

Listing 14-3: Adding new values to the model

When a name is inserted into the `TextField` view and the Save button is pressed, we call a method to store the value and post the notification. To post the notification, we get a reference to the `NotificationCenter` object assigned to the app, define a custom name for the notification ("Update Data"), and post it with the `post()` method.

In the model, the asynchronous `for in` loop defined in the `readNotifications()` method detects that there is a new notification available, performs a new cycle, the number of titles stored in the `titles` property is assigned to the `total` property, and the initial view is updated with the new value.

 Do It Yourself: Create a Multiplatform project. Create a Swift file called ApplicationData.swift for the model in Listing 14-1. Update the `ContentView` view with the code in Listing 14-2. Create a SwiftUI View file called AddBook.swift for the code in Listing 14-3. Remember to inject the `ApplicationData` object into the environment for the app and the previews (Chapter 7, Listing 7-4). Run the application on the iPhone simulator. Press the Add Book button to go to the second scene. Insert a title and press the Save button. The view should be closed and the interface should show the total number of titles inserted so far.

The `Notification` object includes the `userInfo` property, which allows us to attach additional information to the notification. The values allowed to include in the dictionary assigned to this property are Property List values (`NSNumber`, `NSString`, `NSDate`, `NSArray`, `NSDictionary`, `NSData`, and the equivalents in Swift), but other than this, there are no more restrictions on what we can assign to this property. For instance, we could modify our previous example to pass the string inserted by the user and perform an additional task when the notifications contain a specific title. The following are the changes we need to introduce to the `addValue()` method in the `AddBook` view to attach the title to the notification.

```
func addValue(title: String) {
   appData.titles.append(title)

   let center = NotificationCenter.default
   let name = Notification.Name("Update Data")
   let info = ["type": title]
   center.post(name: name, object: nil, userInfo: info)
}
```

Listing 14-4: Adding information to the notification

The code in Listing 14-4 declares a dictionary with the "type" key and the value inserted by the user and assigns it to the `userInfo` argument of the `post()` method. Now, we can check this value from our model every time a notification is received.

```
func readNotifications() async {
   let center = NotificationCenter.default
   let name = Notification.Name("Update Data")

   for await notification in center.notifications(named: name, object:
nil) {
      if let info = notification.userInfo {
         let type = info["type"] as? String
```

```
        if type == "Miracle" {
            print("The Miracle title was inserted")
        }
    }
    await MainActor.run {
        total = titles.count
    }
    }
}
```

Listing 14-5: Reading the value in the notification

The values from the dictionary are returned as values of type **Any**, so we must cast them to the right type. In the **for in** loop of Listing 14-5, we read the value of the "type" key, cast it as a **String**, and then compare it with the string "Miracle". If the values match, we print a message on the console.

 Do It Yourself: Update the **addValue()** method in the **AddBook** view with the code in Listing 14-4, and the **readNotifications()** method in the **ApplicationData** class with the code in Listing 14-5. Run the application on the iPhone simulator. A message should be printed on the console every time you insert the title "Miracle".

If we do not want to post any more notifications, we can stop the process from the **AddBook** view, but if we want to stop processing the notifications from a receiver, we must cancel the task by calling the **cancel()** method, as we did in Chapter 9 (see Listing 9-4).

In the following example, we create a timer in the initializer of the **ApplicationData** class to cancel the task after 10 seconds, so the initial view is no longer updated with any of the values inserted by the user after the time expires.

```
init() {
    let myTask = Task(priority: .background) {
        await readNotifications()
    }
    Timer.scheduledTimer(withTimeInterval: 10, repeats: false) { timer in
        myTask.cancel()
    }
}
```

Listing 14-6: Cancelling the task

 Do It Yourself: Update the **init()** method in the **ApplicationData** class with the code in Listing 14-6. Run the application on the iPhone simulator. Press the Add Book button to insert a title. The initial view should not count any new values after 10 seconds.

(Medium) System Notifications

Besides the notifications posted by our app, the system also posts notifications to the Notification Center all the time to report changes in the interface or the device. There are dozens of notifications available. They work exactly like the custom notifications studied before but are predefined as type properties of UIKit classes. We will probably never use most of the notifications available, but some are very useful. For example, the UIKit framework defines a class called **UIWindow**, used to create the app's windows, that posts notifications to report the state of the keyboard. The following are the most frequently used.

keyboardDidShowNotification—This notification is posted after the keyboard was shown.

keyboardDidHideNotification—This notification is posted after the keyboard was hidden.

Most of the time we don't need to listen to these notifications, SwiftUI provides automatic behavior to adapt the interface to the keyboard. For instance, the following interface presents an image and a text field to allow the user to insert a caption for it. When the user taps on the text field, the keyboard opens, and the image is resized to fit the screen.

```
struct ContentView: View {
   @FocusState var focusTitle: Bool
   @State private var inputTitle: String = ""

   var body: some View {
      VStack {
         Image("spot1")
            .resizable()
            .scaledToFit()
         HStack {
            TextField("Insert Title", text: $inputTitle)
               .textFieldStyle(.roundedBorder)
               .focused($focusTitle)
            Button("Save") {
               focusTitle = false
            }
         }
         Spacer()
      }.padding()
   }
}
```

Listing 14-7: Interface to test the keyboard

The view includes a **@FocusState** property to be able to remove focus from the **TextField** view and close the keyboard. When the keyboard opens, the **Image** view adapts to the space available, and when the keyboard closes, the **Image** view expands back to its initial state.

Figure 14-2: Interface adapting to the keyboard

If we don't want the interface to adapt to the space available, we can embed it in a **ScrollView** view.

```
struct ContentView: View {
   @FocusState var focusTitle: Bool
   @State private var inputTitle: String = ""

   var body: some View {
      ScrollView {
```

```
        VStack {
            Image("spot1")
                .resizable()
                .scaledToFit()
            HStack {
                TextField("Insert Title", text: $inputTitle)
                    .textFieldStyle(.roundedBorder)
                    .focused($focusTitle)
                Button("Save") {
                    focusTitle = false
                }
            }
            Spacer()
        }.padding()
    }
}
}
```

Listing 14-8: Scrolling the interface to make room for the keyboard

The only difference from the previous example is that we have now embedded the views into a **ScrollView** view, so instead of adapting the interface, the system scrolls the views to keep the **TextField** view visible when the keyboard is opened.

Figure 14-3: The interface scrolls to adapt to the keyboard

This is the automatic behavior provided by SwiftUI, but we can still introduce modifications by listening to the keyboard notifications. For instance, when the interface is embedded in a **ScrollView** view, the **TextField** view scrolls enough to become visible, but there is no margin between this view and the keyboard (see Figure 14-3, right). If we want to improve the design, we can apply some modifiers to the views and change the styles when the state of the keyboard changes.

Although we can perform these changes from the views, it is better to do it from the model. For example, the following model listens to keyboard notifications and modifies the value of a **@Published** property to change the offset of the **ScrollView** view by -20 points when the keyboard is opened.

```
import SwiftUI

class ApplicationData: ObservableObject {
    let center = NotificationCenter.default
    @Published var scrollOffset: CGFloat = 0

    init() {
        Task(priority: .background) {
            await receiveNotificationOpen()
        }
```

```
            Task(priority: .background) {
                await receiveNotificationClose()
            }
        }
        func receiveNotificationOpen() async {
            let name = await UIWindow.keyboardDidShowNotification
            for await _ in center.notifications(named: name, object: nil) {
                await MainActor.run {
                    scrollOffset = -20
                }
            }
        }
        func receiveNotificationClose() async {
            let name = await UIWindow.keyboardDidHideNotification
            for await _ in center.notifications(named: name, object: nil) {
                await MainActor.run {
                    scrollOffset = 0
                }
            }
        }
    }
}
```

Listing 14-9: Listening to keyboard notifications

The asynchronous **for in** loop waits for new values to come in. This means that we cannot declared one loop after another because the second loop will never be executed. This is the reason why in this example we have created two tasks, one to listen to the **keyboardDidShowNotification** notification and another to listen to the **keyboardDidHideNotification** notification. When a **keyboardDidShowNotification** notification is received, we assign the value -20 to the **scrollOffset** property, and when a **keyboardDidHideNotification** notification is received, we assign the value 0.

In the view, we can use the value of the **scrollOffset** property to set the **ScrollView** view's offset.

```
struct ContentView: View {
    @EnvironmentObject var appData: ApplicationData
    @FocusState var focusTitle: Bool
    @State private var inputTitle: String = ""

    var body: some View {
        ScrollView {
            VStack {
                Image("spot1")
                    .resizable()
                    .scaledToFit()
                HStack {
                    TextField("Insert Title", text: $inputTitle)
                        .textFieldStyle(.roundedBorder)
                        .focused($focusTitle)
                    Button("Save") {
                        focusTitle = false
                    }
                }
                Spacer()
            }.padding()
        }
        .offset(CGSize(width: 0, height: appData.scrollOffset))
    }
}
```

Listing 14-10: Modifying the interface when the keyboard state changes

Chapter 14 - Notifications

The `ScrollView` view now moves up 20 points when the keyboard is opened and goes back to its original position when it is closed, generating a padding between the views and the keyboard.

 Do It Yourself: Create a Multiplatform project. Create a Swift file called ApplicationData.swift for the model in Listing 14-9. Update the `ContentView` view with the code in Listing 14-10. Download the spot1 image from our website and add it to the Asset Catalog. Remember to inject the `ApplicationData` object into the environment for the app and the previews (Chapter 7, Listing 7-4). Run the application on the iPhone simulator. Tap on the text field to activate the keyboard. You should see the interface scrolling up and a padding between the views and the keyboard.

 IMPORTANT: The names of the keyboard notifications are provided by the `UIWindow` class. The objects created from this class are used to define the interface and therefore they only work on the main thread (the Main Actor). Therefore, to read these values, we must wait with the `await` keyword to avoid a data race (see Chapter 9).

In Chapter 6, we determined the rotation of the device by detecting the Size Classes (see Listing 6-59) or by reading the values produced by the `GeometryReader` view (see Listing 6-60). Although useful, these tools do not apply to all situations. To know for certain the current orientation and detect changes, we need direct access to the device. For this purpose, the UIKit framework defines the `UIDevice` class. This class creates an object that controls the device and provides information about it, including the orientation. The class includes the following notification to report changes.

orientationDidChangeNotification—This notification is posted by the `UIDevice` object when the device's orientation changes.

For accurate detection, the device needs to activate the accelerometer. For this purpose, the `UIDevice` class defines the following methods.

beginGeneratingDeviceOrientationNotifications()—This method enables the accelerometer and begins delivering notifications to communicate changes in the orientation.

endGeneratingDeviceOrientationNotifications()—This method tells the system that the accelerometer is no longer required and stops the delivery of notifications.

And the following are the properties defined by the `UIDevice` class to access the device and return the current orientation.

current—This type property returns the instance of the `UIDevice` class that represents the device in which the app is currently running.

orientation—This property returns a value that determines the current orientation of the device. It is an enumeration of type `UIDeviceOrientation` with the values `unknown`, `portrait`, `portraitUpsideDown`, `landscapeLeft`, `landscapeRight`, `faceUp`, and `faceDown`. The enumeration also includes properties that return a Boolean value to report the main orientation: `isPortrait`, `isLandscape`, and `isFlat`.

As always, we can listen to the notification from the model and perform the necessary changes. In this cases, we have decided to include a `@Published` property to update the views when the device's orientation goes from portrait to landscape and vice versa.

```
import SwiftUI

class ApplicationData: ObservableObject {
    @Published var isLandscape: Bool = false

    init() {
        Task(priority: .background) {
            await receiveNotification()
        }
    }
    func receiveNotification() async {
        let center = NotificationCenter.default
        let name = await UIDevice.orientationDidChangeNotification
        for await _ in center.notifications(named: name, object: nil) {
            await MainActor.run {
                let device = UIDevice.current
                let orientation = device.orientation
                isLandscape = orientation.isLandscape
            }
        }
    }
}
```

Listing 14-11: Detecting changes in the orientation

When an **orientationDidChangeNotification** notification is received, we read the **current** property to get a reference to the **UIDevice** object that represents the device running the app, access the object's **orientation** property, and assign the value of the **isLandscape** property to our property with the same name. If the device is in landscape orientation, the value assigned to this property is **true**, otherwise it is **false**.

In the view, we need to read the **isLandscape** property to organize the views according to the current orientation, but also call the **UIDevice** methods to get the system to start posting notifications when the device is rotated and to stop when is not required anymore. For this purpose, we can apply the **onAppear()** and **onDisappear()** modifiers, as shown next.

```
struct ContentView: View {
    @EnvironmentObject var appData: ApplicationData

    var body: some View {
        Group {
            if !appData.isLandscape {
                VStack(spacing: 0) {
                    HeaderView(isCompact: true)
                    BodyView()
                }
            } else {
                HStack(spacing: 0) {
                    HeaderView(isCompact: false)
                    BodyView()
                }
            }
        }.ignoresSafeArea()
        .onAppear {
            let device = UIDevice.current
            device.beginGeneratingDeviceOrientationNotifications()
        }
        .onDisappear {
            let device = UIDevice.current
            device.endGeneratingDeviceOrientationNotifications()
        }
    }
}
```

```
struct HeaderView: View {
   let isCompact: Bool

   var body: some View {
      Text("Food Menu")
         .frame(minWidth: 0, maxWidth: .infinity, minHeight: 0,
maxHeight: isCompact ? 150 : .infinity)
         .background(Color.yellow)
   }
}
struct BodyView: View {
   var body: some View {
      Text("Content Title")
         .frame(minWidth: 0, maxWidth: .infinity, minHeight: 0,
maxHeight: .infinity)
         .background(Color.gray)
   }
}
```

Listing 14-12: *Adapting the interface to changes in the orientation*

This app is the same as the one created in Chapter 6 (see Listing 6-59), but instead of organizing the views according to the horizontal Size Class, we do it according to the value of the **isLandscape** property from the model. Now the position of the views always depend on the orientation of the device.

Figure 14-4: *Different interface for portrait and landscape orientations*

Do It Yourself: Update the ApplicationData.swift file with the code in Listing 14-11 and the ContentView.swift file with the code in Listing 14-12. Run the application on the iPhone simulator. Rotate the device. You should see different interfaces, as illustrated in Figure 14-4.

(Basic) **14.2 User Notifications**

Another type of notification available is the User Notification. These are notifications that the system shows to the user when the app has an event to report, such as the completion of a task or real-life events that the user wants to be reminded of. There are three different types of User Notifications: alert, badge, and sound. A badge-type notification displays a badge with a number over the app's icon, a sound-type notification plays a sound, and an alert-type notification may be displayed as a banner, an Alert View, or a message on the lock screen, depending on the current state of the device and the configuration set by the user. They can be scheduled all at once or independently. For instance, we can schedule a notification that displays an alert and plays a sound, another that displays an alert and shows a badge, or another that just plays a sound.

IMPORTANT: User Notifications are divided into Local Notifications and Remote Notifications (also known as Push Notifications). Local Notifications are notifications generated by the application running on the device, while Remote Notifications are generated by remote servers and received by the system through the network. In this chapter, we are going to study Local Notifications. For more information on Remote Notifications, visit our website and follow the links for this chapter.

Basic User Notifications Framework

User Notifications are created and managed by classes of the User Notifications framework. The framework includes the **UNUserNotificationCenter** class to create a Notification Center that we can use to schedule and manage user notifications. This is like the Notification Center studied before but specific for User Notifications. The class includes the following type method to retrieve the **UNUserNotificationCenter** object assigned to the app.

current()—This type method returns a reference to the **UNUserNotificationCenter** object assigned to the app.

From the **UNUserNotificationCenter** object, we can manage the notifications. The first step is to request authorization from the user. The class includes the following methods for this purpose.

requestAuthorization(options: UNAuthorizationOptions)—This asynchronous method requests authorization from the user to show notifications and returns a Boolean value to report the result. The **options** argument is a set of properties that determine the type of notifications we want to show. The properties available are **badge**, **sound**, **alert**, **carPlay**, **criticalAlert**, **provisional**, and **announcement**.

notificationSettings()—This asynchronous method returns a **UNNotification-Settings** object with the current settings. The most useful property is **authorizationStatus**, which returns an enumeration value with the authorization status. (The user may change the status of the authorization anytime from the Settings app.) The possible values are **notDetermined**, **denied**, **authorized**, **provisional**, and **ephemeral**.

For the notifications to be sent, they must be added to the User Notification Center. The **UNUserNotificationCenter** class includes the following methods to add and remove them.

add(UNNotificationRequest)—This asynchronous method schedules a new notification in the User Notification Center. The argument is the request for the notification.

removePendingNotificationRequests(withIdentifiers: [String])—This method removes the pending notifications with the identifiers specified by the argument.

The framework includes the **UNMutableNotificationContent** class to store the content of a notification. The following are the properties included in this class to set the values.

title—This property sets or returns the notification's title.

subtitle—This property sets or returns the notification's subtitle.

body—This property sets or returns the notification's message.

badge—This property sets or returns a number to show over the app's icon.

sound—This property sets or returns the sound we want to play when the notification is delivered to the user. It is an object of type **UNNotificationSound**.

userInfo—This property sets or returns a dictionary with the information we want to send with the notification.

These properties define the information the notification is going to show to the user. Some of these properties store strings, except for the **badge** property which takes an **NSNumber** object, and the **sound** property which takes an object of the **UNNotificationSound** class. This class includes the following initializer and property to get the object.

UNNotificationSound(named: UNNotificationSoundName)—This initializer creates a **UNNotificationSound** object with the sound specified by the argument.

default—This type property returns a **UNNotificationSound** object with the sound defined by the system.

The names of the sounds are defined by a structure of type **UNNotificationSoundName**. The structure includes the following initializer.

UNNotificationSoundName(rawValue: String)—This initializer creates a **UNNotificationSoundName** object with the name of the file that contains the sound we want to play with the notification.

The **UNMutableNotificationContent** class also allows us to set the level of interruption. By default, notifications are **active**, which means they are going to turn on the screen and play sound, but they can also be set to **passive** (they do not turn the screen on), **timeSensitive** (they are displayed immediately, but considering user settings), and **critical** (they bypass user settings). The class includes the following property to define the interruption level.

interruptionLevel—This property sets or returns a value that determines the importance and delivery timing of the notification. It is a **UNNotification-InterruptionLevel** enumeration with the values **active** (default), **critical**, **passive**, and **timeSensitive**.

User Notifications are posted to the User Notification Center and then presented by the system when a certain condition is met. These conditions are established by objects called *Triggers*. There are three types of triggers available for Local Notifications: Time Interval, (the notification is delivered after a certain period of time), Calendar (the notification is delivered on a specific date), and Location (the notification is delivered in a specific location). The framework defines three classes to create these triggers: **UNTimeIntervalNotificationTrigger**, **UNCalendarNotificationTrigger**, and **UNLocationNotificationTrigger**.

UNTimeIntervalNotificationTrigger(timeInterval: TimeInterval, **repeats:** Bool)—This initializer creates a Time Interval trigger that will deliver the notification after the period of time determined by the **timeInterval** argument (in seconds). The **repeats** argument determines if the notification will be delivered once or infinite times.

UNCalendarNotificationTrigger(dateMatching: DateComponents, **repeats:** Bool)—This initializer creates a Calendar trigger that delivers the notification at the date determined by the **dateMatching** argument. The **repeats** argument determines if the notification will be delivered once or infinite times.

UNLocationNotificationTrigger(region: CLCircularRegion, **repeats:** Bool)— This initializer creates a Location trigger that delivers the notification when the device is inside a region in the real world determined by the **region** argument. The **repeats** argument determines if the notification will be delivered once or infinite times.

To deliver a notification, we must create a request that contains the notification, an identifier, and a trigger. For this purpose, the framework defines the **UNNotificationRequest** class.

UNNotificationRequest(identifier: String, **content:** UNNotificationContent, **trigger:** UNNotificationTrigger?**)**—This initializer creates a request to deliver the notification specified by the **content** argument and at the time or place specified by the **trigger** argument. The **identifier** argument is a string that we can use later to identify and manage the request.

As we already mentioned, before sending user notifications we must ask the user for permission. Apple recommends doing it only when we really need it. For instance, if our application contains a view with a switch for the user to activate notifications or a button to send them, we should ask permission in this view and not right after the app is launched. The following example illustrates how to do it.

```
import SwiftUI
import UserNotifications

struct ContentView: View {
    @State private var inputMessage: String = ""
    @State private var isButtonDisabled: Bool = false

    var body: some View {
        VStack(spacing: 12) {
            HStack {
                Text("Message:")
                TextField("Insert Message", text: $inputMessage)
                    .textFieldStyle(.roundedBorder)
            }
            HStack {
                Spacer()
                Button("Post Notification") {
                    let message =
inputMessage.trimmingCharacters(in: .whitespaces)
                    if !message.isEmpty {
                        Task(priority: .background) {
                            let center = UNUserNotificationCenter.current()
                            let authorization = await
center.notificationSettings()
                            if authorization.authorizationStatus == .authorized {
                                await sendNotification()
                            }
                        }
                    }
                }.disabled(isButtonDisabled)
            }
            Spacer()
        }.padding()
        .task(priority: .background) {
            do {
                let center = UNUserNotificationCenter.current()
                let authorized = try await
center.requestAuthorization(options: [.alert, .sound])
                await MainActor.run {
                    isButtonDisabled = !authorized
                }
            } catch {
                print("Error: \(error)")
            }
        }
    }
}
```

Listing 14-13: Asking permission to send notifications

This view provides a `TextField` view for the user to insert a message to send with the notification and a button to post it. But before even enabling the button, we must ask for permission with the `requestAuthorization()` method. The task is initiated by the `task()` modifier when the view is loaded. In the closure assigned to this modifier, we get a reference to the `UNUserNotificationCenter` object assigned to our app, ask the user to authorize the app to post notifications of type `alert` and `sound`, and then enable or disable the button on the interface according to the value returned. (Notice that before the value is assigned to the `isButtonDisabled` property, it is inverted with the ! symbol.)

When the `requestAuthorization()` method is called, it creates an Alert View with a message and two buttons to let the user decide what to do, as shown below.

Figure 14-5: *Authorization to deliver notifications*

When the use presses the button to post a notification, we initiate another asynchronous task, this time to check whether the app is still allowed to post notifications. For this purpose, the `UNUserNotificationCenter` class includes the `notificationSettings()` method. We should always consult this method before sending notifications to make sure that the app is still authorized to do it. If the value of the `authorizationStatus` property is equal to `authorized`, it means that we can proceed. The `add()` method used to send a notification is also asynchronous, so after the authorization is confirmed, we call our own asynchronous method to send the notification.

```
func sendNotification() async {
    let content = UNMutableNotificationContent()
    content.title = "Reminder"
    content.body = inputMessage

    let trigger = UNTimeIntervalNotificationTrigger(timeInterval: 30,
repeats: false)
    let id = "reminder-\(UUID())"
    let request = UNNotificationRequest(identifier: id, content: content,
trigger: trigger)

    do {
        let center = UNUserNotificationCenter.current()
        try await center.add(request)
        await MainActor.run {
            inputMessage = ""
        }
    } catch {
        print("Error: \(error)")
    }
}
```

Listing 14-14: *Scheduling a notification*

The process to schedule a notification is simple. We must create an instance of the **UNMutableNotificationContent** class with the values we want the notification to show to the user, create a trigger (in this case we use a Time Interval trigger), create an instance of the **UNNotificationRequest** class with these values to request the delivery of the notification, and finally add the request to the User Notification Center with the **add()** method. Notice that the request identifier must be unique. In our example, we define it with a string that includes the word "reminder" followed by a random value generated by the **UUID()** function.

Figure 14-6: Notification

 Do It Yourself: Create a Multiplatform project. Update the ContentView.swift file with the code in Listing 14-13. Add the method in Listing 14-14 at the end of the **ContentView** structure. The first time you run the application the system will ask you to allow the app to deliver notifications. Press the Allow button. Type a message and press the Post Notification button to post the notification. Press the Home button to close the app. You should see the notification popping up on the screen after 30 seconds.

Notifications can also play a sound. All we need to do is to add the sound file to the project, create the **UNNotificationSound** object with it, and assign it to the **sound** property.

```
func sendNotification() async {
    let content = UNMutableNotificationContent()
    content.title = "Reminder"
    content.body = inputMessage
    content.sound = UNNotificationSound(named:
UNNotificationSoundName(rawValue: "alarm.mp3"))

    let trigger = UNTimeIntervalNotificationTrigger(timeInterval: 30,
repeats: false)
    let id = "reminder-\(UUID())"
    let request = UNNotificationRequest(identifier: id, content: content,
trigger: trigger)

    do {
        let center = UNUserNotificationCenter.current()
        try await center.add(request)
        await MainActor.run {
            inputMessage = ""
        }
    } catch {
        print("Error: \(error)")
    }
}
```

Listing 14-15: Playing a sound

Chapter 14 - Notifications

Do It Yourself: Update the `sendNotification()` method with the code in Listing 14-15. Download the alarm.mp3 file from our website and drag it to your project. Run the application on the iPhone simulator. Insert a message and press the button to post the notification. Go to the Home screen. After 30 seconds, you should see the notification and hear the sound of an alarm.

Basic Media Attachments

In addition to sound, notifications can also include other types of media, such as images and videos. The **UNMutableNotificationContent** class includes the following property to attach media files to the notification.

attachments—This property sets or returns an array of **UNNotificationAttachment** objects with the media files we want to show in the notification.

The attachments are loaded by an object of the **UNNotificationAttachment** class. The class includes the following initializer.

UNNotificationAttachment(identifier: String, **url:** URL, **options:** Dictionary?)—This initializer creates an attachment with the media loaded from the URL specified by the **url** argument. The **identifier** argument is the attachment's unique identifier. And the **options** argument is a dictionary with predefined values to configure the media. The most useful are **UNNotificationAttachmentOptionsThumbnail-ClippingRectKey** to use only a portion of an image, and **UNNotification-AttachmentOptionsThumbnailTimeKey** to select a frame from a video.

To attach an image or a video to the notification, we must create the **UNNotification-Attachment** object and assign it to the content's **attachments** property. This object takes a unique identifier, that we can create as we always do, and the URL of the file that contains the media we want to add to the notification. This means that we need the media in a file or to create the file ourselves. The following example illustrates how to take an image from the Asset Catalog, store it in a file, and assign it to the notification.

```
func sendNotification() async {
   let content = UNMutableNotificationContent()
   content.title = "Reminder"
   content.body = inputMessage

   let idImage = "attach-\(UUID())"
   if let urlImage = await getThumbnail(id: idImage) {
      if let attachment = try? UNNotificationAttachment(identifier:
idImage, url: urlImage, options: nil) {
         content.attachments = [attachment]
      }
   }
   let trigger = UNTimeIntervalNotificationTrigger(timeInterval: 10,
repeats: false)

   let id = "reminder-\(UUID())"
   let request = UNNotificationRequest(identifier: id, content: content,
trigger: trigger)
   do {
      let center = UNUserNotificationCenter.current()
      try await center.add(request)
      await MainActor.run {
         inputMessage = ""
      }
   } catch {
```

```
        print("Error: \(error)")
    }
}
func getThumbnail(id: String) async -> URL? {
    let manager = FileManager.default
    if let docURL = manager.urls(for: .documentDirectory,
in: .userDomainMask).first {
        let fileURL = docURL.appendingPathComponent("\(id).png")
        if let image = UIImage(named: "husky") {
            if let thumbnail = await image.byPreparingThumbnail(ofSize:
CGSize(width: 100, height: 100)) {
                if let imageData = thumbnail.pngData() {
                    if let _ = try? imageData.write(to: fileURL) {
                        return fileURL
                    }
                }
            }
        }
    }
    return nil
}
```

Listing 14-16: Attaching an image to a notification

Because we need to load, process, and save the image in a file, we moved the code to a new method called **getThumbnail()**. In this method, we get the URL of the Documents directory, append the name of the file, then load the image from the Asset Catalog, convert it to data, reduce the size with the **byPreparingThumbnail()** method, and store it (see Chapter 10, Listing 10-21). The file's URL is returned by the method and used by the code to attach the image to the notification. The result is shown below. The image is displayed inside the banner and expanded when the user taps and holds the finger over the notification (or drags the notification down, depending on the state of the application).

Figure 14-7: Media Attachment

Do It Yourself: Update the **sendNotification()** method with the code in Listing 14-16 and add the **getThumbnail()** method below. Download the husky image from our website and add it to the Asset Catalog. Run the application on the iPhone simulator. Insert a message and press the button to post the notification. Go to the Home screen. You should see a notification with the picture of the husky, as in Figure 14-7.

Basic Provisional Notifications

Asking the user for permission can be a bit disruptive for some applications. If we consider that due to the characteristics of our app the user's acceptance to receive notifications may be implicit, we can post provisional notifications. These are called quiet notifications and only show up in the Notification Center (they are not displayed in the Locked or Home screens). They include buttons for the user to decide whether to keep them or turn them off.

To get our app to post provisional notifications, all we need to do is to add the **provisional** option to the **requestAuthorization()** method, as shown next.

```
.task(priority: .background) {
   do {
      let center = UNUserNotificationCenter.current()
      let authorized = try await center.requestAuthorization(options:
[.alert, .sound, .provisional])
      await MainActor.run {
         isButtonDisabled = !authorized
      }
   } catch {
      print("Error: \(error)")
   }
}
```

Listing 14-17: *Scheduling provisional notifications*

If we use provisional notifications, the user is not prompted for authorization. The app is automatically authorized to post notifications, but the status is set as **provisional** instead of **authorized**, so we must consider this condition when we check the status.

```
Button("Post Notification") {
   let message = inputMessage.trimmingCharacters(in: .whitespaces)
   if !message.isEmpty {
      Task(priority: .background) {
         let center = UNUserNotificationCenter.current()
         let authorization = await center.notificationSettings()
         let status = authorization.authorizationStatus
         if status == .authorized || status == .provisional {
            await sendNotification()
         }
      }
   }
}.disabled(isButtonDisabled)
```

Listing 14-18: *Checking the status of a provisional authorization*

Because provisional notifications are only shown on the Notification Center, the user must open the Notification Center to see them and press the Manage button to decide whether to keep them or turn them off.

Figure 14-8: *Provisional notifications in the Notification Center*

Do It Yourself: Update the `task()` modifier in the `ContentView` view with the code in Listing 14-17 and replace the `Button` view with the view in Listing 14-18. Uninstall the app and run it again from Xcode. Post a notification. Go to the Home screen and drag your finger from the bottom to open the Notification Center. You should see the provisional notification, as shown in Figure 14-8.

Basic Notifications Delegate

If the user is working with the app when a notification is delivered, the notification is not displayed on the screen, but we can assign a delegate to the User Notification Center to change this behavior. For this purpose, the framework defines the `UNUserNotificationCenter-Delegate` protocol, which allows us to do two things: we can decide whether to show the notification when the app is running, and also respond to actions performed by the user. For this purpose, the protocol defines the following methods.

userNotificationCenter(UNUserNotificationCenter, **willPresent:** UN-Notification)—This asynchronous method is called by the User Notification Center on the delegate when the application is active and a notification has to be delivered. The method must return a structure of type `UNNotificationPresentationOptions` to indicate how we want to alert the user. The structure includes the type properties **badge**, **banner**, **list**, and **sound**.

userNotificationCenter(UNUserNotificationCenter, **didReceive:** UN-NotificationResponse)—This method is called by the User Notification Center when the user interacts with the notification (performs an action). The **didReceive** argument is an object with information about the notification and the action performed.

When a notification is triggered and the app is being executed, the User Notification Center calls the `userNotificationCenter(UNUserNotificationCenter, willPresent:)` method on its delegate to ask the application what to do. In this method, we can perform any task we want and then return a `UNNotificationPresentationOptions` value to specify the type of notification we want to show.

As always, we can declare any object as the delegate, but it is recommended to use the model. In the following example, we make the model conform the `UNUserNotification-CenterDelegate` protocol, assign it as the delegate of the `UNUserNotificationCenter` object, and implement the `userNotificationCenter(UNUserNotificationCenter, willPresent:)` method to show the notification in a banner while the app is running.

```
import SwiftUI
import UserNotifications
class ApplicationData: NSObject, ObservableObject,
UNUserNotificationCenterDelegate {
   override init() {
      super.init()
      let center = UNUserNotificationCenter.current()
      center.delegate = self
   }
   func userNotificationCenter(_ center: UNUserNotificationCenter,
willPresent notification: UNNotification) async ->
UNNotificationPresentationOptions {
      return [.banner]
   }
}
```

Listing 14-19: Showing notifications while the app is running

As other protocols implemented before, the `UNUserNotificationCenterDelegate` protocol needs the class to inherit from the `NSObject` class (see Chapter 13, Listing 13-11). For the protocol methods to be called, we need to inject an instance of the `ApplicationData` class into the environment, as we did in previous examples, so the object is initialized and assigned as the delegate of the `UNUserNotificationCenter` object.

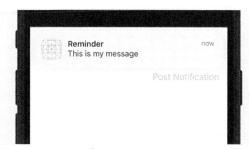

Figure 14-9: *Notifications in an active application*

 Do It Yourself: Create a Swift file called ApplicationData.swift for the model in Listing 14-19. Remember to inject the `ApplicationData` object into the environment for the app (Chapter 7, Listing 7-4). Remove all the changes introduced in the previous section to create provisional notifications or implement the `ContentView` view and the method defined in Listings 14-13 and 14-14. Uninstall the app from the simulator or the device. Run the application again, press the Allow button, and post a notification. After a few seconds, the notification should appear over the app at the top of the screen, as shown in Figure 14-9.

(Basic) Groups

The system automatically groups notifications together by app. For instance, if our application sends multiple notifications to the Notification Center, they will all be grouped together with the last one at the top. This is the automatic behavior, but we can separate them in custom groups using identifiers. The `UNMutableNotificationContent` class includes the following property for this purpose.

threadIdentifier—This property sets or returns a string used to identify each group of notifications.

All the notifications with the same identifier will be grouped together. The following example posts multiple notifications and separates them in two groups called Group One and Group Two.

```
func sendNotification() async {
   let listGroups = ["Group One", "Group Two"]

   for group in listGroups {
      for index in 1...3 {
         let content = UNMutableNotificationContent()
         content.title = "Reminder \(group)"
         content.body = "\(index) - \(inputMessage)"
         content.threadIdentifier = group

         let trigger = UNTimeIntervalNotificationTrigger(timeInterval:
10, repeats: false)

         let id = "reminder-\(UUID())"
         let request = UNNotificationRequest(identifier: id, content:
content, trigger: trigger)
```

```
        do {
            let center = UNUserNotificationCenter.current()
            try await center.add(request)
        } catch {
            print("Error: \(error)")
        }
    }
}
await MainActor.run {
    inputMessage = ""
}
}
```

Listing 14-20: Organizing notifications into groups

For didactic purposes, we defined one array with the name of the groups ("Group One" and "Group Two") and a **for in** loop to post three notifications per group (**1...3**). To be able to identify the notifications and the groups, we include these values in the **title** and **body** of the **UNMutableNotificationContent** object, and to tell the system to which group each notification belongs, we assign the name of the group to the **threadIdentifier** property. In total, we post six notifications in two groups, as shown below.

Figure 14-10: Notifications in two groups

 Do It Yourself: Update the **sendNotification()** method with the code in Listing 14-20. Run the application. Post a notification. Go to the Lock screen. After 10 seconds you should see all the notifications organized in two groups.

(Basic) **Summary**

Users can create notification summaries to get a single alert at a specific time in the day with all the notifications grouped together. A summary can include notifications from one or multiple apps. The tool that allows users to create a summary is available in the Notifications option of the Settings app.

Figure 14-11: Summary option in Settings app

To configure the summary from our application, we must create a category and add that category to the User Notification Center. Categories are objects that define actions and behavior associated to a notification or a group of notifications. The framework offers the **UNNotificationCategory** class to create these objects. The following is the initializer used to configure a summary.

UNNotificationCategory(identifier: String, **actions:** [UNNotificationAction], **intentIdentifiers:** [String], **hiddenPreviewsBodyPlaceholder:** String?, **categorySummaryFormat:** String?, **options:** UNNotificationCategory-Options)—This initializer creates a category to configure a summary. The **identifier** argument is a string that identifies the category, the **actions** argument defines the actions available for the summary, the **intentIdentifiers** argument is an array of strings used to guide Siri to produce a better response, the **hiddenPreviewsBodyPlaceholder** argument is the string to show instead of the notifications when the previews are disabled, the **categorySummaryFormat** argument is the string that describes the summary, and the **options** argument is an array of properties that determine how the notifications associated to the category are going to be handled. The properties available are **custom-DismissAction** (processes the dismiss action) and **allowInCarPlay** (allows car play to show notifications).

The **UNUserNotificationCenter** class includes the following method to register a category in the User Notification Center.

setNotificationCategories(Set**)**—This method configures the User Notification Center to work with the type of notifications and actions we want to support. The argument is the set of categories we want to associate to the notifications center.

When the notifications appeared in a summary, they are sorted according to their relevance. The system determines this relevance for us, but we can suggest a specific order by setting the notification's relevance ourselves. The **UNMutableNotificationContent** class includes the following property for this purpose.

relevanceScore—This property sets or returns a value of type **Double** between 0 and 1 to tell the system how to sort the app's notifications. The notification with the highest relevance gets featured in the notification summary.

The following are the modifications we need to introduce to the **sendNotification()** method to include the notifications in a summary.

```
func sendNotification() async {
   let center = UNUserNotificationCenter.current()
   let groupID = "Group One"
   let totalMessages = 3

   let summaryFormat = "\(totalMessages) messages"
   let category = UNNotificationCategory(identifier: groupID, actions:
[], intentIdentifiers: [], hiddenPreviewsBodyPlaceholder: nil,
categorySummaryFormat: summaryFormat, options: [])
   center.setNotificationCategories([category])

   for index in 1...totalMessages {
      let content = UNMutableNotificationContent()
      content.title = "Reminder"
      content.body = "\(index) - \(inputMessage)"
      content.threadIdentifier = groupID

      let trigger = UNTimeIntervalNotificationTrigger(timeInterval: 10,
repeats: false)
      let id = "reminder-\(UUID())"
```

```
      let request = UNNotificationRequest(identifier: id, content:
content, trigger: trigger)
      do {
         try await center.add(request)
      } catch {
         print("Error: \(error)")
      }
   }
   await MainActor.run {
      inputMessage = ""
   }
}
```

Listing 14-21: *Configuring a summary of notifications*

In this example, we create one group with three notifications. To include the notifications in the summary, we create a category with a summary message that includes the number of notifications included in the summary. The rest of the process is the same as before.

If we just run the application, the notifications are displayed as before, but we can go to the Settings app and set a summary for the app, as shown in Figure 14-11. Below is what the summary created by our app looks like when it is shown to the user.

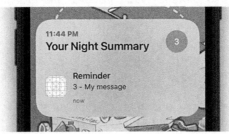

Figure 14-12: *Notifications summary in the Lock screen*

Do It Yourself: Update the `sendNotification()` method with the code in Listing 14-21. Press the Home button, open the Settings app, and set a summary for the application, as shown in Figure 14-11. (Remember to go to the list at the bottom and select the app to include it in the summary.) Run the application and post a notification. You should see a summary in the Lock screen with all the notifications at the time specified in Settings (Figure 14-12).

(Basic) Actions

Notifications can show custom actions in the form of buttons and input fields that the user can interact with to provide feedback without having to open our app. The actions are defined by two classes: **UNNotificationAction** and **UNTextInputNotificationAction**.

UNNotificationAction(identifier: String, **title:** String, **options:** UN-NotificationActionOptions)—This initializer creates an action represented by a custom button. The **identifier** argument is a string that we can use to identify the action, the **title** argument is the text shown on the button, and the **options** argument is a set of properties that determine how the action should be performed. The properties available are **authenticationRequired** (the user is required to unlock the device), **destructive** (the button is highlighted), and **foreground** (the app is opened to perform the action).

UNTextInputNotificationAction(identifier: String, **title:** String, **options:** UNNotificationActionOptions, **textInputButtonTitle:** String, **textInputPlace-**

holder: String)—This initializer creates an action represented by a custom button that when pressed prompts the system to display an input field. In addition to the arguments included by a normal action, these types of actions also include the **textInputButtonTitle** and **textInputPlaceholder** arguments to define the button and the placeholder for the input field.

After the actions are defined, we must create a category to group them together. The **UNNotificationCategory** class includes the following initializer to add actions to a notification.

UNNotificationCategory(identifier: String, **actions:** [UNNotificationAction], **intentIdentifiers:** [String], **options:** UNNotificationCategoryOptions)—This initializer creates a category with the actions specified by the **actions** argument. The **identifier** argument is a string that identifies the category, the **intentIdentifiers** argument is an array of strings used to guide Siri to produce a better response, and the **options** argument is an array of properties that determine how the notifications associated to the category are going to be handled. The properties available are **customDismissAction** (processes the dismiss action) and **allowInCarPlay** (allows car play to show notifications).

When an action is performed, the User Notification Center calls the **userNotification-Center(UNUserNotificationCenter, didReceive:)** method on its delegate. The method receives a **UNNotificationResponse** object with information about the action and the notification. The class includes the following properties to read the values.

actionIdentifier—This property sets or returns a string with the action's identifier.

notification—This property sets or returns a **UNNotification** object representing the notification. The object includes the **date** property to get the date the notification was delivered and the **request** property with a reference to the **UNNotificationRequest** object used to schedule the notification, which in turn offers the **content** property to access the values of the notification.

As an example, we are going to add an action that shows a Delete button when the notification is opened. The following are the modifications we must introduce to the **sendNotification()** method for this purpose.

```
func sendNotification() async {
   let center = UNUserNotificationCenter.current()
   let groupID = "listActions"
   let actionDelete = UNNotificationAction(identifier: "deleteButton",
title: "Delete", options: .destructive)
   let category = UNNotificationCategory(identifier: groupID, actions:
[actionDelete], intentIdentifiers: [], options: [])
   center.setNotificationCategories([category])

   let content = UNMutableNotificationContent()
   content.title = "Reminder"
   content.body = inputMessage
   content.categoryIdentifier = groupID

   let trigger = UNTimeIntervalNotificationTrigger(timeInterval: 10,
repeats: false)
   let id = "reminder-\(UUID())"
   let request = UNNotificationRequest(identifier: id, content: content,
trigger: trigger)
   do {
      try await center.add(request)
      await MainActor.run {
```

```
        inputMessage = ""
      }
   } catch {
      print("Error: \(error)")
   }
}
```

Listing 14-22: Adding an action to a notification

The method defines a **UNNotificationAction** object to create the Delete button, and then a category using this button and the "listActions" identifier. Categories must be added to the User Notification Center with the **setNotificationCategories()** method and then assigned to the notification's **categoryIdentifier** property, as we have done previously.

To respond to the user, we must implement the protocol method on the delegate, as we did in the example of Listing 14-19. Again, we are using our model for this purpose.

```
import SwiftUI
import UserNotifications

class ApplicationData: NSObject, ObservableObject,
UNUserNotificationCenterDelegate {
   override init() {
      super.init()
      let center = UNUserNotificationCenter.current()
      center.delegate = self
   }
   @MainActor
   func userNotificationCenter(_ center: UNUserNotificationCenter,
didReceive response: UNNotificationResponse) async {
      let identifier = response.actionIdentifier
      if identifier == "deleteButton" {
         print("Delete Message")
      }
   }
}
```

Listing 14-23: Processing actions for notifications

Actions are displayed when the user taps and holds the finger over the notification (or drags it down, depending on the current state of the application). In this case, the notification shows a Delete button. If the user presses this button, the User Notification Center calls the delegate method to give our application the chance to perform a task. In our example, we read the **actionIdentifier** property, compare it with the string "deleteButton" to confirm that the user pressed the Delete button, and then print a message on the console in case of success.

Figure 14-13: Actions in a notification

 Do It Yourself: Update the **sendNotification()** method with the code in Listing 14-22 and the ApplicationData.swift file with the code in Listing 14-23. Remember to inject the **ApplicationData** object into the environment

(Chapter 7, Listing 7-4). Run the application, post a notification, and go to the Home screen. Tap and hold the finger on the notification to reveal the Delete button (Figure 14-13). Press the button. You should see a message printed on the console.

 IMPORTANT: After the statements in the `userNotificationCenter(UN-UserNotificationCenter, didReceive:)` method are processed, the system executes a closure in the background to finish the operation. Because the method is asynchronous and the closure must be executed in the main thread (the Main Actor), we must mark the method with the `@MainActor` attribute, as we did in Listing 14-23.

In the last example, we implemented a simple action that shows a button when the notification is expanded, but we can also include an action that shows an input field, so the user can provide feedback right from the screen where the notification is being displayed. The following are the changes we need to introduce to the `sendNotification()` method to add an action of this type.

```
func sendNotification() async {
   let center = UNUserNotificationCenter.current()
   let groupID = "listActions"
   let actionDelete = UNNotificationAction(identifier: "deleteButton",
title: "Delete", options: .destructive)
   let actionInput = UNTextInputNotificationAction(identifier:
"inputField", title: "Message", options: [])

   let category = UNNotificationCategory(identifier: groupID, actions:
[actionDelete, actionInput], intentIdentifiers: [], options: [])
   center.setNotificationCategories([category])

   let content = UNMutableNotificationContent()
   content.title = "Reminder"
   content.body = inputMessage
   content.categoryIdentifier = groupID

   let trigger = UNTimeIntervalNotificationTrigger(timeInterval: 10,
repeats: false)
   let id = "reminder-\(UUID())"
   let request = UNNotificationRequest(identifier: id, content: content,
trigger: trigger)
   do {
      try await center.add(request)
      await MainActor.run {
         inputMessage = ""
      }
   } catch {
      print("Error: \(error)")
   }
}
```

Listing 14-24: Adding an input action to a notification

And the following are the modifications we need to introduce to the delegate method to process this new action.

```
import SwiftUI

class ApplicationData: NSObject, ObservableObject,
UNUserNotificationCenterDelegate {
   override init() {
      super.init()
      let center = UNUserNotificationCenter.current()
```

```
      center.delegate = self
   }
   @MainActor
   func userNotificationCenter(_ center: UNUserNotificationCenter,
didReceive response: UNNotificationResponse) async {
      let identifier = response.actionIdentifier
      if identifier == "deleteButton" {
         print("Delete Message")
      } else if identifier == "inputField" {
         print("Send: \((response as!
UNTextInputNotificationResponse).userText)")
      }
   }
}
```

Listing 14-25: Processing the user's feedback

The text inserted by the user in the text field is sent to the delegate method. The framework offers a special class to represent the response called **UNTextInputNotificationResponse**. To access the value inserted by the user, we must cast the response object to this class and then read its **userText** property, as we did in Listing 14-25. The result is shown below.

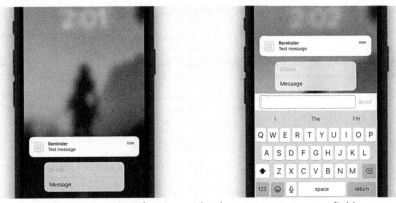

Figure 14-14: Notification with a button to open a text field

 Do It Yourself: Update the **sendNotification()** method with the code in Listing 14-24 and the ApplicationData.swift file with the code in Listing 14-25. Run the application, send a notification, and go to the Home screen. Expand the notification to see the actions. Click the Message button, insert a value, and press the Send button. You should see the same text printed on the console.

(Basic) 14.3 App States

An application can be in three different states: active, inactive, or in the background. The app is active when it is visible and the user can interact with it, inactive when it is visible but not in focus, and in the background when it is still open but not visible anymore. The states are reported by an environment property called **scenePhase**. This property returns an enumeration value of type **ScenePhase**. The values available are **active**, **inactive**, and **background**. To detect the changes in the app's state, we can use the **onChange()** modifier, as shown next.

```
import SwiftUI

@main
struct TestApp: App {
   @Environment(\.scenePhase) var scenePhase
```

```
var body: some Scene {
    WindowGroup {
        ContentView()
            .onChange(of: scenePhase) { phase in
                if phase == .active {
                    print("The app is active")
                } else if phase == .background {
                    print("The app is in the background")
                }
            }
    }
}
```

Listing 14-26: Detecting changes in the app's state

It is recommended to respond to changes in the state of the app from the **App** structure. In this example, we compare the value returned by the **scenePhase** property with the values **active** and **background**, so we can print a message on the console when the state changes between those two. If the app becomes active, the message "The app is active" is printed on the console, and when the app moves to the background, the message "The app is in the background" is printed instead.

 Do It Yourself: Create a Multiplatform project. Update the **App** structure with the code in Listing 14-26. Run the application on the iPhone simulator. You should see the message "The app is active" when the **ContentView** view appears on the screen. Press the Home button to close the app. This time, you should see the message "The app is in the background" on the console.

(Medium) App Delegates

Controlling the app state with the values returned by the **scenePhase** property is more than enough for most situations, but some old frameworks still depend on delegate objects assigned to the application. To control the states of the application and report changes, the UIKit framework defines the **UIApplication** class.

When the user taps on the icon to run the app, the system creates an object of type **UIApplication**. This object starts a loop to keep the application running, checks for events, and report changes in the state of the app. The class includes the following type property to access the object.

shared—This type property returns the instance of the **UIApplication** class assigned to our app.

From this object, we can check the state of the app. The class includes the following property for this purpose.

applicationState—This property returns the app's current state. It is an enumeration of type **State** with the values **active**, **inactive**, and **background**.

We can read this property to get the current state of the app, as we did with the **scenePhase** property before, but some frameworks need more information. For this purpose, the **UIApplication** object can also report changes by calling methods in a delegate object. The UIKit framework includes the **UIApplicationDelegate** protocol to define this delegate. The following are some of the methods included in the protocol.

application(UIApplication, didFinishLaunchingWithOptions: Dictionary)— This is the first method called by the **UIApplication** object. It is called to let us know that all the necessary objects have been instantiated, and the app is ready to work.

application(UIApplication, **configurationForConnecting:** UISceneSession, **options:** UIScene.ConnectionOptions)—This method is called when a new Scene (window) is requested by the system or the user. The method must return a `UISceneConfiguration` object with the Scene's configuration.

application(UIApplication, **didDiscardSceneSessions:** Set)—This method is called when the user discards a Scene (closes a window). The **didDiscardSceneSessions** argument is a set with references to the `UISceneSession` objects representing the Scenes' sessions.

The most useful method defined by the `UIApplicationDelegate` protocol is `application(UIApplication, didFinishLaunchingWithOptions:)`. This method is called when the application is launched and therefore it is usually implemented to initialize values in the model or prepare resources the app needs to work. The following example shows how to implement this method and how to associate the app delegate with our SwiftUI app. The first step is to create a custom class that conforms to the `UIApplicationDelegate` protocol.

```
import UIKit
class CustomAppDelegate: NSObject, UIApplicationDelegate {
   func application(_ application: UIApplication,
didFinishLaunchingWithOptions launchOptions:
[UIApplication.LaunchOptionsKey : Any]? = nil) -> Bool {
      print("App has launched")
      return true
   }
}
```

Listing 14-27: Defining a custom app delegate

Now that we have the delegate class and implemented a protocol method, we must connect our SwiftUI app with it, so the method is called. For this purpose, the SwiftUI framework includes the `@UIApplicationDelegateAdaptor` property wrapper. This property wrapper is created from the `UIApplicationDelegateAdaptor` structure, which includes the following initializer.

UIApplicationDelegateAdaptor(DelegateType.Type)—This initializer creates an instance of the `UIApplicationDelegateAdaptor` structure associated with the class specified by the argument.

The `@UIApplicationDelegateAdaptor` property wrapper creates an instance of the class specified by the argument and assigns it as the app's delegate, so when the app state changes, the methods on this object are called.

```
import SwiftUI

@main
struct TestApp: App {
   @UIApplicationDelegateAdaptor(CustomAppDelegate.self) var appDelegate

   var body: some Scene {
      WindowGroup {
         ContentView()
      }
   }
}
```

Listing 14-28: Assigning the app delegate from a SwiftUI application

Chapter 14 - Notifications

Do It Yourself: Create a Swift file called CustomAppDelegate.swift file for the class in Listing 14-27 and update the **App** structure with the code in Listing 14-28. Run the application on the iPhone simulator. You should see the message "App has launched" on the console.

In some devices, multiple instances of the same application can run at the same time. For example, we may have two instances of the Text Editor on the screen processing two different documents, or two instances of a browser loading two different websites. To control these instances, the UIKit framework defines Scenes.

Some devices, such as iPhones and iPods Touch, can only work with one Scene at a time (one window), but iPads and Mac computers can work with multiple Scenes (multiple windows). These Scenes are managed by the **UIApplication** object. The class includes the following properties to access them.

connectedScenes—This property returns a set with references to the Scenes that are currently connected to the application.

supportsMultipleScenes—This property returns a Boolean value to indicate if the application supports multiple Scenes (multiple instances of the app).

To report the state of a Scene, the **UIApplication** object calls methods on the Scene's delegate, which is defined by the **UIWindowSceneDelegate** protocol. The following are the methods available.

scene(UIScene, **willConnectTo:** UISceneSession, **options:** UIScene.ConnectionOptions)—This method is called when a new Scene is created.

sceneDidDisconnect(UIScene)—This method is called when a Scene was removed.

sceneDidBecomeActive(UIScene)—This method is called when a Scene becomes active and therefore it is responding to user events.

sceneWillResignActive(UIScene)—This method is called when a Scene is about to be moved to the background and stop responding to user events.

sceneWillEnterForeground(UIScene)—This method is called when a Scene is about to become visible and respond to user events.

sceneDidEnterBackground(UIScene)—This method is called when a Scene is no longer visible and does not respond to user events anymore.

The Scenes are configured from the app delegate. For this purpose, the **UIApplication-Delegate** protocol includes the **application(UIApplication, configurationFor-Connecting:, options:)** method. To define the configuration, the UIKit framework includes the **UISceneConfiguration** class.

UISceneConfiguration(name: String?, **sessionRole:** Role)—This initializer creates the object required to configure a Scene. The **name** argument is the identifier we want to assign to the Scene, and the **sessionRole** argument specifies the role of the Scene. It is a structure with the type properties **windowApplication**, **windowExternal-Display**, and **carTemplateApplication**.

This initializer provides the name and the role of the Scene, but we must also declare the name of the class that is going to be used to create the Scene's delegate. For this purpose, the **UISceneConfiguration** class includes the following property.

delegateClass—This property sets or returns the class that is going to be used to create the Scene's delegate.

The first step to define a Scene delegate is to create a custom class that conforms to the **UIWindowSceneDelegate** protocol and implements the protocol methods.

```
import UIKit

class CustomSceneDelegate: NSObject, UIWindowSceneDelegate {
   func scene(_ scene: UIScene, willConnectTo session: UISceneSession,
options connectionOptions: UIScene.ConnectionOptions) {
      print("Scene was created")
   }
}
```

Listing 14-29: Defining a custom Scene delegate

In this example, we implemented a method that is called when the Scene is initialized. To assign this object as the Scene delegate for our app, we must define the Scene configuration from the app delegate, as shown next.

```
import UIKit

class CustomAppDelegate: NSObject, UIApplicationDelegate {
   func application(_ application: UIApplication,
didFinishLaunchingWithOptions launchOptions:
[UIApplication.LaunchOptionsKey : Any]? = nil) -> Bool {
      print("App has launched")
      return true
   }
   func application(_ application: UIApplication,
configurationForConnecting connectingSceneSession: UISceneSession,
options: UIScene.ConnectionOptions) -> UISceneConfiguration {
      let config = UISceneConfiguration(name: "Custom Delegate",
sessionRole: connectingSceneSession.role)
      if connectingSceneSession.role == .windowApplication {
         config.delegateClass = CustomSceneDelegate.self
      }
      return config
   }
}
```

Listing 14-30: Configuring a Scene

In this example, we define the **UISceneConfiguration** object with the name "Custom Delegate" and the role received by the method. If our app is running on a mobile device or a Mac computer, the role received by the method is **windowApplication**. If this is the case, we assign our custom class to the **delegateClass** property and return the configuration. When the app is launched, the configuration is defined, the Scene is created, and an instance of our **CustomSceneDelegate** class is assigned as the Scene's delegate, so we see the message "Scene was created" printed on the console.

 Do It Yourself: Create a Swift file called CustomSceneDelegate.swift for the class in Listing 14-29 and update the **CustomAppDelegate** class with the code in Listing 14-30. Run the application on the iPhone simulator. You should see the message "Scene was created" on the console.

The app delegate is assigned to the app by the **@UIApplicationDelegateAdaptor** property wrapper, but there is no connection between the delegate objects and the **App** structure. If we need to access the model from the delegate methods, we must define the model as a singleton, so we can always access the same instance from a type property. The following example illustrates how to build this programming pattern. The first step is to define the model.

```
import SwiftUI

class ApplicationData: ObservableObject {
   @Published var maintext: String

   static let shared = ApplicationData()

   private init() {
      maintext = "Welcome"
   }
}
```

Listing 14-31: Defining the model as a singleton

This model includes a **@Published** property to define the content of a **Text** view in the interface. The instance of the model is created by a **static** property called **shared**. Every time we need to access the model, we can read this property and always get the same instance (see Singletons in Chapter 3).

As always, we need to inject the model into the environment, but instead of creating a new instance of the **ApplicationData** class, as we have done so far, we must get the instance from the **shared** property.

```
import SwiftUI

@main
struct TestApp: App {
   @UIApplicationDelegateAdaptor(CustomAppDelegate.self) var appDelegate
   @StateObject var appData = ApplicationData.shared

   var body: some Scene {
      WindowGroup {
         ContentView()
            .environmentObject(appData)
      }
   }
}
```

Listing 14-32: Injecting the singleton into the environment

Because the model was defined as a singleton, we can access it from anywhere in the code by reading the **shared** property. For instance, we can get a reference to the model from the app delegate and modify the value of the **maintext** property when the app is launched.

```
import UIKit

class CustomAppDelegate: NSObject, UIApplicationDelegate {
   func application(_ application: UIApplication,
didFinishLaunchingWithOptions launchOptions:
[UIApplication.LaunchOptionsKey : Any]? = nil) -> Bool {
      let appData = ApplicationData.shared
      appData.maintext = "Text From Delegate"
      return true
   }
}
```

Listing 14-33: Modifying the model from the app delegate

To complete the example, we need to define a **Text** view on the interface that shows the content of the **maintext** property, so we can see the new value on the screen.

```
import SwiftUI

struct ContentView: View {
   @EnvironmentObject var appData: ApplicationData

   var body: some View {
      Text(appData.maintext)
         .padding()
   }
}
struct ContentView_Previews: PreviewProvider {
   static var previews: some View {
      ContentView().environmentObject(ApplicationData.shared)
   }
}
```

Listing 14-34: Implementing a model created from a singleton

The procedure to access the model is the same as before. We get a reference from the environment and then read or modify the properties. Now, when the app is launched, the app delegate method is called, the string "Text From Delegate" is assigned to the **maintext** property, and the **Text** view shows it on the screen.

Chapter 15
iCloud

(Basic) **15.1 Data in the Cloud**

These days, users own more than one device. If we create an application that works on multiple devices, we must provide a way for the users to share the data, otherwise they will have to insert the same information on every device they own. But the only way to do it effectively is through a server. Data from one device is stored on a server so that it can be retrieved later from other devices. Setting up a server to run this kind of systems is complicated and costly. To provide a standard solution, Apple created a free system called *iCloud*. iCloud allows applications to synchronize data across devices using Apple servers. The system includes three basic services: Key-Value Storage, to store single values, Document Storage, to store files, and CloudKit Storage, to store structured data in public and private databases.

(Basic) **Enabling iCloud**

iCloud must be enabled for each application. The system requires entitlements to authorize our app to use the service and a container where our app's data will be stored. Fortunately, Xcode can set up everything for us by just selecting an option in the Signing & Capabilities panel, found inside the app's settings window. The panel includes a + button at the top-left corner to add a new capability to the application (Figure 15-1, number 1). The button opens a view with all the capabilities available. The capability is added by clicking on it and pressing Return.

Figure 15-1: *Activating iCloud for our app*

 IMPORTANT: iCloud services are only available to developers that are members of the Apple Developer Program. At the time of this writing, the membership costs $99 US Dollars per year. You also must register your account with Xcode, as explained in Chapter 5 (see Figure 5-3).

After iCloud is added to the app, it is shown on the panel, below the signing section. From here, we can select the services we want to activate and Xcode takes care of creating the entitlements. Figure 15-2, below, shows the panel with the Key-Value storage service activated.

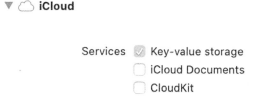

Figure 15-2: *Activating iCloud services*

Do It Yourself: Create a Multiplatform project. Click on the app's settings option at the top of the Navigator Area (Figure 5-4, number 6) and open the Signing & Capabilities panel. Click on the + button at the top-left corner of the panel to add a capability (Figure 15-1, number 1). Select the iCloud option, press return, and check the option Key-value storage (Figure 15-2). This iCloud service is now available in your application.

`Basic` Testing Devices

The best way to test iCloud is by running the app in two different devices, but Apple has made iCloud services available in the simulator as well. Thanks to this feature, we can synchronize data between a device and the simulator to test our app.

For the devices and the simulators to be able to access iCloud services, we must register our iCloud account in the Settings app. We have to go to the Home screen, access the Settings app, tap on the option Sign in to your iPhone/iPad (Figure 15-3, center), and sign in to Apple services with our Apple ID. We must repeat the process for every device or simulator we want to use.

Figure 15-3: *iCloud account in the simulator*

`Basic` 15.2 Key-Value Storage

The Key-Value storage system is the User Defaults system for iCloud. It works the same way, but all the data is stored on iCloud servers instead of the device. We can use it to store the app's preferences, states, or any other value that we need to automatically set on each device owned by the user. Foundation defines the **NSUbiquitousKeyValueStore** class to provide access to this system. The class includes the following methods to store and retrieve values.

set(Value, **forKey:** String**)**—This method stores the value specified by the first argument with the key specified by the **forKey** argument. The class provides versions of this method for every data type we are allowed to store in the system, such as **String**, **Bool**, **Data**, **Double**, **Int64**, dictionaries, arrays, and also Property List values (**NSNumber**, **NSString**, **NSDate**, **NSArray**, **NSDictionary**, **NSData**, and their equivalents in Swift).

bool(forKey: String**)**—This method retrieves a value of type **Bool**.

double(forKey: String**)**—This method retrieves a value of type **Double**.

longLong(forKey: String**)**—This method retrieves a value of type **Int64**.

string(forKey: String**)**—This method retrieves a value of type **String**.

array(forKey: String**)**—This method retrieves an array.

dictionary(forKey: String**)**—This method retrieves a dictionary.

data(forKey: String**)**—This method retrieves a value of type **Data**.

object(forKey: String)—This method retrieves an object.

To store or access a value, we must initialize an **NSUbiquitousKeyValueStore** object and then call any of these methods. The object takes care of establishing the connection with iCloud and downloading or uploading the values, but it doesn't keep the values up-to-date. If a value is modified in one device, the change must be reflected on the others in real time. For this purpose, the **NSUbiquitousKeyValueStore** class defines the following notification.

didChangeExternallyNotification—This notification is posted by the system when a change in the values on the Key-Value storage is detected.

As we already mentioned, the system is used to storing discrete values that represent the user's preferences or the app's status. For example, we may have a stepper that allows the user to set a limit on the number of items the application can manage.

Figure 15-4: *Interface to test Key-Value storage*

The application must initialize the interface with the current value stored in iCloud, but it also has to send the value back when a new one is set by the user, and update it when it is changed from another device. The best way to manage this information is from the model. We need a **@Published** property to store the local value and a few methods to send and receive the value to and from iCloud.

```
import SwiftUI

class ApplicationData: ObservableObject {
   @Published var control: Double = 0
   let storage: NSUbiquitousKeyValueStore

   init() {
      storage = NSUbiquitousKeyValueStore()
      control = storage.double(forKey: "control")
   }
   func valueChanged(value: Double) {
      if control != storage.double(forKey: "control") {
         storage.set(value, forKey: "control")
         storage.synchronize()
      }
   }
   func valueReceived() async {
      let center = NotificationCenter.default
      let name =
NSUbiquitousKeyValueStore.didChangeExternallyNotification
      for await notification in center.notifications(named: name, object:
storage) {
         if notification.name == name {
            await MainActor.run {
               control = storage.double(forKey: "control")
            }
         }
      }
   }
}
```

Listing 15-1: *Storing a value in iCloud*

This model defines a **@Published** property called **control** that we use to keep track of the value set by the stepper, and a normal property to store the **NSUbiquitousKeyValueStore** object necessary to access the values in iCloud. When the observable object is initialized, we create the **NSUbiquitousKeyValueStore** object and load from iCloud a value stored with the "control" key. (If the value doesn't exist, the value returned is 0.)

Next, we define two methods. The **valueChanged()** method is executed every time the value of the **control** property is modified. This method sends the new value to iCloud with the **set()** method and then calls the **synchronize()** method to make sure the system sends it right away. Notice that because we want to send the value only when it is modified by the user, we only do it when the new value is different than the current value. The second method is called **valueReceived()**. This method initializes an asynchronous **for in** loop to listen to the **didChangeExternallyNotification** notification. When the value is modified from another device, the notification is triggered, so we can read the new value from iCloud and update the **control** property.

All the job is done by the model, so the view only needs to include a **Stepper** and a **Text** view to recreate the interface illustrated in Figure 15-4, and implement the **onChange()** and **task()** modifiers to call the methods in the model when necessary.

```
struct ContentView: View {
    @EnvironmentObject var appData: ApplicationData

    var body: some View {
        VStack {
            HStack {
                Stepper("", value: $appData.control)
                    .labelsHidden()
                Text("\
(appData.control.formatted(.number.precision(.fractionLength(0))))")
                    .font(.title)
                Spacer()
            }
            Spacer()
        }.padding()
        .onChange(of: appData.control) { value in
            appData.valueChanged(value: value)
        }
        .task {
            await appData.valueReceived()
        }
    }
}
```

Listing 15-2: Defining the interface to store and read values from iCloud

Do It Yourself: Create a Swift file called ApplicationData.swift for the model in Listing 15-1. Update the **ContentView** view with the code in Listing 15-2. Remember to inject the **ApplicationData** object into the environment for the app and the previews (Chapter 7, Listing 7-4). Run the application on two different devices. Press the stepper's buttons to change the value to 5 on one device. You should see the value changing on the other device (the process may take several seconds). Stop the application from Xcode and run it again. You should see the value 5 on the screen. (Remember to activate the same iCloud account in any of the simulators or devices you try.)

IMPORTANT: The simulator does not update the information automatically. If you modify the value on your device and do not see it changing on the simulator, open the Features menu and select the option Trigger iCloud Sync. This synchronizes the application with iCloud and updates the values right away.

Chapter 15 - iCloud

The same way we can store one value, we can store several. The Key/Value storage service can manage multiple values using different keys, but if we want to simplify our work, we can use a structure to store all the values, encode that structure into data with JSON, and then store only one value in iCloud containing that data. Our next example follows this approach. We define a structure to store the user's name, address and city, and then encode and decode an instance of that structure to store the values in iCloud.

```
import SwiftUI

struct PersonalInfo: Codable {
    var name: String
    var address: String
    var city: String
}
class ApplicationData: ObservableObject {
    @Published var userInfo: PersonalInfo
    let storage: NSUbiquitousKeyValueStore

    init() {
        storage = NSUbiquitousKeyValueStore()

        userInfo = PersonalInfo(name: "", address: "", city: "")
        if let dataInfo = storage.data(forKey: "info") {
            let decoder = JSONDecoder()
            if let info = try? decoder.decode(PersonalInfo.self, from:
dataInfo) {
                userInfo = info
            }
        }
    }
    func setInfo() {
        let encoder = JSONEncoder()
        if let data = try? encoder.encode(userInfo) {
        storage.set(data, forKey: "info")
        }
    }
    func valueReceived() async {
        let center = NotificationCenter.default
        let name =
NSUbiquitousKeyValueStore.didChangeExternallyNotification
        for await notification in center.notifications(named: name, object:
storage) {
            if notification.name == name {
                await MainActor.run {
                    if let dataInfo = storage.data(forKey: "info") {
                        let decoder = JSONDecoder()
                        if let info = try? decoder.decode(PersonalInfo.self,
from: dataInfo) {
                            userInfo = info
                        }
                    }
                }
            }
        }
    }
}
```

Listing 15-3: Storing multiple values in iCloud

The process is the same as before. We read the value from iCloud when the observable object is initialized, and then implement two methods, one to send the **PersonalInfo** structure to iCloud when the user inserts new values, and another to listen to the **didChangeExternallyNotification** notification and update the structure when new values are inserted from a different device. The only difference is in how the value is processed. This time we are dealing with a structure encoded as a JSON value, therefore we need to use a **JSONDecoder** object when a value is received, and a **JSONEncoder** object to send the value to iCloud (see Chapter 10, Listing 10-42).

We need two views for this example: one to show the current values and another to let the user insert new ones. The initial view is simple. All it needs to do is to get the values from the **@Published** property, show them on the screen, and initialize a task to update them every time they are modified from a different device.

```
struct ContentView: View {
    @EnvironmentObject var appData: ApplicationData
    @State private var openSheet: Bool = false

    var body: some View {
        NavigationStack {
            VStack {
                HStack {
                    Text("Name:")
                    Text(appData.userInfo.name)
                    Spacer()
                }
                HStack {
                    Text("Address:")
                    Text(appData.userInfo.address)
                    Spacer()
                }
                HStack {
                    Text("City:")
                    Text(appData.userInfo.city)
                    Spacer()
                }
                Spacer()
            }.padding()
            .navigationBarTitle("Personal Info")
            .toolbar {
                ToolbarItem(placement: .navigationBarTrailing) {
                    Button("Change") {
                        openSheet = true
                    }
                }
            }
            .sheet(isPresented: $openSheet) {
                InsertInfoView(openSheet: $openSheet)
            }
            .task {
                await appData.valueReceived()
            }
        }
    }
}
```

Listing 15-4: Reading multiple values from iCloud

This view includes a button in the navigation bar to open a view called **InsertInfoView** in a sheet. The following is our implementation of this view.

```
import SwiftUI
struct InsertInfoView: View {
    @EnvironmentObject var appData: ApplicationData
    @Binding var openSheet: Bool
    @State private var inputName: String = ""
```

```
@State private var inputAddress: String = ""
@State private var inputCity: String = ""

var body: some View {
    VStack(spacing: 10) {
        TextField("Insert Name", text: $inputName)
            .textFieldStyle(.roundedBorder)
        TextField("Insert Address", text: $inputAddress)
            .textFieldStyle(.roundedBorder)
        TextField("Insert City", text: $inputCity)
            .textFieldStyle(.roundedBorder)
        HStack {
            Spacer()
            Button("Save") {
                appData.userInfo = PersonalInfo(name: inputName, address:
inputAddress, city: inputCity)
                appData.setInfo()
                openSheet = false
            }
        }
        Spacer()
    }.padding()
    .onAppear {
        inputName = appData.userInfo.name
        inputAddress = appData.userInfo.address
        inputCity = appData.userInfo.city
    }
}
}
struct InsertInfoView_Previews: PreviewProvider {
    static var previews: some View {
        InsertInfoView(openSheet: .constant(false))
            .environmentObject(ApplicationData())
    }
}
}
```

Listing 15-5: *Saving multiple values in iCloud*

This is a normal view with three **TextField** views to allow the user to insert and modify the values. Because there might be values already stored in iCloud, we assign the values in the **userInfo** property to **@State** properties to show them to the user when the view appears. If the user presses the button to save the values, we create a new **PersonalInfo** structure and call the **setInfo()** method in the model to encode it and send it to iCloud.

The application is ready. When the user inserts new values, they are sent to iCloud, and when the app is launched or a notification is received, the values in iCloud are downloaded and shown on the screen.

Figure 15-5: *Interface to store multiple values in Key/Value storage*

Do It Yourself: Update the ApplicationData.swift file with the code in Listing 15-3. Update the **ContentView** view with the code in Listing 15-4. Create a SwiftUI View file called InsertInfoView.swift for the code in Listing 15-5. Run the application on two devices. Press the Change button. Insert new values and press Save. Wait a few seconds for the values to appear on the second device.

The Key-Value storage system was developed to store small values. The purpose is to allow users to set preferences or configuration parameters across devices. Although very useful, it presents some limitations, especially on the amount of data we can store (currently no more than 1 Megabyte). An alternative is to activate the iCloud Documents option in the Capabilities panel and upload files instead.

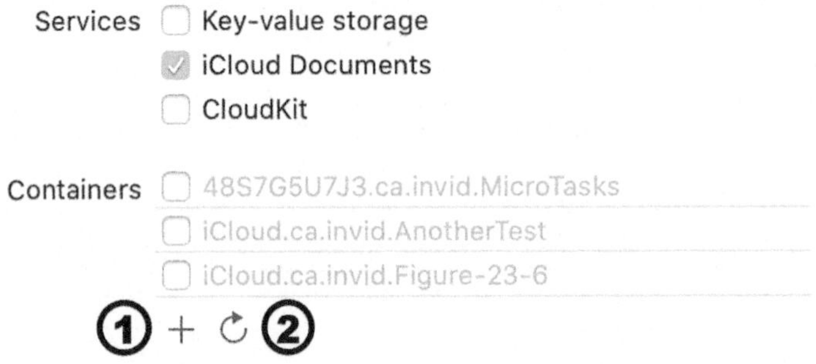

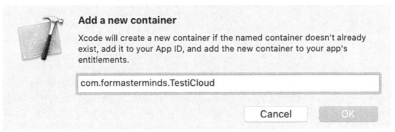

Figure 15-6: *iCloud Documents service*

The operating system uses a container to store iCloud files. This container is a folder in the app's storage space where iCloud files are created. Once a file is added, modified or removed from this container, the system automatically reports the changes to iCloud, so the copies of the app running in other devices can modify their own container to stay synchronized. If the container is not created by Xcode, we have to do it ourselves by pressing the + button (Figure 15-6, number 1). This opens a window to insert the container's name.

Add a new container

Xcode will create a new container if the named container doesn't already exist, add it to your App ID, and add the new container to your app's entitlements.

com.formasterminds.TestiCloud

Cancel   OK

Figure 15-7: *Container's name*

The name must be unique, and the best way to guaranty it is to use the app's bundle identifier. In our example, we use the bundle identifier to create the container for an app called TestiCloud. Once the container is created, we should press the Refresh button to make sure the information is uploaded to Apple servers right away (Figure 15-6, number 2). After this, the container is added and selected as the active container for the application.

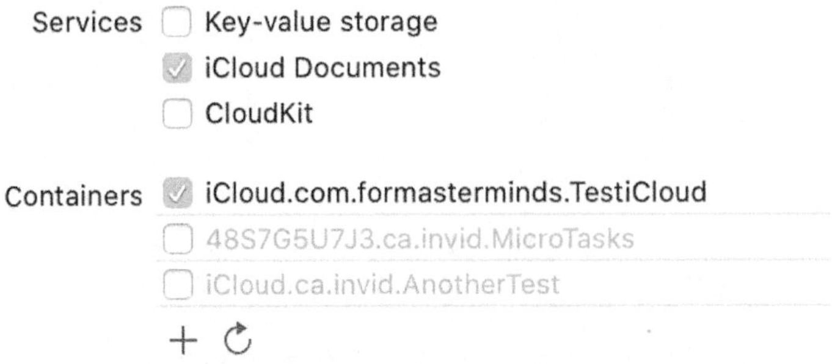

Services ☐ Key-value storage
☑ iCloud Documents
☐ CloudKit

Containers ☑ iCloud.com.formasterminds.TestiCloud
☐ 48S7G5U7J3.ca.invid.MicroTasks
☐ iCloud.ca.invid.AnotherTest

+ ↻

Figure 15-8: *Selected container*

Do It Yourself: Create a Multiplatform project. Click on the app's settings option at the top of the Navigator Area (Figure 5-4, number 6) and open the Signing & Capabilities panel. Click on the + button at the top-left corner of the panel to add a capability (Figure 15-1, number 1). Select the iCloud option, press return, and check the option iCloud Documents. Press the + button to add a container (Figure 15-6, number 1). Insert the app's bundle identifier for the container's name and press the OK button (you can find the bundle identifier on top of the iCloud section). If the name of the container appears in red, press the Refresh button to upload the information to Apple servers (Figure 15-6, number 2).

An iCloud container is called *Ubiquitous Container* because its content is shared with other devices and therefore available everywhere. The `FileManager` class includes properties and methods to work with a ubiquitous container. The following are the most frequently used.

url(forUbiquityContainerIdentifier: String?**)**—This method returns the URL of the app's iCloud container. The **forUbiquityContainerIdentifier** argument is the name of the container we want to access. The value `nil` returns the container assigned by default.

evictUbiquitousItem(at: URL**)**—This method removes the local copy of the document at the URL specified by the **at** argument.

Although the files are stored in a container in the device and synchronized by the system automatically, working with iCloud introduces some challenges that the `FileManager` class cannot overcome. The most important is coordination. Because of the unreliability of network connections, at any moment iCloud may find different versions of the same file. Modifications that were introduced to the file from one device may not have reached iCloud and therefore may later conflict with updates introduced from another device. The application has to decide which version of the file to preserve or what data is more valuable when the file is edited from two different devices at the same time. These issues are not easy to solve and can turn development into a nightmare. Considering all the problems a developer has to face, Apple introduced a class called `UIDocument` designed specifically to manage files for iCloud. The class includes capabilities to coordinate and synchronize files of any size, and features that simplify the manipulation of documents in mobile devices, like progression reports, automatic thumbnail generation, undo manager, and others.

The `UIDocument` class was not designed to be implemented directly in our code; it is like an interface between the app's data and the files we use to store it. To take advantage of this class, we must create a subclass and overwrite some of its methods. Once we define the subclass, we can create the object with the following initializer.

UIDocument(fileURL: URL**)**—This initializer creates a new `UIDocument` object. The **fileURL** argument is a `URL` structure with the location of the file in iCloud's container.

The following are the methods we must override in the subclass of `UIDocument` to provide the data for the file and to retrieve it later.

contents(forType: String**)**—This method is called when the `UIDocument` object needs to store the content of the document on file. The method must return an object with the document's data (usually a `Data` structure). The **forType** argument identifies the type of the file (by default, it is determined from the file's extension).

load(fromContents: Any, **ofType:** String?**)**—This method is called when the `UIDocument` object loads the content of the document from the file. The **fromContents** argument is an object with the file's content (usually a `Data` structure), and the **ofType** argument is a string that identifies the file's type (by default, it is determined from the file's extension).

Once an object is created from our **UIDocument** subclass, we can manage the file from the asynchronous methods provided by the class. The following are the most frequently used.

open()—This asynchronous method asks the **UIDocument** object to open the file and load its content. The method returns a Boolean value to indicate if the operation was successful.

save(to: URL, **for:** SaveOperation)—This asynchronous method asks the **UIDocument** object to save the content of the document on file. The **for** argument is an enumeration value that indicates the type of operation to perform. The values available are **forCreating** (to save the file for the first time) and **forOverwriting** (to overwrite the file's current version). The method returns a Boolean value to indicate if the operation was successful.

close()—This asynchronous method saves any pending changes and closes the document. The method returns a Boolean value to indicate if the operation was successful.

The first thing we have to do to work with documents in iCloud is to define a subclass of **UIDocument**. The following is the one we are going to use for the examples in this chapter.

```
import SwiftUI

class MyDocument: UIDocument {
    var fileContent: Data?

    override func contents(forType typeName: String) throws -> Any {
        return fileContent ?? Data()
    }
    override func load(fromContents contents: Any, ofType typeName:
String?) throws {
        if let data = contents as? Data, !data.isEmpty {
            fileContent = data
        }
    }
}
```

Listing 15-6: Creating the document

The **UIDocument** subclass needs at least three elements: a property to store the file's content, the **contents()** method to provide the data to store in the file, and the **load()** method to get the data back from the file. When the **UIDocument** object is asked to store or load the data in the file, it calls these methods and use the property as a proxy to move the data around. Therefore, every time we want to access the file's content, we must open the document and read this property. In our example, we called it **fileContent**.

(Basic) **Metadata Query**

Accessing the files is also complicated in iCloud. We cannot just get a list of files with methods like **contentsOfDirectory()** from the **FileManager** class because there could be some files that have not been downloaded yet to the device. What we can do instead is to get the information pertaining to the files. This data is called *Metadata*, and refers to all the information associated with a particular file, such as its name, the date it was created, etc. To get the files' metadata, Foundation defines the **NSMetadataQuery** class. This class provides the properties and methods necessary to retrieve the information and watch for updates.

predicate—This property sets or returns the predicate for the query. It is an optional of type **NSPredicate**.

sortDescriptors—This property sets or returns the sort descriptors for the query. It is an array of `NSSortDescriptor` objects.

searchScopes—This property sets or returns a value that indicates the scope of the query. It is an array with constants that represent a predefined scope. The constants available for mobile devices are `NSMetadataQueryUbiquitousDocumentsScope` (searches for all the files in the Documents directory of the iCloud's container) and `NSMetadataQueryUbiquitousDataScope` (searches for all the files that are not in the Documents directory of the iCloud's container).

results—This property returns an array with the query's results. By default, the array contains `NSMetadataItem` objects with the metadata of every file found.

resultCount—This property returns an `Int` with the number of results produced by the query.

result(at: Int**)**—This method returns the `NSMetadataItem` object from the query's results array at the index specified by the **at** argument.

start()—This method initiates the query.

stop()—This method stops the query.

enableUpdates()—This method enables query updates.

disableUpdates()—This method disables query updates.

The `NSMetadataQuery` class also includes some notifications to report when new data is available. The following are the most frequently used.

NSMetadataQueryDidUpdate—This notification is posted when the results of the query change.

NSMetadataQueryDidFinishGathering—This notification is posted when the query finishes getting all the information.

The results of a query are returned by the `results` property in the form of an array of `NSMetadataItem` objects. This is a simple class defined to contain the attributes of a file. The class provides the following method to retrieve the values.

value(forAttribute: String**)**—This method returns the value of the file's attribute determined by the **forAtttribute** argument. The `NSMetadataItem` class defines a list of constants to represent the attributes. The constants available are `NSMetadataItemFS-NameKey` (file's name), `NSMetadataItemDisplayNameKey` (document's name), `NSMetadataItemURLKey` (file's URL), `NSMetadataItemPathKey` (file's path), `NSMetadataItemFSSizeKey` (file's size), `NSMetadataItemFSCreationDateKey` (date of creation), and `NSMetadataItemFSContentChangeDateKey` (date the file was last modified).

(Basic) **Single Document**

The interface for an application capable of processing documents must include a way for the user to select the document and the tools to edit its content. For the following example, we will work with only one document to keep it simple. The initial view includes a button that opens a sheet with a `TextEditor` view for the user to edit the document's content.

Figure 15-9: Interface to edit a document

The codes listed below make up the model we need for this application. The first part, next, initializes the **NSMetadataQuery** object and starts listening to the **NSMetadataQueryDid-FinishGathering** notification to update the document when new information is received.

```
import SwiftUI
class ApplicationData: ObservableObject {
    var document: MyDocument!
    var metaData: NSMetadataQuery!

    init() {
        metaData = NSMetadataQuery()
        metaData.predicate = NSPredicate(format: "%K == %@",
NSMetadataItemFSNameKey, "myfile.dat")
        metaData.searchScopes = [NSMetadataQueryUbiquitousDocumentsScope]

        Task(priority: .high) {
            let center = NotificationCenter.default
            let name = NSNotification.Name.NSMetadataQueryDidFinishGathering
            for await notification in center.notifications(named: name,
object: metaData) {
                if notification.name == name {
                    await createFile()
                }
            }
        }
        metaData.start()
    }
}
```

Listing 15-7: Initializing the model required to store a document in iCloud

Because of the logic of our application, we only need a property to store the reference to the **MyDocument** object we are going to use to access the file and a property to reference the **NSMetadataQuery** object that we will use to search for the files available in the ubiquitous container. In this example, we call these properties **document** and **metaData**.

When the observable object is initialized, we create the **NSMetadataQuery** object, configure the query to search for documents inside the iCloud's container (**NSMetadataQuery-UbiquitousDocumentsScope**), start listening to the **NSMetadataQueryDidFinish-Gathering** notification, and initiate the process with the **start()** method. Because in this example we are working with only one document, we make sure that the query returns the right file with a predicate. The format of the predicate for a query requires comparing the value of a file's attribute with the string we are looking for. The attribute is represented by the constants defined in the **NSMetadataItem** class. In this case, we use the **NSMetadataItemFSNameKey** constant to filter the files by name. (Notice that the value of the constant is introduced in the string with the **%K** placeholder. As explained before, this is called *Dynamic Key* and what it does is to insert the value without quotes.)

The query gets the document and then posts a **NSMetadataQueryDidFinishGathering** notification. When the notification is received, we can get the list of documents in the container and use them. In this example, we execute a method called **createFile()** to perform that task.

```
@MainActor
func createFile() async {
   if metaData.resultCount > 0 {
      let file = metaData.result(at: 0) as! NSMetadataItem
      let fileURL = file.value(forAttribute: NSMetadataItemURLKey) as! URL
      document = MyDocument(fileURL: fileURL)
   } else {
      let manager = FileManager.default
      if let fileURL = manager.url(forUbiquityContainerIdentifier: nil) {
         let documentURL = fileURL.appendingPathComponent("Documents/
myfile.dat")
         document = MyDocument(fileURL: documentURL)
         document.fileContent = Data()
         if manager.fileExists(atPath: documentURL.path) {
            let _ = await document.save(to: documentURL,
for: .forOverwriting)
         } else {
            let _ = await document.save(to: documentURL,
for: .forCreating)
         }
      }
   }
}
```

Listing 15-8: Processing query results

Because in this application we are only working with one document, the `createFile()` method has to perform two tasks. If a file is found, we must create an instance of `MyDocument` and assign it to the `document` property to make it available for the views, but if no file is available, we must create one. To know if the query has found a document, we check the value of the `resultCount` property of the `NSMetadataQuery` object. This property returns the number of documents (files) available. If the number is greater than 0, we get the metadata of the first document on the list with the `result(at:)` method, get its URL with the `value(forAttribute:)` method, and create a `MyDocument` instance with it.

On the other hand, if no document was created yet, the `createFile()` method has to generate the URL and create a new one. To build our document's URL, we get the URL of the app's iCloud container with the `url(forUbiquityContainerIdentifier:)` method provided by the `FileManager` object. The URL returned by this method is the container's root directory, to which we must append the Documents directory and the file's name (Documents/ myfile.dat). With the URL ready, we create a `MyDocument` object, assign an empty `Data` structure to the `fileContent` property to define the document's initial content, and call the `save()` method to store it. If a document in the URL already exists, we call this method with the `forOverwriting` argument to modify it, otherwise, we call it with the `forCreating` argument to create a new one. Internally, the `MyDocument` instance calls the `contents()` method to get the document's content and creates the file inside the container.

 IMPORTANT: In this example, we don't need to check the Boolean value returned by the `save()` and `close()` methods, so we ignore the values with an underscore (_), as we did when working with tuples and **switch** statements in Chapter 2 (see Listing 2-38).

From the views, we must open the document, save the changes, and close it. The following are the methods we need to include in the model for this purpose.

```
@MainActor
func openDocument() async -> String {
   let manager = FileManager.default
```

```
        if let fileURL = manager.url(forUbiquityContainerIdentifier: nil) {
            let documentURL = fileURL.appendingPathComponent("Documents/
myfile.dat")
            document = MyDocument(fileURL: documentURL)
            let success = await document.open()
            if success {
                if let data = document.fileContent {
                    return String(data: data, encoding: .utf8) ?? ""
                }
            }
        }
        return ""
}
@MainActor
func saveDocument(text: String) async {
    let manager = FileManager.default
    if let fileURL = manager.url(forUbiquityContainerIdentifier: nil) {
        let documentURL = fileURL.appendingPathComponent("Documents/
myfile.dat")

        if let data = text.data(using: .utf8) {
            document.fileContent = data
            let _ = await document.save(to: documentURL,
for: .forOverwriting)
        }
    }
}
@MainActor
func closeDocument() async {
    let _ = await document.close()
}
```

Listing 15-9: Updating the document

The **openDocument()** method is called every time the user opens the view to edit the document. In this method, we determine the URL, create the instance of **MyDocument** again, open the document with the **open()** method, read the content and return a string, so the view can show it on the screen. The **saveDocument()** method performs the opposite process; it takes the text inserted by the user, turns it into a **Data** structure with the **data()** method, assigns it to the document, and saves the document in the container.

At the end, we also include a method called **closeDocument()**. The purpose of this method is to close the document after the user finishes introducing the changes.

With these methods, the model is ready. The next step is to provide the views. And as always, they are very simple. The initial view only needs a button to open the editor.

```
struct ContentView: View {
    @State private var editDocument: Bool = false

    var body: some View {
        VStack {
            Text("My Document")
                .padding()
            Button("Open Document") {
                editDocument = true
            }.buttonStyle(.borderedProminent)
                .padding()
        }
        .sheet(isPresented: $editDocument) {
            EditDocumentView()
        }
```

```
        }
    }
```

Listing 15-10: Defining the main interface

The button opens a sheet with a view to edit the document. We call it `EditDocumentView`.

```
struct EditDocumentView: View {
    @EnvironmentObject var appData: ApplicationData
    @Environment(\.dismiss) var dismiss
    @State private var inputText: String = ""

    var body: some View {
        VStack {
            HStack {
                Button("Close") {
                    dismiss()
                }.padding()
                Spacer()
                Button("Save") {
                    Task(priority: .high) {
                        await appData.saveDocument(text: inputText)
                        dismiss()
                    }
                }.padding()
            }
            GroupBox {
                TextEditor(text: $inputText)
            }
        }
        .task {
            inputText = await appData.openDocument()
        }
        .onDisappear {
            Task(priority: .background) {
                await appData.closeDocument()
            }
        }
    }
}
```

Listing 15-11: Editing the document

This view includes a `TextEditor` view to edit the document's content and a button to save it. The editor's content is managed by a `@State` property called `inputText`. When the view is loaded, we initiate a task that calls the `openDocument()` method in the model and assigns the value returned by the method to this property, so the `TextEditor` view is initialized with the document's current content.

When the user taps the Save button to save the changes, we call the `saveDocument()` method in the model to store the new value, and dismiss the view. Notice that we have also implemented the `onDisappear()` modifier to make sure that the document is always closed, no matter how or when the view is dismissed.

Do It Yourself: In the project initiated before to work with iCloud Documents, create a Swift file called MyDocument.swift for the `UIDocument` subclass defined in Listing 15-6. Create another Swift file called ApplicationData.swift for the model in Listing 15-7. Add the methods in Listings 15-8 and 15-9 to the `ApplicationData` class. Update the `ContentView` view with the code in Listing 15-10. Create a SwiftUI View file called EditDocumentView.swift for the view in Listing 15-11. Remember to inject the `ApplicationData` object into the environment for the app and the previews (Chapter 7, Listing 7-4). Run the application in two devices. Press the Open Document button on the first device. Insert a text and press the Save button. Wait a few seconds and press the Open Document button again but on the second device. You should see on the screen the same text inserted from the first device.

(Basic) **Multiple Documents**

In the previous example, we have worked with only one document, but most applications allow users to create and manage all the documents they need. The requirements for working with a single document or many are the same. We must define a query and listen to the notifications to update the data in our model and the interface. But this time we also need to include a structure to store information about each document in the container, so the views can show the list of documents available and users can select the one they want to work with. The following model includes a structure called **FileInfo** for this purpose.

```
import SwiftUI
struct NotificationWrapper: @unchecked Sendable {
    let value: Notification
}
struct FileInfo: Identifiable {
    let id: UUID = UUID()
    var name: String
    var url: URL
}
class ApplicationData: ObservableObject {
    @Published var listOfFiles: [FileInfo] = []
    var document: MyDocument!
    var metaData: NSMetadataQuery!

    init() {
        metaData = NSMetadataQuery()
        metaData.searchScopes = [NSMetadataQueryUbiquitousDocumentsScope]

        Task(priority: .high) {
            let center = NotificationCenter.default
            let name = NSNotification.Name.NSMetadataQueryDidFinishGathering
            for await notification in center.notifications(named: name,
object: metaData) {
                if notification.name == name {
                    await getFiles()
                }
            }
        }
        Task(priority: .high) {
            let center = NotificationCenter.default
            let name = NSNotification.Name.NSMetadataQueryDidUpdate
            for await notification in center.notifications(named: name,
object: metaData) {
                if notification.name == name {
                    let wrapper = NotificationWrapper(value: notification)
                    await updateFiles(notification: wrapper)
                }
            }
        }
        metaData.start()
    }
}
```

Listing 15-12: Working with multiple documents

The model in Listing 15-12 includes a new structure called `FileInfo` and a `@Published` property called `listOfFiles` to store the instances that represent the documents in the container. In addition to the `NSMetadataQueryDidFinishGathering` notification, now we also listen to the `NSMetadataQueryDidUpdate` notification to keep the files up to date. When this notification is received, we execute a method called `updateFiles()`. This method receives the `Notification` object produced by the `notifications()` method to know the changes it needs to perform in the model. Notice that the method is executed in the Main Actor, but the `Notification` object comes from an asynchronous thread. This means that the object is not safe (it can produce a data race). To be able to pass this value to the method without getting warnings and errors from the compiler, we wrap it in a structure called `NotificationWrapper`. (For more information on data races and the `Sendable` protocol, read Chapter 9.)

The rest of the code in the observable object is the same as before, only the methods change. For instance, when the `NSMetadataQueryDidFinishGathering` notification is posted by the `NSMetadataQuery` object, we execute a method called `getFiles()` to process the list of files available in the container.

```
@MainActor
func getFiles() {
   if metaData.resultCount > 0 {
      let files = metaData.results as! [NSMetadataItem]
      for item in files {
          let fileName = item.value(forAttribute: NSMetadataItemFSNameKey)
as! String
          if !listOfFiles.contains(where: { $0.name == fileName }) {
              let documentURL = item.value(forAttribute:
NSMetadataItemURLKey) as! URL
              listOfFiles.append(FileInfo(name: fileName, url:
documentURL))
          }
      }
      listOfFiles.sort(by: { $0.name < $1.name })
   }
}
```

Listing 15-13: Processing the list of files in the container

The `getFiles()` method includes a `for in` loop to go through the list of documents retrieved by the query, get the name of each file, check whether the `listOfFiles` array already contains a file with that name, and add it to the list if necessary.

As we already mentioned, another method we need to add to the model is the one called when a `NSMetadataQueryDidUpdate` notification is received. This notification is posted every time the `NSMetadataQuery` object detects an update in the container (local or remote). In this case, we must respond to a document being added or removed. To detect the type of change, the `NSMetadataQuery` class defines the following constants.

NSMetadataQueryUpdateAddedItemsKey—This constant retrieves an array of `NSMetadataItem` objects that represent the documents added to the container.

NSMetadataQueryUpdateChangedItemsKey—This constant retrieves an array of `NSMetadataItem` objects that represent the documents that were modified.

NSMetadataQueryUpdateRemovedItemsKey—This constant retrieves an array of `NSMetadataItem` objects that represent the documents that were removed from the container.

This information is returned by the `userInfo` property of the `Notification` object produced by the `NSMetadataQueryDidUpdate` notification and passed to the `updateFiles()` method, so we can process the changes accordingly, as shown next.

```
@MainActor
func updateFiles(notification: NotificationWrapper) {
   metaData.disableUpdates()

   let manager = FileManager.default
   if let modifications = notification.value.userInfo {
      if let removed =
modifications[NSMetadataQueryUpdateRemovedItemsKey] as? [NSMetadataItem] {
         for item in removed {
            let name = item.value(forAttribute: NSMetadataItemFSNameKey)
as! String
            if let index = listOfFiles.firstIndex(where: { $0.name ==
name }) {
               listOfFiles.remove(at: index)
            }
         }
      }
      if let added = modifications[NSMetadataQueryUpdateAddedItemsKey]
as? [NSMetadataItem] {
         for item in added {
            let name = item.value(forAttribute: NSMetadataItemFSNameKey)
as! String
            if !listOfFiles.contains(where: { $0.name == name }) {
               if let fileURL =
manager.url(forUbiquityContainerIdentifier: nil) {
                  let documentURL =
fileURL.appendingPathComponent("Documents/\(name)")
                  listOfFiles.append(FileInfo(name: name, url:
documentURL))
               }
            }
         }
         listOfFiles.sort(by: { $0.name < $1.name })
      }
   }
   metaData.enableUpdates()
}
```

Listing 15-14: Updating the container

The **updateFiles()** method in Listing 15-14 receives the wrapper with the **Notification** object, so we can read the notification's **userInfo** property and determine the type of updates performed by the user. If the value is of type **NSMetadataQueryUpdateRemovedItemsKey**, we remove the deleted documents from the **listOfFiles** array, but if the value is of type **NSMetadataQueryUpdateAddedItemsKey**, we create a **FileInfo** structure to represent the file and add it to the **listOfFiles** array as before.

Notice that to avoid simultaneous updates, we disable the **NSMetadataQuery** object momentarily with the **disableUpdates()** method and enable it again with the **enableUpdates()** method when the updates are over.

The remaining methods are those required by the views to process the documents. For instance, we need the following two methods to create and remove files from the container.

```
@MainActor
func createFile(name: String) async {
   let manager = FileManager.default
   if let fileURL = manager.url(forUbiquityContainerIdentifier: nil) {
      let documentURL = fileURL.appendingPathComponent("Documents/\
(name)")
      let document = MyDocument(fileURL: documentURL)
      document.fileContent = Data()
```

Chapter 15 - iCloud

```
         let _ = await document.save(to: documentURL, for: .forCreating)
    }
}
func removeFiles(indexes: IndexSet) async {
    let manager = FileManager.default
    for index in indexes {
        let fileURL = listOfFiles[index].url
        do {
            try manager.removeItem(atPath: fileURL.path)
            await MainActor.run {
                let _ = listOfFiles.remove(at: index)
            }
        } catch {
            print("Error deleting file: \(error)")
        }
    }
}
```

Listing 15-15: Adding and removing documents from the container

The **createFile()** method defines a URL with the file's name, creates an empty document, and saves it in the container. On the other hand, the **removeFiles()** method removes the files selected by the user from the container and the corresponding **FileInfo** structures from the array. This last method receives an **IndexSet** value with the indexes of the documents to be removed. This is the value generated by the **onDelete()** modifier. We iterate through these values with a **for in** loop, get the file's URL from the **url** property, and remove it from the container with the **removeItem()** method and from the **listOfFiles** array with the **remove()** method. Notice that the method is asynchronous. This is required by the system. Every time we remove a file from the ubiquitous container we must do it from a background thread. And this is the reason why we modify the **listOfFiles** property from the Main Actor. (Changes to the interface must always be performed from the main thread.)

The model also needs a few more methods to open, save, and close the documents.

```
@MainActor
func openDocument(url: URL) async -> String {
    document = MyDocument(fileURL: url)
    let success = await document.open()
    if success {
        if let data = document.fileContent {
            return String(data: data, encoding: .utf8) ?? ""
        }
    }
    return ""
}
@MainActor
func saveDocument(url: URL, content: String) async {
    if let data = content.data(using: .utf8) {
        document.fileContent = data
        let _ = await document.save(to: url, for: .forOverwriting)
    }
}
@MainActor
func closeDocument() async {
    let _ = await document.close()
}
```

Listing 15-16: Opening, saving, and closing a document

The model is ready, now we must define the views. For this example, we need three views: one to list the documents available, one to let the user add new documents, and another to edit them. The following are the changes we need to introduce to the **ContentView** view.

```
struct ContentView: View {
    @EnvironmentObject var appData: ApplicationData
    @State private var openSheet: Bool = false

    var body: some View {
        NavigationStack {
            List {
                ForEach(appData.listOfFiles) { file in
                    NavigationLink(destination: EditDocumentView(selectedFile:
file)) {
                        Text(file.name)
                    }
                }
                .onDelete { indexes in
                    Task(priority: .background) {
                        await appData.removeFiles(indexes: indexes)
                    }
                }
            }
            .navigationBarTitle("List of Files")
            .navigationBarTitleDisplayMode(.inline)
            .toolbar {
                ToolbarItem(placement: .navigationBarTrailing) {
                    Button("Create File") {
                        openSheet = true
                    }
                }
            }
            .sheet(isPresented: $openSheet) {
                CreateFileView()
            }
        }
    }
}
```

Listing 15-17: Listing the documents available in the container

This view creates a list with the values in the **listOfFiles** property, applies the **onDelete()** modifier to the **ForEach** view to let the user delete a document, and includes a button in the navigation bar to open a sheet to add new documents. The view opened by the **sheet()** modifier is called **CreateFileView**.

```
struct CreateFileView: View {
    @EnvironmentObject var appData: ApplicationData
    @Environment(\.dismiss) var dismiss
    @State private var inputFileName: String = ""
    @State private var buttonDisabled: Bool = false

    var body: some View {
        VStack {
            HStack {
                Button("Close") {
                    dismiss()
                }
                Spacer()
                Button("Create") {
                    let fileName =
inputFileName.trimmingCharacters(in: .whitespaces)
                    if !fileName.isEmpty && !
appData.listOfFiles.contains(where: { $0.name == fileName }) {
                        buttonDisabled = true

                        Task(priority: .high) {
```

```
                await appData.createFile(name: fileName)
                dismiss()
            }
        }
    }.disabled(buttonDisabled)
}.padding()
TextField("Insert name and extension", text: $inputFileName)
    .textFieldStyle(.roundedBorder)
    .autocapitalization(.none)
    .disableAutocorrection(true)
    .padding()
Spacer()
            }
        }
    }
}
```

Listing 15-18: Creating new documents

This view includes a **TextField** view to let the user insert the name of the document and a button to save it. When the user presses the Save button, the code checks whether a file with that name already exists in the **listOfFiles** array, disables the button to show to the user that the action is being processed, and calls the **createFile()** method to add it to the container.

The **ForEach** loop in the **ContentView** view includes a **NavigationLink** view for the rows. This navigation link opens the **EditDocumentView** view to allow the user to edit the selected document. The following are the changes we need to introduced to this view for our example.

```
struct EditDocumentView: View {
    @EnvironmentObject var appData: ApplicationData
    @Environment(\.dismiss) var dismiss
    @State private var inputText: String = ""
    let selectedFile: FileInfo

    var body: some View {
        GroupBox {
            TextEditor(text: $inputText)
        }
        .navigationBarTitle(selectedFile.name)
        .navigationBarTitleDisplayMode(.inline)
        .toolbar {
            ToolbarItem(placement: .navigationBarTrailing) {
                Button("Save") {
                    Task(priority: .high) {
                        await appData.saveDocument(url: selectedFile.url,
content: inputText)
                        dismiss()
                    }
                }
            }
        }
        .task {
            inputText = await appData.openDocument(url: selectedFile.url)
        }
        .onDisappear {
            Task(priority: .background) {
                await appData.closeDocument()
            }
        }
    }
}
struct EditDocumentView_Previews: PreviewProvider {
    static var previews: some View {
        NavigationStack {
```

```
        EditDocumentView(selectedFile: FileInfo(name: "", url:
URL(fileURLWithPath: "")))
            .environmentObject(ApplicationData())
        }
    }
}
```

Listing 15-19: *Displaying the document's content*

This view receives a value of type **FileInfo** with the information of the file selected by the user. As soon as the view is loaded, we initiate an asynchronous task to open the document for this file and assign the content to the **TextEditor** view so the user can see it and modify it.

Figure 15-10: *Interface to read and save multiple documents*

 Do It Yourself: Update the ApplicationData.swift file with the code in Listing 15-12 and the methods in Listings 15-13, 15-14, 15-15, and 15-16. Update the **ContentView** view with the code in Listing 15-17. Create a SwiftUI View file called CreateFileView.swift for the view in Listing 15-18, and update the **EditDocumentView** view with the code in Listing 15-19. Run the application simultaneously in two devices. Press the Create File button to add a document. You should see the document listed on both devices. Slide the row to the left and press the Delete button. The document should be removed in both devices.

Basic) 15.4 CloudKit

CloudKit is a database system in iCloud. Using this system, we can store structured data online with different levels of accessibility. The system offers three types of databases to determine who has access to the information.

- **Private Database** to store data that is accessible only to the user.
- **Public Database** to store data that is accessible to every user running the app.
- **Shared Database** to store data the user wants to share with other users.

CloudKit databases have specific purposes and functionalities. The Private database is used when we want the user to be able to share private information among his or her own devices (only the user can access the information stored in this database), and the Public and Shared databases are used to share information between users. (The information stored in the Public database is accessible to all the users running our app, and the information stored in the Shared database is accessible to the users the user decides to share the data with.)

The data is stored in the database as records and records are stored in zones. The Private and Public databases include a default zone, but the Private and Shared databases also work with custom zones (called Shared Zones in a Shared database), as illustrated below.

Private Database	Public Database	Shared Database

Private Database

Record

Custom Zone

Record

Record

Public Database

Record

Record

Record

Record

Shared Database

Shared Zone

Record

Record

Figure 15-11: Databases configuration

(Basic) **Enabling CloudKit**

As we did with the rest of the iCloud services, the first step to use CloudKit is to activate it from the Signing & Capabilities panel.

Services ☐ Key-value storage
☐ iCloud Documents
☑ CloudKit

Containers ☑ iCloud.com.formasterminds.TestCloudKit
☐ 48S7G5U7J3.ca.invid.MicroTasks
☐ iCloud.ca.invid.AnotherTest
+ ↻

Figure 15-12: CloudKit service

CloudKit requires a container to manage the databases. If the container is not automatically generated by Xcode when we activate the CloudKit service, we must create it ourselves, as we did before for the iCloud Documents service (see Figures 15-6 and 15-7).

Because CloudKit uses Remote Notifications to report changes in the databases, when we activate CloudKit, Xcode automatically includes an additional service called *Push Notifications*.

⌐• **Push Notifications**   ×

Figure 15-13: Push Notifications

Remote Notifications are like the Local Notifications introduced in Chapter 14, but instead of being posted by the app they are sent from a server to inform our app or the user that something changed or needs attention. The Remote Notifications posted by CloudKit are sent from Apple servers when something changes in a database. Because this may happen not only when the user is working with the app but also when the app is in the background, to get these notifications, we must add the Background Mode capability and activate two services called *Background Fetch* and *Remote Notifications*.

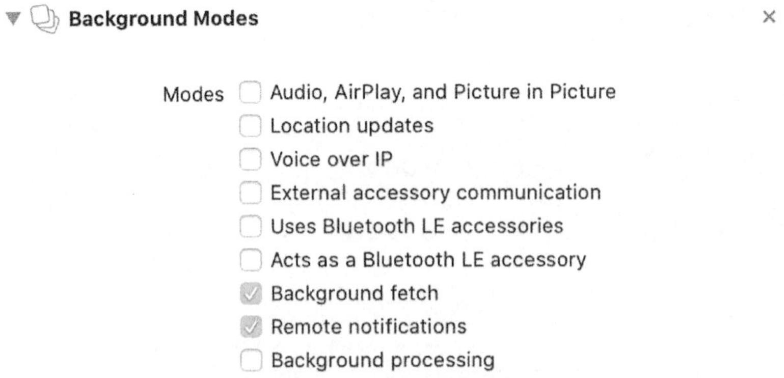

Modes ☐ Audio, AirPlay, and Picture in Picture
      ☐ Location updates
      ☐ Voice over IP
      ☐ External accessory communication
      ☐ Uses Bluetooth LE accessories
      ☐ Acts as a Bluetooth LE accessory
      ☑ Background fetch
      ☑ Remote notifications
      ☐ Background processing

Figure 15-14: Background Mode

Do It Yourself: Create a Multiplatform project. Click on the app's settings option at the top of the Navigator Area (Figure 5-4, number 6) and open the Signing & Capabilities panel. Click on the + button at the top-left corner of the panel to add a capability. Select the iCloud option and press return. Repeat the process to add the Background Modes capability. In the Background Modes section, check the options Background fetch and Remote Notifications (Figure 15-14). In the iCloud section, check the option CloudKit (Figure 15-12). Press the + button to add a container. Insert the app's bundle identifier for the container's name and press the OK button (you can find the bundle identifier at the top of the panel). If the name of the container appears in red, press the Refresh button to upload the information to Apple servers.

(Basic) ## Implementing CloudKit

Although we can access a CloudKit database and manually create, modify and delete records, as we will see later, this requires us to take care not only of the process of keeping the database up to date, but also check for errors and synchronize devices. Because these tasks are usually the same for most applications, Apple provides an API that works along with Core Data to automatically share the data stored on the device with a CloudKit database. All we need to do is to create the Core Data stack with the **NSPersistentCloudKitContainer** class instead of the **NSPersistentContainer** class. After this, the Core Data's Persistent Store is automatically synchronized with CloudKit servers and the data is available on every device logged in to the same iCloud account. The **NSPersistentCloudKitContainer** class is a subclass of the **NSPersistentContainer** class and therefore it includes the same initializer.

NSPersistentCloudKitContainer(name: String)—This initializer creates a Persistent Store with the name specified by the **name** argument.

In addition to common properties, like the **viewContext** property to return a reference to the context, this subclass also includes the following methods in case our application needs to retrieve records manually.

record(for: NSManagedObjectID)—This method returns a **CKRecord** object with the record that corresponds to the Core Data object specified by the **for** argument. The argument is the object's identifier (returned by the **objectID** property). If no record is found, the method returns **nil**.

records(for: [NSManagedObjectID])—This method returns an array of **CKRecord** objects with the records that correspond to the Core Data objects specified by the **for** argument. The argument is an array of identifiers (returned by the **objectID** property).

recordID(for: NSManagedObjectID**)**—This method returns a **CKRecord.ID** value with the identifier of the record that corresponds to the Core Data object specified by the **for** argument. The argument is the object's identifier (returned by the **objectID** property).

recordIDs(for: [NSManagedObjectID]**)**—This method returns an array of **CKRecord.ID** values with the identifiers of the records that correspond to the Core Data objects specified by the **for** argument. The argument is an array of object identifiers (returned by the **objectID** property).

Thanks to this amazing API, creating an application that stores information locally with Core Data and synchronizes the data with a CloudKit database is extremely simple. All we have to do is to define the Core Data stack with the **NSPersistentCloudKitContainer** class and then create the Core Data application as always. As an example, we are going to create an application that stores countries and cities. We need two entities called Cities and Countries. The Cities entity needs an attribute of type String called *name* and a To-One relationship called *country*.

Figure 15-15: Cities entity

And the Countries entity needs an attribute of type String called *name* and a To-Many relationship called *cities*, as shown below.

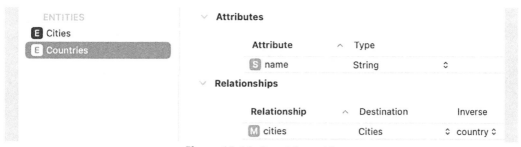

Figure 15-16: Countries entity

There is one more requirement for the model to be ready to work with CloudKit. We must select the Configuration (Figure 15-17, number 1) and check the option Used with CloudKit in the Data Model Inspector panel (Figure 15-17, number 2). This makes sure that if we create other configurations later, the system knows which one must be synchronized with CloudKit servers.

Figure 15-17: Used with CloudKit option

Do It Yourself: Create a Core Data model from the File menu (Chapter 10, Figure 10-20). Add two entities to the model called Countries and Cities with their respective attributes and relationships, as shown in Figures 15-14 and 15-15. Select the Default configuration (Figure 15-17, number 1), open the Data Model Inspector panel on the right, and check the Used with CloudKit option (Figure 15-17, number 2).

 IMPORTANT: If we later want to create additional Entities to store information only on the device, we can add a new configuration to the Core Data model, assign the Entities to that configuration, and keep the Used with CloudKit option unchecked. All the objects stored for those Entities will not be synchronized with CloudKit.

Once the application is configured to work with CloudKit and the Core Data model is ready, we can work on our code. First, we must initialize the Core Data stack as we did before but using the `NSPersistentCloudKitContainer` class instead (see Listing 10-56).

```
import SwiftUI
import CoreData

class ApplicationData: ObservableObject {
    let container: NSPersistentCloudKitContainer

    static var preview: ApplicationData = {
        let model = ApplicationData(preview: true)
        return model
    }()
    init(preview: Bool = false) {
        container = NSPersistentCloudKitContainer(name: "Model")
        if preview {
            container.persistentStoreDescriptions.first!.url =
URL(fileURLWithPath: "/dev/null")
        }
        container.viewContext.automaticallyMergesChangesFromParent = true
        container.loadPersistentStores(completionHandler:
{ (storeDescription, error) in
            if let error = error as NSError? {
                fatalError("Unresolved error \(error), \(error.userInfo)")
            }
        })
    }
}
```

Listing 15-20: Preparing Core Data to work with CloudKit

The `persistentContainer` property is set as before, but instead of returning an `NSPersistentContainer` value it returns an `NSPersistentCloudKitContainer` value to synchronize the Persistent Store with CloudKit servers.

As always, we need to inject the context into the environment from the **App** structure.

```
import SwiftUI

@main
struct TestApp: App {
    @StateObject var appData = ApplicationData()

    var body: some Scene {
        WindowGroup {
            ContentView()
                .environment(\.managedObjectContext,
appData.container.viewContext)
```

```
            }
        }
    }
}
```

Listing 15-21: Injecting the context into the environment

And that's all it takes. From now on, every change introduced in the Persistent Store is going to be uploaded to CloudKit and every device running the application is going to be automatically synchronized. All that is left is to design the views to display the objects or add new ones. Here is the initial view for our example.

```
import SwiftUI
import CoreData

struct ContentView: View {
   @Environment(\.managedObjectContext) var dbContext
   @FetchRequest(sortDescriptors: [SortDescriptor(\Countries.name, order:
.forward)]) var listCountries: FetchedResults<Countries>
   @State private var openSheet: Bool = false

   var body: some View {
      NavigationStack {
         List {
            ForEach(listCountries) { country in
               NavigationLink(destination:
ShowCitiesView(selectedCountry: country)) {
                  Text(country.name ?? "Undefined")
               }
            }
         }
         .navigationBarTitle("Countries")
         .toolbar {
            ToolbarItem(placement: .navigationBarTrailing) {
               Button("Add Country") {
                  openSheet = true
               }
            }
         }
         .sheet(isPresented: $openSheet) {
            InsertCountryView()
         }
      }
   }
}
struct ContentView_Previews: PreviewProvider {
   static var previews: some View {
      ContentView()
         .environment(\.managedObjectContext,
ApplicationData.preview.container.viewContext)
   }
}
```

Listing 15-22: Listing the countries stored in the Persistent Store

This view defines a **@FetchRequest** property to load the objects of type **Countries** from the Persistent Store and then lists the values with a **List** view. As previous examples, the view includes a button to open the **InsertCountryView** view to let the user insert a new country.

```
import SwiftUI
import CoreData

struct InsertCountryView: View {
   @Environment(\.managedObjectContext) var dbContext
```

```
@Environment(\.dismiss) var dismiss
@State private var inputName: String = ""

var body: some View {
    VStack {
        HStack {
            Text("Country:")
            TextField("Insert Country", text: $inputName)
                .textFieldStyle(.roundedBorder)
        }
        HStack {
            Spacer()
            Button("Save") {
                let text = inputName.trimmingCharacters(in: .whitespaces)
                if !text.isEmpty {
                    let newCountry = Countries(context: dbContext)
                    newCountry.name = text
                    do {
                        try dbContext.save()
                    } catch {
                        print("Error saving country")
                    }
                    dismiss()
                }
            }
        }
        Spacer()
    }.padding()
}
}
struct InsertCountryView_Previews: PreviewProvider {
    static var previews: some View {
        InsertCountryView()
            .environment(\.managedObjectContext,
ApplicationData.preview.container.viewContext)
    }
}
```

Listing 15-23: Inserting new countries in the Persistent Store

There is also nothing new in this view. We create a new **Countries** object with the value inserted by the user when the Save button is pressed and save the context with the **save()** method, but because the application is connected to CloudKit the system automatically creates a record from the **Countries** object and uploads it to CloudKit servers.

The following is the **ShowsCitiesView** view opened when a country is selected by the user.

```
import SwiftUI
import CoreData
struct ShowCitiesView: View {
    @FetchRequest(sortDescriptors: [], predicate: NSPredicate(format:
"FALSEPREDICATE")) var listCities: FetchedResults<Cities>
    @State private var openSheet: Bool = false
    let selectedCountry: Countries?

    init(selectedCountry: Countries?) {
        self.selectedCountry = selectedCountry
        if selectedCountry != nil {
            _listCities = FetchRequest(sortDescriptors:
[SortDescriptor(\Cities.name, order: .forward)], predicate:
NSPredicate(format: "country = %@", selectedCountry!),
animation: .default)
        }
    }
```

```
    var body: some View {
        List {
            ForEach(listCities) { city in
                Text(city.name ?? "Undefined")
            }
        }
        .navigationBarTitle(selectedCountry?.name ?? "Undefined")
        .toolbar {
            ToolbarItem(placement: .navigationBarTrailing) {
                Button("Add City") {
                    openSheet = true
                }
            }
        }
        .sheet(isPresented: $openSheet) {
            InsertCityView(country: selectedCountry)
        }
    }
}
struct ShowCitiesView_Previews: PreviewProvider {
    static var previews: some View {
        NavigationStack {
            ShowCitiesView(selectedCountry: nil)
                .environment(\.managedObjectContext,
ApplicationData.preview.container.viewContext)
        }
    }
}
```

Listing 15-24: Listing the cities stored in the Persistent Store

This view lists the cities with a **List** view, as we did before for the countries, but because we only need to show the cities that belong to the selected country, we initialize the **@FetchRequest** property wrapper with a false predicate and then use the **Countries** object returned by the **selectedCountry** property to create a new **FetchRequest** structure with a predicate that filters the cities by country (see Listing 10-68).

The **ShowCitiesView** view also includes a button to let the user insert new cities. The following is the view opened by the **sheet()** modifier when the button is pressed.

```
import SwiftUI
import CoreData

struct InsertCityView: View {
    @Environment(\.managedObjectContext) var dbContext
    @Environment(\.dismiss) var dismiss
    @State private var inputName: String = ""
    let country: Countries?

    var body: some View {
        VStack {
            HStack {
                Text("City:")
                TextField("Insert City", text: $inputName)
                    .textFieldStyle(.roundedBorder)
            }
            HStack {
                Spacer()
                Button("Save") {
                    let text = inputName.trimmingCharacters(in: .whitespaces)
                    if !text.isEmpty {
                        let newCity = Cities(context: dbContext)
                        newCity.name = text
                        newCity.country = country
```

```
                do {
                    try dbContext.save()
                } catch {
                    print("Error saving city")
                }
                dismiss()
            }
        }
    }
    Spacer()
}.padding()
            }
        }
struct InsertCityView_Previews: PreviewProvider {
    static var previews: some View {
        InsertCityView(country: nil)
            .environment(\.managedObjectContext,
ApplicationData.preview.container.viewContext)
    }
}
```

Listing 15-25: Inserting new cities in the Persistent Store

Again, we just create a new **Cities** object with the value inserted by the user when the Save button is pressed and the system takes care of creating the record an uploading it to CloudKit.

The application shows the list of countries and cities stored in the Persistent Store, and allows the user to insert new values, as previous Core Data applications, but now all the information is uploaded to CloudKit servers and automatically shared with other devices.

Figure 15-18: Working with CloudKit

Do It Yourself: Create a Swift file called ApplicationData.swift for the model in Listing 15-20. Remember to assign the name of your Core Data model to the **NSPersistentCloudKitContainer** initializer. Update the **App** structure with the code in Listing 15-21 and the ContentView.swift file with the code in Listing 15-22. Create SwiftUI View files called InsertCountryView.swift, ShowCitiesView.swift, and InsertCityView.swift for the codes in Listings 15-23, 15-24, and 15-25. Run the application in two devices. Press the Add Country button and insert a new country. After a few seconds, you should see the same value appear on the second device. Repeat the process for the cities.

(Basic) **Custom Implementation**

Of course, we can also implement CloudKit on our own. This requires accessing the container and the database, and manually managing the records inside. First, we need access to the CloudKit container. This is a space in Apple's servers designated to our app. The framework provides a class called **CKContainer** to access the container and the databases it contains. Because an app may have more than one container, the class includes an initializer to get a reference to a specific container and a type method to get a reference to the container by default.

CKContainer(identifier: String**)**—This initializer creates the **CKContainer** object that references the container identified with the name specified by the **identifier** argument. It is required when working with multiple containers or the container's name is different from the Bundle's identifier.

default()—This type method returns the **CKContainer** object that references the container by default (the container named after the Bundle's identifier).

Container objects provide the following properties to get access to the databases.

privateCloudDatabase—This property returns a **CKDatabase** object with a reference to the user's Private database.

publicCloudDatabase—This property returns a **CKDatabase** object with a reference to the app's Public database.

sharedCloudDatabase—This property returns a **CKDatabase** object with a reference to the user's Shared database.

(Basic) **Records**

Once we have decided which database we are going to use, we must generate records to store the user's data. Records are objects that store information as key/value pairs, like dictionaries. These objects are classified by types to determine the characteristics of the record. For example, if we want to store records that contain information about books, we can use the type "Books", and if later we want to store records with information about authors, we can use the type "Authors". (A type is analog to the Entities in Core Data.) The framework provides the **CKRecord** class to create and manage records. The class includes the following initializer.

CKRecord(recordType: String, **recordID:** CKRecord.ID**)**—This initializer creates a **CKRecord** object of the type and with the ID specified by the arguments. The **recordType** argument is a custom identifier for the type, and the **recordID** argument is the record's identifier.

Records are identified with an ID that includes a name and a reference to the zone the record belongs to. (If a custom ID is not specified, the record is stored with an ID generated by CloudKit.) To create and access the ID and its values, the **CKRecord** class defines the **ID** class with the following initializers and properties.

CKRecord.ID(recordName: String**)**—This initializer creates a **CKRecord.ID** object to identify a record. The **recordName** argument is the name we want to give to the record (it must be unique).

CKRecord.ID(recordName: String, **zoneID:** CKRecordZone.ID**)**—This initializer creates a **CKRecord.ID** object to identify a record stored with the name and in the zone specified by the arguments. The **recordName** argument is the name we want to give to the record, and the **zoneID** argument is the identifier of the custom zone where we want to store it.

recordName—This property returns a string with the name of the record.

zoneID—This property returns a **CKRecordZone.ID** object with the ID of the zone the record belongs to.

The **CKRecord** class offers properties to set or get the record's ID and other attributes. The following are the most frequently used.

recordID—This property returns the **CKRecord.ID** object that identifies the record.

recordType—This property returns a string that determines the record's type.

recordChangeTag—This property returns a string with the tag assigned to the record (each record is assigned a tag by the server).

creationDate—This property returns a **Date** value with the date in which the record was created.

modificationDate—This property returns a **Date** value that indicates the last time the record was modified.

Because the values of a record are stored as key/value pairs, we can use square brackets to read and modify them (as we do with dictionaries), but the class also includes the following methods.

setObject(Value?, **forKey:** String**)**—This method sets or updates a value in the record. The fist argument is the value we want to store, and the **forKey** argument is the key we want to use to identify the value. The value must be any of the following types: **NSString**, **NSNumber**, **NSData**, **NSDate**, **NSArray**, **CLLocation**, **CKAsset**, and **Reference**.

object(forKey: String**)**—This method returns the value associated with the key specified by the **forKey** argument. The value is returned as a generic **CKRecordValue** type that we must cast to the right data type.

Basic Zones

As illustrated in Figure 15-11, the Public database can only store records in a default zone, but the Private and Shared databases can include custom zones. In the case of the Private database, the custom zones are optional (although they are required for synchronization, as we will see later).

Zones are like sections inside a database to separate records that are not directly related. For example, we may have an app that stores locations, like the names of countries and cities, but also allows the user to store a list of Christmas gifts. In cases like this, we can create a zone to store the records that include information about countries and cities and another zone to store the records that include information about the gifts. The CloudKit framework provides the **CKRecordZone** class to represent these zones. The class includes an initializer to create custom zones and a type method to get a reference to the zone by default.

CKRecordZone(zoneName: String**)**—This initializer creates a **CKRecordZone** object to represent a zone with the name specified by the **zoneName** argument.

default()—This type method returns the **CKRecordZone** object that represents the zone by default.

Basic Query

When we want to access data stored in CloudKit, we must download the records from the database and read their values. Records may be fetched from a database one by one using their ID or in a batch using a query. To define a query, the framework provides the **CKQuery** class. The class includes the following initializer and properties.

CKQuery(recordType: String, **predicate:** NSPredicate)—This initializer creates a **CKQuery** object to fetch multiple records from a database. The **recordType** argument specifies the type of records we want to fetch, and the **predicate** argument determines the matching criteria we want to use to select the records.

recordType—This property sets or returns a string that determines the type of records we want to fetch.

predicate—This property sets or returns an **NSPredicate** object that defines the matching criteria for the query.

sortDescriptors—This property sets or returns an array of **NSSortDescriptor** objects that determine the order of the records returned by the query.

(Basic) **Asynchronous Operations**

CloudKit is an online service and therefore any task may take time to process. For this reason, the CloudKit framework uses asynchronous operations to access the information on the servers. An operation must be created for every process we want to perform on a database, including storing, reading, and organizing records.

These operations are like Swift asynchronous tasks but created from classes defined in the Foundation framework. The CloudKit framework includes its own subclasses of the Foundation classes to define operations. There is a base class called **CKDatabaseOperation**, and then several subclasses for every operation we need. Once an operation is defined, it must be added to the **CKDatabase** object that represents the database we want to modify. The **CKDatabase** class offers the following method for this purpose.

add(CKDatabaseOperation)—This method executes the operation specified by the argument on the database. The argument is an object of a subclass of the **CKDatabaseOperation** class.

Although we can create single operations and assign them to the database, as we will see later, the **CKDatabase** class also offers convenient methods to generate and execute the most common. The following are the methods available to process records.

record(for: CKRecord.ID)—This asynchronous method fetches the record with the ID specified by the **for** argument. The method returns a **CKRecord** object with the record, or an error if the record is not found.

save(CKRecord)—This asynchronous method stores a record in the database. (If the record exists, it is updated.) The argument is a reference to the record we want to store.

deleteRecord(withID: CKRecord.ID)—This asynchronous method deletes from the database the record with the identifier specified by the **withID** argument.

The following are the methods provided by the **CKDatabase** class to process zones.

recordZone(for: CKRecordZone.ID)—This asynchronous method fetches the zone with the ID specified by the **for** argument. The method returns a **CKRecordZone** object representing the zone that was fetched or an error if the zone is not found.

allRecordZones()—This asynchronous method fetches all the zones available in the database. The method returns an array of **CKRecordZone** objects representing the zones that were fetched or an error if no zones are found.

save(CKRecordZone)—This asynchronous method creates a zone in the database. The argument is the object representing the zone we want to create.

deleteRecordZone(withID: CKRecordZone.ID**)**—This asynchronous method deletes from the database the zone with the ID specified by the **withID** argument.

To fetch multiple records, the **CKDatabase** class includes the following convenient methods.

records(matching: CKQuery, **inZoneWith:** CKRecordZone.ID?, **desiredKeys:** [CKRecord.FieldKey]?, **resultsLimit:** Int**)**—This asynchronous method performs the query specified by the **matching** argument in the zone specified by the **inZoneWith** argument. The **desiredKeys** argument is an array of the values we want the records to include, and the **resultsLimit** argument determines the number of records we want to fetch (the value 0 returns all the records that match the query). The method returns a tuple with two values called **matchResults** and **queryCursor**. The **matchResults** value is an array of tuples with two values: the record identifier and a **Result** with the records and errors found. On the other hand, the **queryCursor** value is a cursor we can use to fetch more records that match this query.

records(continuingMatchFrom: Cursor, **desiredKeys:** Dictionary, **resultsLimit:** Int**)**—This asynchronous method creates an operation that fetches records starting from the cursor specified by the **continuingMatchFrom** argument. The cursor is an object that configures a query to retrieve the remaining results of a previous query. The **desiredKeys** argument is an array of the values we want the records to include, and the **resultsLimit** argument determines the number of records we want to fetch (the value 0 returns all the records that match the query). The method returns a tuple with two values called **matchResults** and **queryCursor**. The **matchResults** value is an array of tuples with two values: the record identifier and a **Result** enumeration value with the records and errors found. On the other hand, the **queryCursor** value is a cursor we can use to fetch more records that match this query.

Medium Batch Operations

Although the methods provided by the **CKDatabase** class are very convenient and easy to implement, they only perform one request at a time. The problem is that CloudKit servers have a limit on the number of operations we can perform per second (currently 40 requests per second are allowed), so if our application relies heavily on CloudKit, at one point some of the requests might be rejected if we send them one by one. The solution is to create operations that allow us to perform multiple requests at once. The CloudKit framework defines three subclasses of the **CKDatabaseOperation** class for this purpose. The **CKModifySubscriptionsOperation** class creates an operation to add or modify subscriptions, the **CKModifyRecordZones-Operation** class is used to add or modify record zones, and the **CKModifyRecordsOperation** class is for adding and modifying records.

CKModifySubscriptionsOperation(subscriptionsToSave: [CKSubscription], **subscriptionIDsToDelete:** [CKSubscription.ID]**)**—This initializer returns an operation that adds or modifies one or more subscriptions. The **subscriptionsToSave** argument is an array with the subscriptions we want to add or modify, and the **subscriptionIDsToDelete** argument is an array with the IDs of the subscriptions we want to delete from the server.

CKModifyRecordZonesOperation(recordZonesToSave: [CKRecordZone], **recordZoneIDsToDelete:** [CKRecordZone.ID]**)**—This initializer returns an operation that adds or modifies one or more record zones. The **recordZonesToSave** argument is an array with the record zones we want to add or modify, and the **recordZoneIDsToDelete** is an array with the IDs of the record zones we want to delete from the server.

CKModifyRecordsOperation(recordsToSave: [CKRecord], **recordIDsTo-Delete:** [CKRecord.ID])—This operation adds or modifies one or more records. The **recordsToSave** argument is an array with the records we want to add or modify, and the **recordIDsToDelete** argument is an array with the IDs of the records we want to delete from the server.

These operations must be initialized first and then added to the database with the **add()** method of the **CKDatabase** class. Each initializer offers the options to modify elements and remove them. If we only need to perform one task, the other can be omitted with the value **nil**.

(Basic) References

Records of different types are usually related. For example, along with records of type Countries we may have records of type Cities to store information about the cities of each country. To create these relationships, records include references. References are objects that store information about a connection between one record and another. They are created from the **Reference** class defined inside the **CKRecord** class. The following are its initializers.

CKRecord.Reference(recordID: CKRecord.ID, **action:** CKRecord.ReferenceAction)—This initializer creates a **Reference** object pointing to the record identified with the ID specified by the **recordID** argument. The **action** argument is an enumeration that determines what the database should do with the record when the record that is referencing is deleted. The possible values are **none** (nothing is done) and **deleteSelf** (when the record referenced by the reference is deleted, the record with the reference is deleted as well).

CKRecord.Reference(record: CKRecord, **action:** CKRecord.ReferenceAction) —This initializer creates a **Reference** object pointing to the record specified by the **record** argument. The **action** argument is an enumeration that determines what the database should do with the record when the record that is referencing is deleted. The possible values are **none** (nothing is done) and **deleteSelf** (when the record referenced by the reference is deleted, the record with the reference is deleted as well).

References in CloudKit are called *Back References* because they are assigned to the record that is the children of another record. Following our example, the reference should be assigned to the city and not the country, as illustrated next.

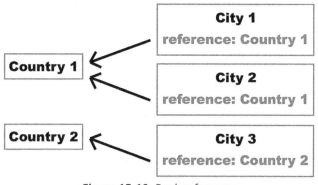

Figure 15-19: Back references

(Basic) CloudKit Dashboard

CloudKit creates a model of our app's database on its servers as records are added to the database. For example, if our app stores records of type "Books", the first time a record is created, CloudKit adds the type "Books" to the list of record types available for our app and creates fields to represent each of the values in the record. This way, the system sets up the database's structure from the data we store during development, saving us the trouble of configuring the database beforehand. (We do not have to create a model as we do with Core Data.) But there are some configuration parameters that the system cannot determine and we need to set up ourselves. For this purpose, Apple provides the CloudKit dashboard. This is an online control panel that we can use to manage the CloudKit databases, add, update, or remove records, and configure the schema.

The panel is available at **icloud.developer.apple.com/dashboard/** or by clicking on the CloudKit Dashboard button at the bottom of the iCloud section in the Signing & Capabilities panel. The dashboard's home page includes four buttons to access the tools available. We can configure the database, check how our database is performing, check user activity, and manage our account.

Figure 15-20: *Buttons in the main menu*

If we click on the CloudKit Database button, a panel is loaded to edit the database. The panel includes an option at the top to select the container (Figure 15-21, number 1), a bar on the left to edit the data and the schema, and a bar on the right to show and edit the values.

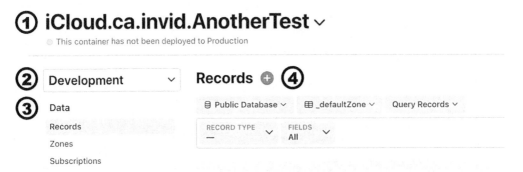

Figure 15-21: *Database panel*

The bar on the left includes a button to select from two configurations: Development and Production (Figure 15-21, number 2). The Development option shows the configuration of the database used during development. This is the database we use as we develop our app. The Production option shows the configuration of the database that we are going to deliver with our app (the one that is going to be available to our users).

During development, we can store information in the database for testing. Below the configuration option is the Data section (Figure 15-21, number 3) where we can edit the data stored by our application, including records, zones, and subscriptions. The panel also offers an option on the right to add records (Figure 15-21, number 4), and buttons to select the database we want to access (Public, Private, or Shared), select the zone, and indicate how we want to access the records.

IMPORTANT: Notice that the Public Database is selected by default. If you want to see the records stored by the examples in this chapter, you need to click on this button and select the Private Database instead.

As we already explained, the schema (the database model) is automatically generated by CloudKit servers when we save records from our app during development. For instance, if our app creates a Books record, the server creates a record type called Books and adds it to the database model. In theory, this is enough to create the model, but in practice we always need to erase record types or values that we don't use anymore and add or modify others that the app may need later. For this purpose, the dashboard provides access to the schema on the left-side bar.

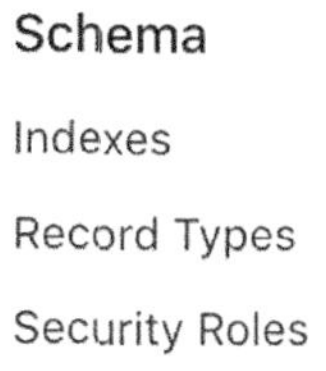

Schema

Indexes

Record Types

Security Roles

Figure 15-22: Database schema

From the Record Types option, we can add, modify, or delete record types (Entities) and their values (Attributes). The option to add a new record type is at the top of the panel (Figure 15-23, number 1), and the record types already created are listed below (Figure 15-23, number 2).

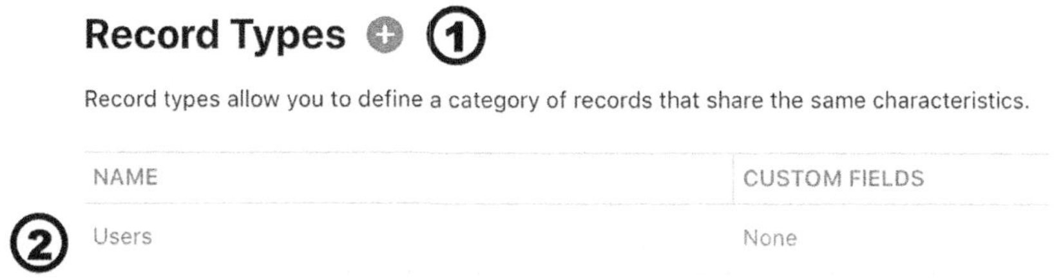

Record Types ⊕ ①

Record types allow you to define a category of records that share the same characteristics.

NAME	CUSTOM FIELDS
② Users	None

Figure 15-23: Record types

(Basic) **Custom CloudKit Application**

Using the tools introduced above, we can implement CloudKit on our own, but there are several ways to do it. It all depends on the characteristics of our application and what we want to achieve. An alternative is to centralize all the logic in the model. For instance, the following is a possible implementation of the application created before with Core Data to store countries and cities.

```
import SwiftUI
import CloudKit
struct Country {
   var name: String?
   var record: CKRecord
}
struct City {
   var name: String?
   var record: CKRecord
}
struct CountryViewModel: Identifiable {
   var id: CKRecord.ID
   var country: Country

   var countryName: String {
```

```
            return country.name ?? "Undefined"
      }
}
struct CityViewModel: Identifiable {
      var id: CKRecord.ID
      var city: City

      var cityName: String {
            return city.name ?? "Undefined"
      }
}
class ApplicationData: ObservableObject {
      @Published var listCountries: [CountryViewModel] = []
      @Published var listCities: [CityViewModel] = []
      var database: CKDatabase!

      init() {
            let container = CKContainer.default()
            database = container.privateCloudDatabase

            Task(priority: .high) {
                  await readCountries()
            }
      }
      func insertCountry(name: String) async {
            let id = CKRecord.ID(recordName: "idcountry-\(UUID())")
            let record = CKRecord(recordType: "Countries", recordID: id)
            record.setObject(name as NSString, forKey: "name")

            do {
                  try await database.save(record)
                  await MainActor.run {
                        let newCountry = Country(name: record["name"], record:
record)
                        let newItem = CountryViewModel(id: record.recordID, country:
newCountry)
                        listCountries.append(newItem)
                        listCountries.sort(by: { $0.countryName < $1.countryName })
                  }
            } catch {
                  print("Error: \(error)")
            }
      }
      func insertCity(name: String, country: CKRecord.ID) async {
            let id = CKRecord.ID(recordName: "idcity-\(UUID())")
            let record = CKRecord(recordType: "Cities", recordID: id)
            record.setObject(name as NSString, forKey: "name")

            let reference = CKRecord.Reference(recordID: country,
action: .deleteSelf)
            record.setObject(reference, forKey: "country")

            do {
                  try await database.save(record)
                  await MainActor.run {
                        let newCity = City(name: record["name"], record: record)
                        let newItem = CityViewModel(id: record.recordID, city:
newCity)
                        listCities.append(newItem)
                        listCities.sort(by: { $0.cityName < $1.cityName })
                  }
            } catch {
                  print("Error: \(error)")
            }
      }
      func readCountries() async {
            let predicate = NSPredicate(format: "TRUEPREDICATE")
```

```
        let query = CKQuery(recordType: "Countries", predicate: predicate)
        do {
            let list = try await database.records(matching: query,
inZoneWith: nil, desiredKeys: nil, resultsLimit: 0)
            await MainActor.run {
                listCountries = []
                for (_, result) in list.matchResults {
                    if let record = try? result.get() {
                        let newCountry = Country(name: record["name"], record:
record)
                        let newItem = CountryViewModel(id: record.recordID,
country: newCountry)
                        listCountries.append(newItem)
                    }
                }
                listCountries.sort(by: { $0.countryName < $1.countryName })
            }
        } catch {
            print("Error: \(error)")
        }
    }
    func readCities(country: CKRecord.ID) async {
        let predicate = NSPredicate(format: "country = %@", country)
        let query = CKQuery(recordType: "Cities", predicate: predicate)
        do {
            let list = try await database.records(matching: query,
inZoneWith: nil, desiredKeys: nil, resultsLimit: 0)
            await MainActor.run {
                listCities = []
                for (_, result) in list.matchResults {
                    if let record = try? result.get() {
                        let newCity = City(name: record["name"], record:
record)
                        let newItem = CityViewModel(id: record.recordID, city:
newCity)
                        listCities.append(newItem)
                    }
                }
                listCities.sort(by: { $0.cityName < $1.cityName })
            }
        } catch {
            print("Error: \(error)")
        }
    }
}
```

Listing 15-26: Defining a model for CloudKit

We begin by defining two structures, **Country** and **City**, to store the name of the country and city, and also a reference to the record downloaded from the CloudKit database, and two more for our view model, **CountryViewModel** and **CityViewModel**. These view models identify each value by the record ID (**CKRecord.ID**) and include a computed property to return a string with the name.

The observable object defines the **@Published** properties we need to store the data locally and show it to the user. The **listCountries** property is an array with the list of countries already inserted in the database, and the **listCities** property is another array with the list of cities available for a specific country. Another property included in this class is **database**. This property stores a reference to the CloudKit's database, so we can access it from anywhere in the code. The property is initialized in the **init()** method with a reference to the Private Database.

(We use the private database because we only want the user to be able to share the data between his or her own devices.)

The observable object also includes methods to add and read records. For instance, the **insertCountry()** and **insertCity()** methods are going to be called from the views when the user inserts a new country or city. Their task is to create the records and upload them to CloudKit. The process begins by defining a record ID, which is a unique value that identifies each record. For the countries, we use the string "idcountry" followed by a random value generated by the **UUID()** function. Using this ID, we create a **CKRecord** object of type Countries, then add a property called "name" with the value received by the method, and finally save it in CloudKit servers with the **save()** method of the **CKDatabase** object. This method generates an operation that communicates with the servers asynchronously. If there is no error, we add the record to the **listCountries** property, which updates the views and the screen.

The method to add a city is the same, with the exceptions that we must define the type of records as Cities and add an extra attribute to the record with a reference to the country the city belongs to. For this purpose, we create a **Reference** object with the country's record ID received by the method and an action of type **deleteSelf**, so when the record of the country is deleted, this record is deleted as well.

Next are the methods we need to implement to read the countries and cities already stored in the database. In the **readCountries()** method, we define a predicate with the TRUEPREDICATE keyword and a query for records of type Countries. The record type asks the server to only look for records of type Countries, and the TRUEPREDICATE keyword determines that the predicate will always return true, so we get back all the records available. If the query doesn't return any errors, we get the records from the **matchResults** value and add them to the **listCountries** array to update the views.

The **readCities()** method is very similar, except that this time we are getting the list of cities that belong to the country selected by the user. (The view that shows the cities only opens when the user taps on a row to select a country.) The rest of the process is the same. We get the records that represent the cities, create the **CityViewModel** structures with them, and store them in the **listCities** array.

 IMPORTANT: This example assumes that you have assigned the bundle's name to the container and therefore we get a reference to the container with the **default()** type method. If the name assigned to the container is different than the bundle's, you can specify it with the **CKContainer** initializer, as in **CKContainer(identifier: "iCloud.com.mydomain.MyContainer")**.

For the interface, we need a total of four views: a view to show the list of countries, a view to allow the user to insert a new country, a view to show the list of cities that belong to the selected country, and another view to allow the user to insert a new city. The following is the initial view.

```
struct ContentView: View {
    @EnvironmentObject var appData: ApplicationData
    @State private var openSheet: Bool = false

    var body: some View {
        NavigationStack {
            List {
                ForEach(appData.listCountries) { country in
                    NavigationLink(destination:
ShowCitiesView(selectedCountry: country)) {
                        Text(country.countryName)
                    }
                }
            }
            .navigationBarTitle("Countries")
            .toolbar {
```

```
            ToolbarItem(placement: .navigationBarTrailing) {
                Button("Add Country") {
                    openSheet = true
                }
            }
        }
        .sheet(isPresented: $openSheet) {
            InsertCountryView()
        }
      }
    }
  }
}
struct ContentView_Previews: PreviewProvider {
    static var previews: some View {
        ContentView().environmentObject(ApplicationData())
    }
}
```

The countries stored in the CloudKit database are retrieved by the **readCountries()** method in our model. This method is called when the observable object is initialized, so all the view has to do is to list the countries stored in the **listCountries** property.

To let the user add a new country, the view includes a **sheet()** modifier that opens the **InsertCountryView** view. The following is our implementation of this view.

```
import SwiftUI
import CloudKit

struct InsertCountryView: View {
    @EnvironmentObject var appData: ApplicationData
    @Environment(\.dismiss) var dismiss
    @State private var inputName: String = ""
    @State private var buttonDisabled: Bool = false

    var body: some View {
        VStack {
            HStack {
                Text("Country:")
                TextField("Insert Country", text: $inputName)
                    .textFieldStyle(.roundedBorder)
            }
            HStack {
                Spacer()
                Button("Save") {
                    let text = inputName.trimmingCharacters(in: .whitespaces)
                    if !text.isEmpty {
                        buttonDisabled = true

                        Task(priority: .high) {
                            await appData.insertCountry(name: text)
                            dismiss()
                        }
                    }
                }.disabled(buttonDisabled)
            }
            Spacer()
        }.padding()
    }
}
struct InsertCountryView_Previews: PreviewProvider {
    static var previews: some View {
        InsertCountryView().environmentObject(ApplicationData())
```

```
        }
    }
```

Listing 15-28: Storing countries in the Private database

This view includes a **TextField** view to insert the name of the country and a button to save it in the database. When the button is pressed, we call the **insertCountry()** method in the model. The method creates the record with the value inserted by the user and calls the **save()** method on the database to store it in CloudKit servers.

Next is the view necessary to show the list of cities available for each country. The view is called **ShowCitiesView** and opens when the user taps on a row in the initial view to select a country.

```
import SwiftUI
import CloudKit

struct ShowCitiesView: View {
    @EnvironmentObject var appData: ApplicationData
    @State private var openSheet: Bool = false
    let selectedCountry: CountryViewModel

    var body: some View {
        VStack {
            List {
                ForEach(appData.listCities) { city in
                    Text(city.cityName)
                }
            }
        }
        .navigationBarTitle(selectedCountry.countryName)
        .toolbar {
            ToolbarItem(placement: .navigationBarTrailing) {
                Button("Add City") {
                    openSheet = true
                }
            }
        }
        .sheet(isPresented: $openSheet) {
            InsertCityView(country: selectedCountry.id)
        }
        .task {
            await appData.readCities(country: selectedCountry.id)
        }
    }
}
struct ShowCitiesView_Previews: PreviewProvider {
    static var previews: some View {
        ShowCitiesView(selectedCountry: CountryViewModel(id:
CKRecord.ID(recordName: "Test"), country: Country(name: "Test", record:
CKRecord(recordType: "Cities", recordID: CKRecord.ID(recordName:
"Test")))))
            .environmentObject(ApplicationData())
    }
}
```

Listing 15-29: Listing the cities of a country

This view includes a property of type **CountryViewModel** called **selectedCountry** to receive the information about the selected country. Form this property, we get the country's record ID and call the **readCities()** method in the model when the view appears to retrieve the cities available for that country. The view creates a list with these values and then includes a

sheet() modifier to let the user add more. The modifier opens a view called **InsertCityView** for this purpose.

```
import SwiftUI
import CloudKit

struct InsertCityView: View {
   @EnvironmentObject var appData: ApplicationData
   @Environment(\.dismiss) var dismiss

   @State private var inputName: String = ""
   @State private var buttonDisabled: Bool = false
   let country: CKRecord.ID

   var body: some View {
      VStack {
         HStack {
            Text("City:")
            TextField("Insert City", text: $inputName)
               .textFieldStyle(.roundedBorder)
         }
         HStack {
            Spacer()
            Button("Save") {
               let text = inputName.trimmingCharacters(in: .whitespaces)
               if !text.isEmpty {
                  buttonDisabled = true

                  Task(priority: .high) {
                     await appData.insertCity(name: text, country:
self.country)
                     dismiss()
                  }
               }
            }.disabled(buttonDisabled)
         }
         Spacer()
      }.padding()
   }
}
struct InsertCityView_Previews: PreviewProvider {
   static var previews: some View {
      InsertCityView(country: CKRecord.ID(recordName: "Test"))
         .environmentObject(ApplicationData())
   }
}
```

Listing 15-30: Storing cities in the Private Database

The view receives the country's record ID to know which country the city belongs to, and then calls the **insertCity()** method in the model with the name inserted by the user and this ID to create a Cities record connected to that Countries record in the CloudKit database.

Do It Yourself: Create a new Multiplatform project. Open the Signing & Capabilities panel, add the iCloud capability, and check the CloudKit option (Figure 15-11). Add a container with the app's bundle as the name. Add the Background Modes capability and check the options Background fetch and Remote Notifications. Create a Swift file called ApplicationData.swift for the model in Listing 15-26. Update the **ContentView** view with the code in Listing 15-27. Create SwiftUI View files with the names InsertCountryView.swift, ShowCitiesView.swift, and InsertCityView.swift for the codes in Listings 15-28, 15-29, and 15-30, respectively. Remember to inject the **ApplicationData**

object into the environment for the app and the previews (Chapter 7, Listing 7-4). Run the application on a device and press the Add Country button to insert a country. Select the country and press the Add City button to add a city.

The application is ready. When the user inserts a new value, the code creates a record and uploads it to CloudKit servers, but if we stop and start the application again, the countries are not shown on the screen anymore. This is because we haven't defined the required indexes.

CloudKit automatically creates indexes for every key we include in the records, except for the record's identifier. Therefore, when we query the Cities records by their country attribute to get the cities that belong to the country selected by the user, CloudKit knows how to find and return those records, but when we try to retrieve the Countries records without a predicate, CloudKit tries to fetch them by the record identifiers and fails because there is no index associated to that attribute (called *recordName*). To create an index for this attribute, we need to go to the dashboard, click on the Indexes option in the Schema section, and click on the Countries record type to modify it.

When we click on a record, the panel shows the list of indexes available. By default, the Countries records contains three indexes for the name attribute, but no index for the record's identifier.

"Countries" Indexes

FIELD	INDEX TYPE	
name	QUERYABLE	⊖
name	SEARCHABLE	⊖
name	SORTABLE	⊖

Figure 15-24: *Record's indexes*

To add an index, we must press the Add Basic Index button at the bottom of the list. The panel opens a form to create a new index.

Figure 15-25: *Index configuration*

There are three types of indexes: Queryable (it can be included in a query), Searchable (it can be searched), and Sortable (it can be sorted). By default, all these indexes are associated to custom attributes but not to the record's identifier. When we query the database from the `readCountries()` method in the model, we do not specify any field in the predicate and therefore the system fetches the records by their identifiers, which is described in the database as recordID (recordName). For this reason, to retrieve the countries in our example, we must add a Queryable index to the recordName field of the Countries record type, as shown in figure 15-25.

Once we select the recordName field and the Queryable index, we can press the Save button to save the changes. Now, if we run the application again from Xcode, the records added to the database are shown on the screen.

Do It Yourself: Open the CloudKit dashboard (icloud.developer.apple.com/ dashboard/), select your app's container, click on the Indexes option in the Schema section. Click on the record type Countries, click on the Add Basic Index button, and add the index for the recordName field, as shown in Figure 15-25. (You may have to wait a few seconds for the record type to be created after a new record is added from the app.) Press the Save Changes button to save the changes and run the application again. You should see on the screen the countries you have inserted before.

(Basic) ## Assets

Records may also include files, and the files may contain anything from pictures to sound or even videos. To add a file to a record, we must create an asset with the **CKAsset** class. The class includes the following initializer.

CKAsset(fileURL: URL)—This initializer creates a **CKAsset** object with the content of the file in the location determined by the **fileURL** argument.

The assets are added to a record with a key, as any other value. For our example, we are going to store a picture in the record of every city and add a view to show the picture when the city is selected.

Figure 15-26: *Interface to work with assets*

The following are the changes we have to introduce to the **insertCity()** method in the model to get the URL of the image and assign the asset to the record.

```
func insertCity(name: String, country: CKRecord.ID) async {
   let id = CKRecord.ID(recordName: "idcity-\(UUID())")
   let record = CKRecord(recordType: "Cities", recordID: id)
   record.setObject(name as NSString, forKey: "name")

   let reference = CKRecord.Reference(recordID: country,
action: .deleteSelf)
   record.setObject(reference, forKey: "country")

   let bundle = Bundle.main
   if let fileURL = bundle.url(forResource: "Toronto", withExtension:
"jpg") {
      let asset = CKAsset(fileURL: fileURL)
      record.setObject(asset, forKey: "picture")
   }
   do {
      try await database.save(record)
      await MainActor.run {
         let newCity = City(name: record["name"], record: record)
```

```
            let newItem = CityViewModel(id: record.recordID, city: newCity)
            listCities.append(newItem)
            listCities.sort(by: { $0.cityName < $1.cityName })
        }
    } catch {
        print("Error: \(error)")
    }
}
```

Listing 15-31: Storing assets

In the new **insertCity()** method introduced in Listing 15-31, we get the URL of an image included in the project called Toronto, create a **CKAsset** object with it, and assign the object to the record of every city with the "picture" key. Now, besides the name, a file with this image will be stored for every city inserted by the user. To get the asset back, we must add a computed property to the view model, as shown next.

```
struct CityViewModel: Identifiable {
    let id: CKRecord.ID
    let city: City

    var cityName: String {
        return city.name ?? "Undefined"
    }
    var cityPicture: UIImage {
        if let asset = city.record["picture"] as? CKAsset, let fileURL =
asset.fileURL {
            if let picture = UIImage(contentsOfFile: fileURL.path) {
                return picture
            }
        }
        return UIImage(named: "nopicture")!
    }
}
```

Listing 15-32: Preparing the image for the view

How to read the assets stored in the record depends on the type of content managed by the asset. In this example, we must use the asset's URL to create a **UIImage** object to show the image to the user. For this purpose, the **cityPicture** property introduced in Listing 15-32 reads the value in the record with the "picture" key, casts it as a **CKAsset** object, and gets the asset's URL from the **fileURL** property. If the process is successful, we create a **UIImage** object with the image in this URL and return it, otherwise, we return a **UIImage** object with a placeholder image (nopicture).

The following are the modifications we must introduce to the **ShowCitiesView** view to provide the **NavigationLink** view required for the user to be able to select a city and open a view to see the city's picture.

```
List {
    ForEach(appData.listCities) { city in
        NavigationLink(destination: ShowPictureView(selectedCity: city)) {
            Text(city.cityName)
        }
    }
}
```

Listing 15-33: Opening a view to show the asset

The **NavigationLink** view in Listing 15-33 opens a view called **ShowPictureView** to show the city's picture. The following is our implementation of this view.

```
import SwiftUI
import CloudKit

struct ShowPictureView: View {
   @EnvironmentObject var appData: ApplicationData
   let selectedCity: CityViewModel

   var body: some View {
      VStack {
         Image(uiImage: selectedCity.cityPicture)
            .resizable()
            .scaledToFit()
         Spacer()
      }.navigationBarTitle(selectedCity.cityName)
   }
}
struct ShowPictureView_Previews: PreviewProvider {
   static var previews: some View {
      ShowPictureView(selectedCity: CityViewModel(id:
CKRecord.ID(recordName: "Test"), city: City(name: "Test", record:
CKRecord(recordType: "Cities", recordID: CKRecord.ID(recordName:
"Test")))))
         .environmentObject(ApplicationData())
   }
}
```

Listing 15-34: Showing the asset

This view receives the information about the selected city through the **selectedCity** property. From this property, we get the city's picture and name and show them to the user. As a result, every time the user selects a city, the asset is turned into an image and displayed on the screen.

Do It Yourself: Update the **insertCity()** method in the **ApplicationData** class with the code in Listing 15-31, the **CityViewModel** structure in the model with the code in Listing 15-32, and the **ShowCitiesView** view with the code in Listing 15-33. Download the nopicture and the Toronto images from our website. Add the nopicture image to the Asset Catalog and the Toronto file to the project (we read this file from the bundle). Create a SwiftUI View file with the name ShowPictureView.swift for the code in Listing 15-34. Run the application on a device, select a country and add a new city. Select the city. You should see the Toronto image on the screen. In this example, we always load the same image from the bundle. We will study how to get images from the Photo Library and take photos from the camera in Chapter 18.

Basic Subscriptions

The previous examples fetch the records available and show them on the screen every time the app is launched. This means that records added to the database from another device will not be visible until the app is launched again. This is not the behavior expected by the user. When working with applications that store information online, users expects the information to be updated as soon as it becomes available. To provide this feature, CloudKit uses subscriptions.

Subscriptions are queries stored by our application in CloudKit servers. When a change occurs in the database, the query detects the modification and triggers the delivery of a Remote Notification from the iCloud servers to the copy of the app that registered the subscription.

Database subscriptions are created from the **CKDatabaseSubscription** class (a subclass of a generic class called **CKSubscription**). The class includes the following initializer.

CKDatabaseSubscription(subscriptionID: String**)**—This initializer creates a `CKDatabaseSubscription` object that represents a subscription with the ID specified by the **subscriptionID** argument.

Subscriptions are also added to CloudKit servers with operations. The `CKDatabase` class offers convenient methods to create them.

save(CKSubscription**)**—This asynchronous method stores in the servers the subscription specified by the argument.

deleteSubscription(withID: String**)**—This asynchronous method removes from the server the subscription with the identifier specified by the **withID** argument.

After a subscription is registered on the server, we must listen to Remote Notifications and download the changes. The first thing our application needs to do to be able to receive these notifications is to register with the iCloud servers. The `UIApplication` class offers the following method for this purpose.

registerForRemoteNotifications()—This method registers the app in iCloud servers to receive Remote Notifications. A token is generated to identify each copy of our app, so the notifications are delivered to the right user.

To report to our application that a Remote Notification was received, the `UIApplication` object calls a method in the app's delegate (see App Delegates in Chapter 14). The following is the method defined by the `UIApplicationDelegate` class for this purpose.

application(UIApplication, **didReceiveRemoteNotification:** Dictionary, **fetchCompletionHandler:** Block**)**—This method is called by the application on its delegate when a Remote Notification is received. The **didReceiveRemoteNotification** argument is a dictionary with information about the notification, and the **fetch-CompletionHandler** argument is a closure that we must execute after all the custom tasks are performed. The closure must be called with a value that describes the result of the operation. For this purpose, UIKit offers the `UIBackgroundFetchResult` enumeration with the values `newData` (new data was downloaded), `noData` (no data was downloaded), and `failed` (the app failed to download the data).

Setting up a subscription on CloudKit servers requires us to follow several steps. To begin with, we must call the `registerForRemoteNotifications()` method of the `UIApplication` object as soon as the application is launched to tell the system that we want to register the application to receive Remote Notifications from iCloud servers (Apple's Push Notification service). For this purpose, we must create a custom class that conform to the `UIApplication-Delegate` protocol and implement the `application(UIApplication, didFinish-LaunchingWithOptions:)` method, as we did in the example of Listing 14-27. If the registration is successful, the system calls the delegate method introduced above every time a notification is received, so we need to implement that method as well, as shown next.

```
import UIKit
import CloudKit

class CustomAppDelegate: NSObject, UIApplicationDelegate {
   let appData = ApplicationData.shared

   func application(_ application: UIApplication,
didFinishLaunchingWithOptions launchOptions:
[UIApplication.LaunchOptionsKey : Any]? = nil) -> Bool {
      application.registerForRemoteNotifications()
```

```
     Task(priority: .background) {
         await appData.configureDatabase()
     }
     return true
}
func application(_ application: UIApplication,
didReceiveRemoteNotification userInfo: [AnyHashable : Any],
fetchCompletionHandler completionHandler: @escaping
(UIBackgroundFetchResult) -> Void) {
     let notification = CKNotification(fromRemoteNotificationDictionary:
userInfo) as? CKDatabaseNotification
     guard notification != nil else {
         completionHandler(.failed)
         return
     }
     appData.checkUpdates(finishClosure: { (result) in
         completionHandler(result)
     })
}
}
```

Listing 15-35: Processing Remote Notifications from a custom app delegate

When the application is launched, we perform two operations. We call the **registerForRemoteNotifications()** method on the **UIApplication** object to register the application with iCloud servers and execute a method called **configureDatabase()** that we are going to define later in our **ApplicationData** class to create the subscription and the custom zone for the first time.

The **registerForRemoteNotifications()** method prepares the application to receive notifications, but the notifications are processed by the second delegate method. The first thing we have to do in this method is to check whether the notification received is a notification sent by a CloudKit server. For this purpose, the CloudKit framework includes the **CKNotification** class with properties we can use to process the dictionary and read its values. The class includes the following initializer.

CKNotification(fromRemoteNotificationDictionary: Dictionary)—This
initializer creates a **CKNotification** object from the information included in the notification (the value of the **userInfo** parameter in the delegate method).

Because CloudKit servers can send other types of notifications, we also check whether the notification received is of type **CKDatabaseNotification**. In case of success, we proceed to download the data. But before, we must consider that the system requires us to report the result of the operation. Notifications may be received when the application is closed or in the background. If this happens, the system launches our application and puts it in the background to allow it to contact the servers and process the information. But because this process consumes resources, the system needs to know when the operation is over and therefore it requires us to report it by calling the closure received by the **completionHandler** parameter with a value of the **UIBackgroundFetchResult** enumeration that determines what happened (**newData** if we downloaded new data, **noData** if there was nothing to download, and **failed** if the process failed). By calling the closure, we tell the system that the process is over, but because the operations are performed asynchronously, we cannot do it until they are finished. That's the reason why, in the example of Listing 15-35, we execute a method in the model called **checkUpdates()** that takes a closure. This method downloads the new information and executes the closure when finished. This way, we can call the **completionHandler** closure after all the operations have been processed.

IMPORTANT: The `UIApplicationDelegate` class also defines an asynchronous method to receive remote notifications called `application` `(UIApplication, didReceiveRemoteNotification: Dictionary)`. In this example, we are using concurrent operations, but if you need to perform asynchronous operations, you may implement this method instead.

Of course, the protocol methods defined in Listing 15-35 are only called if we assigned the class as the app delegate with the `@UIApplicationDelegateAdaptor` property wrapper from the `App` structure.

```
import SwiftUI

@main
struct TestApp: App {
    @UIApplicationDelegateAdaptor(CustomAppDelegate.self) var appDelegate
    @StateObject var appData = ApplicationData.shared

    var body: some Scene {
        WindowGroup {
            ContentView()
                .environmentObject(appData)
        }
    }
}
```

Listing 15-36: Assigning the app's delegate

Because we are working with an app delegate, we need our model to be a singleton, so we can reference it from anywhere in our code (see Singletons in Chapter 3). The following are the new properties we need to include in our model and the changes required by the initializer. (This example assumes that we are working with the model introduced in Listing 15-26.)

```
class ApplicationData: ObservableObject {
    @AppStorage("subscriptionSaved") var subscriptionSaved: Bool = false
    @AppStorage("zoneCreated") var zoneCreated: Bool = false
    @AppStorage("databaseToken") var databaseToken: Data = Data()
    @AppStorage("zoneToken") var zoneToken: Data = Data()

    @Published var listCountries: [CountryViewModel] = []
    @Published var listCities: [CityViewModel] = []
    var database: CKDatabase!

    static let shared = ApplicationData()

    private init() {
        let container = CKContainer.default()
        database = container.privateCloudDatabase

        Task(priority: .high) {
            await readCountries()
        }
    }
}
```

Listing 15-37: Defining the properties to control the subscription and the custom zone

Subscriptions only report changes in customs zones. Therefore, if we want to receive notifications, in addition to creating the subscription we also have to create a record zone and store all our records in it. Therefore, the first thing we do in the model in Listing 15-37 is to store two Boolean values in the App Storage system called "subscriptionSaved" and "zoneCreated". These values will be used later to know whether we have already created the subscription and the custom zone.

This model also includes two additional **@AppStorage** properties that we will use later to keep track of the current updates received from the server, and a **static** property to provide a unique instance we can access from anywhere in the code.

The next step is to implement the methods in charge of contacting the CloudKit servers and processing the information. From the application's delegate, we called two methods in the model: the **configureDatabase()** method to create the subscription and the zone, and the **checkUpdates()** method to download and process the information. The following is our implementation of the **configureDatabase()** method.

```
func configureDatabase() async {
   if !subscriptionSaved {
      let newSubscription = CKDatabaseSubscription(subscriptionID:
"updatesDatabase")
      let info = CKSubscription.NotificationInfo()
      info.shouldSendContentAvailable = true
      newSubscription.notificationInfo = info

      do {
         try await database.save(newSubscription)
         await MainActor.run {
            subscriptionSaved = true
         }
      } catch {
         print("Error: \(error)")
      }
   }
   if !zoneCreated {
      let newZone = CKRecordZone(zoneName: "listPlaces")
      do {
         try await database.save(newZone)
         await MainActor.run {
            zoneCreated = true
         }
      } catch {
         print("Error: \(error)")
      }
   }
}
```

Listing 15-38: Configuring the database

The first thing we do in the **configureDatabase()** method is to check the value of the **subscriptionSaved** property to know if a subscription was already created. If not, we use the **CKDatabaseSubscription** initializer to create a subscription with the name "updatesDatabase" and then define the **notificationInfo** property to configure the notifications that are going to be sent by the server. For this purpose, the framework defines the **CKNotificationInfo** class. This class includes multiple properties to configure Remote Notifications for CloudKit, but database subscriptions only require us to set the **shouldSendContentAvailable** property with the value **true**. After this, the subscription is saved on the server with the **save()** method of the **CKDatabase** object and the value **true** is assigned to the **subscriptionSaved** property if the operation is successful.

We follow the same procedure to create the custom zone. We check the value of the **zoneCreated** property to know if there is a custom zone already on the server, and if not, we create one called "listPlaces" to store our records. If the operation is successful, we assign the value **true** to the **zoneCreated** property to indicate that the zone was already created.

Next, we must define the **checkUpdates()** method to download and process the changes in the database. But first, we need to think about how we are going to organize our code. Every process executed in CloudKit servers is performed by asynchronous operations. This means that we need to think about the order in which the operations are executed. For some, the order doesn't matter, but for others it is crucial. For instance, we cannot store records in a zone before the zone is created. As we have seen in Chapter 9, we can use Swift concurrency to control the order in which tasks are performed, but CloudKit operations are already concurrent. Therefore, depending on the requirements of our application, it may be better to just implement closures that execute code after the operations are over, and this is the approach we take in this example.

The procedure is as follows. Every time we call the **checkUpdates()** method to download the data, we send a closure to the method with the code we want to execute once the operation is over. This way, we make sure that the operations are over before doing anything else.

```
func checkUpdates(finishClosure: @escaping (UIBackgroundFetchResult) ->
Void) {
    Task(priority: .high) {
        await configureDatabase()
        downloadUpdates(finishClosure: finishClosure)
    }
}
```

Listing 15-39: Initiating the process to get the updates from the server

The **checkUpdates()** method calls the **configureDatabase()** method again to make sure that the database is configured properly.

To simplify the code, we moved the statements to an additional method called **downloadUpdates()**. So after we confirm that the zone was created, we call this method with a reference to the closure received by the **checkUpdates()** method. (We pass the closure from one method to another so we can execute it after all the operations are over, as we will see next.)

 IMPORTANT: Passing closures from one method to another is a way to control the order in which the code is executed when we use concurrent operations. We chose this programming pattern for this example because it simplifies the code, but as we mentioned before, in some cases may be better to implement Swift concurrency.

Before implementing the **downloadUpdates()** method and process the changes in the database, we ought to study the operations provided by the CloudKit framework for this purpose. The operation to fetch the list of changes available in the database is created from a subclass of the **CKDatabaseOperation** class called **CKFetchDatabaseChangesOperation**. This class includes the following initializer.

CKFetchDatabaseChangesOperation(previousServerChangeToken: CK-
ServerChangeToken?)—This initializer creates an operation to fetch changes from a database. The argument is a token that determines which changes were already fetched. If we specify a token, only the changes that occurred after the token was created are fetched.

The class also includes properties to define completion handlers (closures) for every step of the process.

recordZoneWithIDChangedBlock—This property sets a closure that is executed to report which zones present changes. The closure receives a value of type **CKRecordZone.ID** with the identifier of the zone that changed.

changeTokenUpdatedBlock—This property sets a closure that is executed to provide the last database token. The closure receives an object of type **CKServerChangeToken** with the current token that we can store to send to subsequent operations.

fetchDatabaseChangesResultBlock—This property sets a closure that is executed when the operation is over. The closure receives a **Result** enumeration to report the success or failure of the operation. The enumeration value includes a tuple and a **CKError** value to report errors. The tuple includes two values: a **CKServerChangeToken** object with the last token and a Boolean value that indicates if there are more changes available.

After the completion of the **CKFetchDatabaseChangesOperation** operation, we must perform another operation to download the changes. For this purpose, the framework includes the **CKFetchRecordZoneChangesOperation** class with the following initializer.

CKFetchRecordZoneChangesOperation(recordZoneIDs: [CKRecordZone.ID], **configurationsByRecordZoneID:** Dictionary)—This initializer creates an operation to download changes from a database. The **recordZoneIDs** argument is an array with the IDs of all the zones that present changes, and the **configurationsByRecordZoneID** argument is a dictionary with configuration values for each zone. The dictionary takes **CKRecordZone.ID** objects as keys and options determined by an object of the **ZoneConfiguration** class included in the **CKFetchRecordZoneChangesOperation** class. The class includes three properties to define the options: **desiredKeys** (array of strings with the keys we want to retrieve), **previousServerChangeToken** (**CKServerChangeToken** object with the current token), and **resultsLimit** (integer that determines the number of records to retrieve).

The **CKFetchRecordZoneChangesOperation** class also includes properties to define completion handlers (closures) for every step of the process.

recordWasChangedBlock—This property sets a closure that is executed when a new or updated record is downloaded. The closure receives two values: a **CKRecord.ID** with the identifier of the record that changed, and a **Result** enumeration value to report the success or failure of the operation. The enumeration includes two values: a **CKRecord** object with the record that changed and a **CKError** value to report errors.

recordWithIDWasDeletedBlock—This property sets a closure that is executed when the operation finds a deleted record. The closure receives two values: a **CKRecord.ID** object with the identifier of the record that was deleted, and a string with the record's type.

recordZoneChangeTokensUpdatedBlock—This property sets a closure that is executed when the change token for the zone is updated. The closure receives three values: a **CKRecordZone.ID** with the identifier of the zone associated to the token, a **CKServerChangeToken** object with the current token, and a **Data** structure with the last token sent by the app to the server.

recordZoneFetchResultBlock—This property sets a closure that is executed when the operation finishes downloading the changes of a zone. The closure receives two values: a **CKRecordZone.ID** with the zone's identifier, and a **Result** enumeration value to report the success or failure of the operation. The enumeration includes two values: a tuple and a **CKError** value to report errors. In turn, the tuple includes three values: a **CKServerChangeToken** object with the current token, a **Data** structure with the last token sent to the server, and a Boolean value that indicates if there are more changes available.

fetchRecordZoneChangesResultBlock—This property sets a closure that is executed after the operation is over. The closure receives a **Result** enumeration value to report errors.

CloudKit servers use tokens to know which changes were already sent to every instance of the app, so the information is not downloaded twice from the same device. If a device stores or modifies a record, the server generates a new token, so the next time a device accesses the servers only the changes introduced after the last token was created will be downloaded.

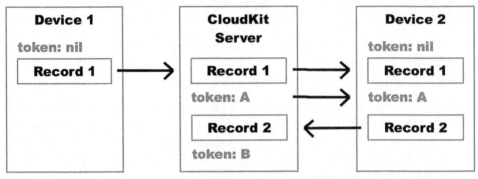

Figure 15-27: *Tokens*

In the process depicted in Figure 15-27, the app in Device 1 stores a new record in the server (Record 1). To report the changes, the server generates a new token (A). When the app in Device 2 connects to the server, the server detects that this device does not have the latest token, so it returns Record 1 and the current token (A) to update the state in this device. If later the user decides to create a new record from Device 2 (Record 2), a new token will be created (B). The next time Device 1 connects to the server, it will find that its token is different from the server's token, so it will download the modifications inserted after token A.

Tokens are great because they allow us to only get the latest changes, but this process is not automatic, we are responsible of storing the current tokens and preserve the state of our app. The server creates a token for the database and a token for each of the custom zones. For our example, we need two tokens: one to keep track of the changes in the database and another for the custom zone created by the **configureDatabase()** method. To work with these values, we are going to use two variables called **changeToken**, for the database token, and **fetchChangeToken**, for the token of our custom zone, and we are going to store them permanently with the **@AppStorage** properties defined before in the model (**databaseToken** and **zoneToken**). All this process is performed by the **downloadUpdates()** method.

```
func downloadUpdates(finishClosure: @escaping (UIBackgroundFetchResult)
-> Void) {
    var changeToken: CKServerChangeToken!
    var changeZoneToken: CKServerChangeToken!
    if let token = try? NSKeyedUnarchiver.unarchivedObject(ofClass:
CKServerChangeToken.self, from: databaseToken) {
        changeToken = token
    }
    if let token = try? NSKeyedUnarchiver.unarchivedObject(ofClass:
CKServerChangeToken.self, from: zoneToken) {
        changeZoneToken = token
    }
    var zonesIDs: [CKRecordZone.ID] = []
    let operation =
CKFetchDatabaseChangesOperation(previousServerChangeToken: changeToken)
    operation.recordZoneWithIDChangedBlock = { zoneID in
        zonesIDs.append(zoneID)
    }
    operation.changeTokenUpdatedBlock = { token in
        changeToken = token
    }
```

```swift
operation.fetchDatabaseChangesResultBlock = { result in
    guard let values = try? result.get() else {
        finishClosure(UIBackgroundFetchResult.failed)
        return
    }
    if zonesIDs.isEmpty {
        finishClosure(UIBackgroundFetchResult.noData)
    } else {
        changeToken = values.serverChangeToken

        let configuration =
CKFetchRecordZoneChangesOperation.ZoneConfiguration()
        configuration.previousServerChangeToken = changeZoneToken
        let fetchOperation =
CKFetchRecordZoneChangesOperation(recordZoneIDs: zonesIDs,
configurationsByRecordZoneID: [zonesIDs[0]: configuration])

        fetchOperation.recordWasChangedBlock = { recordID, result in
            guard let record = try? result.get() else {
                print("Error")
                return
            }
            if record.recordType == "Countries" {
            Task(priority: .high) {
                let index = self.listCountries.firstIndex(where: { item in
                    return item.id == record.recordID
                })
                await MainActor.run {
                    let newCountry = Country(name: record["name"],
record: record)
                    let newItem = CountryViewModel(id: record.recordID,
country: newCountry)
                    if index != nil {
                        self.listCountries[index!] = newItem
                    } else {
                        self.listCountries.append(newItem)
                    }
                    self.listCountries.sort(by: { $0.countryName <
$1.countryName })
                }
            }
            }
        }
        fetchOperation.recordWithIDWasDeletedBlock = { recordID,
recordType in
            if recordType == "Countries" {
            Task(priority: .high) {
                let index = self.listCountries.firstIndex(where:
{(item) in
                    return item.id == recordID
                })
                await MainActor.run {
                    if index != nil {
                        self.listCountries.remove(at: index!)
                    }
                    self.listCountries.sort(by: { $0.countryName <
$1.countryName })
                }
            }
            }
        }
        fetchOperation.recordZoneChangeTokensUpdatedBlock = { zoneID,
token, data in
            changeZoneToken = token
```

```
            }
        fetchOperation.recordZoneFetchResultBlock = { zoneID, result in
            guard let values = try? result.get() else {
                print("Error")
                return
            }
            changeZoneToken = values.serverChangeToken
        }
        fetchOperation.fetchRecordZoneChangesResultBlock = { result in
            switch result {
                case .failure(_):
                    finishClosure(UIBackgroundFetchResult.failed)
                    return
                default:
                    break
            }
            if changeToken != nil {
                if let data = try?
NSKeyedArchiver.archivedData(withRootObject: changeToken!,
requiringSecureCoding: false) {
                    Task(priority: .high) {
                        await MainActor.run {
                            self.databaseToken = data
                        }
                    }
                }
            }
            if changeZoneToken != nil {
                if let data = try?
NSKeyedArchiver.archivedData(withRootObject: changeZoneToken!,
requiringSecureCoding: false) {
                    Task(priority: .high) {
                        await MainActor.run {
                            self.zoneToken = data
                        }
                    }
                }
            }
            finishClosure(UIBackgroundFetchResult.newData)
        }
        self.database.add(fetchOperation)
    }
    }
    database.add(operation)
}
```

Listing 15-40: Downloading the updates from the server

This is a very long method that we need to study piece by piece. As mentioned before, we start by defining the properties we are going to use to store the tokens (one for the database and another for the custom zone). Next, we check if there are tokens already stored in the **@AppStorage** properties. Because the tokens are instances of the **CKServerChangeToken** class, we cannot store their values directly in App Storage, we must first convert them into **Data** structures. This is the reason why, when we read the values, we cast them as **Data** with the **as?** operator and then unarchive them with the **unarchivedObject()** method of the **NSKeyedUnarchiver** class (see Archiving in Chapter 10).

Next, we configure the operations necessary to get the updates from the server. We must perform two operations on the database, one to download the list of changes available and another to download the actual changes and show them to the user. The operations are performed and then the results are reported to the closures assigned to their properties.

The first operation we need to perform is the `CKFetchDatabaseChangesOperation` operation. The initializer requires the previous token to get only the changes that are not available on the device, so we pass the value of the `changeToken` property. Next, we define the closures for each of its properties. This operation includes three properties, one to report the zones that changed, one to report the creation of a new database token, and another to report the conclusion of the operation. The first property defined in our example is `recordZoneWithIDChangedBlock`. The closure assigned to this property is executed every time the system finds a zone whose content has changed. In this closure, we add the zone ID to an array to keep a reference of each zone that changed.

Something similar happens with the closure assigned next to the `changeTokenUpdated-Block` property. This closure is executed every time the system decides to perform the operation again to download the changes in separate processes. To make sure that we only receive the changes that we did not process yet, we use this closure to update the `changeToken` property with the current token.

The last property we have defined for this operation is `fetchDatabaseChangesResult-Block`. The closure assigned to this property is executed to let the app know that the operation is over, and this is how we know that we have all the information we need to begin downloading the changes with the second operation. This closure receives a `Result` enumeration value, which includes a tuple with two values and an `Error` value to report errors. If no values are returned, we execute the `finishClosure` closure with the value `failed` and the operation is over. On the other hand, if there are values available, we check if the `zoneIDs` array contains any zone ID. If it is empty, it means that there are no changes available and therefore we execute the `finishClosure` closure with the value `noData`, but if the array is not empty, we store the last token in the `changeToken` variable and configure the `CKFetchRecordZoneChanges-Operation` operation to download the changes.

The `CKFetchRecordZoneChangesOperation` operation is performed over the zones that changed, so we must initialize it with the array of zone identifiers generated by the previous operation. The initializer also requires a dictionary with the zone identifiers as keys and `ZoneConfiguration` objects that include the previous token for each zone as values. Because in this example we only work with one zone, we read the first element of the `zonesIDs` array to get the identifier of our custom zone and provide a `ZoneConfiguration` object with the current token for the zone stored in the `changeZoneToken` variable.

This operation works like the previous one. The changes are fetched, and the results are reported to the closures assigned to its properties. The first property declared in Listing 15-40 is `recordWasChangedBlock`. The closure assigned to this property is called every time a new or updated record is received. Here, we check if the record is of type Countries and store it in the corresponding array. When the record is of type Countries, we use the `firstIndex(where:)` method to look for duplicates. If the record already exists in the array, we update its values, otherwise, we add the record to the list.

The closure of the `recordWithIDWasDeletedBlock` property defined next is executed every time the app receives the ID of a deleted record (a record that was deleted from the CloudKit database). In this case, we do the same as before but instead of updating or adding the record we remove it from the list with the `remove()` method.

The closures assigned to the next two properties, `recordZoneChangeTokensUpdated-Block` and `recordZoneFetchResultBlock`, are executed when the process completes a cycle, either because the system decides to download the data in multiple processes, or the operation finished fetching the changes in a zone. Depending on the characteristics of our application, we may need to perform some tasks in these closures, but in our example, we just store the current token in the `changeZoneToken` variable so the next time the operation is performed we only get the changes we have not downloaded yet.

Finally, the closure assigned to the `fetchRecordZoneChangesResultBlock` property is executed to report that the operation is over. The closure receives a `Result` value to report errors. If there is an error, we call the **finishClosure** closure with the value **failed** to tell the system that the operation failed, otherwise, we store the current tokens in the **@AppStorage** properties and call the **finishClosure** closure with the value **newData**, to tell the system that new data has been downloaded. Notice that to store the tokens we must turn them into **Data** structures and encode them with the **archivedData()** method of the **NSKeyedArchiver** class (see Archiving in Chapter 10).

Lastly, after the definition of each operation and their properties, we call the **add()** method of the **CKDatabase** object to add them to the database.

There is one more change we must perform in our model for the subscription to work. So far, we have stored the records in the zone by default, but as we already mentioned, subscriptions require the records to be stored in a custom zone. The following are the changes we must introduce to the **insertCountry()** and **insertCity()** methods to store the records inside the listPlaces zone created before.

```
func insertCountry(name: String) async {
   await configureDatabase()

   let text = name.trimmingCharacters(in: .whitespaces)
   if !text.isEmpty {
      let zone = CKRecordZone(zoneName: "listPlaces")
      let id = CKRecord.ID(recordName: "idcountry-\(UUID())", zoneID:
zone.zoneID)
      let record = CKRecord(recordType: "Countries", recordID: id)
      record.setObject(text as NSString, forKey: "name")

      do {
         try await database.save(record)
         await MainActor.run {
            let newCountry = Country(name: record["name"], record:
record)
            let newItem = CountryViewModel(id: record.recordID, country:
newCountry)
            listCountries.append(newItem)
            listCountries.sort(by: { $0.countryName < $1.countryName })
         }
      } catch {
         print("Error: \(error)")
      }
   }
}
func insertCity(name: String, country: CKRecord.ID) async {
   await configureDatabase()

   let text = name.trimmingCharacters(in: .whitespaces)
   if !text.isEmpty {
      let zone = CKRecordZone(zoneName: "listPlaces")
      let id = CKRecord.ID(recordName: "idcity-\(UUID())", zoneID:
zone.zoneID)
      let record = CKRecord(recordType: "Cities", recordID: id)
      record.setObject(text as NSString, forKey: "name")

      let reference = CKRecord.Reference(recordID: country,
action: .deleteSelf)
      record.setObject(reference, forKey: "country")

      let bundle = Bundle.main
      if let fileURL = bundle.url(forResource: "Toronto", withExtension:
"jpg") {
         let asset = CKAsset(fileURL: fileURL)
         record.setObject(asset, forKey: "picture")
      }
```

```
        do {
            try await database.save(record)
            await MainActor.run {
                let newCity = City(name: record["name"], record: record)
                let newItem = CityViewModel(id: record.recordID, city:
newCity)
                listCities.append(newItem)
                listCities.sort(by: { $0.cityName < $1.cityName })
            }
        } catch {
            print("Error: \(error)")
        }
    }
}
```

Listing 15-41: *Storing the records in a custom zone*

All we have to do to store a record in a custom zone is to create the **CKRecordZone** object and assign its ID to the record ID by including it in the initializer of the **CKRecord.ID** object.

Notice that the first thing we do in both methods is to call the **configureDatabase()** method. We call this method again, so every time a record is inserted, we check that the subscription and the zone were already added to the database.

 Do It Yourself: Create a Swift file called CustomAppDelegate.swift for the class in Listing 15-35. Update the **App** structure with the code in Listing 15-36. Update the **ApplicationData** class with the properties and initializer of Listing 15-37. Add the methods of Listings 15-38, 15-39, and 15-40 to the **ApplicationData** class. Update the **insertCountry()** and **insertCity()** methods of the **ApplicationData** class with the code in Listing 15-41. Update the **PreviewProvider** structures for each view to load the model from the **shared** property (**environmentObject(ApplicationData.shared)**). Run the application in two different devices and insert a new country. You should see the country appear on the screen of the second device.

 IMPORTANT: Remote Notifications can only be tested on a real device (they do not work on the simulator). If you only have one device, you can test your applications by adding records from the CloudKit dashboard.

(Medium) Errors

Errors are an important part of CloudKit. The service is highly dependent on the network and how reliable it is. If the device is disconnected or the connection is not good enough, the operations might not be performed or data might be lost. CloudKit does not provide a standard solution for these situations, it just returns an error and expects our app to solve the problem. If the user creates a new record but at that moment the device is disconnected from the Internet, our app is responsible for registering the incident and trying again later.

The most common error is related to the user's iCloud account. Every user must have an iCloud account to access CloudKit servers. If an iCloud account is not set on the device or has restrictions due to Parental Control or Device Management, the app will not be able to connect to the servers. The **CKContainer** class offers the following method to check the status of the user's account.

accountStatus()—This asynchronous method attempts to access the user's iCloud account and returns a **CKAccountStatus** enumeration to report the current state. The enumeration includes the values **couldNotDetermine**, **available**, **restricted**, and **noAccount**.

If the status of the iCloud account changes while the app is running, the system posts a notification that we can use to perform updates and synchronization tasks.

CKAccountChanged—This notification is posted by the system when the status of the user's iCloud account registered on the device changes.

We should always check if the servers are available before trying to perform an operation and warn the user about it. For instance, we can modify the `insertCountry()` method in our model to check the status of the connection before introducing a new record.

```
func insertCountry(name: String) async {
   await configureDatabase()

   do {
      let container = CKContainer.default()
      let status = try await container.accountStatus()
      if status != CKAccountStatus.available {
         print("iCloud Not Available")
         return
      }
   } catch {
      print("Error: \(error)")
      return
   }
   let text = name.trimmingCharacters(in: .whitespaces)
   if !text.isEmpty {
      let zone = CKRecordZone(zoneName: "listPlaces")
      let id = CKRecord.ID(recordName: "idcountry-\(UUID())", zoneID:
zone.zoneID)
      let record = CKRecord(recordType: "Countries", recordID: id)
      record.setObject(text as NSString, forKey: "name")

      do {
         try await database.save(record)
         await MainActor.run {
            let newCountry = Country(name: record["name"], record:
record)
            let newItem = CountryViewModel(id: record.recordID, country:
newCountry)
            listCountries.append(newItem)
            listCountries.sort(by: { $0.countryName < $1.countryName })
         }
      } catch {
         print("Error: \(error)")
      }
   }
}
```

Listing 15-42: Checking CloudKit availability

This example checks the status of the account and prints a message on the console if an error occurs or the status is other than **available**. If an error occurs, the code returns from the function without letting the user insert the new record.

 Do It Yourself: Update the `insertCountry()` method in the `ApplicationData` class with the code in Listing 15-42. Run the application on a device and activate Airplane Mode from Settings. Add a new country. You should see a **CKError** on the console that reads "Network Unavailable".

In the last example, we just checked whether an error occurred or not and proceeded accordingly, but we can also identify the type of error returned by the operation. Errors are structures that conform to the **Error** protocol. Every time we want to read an error, we must cast it to the right type. In CloudKit, the errors are of type **CKError**, a structure that includes the following property to return the error code.

code—This property returns a value that identifies the error. The property is of type **CKError.Code**; an enumeration defined by the **CKError** structure with values that represent all the errors produced by CloudKit. The list of values available is extensive. The most frequently used are **partialFailure**, **networkUnavailable**, **networkFailure**, **serviceUnavailable**, **unknownItem**, **operationCancelled**, **changeToken-Expired**, **quotaExceeded**, **zoneNotFound**, and **limitExceeded**.

The following example implements the **recordZone()** method of the **CKDatabase** object to check whether a zone exists in the database. In the **catch** block, we cast the value of the **error** parameter as a **CKError** structure and then compare the value of its **code** property with the value **zoneNotFound** of the **Code** enumeration. If the values match, it means that the zone we tried to access does not exist.

```
func checkZones() async {
   let newZone = CKRecordZone(zoneName: "myNewZone")
   do {
      try await database.recordZone(for: newZone.zoneID)
   } catch {
      if let error = error as? CKError {
         if error.code == CKError.Code.zoneNotFound {
            print("Not found")
         } else {
            print("Zone Found")
         }
      }
   }
}
```

Listing 15-43: Checking for errors

 Do It Yourself: Add the **checkZones()** method in Listing 15-43 to the **ApplicationData** class. Call this method from the initializer (**checkZones()**). Run the application again. You should see the message "Not Found" on the console because we are trying to access a zone with a different name than the one we have created before.

(Basic) ## Deploy to Production

In CloudKit's dashboard, at the bottom of the panel on the left, there is a list of options to work with the database schema. We can export the schema, import a schema from our computer, reset the schema to start from scratch, and deploy the schema to production. This last option is the one we need to select when we want to prepare our app for distribution (to be sold in the App Store).

The Deploy Schema Changes option opens a panel where we can see the features that are going to be transferred to the Production environment. This includes record types and indexes, but it does not include records (values added for testing). If we agree, we must press the Deploy button to finish the process, and our database in CloudKit will be ready for distribution.

IMPORTANT: The Production environment is used by apps that are submitted to Apple for distribution. This step is required for your application to be published in the App Store. If you don't deploy the changes to production, the database is not going to be available to your users. To learn how to submit your app to the App Store, read Chapter 20.

Chapter 16
Framework Integration

16.1 Integration with UIKit

SwiftUI is a new framework and therefore not everything we need to build a professional application is available. For mobile applications, this means that sometimes we must resort to the tools provided by the UIKit framework.

We have introduced UIKit before. This is the framework SwiftUI implements in the background to build most of the views and controls. Some UIKit classes are used to run the application (**UIApplication**), to load images (**UIImage**), to manage the device (**UIDevice**), the window (**UIWindow**), and some to define the delegates used to set up the application and the Scenes (**UIApplicationDelegate** and **UIWindowSceneDelegate**). And, of course, the framework provides all the tools we need to create the interface, including two basic classes to create and manage the views: **UIView** and **UIViewController**.

These last two classes, **UIView** and **UIViewController**, are the ones we need to implement if we want to add UIKit features to our SwiftUI interface. Subclasses of the **UIView** class are used to present information on the screen, such as labels and images, and to create controls, such as buttons, sliders and switches. On the other hand, subclasses of the **UIViewController** class are designed to present the views and include the functionality necessary to process their values and interact with the user. To integrate these tools into the SwiftUI interface, the SwiftUI framework defines two protocols: **UIViewRepresentable** and **UIViewControllerRepresentable**.

Basic **Representable View**

The **UIViewRepresentable** protocol defines a structure that acts as a wrapper for objects created from the **UIView** class or its subclasses. A structure that conforms to this protocol can present a UIKit view within a SwiftUI interface. To create and manage the UIKit view, the structure must implement the following methods.

makeUIView(context: Context)—This method creates the UIKit view and returns it. The **context** argument is a reference to a structure of type **UIViewRepresentable-Context** that provides information about the state of the view.

updateUIView(UIViewType, **context:** Context)—This method updates the UIKit view with information provided by the SwiftUI interface through a **Binding** property. The first argument is a reference to the UIKit view, and the **context** argument is a reference to a structure of type **UIViewRepresentableContext** that provides information about the state of the view.

dismantleUIView(UIViewType, **coordinator:** Coordinator)—This type method prepares the view to be dismissed. The first argument is a reference to the UIKit view, and the **coordinator** argument is the object that sends values back to the SwiftUI interface.

makeCoordinator()—This method creates the object that communicates information from the UIKit view back to the SwiftUI interface.

To include a **UIView** object in a SwiftUI interface (or an object created from any of its subclasses), we must define a structure that conforms to the **UIViewRepresentable** protocol and implement the methods listed above. The **makeUIView()** and **updateUIView()** methods are mandatory. In the **makeUIView()** method, we must create the instance of the UIKit view and return it, and the `updateUIView()` method is used to update the view with values coming from the SwiftUI interface.

The following example creates a UIKit view with a blue background and includes it in a SwiftUI interface. We only need the `makeUIView()` method to create the UIKit view, but we also have to implement the `updateUIView()` method because it is required by the protocol.

```
import SwiftUI

struct MyCustomView: UIViewRepresentable {
    func makeUIView(context: Context) -> some UIView {
        let view = UIView()
        view.backgroundColor = UIColor(.blue)
        return view
    }
    func updateUIView(_ uiView: UIViewType, context: Context) {
    }
}
```

Listing 16-1: Preparing a UIKit view to work with SwiftUI

The `makeUIView()` method is called every time a new instance of the `MyCustomView` structure is created. In this method, we create the `UIView` view, give it a blue background, and return it. Therefore, every time we create an instance of the `MyCustomView` structure, a `UIView` is created and included in our SwiftUI interface, as in the following example.

```
struct ContentView: View {
    var body: some View {
        VStack {
            MyCustomView()
                .frame(width: 200, height: 150)
                .padding()
            Spacer()
        }
    }
}
```

Listing 16-2: Showing a UIKit view within a SwiftUI view

A representable view has a flexible size by default, but we can use SwiftUI modifiers to change it. In this example, we use the `frame()` modifier to assign a fixed width and height.

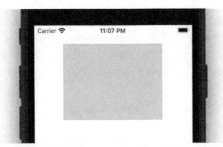

Figure 16-1: UIKit view in a SwiftUI interface

A `UIView` object creates an empty view, but we can also implement views that take user's input, such as input fields, switches, and more. To pass values from the SwiftUI view to the UIKit view, we use the `updateUIView()` method, but if we want to send values from the UIKit view to the SwiftUI interface, we must implement the `makeCoordinator()` method. From this method, we must create an instance of a coordinator object and return it. A coordinator is an object that can send information back from the UIKit view to the SwiftUI interface, usually by modifying

Binding properties. How to process these values depends on the type of UIKit view we are working with. For instance, a **UITextView** view creates an input field for the user to type multiple lines of text, like the **TextEditor** view in SwiftUI. This view reports changes by calling delegate methods. Therefore, to get the text inserted by the user in a **UITextView** view and process it in SwiftUI, we must create a coordinator class that conforms to the **UITextViewDelegate** protocol and implements its methods. The following example illustrates how to create a **UIViewRepresentable** structure to work with this class.

```
import SwiftUI
struct TextView: UIViewRepresentable {
   @Binding var input: String

   func makeUIView(context: Context) -> UITextView {
      let view = UITextView()
      view.backgroundColor = UIColor.yellow
      view.font = UIFont.systemFont(ofSize: 17)
      view.delegate = context.coordinator
      return view
   }
   func updateUIView(_ uiView: UITextView, context: Context) {
      uiView.text = input
   }
   func makeCoordinator() -> CoordinatorTextView {
      return CoordinatorTextView(input: $input)
   }
}
class CoordinatorTextView: NSObject, UITextViewDelegate {
   @Binding var inputCoordinator: String

   init(input: Binding<String>) {
      self._inputCoordinator = input
   }
   func textViewDidChange(_ textView: UITextView) {
      inputCoordinator = textView.text
   }
}
```

Listing 16-3: Sending and receiving values from the SwiftUI view

This example creates a **UIViewRepresentable** structure called **TextView**. The structure includes a **Binding** property called **input** to receive and pass the values to the SwiftUI view.

Below the definition of the **TextView** structure we define a class called **CoordinatorTextView**. This is our view coordinator and its job is to send values back to the SwiftUI view. For this purpose, we initialize it with a **Binding** property that is going to be associated with the **input** property defined by the **TextView** structure, and then implement a delegate method that is executed when a character is inserted or removed by the user. The method receives the current text in the input field, so we assign it to the **Binding** property to send it back to the SwiftUI view.

The **CoordinatorTextView** object is created from the **makeCoordinator()** method when the **UIViewRepresentable** structure is initialized, so the structure is ready from the beginning to receive and send values.

The view is implemented in the SwiftUI interface as before. All we need to add now is a **@State** property to store and pass the value to the **input** property.

```
struct ContentView: View {
   @State private var inputText: String = "Initial text"
   var body: some View {
```

```
VStack {
    HStack {
        Text(inputText)
        Spacer()
        Button("Clear") {
            inputText = ""
        }
    }
    TextView(input: $inputText)
}.padding()
}
}
```

Listing 16-4: Receiving and sending values to a UIKit view

This view defines a `@State` property called `inputText`, a `Text` view to show its value, a button to replace the current value with an empty string, and an instance of our `TextInput` view. This view receives a reference to the `inputText` property, so the property is connected to the `input` property in the representable view and we can pass values back and forth.

When the user types or removes a character from the text view, the representable view calls the `textViewDidChange()` method in the coordinator and the method assigns the current value in the text view to the `inputCoordinator` property, and hence to the `input` property. This means that the value is now available in the view's `@State` property and the `Text` view can show it on the screen.

On the other hand, when the user presses the Clear button, we assign an empty string to the `@State` property, the system executes the `updateUIView()` method in the representable view, and the value of the `Binding` property connected to the `@State` property is assigned to the view, so the text view is cleared.

Figure 16-2: `UITextView` *view in a SwiftUI interface*

 Do It Yourself: Create a Multiplatform project. Create a Swift file called TextView.swift for the code in Listing 16-3. Update the `ContentView` view with the code in Listing 16-4. Run the application on the iPhone simulator. Insert a text. You should see the text changing at the top. Press the Clear button. You should see the text removed from the text view and the view at the top.

 IMPORTANT: A `UIViewRepresentable` structure can represent any UIKit view we want. The implementation always depends on the view we want to use. We will see more examples in following chapters. To learn more about UIKit and UIKit views, read our book **UIKit for Masterminds** (www.formasterminds.com).

(Basic) **Representable View Controller**

The `UIViewControllerRepresentable` protocol defines a structure that acts as a wrapper for objects created from the `UIViewController` class or its subclasses. This class presents a view that can include other views to define the interface for a window or the entire screen, like the views defined by SwiftUI View files. A structure that conforms to the `UIViewController-Representable` protocol can present these view controllers within a SwiftUI interface. To create and manage the view controller, the structure must implement the following methods.

makeUIViewController(context: Context)—This method creates the UIKit view controller and returns it. The **context** argument is a reference to a structure of type **UIViewControllerRepresentableContext** that provides information about the state of the view controller.

updateUIViewController(UIViewControllerType, **context:** Context)—This method updates the UIKit view controller with information provided by the SwiftUI interface. The first argument is a reference to the UIKit view controller, and the **context** argument is a reference to a structure of type **UIViewControllerRepresentable-Context** that provides information about the state of the view controller.

dismantleUIViewController(UIViewControllerType, **coordinator:** Coordinator)—This type method prepares the view controller to be dismissed. The first argument is a reference to the UIKit view controller, and the **coordinator** argument is the object that sends values back to the SwiftUI interface.

makeCoordinator()—This method creates the object that communicates information from the UIKit view controller back to the SwiftUI interface.

A UIKit view controller is created from a subclass of the **UIViewController** class. The file is created from the File menu, as any other, but the option we need to select to get a subclass of a UIKit class is called Cocoa Touch Class. Once this option is selected, Xcode shows a window where we can insert the name of the file and the class from which we want to create our subclass. For our example, we have created a class called **DetailViewController** that inherits from the **UIViewController** class.

```
import UIKit
class DetailViewController: UIViewController {
    override func viewDidLoad() {
        super.viewDidLoad()
        let label = UILabel()
        label.frame = CGRect(x: 20, y: 16, width: 250, height: 30)
        label.font = UIFont.systemFont(ofSize: 30)
        label.text = "Hello World!"
        view.addSubview(label)
    }
}
```

Listing 16-5: Creating a UIKit view controller

When the view controller class is instantiated, it creates a view to represent the interface, assigns it to the **view** property, and calls the **viewDidLoad()** method to tell our code that the view is ready. In this method, we can perform all the initialization tasks we need. In our example, we create a **UILabel** object to display a text on the screen. This object works like the SwiftUI **Text** view, but it requires some configuration. In our example, we give it a position and size by assigning a **CGRect** value to the **frame** property, define a font with a size of 30 pixels, give it the text to display, and then add it to the view controller's view with the **addSubview()** method.

Now that we have the view controller, we need to create a representable view to turn it into a SwiftUI view, as in the following example.

```
import SwiftUI
struct MyViewController: UIViewControllerRepresentable {
    func makeUIViewController(context: Context) -> DetailViewController {
        let controller = DetailViewController()
        return controller
    }
```

```
    func updateUIViewController(_ uiViewController: UIViewControllerType,
context: Context) {
    }
}
```

Listing 16-6: Creating the representable view for a UIKit view controller

The **UIViewControllerRepresentable** protocol works like the **UIViewRepresentable** protocol. We define a structure that conforms to it and then include the methods we need to create and update the view. In our example, we only define the **makeUIViewController()** method because all we need is to create an instance of our view controller to present it on the screen. The following SwiftUI view loads this view controller inside a **NavigationStack** view when the user presses a button.

```
struct ContentView: View {
    var body: some View {
        NavigationStack {
            VStack {
                NavigationLink("Open UIKit View", destination: {
                    MyViewController()
                }).buttonStyle(.borderedProminent)
                Spacer()
            }.padding()
        }
    }
}
```

Listing 16-7: Loading a UIKit view controller from a SwiftUI view

This view includes a **NavigationLink** view that loads an instance of the **MyViewController** structure, so we can navigate from the initial view to the view controller created by this structure, as we do with normal SwiftUI views.

Figure 16-3: UIKit view controller in a SwiftUI interface

 Do It Yourself: Select the File option from the menu at the top of the screen to create a new file. Click on the Cocoa Touch Class icon in the iOS section to create a UIKit file. Select the **UIViewController** class from the Subclass option. Insert the name DetailViewController and press Next to save it. Update the **DetailViewController** class with the code in Listing 16-5. Create a Swift file called MyViewController.swift for the code in Listing 16-6. Update the **ContentView** view with the code in Listing 16-7. Run the application on the iPhone simulator. Press the button to open the UIKit view controller. We will see some practical examples on how to implement Representable Views and Representable View Controllers in the following chapters.

Chapter 17
Web

(Basic) **17.1 Web**

Apps can allow the user to access the web, but there are different ways to do it. We can provide links for the user to open a document in the browser, embed a predefined browser into the app's interface, or load data in the background, process it, and show the result to the user.

(Basic) **Links**

A link is a text or an image associated with a URL that indicates the location of a document. When the user clicks or taps the link, the document is opened. Links were designed for the web, but we can add them to our applications and let the system decide where to open the document (a browser or another app). SwiftUI includes the `Link` view to create them.

Link(String, destination: URL)—This initializer creates a button to open a link. The first argument specifies the button's title, and the **destination** argument is a `URL` structure with the location of the document we want to open. If we want to use views to represent the label, we can implement the initializer `Link(destination:, label:)`.

The following example opens the www.formasterminds.com website when the button is pressed. The code defines a `@State` property to store the URL and initializes it with the one we want to open. Using this value, we create the `URL` structure and assign it to the `Link` view. When the button is pressed, the system reads the URL, detects that it is a web address, and opens the browser to load the website.

```
struct ContentView: View {
   @State private var searchURL = "https://www.formasterminds.com"

   var body: some View {
      VStack {
         Link("Open Web", destination: URL(string: searchURL)!)
            .buttonStyle(.borderedProminent)
         Spacer()
      }.padding()
   }
}
```

Listing 17-1: Opening a website

Figure 17-1: Link

Do It Yourself: Create a Multiplatform project. Update the **ContentView** view with the code in Listing 17-1. Run the application and press the button. The system should open an external browser and load the website.

In this example, we have defined the URL in code, but sometimes the URL is provided by the user or taken from another document. In cases like this, the URL may contain characters that are not allowed and can cause the location to be impossible to identify. To make sure that the URL is valid, we must turn unsafe characters into percent-encoding characters. These are characters represented by the % sign followed by an hexadecimal number. The **String** structure includes the following method for this purpose.

addingPercentEncoding(withAllowedCharacters: CharacterSet)—This method returns a string with all the characters in the set specified by the argument replaced by percent-encoded characters. The **withAllowedCharacters** argument is a structure with type properties to create instances that represent common sets. The ones available for URLs are **urlFragmentAllowed**, **urlHostAllowed**, **urlPassword-Allowed**, **urlPathAllowed**, **urlQueryAllowed**, and **urlUserAllowed**.

This method is implemented by the **NSString** class, but we can use it from any instance of the **String** structure. This means that all we need is to apply the method to the URL we want to check and assign that URL to the **Link** view. The problem is that this view takes a URL that is ready to be processed, so we must first check the value from a computed property or a method. To simplify the process, the environment includes a property called **openURL** that returns a method we can use to open a URL, and therefore we can include it in a control or any operation we want. For instance, the following example implements a **Button** view that replaces invalid characters in the URL with percent-encoded characters and then executes the **openURL()** method to open it.

```
struct ContentView: View {
    @Environment(\.openURL) var openURL
    @State private var searchURL = "https://www.formasterminds.com"

    var body: some View {
        VStack {
            Button("Open Web") {
                if let url =
searchURL.addingPercentEncoding(withAllowedCharacters: .urlQueryAllowed)
{
                    openURL(URL(string: url)!)
                }
            }.buttonStyle(.borderedProminent)
            Spacer()
        }.padding()
    }
}
```

Listing 17-2: Encoding URLs

In this example, we process a URL that we know it works, but this is not always the case. URLs are usually taken from external sources or provided by the user. In cases like this, we not only have to encode the values with the **addingPercentEncoding()** method but also check that all the components of the URL are in place. For instance, if the user only writes the domain (www.formasterminds.com) without the protocol (https), we must build the full URL before trying to open it. To read, create, or modify URL components, the Foundation framework defines the **URLComponents** structure. The structure includes the following initializer.

URLComponents(string: String)—This initializer creates a `URLComponents` structure with the components from the URL specified by the **string** argument.

The structure includes several properties to read and modify the components. The following are the most frequently used.

scheme—This property sets or returns the URL's protocol (e.g., "http").

host—This property sets or returns the URL's domain (e.g., "www.google.com").

path—This property sets or returns the URL's components after the domain (e.g., "/index.php").

query—This property sets or returns the URL's parameters (e.g., "id=22").

queryItems—This property sets or returns an array of `URLQueryItem` structures containing each of the parameters included in the URL.

The `URLComponents` structure also includes the following property to return a string with the URL created from the components.

string—This property returns a string with the URL built from the values of the components.

In the following example, we allow the user to insert a URL, but we assign the https protocol to the URL to make sure it is always included.

```
struct ContentView: View {
    @Environment(\.openURL) var openURL
    @State private var searchURL = ""

    var body: some View {
        VStack {
            TextField("Insert URL", text: $searchURL)
                .textFieldStyle(.roundedBorder)
                .autocapitalization(.none)
                .disableAutocorrection(true)
            Button("Open Web") {
                if !searchURL.isEmpty {
                    var components = URLComponents(string: searchURL)
                    components?.scheme = "https"
                    if let newURL = components?.string {
                        if let url =
newURL.addingPercentEncoding(withAllowedCharacters: .urlQueryAllowed) {
                            openURL(URL(string: url)!)
                        }
                    }
                }
            }.buttonStyle(.borderedProminent)
            Spacer()
        }.padding()
    }
}
```

Listing 17-3: Encoding custom URLs

The `URLComponents` structure takes a string with the URL, extracts the components, and assigns them to the structure's properties, so we can read or modify them. In this example, we assign the "https" string to the **scheme** property to make sure the URL is valid and can be processed by the system. Once the components are ready, we get the full URL from the **string** property, replace invalid characters with percent-encoded characters, and open it.

Figure 17-2: Custom URLs

Safari View Controller

Links provide access to the web from our app, but they open the document in an external application. Considering how important it is for our application to capture the user's attention, Apple includes a framework called SafariServices. This framework allows us to incorporate the Safari browser into our app to offer a better experience to our users. The framework includes the **SFSafariViewController** class to create a view controller that incorporates its own view to display web pages and tools for navigation.

SFSafariViewController(url: URL, **configuration:** Configuration)—This initializer creates a new Safari view controller that automatically loads the website indicated by the **url** argument. The **configuration** argument is a property of an object of the **Configuration** class included in the **SFSafariViewController** class. The properties available are **entersReaderIfAvailable** and **barCollapsingEnabled**.

The **SFSafariViewController** class creates a UIKit view controller. Therefore, we must define a representable view controller with the **UIViewControllerRepresentable** protocol to add it to our SwiftUI interface, as in the following example. (For more information about representable view controllers, read Chapter 16.)

```
import SwiftUI
import SafariServices

struct SafariBrowser: UIViewControllerRepresentable {
    @Binding var searchURL: URL

    func makeUIViewController(context: Context) -> SFSafariViewController {
        let safari = SFSafariViewController(url: searchURL)
        return safari
    }
    func updateUIViewController(_ uiViewController:
SFSafariViewController, context: Context) {}
}
```

Listing 17-4: Creating a Safari Browser

This structure creates a view controller that contains a functional Safari browser. In the following example, we open this view in a sheet.

```
struct ContentView: View {
    @State private var searchURL: URL = URL(string: "https://
www.formasterminds.com")!
    @State private var openSheet: Bool = false

    var body: some View {
        VStack {
            Button("Open Browser") {
                openSheet = true
            }.buttonStyle(.borderedProminent)
```

```
            Spacer()
        }.padding()
        .sheet(isPresented: $openSheet) {
            SafariBrowser(searchURL: $searchURL)
        }
    }
}
```

Listing 17-5: Opening a Safari Browser

This view defines a **@State** property of type **URL** that is initialized with the URL https://www.formasterminds.com. When the button is pressed, a **SafariBrowser** view is initialized with this value, the browser is opened in a sheet, and the website is loaded.

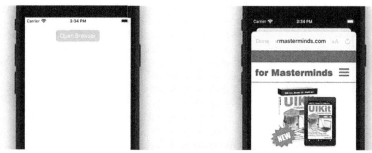

Figure 17-3: Safari browser

 Do It Yourself: Create a Multiplatform project. Create a Swift file called SafariBrowser.swift for the code in Listing 17-4. Update the **ContentView** view with the code in Listing 17-5. Run the application on the iPhone simulator and press the button. You should see the Safari browser in a sheet with the www.formasterminds.com website.

The **SFSafariViewController** class also offers the following properties for configuration.

dismissButtonStyle—This property sets or returns a value that determines the type of button the view controller is going to show to dismiss the view. It is an enumeration of type **DismissButtonStyle** with the values **done** (default), **close**, and **cancel**.

preferredBarTintColor—This property sets or returns a **UIColor** value that determines the color of the bars.

preferredControlTintColor—This property sets or returns a **UIColor** value that determines the color of the controls.

The following example takes advantage of these properties to match the colors of the browser with the colors of the www.formasterminds.com website.

```
import SwiftUI
import SafariServices

struct SafariBrowser: UIViewControllerRepresentable {
    @Binding var searchURL: URL

    func makeUIViewController(context: Context) -> SFSafariViewController {
        let safari = SFSafariViewController(url: searchURL)
        safari.dismissButtonStyle = .close
        safari.preferredBarTintColor = UIColor(red: 81/255, green: 91/255,
blue: 119/255, alpha: 1.0)
        safari.preferredControlTintColor = UIColor.white
```

```
        return safari
    }
    func updateUIViewController(_ uiViewController:
SFSafariViewController, context: Context) {}
}
```

Listing 17-6: Configuring the view controller

The code in Listing 17-6 also modifies the **dismissButtonStyle** property to change the type of button displayed by the browser. Instead of Done, the button now says Close.

Figure 17-4: Custom Safari view controller

When the user scrolls the page, the controller collapses the bars to make room for the content. This makes difficult for the user to dismiss the view or access the tools. If we think that it is more appropriate for our app to always keep the bars at the original size, we can initialize the controller with a **Configuration** object. This class is defined inside the **SFSafariView-Controller** class and includes the following property to configure the bars.

barCollapsingEnabled—This property sets or returns a Boolean value that determines whether the navigation bars are collapsed or not.

Once the **Configuration** object is created, we can configure the property and assign it to the Safari View Controller from the controller's initializer.

```
import SwiftUI
import SafariServices

struct SafariBrowser: UIViewControllerRepresentable {
    @Binding var searchURL: URL

    func makeUIViewController(context: Context) -> SFSafariViewController {
        let config = SFSafariViewController.Configuration()
        config.barCollapsingEnabled = false
        let safari = SFSafariViewController(url: searchURL, configuration:
config)
        return safari
    }
    func updateUIViewController(_ uiViewController:
SFSafariViewController, context: Context) {}
}
```

Listing 17-7: Preserving the bars at their original size

Do It Yourself: Update the **SafariBrowser** structure with the code in Listing 17-7. Run the application and scroll the page. The bars should stay at the same size and the buttons should always be visible.

Chapter 17 - Web

The framework also defines the **SFSafariViewControllerDelegate** protocol, so we can assign a delegate to the Safari View Controller to control the process. The following are some of the methods defined by this protocol.

safariViewController(SFSafariViewController, **didCompleteInitialLoad:** Bool**)**—This method is called by the controller when the initial website finishes loading.

safariViewControllerDidFinish(SFSafariViewController**)**—This method is called by the controller when the view is dismissed (the user pressed the Done button).

The Safari View Controller includes the **delegate** property to assign a delegate. The following example creates a coordinator, assigns it as the view's delegate, and implements the **safariViewControllerDidFinish()** method to deactivate the button on the interface when the user dismisses the view. (The user is only able to open the view once.)

```
import SwiftUI
import SafariServices

struct SafariBrowser: UIViewControllerRepresentable {
   @Binding var disable: Bool
   @Binding var searchURL: URL

   func makeUIViewController(context: Context) -> SFSafariViewController {
      let config = SFSafariViewController.Configuration()
      config.barCollapsingEnabled = false
      let safari = SFSafariViewController(url: searchURL, configuration:
config)
      safari.delegate = context.coordinator
      return safari
   }
   func updateUIViewController(_ uiViewController:
SFSafariViewController, context: Context) {}
   func makeCoordinator() -> SafariCoordinator {
      SafariCoordinator(disableCoordinator: $disable)
   }
}
class SafariCoordinator: NSObject, SFSafariViewControllerDelegate {
   @Binding var disableCoordinator: Bool

   init(disableCoordinator: Binding<Bool>) {
      self._disableCoordinator = disableCoordinator
   }
   func safariViewControllerDidFinish(_ controller:
SFSafariViewController) {
      disableCoordinator = true
   }
}
```

Listing 17-8: Assigning a delegate to the Safari View Controller

In the view, we need to define a **@State** property to store the Boolean value and implement the **disable()** modifier on the **Button** view to enable or disable the button depending on this value.

```
struct ContentView: View {
   @State private var searchURL: URL = URL(string: "https://
www.formasterminds.com")!
   @State private var openSheet: Bool = false
   @State private var disableButton: Bool = false

   var body: some View {
```

```
    VStack {
        Button("Open Browser") {
            openSheet = true
        }.buttonStyle(.borderedProminent)
        .disabled(disableButton)
        Spacer()
    }.padding()
    .sheet(isPresented: $openSheet) {
        SafariBrowser(disable: $disableButton, searchURL: $searchURL)
    }
}
}
```

Listing 17-9: Disabling the button from the Safari View Controller delegate

In this example, we include a state property of type `Bool` called `disableButton` and pass it to the representable view controller, so we can modify its value from the coordinator. When the Safari View Controller is dismissed, the `safariViewControllerDidFinish()` method is executed, the value `true` is assigned to the `disableButton` property, and therefore the user is not allowed to press the button again.

 Do It Yourself: Update the SafariBrowser.swift file with the code in Listing 17-8 and the `ContentView` view with the code in Listing 17-9. Run the application on the iPhone simulator and press the button. Press the Done button to close the Safari View Controller. The button should be disabled.

⸨ Basic ⸩ WebKit Framework

For some applications, the options for customization included in the Safari view controller are not enough. To provide more alternatives, Apple offers the WebKit framework. With this framework we can display web content within a view. The view is defined by a subclass of the `UIView` class called `WKWebView`. The class provides the following properties and methods to manage the content.

title—This property returns a string with the document's title.

url—This property returns a `URL` structure with the document's URL.

isLoading—This property returns a Boolean value that determines if the view is in the process of loading a URL or not.

canGoBack—This property returns a Boolean value that determines if the view can navigate to the previous page.

canGoForward—This property returns a Boolean value that determines if the view can navigate to the next page.

estimatedProgress—This property returns a value of type `Double` between 0.0 and 1.0 that determines the fraction of the content that has been already loaded.

load(URLRequest**)**—This method loads the content of a URL. The argument is an object with the request for the URL we want to open.

goBack()—This method navigates to the previous page on the navigation history.

goForward()—This method navigates to the next page on the navigation history.

go(to: WKBackForwardListItem**)**—This method navigates to the web page indicated by the argument. The **to** argument is an object that represents a web page in a navigation list.

reload()—This method reloads the current page (it refreshes the web page).

stopLoading()—This method asks the view to stop loading the content.

To load a website, we must create a request. The UIKit framework offers the `URLRequest` structure for this purpose. The structure includes the following initializer.

URLRequest(url: URL, **cachePolicy:** CachePolicy, **timeoutInterval:** TimeInterval)—This initializer creates a request to load the URL specified by the **url** argument. The **cachePolicy** argument is an enumeration that determines how the request will work with the cache. The possible values are: `useProtocolCachePolicy` (default), `reloadIgnoringLocalCacheData`, `reloadIgnoringLocalAndRemoteCacheData`, `returnCacheDataElseLoad`, `returnCacheDataDontLoad`, and `reloadRevalidatingCacheData`. The **timeoutInterval** argument is the maximum time allowed for the system to process the request (60.0 by default). Only the first argument is required, the rest of the arguments are defined with values by default.

A WebKit view can report the state of the content through a delegate. For this purpose, the framework defines the `WKNavigationDelegate` protocol. The following are some of the methods included in this protocol.

webView(WKWebView, **decidePolicyFor:** WKNavigationAction, **decisionHandler:** Closure)—This method is called on the delegate to determine if the view should process a request. The **decidePolicyFor** argument is an object with information about the request, and the **decisionHandler** argument is a closure that we must execute to report our decision. The closure takes a value of type `WKNavigationActionPolicy`, an enumeration with the properties `cancel` and `allow`.

webView(WKWebView, **didStartProvisionalNavigation:** WKNavigation!)—This method is called on the delegate when the view begins loading new content.

webView(WKWebView, **didFinish:** WKNavigation!)—This method is called on the delegate when the view finishes loading the content.

webView(WKWebView, **didFailProvisionalNavigation:** WKNavigation!, **withError:** Error)—This method is called on the delegate when an error occurs loading the content.

webView(WKWebView, **didReceiveServerRedirectForProvisionalNavigation:** WKNavigation!)—This method is called on the delegate when the server redirects the navigator to a different destination.

The WebKit view is a UIKit view and therefore we must use the `UIViewRepresentable` protocol to create it. Once the representable view is defined, the process to load a website in a WebKit view is simple; we provide the URL, create a request, and ask the view to load it.

```
import SwiftUI
import WebKit

struct WebView: UIViewRepresentable {
   let searchURL: URL

   func makeUIView(context: Context) -> WKWebView {
      let view = WKWebView()
      let request = URLRequest(url: searchURL)
      view.load(request)
      return view
   }
}
```

```
    func updateUIView(_ uiView: WKWebView, context: Context) {}
}
```

Listing 17-10: *Loading a website with a WebKit View*

This example prepares the request with the URL received from the SwiftUI interface and loads the website with the **load()** method. Because we always load the same website, the view just has to define the URL and pass it to the **WebView** instance.

```
struct ContentView: View {
   var body: some View {
      WebView(searchURL: URL(string: "https://www.google.com")!)
   }
}
```

Listing 17-11: *Showing the WebKit view*

Do It Yourself: Create a Multiplatform project. Create a Swift file called WebView.swift for the code in Listing 17-10. Update the **ContentView** view with the code in Listing 17-11. Run the application on the iPhone simulator. You should see Google's website on the screen.

IMPORTANT: In the example of Listing 17-11, we open a secure URL (a URL that begins with the prefix https://) because these are the URLs allowed by default. As we have seen in Chapter 9, Apple implements a system called App Transport Security (ATS) to block insecure URLs. If you want to allow users to load insecure URLs with a **WKWebView** view, you must configure the ATS system with the Allow Arbitrary Loads option (see Figure 9-3).

With a **WKWebView** view, we can load any website we want, including those specified by the user. We just need to provide a way for the user to insert a URL, as we did in previous examples, and then execute the **load()** method again to load it. For this purpose, the following view includes a **TextField** view and a button. When the button is pressed, we call a method in the **WebView** structure to update the view with the URL inserted by the user.

```
import SwiftUI

class ContentData: ObservableObject {
   @Published var inputURL: String = ""
}
struct ContentView: View {
   @ObservedObject var contentData = ContentData()
   var webView: WebView!

   init() {
      webView = WebView(inputURL: $contentData.inputURL)
   }
   var body: some View {
      VStack {
         HStack {
            TextField("Insert URL", text: $contentData.inputURL)
               .autocapitalization(.none)
               .disableAutocorrection(true)
            Button("Load") {
               let text =
contentData.inputURL.trimmingCharacters(in: .whitespaces)
               if !text.isEmpty {
                  webView.loadWeb(web: text)
               }
```

```
            }
        }.padding(5)
        webView
      }
    }
  }
}
```

Listing 17-12: Allowing the user the insert a URL

In this example, we include a property called `webView` to store a `WebView` structure. The property is initialized with a new instance and then used to call methods on the structure and present the view on the screen.

The URL inserted by the user is stored in a property called `inputURL`, which is passed to the `WebView` structure. This is to be able to update the value of the text field every time the user navigates to a new page. Notice that to be able to pass the `inputURL` property to the view in the initializer, we had to declare it as a `@Published` property inside an observable object.

The `WebView` structure for this example has to create the `WKWebView` view and implement the methods to load new URLs and keep the views updated.

```
import SwiftUI
import WebKit

struct WebView : UIViewRepresentable {
    @Binding var inputURL: String
    let view: WKWebView = WKWebView()

    func makeUIView(context: Context) -> WKWebView  {
        view.navigationDelegate = context.coordinator
        let request = URLRequest(url: URL(string: "https://
www.google.com")!)
        view.load(request)
        return view
    }
    func updateUIView(_ uiView: WKWebView, context: Context) {}

    func loadWeb(web: String) {
        var components = URLComponents(string: web)
        components?.scheme = "https"
        if let newURL = components?.string {
            if let url = newURL.addingPercentEncoding(withAllowedCharacters:
.urlQueryAllowed) {
                if let loadURL = URL(string: url) {
                    let request = URLRequest(url: loadURL)
                    view.load(request)
                }
            }
        }
    }
    func makeCoordinator() -> CoordinatorWebView {
        return CoordinatorWebView(input: $inputURL)
    }
}
class CoordinatorWebView: NSObject, WKNavigationDelegate {
    @Binding var inputURL: String

    init(input: Binding<String>) {
        self._inputURL = input
    }
    func webView(_ webView: WKWebView, didCommit navigation:
WKNavigation!) {
        if let webURL = webView.url {
```

```
        inputURL = webURL.absoluteString
      }
   }
}
```

Listing 17-13: Updating the `WKWebView` *with the URLs inserted by the user*

We have introduced several modifications in this **WebView** structure to be able to load multiple URLs. First, we instantiate the **WKWebView** view outside the **makeUIView()** method to be able to access it from our custom methods. In the **makeUIView()** method, we declare the coordinator as the delegate of the view by assigning a reference of the coordinator to the view's **navigationDelegate** property, and then the request is created and load it. The view is now initialized, and it will call methods on the coordinator to report changes. But before implementing the coordinator, we define the **loadWeb()** method to load the URL inserted by the user. This is the method executed when the user taps the Load button next to the text field. The method receives a string, prepares the URL, and loads it with the **load()** method.

The URLs inserted by the user are loaded and their content is shown on the screen. Now we must do the opposite, we need to update the URL in the text field when the content of the view changes. This happens when the user taps on the links on a page to navigate to another. For this purpose, we make the coordinator conform to the **WKNavigationDelegate** protocol and implement the **webView(WKWebView, didCommit:)** method. This method is called by the **WKWebView** view when it is loading new content. Here, we get the current URL from the view's **url** property and assign it to the **inputURL** property, which modifies the value in the **TextField** view, so the URL in this field matches the website being displayed on the screen.

 Do It Yourself: Update the ContentView.swift file with the code in Listing 17-12 and the WebView.swift file with the code in Listing 17-13. Run the application on the iPhone simulator. Insert a URL and press the Load button. The view should load the URL and show the website. Click on a link to navigate to another page. The URL in the text field should match the address of the page on the screen.

In the app we have built so far, the user can visit any URL and navigate by clicking on the links, but our interface doesn't offer the possibility to move back or forward in the navigation history. The **WKWebView** class offers several methods to control the content. For instance, there is the **goBack()** method to go back to the previous page, the **goForward()** method to go to the page we came back from, and the **reload()** method to refresh the page. To execute these methods, we are going to add three buttons below the navigation bar.

```
import SwiftUI

class ContentData: ObservableObject {
   @Published var inputURL: String = ""
   @Published var backDisabled: Bool = true
   @Published var forwardDisabled: Bool = true
}
struct ContentView: View {
   @ObservedObject var contentData = ContentData()
   var webView: WebView!

   init() {
      webView = WebView(inputURL: $contentData.inputURL, backDisabled:
$contentData.backDisabled, forwardDisabled: $contentData.forwardDisabled)
   }
   var body: some View {
      VStack {
```

```
        HStack {
            TextField("Insert URL", text: $contentData.inputURL)
            Button("Load") {
                let text =
contentData.inputURL.trimmingCharacters(in: .whitespaces)
                if !text.isEmpty {
                    webView.loadWeb(web: text)
                }
            }
        }.padding(5)

        HStack {
            Button(action: {
                webView.goBack()
            }, label: {
                Image(systemName: "arrow.left.circle")
                    .font(.title)
            }).disabled(contentData.backDisabled)
            Button(action: {
                webView.goForward()
            }, label: {
                Image(systemName: "arrow.right.circle")
                    .font(.title)
            }).disabled(contentData.forwardDisabled)
            Spacer()
            Button(action: {
                webView.refresh()
            }, label: {
                Image(systemName: "arrow.clockwise.circle")
                    .font(.title)
            })
        }.padding(5)
        webView
    }
    }
}
```

Listing 17-14: Providing buttons for navigation

This view defines two more **@Published** properties in the observable object to determine whether the back and forward buttons should be enabled or not. When the view is displayed for the first time, the buttons should be disabled because only one document was loaded into the view, but after a new document is loaded, we have to enable the buttons to let the user go back and forth in the navigation history. For this purpose, we must pass the properties to the **WebView** structure and modify their values from the coordinator every time a document is loaded.

```
import SwiftUI
import WebKit

struct WebView: UIViewRepresentable {
    @Binding var inputURL: String
    @Binding var backDisabled: Bool
    @Binding var forwardDisabled: Bool

    let view: WKWebView = WKWebView()

    func makeUIView(context: Context) -> WKWebView  {
        view.navigationDelegate = context.coordinator
        let request = URLRequest(url: URL(string: "https://
www.google.com")!)
        self.view.load(request)
        return view
    }
```

```
    func updateUIView(_ uiView: WKWebView, context: Context) {}

    func loadWeb(web: String) {
        var components = URLComponents(string: web)
        components?.scheme = "https"
        if let newURL = components?.string {
            if let url = newURL.addingPercentEncoding(withAllowedCharacters:
.urlQueryAllowed) {
                if let loadURL = URL(string: url) {
                    let request = URLRequest(url: loadURL)
                    view.load(request)
                }
            }
        }
    }
    func goBack(){
        view.goBack()
    }
    func goForward(){
        view.goForward()
    }
    func refresh(){
        view.reload()
    }
    func makeCoordinator() -> CoordinatorWebView {
        return CoordinatorWebView(input: $inputURL, back: $backDisabled,
forward: $forwardDisabled)
    }
}
class CoordinatorWebView: NSObject, WKNavigationDelegate {
    @Binding var inputURL: String
    @Binding var backDisabled: Bool
    @Binding var forwardDisabled: Bool

    init(input: Binding<String>, back: Binding<Bool>, forward:
Binding<Bool>) {
        self._inputURL = input
        self._backDisabled = back
        self._forwardDisabled = forward
    }
    func webView(_ webView: WKWebView, didCommit navigation:
WKNavigation!) {
        if let webURL = webView.url {
            inputURL = webURL.absoluteString
            backDisabled = !webView.canGoBack
            forwardDisabled = !webView.canGoForward
        }
    }
}
```

Listing 17-15: Navigating back and forth in the navigation history

This code adds three methods to the **WebView** structure to perform the actions selected by the user (moving backward, forward, or refreshing the page). In the **webView(WKWebView, didFinish:)** method, we update the URL in the text field, as before, but also modify the state of the buttons with the values of the **canGoBack** and **canGoForward** properties, so they are only enabled when there is a page to open.

Figure 17-5: Buttons for navigation

 Do It Yourself: Update the ContentView.swift file with the code in Listing 17-14 and the WebView.swift file with the code in Listing 17-15. Run the application on the iPhone simulator. Search a term in Google. Click on a link and press the back button. The view should go back to the previous page.

 IMPORTANT: The WebKit framework also offers tools to process cookies and JavaScript code, which allow you to interact with the document's content. The topic is beyond the scope of this book. For more information, visit our website and follow the links for this chapter.

(Basic) **Web Content**

The Safari view controller and the WebKit view were designed to show content to the user, but the capacity to integrate that content with our app is limited. Sometimes all we need is to extract a piece of information from a document or process the data instead of showing the entire content as it is. In cases like this, we must load the document in the background and analyze it to extract only what we need.

Foundation includes a group of classes to get the content referenced by a URL. The main class is called **URLSession**. This class creates a session that manages an HTTP connection to obtain data, and download or upload files. The following are some of the properties and initializers provided by the class to create the session.

shared—This type property returns a standard session with a configuration by default that is suitable to perform basic requests.

URLSession(configuration: URLSessionConfiguration)—This initializer creates a new session with the configuration set by the argument. The **configuration** argument is an object that specifies the session's behavior.

URLSession(configuration: URLSessionConfiguration, **delegate:** URLSessionDelegate?, **delegateQueue:** OperationQueue?)—This initializer creates a new session with the configuration set by the arguments. The **configuration** argument is an object that specifies the session's behavior, the **delegate** argument is a reference to the delegate object we want to assign to the session, and the **delegateQueue** argument is the queue in which the delegate methods are going to be executed.

The session sets up the connection, but it does not perform any tasks. To download or upload data we must implement the following methods defined in the **URLSession** class.

data(from: URL, **delegate:** URLSessionTaskDelegate?)—This asynchronous method adds a task to the session to download the data at the URL indicated by the **from** argument. The **delegate** argument is the delegate object used by the task to report updates during the process. The method returns a tuple with two values: a **Data** structure with the data returned by the server and a **URLResponse** object with the status of the request.

download(from: URL, delegate: URLSessionTaskDelegate?)—This asynchronous method adds a task to the session to download the file at the URL indicated by the **from** argument. The **delegate** argument is the delegate object used by the task to report updates during the process. The method returns a tuple with two values: a **URL** structure that indicates the location of the downloaded file and a **URLResponse** object with the status of the request.

The following are the methods defined by the class to upload data and files.

upload(for: URLRequest, from: Data, delegate: URLSessionTaskDelegate?) —This asynchronous method adds a task to the session to upload the data indicated by the **from** argument. The **delegate** argument is the delegate object used by the task to report updates during the process. The method returns a tuple with two values: a **Data** structure with the data returned by the server and a **URLResponse** object with the status of the request.

upload(for: URLRequest, fromFile: URL, delegate: URLSessionTask-Delegate?)—This asynchronous method adds a task to the session to upload the file in the URL indicated by the **fromFile** argument. The **delegate** argument is the delegate object used by the task to report updates during the process. The method returns a tuple with two values: a **Data** structure with the data returned by the server and a **URLResponse** object with the status of the request.

These methods are asynchronous. When the data finishes downloading or uploading, they return the result. For example, if we use the **data()** method to get data from a website, the value returned includes a value with the data and an object of type **URLResponse** with the status of the request. When we access a URL using the HTTP protocol, the response is represented by an object of type **HTTPURLResponse** (a subclass of **URLResponse**). This class includes the **statusCode** property to return a code that determines the status of the request. There are several codes available to report things like the success of the request (200) or more drastic situations like when the website has been moved to a different address (301). If all we want is to make sure that the data was downloaded correctly, we can check if the value of the **statusCode** property is equal to 200 before processing anything. The following example shows how to perform a basic request.

```
import SwiftUI

class ApplicationData: ObservableObject {
   @Published var webContent: String = ""
   @Published var buttonDisabled: Bool = false

   func loadWeb() async {
      buttonDisabled = true

      let session = URLSession.shared
      let webURL = URL(string: "https://www.yahoo.com")
      do {
         let (data, response) = try await session.data(from: webURL!)
         if let resp = response as? HTTPURLResponse {
            let status = resp.statusCode
            if status == 200 {
               if let content = String(data: data, encoding:
String.Encoding.ascii) {
```

```
                await MainActor.run {
                    webContent = content
                    buttonDisabled = false
                }
                print(content)
            }
        } else {
            print("Error: \(status)")
        }
    }
} catch {
    print("Error: \(error)")
}
    }
}
```

Listing 17-16: Loading a remote document

This model loads the content of the website at www.yahoo.com and assigns it to the **webContent** property. The process is performed by the **loadWeb()** method. The method defines the request with the https://www.yahoo.com URL, and then calls the **data()** method on the session to download the page. The method downloads the content at that address, checks whether the process was successful (200), gets a string from the data, and updates the **webContent** property with this value to make it available for the view. The following is a simple view to process this data.

```
struct ContentView: View {
    @EnvironmentObject var appData: ApplicationData

    var body: some View {
        VStack {
            Button("Load Web") {
                Task(priority: .high) {
                    await appData.loadWeb()
                }
            }.disabled(appData.buttonDisabled)
            Text("Total Characters: \(appData.webContent.count)")
                .padding()
            Spacer()
        }.padding()
    }
}
```

Listing 17-17: Displaying the document's content

The content returned by the www.yahoo.com domain is extensive. For didactic purposes, we print it on the console and display on the screen the number of characters in the string, but a professional application usually processes the value to extract information.

 Do It Yourself: Create a Multiplatform project. Create a Swift file called ApplicationData.swift for the code in Listing 17-16. Update the **ContentView** view with the code in Listing 17-17. Remember to inject the **ApplicationData** object into the environment for the app and the previews (Chapter 7, Listing 7-4). Run the application on the iPhone simulator. Press the Load Web button. After a few seconds, you should see the document downloaded from www.yahoo.com printed on the console and the number of characters on the screen.

A standard session like the one we used in this example comes with a configuration by default that is suitable for most situations, but a custom session requires its own configuration. To configure a session, Foundation provides a class called **URLSessionConfiguration**. The following is the type property we can use to get a configuration object with values by default.

default—This property returns a **URLSessionConfiguration** object with default settings.

Once we get an object with a standard configuration, we can adapt it to the requirements of our application. The following are some of the properties offered by the **URLSession-Configuration** class to modify the configuration.

allowsCellularAccess—This property sets or returns a Boolean value that determines if the connection should be made when the device is connected to a cellular network.

timeoutIntervalForRequest—This property sets or returns a **TimeInterval** value (a typealias of **Double**) that determines the number of seconds the session should wait for a request to be answered. The value by default is 60.

waitsForConnectivity—This property sets or returns a Boolean value that determines if the session should wait to perform the request until the device gets connected to the network. The value by default is **false**.

Working with custom sessions only requires us to change how the session is initialized, but the rest of the code remains the same.

```
import SwiftUI

class ApplicationData: ObservableObject {
    @Published var webContent: String = ""
    @Published var buttonDisabled: Bool = false

    func loadWeb() async {
        buttonDisabled = true

        let config = URLSessionConfiguration.default
        config.waitsForConnectivity = true
        let session = URLSession(configuration: config)

        let webURL = URL(string: "https://www.yahoo.com")
        do {
            let (data, response) = try await session.data(from: webURL!)
            if let resp = response as? HTTPURLResponse {
                let status = resp.statusCode
                if status == 200 {
                    if let content = String(data: data, encoding:
String.Encoding.ascii) {
                        await MainActor.run {
                            webContent = content
                            buttonDisabled = false
                        }
                        print(content)
                    }
                } else {
                    print("Error: \(status)")
                }
            }
        } catch {
            print("Error: \(error)")
        }
    }
```

```
        }
    }
```

Listing 17-18: Instantiating a custom session

In this example, we haven't implemented the **delegate** argument of the **data()** method. This argument is optional, but we can declare it if we need to respond and process updates. The framework defines the **URLSessionTaskDelegate** protocol to create this delegate. The following are some of the methods included in the protocol.

urlSession(URLSession, **task:** URLSessionTask, **didReceive:** URL-AuthenticationChallenge, **completionHandler:** Closure)—This method is called on the delegate when authentication is requested by the server. Our implementation must call the completion handler received by the method with two arguments that define the settings and credentials.

urlSession(URLSession, **task:** URLSessionTask, **willPerformHTTP-Redirection:** HTTPURLResponse, **newRequest:** URLRequest, **completion-Handler:** Block)—This method is called on the delegate when the server redirected the connection to another URL. Our implementation must call the completion handler received by the method with an argument that defines the new request (the value of the **newRequest** argument) or the value **nil** if we do not want to follow the redirection.

Some websites, like www.yahoo.com, automatically send the user to a different address that contains a version of the website that is customized based on the user's location and preferences. This means that the URL we provide does not represent the final destination; the server does not return any data but instead redirects the user to another document. In cases like this, we can define a custom session with a delegate and then implement the method of the **URLSession-TaskDelegate** protocol to determine what we want to do when the server is redirecting our application.

```
import SwiftUI

class ApplicationData: NSObject, URLSessionTaskDelegate, ObservableObject {
    @Published var webContent: String = ""
    @Published var buttonDisabled: Bool = false

    func loadWeb() async {
        buttonDisabled = true

        let session = URLSession.shared
        let webURL = URL(string: "https://www.yahoo.com")
        do {
            let (data, response) = try await session.data(from: webURL!,
delegate: self)
            if let resp = response as? HTTPURLResponse {
                let status = resp.statusCode
                if status == 200 {
                    if let content = String(data: data, encoding:
String.Encoding.ascii) {
                        await MainActor.run {
                            webContent = content
                            buttonDisabled = false
                        }
                    }
                } else {
                    print("Error: \(status)")
                }
            }
```

```
    } catch {
      print("Error: \(error)")
    }
  }
  func urlSession(_ session: URLSession, task: URLSessionTask,
willPerformHTTPRedirection response: HTTPURLResponse, newRequest request:
URLRequest) async -> URLRequest? {
    print(request.url ?? "No URL")
    return request
  }
}
```

Listing 17-19: Redirecting the user

 Do It Yourself: Update the `ApplicationData` class with the code in Listing 17-19. Run the application on the iPhone simulator. Press the Load Web button. You should see the URL to which the user was redirected printed on the console.

Web documents, like the one returned by www.yahoo.com, are written in HTML. This is a simple programming language used by every website to organize information. Extracting data from these documents can be tedious and error prone. That is the reason why websites usually provide additional services to share data in JSON format. These JSON documents are dynamically generated and contain only the information requested by the application. For instance, the website www.openweathermap.org offers a service that generates JSON documents with information about the weather (https://openweathermap.org/api).

To illustrate how to access and process the documents produced by these services, we are going to read posts from a website called JSONPlaceholder (jsonplaceholder.typicode.com) that generates phony documents. The process doesn't require anything new. We must load the document with a `URLSession` and then decode it with a `JSONDecoder` object.

```
import SwiftUI

struct Post: Codable, Identifiable {
   var id: Int
   var userId: Int
   var title: String
   var body: String
}
class ApplicationData: ObservableObject {
   @Published var listOfPosts: [Post] = []

   init() {
      Task(priority: .high) {
         await loadJSON()
      }
   }
   func loadJSON() async {
      let session = URLSession.shared
      let webURL = URL(string: "https://jsonplaceholder.typicode.com/
posts")

      do {
         let (data, response) = try await session.data(from: webURL!)
         if let resp = response as? HTTPURLResponse {
            let status = resp.statusCode
            if status == 200 {
               let decoder = JSONDecoder()
               if let posts = try? decoder.decode([Post].self, from:
data) {

                  await MainActor.run {
```

```
                listOfPosts = posts
            }
        }
    } else {
        print("Error: \(status)")
    }
}
} catch {
    print("Error: \(error)")
}
}
}
}
```

Listing 17-20: Loading a JSON document

As we have learned in Chapter 10, to decode a JSON document we must define a structure that matches the JSON values one by one. The https://jsonplaceholder.typicode.com/posts URL returns a list of posts, each one with four values: an integer with the user's identifier, another integer with the post's identifier, a string with the title, and a string with the message. To store these values, the model in Listing 17-20 defines the **Post** structure. The structure conforms to the **Codable** protocol to be able to decode it, and to the **Identifiable** protocol to be able to list the instances with a **List** view.

The process to download the document is the same as before. We get the session, call the **data()** method on it, decode the data into an array of **Post** structures with a **JSONDecoder** object, and store the values in the **listOfPosts** property to update the view. Because the document is downloaded when the model is initialized, all we have to do in the view is to list the values.

```
struct ContentView: View {
    @EnvironmentObject var appData: ApplicationData

    var body: some View {
        VStack {
            List {
                ForEach(appData.listOfPosts) { post in
                    VStack(alignment: .leading) {
                        Text(post.title).bold()
                        Text(post.body)
                    }.padding(5)
                }
            }.listStyle(.plain)
        }.padding()
    }
}
```

Listing 17-21: Listing the values from the document

 Do It Yourself: Update the ApplicationData.swift file from the previous project with the code in Listing 17-20 and the **ContentView** view with the code in Listing 17-21. Run the application. You should see 100 messages on the screen. To see the structure of the JSON file returned from the URL https://jsonplaceholder.typicode.com/posts, insert the URL in your browser.

Chapter 18
Media

(Basic) **18.1 Pictures**

These days, personal devices are mainly used to process images, videos, and sound, and Apple devices are no exception. SwiftUI can display an image with an `Image` view, but it requires the assistance of other frameworks to process the image, present a video on the screen, or play sounds. In this chapter, we introduce some of the tools provided by Apple for this purpose.

(Basic) **Photos Picker**

SwiftUI includes the `PhotosPicker` structure to generate a view that allows the user to select one or multiple pictures from the Photo Library. The following is the view's initializer.

PhotosPicker(selection: Binding, **maxSelectionCount:** Int?, **selection-Behavior:** PhotosPickerSelectionBehavior, **matching:** PHPickerFilter?, **preferredItemEncoding:** EncodingDisambiguationPolicy, **photoLibrary:** PHPhotoLibrary, **label:** Closure)—This initializer creates a `PhotosPicker` view with the configuration specified by the arguments. The **selection** argument is the `Binding` property that stores the references to the selected items. The **maxSelectionCount** argument is the maximum number of items we want to user to be able to select. The **selectionBehavior** argument determines if the selection is going to be numbered or not. It is a structure with the type properties `default` and `ordered`. The **matching** argument determines the type of items the view should include. It is a structure with the type properties `bursts`, `cinematicVideos`, `depthEffectPhotos`, `images`, `livePhotos`, `panoramas`, `screenRecordings`, `screenshots`, `slomoVideos`, `timelapseVideos`, and `videos`. The **preferredItemEncoding** argument determines the encoding to use to process the items. It is a structure with the type properties `automatic` (default), `current`, and `compatible`. The **photoLibrary** argument provides access to the library. It is a structure with the type method `shared()`. And the **label** argument is a closure that provides the label for the button generated by the view.

Because it may take time to retrieve the items, the picker does not return the images or videos directly, it returns a reference to the items that we can use to retrieve them later. The framework defines the `PhotosPickerItem` structure for this purpose. The structure includes the following property and method to access the media.

itemIdentifier—This property returns a string with the item's identifier.

loadTransferable(type: Type)—This asynchronous method loads the item and assigns it to an instance of the data type specified by the **type** argument. The data type assigned to this argument must conform to the `Transferable` protocol.

The `PhotosPicker` structure and all the data types required to read and retrieve items from the library are defined in the PhotosUI framework, that we must import along with SwiftUI. Another requirement of the structure is a state property to store the selected items. If we want to allow the user to select multiple items, the property must store an array of `PhotosPickerItem` structures, but if we want the user to select only one item, the property only needs to store one optional `PhotosPickerItem` structure, as shown next.

```
import SwiftUI
import PhotosUI
struct ContentView: View {
    @State private var selected: PhotosPickerItem?
    @State private var picture: UIImage?

    var body: some View {
        NavigationStack {
            VStack {
                Image(uiImage: picture ?? UIImage(named: "nopicture")!)
                    .resizable()
                    .scaledToFit()
                Spacer()
            }
            .toolbar {
                ToolbarItem(placement: .navigationBarTrailing) {
                    PhotosPicker(selection: $selected, matching: .images,
photoLibrary: .shared()) { Text("Select a photo") }
                }
            }
            .onChange(of: selected) { item in
                Task(priority: .background) {
                    if let data = try? await item?.loadTransferable(type:
Data.self) {
                        picture = UIImage(data: data)
                    }
                }
            }
        }
    }
}
```

Listing 18-1: *Creating a Photo picker*

Most of the arguments in the **PhotosPicker** initializer are optional. For this example, we only need to tell the picker where to store the references to the selected items, the type of items we want to show to the user (**images**), and where to get them (the shared library). The **PhotosPicker** structure creates a button that opens a view to select the items when pressed, so we add it to the navigation bar.

When an item is selected, a reference is stored in the state property. This means that we can monitor that property for changes. In this example, we use the **onChange()** modifier. If a new image is selected, we start an asynchronous task to call the **loadTransferable()** method on the selected item. This method loads the image, turns it into a **Data** structure, and returns it. If the process is successful, we use the data to initialize a **UIImage** object and assign it to a **picture** property to show it on the screen.

Figure 18-1: *Photo Library's interface (center)*

Do It Yourself: Create a Multiplatform project. Update the `ContentView` view with the code in Listing 18-1. Download the image nopicture from our website and add it to the Asset Catalog. Press the Select a photo button. Tap on a picture to select it. The image should be assigned to the `Image` view and displayed on the screen, as shown in Figure 18-1.

 IMPORTANT: In this example, we have used the `Data` structure to transfer the value with the `loadTransferable()` method. We could have used an `Image` view instead, but at the moment of writing this data type can only receive PNG images. For more information on the `Transferable` protocol, read the Drag and Drop Gesture section in Chapter 12.

By assigning an array of `PhotosPickerItem` structures to the state property, we can allow the user to select multiple items, but there are a few things we must consider. One of the things we have to think about is how we are going to remove items from the list when they are deselected by the user. We could clear the array and load every item again, but some items may take a while to load. Another alternative is to store the items in a separate array and compare values to only remove the items that have been deselected but keep the rest. This is the approach we follow in the following example. For this purpose, we need a model with a structure to store the images along with their identifiers.

```
import SwiftUI
import PhotosUI
struct ItemsData: Identifiable {
   var id: String
   var image: UIImage
}
class ApplicationData: ObservableObject {
   @Published var listPictures: [ItemsData] = []
   @Published var selected: [PhotosPickerItem] = []

   func removeDeselectedItems() {
      listPictures = listPictures.filter { value in
         if selected.contains(where: { $0.itemIdentifier == value.id }) {
            return true
         } else {
            return false
         }
      }
   }
   func addSelectedItems() {
      for item in selected {
         Task(priority: .background) {
            if let data = try? await item.loadTransferable(type:
Data.self) {
               if let id = item.itemIdentifier, let image = UIImage(data:
data) {
                  if !listPictures.contains(where: { $0.id == id }) {
                     let newPicture = ItemsData(id: id, image: image)
                     await MainActor.run {
                        listPictures.append(newPicture)
                     }
                  }
               }
            }
         }
      }
   }
}
```

Listing 18-2: Defining the model for multiple selection

The model includes two **@Published** properties, one to store an array of **ItemsData** structures to supply the currently selected images to the views, and one with an array of **PhotosPickerItem** structures for the **PhotosPicker** view to store the references of the items the user selects from the Photo Library.

There are also two methods in the model: **removeDeselectedItems()** and **addSelectedItems()**. Both will be executed from the view every time the user modifies the selection (Every time the value of the **selected** property changes). The **removeDeselected-Items()** method iterates through the items in the **listPictures** array to check which ones are still selected by the user, so any item that has been deselected is not included on the list anymore. On the other hand, the **addSelectedItems()** method adds to the **listPictures** array the items that the user has added to the selection. The view can now use the **listPictures** array to show the selected images on the screen, and call these methods every time the selection is modified.

```
struct ContentView: View {
    @EnvironmentObject var appData: ApplicationData

    let guides = [
        GridItem(.flexible()),
        GridItem(.flexible()),
        GridItem(.flexible())
    ]
    var body: some View {
        NavigationStack {
            ScrollView {
                LazyVGrid(columns: guides) {
                    ForEach(appData.listPictures) { item in
                        Image(uiImage: item.image)
                            .resizable()
                            .scaledToFit()
                    }
                }
            }.padding()
            .toolbar {
                ToolbarItem(placement: .navigationBarLeading) {
                    Button("Deselect") {
                        appData.selected = []
                    }
                }
                ToolbarItem(placement: .navigationBarTrailing) {
                    PhotosPicker(selection: $appData.selected,
maxSelectionCount: 4, selectionBehavior: .ordered, matching: .images,
photoLibrary: .shared()) { Text("Select Photos") }
                }
            }
            .onChange(of: appData.selected) { items in
                appData.removeDeselectedItems()
                appData.addSelectedItems()
            }
        }
    }
}
```

Listing 18-3: Allowing the user to perform multiple selections

In this example, we have configured the picker to allow the selection of a maximum of 4 items, but this is not necessary. If no limit is declared, the picker allows users to select all the items they want. The result is shown below.

Figure 18-2: Multiple selection

Do It Yourself: Create a Swift file called ApplicationData.swift for the model in Listing 18-2. Update the `ContentView` view with the code in Listing 18-3. Remember to inject the `ApplicationData` object into the environment for the app and the previews (Chapter 7, Listing 7-4). Run the application on a device. Press the Select Photo button and select multiple pictures. You should see the selected pictures on the list, as shown in Figure 18-2. At the moment of writing, the state property is not modified when all the items are deselected. If that's still the case, you can add a button to remove all the items and clean the selection, as we did in this example.

(Basic) Camera

One of the most common uses of mobile devices is to take and store photos, and that is why no device is sold without a camera anymore. Because of how normal it is for an application to access the camera and manage pictures, UIKit offers a controller with built-in functionality that provides all the tools necessary for the user to take pictures and record videos. The class to create this controller is called `UIImagePickerController`. The following are the properties included in this class for configuration.

sourceType—This property sets or returns a value that determines the type of source we want to use to get the pictures. It is an enumeration called `SourceType` included in the `UIImagePickerController` class. Currently, only the value **camera** is available.

mediaTypes—This property sets or returns a value that determines the type of media we want to work with. It takes an array of strings with values that represent every media we want to use. The most common are public.image for pictures and public.movie for videos.

cameraCaptureMode—This property sets or returns a value that determines the capture mode used by the camera. It is an enumeration called `CameraCaptureMode` included in the `UIImagePickerController` class. The values available are **photo** and **video**.

cameraFlashMode—This property sets or returns a value that determines the flash mode used by the camera. It is an enumeration called `CameraFlashMode` included in the `UIImagePickerController` class. The values available are **on**, **off**, and **auto**.

allowsEditing—This property sets or returns a Boolean value that determines if the user is allowed to edit the image.

videoQuality—This property sets or returns a value that determines the quality of the recorded video. It is an enumeration called `QualityType` included in the `UIImagePickerController` class. The values available are **typeHigh**, **typeMedium**, **typeLow**, **type640x480**, **typeIFrame960x540**, and **typeIFrame1280x720**.

The **UIImagePickerController** class also offers the following type methods to detect the source available and the type of media it can manage.

isSourceTypeAvailable(SourceType**)**—This type method returns a Boolean value that indicates if the source specified by the argument is supported by the device. The argument is an enumeration called **SourceType** included in the **UIImagePicker-Controller** class. At this moment, only the value **camera** is available.

availableMediaTypes(for: SourceType**)**—This type method returns an array with strings that represent the media types available for the source specified by the argument. The argument is an enumeration called **SourceType** included in the **UIImagePicker-Controller** class. At this moment, only the value **camera** is available.

isCameraDeviceAvailable(CameraDevice**)**—This type method returns a Boolean value that indicates if the camera specified by the argument is available on the device. The argument is an enumeration called **CameraDevice** included in the **UIImagePicker-Controller** class. The values available are **rear** and **front**.

The **UIImagePickerController** class creates a new view where the user can take pictures or record videos. After the image or the video are created, the view must be dismissed, and the media processed. The way our code gets access to the media and knows when to dismiss the view is through a delegate that conforms to the **UIImagePickerControllerDelegate** protocol. The protocol includes the following methods.

imagePickerController(UIImagePickerController, **didFinishPickingMedia-WithInfo:** Dictionary**)**—This method is called on the delegate when the user finishes taking the image or recording the video. The second argument contains a dictionary with the information about the media. The values in the dictionary are identified with properties of the **InfoKey** structure included in the **UIImagePickerController** class. The properties available are **cropRect**, **editedImage**, **imageURL**, **livePhoto**, **mediaMetadata**, **mediaType**, **mediaURL**, and **originalImage**.

imagePickerControllerDidCancel(UIImagePickerController**)**—This method is called on the delegate when the user cancels the process.

An image picker can be presented with a sheet or a popover, but if we want the view to occupy the entire screen, we can embed it in a **NavigationStack** view and present it with a **NavigationLink**. This is the approach we take in the following example. The interface includes a button to open the image picker and an **Image** view to display the picture taken by the user.

Figure 18-3: Interface to work with the camera

IMPORTANT: To access the camera, you must ask authorization to the user. The process is automatic, but you have to add the "Privacy - Camera Usage Description" option to the Info panel in the app's settings with the message you want to show to the user (see Chapter 5, Figure 5-34).

The image picker controller is a UIKit view controller and therefore it is incorporated into the SwiftUI interface with a representable view controller. To be able to process the image taken by the camera, we need to include a coordinator and implement the delegate methods. This coordinator must conform to two protocols: **UINavigationControllerDelegate** and **UIImagePickerControllerDelegate**, as shown in the following example.

```
import SwiftUI
struct ImagePicker: UIViewControllerRepresentable {
    @Binding var path: NavigationPath
    @Binding var picture: UIImage?

    func makeUIViewController(context: Context) -> UIImagePickerController {
        let mediaPicker = UIImagePickerController()
        mediaPicker.delegate = context.coordinator
        if UIImagePickerController.isSourceTypeAvailable(.camera) {
            mediaPicker.sourceType = .camera
            mediaPicker.mediaTypes = ["public.image"]
            mediaPicker.allowsEditing = false
            mediaPicker.cameraCaptureMode = .photo
        } else {
            print("The media is not available")
        }
        return mediaPicker
    }
    func updateUIViewController(_ uiViewController:
UIImagePickerController, context: Context) {}

    func makeCoordinator() -> ImagePickerCoordinator {
        ImagePickerCoordinator(path: $path, picture: $picture)
    }
}
class ImagePickerCoordinator: NSObject, UINavigationControllerDelegate,
UIImagePickerControllerDelegate {
    @Binding var path: NavigationPath
    @Binding var picture: UIImage?

    init(path: Binding<NavigationPath>, picture: Binding<UIImage?>) {
        self._path = path
        self._picture = picture
    }
    func imagePickerController(_ picker: UIImagePickerController,
didFinishPickingMediaWithInfo info: [UIImagePickerController.InfoKey :
Any]) {
        if let newpicture = info[.originalImage] as? UIImage {
            picture = newpicture
        }
        path = NavigationPath()
    }
    func imagePickerControllerDidCancel(_ picker: UIImagePickerController) {
        path = NavigationPath()
    }
}
```

Listing 18-4: Creating the Image Picker Controller to take pictures

This representable view controller creates an instance of the **UIImagePickerController** class and assigns the **ImagePickerCoordinator** object as its delegate. Next, it checks if the camera is available and configures the controller in case of success or shows a message on the console otherwise. The value **camera** is assigned to the **sourceType** property to tell the controller that we are going to get the picture from the camera, an array with the value public.image is assigned to the **mediaTypes** property to set images as the media we want to retrieve, the **allowEditing** property is set as **false** to not let the user edit the image, and the value **photo** is assigned to the **cameraCaptureMode** property to allow the user only to take pictures.

The camera's interface includes buttons to control the camera and take the picture. After the user takes the picture, a new set of buttons appear to allow the user select the picture or take another one. If the user decides to use the current picture, the controller calls the **imagePickerController(didFinishPickingMediaWithInfo:)** method on its delegate to report the action. This method receives a parameter called **info** that we can read to get the media returned by the controller and process it (store it in a file, Core Data, or show it on the screen). In our example, we read the value of the **originalImage** key to get a **UIImage** object that represents the image taken by the user and assign this object to a state property to make it available for the view. Notice that we have also implemented the **imagePickerController-DidCancel()** method in the coordinator to dismiss the controller when the user presses the Cancel button.

The view must include a button to open the Image Picker Controller and an **Image** view to show the picture taken by the user.

```
import SwiftUI

class ContentData: ObservableObject {
    @Published var path = NavigationPath()
    @Published var picture: UIImage?
}
struct ContentView: View {
    @ObservedObject var contentData = ContentData()
    var ImagePickerView: ImagePicker!

    init() {
        ImagePickerView = ImagePicker(path: $contentData.path, picture:
$contentData.picture)
    }
    var body: some View {
        NavigationStack(path: $contentData.path) {
            VStack {
                HStack {
                    Spacer()
                    NavigationLink("Get Picture", value: "Open Picker")
                }.navigationDestination(for: String.self, destination: { _ in
                    ImagePickerView
                })
                Image(uiImage: contentData.picture ?? UIImage(named:
"nopicture")!)
                    .resizable()
                    .scaledToFill()
                    .frame(minWidth: 0, maxWidth: .infinity, minHeight: 0,
maxHeight: .infinity)
                    .clipped()
                Spacer()
            }.padding()
        }.statusBarHidden()
    }
}
```

Listing 18-5: Defining the interface to take pictures

Chapter 18 - Media

This view creates an instance of the **ImagePicker** structure and declares it as the destination of a **NavigationLink** button. When the button is pressed, the view opens. If the user takes a picture and decides to use it, the picture is assigned to the **picture** property by the delegate method and the **Image** view is updated to display it on the screen.

Do It Yourself: Create a Multiplatform project. Create a Swift file called ImagePicker.swift for the code in Listing 18-4. Update the ContentView.swift file with the code in Listing 18-5. Download the image nopicture from our website and add it to the Asset Catalog. Add the "Privacy - Camera Usage Description" option to the Info panel in the app's settings with the text you want to show to the user. Run the application on a device and press the button. Take a picture and press the button to use it. You should see the photo on the screen.

(Basic) Storing Pictures

In the previous example, we show the picture on the screen, but we can store it in a file or in the Core Data's Persistent Store. An alternative, sometimes useful when working with the camera, is to store the picture in the device's Photo Library so that it is accessible to other applications. The UIKit framework offers two functions to store images and videos.

UIImageWriteToSavedPhotosAlbum(UIImage, Any?, Selector?, Unsafe-MutableRawPointer?**)**—This function adds the image specified by the first argument to the camera roll. The second argument is a reference to the object that contains the method we want to execute when the process is over, the third argument is a selector that represents that method, and the last argument is an object with data to pass to the method.

UISaveVideoAtPathToSavedPhotosAlbum(String, Any?, Selector?, UnsafeMutableRawPointer?**)**—This function adds the video to the camera roll at the path indicated by the first argument. The second argument is a reference to the object that contains the method we want to execute when the process is over, the third argument is a selector that represents that method, and the last argument is an object with additional data for the method.

IMPORTANT: To store pictures or videos in the device, we must ask the user's authorization. As always, this is done from the Info panel in the app's settings. In this case, we must add the "Privacy - Photo Library Additions Usage Description" option with the message we want to show to the user when authorization is requested.

These are old functions defined in Objective-C and therefore require some parameters that are not common to SwiftUI applications. But if all we want is to store the image, we can declare the first argument and define the rest as **nil**. For instance, we can add a button at the top of the screen to the previous application that opens an Alert view with two buttons, one to cancel the operation and another to save the current picture to the Photo Library. When the button to save the picture is pressed, we can call the **UIImageWriteToSavedPhotosAlbum()** function with a reference to the **picture** property, and the picture will be saved.

```
import SwiftUI
class ContentData: NSObject, ObservableObject {
   @Published var path = NavigationPath()
   @Published var picture: UIImage?
}
struct ContentView: View {
   @ObservedObject var contentData = ContentData()
```

```
    @State private var showAlert: Bool = false
    var ImagePickerView: ImagePicker!

    init() {
        ImagePickerView = ImagePicker(path: $contentData.path, picture:
$contentData.picture)
    }
    var body: some View {
        NavigationStack(path: $contentData.path) {
            VStack {
                HStack {
                    Button("Share Picture") {
                        showAlert = true
                    }.disabled(contentData.picture == nil ? true : false)
                    Spacer()
                    NavigationLink("Get Picture", value: "Open Picker")
                }.navigationDestination(for: String.self, destination: { _ in
                    ImagePickerView
                })
                .alert("Save Picture", isPresented: $showAlert, actions: {
                    Button("Cancel", role: .cancel, action: {
                        showAlert = false
                    })
                    Button("YES", role: .none, action: {
                        if let picture = contentData.picture {
                            UIImageWriteToSavedPhotosAlbum(picture, nil, nil,
nil)
                        }
                    })
                }, message: { Text("Do you want to store the picture in the
Photo Library?") })

                Image(uiImage: contentData.picture ?? UIImage(named:
"nopicture")!)
                    .resizable()
                    .scaledToFill()
                    .frame(minWidth: 0, maxWidth: .infinity, minHeight: 0,
maxHeight: .infinity)
                    .clipped()
                Spacer()
            }.padding()
        }.statusBarHidden()
    }
}
```

Listing 18-6: Showing an Alert view when a picture is saved

The process is the same as before. The image picker controller allows the user to take a picture and then calls the delegate method to process it. The picture is assigned to the **picture** property to display it on the screen, but now we have an additional button to save the picture to the Photo Library.

 Do It Yourself: Update the ContentView.swift file with the code in Listing 18-6. Add the "Privacy - Photo Library Additions Usage Description" option to the Info panel in the app's settings to get access to the Photo Library. (Remember that you also need the "Privacy - Camera Usage Description" option to access the camera, as before.) Run the application on a device and take a picture. You should see the picture on the screen. Press the Share Picture button. You should see an Alert View with the message "Picture Saved" and the picture should be available in your Photo Library.

Another way to share information with other applications is a share sheet. This is a sheet provided by the system that includes icons to open the applications we can share content with. SwiftUI includes the following view to open the sheet.

ShareLink(String, **item:** Item, **subject:** Text?, **message:** Text?, **preview:** SharePreview**)**—This initializer creates a button that presents a sheet to select the application with which we want to share the data. The first argument is the button's title. The **item** argument is the value we want to share. (The value must conform to the `Transferable` protocol.) The **subject** argument is the item's title. The **message** argument is the item's description. And the **preview** argument is a structure that provides a representation of the item.

If we want to share an image, we must provide a preview. SwiftUI includes the `Share-Preview` structure for this purpose.

SharePreview(String, **image:** Image**)**—This initializer creates a representation of the item to share. The first argument is the description of the item, and the **image** argument is an `Image` view that visually represents the item.

Share links are frequently used to share text, but they can share any type of value we want as long as it conforms to the `Transferable` protocol. For instance, we can share the picture taken by the camera.

```
struct ContentView: View {
   @ObservedObject var contentData = ContentData()
   var ImagePickerView: ImagePicker!
   init() {
      ImagePickerView = ImagePicker(path: $contentData.path, picture:
$contentData.picture)
   }
   var body: some View {
      NavigationStack(path: $contentData.path) {
         VStack {
            HStack {
               if let picture = contentData.picture {
                  let photo = Image(uiImage: picture)
                  ShareLink("Share Picture", item: photo, preview:
SharePreview("Photo", image: photo))
               }
               Spacer()
               NavigationLink("Get Picture", value: "Open Picker")
            }.navigationDestination(for: String.self, destination: { _ in
               ImagePickerView
            })
            Image(uiImage: contentData.picture ?? UIImage(named:
"nopicture")!)
               .resizable()
               .scaledToFill()
               .frame(minWidth: 0, maxWidth: .infinity, minHeight: 0,
maxHeight: .infinity)
               .clipped()
            Spacer()
         }.padding()
      }.statusBarHidden()
   }
}
```

Listing 18-7: Sharing the image with other applications

The **ShareLink** view creates a button with a predefined label that includes an SF Symbol on the left. In this example, we place it at the top left corner, but only show it when there is a picture to share (when the user has already taken a picture with the camera). If the button is pressed, the system opens a small sheet with icons that represent the apps with which we can share information, and if we scroll the sheet up, options are revealed to perform additional actions like copy and print the data. For instance, if we have the Facebook app installed, we can post a message with our picture, as shown below.

Figure 18-4: Share sheet

 Do It Yourself: Update the **ContentView** view from the previous example with the code in Listing 18-7. Run the application on a device. Press the Get Picture button and take a picture. Press the Share Picture button. You should see the share sheet at the bottom of the screen. Select an app to share the image.

Medium **Custom Camera**

The **UIImagePickerController** controller is built from classes defined in the AV Foundation framework. This framework provides the code necessary to process media and control input devices, like the camera and the microphone. So we can use the classes in this framework directly to build our own controller and customize the process and the interface.

Creating our own controller to access the camera and retrieve information demands the coordination of several systems. We need to configure the input from the camera and the microphone, process the data received from these inputs, show a preview to the user, and generate the output in the form of an image, live photo, video, or audio. Figure 18-5 illustrates all the elements involved.

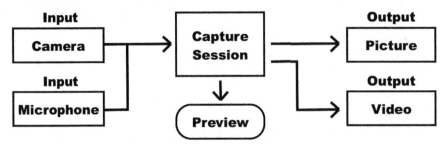

Figure 18-5: System to capture media

The first thing we need to do to build this structure is to determine the input devices. The AV Foundation framework defines the **AVCaptureDevice** class for this purpose. An instance of this class can represent any type of input device, including cameras and microphones. The following are some of the methods included in the class to access and manage a device.

default(for: AVMediaType)—This type method returns an **AVCaptureDevice** object that represents the default capture device for the media specified by the argument. The **for** argument is a structure of type **AVMediaType** with properties to define the type of media. The properties available to work with the cameras and microphones are **video** and **audio**.

requestAccess(for: AVMediaType)—This asynchronous type method asks the user for permission to access the device. The **for** argument is a structure of type **AVMediaType** with properties to define the type of media. The properties available to work with the cameras and microphones are **video** and **audio**.

authorizationStatus(for: AVMediaType)—This type method returns a value that determines the status of the authorization to use the device. The **for** argument is a structure of type **AVMediaType** with properties to define the type of media. The properties available to work with the cameras and microphones are **video** and **audio**. The method returns an enumeration of type **AVAuthorizationStatus** with the values **notDetermined**, **restricted**, **denied**, and **authorized**.

An instance of the **AVCaptureDevice** class represents a capture device. To define this device as an input device, we must create an object that controls the ports and connections. The framework defines the **AVCaptureDeviceInput** class for this purpose. The class includes the following initializer to create the input object for the device.

AVCaptureDeviceInput(device: AVCaptureDevice)—This initializer creates an input for the device specified by the **device** argument.

In addition to inputs, we also need outputs to process the data captured by the device. The framework defines subclasses of a base class called **AVCaptureOutput** to describe the outputs. There are several subclasses available, such as **AVCaptureVideoDataOutput** to process the frames of a video, and **AVCaptureAudioDataOutput** to get the audio, but the most frequently used is the **AVCapturePhotoOutput** class used to capture a single video frame (take a picture). This class works with a delegate that conforms to the **AVCapturePhotoCaptureDelegate** protocol, which among other methods defines the following to return a still image.

photoOutput(AVCapturePhotoOutput, **didFinishProcessingPhoto:** AVCapturePhoto, **error:** Error?)—This method is called on the delegate after the image is captured. The **didFinishProcessingPhoto** argument is a container with information about the image, and the **error** argument is used to report errors.

To control the flow of data from input to output, the framework defines the **AVCaptureSession** class. From an instance of this class, we can control the inputs and outputs and determine when the process begins and ends by calling the following methods.

addInput(AVCaptureInput)—This method adds an input to the capture session. The argument represents the input device we want to add.

addOutput(AVCaptureOutput)—This method adds an output to the capture session. The argument represents the output we want to generate from the capture session.

startRunning()—This method starts the capture session.

stopRunning()—This method stops the capture session.

The framework also defines the **AVCaptureVideoPreviewLayer** class to show a preview to the user. This class creates a sublayer to display the video captured by the input device. The class includes the following initializer and properties to create and manage the preview layer.

AVCaptureVideoPreviewLayer(session: AVCaptureSession)—This initializer creates an **AVCaptureVideoPreviewLayer** object with a preview layer connected to the capture session defined by the **session** argument.

videoGravity—This property defines how the video adjust its size to the size of the preview layer. It is an enumeration of type **AVLayerVideoGravity** with the values **resizeAspect**, **resizeAspectFill**, and **resize**.

connection—This property returns an object of type **AVCaptureConnection** that defines the connection between the capture session and the preview layer.

The input, output, and preview layers are connected to the capture session by objects of the **AVCaptureConnection** class. The class manages the information for the connection, including ports and data. The following are some of the properties provided by this class.

videoOrientation—This property sets or returns the orientation of the video. It is an enumeration of type **AVCaptureVideoOrientation** with the values **portrait**, **portraitUpsideDown**, **landscapeRight**, and **landscapeLeft**.

isVideoOrientationSupported—This property returns a Boolean value that determines whether it is possible to set the video orientation or not.

The interface we are going to create for this example is similar to the previous ones. We need a button to open the view that allows the user to take a picture with the camera, and an **Image** view to show it on the screen.

Figure 18-6: Interface for a custom camera

The process to activate the camera and get the picture taken by the user is independent of the interface, but if we want to let the user see the image coming from the camera, we must create a preview layer and add it to a UIKit view. As we have seen before, UIKit views are created from the **UIView** class, so we need to define a representable view (see Chapter 16).

```
import SwiftUI
struct CustomPreviewLayer: UIViewRepresentable {
   let view = UIView()
   func makeUIView(context: Context) -> UIView {
      return view
   }
   func updateUIView(_ uiView: UIView, context: Context) { }
}
```

Listing 18-8: Defining a UIView *to show the camera's preview video*

For this example, we are going to manage all the logic for the camera in a model. The following are the basic elements we need to set up the system.

```swift
import SwiftUI
import AVFoundation

class ViewData {
    var captureSession: AVCaptureSession!
    var stillImage: AVCapturePhotoOutput!
    var previewLayer: AVCaptureVideoPreviewLayer!
    var imageOrientation: UIImage.Orientation!
}
class ApplicationData: NSObject, ObservableObject,
AVCapturePhotoCaptureDelegate {
    @Published var path = NavigationPath()
    @Published var picture: UIImage?

    var cameraView: CustomPreviewLayer!
    var viewData: ViewData

    override init() {
        cameraView = CustomPreviewLayer()
        viewData = ViewData()
        super.init()

        Task(priority: .background) {
            await receiveNotification()
        }
    }
    func receiveNotification() async {
        let center = NotificationCenter.default
        let name = await UIDevice.orientationDidChangeNotification
        for await _ in center.notifications(named: name, object: nil) {
            if viewData.captureSession != nil {
                await MainActor.run {
                    viewData.previewLayer.frame = cameraView.view.bounds
                    let videoOrientation = getCurrentOrientation()
                    let connection = viewData.previewLayer.connection
                    connection?.videoOrientation = videoOrientation
                }
            }
        }
    }
}
```

Listing 18-9: Defining the properties we need to manage the camera

This code is only the first part of our model, we still need to add a few methods to activate and control the camera, but it provides the set of properties we need to store references to every element of the system and instantiate the **UIView** view we need to show the preview layer. Because these properties are required by multiple methods, we declare them in a separate class called **ViewData**. When the model is initialized, we create an instance of this class and the representable view (**CustomPreviewLayer**), and then run an asynchronous method to listen to the **orientationDidChangeNotification** notification to be able to adapt the size and orientation of the preview when the device's orientation changes (see Chapter 14, Listing 14-11).

The next step is to define a method to ask for the user's permission to access the camera. This is done automatically when we use a **UIImagePickerController** controller, but we have to do it ourselves in a custom controller using the type methods provided by the **AVCaptureDevice** class. The following is the method we must add to our model for this purpose.

```
func getAuthorization() async {
    let granted = await AVCaptureDevice.requestAccess(for: .video)
    await MainActor.run {
        if granted {
            self.prepareCamera()
        } else {
            print("Not Authorized")
        }
    }
}
```

Listing 18-10: Asking for permission to use the camera

The **requestAccess()** method is asynchronous; it waits for the user to respond and returns a value of type **Bool** to report the result. If the user grants access, we execute a method called **prepareCamera()**. This is where we begin to build the network of objects introduced in Figure 18-5. The method must get a reference to the current capture device for video and create the inputs and outputs we need to capture a still image (to take a picture).

```
func prepareCamera() {
    viewData.captureSession = AVCaptureSession()
    if let device = AVCaptureDevice.default(for: AVMediaType.video) {
        if let input = try? AVCaptureDeviceInput(device: device) {
            viewData.captureSession.addInput(input)
            viewData.stillImage = AVCapturePhotoOutput()
            viewData.captureSession.addOutput(viewData.stillImage)
            showCamera()
        } else {
            print("Not Authorized")
        }
    } else {
        print("Not Authorized")
    }
}
```

Listing 18-11: Initializing the camera

We can create and add to the session all the inputs and outputs we need, in any order, but because the **AVCaptureDeviceInput()** initializer throws an error, we use it first. This initializer creates an object that manages the input for the capture device. If the initializer is successful, we add it to the capture session with the **addInput()** method and then create the output. For this example we have decided to use the session to capture a still image, so we use the **AVCapturePhotoOutput** class to create the output and add it to the session with the **addOutput()** method.

After adding the inputs and outputs to the capture session, the **prepareCamera()** method executes an additional method called **showCamera()** to generate the preview layer and show the video coming from the camera on the screen. In this method, we must create the layer and set its size and orientation.

```
func showCamera() {
    let width = cameraView.view.bounds.size.width
    let height = cameraView.view.bounds.size.height

    viewData.previewLayer = AVCaptureVideoPreviewLayer(session:
viewData.captureSession)
    viewData.previewLayer.videoGravity = .resizeAspectFill
    viewData.previewLayer.frame = CGRect(x: 0, y: 0, width: width, height:
height)
```

Chapter 18 - Media

```
    let videoOrientation = getCurrentOrientation()
    let connection = viewData.previewLayer.connection
    connection?.videoOrientation = videoOrientation

    let layer = cameraView.view.layer
    layer.addSublayer(viewData.previewLayer)
    Task(priority: .background) {
        viewData.captureSession.startRunning()
    }
}
```

Listing 18-12: Showing the video from the camera on the screen

The **AVCaptureVideoPreviewLayer()** initializer creates a layer that we have to adjust to the size of its view and add as a sublayer of the view's layer. But setting the position and size of the layer does not determine how its content is going to be shown. The video coming from the camera could have a different size and orientation. How the video is going to adjust to the size of the layer is determined by the value of the layer's **videoGravity** property, and the orientation is set in the connection established between the capture session and the preview layer. That is why, after setting the value of the **videoGravity** property and the layer's frame, we get a reference to the connection from the layer's **connection** property. By modifying the **videoOrientation** property of the connection, we can adjust the orientation according to the device's orientation and finally add the sublayer to the view's layer with the **addSublayer()** method. Once the sublayer is ready, the capture session is initiated with the **startRunning()** method. (The system requires this method to be executed in a background thread.)

The device's orientation is not only required to define the orientation of the preview layer, but also the orientation of the image taken by the camera. In our example, the value of the **videoOrientation** property is determined by a method called **getCurrentOrientation()**. This method returns the **AVCaptureVideoOrientation** value we need to set the orientation of the preview layer and stores a **UIImage.Orientation** value in the **imageOrientation** property to set the image orientation later.

```
func getCurrentOrientation() -> AVCaptureVideoOrientation {
    var currentOrientation: AVCaptureVideoOrientation!
    let deviceOrientation = UIDevice.current.orientation

    switch deviceOrientation {
        case .landscapeLeft:
            currentOrientation = AVCaptureVideoOrientation.landscapeRight
            viewData.imageOrientation = .up
        case .landscapeRight:
            currentOrientation = AVCaptureVideoOrientation.landscapeLeft
            viewData.imageOrientation = .down
        case .portrait:
            currentOrientation = AVCaptureVideoOrientation.portrait
            viewData.imageOrientation = .right
        case .portraitUpsideDown:
            currentOrientation =
AVCaptureVideoOrientation.portraitUpsideDown
            viewData.imageOrientation = .left
        default:
            if UIDevice.current.orientation.isLandscape {
                currentOrientation = AVCaptureVideoOrientation.landscapeRight
                viewData.imageOrientation = .up
            } else {
                currentOrientation = AVCaptureVideoOrientation.portrait
                viewData.imageOrientation = .right
            }
    }
```

```
        break
    }
    return currentOrientation
}
```

Listing 18-13: Detecting the device's orientation

 IMPORTANT: The camera always encodes the image in its native orientation, which is landscape-right. In consequence, when the device is in portrait mode, we have to set the orientation of the image to right, when it is in landscape-left mode, we have to set the image's orientation to down, and when it is in landscape-right mode, we have to set it to up. Also, the landscape orientation of the video is the opposite of the device, therefore when the device is in the landscape-right orientation, the video orientation is landscape-left, and vice versa.

At this point, the video is playing on the screen and the system is ready to perform a capture. The process to capture an image is initiated by the output object. The **AVCapturePhotoOutput** class we use to capture a still image offers the following method for this purpose.

capturePhoto(with: AVCapturePhotoSettings, **delegate:** AVCapturePhoto-CaptureDelegate)—This method initiates a photo capture with the settings specified by the **with** argument. The **delegate** argument is a reference to the object that implements the methods of the **AVCapturePhotoCaptureDelegate** protocol to receive the data generated by the output.

The type of photo captured by the output is determined by an **AVCapturePhotoSettings** object. The class includes multiple initializers. The following are the most frequently used.

AVCapturePhotoSettings()—This initializer creates an **AVCapturePhotoSettings** object with the format by default.

AVCapturePhotoSettings(format: Dictionary)—This initializer creates a **AVCapturePhotoSettings** object with the format specified by the **format** argument. The argument is a dictionary with keys and values to set the characteristics of the image. Some of the keys available are **kCVPixelBufferPixelFormatTypeKey** (uncompressed format), **AVVideoCodecKey** (compressed format), **AVVideoQualityKey** (quality).

The following are the properties available in this class to configure the image and the preview.

previewPhotoFormat—This property sets or returns a dictionary with keys and values that determine the characteristics of the preview image. The keys available are **kCVPixelBufferPixelFormatTypeKey** (uncompressed format), **kCVPixelBuffer-WidthKey** (width) and **kCVPixelBufferHeightKey** (height).

flashMode—This property sets or returns the flash mode used when the image is captured. It is an enumeration of type **FlashMode** with the values **on**, **off**, and **auto**.

isHighResolutionPhotoEnabled—This property is a Boolean value that determines if the image is going to be taken in high resolution.

To capture an image, we have to define the settings with an **AVCapturePhotoSettings** object, call the **capturePhoto()** method of the **AVCapturePhotoOutput** object, and define the delegate method that is going to receive the image. The following is the method we need to add to the model to take the picture.

```
func takePicture() {
   let settings = AVCapturePhotoSettings()
   viewData.stillImage.capturePhoto(with: settings, delegate: self)
}
```

Listing 18-14: Taking a picture

When the user presses the button to take the picture, the **takePicture()** method is executed and the **capturePhoto()** method is called to ask the output object to capture an image. After the image is captured, this object sends the result to a delegate method. Notice that we declared the **ApplicationData** class as the delegate object (see Listing 18-9), so we can declare the delegate method in the model. The following is our implementation of this method.

```
func photoOutput(_ output: AVCapturePhotoOutput, didFinishProcessingPhoto
photo: AVCapturePhoto, error: Error?) {
   let scene = UIApplication.shared.connectedScenes.first as?
UIWindowScene
   let scale = scene?.screen.scale ?? 1

   if let imageData = photo.cgImageRepresentation() {
      picture = UIImage(cgImage: imageData, scale: scale, orientation:
viewData.imageOrientation)
      path = NavigationPath()
   }
}
```

Listing 18-15: Processing the image

The **photoOutput(AVCapturePhotoOutput, didFinishProcessingPhoto:)** method receives the picture produced by the camera. The value received by this method is an object of type **AVCapturePhoto**, which is a container with information about the image. The class includes two convenient methods to get the data representing the image.

fileDataRepresentation()—This method returns a data representation of the image that we can use to create a **UIImage** object.

cgImageRepresentation()—This method returns the image as a **CGImage** object (Core Graphics).

In our example, we have implemented the **cgImageRepresentation()** method because the **UIImage** class defines a convenient initializer to create an image from a **CGImage** object that includes the scale and orientation. We get the orientation from the **imageOrientation** property set by the **getCurrentOrientation()** method, but the image is created to the scale of the screen, so we need to access the screen to get the current scale. The screen is managed by an object of the **UIScreen** class that is automatically created for the device and assigned to a property of the Scene. Therefore, to access the screen and get the scale, we must read the **UIWindowScene** object that controls the current Scene from the **connectedScenes** property of the **UIApplication** object. We have introduced this object in Chapter 14. It is created by the system to control the application. The object is accessible from a type property provided by the class called **shared** and it includes the **connectedScenes** property to return references to all the Scenes opened for the app. In this example, we are developing an application for mobile devices, so all we need is to access the first Scene available. The **UIWindowScene** object includes the **screen** property to return a reference to the **UIScreen** object that represents the screen, and the **UIScreen** object includes the **scale** property to return the current scale and the **bounds** property to return the screen's size, among others. With these values, we create the **UIImage** object and assign it to the **picture** property to update the view, which receives this object and displays the image on the screen, as shown next.

```
struct ContentView: View {
    @EnvironmentObject var appData: ApplicationData

    var body: some View {
        NavigationStack(path: $appData.path) {
            VStack {
                HStack {
                    Spacer()
                    NavigationLink("Take Picture", value: "Open Camera")
                }
                .navigationDestination(for: String.self, destination: { _ in
                    CustomCameraView()
                })
                Image(uiImage: appData.picture ?? UIImage(named:
"nopicture")!)
                    .resizable()
                    .scaledToFit()
                    .frame(minWidth: 0, maxWidth: .infinity, minHeight: 0,
maxHeight: .infinity)
                    .clipped()
                Spacer()
            }.padding()
            .navigationBarHidden(true)
        }.statusBar(hidden: true)
    }
}
```

Listing 18-16: Showing the image

There is nothing new in this view, with the exception that now instead of opening a **UIImagePickerController** with a standard interface, we open a view that has to provide the buttons and custom controls required for the user to take a picture. The following is our implementation of this view.

```
import SwiftUI
struct CustomCameraView: View {
    @EnvironmentObject var appData: ApplicationData

    var body: some View {
        ZStack {
            appData.cameraView
            VStack {
                Spacer()
                HStack {
                    Button("Cancel") {
                        appData.path = NavigationPath()
                    }
                    Spacer()
                    Button("Take Picture") {
                        appData.takePicture()
                    }
                }.padding()
                .frame(height: 80)
                .background(Color(red: 0.9, green: 0.9, blue: 0.9, opacity:
0.8))
            }
        }
        .edgesIgnoringSafeArea(.all)
        .frame(minWidth: 0, maxWidth: .infinity, minHeight: 0,
maxHeight: .infinity)
        .navigationBarHidden(true)
        .onAppear {
```

```
        let device = UIDevice.current
        device.beginGeneratingDeviceOrientationNotifications()

        Task(priority: .high) {
            await appData.getAuthorization()
        }
    }
    .onDisappear {
        let device = UIDevice.current
        device.endGeneratingDeviceOrientationNotifications()
    }
  }
}
```

Listing 18-17: *Taking a picture*

As illustrated in Figure 18-6, this view includes our **UIView** to show the video coming from the camera and another view on top to provide two buttons, one to cancel the process and dismiss the view, and another to take a picture. When the view appears on the screen, we call the **getAuthorization()** method to start the process. If the user presses the Take Picture button, we call the **takePicture()** method to capture the image. Once the image is processed, the view is dismissed by the delegate method, and the picture is shown on the screen.

Do It Yourself: Create a Multiplatform project. Download the nopicture image from our website and add it to the Asset Catalog. Create a Swift file called CustomPreviewLayer.swift for the code in Listing 18-8, and another called ApplicationData.swift for the model in Listing 18-9. Add to the model the methods in Listings 18-10, 18-11, 18-12, 18-13, 18-14 and 18-15. Update the **ContentView** view with the code in Listing 18-16. Create a SwiftUI View file called CustomCameraView.swift for the view in Listing 18-17. Remember to add the option "Privacy - Camera Usage Description" to the Info panel in the app's settings and to inject the **ApplicationData** object into the environment for the app and the previews (Chapter 7, Listing 7-4). Run the application on a device and take a picture.

Basic 18.2 Video

Recording and playing videos is probably as important to users as taking and displaying pictures. As with images, Apple frameworks include pre-built tools for playing videos and creating a custom video player.

Basic Video Player

SwiftUI defines the **VideoPlayer** view to play videos. This view provides all the controls required to play, stop, and move the video back and forth. The view includes the following initializer.

VideoPlayer(player: AVPlayer?, **videoOverlay:** Closure)—This initializer creates a video player to play the video provided by the argument. The **player** argument is the object in charge of playing the media, and the **videoOverlay** argument provides the views we want to show on top of the video.

The **VideoPlayer** view presents the interface for the user to control the video, but the video is played by an object of the **AVPlayer** class. The class includes the following initializer.

AVPlayer(url: URL)—This initializer creates an **AVPlayer** object to play the media in the URL indicated by the **url** argument.

The **AVPlayer** class also includes properties and methods to control the video programatically.

volume—This property sets or returns a value that determines the player's volume. It is a value of type **Float** between 0.0 and 1.0.

isMuted—This property is a Boolean value that determines whether the player's audio is muted or not.

rate—This property sets or returns a **Float** value that determines the rate at which the media is being played. A value of 0.0 pauses the video and 1.0 sets the normal rate.

play()—This method begins playback.

pause()—This method pauses playback.

addPeriodicTimeObserver(forInterval: CMTime, **queue:** DispatchQueue?, **using:** Closure)—This method adds an observer that executes a closure every certain period of time. The **forInterval** argument determines the time between executions, the **queue** argument is the queue in which the closure should be executed (the main thread is recommended), and the **using** argument is the closure we want to execute. The closure receives a value of type **CMTime** with the time at which the closure was called.

The **VideoPlayer** view requires an **AVPlayer** object to play the video, and this object loads the video from a URL. The best way to prepare this information is with a model. In the following model, we get the URL of a video in the bundle called videotrees.mp4, and create an **AVPlayer** object with this value.

```
import SwiftUI
import AVKit

class ApplicationData: ObservableObject {
    @Published var player: AVPlayer!

    init() {
        let bundle = Bundle.main
        if let videoURL = bundle.url(forResource: "videotrees",
withExtension: "mp4") {
            player = AVPlayer(url: videoURL)
        }
    }
}
```

Listing 18-18: Preparing the video to be played

The **VideoPlayer** view and the **AVPlayer** class are defined in the AVKit framework. In this example, we import the framework and store the **AVPlayer** object in a **@Published** property to make it available for the view. In the view, we need to check this property and show the **VideoPlayer** view if there is a video to play.

```
import SwiftUI
import AVKit

struct ContentView: View {
    @EnvironmentObject var appData: ApplicationData

    var body: some View {
        if appData.player != nil {
            VideoPlayer(player: appData.player)
                .ignoresSafeArea()
        } else {
            Text("Video not available")
```

```
      }
   }
}
```

Listing 18-19: Playing a video

Figure 18-7: Standard video player

 Do It Yourself: Create a Multiplatform project. Download the videotrees.mp4 file from our website and add it to your project (make sure that the target is selected). Create a Swift file called ApplicationData.swift for the model in Listing 18-18. Update the `ContentView` view with the code in Listing 18-19. Remember to inject the `ApplicationData` object into the environment for the app and the previews (Chapter 7, Listing 7-4). Run the application in the iPhone simulator. Press play to play the video.

In the previous example, the video doesn't play until the user presses the play button. But we can implement the `AVPlayer` properties and methods to control the video programatically. For instance, the following example starts the video as soon as the view is loaded.

```
struct ContentView: View {
   @EnvironmentObject var appData: ApplicationData

   var body: some View {
      if appData.player != nil {
         VideoPlayer(player: appData.player)
            .onAppear {
               appData.player.play()
            }
            .ignoresSafeArea()
      } else {
         Text("Video not available")
      }
   }
}
```

Listing 18-20: Automatically playing a video

The initializer of the `VideoPlayer` view can also include an argument that takes a closure to add a layer of views over the video. For instance, in the following example we implement this initializer to add a label with the video's title at the top.

```
struct ContentView: View {
   @EnvironmentObject var appData: ApplicationData

   var body: some View {
      if appData.player != nil {
         VideoPlayer(player: appData.player, videoOverlay: {
            VStack {
               Text("Title: Trees at the park")
                  .font(.title)
```

```
                    .padding([.top, .bottom], 8)
                    .padding([.leading, .trailing], 16)
                    .foregroundColor(.black)
                    .background(.ultraThinMaterial)
                    .cornerRadius(10)
                    .padding(.top, 8)
                Spacer()
            }
        })
        .ignoresSafeArea()
    } else {
        Text("Video not available")
    }
}
}
```

Listing 18-21: Presenting views over the video

The views returned by the closure are placed over the video but below the controls, so they cannot take input from the user, but we can use them to provide additional information, as in this case. The result is shown below.

Figure 18-8: Overlay views

(Medium) Custom Video Player

In addition to all the code necessary for the **VideoPlayer** view to work, the AVFoundation framework also offers classes to create each component of the structure required to play media. There is a class in charge of the asset (video or audio), a class in charge of providing the media to the player, a class in charge of playing the media, and a class in charge of displaying the media on the screen. Figure 18-9 illustrates this structure.

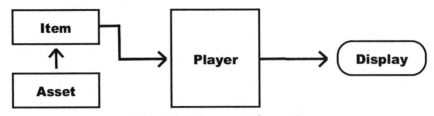

Figure 18-9: System to play media

The media to be played is provided as an asset. An asset is composed of one or more tracks of media, including video, audio, subtitles, etc. The AVFoundation framework defines a class called **AVAsset** to load an asset. The class includes the following initializer.

AVURLAsset(url: URL)—This initializer creates an **AVURLAsset** object with the media in the location indicated by the **url** argument. The argument is a **URL** structure with the location of a local or remote resource.

Chapter 18 - Media

An asset contains static information and cannot manage its state when it is being played. To control the asset, the framework defines the **AVPlayerItem** class. With this class, we can reference an asset and manage the timeline. The class includes multiple initializers. The following is the most frequently used.

AVPlayerItem(asset: AVAsset)—This initializer creates an **AVPlayerItem** object to represent the asset defined by the **asset** argument.

The **AVPlayerItem** class also includes properties and methods to control the status of the asset. The following are the most frequently used.

status—This property returns a value that indicates the status of the player item. It is an enumeration called **Status** included in the **AVPlayerItem** class. The values available are **unknown**, **readyToPlay**, and **failed**.

duration—This property returns a value that indicates the duration of the player item. It is a structure of type **CMTime**.

currentTime()—This method returns a **CMTime** value with the current time.

seek(to: CMTime)—This asynchronous method moves the playback cursor to the time specified by the **to** argument and returns a Boolean value that determines whether the seek operation is finished or not.

The **AVPlayerItem** object manages the information necessary for playback but it does not play the media; this is done by an instance of the **AVPlayer** class. This is the same class we used before to load a video for the **VideoPlayer** view. The class includes the following initializer to create a player from an **AVPlayerItem** object.

AVPlayer(playerItem: AVPlayerItem?)—This initializer creates an **AVPlayer** object to play the media represented by the **playerItem** argument.

The last object required by the structure is the one in charge of displaying the media. This is a subclass of the **CALayer** class called **AVPlayerLayer** that provides the code necessary to draw the frames on the screen. The class includes the following initializer and property to create and configure the layer.

AVPlayerLayer(player: AVPlayer)—This initializer creates an **AVPlayerLayer** object associated with the player specified by the **player** argument.

videoGravity—This property defines how the video adjusts its size to the preview layer's size. It is a **AVLayerVideoGravity** structure with the type properties **resize**, **resizeAspect**, and **resizeAspectFill**.

All these classes define the system we need to play media, but we also need a way to control time. Because the precision of floating-point values is not suitable for media playback, the framework implements, among other things, the **CMTime** structure from an old framework called Core Media. The structure contains multiple values to represent time as a fraction. The most important are **value** and **timescale**, which represent the numerator and denominator, respectively. For example, if we want to create a **CMTime** structure to represent 0.5 seconds, we may declare 1 as the numerator and 2 as the denominator (1 divided by 2 is equal to 0.5). The class includes initializers and type properties to create these values. The following are the most frequently used.

CMTime(value: CMTimeValue, **timescale:** CMTimeScale)—This initializer creates a **CMTime** structure with the values specified by the **value** and **timescale** arguments. The arguments are integers of type **Int64** and **Int32**, respectively.

CMTime(seconds: Double, **preferredTimescale:** CMTimeScale)—This initializer creates a `CMTime` structure from a floating-point value that represents the time in seconds. The **seconds** argument determines the seconds we want to assign to the structure, and the **preferredTimescale** argument determines the scale we want to use. A value of 1 preserves the value in seconds assigned to the first argument.

zero—This type property returns a `CMTime` structure with the value 0.

The `CMTime` structure also includes multiple properties to set and retrieve the values. The following are the most frequently used.

seconds—This property returns the time of a `CMTime` structure in seconds. It is of type `Double`.

value—This property returns the value of a `CMTime` structure.

timescale—This property returns the time scale of a `CMTime` structure.

To create a custom video player, we must load the asset (`AVURLAsset`), create the item to manage the asset (`AVPlayerItem`), add the item to the player (`AVPlayer`), and associate the player to a layer to display the media on the screen (`AVPlayerLayer`). But playing the media requires an additional step. The media does not become immediately available, it has to be loaded and prepared for playback, so we cannot play it right away, we must wait until it is ready. The media status is reported by the `status` property of the `AVPlayerItem` object, so we must observe the value of this property to start playing the media only after it is equal to `readyToPlay`. This requires the use of a technique called KVO (Key-Value Observing). KVO was developed in Objective-C and it is used to turn an object into an observer of a property. When the value of that property changes, the object executes a method to report the change. The methods to add, remove, and respond to an observer are defined in the `NSObject` class. The following are the three methods involved in the process.

addObserver(NSObject, **forKeyPath:** String, **options:** NSKeyValue-ObservingOptions, **context:** UnsafeMutableRawPointer?)—This method adds an observer to the object. The first argument is the object that responds to the notification, the **forKeyPath** argument is a string with the name or the path to the property we want to observe, the **options** argument is an enumeration that determines the values that are going to be sent to the method that responds to the notification (possible values are **new**, **old**, **initial**, and **prior**), and the **context** argument is a generic value that identifies the observer (used when a class and its subclasses observe the same property).

removeObserver(NSObject, **forKeyPath:** String)—This method removes an observer. The arguments are the same values specified in the `addObserver()` method when the observer was added.

observeValue(forKeyPath: String?, **of:** Any?, **change:** Dictionary?, **context:** UnsafeMutableRawPointer?)—This method is called by the observer to report a change in the value of the observed property.

The following example implements these methods to listen to the `status` property of the `AVPlayerItem` object. As before, we need a representable view with an empty `UIView` object to present the video on the screen.

```
import SwiftUI
struct CustomPlayerView: UIViewRepresentable {
   var view = UIView()
```

```
   func makeUIView(context: Context) -> UIView {
      return view
   }
   func updateUIView(_ uiView: UIView, context: Context) { }
}
```

Listing 18-22: Building a custom video player

The next step is to build the video player and then call the **play()** method from the **observeValue()** method to start playing the video as soon as it is ready.

```
import SwiftUI
import AVFoundation
class ViewData: NSObject {
   var playerItem: AVPlayerItem!
   var player: AVPlayer!
   var playerLayer: AVPlayerLayer!

   func setObserver() {
      playerItem.addObserver(self, forKeyPath: "status", options: [],
context: nil)
   }
   override func observeValue(forKeyPath keyPath: String?, of object:
Any?, change: [NSKeyValueChangeKey : Any]?, context:
UnsafeMutableRawPointer?) {
      if playerItem.status == .readyToPlay {
         playerItem.removeObserver(self, forKeyPath: "status")
         player.play()
      }
   }
}
class ApplicationData: ObservableObject {
   var customVideoView: CustomPlayerView!
   var viewData: ViewData

   init() {
      customVideoView = CustomPlayerView()
      viewData = ViewData()
      let bundle = Bundle.main
      let videoURL = bundle.url(forResource: "videotrees", withExtension:
"mp4")
      let asset = AVURLAsset(url: videoURL!)
      viewData.playerItem = AVPlayerItem(asset: asset)
      viewData.player = AVPlayer(playerItem: viewData.playerItem)
      viewData.playerLayer = AVPlayerLayer(player: viewData.player)
      let scene = UIApplication.shared.connectedScenes.first as?
UIWindowScene
      let screenSize = scene?.screen.bounds ?? .zero
      viewData.playerLayer.frame = screenSize
      let layer = customVideoView.view.layer
      layer.addSublayer(viewData.playerLayer)
      viewData.setObserver()
      Task(priority: .background) {
         await receiveNotification()
      }
   }
   func receiveNotification() async {
      let center = NotificationCenter.default
      let name = await UIDevice.orientationDidChangeNotification
      for await _ in center.notifications(named: name, object: nil) {
         if viewData.playerItem != nil {
            await MainActor.run {
               viewData.playerLayer.frame = customVideoView.view.bounds
            }
```

```
            }
        }
    }
}
```

Because the observer methods are defined in the **NSObject** class, they can only be implemented in a class that inherits from **NSObject**. For this reason, we set up and respond to the observer in the **ViewData** class. First, we define the three properties we need to store the player item, the player, and the layer, then we define a method that sets an observer for the **status** property of the **AVPlayerItem** object, and finally we respond to that observer with the **observeValue()** method. If the current status is **readyToPlay**, we remove the observer and play the video.

To set up the video player, we load the video from the bundle and create the player structure as soon as the model is initialized. The player is associated with an **AVPlayerLayer** layer and the layer is added as a sublayer of the **UIView** view. The size of this layer is set as the size of the screen or the view, depending on what values are available at the moment.

In the interface, we only need to present the representable view. The video is shown full screen, it adapts to the screen orientation, and it is played as soon as the view is loaded.

```
struct ContentView: View {
    @EnvironmentObject var appData: ApplicationData

    var body: some View {
        appData.customVideoView
            .ignoresSafeArea()
    }
}
```

Listing 18-24: Showing a video

Do It Yourself: Create a Multiplatform project. Download the videotrees.mp4 file from our website and add it to your project. (Remember to check the option Add to Target.) Create a Swift file called CustomPlayerView.swift for the code in Listing 18-22 and another called ApplicationData.swift for the model in Listing 18-23. Update the **ContentView** view with the code in Listing 18-24. Run the application on the iPhone simulator. The video should autoplay.

The previous example plays the video, but it does not provide any tools for the user to control it. The **AVPlayer** class includes methods to play, pause, and check the state of the media, but we are responsible for creating the interface, as we do in the following example.

Figure 18-10: Controls for a custom video player

How we control the process and respond to the interface depends on the requirements of our application. For this example, we have decided to define two states, one to indicate if the video is playing or not, and another to determine the size of the progress bar. The following are the changes we must introduce to our model to allow the user to play and pause the video and to update the progress bar.

```swift
import SwiftUI
import AVFoundation

class ViewData: NSObject {
   var playerItem: AVPlayerItem!
   var player: AVPlayer!
   var playerLayer: AVPlayerLayer!
}
class ApplicationData: ObservableObject {
   @Published var playing: Bool = false
   @Published var progress: CGFloat = 0
   var customVideoView: CustomPlayerView!
   var viewData: ViewData

   init() {
      customVideoView = CustomPlayerView()
      viewData = ViewData()

      let bundle = Bundle.main
      let videoURL = bundle.url(forResource: "videotrees", withExtension:
"mp4")
      let asset = AVURLAsset(url: videoURL!)
      viewData.playerItem = AVPlayerItem(asset: asset)
      viewData.player = AVPlayer(playerItem: viewData.playerItem)
      viewData.playerLayer = AVPlayerLayer(player: viewData.player)

      let scene = UIApplication.shared.connectedScenes.first as?
UIWindowScene
      let screenSize = scene?.screen.bounds ?? .zero
      viewData.playerLayer.frame = screenSize
      let layer = customVideoView.view.layer
      layer.addSublayer(viewData.playerLayer)

      let interval = CMTime(value: 1, timescale: 2)
      viewData.player.addPeriodicTimeObserver(forInterval: interval,
queue: DispatchQueue.main, using: { time in
         let duration = self.viewData.playerItem.duration
         let position = time.seconds / duration.seconds
         self.progress = CGFloat(position)
      })
      Task(priority: .background) {
         await receiveNotification()
      }
   }
   func receiveNotification() async {
      let center = NotificationCenter.default
      let name = await UIDevice.orientationDidChangeNotification
      for await _ in center.notifications(named: name, object: nil) {
         if viewData.playerItem != nil {
            await MainActor.run {
               viewData.playerLayer.frame = customVideoView.view.bounds
            }
         }
      }
   }
   func playVideo() {
      if viewData.playerItem.status == .readyToPlay {
         if playing {
            viewData.player.pause()
            playing = false
         } else {
            viewData.player.play()
            playing = true
         }
      }
```

```
        }
    }
```

Listing 18-25: Preparing the video player

In this example, we include a method called **playVideo()** to execute when the user presses the Play button. The method checks whether the media can be played or not, and then performs an action according to the value of the **playing** property. If the video is playing, we pause it, and if it is paused, we play it. In either case, we update the value of the **playing** property to reflect the new state.

To calculate the size of the progress bar, we must implement an observer. But this is not a KVO observer like the one implemented before. Normal observers are not fast enough, so the AVFoundation framework offers the **addPeriodicTimeObserver()** method to create an observer that provides a more accurate response. The method requires a **CMTime** value to determine the frequency at which the code will be executed, a reference to the main queue, and a closure with the code we want to execute every time the observer is triggered. In this example, we create a **CMTime** value to represent a time of 0.5 seconds, and then use it in the call of the **addPeriodicTimeObserver()** method to register the observer. After this, the closure provided to the observer will be executed every 0.5 seconds during playback. In this closure, we get the current time and the duration of the video in seconds and calculate the progression by turning seconds into a value between 0.0 and 1.0 that we can later convert into points to display the progress bar on the screen.

 IMPORTANT: The **addPeriodicTimeObserver()** method doesn't work with Swift concurrency. Instead, it requires the thread to be defined by a **DispatchQueue** object. This is an old class defined by the Dispatch framework to create asynchronous tasks. The class includes a type property called **main** to define a task for the main queue (the Main Actor), and this is how we make sure that the closure assigned to this method runs in the main thread.

The player is ready. It is time to define the interface. In this occasion, we need to present the representable view inside a **ZStack** so we can display a toolbar on top (see Figure 18-10).

```
struct ContentView: View {
    @EnvironmentObject var appData: ApplicationData

    var body: some View {
        ZStack {
            appData.customVideoView
                .ignoresSafeArea()
            VStack {
                Spacer()
                HStack {
                    Button(appData.playing ? "Pause" : "Play") {
                        appData.playVideo()
                    }.frame(width: 70)
                    .foregroundColor(.black)
                    GeometryReader { geometry in
                        HStack {
                            Rectangle()
                                .fill(Color(red: 0, green: 0.4, blue: 0.8,
opacity: 0.8))
                                .frame(width: geometry.size.width *
appData.progress, height: 20)
                            Spacer()
                        }
                    }.padding(.top, 15)
                }
                .padding([.leading, .trailing])
```

```
            .frame(height: 50)
            .background(Color(red: 0.9, green: 0.9, blue: 0.9, opacity: 0.8))
        }
      }
    }
  }
}
```

Listing 18-26: Playing and pausing the video

The toolbar includes a button and a **Rectangle** view that represents the progress bar. The label for the button depends on the value of the **playing** property. If the video is playing, we show the text "Pause" and when it is paused, we show the text "Play". To calculate the size of the **Rectangle** view that represents the progress bar, we embed the view in a **GeometryReader** and then multiply its width by the value of the **progress** property. Because this property contains a value between 0.0 and 1.0, the operation returns the value we need to set the width of the bar and show the progression on the screen.

 Do It Yourself: Update the model with the code in Listing 18-25 and the **ContentView** view with the code in Listing 18-26. Run the application. You should see the video player illustrated in Figure 18-10.

The observer added by the **addPeriodicTimeObserver()** method is not the only way to get information from the player over time. The **AVPlayerItem** class also defines several notifications to report events that happen during media playback. For example, we can listen to the **AVPlayerItemDidPlayToEndTime** notification to know when the video finishes playing. For this purpose, we need to define a method in the model to listen and respond to the notification, and a task to call this method as soon as the representable view is created. The following is the task we need to add in the **ApplicationData**'s initializer.

```
Task(priority: .background) {
  await rewindVideo()
}
```

Listing 18-27: Executing an asynchronous method to detect the end of the video

In the **rewindVideo()** method, we must listen to the **AVPlayerItemDidPlayToEndTime** notification and prepare the video to be played again. For this purpose, the **AVPlayerItem** class offers the **seek()** method. This method moves the playback to the time specified by the argument and executes a closure after the process is over. In this case, we are going to use a **CMTime** value of 0 to move the playback to the beginning of the video and then reset the **playing** and **progress** properties to allow the user to play the video again.

```
func rewindVideo() async {
  let center = NotificationCenter.default
  let name = NSNotification.Name.AVPlayerItemDidPlayToEndTime
  for await _ in center.notifications(named: name, object: nil) {
    let finished = await viewData.playerItem.seek(to: CMTime.zero)
    if finished {
      await MainActor.run {
        playing = false
        progress = 0
      }
    }
  }
}
```

Listing 18-28: Rewinding the video

Do It Yourself: Add the task in Listing 18-27 at the end of the `ApplicationData`'s initializer. Add the method in Listing 18-28 to the end of the `ApplicationData` class. Run the application on the iPhone simulator. Press play and wait until the video is over. The player should reset itself and you should be able to play the video again.

If we want to play multiple videos in sequence, we could use the `AVPlayerItemDidPlay-ToEndTime` notification to assign a new asset to the `AVPlayer` object, but the framework offers a subclass of the `AVPlayer` class called `AVQueuePlayer` designed specifically to manage a list of videos. The class creates a playlist from an array of `AVPlayerItem` objects. The following are the initializer and some of its methods.

AVQueuePlayer(items: [AVPlayerItem])—This initializer creates a play list with the items specified by the **items** argument.

advanceToNextItem()—This method advances the playback to the next item on the list.

insert(AVPlayerItem, **after:** AVPlayerItem?**)**—This method inserts a new item on the list.

remove(AVPlayerItem**)**—This method removes an item from the list.

An `AVQueuePlayer` object replaces the `AVPlayer` object used to represent the media. All we have to do to play a sequence of videos is to create the `AVPlayerItem` object for each video and an `AVQueuePlayer` object to replace the `AVPlayer` object we have used so far, as in the following example.

```
import SwiftUI
import AVFoundation
class ViewData: NSObject {
   var playerItem1: AVPlayerItem!
   var playerItem2: AVPlayerItem!
   var player: AVQueuePlayer!
   var playerLayer: AVPlayerLayer!

   func setObserver() {
      playerItem1.addObserver(self, forKeyPath: "status", options: [],
context: nil)
   }
   override func observeValue(forKeyPath keyPath: String?, of object:
Any?, change: [NSKeyValueChangeKey : Any]?, context:
UnsafeMutableRawPointer?) {
      if playerItem1.status == .readyToPlay {
         playerItem1.removeObserver(self, forKeyPath: "status")
         player.play()
      }
   }
}
class ApplicationData: ObservableObject {
   @Published var playing: Bool = false
   @Published var progress: CGFloat = 0
   var customVideoView: CustomPlayerView!
   var viewData: ViewData

   init() {
      customVideoView = CustomPlayerView()
      viewData = ViewData()

      let bundle = Bundle.main
      let videoURL1 = bundle.url(forResource: "videotrees",
withExtension: "mp4")
```

```
        let videoURL2 = bundle.url(forResource: "videobeaches",
withExtension: "mp4")
        let asset1 = AVURLAsset(url: videoURL1!)
        let asset2 = AVURLAsset(url: videoURL2!)
        viewData.playerItem1 = AVPlayerItem(asset: asset1)
        viewData.playerItem2 = AVPlayerItem(asset: asset2)
        viewData.player = AVQueuePlayer(items: [viewData.playerItem1,
viewData.playerItem2])
        viewData.playerLayer = AVPlayerLayer(player: viewData.player)

        let scene = UIApplication.shared.connectedScenes.first as?
UIWindowScene
        let screenSize = scene?.screen.bounds ?? .zero
        viewData.playerLayer.frame = screenSize
        let layer = customVideoView.view.layer
        layer.addSublayer(viewData.playerLayer)
        viewData.setObserver()

        Task(priority: .background) {
            await receiveNotification()
        }
    }
    func receiveNotification() async {
        let center = NotificationCenter.default
        let name = await UIDevice.orientationDidChangeNotification
        for await _ in center.notifications(named: name, object: nil) {
            if viewData.player != nil {
                await MainActor.run {
                    viewData.playerLayer.frame = customVideoView.view.bounds
                }
            }
        }
    }
}
```

Listing 18-29: Playing a list of videos

This example assumes that we are using the simple **ContentView** view defined in Listing 18-24. The code loads two videos, videotrees.mp4 and videobeaches.mp4, and then creates two **AVURLAsset** objects and two **AVPlayerItem** objects to represent them. The **AVQueuePlayer** object is define next to play both videos in sequence. Notice that because the interface we are using for this example does not include a button to play the videos, we add an observer to the first video and call the **play()** method as soon as it is ready.

 Do It Yourself: Update the ApplicationData.swift file with the code in Listing 18-29. This example was designed to work with the **ContentView** view defined in Listing 18-24. Download the videobeaches.mp4 and videotrees.mp4 videos from our website and add them to your project. (Remember to check the option Add to Target.) Run the application. The videos should be played one after another.

(Basic) ## 18.3 Color Picker

Along with all the tools provided by SwiftUI and UIKit to control the camera, play videos, and manage pictures, SwiftUI also includes the **ColorPicker** view to allow the user to pick a color. The view creates a button that opens a predefined interface with tools to select and configure a color. The following is the view's initializer.

ColorPicker(String, selection: Binding, **supportsOpacity:** Bool)—This initializer creates a color picker. The first argument provides the label to show next to the button, the **selection** argument is a **Binding** property that stores a **Color** view with the color selected by the user, and the **supportsOpacity** argument determines whether the user will be allowed to set the color's opacity. The value by default is **true**.

The implementation of the color picker is simple. We define a **@State** property with a **Color** view, and then use it to initialize the **ColorPicker** view, so every time the user selects a color, it is stored in this property and we can use it to modify other views. For instance, in the following example we use the value of the property to change the interface's background color.

```
struct ContentView: View {
    @State private var selectedColor: Color = .white

    var body: some View {
        VStack {
            ColorPicker("Select a Color", selection: $selectedColor)
                .padding()
            Spacer()
        }.background(selectedColor)
    }
}
```

Listing 18-30: *Showing a color picker*

The **ColorPicker** view shows a button that opens an interface for the user to select a color. Once the user performs the selection, the color is automatically assigned to the state property. This means that the user can change the selection as many times as he or she wants, but only the last selected color is preserved by the property.

Figure 18-11: *Color picker*

 Do It Yourself: Create a Multiplatform project. Update the **ContentView** view with the code in Listing 18-30. Run the application on the iPhone simulator and press the color picker button. Select a color. You should see the color of the interface change, as shown in Figure 18-11.

Chapter 19
Multiplatform Applications

Basic **19.1 Mac Apps**

SwiftUI is available for every platform. With SwiftUI we can program applications for iPhones, iPads, Mac computers, the Apple Watch, and Apple TV. But this doesn't mean we can use the same code. The system for IPhones and iPads is the same, but Mac computers, the Apple Watch and Apple TV require a separate set of frameworks. The good news is that Xcode is capable of compiling the same application for multiple devices. All we need to do is to create the Swift files as we have done so far, and then declare platform specific code.

The first step is to configure the target to tell Xcode the platforms our app supports. If we create our project with the Multiplatform App template, it comes configured to work for iPhones, iPads, and Macs.

⌄ **Supported Destinations**

Destination	SDK
📱 iPhone	iOS
▢ iPad	iOS
▢ Mac	macOS

+ —

Figure 19-1: Supported platforms

The panel includes a + button at the bottom to add more platforms and configurations. For instance, to create applications for Mac computers, we have three options available: Mac, Mac Catalyst, and Designed for iPad.

Figure 19-2: Mac destinations

With the Mac option we can create a Mac application with SwiftUI and have access to all the macOS exclusive features. This is the option set by default and the one recommended for new applications. The Mac Catalyst option can adapt an iPad app to the Mac, and therefore it is recommended to convert our existent iPad apps to Mac apps. And the Designed for iPad option allows us to run our iPad apps on Macs with no modifications (not recommended).

As mentioned in Chapter 5, Xcode includes buttons on the toolbar to select the app's scheme and the destination, which includes simulators, real devices, and options to execute the app on the Mac. To run the app on our computer, the option is called My Mac. (The My Mac Rosetta option is used to run applications that were developed to work on Intel processors.)

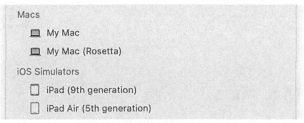

Figure 19-3: My Mac option

Xcode also allows us to provide images for each platform. The options are available from the Attributes Inspector panel when we select a set in the Asset Catalog. For instance, if we select an image set and activate the Mac option from this panel (Figure 19-4, number 1), the set includes placeholders to add images that will only be available when the app is running on the Mac.

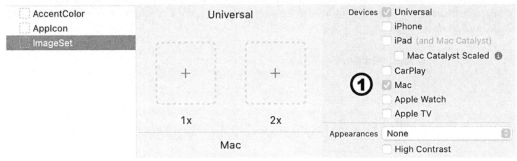

Figure 19-4: Mac images

Basic Conditional Code

Although the system can automatically build the application for each platform, it is our responsibility to discriminate platform-specific code. One alternative is to use conditional compilation. These conditionals are checked before the code is compiled and, therefore, we can use them to select the code we want to implement according to the target platform.

Conditional compilation in Swift is done using the `#if`, `#else`, and `#endif` keywords. The `#if` and `#else` keywords work like the Swift conditionals `if else`, but because the statements are not delimited by a block, the `#endif` keyword is required to signal the end of the code.

There are several parameters we can use to set the condition, but to detect whether the application is being compiled for iOS or macOS, we can use the `os()` instruction and the values `iOS` and `macOS`, as in the following example.

```swift
import SwiftUI

struct ContentView: View {
   var body: some View {
      VStack {
         #if os(macOS)
            Text("Mac Application")
         #else
            Text("Mobile Application")
         #endif
      }.frame(width: 500, height: 350)
   }
}
```

Listing 19-1: Detecting the platform before compiling

Chapter 19 - Multiplatform Applications

This is a very simple example but illustrates how to work with these types of conditionals. If we run this project on a mobile device, we get the message "Mobile Application", but on the Mac, we get a window of a size of 500 by 350 points with the message "Mac Application".

Figure 19-5: Mac application

 Do It Yourself: Create a Multiplatform project. Update the `ContentView` view with the code in Listing 19-1. From the Xcode's toolbar, click on the My Mac option (Figure 19-3). Press the Play button to run the application. You should see a window with a message at the center, as illustrated in Figure 19-5.

In the previous example, we applied the `frame()` modifier to every platform, but we can use the `#if #else` keywords to discriminate any code we want, including views and modifiers. In the following example, we apply different colors to a `Text` view depending on the platform.

```
struct ContentView: View {
    var body: some View {
        VStack {
            Text("My Application")
            #if os(macOS)
                .foregroundColor(.red)
            #else
                .foregroundColor(.green)
            #endif
        }.frame(width: 500, height: 350)
    }
}
```

Listing 19-2: Applying different modifiers to each platform

When the differences between platforms is substantial, instead of selecting single views or modifiers, we can load entire views designed specifically for iOS or macOS. The SwiftUI View files are created as always and we can use conditional compiling to load them, but to avoid Xcode reporting other errors, we must declare that the files should only be compiled for a specific platform. This is done from the Build Phases panel in the app's settings. There is a section called Compile Sources where we can select a file and check the system we want to compile that file for.

Figure 19-6: Platform selection

In this example, we have a view called **MobileDetailView** that we want to shown in any platform, but another view called **MacDetailView** that was designed specifically for Macs.

After we tell Xcode to compile the **MacDetailView** view only for macOS, we must tell the compiler which view to implement in the interface with the **#if #else** conditionals. For instance, the following application defines a universal interface with two columns, but it loads different views on the second column depending on the platform.

```
struct ContentView: View {
    @State private var visibility: NavigationSplitViewVisibility
= .automatic
    var body: some View {
        NavigationSplitView(columnVisibility: $visibility, sidebar: {
            MenuView()
        }, detail: {
            #if os(macOS)
                MacDetailView()
            #else
                MobileDetailView()
            #endif
        })
    }
}
```

Listing 19-3: Defining a multiplatform interface

If we open this application on an iPad or a Mac, the system loads the **ContentView** view first, and then creates two columns. The content of the column on the left is defined by the **MenuView** view, but the content of the column on the right depends on the platform. If the application is compiled for Mac computers, the system shows the **MacDetailView**, but if it is compiled for iPhones and iPads, the system loads the **MobileDetailView** instead.

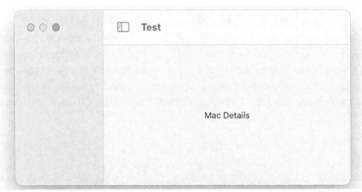

Figure 19-7: Multiplatform interface on a Mac

Do It Yourself: Update the `ContentView` view with the code in Listing 19-3. Create SwiftUI View files called MenuView.swift, MacDetailView.swift , and MobileDetailView.swift. Assign different strings to the `Text` views included by the template inside these views. Select the first item at the top of the Navigator Area to open the app's settings (Figure 5-4, number 6). Open the Build Phases panel and go to the Compile Sources section. Click the Filters button and select only macOS for the MacDetailView.swift file (Figure 19-6). Run the application on the Mac. You should see the content of the `MacDetailView` view on the right, as shown in Figure 19-7.

Basic Menu

Mac applications include a menu bar that is displayed at the top of the screen for easy access to the application's key features.

Figure 19-8: *Standard menu*

The options included with the menu are predefined by the system and provide basic functionality to the app. To introduce changes and add custom functionality, SwiftUI includes the following modifier.

commands(content: Closure)—This modifier modifies the Scene to include the menus and options defined by the closure assigned to the **content** argument.

This modifier is applied to the Scene (the `WindowGroup` structure in the `App` structure) and returns a new Scene with the menu bar configured by the closure. To define the menus and the options from this closure, SwiftUI includes the `CommandMenu` and `CommandGroup` structures. The `CommandMenu` structure is used to create new menus. The following is the structure's initializer.

CommandMenu(String, **content:** Closure)—This structure creates a menu to add to the menu bar. The first argument specifies the menu's title, and the closure assigned to the **content** argument defines the menu's option. The new menu is inserted between the View and Window menus.

To modify the options of standard menus, we can use the `CommandGroup` structure instead. The following are the structure's initializers.

CommandGroup(after: CommandGroupPlacement, **addition:** Closure)—This structure defines a menu option. The **after** argument is a structure that specifies the option after which the new option will be added. The option is defined by the closure assigned to the **addition** argument.

CommandGroup(before: CommandGroupPlacement, **addition:** Closure)— This structure defines a menu option. The **before** argument is a structure that specifies the option before which the new option will be added. The option is defined by the closure assigned to the **addition** argument.

CommandGroup(replacing: CommandGroupPlacement, **addition:** Closure) —This structure defines a menu option. The **replacing** argument is a structure that specifies the option that will be replaced by the new option. The option is defined by the closure assigned to the **addition** argument.

The `CommandGroup` structure determines the position of the new option based on the position of a standard option. The standard options are represented by a `CommandGroupPlacement` structure. The structure includes type properties to return instances that represent all the standard options available. The properties are `appInfo`, `appSettings`, `appTermination`, `appVisibility`, `systemServices`, `importExport`, `newItem`, `printItem`, `saveItem`, `pasteboard`, `textEditing`, `textFormatting`, `undoRedo`, `sidebar`, `toolbar`, `singleWindowList`, `windowArrangement`, `windowList`, `windowSize`, and `help`.

Because the `commands()` modifier applies to the Scene, we can only implement it in the `App` structure. For instance, in the following example we use it to add a new menu to the menu bar.

```
import SwiftUI

@main
struct TestApp: App {
   var body: some Scene {
      WindowGroup {
         ContentView()
      }
      #if os(macOS)
      .commands {
         CommandMenu("Options") {
            Button("Option 1") {
               print("This is the option 1")
            }
            Button("Option 2") {
               print("This is the option 2")
            }
         }
      }
      #endif
   }
}
```

Listing 19-4: *Adding a menu to the menu bar*

The menu options are generated with `Button` views. In this example, we include two: Option 1 and Option 2. The new menu is added between the View and Window menus, as shown below.

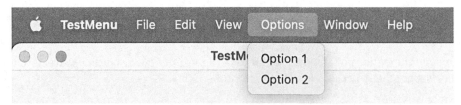

Figure 19-9: *Custom menu*

 Do It Yourself: Create a Multiplatform project. Update the `App` structure with the code in Listing 19-4. Run the application on the Mac. You should see the Options menu in the menu bar with two options. When selected, these options print a message on the console, but you can use them for anything you want, such as modifying a state property to update the interface or executing a method in the model, as we will see later.

Menu options may be connected to keys on the keyboard, so when the user presses the keys, the action associated with the option is executed. SwiftUI offers the following modifier to create these keyboard shortcuts.

Chapter 19 - Multiplatform Applications

keyboardShortcut(KeyEquivalent, **modifiers:** EventModifiers)—This modifier assigns a keyboard shortcut to a menu option. The first argument can be a string representation of the key (e.g., "A") or a function key represented by a `KeyEquivalent` structure. The **modifiers** argument is an array of key modifiers that must be pressed along with the main key to perform the action. The structure includes type properties to return instances for every modifier key available. The properties are `all`, `capsLock`, `command`, `control`, `numericPad`, `option`, and `shift`.

The `KeyEquivalent` structure can be represented by a string, and the string can include a letter, a number, or a punctuation character. The structure also includes type properties to return instances that represent function keys. The properties available are `upArrow`, `downArrow`, `leftArrow`, `rightArrow`, `clear`, `delete`, `deleteForward`, `end`, `escape`, `home`, `pageDown`, `pageUp`, `return`, `space`, and `tab`. The following example creates a shortcut for the second option with the A and Shift keys.

```
.commands {
   CommandMenu("Options") {
      Button("Option 1") {
         print("This is the option 1")
      }
      Button("Option 2") {
         print("This is the option 2")
      }.keyboardShortcut("A", modifiers: [.shift])
   }
}
```

Listing 19-5: Assigning a keyboard shortcut to a menu option

Do It Yourself: Update the `commands()` modifier with the code in Listing 19-5. Run the application on the Mac. Press the Shift + A keys. You should see the message of Option 2 printed on the console.

IMPORTANT: You can add all the options you want to a menu. If you need to separate the options in groups, use a `Divider` view between `Button` views to draw a line.

In addition to our own menus, we can also add options to the standard menus or replace the options provided by the system with the `CommandGroup` structure. This structure defines three initializers that we can use to insert a new option before or after a system option, and also replace an existing one. For instance, the system includes an option in the File menu called New Window. This option is represented by the `newItem` property defined by the `CommandGroupPlacement` structure. The following example shows how to use this property to add an option to the File menu after the New Window option.

```
.commands {
   CommandGroup(after: .newItem, addition: {
      Button("Option 1") {
         print("This is option 1")
      }
   })
}
```

Listing 19-6: Adding options to a standard menu

Figure 19-10: Custom option added to a standard menu

If instead we want to remove a standard option, all we need to do is to assign an empty closure to the **addition** argument. For instance, the following example adds a new option after the **newItem** option and them removes this option from the menu. (Notice that the removal must be performed first.)

```
.commands {
   CommandGroup(replacing: .newItem, addition: {})
   CommandGroup(after: .newItem, addition: {
      Button("Option 1") {
         print("This is option 1")
      }
   })
}
```

Listing 19-7: Removing options

Figure 19-11: Standard option removed

We can also add submenus to a menu by using a **Picker** view instead of a **Button** view. For this purpose, we need a property in the model to store the current state.

```
import SwiftUI

class ApplicationData: ObservableObject {
   @Published var selectedOption: Int = 1
}
```

Listing 19-8: Defining a property in the model to store the index of the selected option

The **@Published** property in this model stores an integer value that we will use to identify the options in the picker with a **tag()** modifier. When an option is selected, the value in the **tag()** modifier is assigned to the **@Published** property in the model, so views know which option is currently selected.

```
import SwiftUI

@main
struct TestApp: App {
   @StateObject var appData = ApplicationData()
```

```
var body: some Scene {
    WindowGroup {
        ContentView()
            .environmentObject(appData)
    }
    #if os(macOS)
    .commands {
        CommandGroup(after: .newItem, addition: {
            Picker("Options", selection: $appData.selectedOption) {
                Text("Option 1").tag(1)
                Text("Option 2").tag(2)
                Text("Option 3").tag(3)
            }
        })
    }
    #endif
}
}
```

Listing 19-9: Adding a submenu

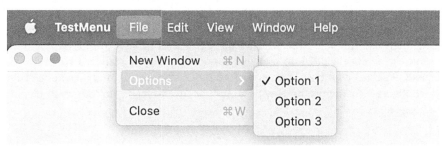

Figure 19-12: Submenu

 Do It Yourself: Create a Swift file called ApplicationData.swift for the model in Listing 19-8. Update the **App** structure with the code in Listing 19-9. Run the application on the Mac. Open the File menu and select an option. The option should remain selected.

SwiftUI includes structures that add predefined commands to the menu bar. The structures currently available are **SidebarCommands**, **TextEditingCommands**, **TextFormatting-Commands**, **ToolbarCommands**, and **ImportFromDevicesCommands**. Probably the most interesting is **ImportFromDevicesCommands**, which adds a submenu to allow the user to import resources from nearby devices. For instance, we can load and process an image in our Mac application that is taken by the camera of an iPhone.

The option is added by the structure, but to process the data, we must apply the following modifier to a view.

importableFromServices(for: Type, **action:** Closure)—This modifier imports data of the type specified by the first argument. The **action** argument provides a closure to process the data.

To add one of these menu options, all we need to do is to include an instance of the structure in the closure assigned to the **commands()** modifier. The following example adds the option to import resources from external devices.

```
.commands {
   ImportFromDevicesCommands()
}
```

Listing 19-10: Adding predefined options to import resources

Figure 19-13: Option to import an image from iPhones or iPads

The process to receive the data is similar to the one we used before to process drag and drop operations (see Drag and Drop Gesture in Chapter 12). We must apply the modifier, specify a data type that conforms to the **Transferable** protocol to determine the type of data we want to accept, and then use the value received by the closure to process the data. But because the devices send the images in JPEG format, we cannot implement standard types like **Image** or **Data**. Instead, we must create a custom structure that conforms to the **Transferable** protocol and it is configured to import data with a **jpeg** content type. For our example, we call it **ImageRepresentation**.

```
import SwiftUI
#if os(macOS)
struct ImageRepresentation: Transferable {
   let image: NSImage

   static var transferRepresentation: some TransferRepresentation {
      DataRepresentation(importedContentType: .jpeg, importing: { data in
         if let newImage = NSImage(data: data) {
            return ImageRepresentation(image: newImage)
         } else {
            return ImageRepresentation(image: NSImage(named:
"nopicture")!)
         }
      })
   }
}
#endif

struct ContentView: View {
   @State private var MyPicture = Image("nopicture")

   var body: some View {
      VStack {
         MyPicture
            .resizable()
            .scaledToFit()
      }.frame(width: 500, height: 350)
         #if os(macOS)
         .importableFromServices(for: ImageRepresentation.self, action:
{ elements in
         if let value = elements.first {
```

Chapter 19 - Multiplatform Applications

```
            MyPicture = Image(nsImage: value.image)
            return true
         }
         return false
      })
      #endif
   }
}
```

Listing 19-11: Importing an image form an external device

The macOS system does not implement the `UIImage` class to store images, but the `NSImage` class. Therefore, the `ImageRepresentation` structure includes a property to store a value of this type with the image received from the device. When a value is received, the `importableFromServices()` modifier reads this property, creates an `Image` view with the value, and assigns it to a `@State` property to show the image on the screen.

 Do It Yourself: Update the `commands()` modifier in the `App` structure with the code in Listing 19-10 and the ContentView.swift file with the code in Listing 19-11. Run the application on the Mac. In the File menu, you should see the option Import from iPhone or iPad (Figure 19-13). Select the option Take Photo. Your cellphone should automatically open the camera. Take a picture. The image should appear on the screen. For more information on the `Transferable` protocol, see Drag and Drop Gesture in Chapter 12.

The options in a menu can be disabled. To disable an option, all we need to do is to apply the `disabled()` modifier to the `Button` view that represents the option and connect it with a state in the model that we can use to enable or disable the option when a condition is met. For instance, we can disable the option when no text was inserted in a `TextField` view. To manage the value, we need a `@Published` property in the model.

```
class ApplicationData: ObservableObject {
   @Published var inputMessage: String = ""
}
```

Listing 19-12: Defining a state to enable and disable a menu option

Now we can disable the option in the menu when this property is empty.

```
.commands {
   CommandGroup(after: .newItem, addition: {
      Button("Option 1") {
         print("This is option 1")
      }.disabled(appData.inputMessage.isEmpty)
   })
}
```

Listing 19-13: Enabling and disabling a menu option

To complete the example, we need to include a `TextField` view in our view that works with the `@Published` property in the model.

```
struct ContentView: View {
    @EnvironmentObject var appData: ApplicationData

    var body: some View {
        VStack {
            TextField("Insert your Name", text: $appData.inputMessage)
            Spacer()
        }.padding()
        .frame(width: 500, height: 350)
    }
}
```

Listing 19-14: Defining a `TextField` view to enable and disable the option

When the user inserts a value in the text field, the option is enabled, but it is immediately disabled when the field is empty.

Figure 19-14: Option disabled

Do It Yourself: Update the **ApplicationData** class with the code in Listing 19-12, the **commands()** modifier in the **App** structure with the code in Listing 19-13, and the **ContentView** view with the code in Listing 19-14. Run the application on the Mac. Open the File menu. The option should be disabled. Insert a text in the text field and open the menu again. Now the option should be enabled.

In the last example, we disable the option if a condition is not met, but often options are enabled or disabled depending on which element on the interface is focused. For example, we may have two **TextField** views, but the action can only be performed when the user is working on one of them (the text field is focused). In Chapter 6, we have learned how to handle focus changes in a view, but to pass the focus state from one view to another, or as in this case, from a view to the menu bar, we need to implement a structure called **FocusedValues**. This structure is a collection of values managed by the system that contains the state of the focused view. Each state is identified by a structure that conforms to the **FocusedValueKey** protocol, which only requirement is a typealias with the name **Value** and the data type of the value managed by the view we want to monitor. Once we have this structure, we need to add a property of this type to the **FocusedValues** structure with an extension, as in the following example.

```
import SwiftUI

struct AddressKey : FocusedValueKey {
    typealias Value = String
}
extension FocusedValues {
    var address: AddressKey.Value? {
        get { self[AddressKey.self] }
        set { self[AddressKey.self] = newValue }
    }
}
```

```
class ApplicationData: ObservableObject {
    @Published var inputMessage: String = ""
    @Published var inputAddress: String = ""
}
```

Listing 19-15: Storing a focus state in the FocusedValues *structure*

In this example, we define a structure called **AddressKey** that conforms to the **FocusedValueKey** protocol with a typealias of **String** called **Value**, so we can store the values managed by the **TextField** view. Next, we define an extension of the **FocusedValues** structure to include our own property. We call this property **address**. The data type is the **Value** type defined by the previous structure, but set as an optional. This is so the system can assign the value **nil** to the property when the view is not focused. The property includes a setter and a getter to set and return the value in the collection with our structure as the key.

Now we need to set and read this focus state from the view and the **App** structure. To set the focus state, SwiftUI includes the following modifier.

focusedValue(WritableKeyPath, Value**)**—This modifier stores a value in the **FocusedValues** structure. The first argument is the key path of the property in the **FocusedValues** structure we want to use to store the value, and the second argument is the value we want to store (usually the view's state).

To observe the value from the focused view, SwiftUI includes the **@FocusedValue** property wrapper. This property wrapper is created from the **FocusedValue** structure, which includes the following initializer.

FocusedValue(KeyPath**)**—This initializer creates a structure to observe the values from a focused view. The argument is the key path of the property in the **FocusedValues** structure that stores the state we want to observe.

To store the focus state of a view in the **FocusedValues** structure, all we need to do is to apply the **focusedValue()** modifier to the view. In the following example, we do it to the **TextField** view that allows the user to insert an address.

```
struct ContentView: View {
    @EnvironmentObject var appData: ApplicationData

    var body: some View {
        VStack {
            TextField("Insert your Name", text: $appData.inputMessage)
                .padding()
            TextField("Insert Address", text: $appData.inputAddress)
                .padding([.leading, .trailing])
                .focusedValue(\.address, appData.inputAddress)
            Spacer()
        }.padding()
        .frame(width: 500, height: 350)
    }
}
```

Listing 19-16: Passing the focus state to the FocusedValues *structure*

When the second **TextField** view is focused, the **focusedValue()** modifier assigns the value of the **inputAddress** property to the **address** property of the **FocusedValues** structure, so the value is available for other views. Now we can observe this value from the **App** structure with the **@FocusedValue** property wrapper.

```
import SwiftUI

@main
struct TestApp: App {
   @StateObject var appData = ApplicationData()
   @FocusedValue(\.address) var addressValue: String?

   var body: some Scene {
      WindowGroup {
         ContentView()
            .environmentObject(appData)
      }
      #if os(macOS)
      .commands {
         CommandGroup(after: .newItem, addition: {
            Button("Option 1") {
               print("This is option 1")
            }.disabled(addressValue == nil)
         })
      }
      #endif
   }
}
```

Listing 19-17: Disabling a menu option according to the focus state of a view

The view defines a property called `addressValue`, which contains the value of the address property of the `FocusedValues` structure. If the `TextField` view that allows the user to insert an address is focused (the user is typing on it), this property contains the value inserted by the user, otherwise, the property returns `nil`, so we can enable or disable the menu option accordingly.

 Do It Yourself: Update the ApplicationData.swift file with the code in Listing 19-15, the `ContentView` view with the code in Listing 19-16, and the `App` structure with the code in Listing 19-17. Run the application on the Mac. Click on the first text field. Open the File menu. The option should be disabled. Click on the second text field to select it. Now the option should be enabled.

 IMPORTANT: SwiftUI also includes the `@FocusedBinding` property wrapper to observe the value of a `Binding` property. This is useful when we need to change the state of a view from the menu. There is also a modifier called `focusedSceneValue()` to store the focus of a Scene instead of a single view. For more information, visit our website and follow the links for this chapter.

(Basic) **Toolbar**

Instead of Navigation Bars, Mac applications use a toolbar at the top of the window where we can add all the items we need. The toolbar is added at the top of the right column in a two column design created with a `NavigationSplitView` view. This means that we can use the `navigationTitle()` modifier to show a title, but SwiftUI also allows us to add a subtitle for macOS applications with the following modifier.

navigationSubtitle(String**)**—This modifier adds a subtitle to the toolbar of a Mac application. The argument is the text we want to assign to the subtitle.

Like the Navigation Bar, the toolbar in a Mac application can also contain buttons. The buttons are incorporated with the same `toolbar()` modifier implemented before. For instance, the following application defines a `NavigationSplitView` view with two views, one to create the content for the left column, and another for the right.

```
struct ContentView: View {
   var body: some View {
      NavigationSplitView(sidebar: {
         MenuView()
      }, detail: {
         DetailView()
      })
   }
}
```

Listing 19-18: Defining a two-column interface

The `MenuView` view defines the left column and only needs some content for this example. On the other hand, the `DetailView` view is the one that shows the toolbar and where we should define the toolbar items, as in the following example.

```
import SwiftUI

struct DetailView: View {
   var body: some View {
      VStack {
         Text("Details")
      }
      .toolbar {
         ToolbarItem(placement: .automatic) {
            Button(action: {
                  print("Adding Book")
               }, label: {
                  Label("Add Book", systemImage: "plus")
               })
         }
      }
      .navigationTitle("My Title")
      #if os(macOS)
      .navigationSubtitle("My Subtitle")
      #endif
   }
}
```

Listing 19-19: Adding items to the toolbar for a Mac application

This view defines the title and subtitle and adds a button with an SF Symbol to the bar. We use the `automatic` value to place it, which positions the button on the right, but we could also have applied the `principal` value, which positions the buttons at the center.

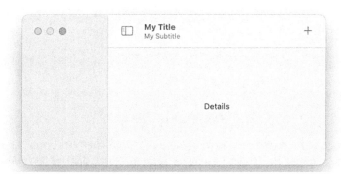

Figure 19-15: Mac toolbar

Do It Yourself: Create a Multiplatform project. Update the `ContentView` view with the code in Listing 19-18. Create two SwiftUI View files called MenuView.swift and DetailView.swift. Leave the `MenuView` view with a single `Text` view, but modify the `DetailView` view with the code in Listing 19-19. Run the application on the Mac. You should see a toolbar with a title and a subtitle, as illustrated in Figure 19-15.

Basic ## Mac Modifiers

SwiftUI defines a few modifiers that are exclusive for Mac applications. The following are the most frequently used.

help(String**)**—This modifier creates a tooltip. (A tooltip is a message that appears next to the view when the mouse is positioned on top of it for a few seconds.)

collapsible(Bool**)**—This modifier determines if a section of a `List` view of type sidebar can be collapsed by the user.

There is also a type method to create a list with alternate backgrounds.

inset(alternatesRowBackgrounds: Bool**)**—This type method assigns the `inset` style to the `List` view. The **alternatesRowBackgrounds** argument determines whether the views are going to be displayed with alternate backgrounds.

The `help()` modifier is simple. All it does is to show a label when the mouse moves over the view and remains in that position for a few seconds. Its purpose is to help the user discover all the tools and learn how to use them. For instance, we can apply it to show a message for the Add Book button added to the toolbar in the previous example.

```
.toolbar {
   ToolbarItem(placement: .automatic) {
      Button(action: {
         print("Adding Book")
      }, label: {
         Label("Add Book", systemImage: "plus")
      })
      .help("Press this button to add a book")
   }
}
```

Listing 19-20: *Showing a tooltip for a button*

If we position the mouse over the button, after a few seconds, the system shows a small label with the text "Press this button to add a book".

Figure 19-16: *Tooltip*

The `collapsible()` modifier and the `inset()` type method apply to `List` views. The `collapsible()` modifier is used to collapse sections in a sidebar list, while the `inset()` method returns a style for the list that highlights rows to make them easy to identify.

Chapter 19 - Multiplatform Applications

To test these two features, we are going to create a small app that shows a list of items selected from a category. The following is the model with some testing values.

```
import SwiftUI

struct ConsumableItems: Identifiable, Hashable {
   let id = UUID()
   var name: String
   var items: [String]
}
struct ConsumableSections: Identifiable, Hashable {
   let id = UUID()
   var name: String
   var sectionItems: [ConsumableItems]
}
class ApplicationData: ObservableObject {
   @Published var listOfItems: [ConsumableSections]

   init() {
      let items1 = ConsumableItems(name: "Fruits", items: ["Apples",
"Avocado", "Bananas", "Blueberries", "Grapes", "Lemons", "Oranges",
"Peaches"])
      let items2 = ConsumableItems(name: "Dairy", items: ["Milk",
"Butter", "Cheese", "Yogurt", "Cream", "Ice Cream"])
      let items3 = ConsumableItems(name: "Juice", items: ["Apple",
"Orange", "Grape"])

      listOfItems = [
         ConsumableSections(name: "Foods", sectionItems: [items1,
items2]),
         ConsumableSections(name: "Beverages", sectionItems: [items3])
      ]
   }
}
```

Listing 19-21: Defining a model with data organized in sections

The model defines two structures, one to store an array of items, and another to define the sections. In the initializer, we define the **@Published** property we need to store the values and initialize it with two sections and three lists of values.

Now, we need to organize the interface. The **NavigationSplitView** view needs a view to list the categories on the left and another to show the list of items on the right.

```
struct ContentView: View {
   @State private var selected: ConsumableItems?
   @State private var visibility: NavigationSplitViewVisibility
= .automatic

   var body: some View {
      NavigationSplitView(columnVisibility: $visibility, sidebar: {
         MenuView(selected: $selected)
      }, detail: {
         let item = selected ?? ConsumableItems(name: "", items: [])
         DetailView(items: item)
      })
   }
}
```

Listing 19-22: Defining a two columns interface

The `DetailView` view receives a `ConsumableItems` structure with the values to show on the list. In this example, we check whether there is an item already selected by the user and send it to the `DetailView` view. If no item was selected, we send an empty structure instead.

The `MenuView` view must list the categories in sections and allow the user to select one, as shown next.

```
import SwiftUI

struct MenuView: View {
   @EnvironmentObject var appData: ApplicationData
   @Binding var selected: ConsumableItems?

   var body: some View {
      List(selection: $selected) {
         ForEach(appData.listOfItems) { sections in
            Section(header: Text(sections.name)) {
               ForEach(sections.sectionItems) { item in
                  NavigationLink(item.name, value: item)
               }
            }
            #if os(macOS)
            .collapsible(true)
            #endif
         }
      }.listStyle(.sidebar)
   }
}
struct MenuView_Previews: PreviewProvider {
   static var previews: some View {
      MenuView(selected: .constant(nil))
         .environmentObject(ApplicationData())
   }
}
```

Listing 19-23: Defining collapsable sections

This example applies the `collapsible()` modifier to the `Section` view, so the user can collapse or expand each section on the list. Notice that for the `collapsible()` modifier to work, the style of the list must be `sidebar`.

The list is created from the `ConsumableSections` structures returned by the `listOfItems` property, and each section is created from the values in the structure's `sectionItems` property. When the user selects a row, the `ConsumableItems` structure is passed to the `DetailView` view and the values are displayed on the list, as shown next.

```
import SwiftUI

struct DetailView: View {
   @EnvironmentObject var appData: ApplicationData
   let items: ConsumableItems

   var body: some View {
      List {
         ForEach(items.items, id: \.self) { item in
            Text(item)
         }
      }
      #if os(macOS)
      .listStyle(.inset(alternatesRowBackgrounds: true))
      #endif
      .toolbar {
         ToolbarItem(placement: .automatic) {
```

Chapter 19 - Multiplatform Applications

```
            Button(action: {
                print("Adding Item")
            }, label: {
                Label("Add Item", systemImage: "plus")
            })
        }
    }
    .navigationTitle("My Title")
    #if os(macOS)
    .navigationSubtitle("My Subtitle")
    #endif
    }
}
struct DetailView_Previews: PreviewProvider {
    static var previews: some View {
        DetailView(items: ConsumableItems(name: "", items: []))
            .environmentObject(ApplicationData())
    }
}
```

Listing 19-24: *Highlighting alternate rows*

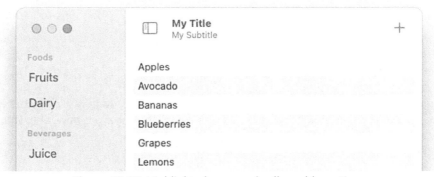

Figure 19-17: *Highlighted rows and collapsable sections*

 Do It Yourself: Add to the previous project a Swift file called ApplicationData.swift for the model in Listing 19-21. Update the `ContentView` view with the code in Listing 19-22. Create two SwiftUI View files called MenuView.swift and DetailView.swift for the views in Listings 19-23 and 19-24. Remember to inject the `ApplicationData` object into the environment for the app and the previews (Chapter 7, Listing 7-4). Run the application on the Mac. You should see something like Figure 19-17. Click on the sections to expand or collapse them.

(Basic) ## Scenes

As explained in Chapter 5, to create an application we must first define a Scene. SwiftUI includes several structures to create standard Scenes for every system. For Multiplatform applications we have been using the `WindowGroup` structure, which is capable of managing one or more instances of our app across all Apple platforms. In Chapter 10, we have introduced the `DocumentGroup` structure to create an application to manage internal and external documents. But there are more. For instance, the framework includes the `Window` structure to create a Scene with only one window.

Window(String, **id:** String, **content:** Closure)—This structure creates a Scene to present a single window. The first argument defines the window's title, the **id** argument defines the window's identifier, and the **content** argument is a closure that provides the Scene's content.

The `Window` structure creates a single independent Scene, and therefore it is useful for applications that cannot allow the user to open multiple windows, like video games, but can also be composed together with other Scenes to present an auxiliary window, as in the following example.

```
import SwiftUI

@main
struct TestApp: App {
   var body: some Scene {
      WindowGroup {
         ContentView()
      }
      #if os(macOS)
      Window("My Window", id: "mywindow") {
         AuxiliaryView()
      }
      #endif
   }
}
```

Listing 19-25: Opening an auxiliary window

To create an auxiliary window, the `Window` structure is applied along with the `WindowGroup` structure, so the app's main window is created as always, but now we have an option in the Window menu to open the auxiliary window.

Merge All Windows

My Window

Bring All to Front

✓ Test

Figure 19-18: Option to open an auxiliary window

Do It Yourself: Create a Multiplatform project. Update the **App** structure with the code in Listing 19-25. Create a new SwiftUI View file called AuxiliaryView.swift with a single **Text** view. Run the application on the Mac. Open the Window menu. You should see an option with the name of the window, as shown in Figure 19-18 (My Window).

The menu option is automatically added to the Window menu when we include a `Window` Scene in the **App** structure, but most users don't know that the option even exists. To provide a better alternative, the Environment includes the following property to open the window programmatically.

openWindow—This property creates an action that presents a window. The property contains an instance of the **OpenWindowAction** structure that exposes a handler we can call to perform the action. There are two options available: we can call it with the **id** argument to open a window with a specific identifier (**openWindow(id: String)**), or with the **value** argument to open a window presented by the `WindowGroup` structure that can process that value type (`openWindow(value: Value)`).

Just like we did with other Environment properties, such as `dismiss` and `dismissSearch`, we must define an `@Environment` property and then call it to perform the action. The following is the `ContentView` view we need to open the auxiliary view created in the previous example.

```
struct ContentView: View {
   @Environment(\.openWindow) var openWindow

   var body: some View {
      VStack {
         Text("Hello, world!")
         Button("Open Auxiliary Window") {
            openWindow(id: "mywindow")
         }
      }.frame(width: 500, height: 300)
   }
}
```

Listing 19-26: Opening a window programmatically

The interface includes a `Button` view to open the auxiliary window. When the button is pressed, we perform the action with the **id** argument to open the window identified with the string mywindow. The result is shown below.

Figure 19-19: Auxiliary window

So far, we have opened the window with a standard configuration, but we can specify some attributes with the following modifiers.

defaultPosition(UnitPoint**)**—This modifier specifies the window's initial position relative to the screen. The argument is a structure with the type properties **topLeading**, **top**, **topTrailing**, **leading**, **center**, **trailing**, **bottomLeading**, **bottom**, and **bottomTrailing**.

defaultSize(width: CGFloat, **height:** CGFloat**)**—This modifier specifies the window's size by default. The arguments determine the width and height.

commandsRemoved()—This modifier removes the standard menu option created by the system for a new window.

These modifiers are applied to the Scene in the **App** structure. In the following example, we assign the auxiliary window a size of 200 by 200 points, position it at the top left corner of the screen, and remove the menu option generated by the system to open it.

```
Window("My Window", id: "mywindow") {
   AuxiliaryView()
}
.defaultSize(width: 200, height: 200)
.defaultPosition(.topLeading)
.commandsRemoved()
```

Listing 19-27: Configuring the auxiliary window

 Do It Yourself: Update the `Window` structure in the previous example with the code in Listing 19-27. Run the application on the Mac. Open the Window menu. The option to open the auxiliary window should be gone. (At the moment of writing, the option to define the position is not contemplated by the system.)

Another structure provided by SwiftUI to create a Scene for macOS applications is `Settings`. This structure creates a Scene that presents an interface for the user to modify the app's settings. The Scene is declared in the `App` structure along with the `WindowGroup` Scene, but it is displayed on the screen when the user selects the Preferences option from the app's menu.

Settings(content: Closure)—This structure creates a Scene to present the app's settings. The **content** argument is a closure with the views that render the Scene.

In the following example, we create a simple `Settings` Scene with a `Stepper` view for the user to set a number, and a `Text` view to show the current number on the screen. The value is stored in the App Storage system with the `@AppStorage` property wrapper, so we can read it later from the views to configure the interface.

```
import SwiftUI
@main
struct TestApp: App {
   @AppStorage("totalItems") var totalItems: Int = 0

   var body: some Scene {
      WindowGroup {
         ContentView()
      }
      Settings {
         HStack {
            Stepper("Total Items", value: $totalItems)
            Text(String(totalItems))
               .font(.title.bold())
         }.frame(width: 200, height: 150)
      }
   }
}
```

Listing 19-28: Defining a Settings *Scene*

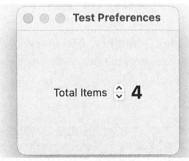

Figure 19-20: Settings Scene

Chapter 19 - Multiplatform Applications

Do It Yourself: Update the `App` structure from the previous example with the code in Listing 19-28. Run the application on the Mac. Open the app's menu and click on the Preferences option. You should see a small window appear on the screen, as shown in Figure 19-20.

Finally, there is one more structure to create a Scene for macOS applications called `MenuBarExtra`. This structure creates a Scene that adds a control to the system's menu bar.

MenuBarExtra(String, **systemImage:** String, **isInserted:** Binding, **content:** Closure**)**—This structure creates a Scene that adds a control to the system's menu bar. The first argument is the control's title, the **systemImage** argument is the SF Symbol we want to use to represent the control, the **isInserted** argument is a Boolean `Binding` property that determines if the control is displayed or not, and the **content** argument is the closure that defines the menu or the view to show when the control is selected.

There are two different styles for the control. We can open a menu with options created by `Button` views, or a view with a custom interface. The following modifier selects the style.

menuBarExtraStyle(MenuBarExtraStyle**)**—This modifier specifies the style of the content shown by the control. The argument is a structure that conforms to the `MenuBarExtraStyle` protocol. The framework includes three structures to define the styles. These structures include the type properties `automatic`, `menu`, and `window`.

By default, the style is set to `automatic`, which means the control will open a menu. To define the options for the menu, we include `Button` and `Divider` views, as shown next.

```
import SwiftUI
@main
struct TestApp: App {
   var body: some Scene {
      WindowGroup {
         ContentView()
      }
      #if os(macOS)
      MenuBarExtra("My Control", systemImage: "phone") {
         Button("Option 1") {
            print("Option 1")
         }
         Button("Option 2") {
            print("Option 2")
         }
         Divider()
         Button("Quit") {
            NSApplication.shared.terminate(nil)
         }
      }
      #endif
   }
}
```

Listing 19-29: *Inserting a control in the system's menu bar*

Most Scenes include a predefined menu with standard options, including one to close the application. This is not the case for the Scene created by the `MenuBarExtra` structure. In this case, we have to do it programmatically. Applications in macOS are managed by an instance of the `NSApplication` class. The class includes the type property `shared` to return this instance, and the instance includes the `terminate()` method to close the application. And this is all we need to create our own option to allow the user to quit the app.

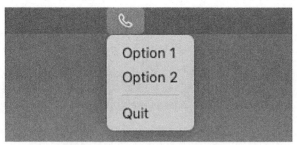

Figure 19-21: Control with a menu

To show a view instead of a menu, we must apply the `menuBarExtraStyle()` modifier with the `window` value and replace the buttons with a single view and its content.

```
MenuBarExtra("My Menu", systemImage: "phone") {
   VStack {
      HStack {
         Spacer()
         Button(action: {
            NSApplication.shared.terminate(nil)
         }, label: {
            Image(systemName: "xmark.circle")
         })
      }.padding()
      Button("Option 1") {
         print("Option 1")
      }.buttonStyle(.borderedProminent)
      Button("Option 2") {
         print("Option 2")
      }.buttonStyle(.borderedProminent)
      Spacer()
   }.frame(width: 200, height: 180)
}.menuBarExtraStyle(.window)
```

Listing 19-30: Defining a control to open a view

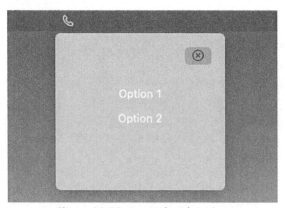

Figure 19-22: Control with a view

Basic Scene Storage

iPads and Mac computers can open multiple instances of an application in separate windows (Scenes). iPads offer multiple alternatives to open the app in a new window. The easiest way to do it is to split the screen with the bottoms at the top and open the app again (see Chapter 12, Figure 12-4). On the Mac is even easier, the option is available on the File menu.

Figure 19-23: Option to create a new window

When we open a new instance of our app (a new window), the `WindowGroup` structure creates a new Scene. Each Scene implements the same views and work with the same model. This means that all the Scenes will present the same values and share the same initial state. But this is not always appropriate. Users often expect the window to be in the state it was before the app was closed or control different information on each window. To store information pertaining to a Scene, SwiftUI includes the `@SceneStorage` property wrapper. This is like the `@AppStorage` property wrapper but instead of storing values for the app, it stores values for the Scene.

In the following example, we create an application that allows the user to select a picture. The index of the selected picture is permanently stored in a `@SceneStorage` property, so the value is restored when the app is launched again. First, we need to define a model with the list of pictures available.

```
import SwiftUI

class ApplicationData: ObservableObject {
    @Published var picturesList: [String]

    init() {
        picturesList = ["bagels", "brownies", "butter", "cheese", "coffee",
"cookies", "donuts", "granola", "juice", "lemonade", "lettuce", "milk",
"oatmeal", "potato", "tomato", "yogurt"]
    }
}
```

Listing 19-31: Defining the model to test multiple Scenes

The interface must include a `Picker` view to select the picture and an `Image` view to show the selected picture on the screen.

```
struct ContentView: View {
    @EnvironmentObject var appData: ApplicationData
    @SceneStorage("selection") var selection: Int = 0

    var body: some View {
        VStack {
            HStack(alignment: .top, spacing: 20) {
                Picker("Select", selection: $selection) {
                    ForEach(appData.picturesList.indices, id: \.self) { index in
                        Button(appData.picturesList[index].capitalized, action:{
                            selection = index
                        }).tag(index)
                    }
                }.frame(width: 200, height: 150, alignment: .top)
                Image(appData.picturesList[selection])
                    .resizable()
                    .scaledToFit()
                    .frame(width: 200, height: 150)
            }
        }.padding(20)
```

```
        }
    }
}
```

Listing 19-32: Storing the state of the Scene

Every time the user selects a different value, the `Picker` view stores that value in the `selection` property and, therefore, the value is preserved. If we close and open the app again, the initial value will be the one we selected before the app was closed. And because we are using the `@SceneStorage` property to set the `Picker` view, the selection is unique for each Scene.

Figure 19-24: Scene with custom values

 Do It Yourself: Create a Multiplatform project. Download the thumbnails from our website and add them to the Asset Catalog. Create a Swift file called ApplicationData.swift for the model in Listing 19-31. Update the `ContentView` view with the code in Listing 19-32. Remember to inject the `ApplicationData` object into the environment for the app and the previews (Chapter 7, Listing 7-4). Run the application on the Mac. Select a picture. You should see the selected picture on the screen. Stop the app from Xcode and run it again. The selected picture should be shown on the screen again. Open the File menu and click on the New Window option to open a new window. You should be able to select different pictures from each window.

 IMPORTANT: There are multiple ways to restore the state of the app and the windows. For more information and to learn about advanced options, visit our website and follow the links for this chapter.

Chapter 20
App Store

(Basic) **20.1 Publishing**

At the beginning of this book, we talked about Apple's strict control over the applications users can access. Applications for Mac computers can be sold separately, but mobile applications can only be sold in the App Store. The tools to submit our application to the App Store are provided by Xcode, but there are a series of requirements we need to satisfy for our app to be published and become available to users.

- We need an Apple Developer Program membership.
- We need a Distribution Certificate.
- We need a Provisioning Profile for distribution.
- We need an App ID to identify the application.
- We must register the app in the App Store Connect website.
- We must create an archive with our app for each platform to send to Apple servers.
- We must upload the archive to App Store Connect for review.

(Basic) **Apple Developer Program**

Developing and testing can be done with a free account, but publishing our app requires a membership to the Apple Developer Program. The option to enroll in this program is available on the **developer.apple.com** website. We must click on the Discover/Program options at the top of the screen, press the Enroll button, and follow the instructions to register an account for an Individual or an organization. At the time of writing, the membership costs USD 99 per year.

(Basic) **Certificates, Provisioning Profiles, and Identifiers**

Apple wants to make sure that only authorized apps are running on its devices, so it requests developers to add a cryptographic signature to each application. There are three values that are necessary to authorize the app: certificates, provisioning profiles, and identifiers. Basically, a certificate identifies the developer that publishes the application, the provisioning profile identifies the device that is allowed to run the application, and an identifier, called *App ID*, identifies the application. These values are packed along with the application's files and therefore Apple always knows who developed the app, who is authorized to run it, and in which devices.

Xcode automatically generates these values for us, so we do not have to worry about them, but Apple offers a control panel in our developer account in case we need to do it manually (the option is not available for free members). Figure 20-1 shows the menu we see after we go to developer.apple.com, click on Account, and select the option Certificates, IDs & Profiles.

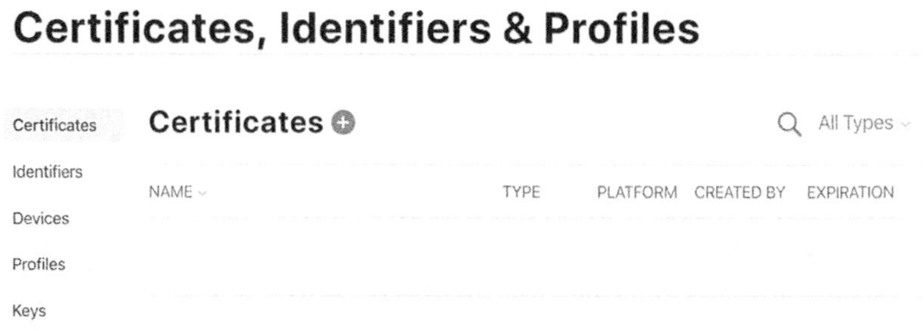

Certificates, Identifiers & Profiles

Certificates	**Certificates** ⊕				Q All Types ⌄
Identifiers					
	NAME ⌄	TYPE	PLATFORM	CREATED BY	EXPIRATION
Devices					
Profiles					
Keys					

Figure 20-1: Web page to manage certificates, provisioning profiles, and identifiers

In this page, we can create, edit, or remove certificates, provisioning profiles and identifiers. The page contains two panels. The left panel offers a list of options to select the type of values we want to work with, and the right panel shows the list of values available and buttons to create new ones. When a value is selected, a new panel opens with tools to edit it.

Basic Icons

Before submitting the app to the App Store, we need to provide the resources Apple needs to make our app available to the public. An important resource we must include in our project are the app's icons. Icons are the little images that the user taps or clicks to launch the app. By default, the Asset Catalog includes a set called *AppIcon* to manage the icons for the application. The set includes placeholders for every icon we need and for every scale and device available.

Icons may be created with any image editing software available on the market. A file must be created for every size required. For example, the first two placeholders require images of 20 points, which means that we need to create an image of a size of 40x40 pixels for the 2x scale and an image of a size of 60x60 pixels for the 3x scale. After all the images are created, we must drag them to the corresponding squares, as we do with any other image. Figure 20-2, below, shows what the AppIcon set may look like once all the icons are provided (sample files are available on our website).

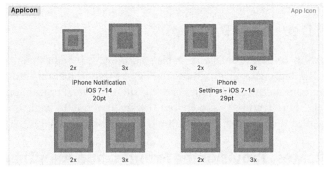

Figure 20-2: AppIcon set with the icons for iPhones and iPads

Basic Launch Screen

The launch screen is the first screen the user sees when the app is launched. No matter the size, applications always take a few seconds to load. The launch screen is required to give the user the impression that the app is responsive.

We can define two aspects of the launch screen: the background color and an image. The values are specified from the Info panel in the app's settings. The option is called Launch Screen. When we press the + button on this key, Xcode shows a list of options to choose from.

Figure 20-3: Launch Screen options

There are two options available to define the content and four to configure the screen. The Background color option specifies the name of the Color Set in the Asset Catalog we want to use to define the screen's background color, and the Image Name option specifies the name of the

Image Set that contains the image we want to display. For configuration, we have the Image respects safe area insets to determine the behavior of the image regarding the safe area, and the Show Navigation bar, Show Tab bar, and Show Toolbar options to determine whether these bars are going to be shown while the app is launched.

For instance, below is what we see if we include a background color and an image. This requires the Asset Catalog to include an Image Set called *launchLogo* and a Color Set called *launchColor*.

Launch Screen		Dictionary	(2 items)
Image Name		String	launchLogo
Background color		String	launchColor

Figure 20-4: Launch Screen configuration

Apple's guidelines recommend creating a launch screen that closely resembles the first screen of your app. For instance, if the app's interface background is yellow, we should assign to the launch screen a yellow background as well. In our example, we define two sets in the Asset Catalog. The launchLogo set includes a PNG image with a logo, and the launchColor set defines a yellow color for the light and dark appearances. The result is shown below.

Figure 20-5: Launch screen for our app

(Basic) **App Store Connect**

The first step to submit our application is to create a record on Apple's servers. Apple has designated a website for this purpose, available at **appstoreconnect.apple.com**. To login, we must use the same Apple ID and password we use to access our account at developer.apple.com. Figure 20-6 illustrates the options available after logging in.

Figure 20-6: App Store Connect menu

From this panel, we can insert our financial information (Agreements, Tax, and Banking), publish our apps (My Apps), and see how the business is going (Sales and Trends). The first step is to create a record for the app we want to publish from the My Apps option. When we click on this icon, a new window shows the list of our apps and a + button at the top to add more.

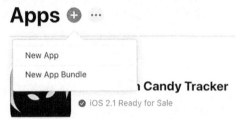

Figure 20-7: Menu to add apps to our account

To add a new app, we must select the New App option and insert the app's information. The first window asks for the platform we have developed the app for (in our case, iOS and macOS), the application's name, the primary language, the bundle ID, and a custom ID (SKU) that can help us identify the app later. The name and language are values we already have, and the SKU is a custom string, but the Bundle ID is a value generate by Xcode. Xcode creates a Bundle ID and submits it to Apple servers when we enable services from the capabilities panel. If our app does not use any of these services, we can register a new Bundle ID from developer.apple.com.

Figure 20-8: Bundle ID and SKU identifier

After these values are inserted, we can press the Create button and complete the rest of the information. This includes the app's description, screenshots, and personal information. We also must select the option Pricing and Availability on the left panel to set the price and where the application will be available. Once all the information is provided, we can finally press the Save button and go back to Xcode to upload the files.

(Basic) **Submitting the Application**

The application and resources must be compiled for each platform in a single archive and then submitted to App Store Connect. We must create an archive for iOS devices and another for macOS. The option is available on the Xcode's Product menu, but it is only enabled when the appropriate device is selected from the Schemes. We can select a real device connected to the computer, or we can use the Any iOS Device option for iOS apps or the Any Mac option for macOS (Figure 20-9, number 1).

Figure 20-9: Archive option

After we click on the Archive option (Figure 20-9, number 2), Xcode compiles the application and creates the archive. The next window shows the archive and offers buttons to validate and submit the app.

Figure 20-10: *List of archives created for our app*

Figure 20-10 shows an archive created for an application called Test (number 1). The item representing the archive includes the date it was created, the app's version, and the number of the build. (We can send multiple builds to App Store Connect and later decide which one we want Apple to review.)

 IMPORTANT: The app's version and the number of the build (archive) are determined from the app's settings (by default, both values are set to 1.0). If we want to specify a different version, we must declare the numbers separated by one or two periods (e.g., 1.0 or 1.2.5). The values represent different revisions of our app, with the order of relevance from left to right. The values are arbitrary, but we are required to change them every time an update is published to the App Store to reflect how big the update is.

Although it is not required, we should always validate the archive before submitting the app. The process allows Xcode to detect errors and suggest how to fix them. To begin the validation process, we can press the Validate App button (Figure 20-10, number 3). The first window presents options to tell Xcode how to configure the archive and what to include.

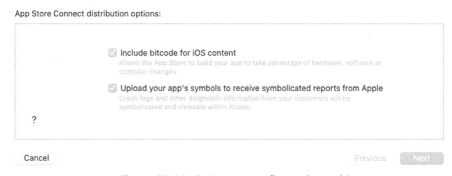

Figure 20-11: *Options to configure the archive*

All the options are recommended. The first one asks Xcode to include code that improves the app's performance, and the second one uploads the necessary information for Apple to be able to report errors and perform diagnostics.

The next window allows us to select how we want to sign the app. With automatic signing, we let Xcode take care of everything for us (recommended).

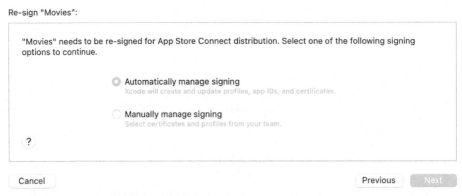

Re-sign "Movies":

"Movies" needs to be re-signed for App Store Connect distribution. Select one of the following signing options to continue.

Automatically manage signing
Xcode will create and update profiles, app IDs, and certificates.

Manually manage signing
Select certificates and profiles from your team.

?

Cancel   Previous   Next

Figure 20-12: Option to select automatic signing

The last window displays a summary and provides a button to initiate the validation process. Once this process is over, if no errors are found, we can finally submit our app to Apple servers by pressing the Distribute App button (Figure 20-10, number 2).

As we already mentioned, we may submit multiple archives to the server (builds). For this reason, we must go back to the App Store Connect website, open the description of our application, and select the archive we just uploaded (it may take a few minutes to be available). Figure 20-13, below, shows the option with the archive uploaded for an app in its version 3.3.

Build

BUILD	VERSION	HAS APP CLIP
1	3.3	NO

Figure 20-13: Selecting the build to send to the App Store

After the archive is selected, we can press the Save button to save the app's description. If all the required information was provided, we can finally press the Submit for Review button at the top of the page to submit the application. The system asks a few questions and then the application is sent to Apple for review (the message Waiting for Review is shown below the app's title).

The process takes a few days to complete. If the app is approved, Apple sends us an email to let us know that the app has become available in the App Store.

Index